PHILIP'S

CW00467627

STREE

Derbyshire

Buxton, Chesterfield, Derby, Matlock, Swadlincote

www.philips-maps.co.uk

First published in 1995 by

Philip's, a division of
Octopus Publishing Group Ltd
www.octopusbooks.co.uk
2-4 Heron Quays, London E14 4JP
An Hachette Livre UK Company
www.hachettelivre.co.uk

Third colour edition 2006
Second impression with revisions 2008
DBYCB

ISBN 978-0-540-08845-4 (pocket)

© Philip's 2008

Ordnance Survey®

This product includes mapping data licensed from
Ordnance Survey® with the permission of the
Controller of Her Majesty's Stationery Office.

© Crown copyright 2008. All rights reserved.
Licence number 100011710.

Contents

III **Key to map symbols**

IV **Key to map pages**

VI **Route planning**

X **Administrative and Postcode boundaries**

1 **Street maps** at 2⅔ inches to 1 mile

266 **Street maps of centres of Chesterfield and Derby** at 5⅓ inches to 1 mile

268 **Index** of towns and villages

271 **Index** of streets, hospitals, industrial estates, railway stations, schools, shopping centres, universities and places of interest

Digital Data

The exceptionally high-quality mapping found in this atlas is available as digital data in TIFF format, which is easily convertible to other bitmapped (raster) image formats.

The index is also available in digital form as a standard database table. It contains all the details found in the printed index together with the National Grid reference for the map square in which each entry is named.

For further information and to discuss your requirements, please contact
james.mann@philips-maps.co.uk

On-line route planner

For detailed driving directions and estimated driving times visit our free route planner at
www.philips-maps.co.uk

III

Symbol	Description
	Motorway with junction number
	Primary route – dual/single carriageway
	A road – dual/single carriageway
	B road – dual/single carriageway
	Minor road – dual/single carriageway
	Other minor road – dual/single carriageway
	Road under construction
	Tunnel, covered road
	Rural track, private road or narrow road in urban area
	Gate or obstruction to traffic (restrictions may not apply at all times or to all vehicles)
	Path, bridleway, byway open to all traffic, road used as a public path
	Pedestrianised area
DY7	**Postcode boundaries**
	County and unitary authority boundaries
	Railway, tunnel, railway under construction
	Tramway, tramway under construction
	Miniature railway
Walsall	**Railway station**
	Private railway station
South Shields	**Metro station**
	Tram stop, tram stop under construction
	Bus, coach station

Symbol	Description
◆	**Ambulance station**
◆	**Coastguard station**
◆	**Fire station**
◆	**Police station**
+	**Accident and Emergency entrance to hospital**
H	**Hospital**
+	**Place of worship**
i	**Information Centre** (open all year)
	Shopping Centre
P P&R	**Parking, Park and Ride**
PO	**Post Office**
⚊ ⚊	**Camping site, caravan site**
▶ ✕	**Golf course, picnic site**
Prim Sch	**Important buildings, schools, colleges, universities and hospitals**
	Built up area
	Woods
River Medway	**Water name**
	River, weir, stream
	Canal, lock, tunnel
	Water
	Tidal water
Church	**Non-Roman antiquity**
ROMAN FORT	**Roman antiquity**
87	**Adjoining page indicators and overlap bands**
237	The colour of the arrow and the band indicates the scale of the adjoining or overlapping page (see scales below)

Acad	Academy
Allot Gdns	Allotments
Cemy	Cemetery
C Ctr	Civic Centre
CH	Club House
Coll	College
Crem	Crematorium
Ent	Enterprise
Ex H	Exhibition Hall
Ind Est	Industrial Estate
IRB Sta	Inshore Rescue Boat Station
Inst	Institute
Ct	Law Court
L Ctr	Leisure Centre
LC	Level Crossing
Liby	Library
Mkt	Market
Meml	Memorial
Mon	Monument
Mus	Museum
Obsy	Observatory
Pal	Royal Palace
PH	Public House
Recn Gd	Recreation Ground
Resr	Reservoir
Ret Pk	Retail Park
Sch	School
Sh Ctr	Shopping Centre
TH	Town Hall/House
Trad Est	Trading Estate
Univ	University
W Twr	Water Tower
Wks	Works
YH	Youth Hostel

■ The small numbers around the edges of the maps identify the 1 kilometre National Grid lines

■ The dark grey border on the inside edge of some pages indicates that the mapping does not continue onto the adjacent page

Enlarged mapping only

Symbol	Description
	Railway or bus station building
	Place of interest
	Parkland

The scale of the maps on the pages numbered in blue is 4.2 cm to 1 km • 2⅔ inches to 1 mile • 1: 23810

0	¼	½	¾	1 mile
0	250 m	500 m	750 m	1 kilometre

The scale of the maps on pages numbered in red is 8.4 cm to 1 km • 5⅓ inches to 1 mile • 1: 11900

0	220 yards	440 yards	660 yards	½ mile
0	125 m	250 m	375 m	½ kilometre

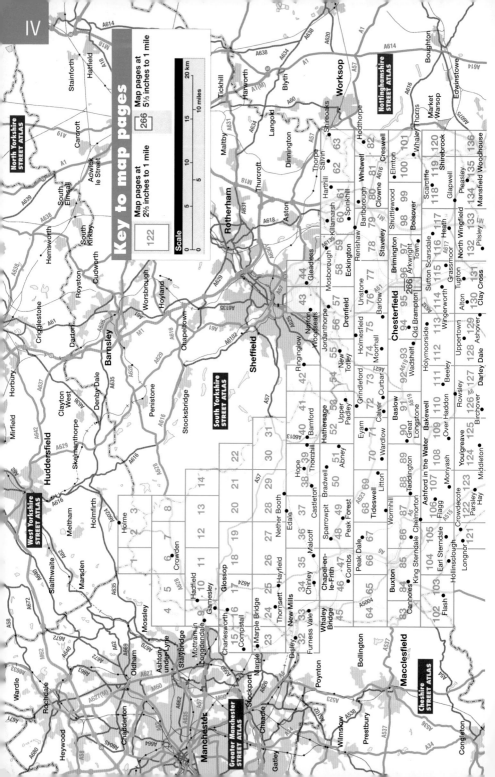

IV

Key to map pages

North Yorkshire STREET ATLAS

Nottinghamshire STREET ATLAS

South Yorkshire STREET ATLAS

West Yorkshire STREET ATLAS

Greater Manchester STREET ATLAS

Cheshire STREET ATLAS

Map pages at 2⅓ inches to 1 mile

122

Map pages at 5⅓ inches to 1 mile

266

Map pages to 1 mile

Scale

0   5   10   15   20 km

0   5   10 miles

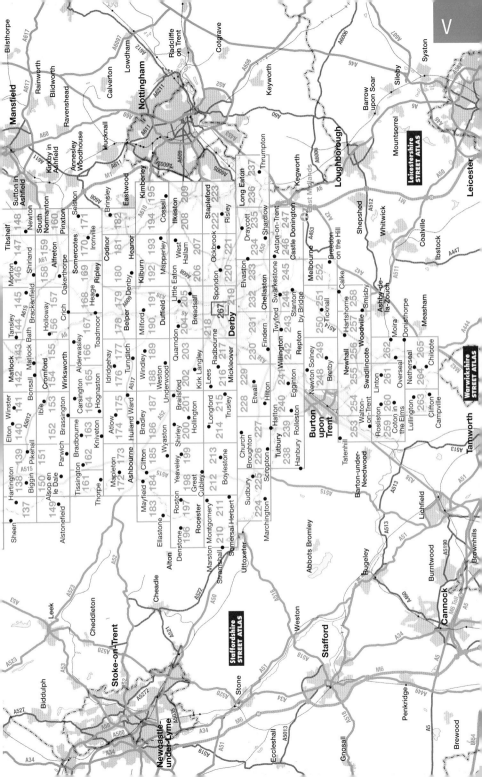

Route planning

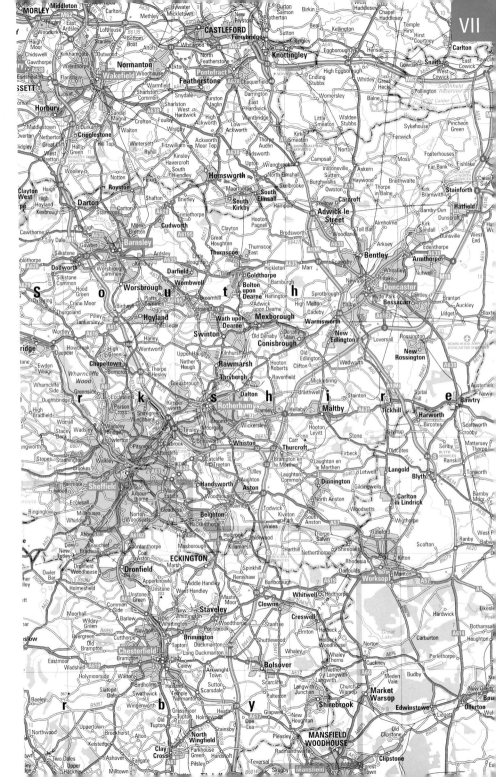

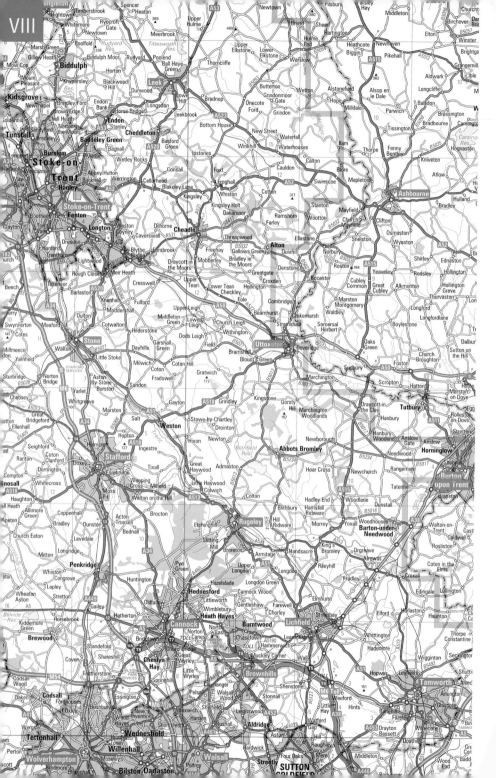

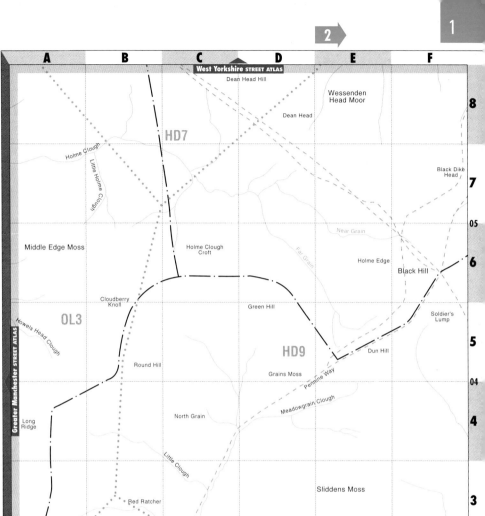

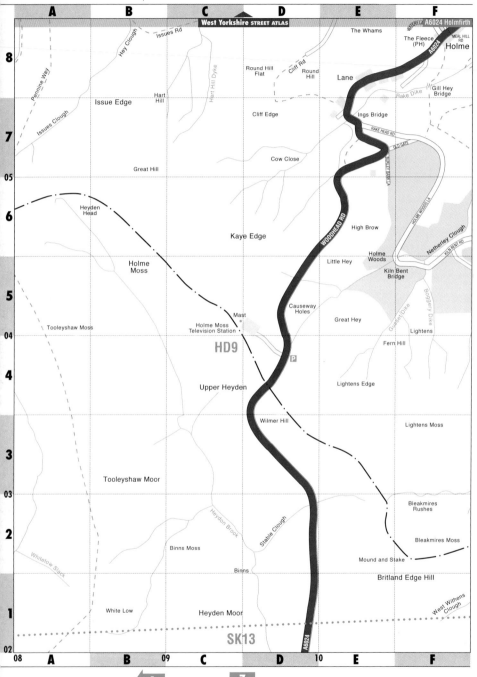

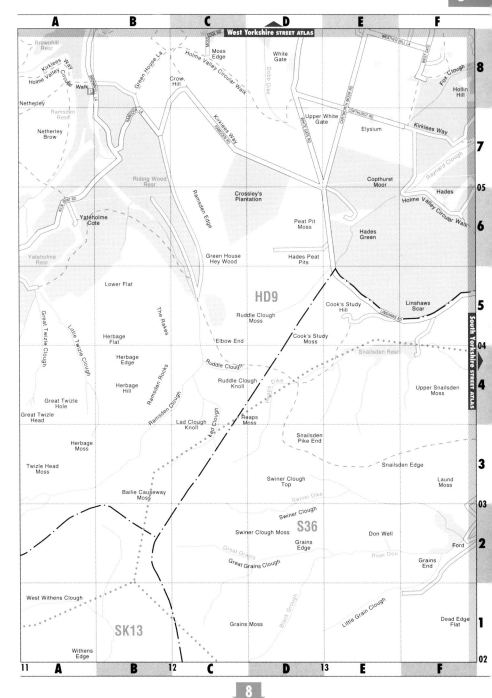

South Yorkshire STREET ATLAS

A | **B** | **C** | **D** | **E** | **F**

Brownhill Resr

Kirklees Valley Way

Holme Valley Circular Walk

Netherley

Netherley Brow

Ramsden Resr

BROWNHILL LA

Green House La

Holme Valley Circular Walk

Crow Hill

Moss Edge

Moss Edge RD

Dobb Dike

White Gate

WEATHER HILL LA

WEST GATE

Fox Clough

Hollin Hill

Kirklees Way

Upper White Gate

WHITE GATE RD

COPTHURST RD

CART MOOR RD

Elysium

Kirklees Way

Raynard Clough

Kirklees Way

RAMSDEN RD

KILN BENT RD

Riding Wood Resr

Ramsden Edge

Crossley's Plantation

Copthurst Moor

Hades

Holme Valley Circular Walk

Yateholme Cote

Peat Pit Moss

Hades Green

Yateholme Resr

Green House Hey Wood

Hades Peat Pits

Lower Flat

The Rakes

HD9

Ruddle Clough Moss

Cook's Study Hill

LINSHAWS RD

Linshaws Scar

5

05

04

Great Twizle Clough

Little Twizle Clough

Herbage Flat

Herbage Edge

Herbage Hill

Elbow End

Ruddle Clough

Cook's Study Moss

Snailsden Resr

Ramsden Rocks

Ramsden Clough

Ruddle Clough Knoll

Dike

Dike

Upper Snailsden Moss

4

Great Twizle Hole

Great Twizle Head

Lad Clough Knoll

Lad Clough

Lad Clough

Reaps Moss

Snailsden Pike End

Snailsden Edge

Herbage Moss

Twizle Head Moss

Bailie Causeway Moss

Swiner Clough Top

Swiner Dike

Laund Moss

3

03

Swiner Clough

S36

Swiner Clough Moss

Great Grains

Great Grains Clough

Swiner Clough Moss

Grains Edge

Don Well

River Don

Grains End

Ford

2

West Withens Clough

Black Grough

Grains Moss

Little Grain Clough

Dead Edge Flat

1

02

SK13

Withens Edge

A | **B** | 12 | **C** | **D** | 13 | **E** | **F**

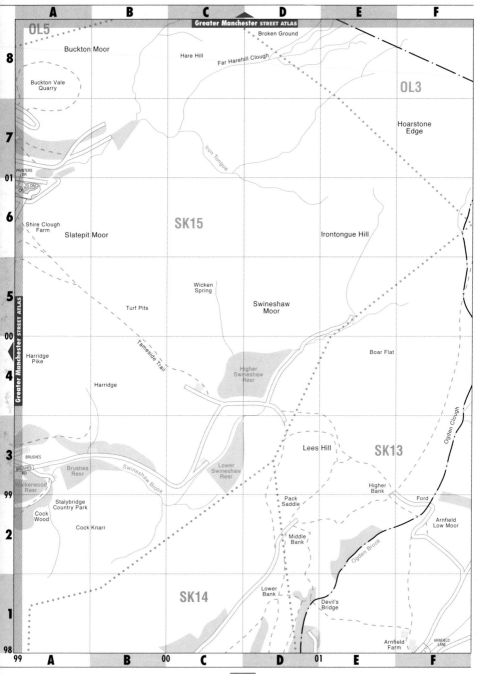

OL5

Buckton Moor

Buckton Vale
Quarry

Broken Ground

Hare Hill

Far Harehill Clough

OL3

Hoarstone
Edge

Iron Tongue

PRINTERS
DR

Shire Clough
Farm

Slatepit Moor

SK15

Irontongue Hill

Wicken
Spring

Swineshaw
Moor

Turf Pits

Tameside Trail

Boar Flat

Harridge
Pike

Higher
Swineshaw
Resr

Harridge

Ogden Clough

Lees Hill

SK13

BRUSHES

Brushes
Resr

Swineshaw Brook

Lower
Swineshaw
Resr

Higher
Bank

Ford

BRUSHES
RD

Walkerwood
Resr

Pack
Saddle

Arnfield
Low Moor

Cock
Wood

Stalybridge
Country Park

Cock Knarr

Middle
Bank

Ogden Brook

SK14

Lower
Bank

Devil's
Bridge

Arnfield
Farm

ARNFIELD
LANE

99   A   B   00   C   D   01   E   F

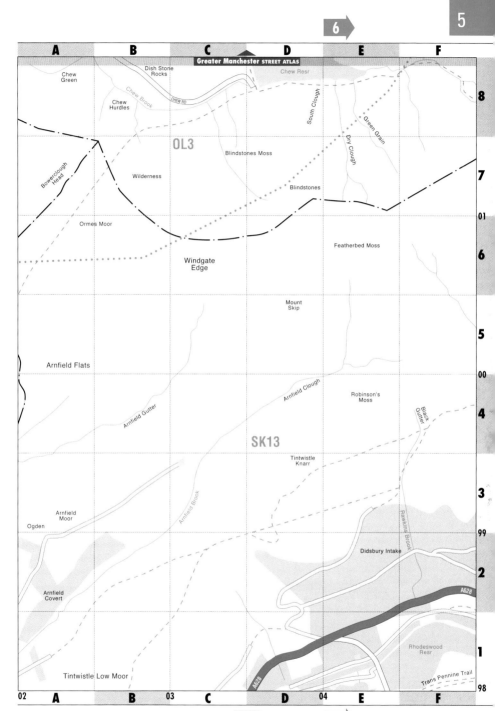

Chew
Green

Dish Stone
Rocks

Chew Resr

Chew Brook

CHEW RD

Chew
Hurdles

South Clough

8

OL3

Blindstones Moss

Green Grain

Bowerclough
Head

Wilderness

Dry Clough

7

Blindstones

01

Ormes Moor

Featherbed Moss

6

Windgate
Edge

Mount
Skip

5

Arnfield Flats

00

Arnfield Clough

Robinson's
Moss

Black
Gutter

4

Arnfield Gutter

SK13

Tintwistle
Knarr

Rawkins Brook

3

Arnfield Brook

99

Arnfield
Moor

Ogden

Didsbury Intake

2

Arnfield
Covert

A628

Rhodeswood
Resr

1

Tintwistle Low Moor

A628

Trans Pennine Trail

98

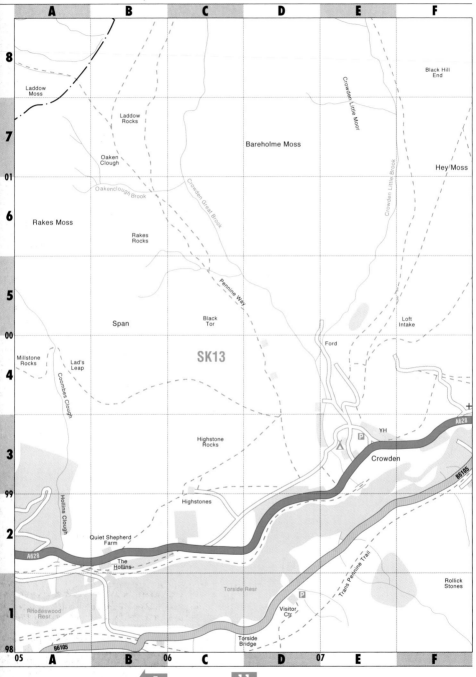

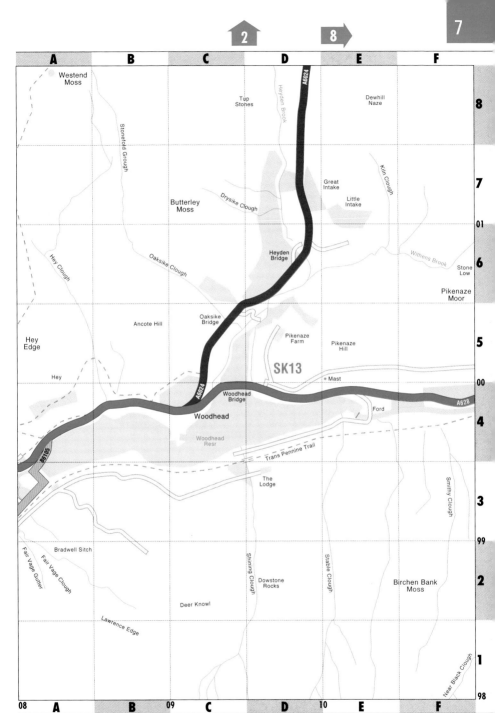

	A	B	C	D	E	F	

8

Westend Moss

Tup Stones

Dewhill Naze

Stonefold Grough

A6024

Heyden Brook

7

Butterley Moss

Drysike Clough

Great Intake

Kin Clough

01

Oaksike Clough

Heyden Bridge

Little Intake

Withens Brook

6

Hey Clough

Stone Low

Pikenaze Moor

Hey Edge

Ancote Hill

Oaksike Bridge

Pikenaze Farm

Pikenaze Hill

5

Hey

A6024

Mast

00

Woodhead Bridge

SK13

Ford

A628

Woodhead

4

A6105

Woodhead Resr

Trans Pennine Trail

3

The Lodge

Smithy Clough

Bradwell Sitch

99

Fair Vage Gutter

Fair Vage Clough

Shining Clough

Dowstone Rocks

Stable Clough

Birchen Bank Moss

2

Deer Knowl

Lawrence Edge

Near Black Clough

1

98

08	A	B	09	C	D	10	E	F

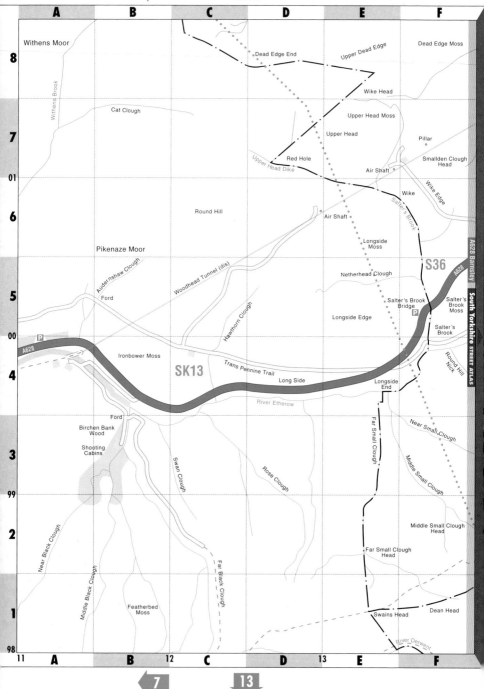

A   B   C   D   E   F

Withens Moor

8

Withens Brook

Dead Edge End

Upper Dead Edge

Dead Edge Moss

Wike Head

Cat Clough

7

Upper Head Moss

Upper Head

Pillar

01

Upper Head Dike

Red Hole

Air Shaft

Smallden Clough Head

Wike

Wike Edge

Round Hill

6

Air Shaft

Salter's Brook

Longside Moss

Pikenaze Moor

Audernshaw Clough

Netherhead Clough

S36

A628 Barnsley | South Yorkshire STREET ATLAS

5

Ford

Woodhead Tunnel (dis)

Hawthorn Clough

Longside Edge

Salter's Brook Bridge

Salter's Brook Moss

Salter's Brook

A628

00

P

A628

P

Ironbower Moss

SK13

Trans Pennine Trail

Long Side

Longside End

Round Hill Nick

4

River Etherow

Near Small Clough

Ford

Birchen Bank Wood

Far Small Clough

Middle Small Clough

Shooting Cabins

Swan Clough

Rose Clough

3

99

Near Black Clough

Middle Black Clough

Far Black Clough

Featherbed Moss

Middle Small Clough Head

2

Far Small Clough Head

Swains Head

Dean Head

1

River Derwent

98

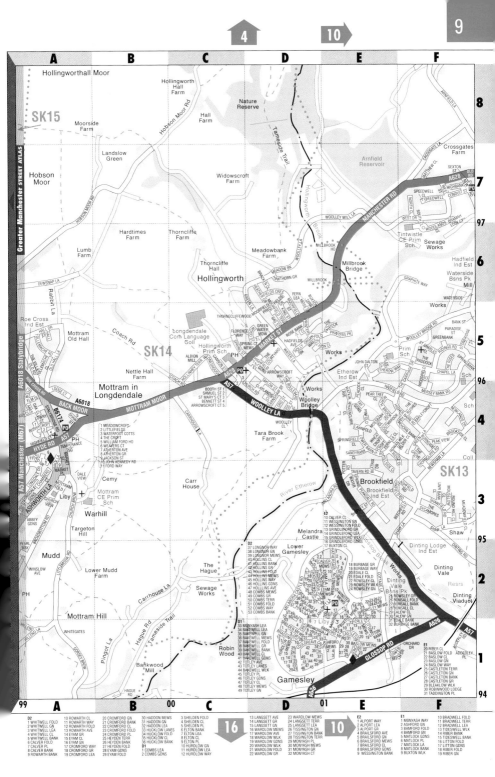

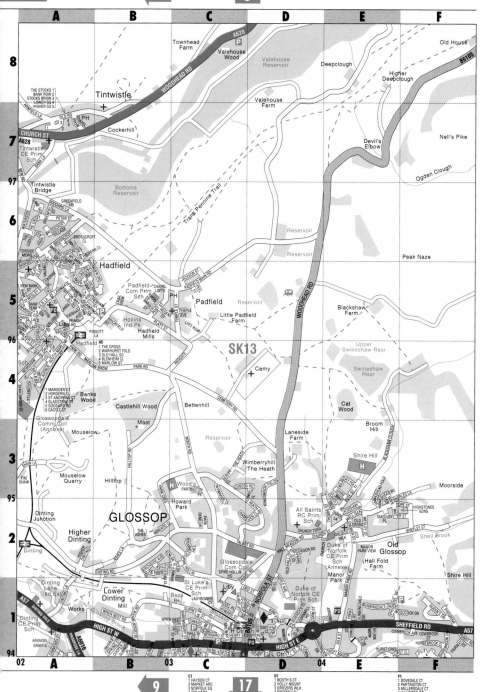

C1
1 HAYDEN CT
2 MARKET ARC
3 NORFOLK SQ
4 THE YARD
5 VICTORIA ST
6 CENTRAL STORE

D1
1 BOOTH'S CT
2 HOLLY MOUNT
3 DROVERS WLK
4 REGENCY CL

F1
1 DOVEDALE CT
2 PARTINGTON CT
3 MILLERSDALE CT
4 HILLWOOD DR
5 HATHERSAGE DR

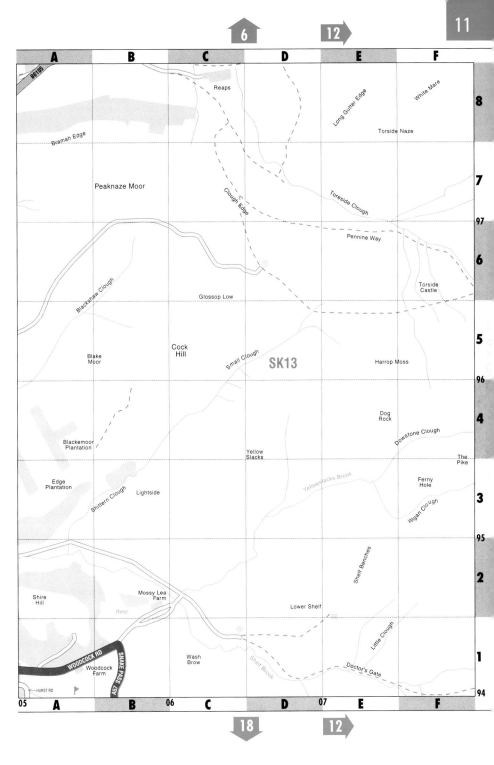

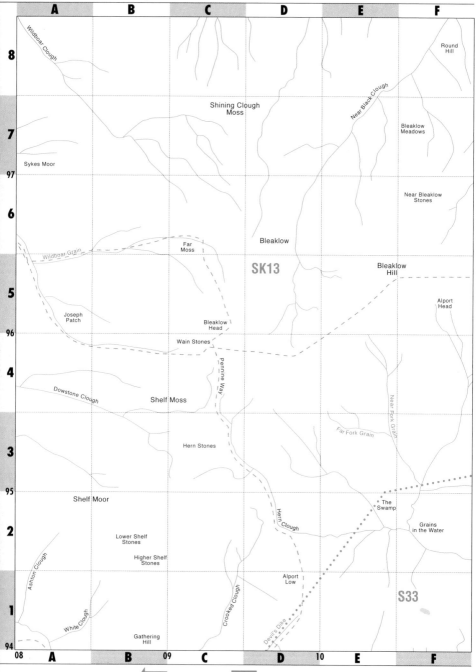

A · B · C · D · E · F

Black
Moss

Middle Black Clough

Featherbed
Moss

8

White
Stones

Swains
Greave

7

97

Barrow
Stones

Barrow Clough

SK13

6

Bleaklow
Stones

Grinah
Stones

Round
Hill

5

96

Westend
Head

Grinah Grain

4

Crap Grain

The Ridge

Ridgewalk Moor

3

95

S33

River Westend

2

Ravens Clough

1

94

Over Wood
Moss

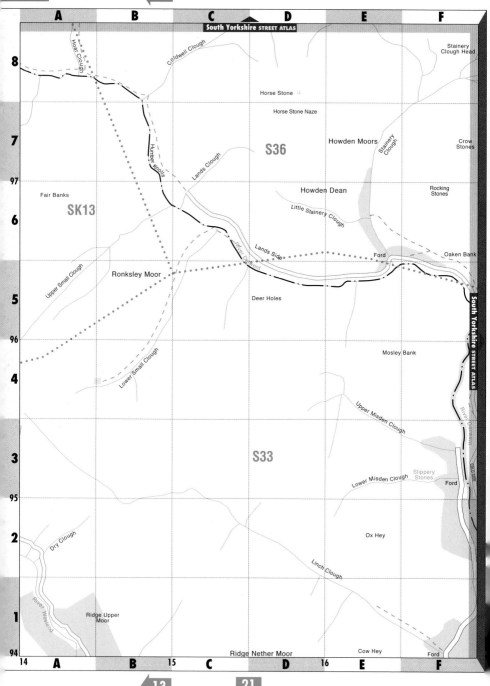

	A	B	C	D	E	F

South Yorkshire STREET ATLAS

8

Hoar Clough

Coldwell Clough

Stainery Clough Head

Horse Stone

Horse Stone Naze

7

S36

Howden Moors

Stainery Clough

Crow Stones

Humber Knolls

Lands Clough

97

Fair Banks

Howden Dean

Rocking Stones

SK13

Little Stainery Clough

6

River Derwent

Lands Side

Ford

Oaken Bank

Upper Small Clough

Ronksley Moor

Deer Holes

5

96

Mosley Bank

4

Lower Small Clough

Upper Misden Clough

River Derwent

3

S33

Lower Misden Clough

Slippery Stones

Ford

COLD SIDE

95

2

Dry Clough

Ox Hey

Linch Clough

River Westend

1

Ridge Upper Moor

94

Ridge Nether Moor

Cow Hey

Ford

South Yorkshire STREET ATLAS

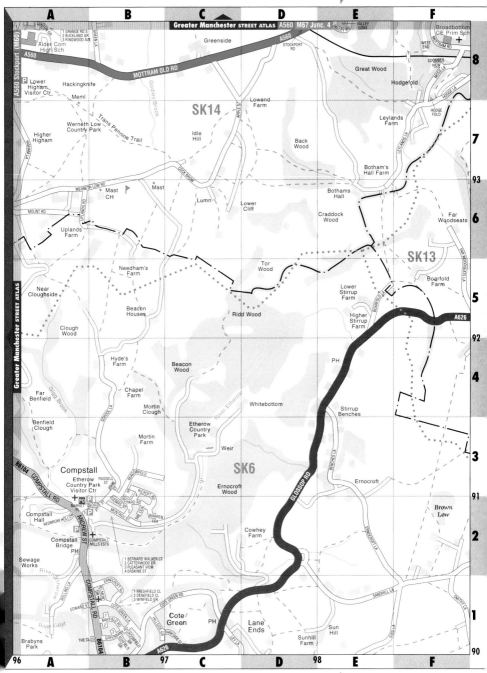

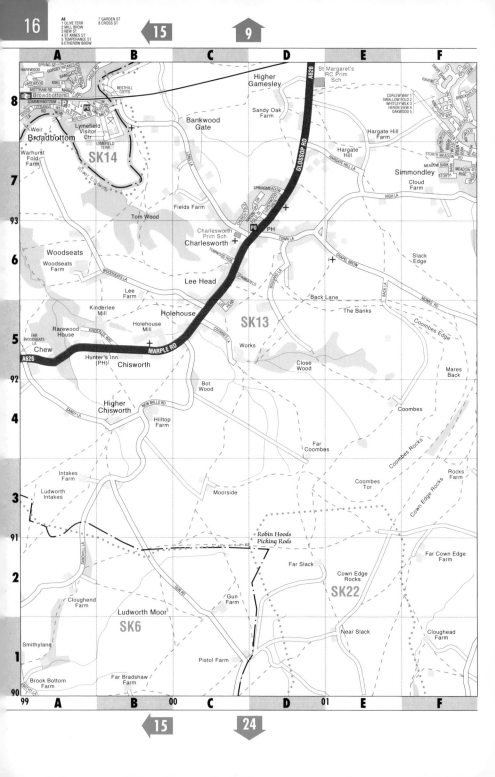

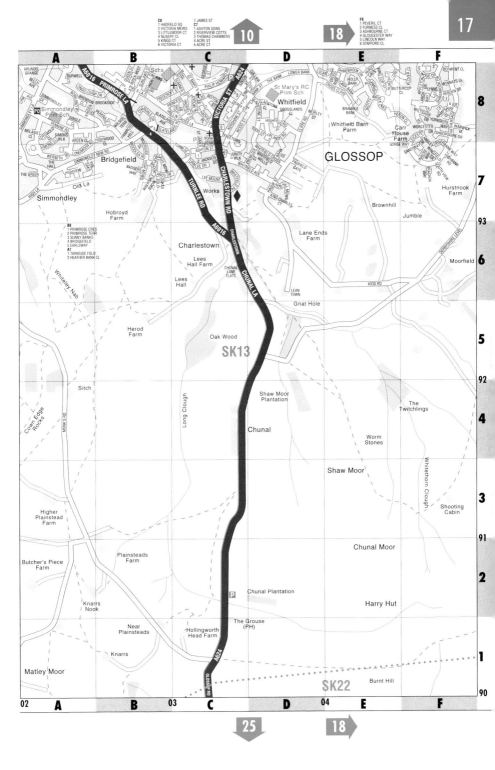

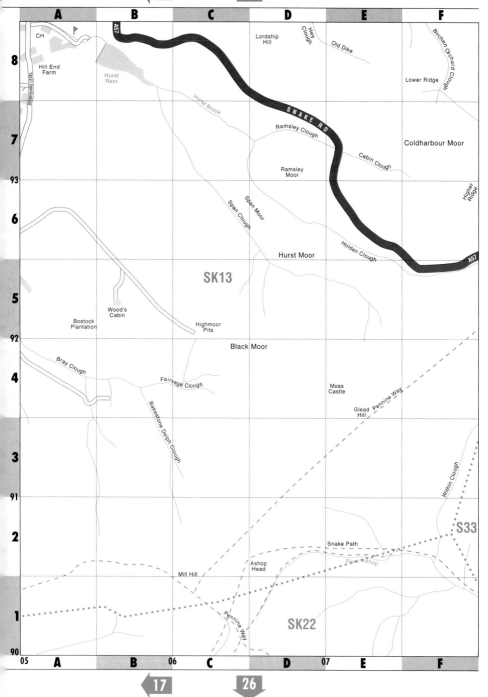

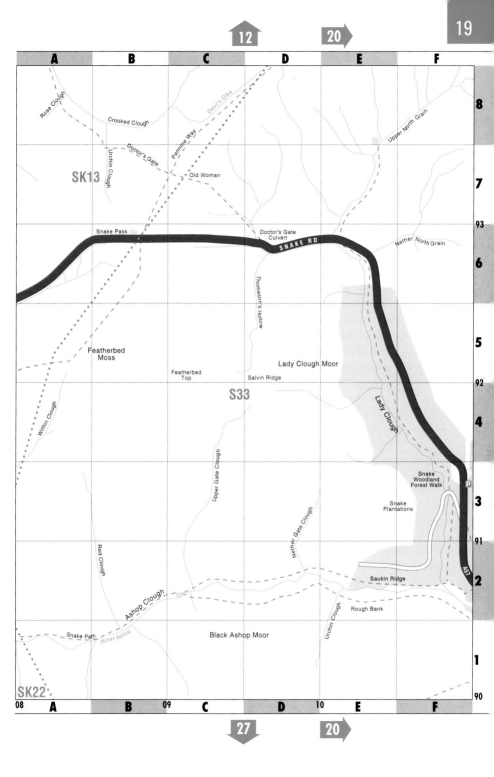

19
13

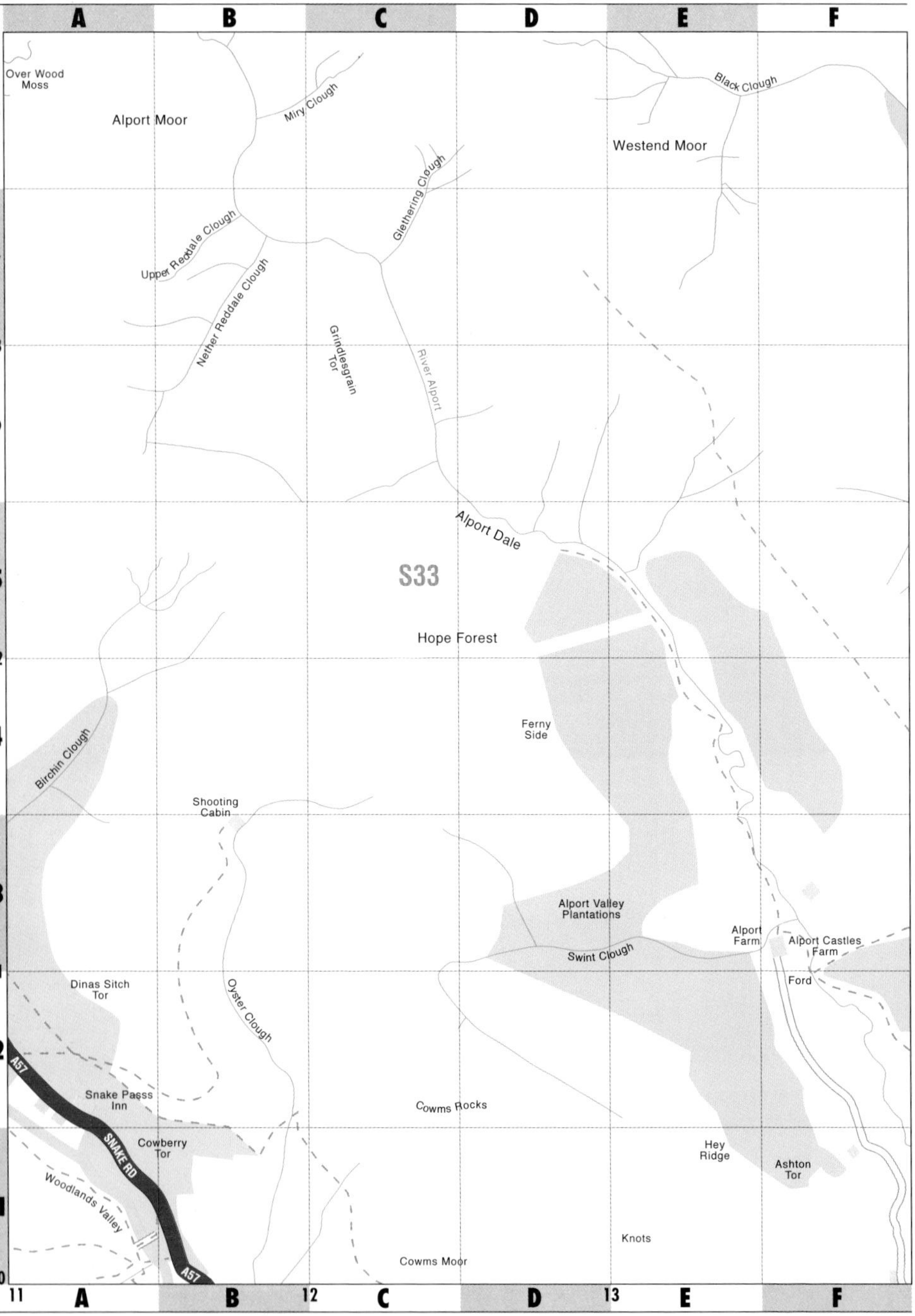

| | A | B | C | D | E | F |

Over Wood Moss

Alport Moor

Miry Clough

Black Clough

Westend Moor

Glethering Clough

Upper Reddale Clough

Nether Reddale Clough

Grindlesgrain Tor

River Alport

Alport Dale

S33

Hope Forest

Ferny Side

Birchin Clough

Shooting Cabin

Alport Valley Plantations

Alport Farm

Alport Castles Farm

Swint Clough

Ford

Oyster Clough

Dinas Sitch Tor

A57

Snake Pass Inn

Cowberry Tor

Cowms Rocks

Hey Ridge

Ashton Tor

SNAKE RD

Woodlands Valley

A57

Knots

Cowms Moor

| 11 | A | B | 12 | C | D | 13 | E | F |

19
28

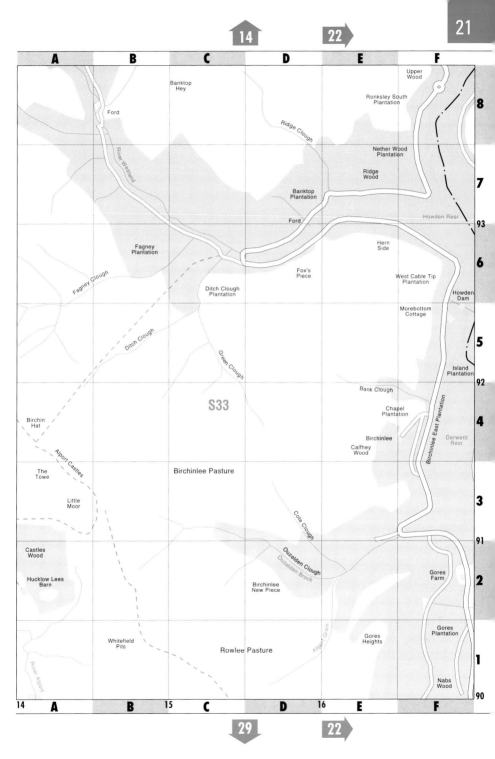

21

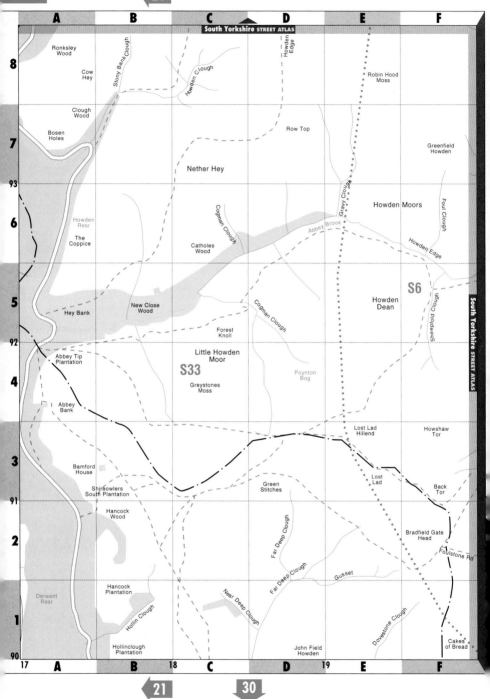

South Yorkshire STREET ATLAS

8

Ronksley Wood

Cow Hey

Stony Bank Clough

Howden Clough

Howden Edge

Robin Hood Moss

Clough Wood

Row Top

Greenfield Howden

7

Bosen Holes

93

Nether Hey

Gravy Clough

Howden Moors

Foul Clough

6

Howden Resr

Cogman Clough

Catholes Wood

Abbey Brook

Howden Edge

S6

The Coppice

5

Hey Bank

New Close Wood

Cogman Clough

Howden Dean

Sheepfold Clough

92

Abbey Tip Plantation

Forest Knoll

Little Howden Moor

Poynton Bog

4

S33

Greystones Moss

Abbey Bank

Lost Lad Hillend

Howshaw Tor

3

Bamford House

Green Stitches

Lost Lad

Back Tor

91

Shireowlers South Plantation

Hancock Wood

Bradfield Gate Head

2

Far Deep Clough

Far Deep Clough

Foulstone Rd

Hancock Plantation

Gusset

Derwent Resr

Hollin Clough

Near Deep Clough

Dovestone Clough

1

Hollinclough Plantation

John Field Howden

Cakes of Bread

90

21   30

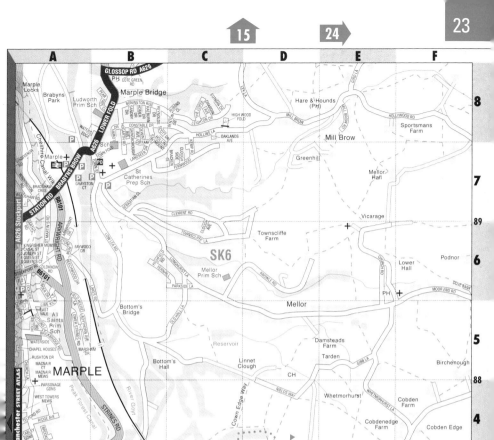

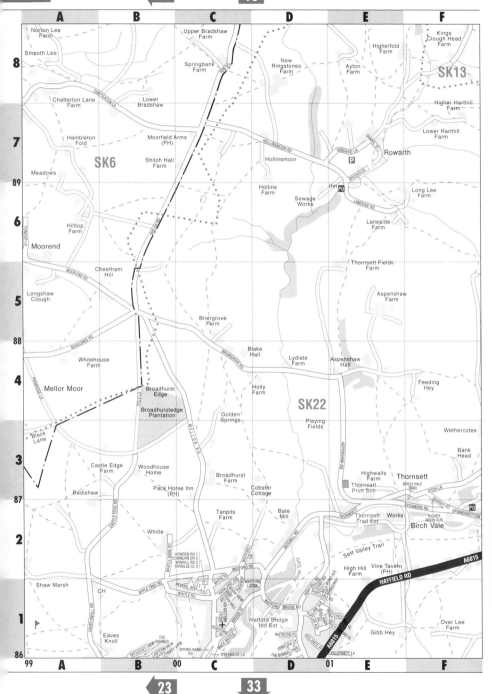

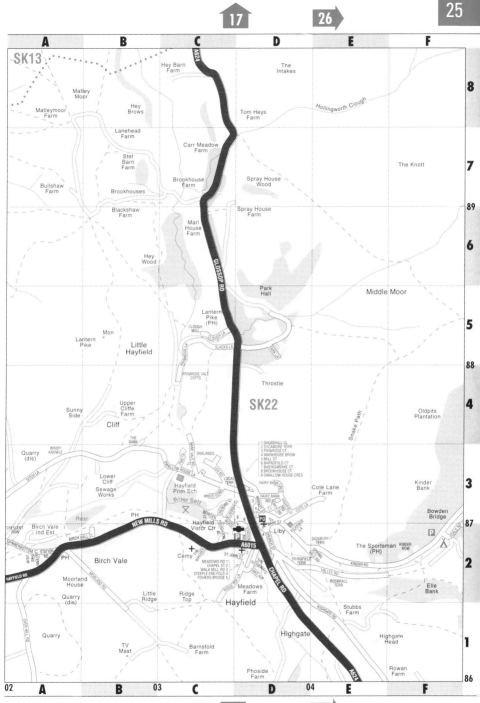

17
26

SK13

| | A | B | C | D | E | F |

Hey Barn Farm

The Intakes

Matley Moor

Hey Brows

Matleymoor Farm

Hollingworth Clough

8

Tom Heys Farm

Lanehead Farm

Carr Meadow Farm

The Knott

7

Stet Barn Farm

Spray House Wood

Brookhouse Farm

Bullshaw Farm

Brookhouses

89

Blackshaw Farm

Spray House Farm

Marl House Farm

6

Hey Wood

Park Hall

Middle Moor

Lantern Pike (PH)

5

Lantern Pike

Mon

Little Hayfield

CLOUGH MILL

CLOUGH LA

SLACKS LA

GLOSSOP RD

PRIMROSE LA

PARK LA

PRIMROSE VALE COTTS

88

Sunny Side

Upper Cliffe Farm

Throstle

SK22

Oldpits Plantation

4

Cliff

THE BANK

Quarry (dis)

WINDY KNOWLE

Lower Cliff

Sewage Works

OAKLANDS

1 SHUDEHILL CL
2 SYCAMORE TERR
3 PRIMROSE CT
4 WARNHOUSE BROW
5 MILL ST
6 BARNSFOLD CT
7 BASINGWERKE CT
8 BROOKHOUSE CT
9 SWALLOW HOUSE CRES

Kinder Bank

SITCH LA

SWALLOW HOUSE LA

BANK HALL RD

LEA RD

LUCAS TERR

WOOD GDNS

FAIRY BANK

Cote Lane Farm

Bowden Bridge

3

Hayfield Prim Sch

River Sett

FAIRY BANK

MARKET ST

COTE LA

87

Resr

PH

CRESENT ROW

Birch Vale Ind Est

NEW MILLS RD

Hayfield Vistor Ctr

Liby

DIDSBURY TERR

The Sportsman (PH)

KINDER ROW

BIRCH HALL CL

BOWDEN QUEEN

A6015

ST JOHN'S ST

SPRING

VALE RD

KINDER RD

2

SPINNERBOTTOM VIEW

LATE FIELD

STATION RD

PH

Birch Vale

Cemy

MEADOWS RD 1
CHAPEL ST 2
WALK MILL RD 3
STEEPLE END FOLD 4
FISHERS BRIDGE 5

St JOHN'S

CHAPEL RD

SPRINGFIELD TERR

ROCKHALL TERR

Elle Bank

HAYFIELD RD

Moorland House

MORLAND RD

Little Ridge

Ridge Top

Meadows Farm

Hayfield

RIDGE LA

HIGHGATE RD

Stubbs Farm

Highgate Head

Quarry (dis)

DYER HILL RD

Quarry

TV Mast

Barnsfold Farm

Highgate

Rowan Farm

1

Phoside Farm

A624

86

| 02 | A | B | 03 | C | D | 04 | E | F |

34
26

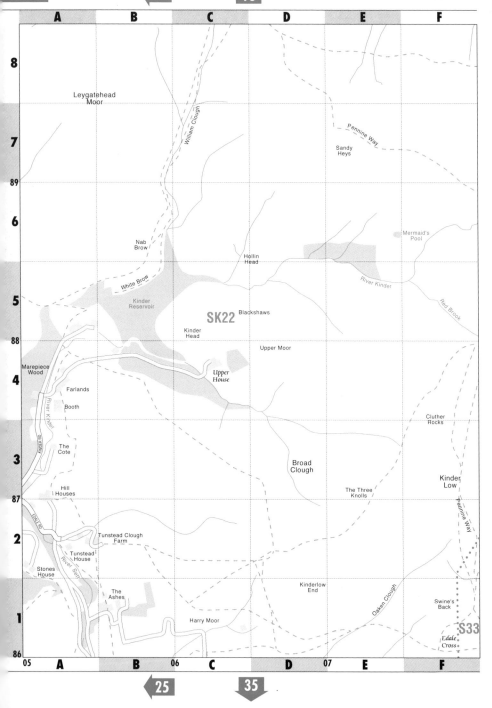

	A	B	C	D	E	F

8

Leygatehead Moor

William Clough

7

Pennine Way

Sandy Heys

89

6

Nab Brow

Mermaid's Pool

Hollin Head

White Brow

River Kinder

Red Brook

5

Kinder Reservoir

SK22 Blackshaws

Kinder Head

88

Upper Moor

Marepiece Wood

Upper House

4

Farlands

Cluther Rocks

Booth

3

The Cote

Broad Clough

Kinder Low

Hill Houses

87

The Three Knolls

Pennine Way

2

Tunstead Clough Farm

Tunstead House

River Sett

Stones House

Kinderlow End

Oaken Clough

Swine's Back

The Ashes

S33

1

Harry Moor

Edale Cross

86

05	A		B	06	C		D	07	E		F

River Kinder

EDALE RD

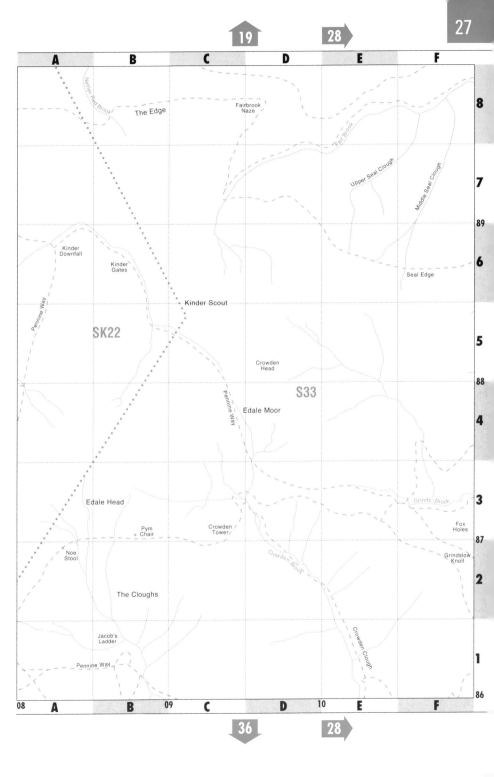

A   B   C   D   E   F

8

The Edge

Fairbrook
Naze

Nether Red Brook

Fair Brook

7

Upper Seal Clough

Middle Seal Clough

89

6

Kinder
Downfall

Kinder
Gates

Seal Edge

Pennine Way

Kinder Scout

SK22

5

Crowden
Head

88

S33

4

Pennine Way

Edale Moor

3

Edale Head

Grinds Brook

Pym
Chair

Crowden
Tower

Fox
Holes

87

Noe
Stool

Crowden Brook

Grindslow
Knoll

2

The Cloughs

Jacob's
Ladder

Crowden Clough

1

Pennine Way

86

08   A   B   09   C   D   10   E   F

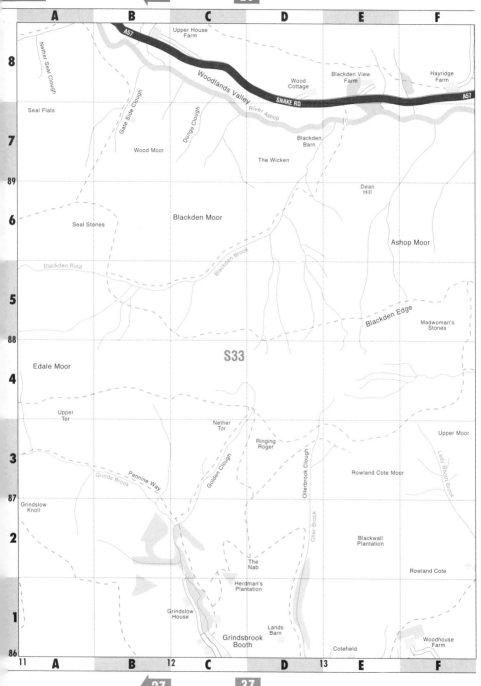

	A	B	C	D	E	F

8

Nether Seal Clough

A57

Upper House Farm

Woodlands Valley

Wood Cottage

Blackden View Farm

Hayridge Farm

SNAKE RD

A57

7

Seal Flats

Gate Side Clough

Dunge Clough

River Ashop

Blackden Barn

Wood Moor

The Wicken

89

Dean Hill

6

Seal Stones

Blackden Moor

Blackden Brook

Ashop Moor

Blackden Rind

5

Blackden Edge

Madwoman's Stones

88

S33

4

Edale Moor

Upper Tor

Nether Tor

Ringing Roger

Upper Moor

3

Grinds Brook

Pennine Way

Golden Clough

Ollerbrook Clough

Rowland Cote Moor

Lady Booth Brook

87

Grindslow Knoll

Oller Brook

2

Blackwall Plantation

Rowland Cote

The Nab

Herdman's Plantation

1

Grindslow House

Lands Barn

Grindsbrook Booth

Cotefield

Woodhouse Farm

86

11	A	B	12	C	D	13	E	F

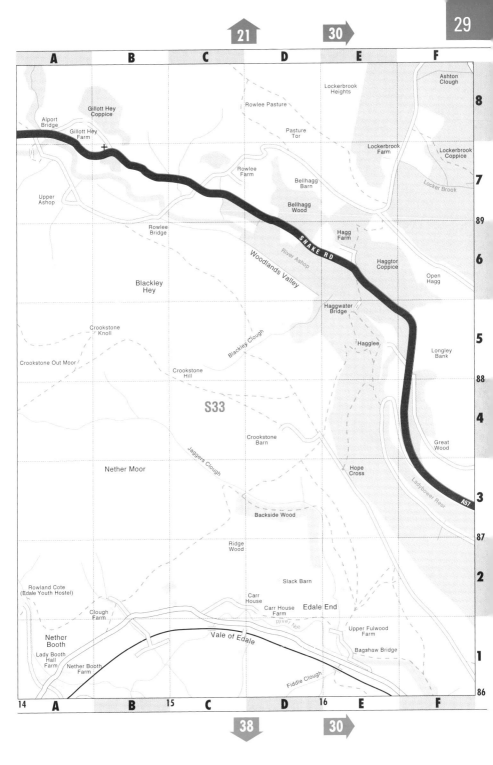

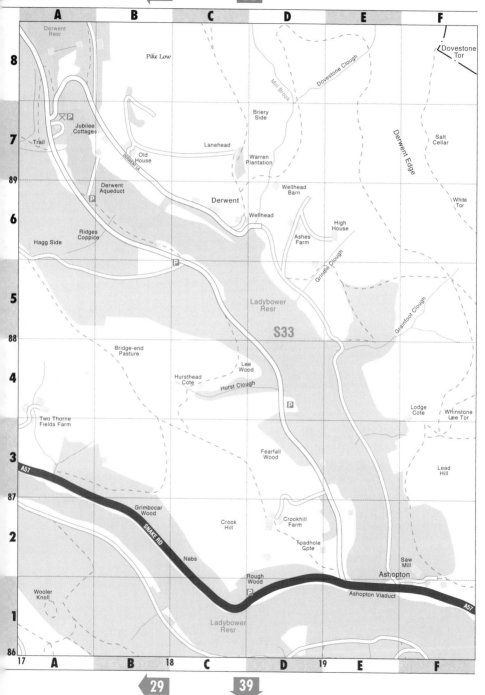

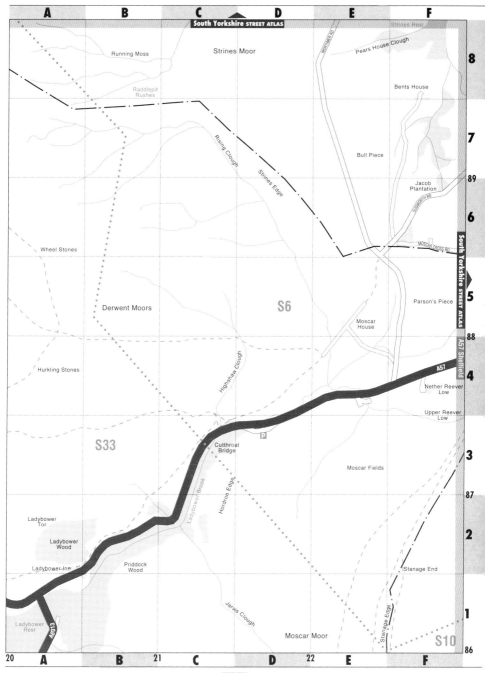

Strines Resr

Running Moss

Strines Moor

Pears House Clough

8

Raddlepit
Rushes

Bents House

Rising Clough

Strines Edge

Bull Piece

7

Jacob
Plantation

89

6

Wheel Stones

MOSCAR CROSS RD

Derwent Moors

S6

Parson's Piece

5

Moscar
House

88

Hurkling Stones

Highshaw Clough

A57

Nether Reever
Low

4

Upper Reever
Low

S33

Cutthroat
Bridge

Moscar Fields

3

Ladybower Brook

Hordron Edge

87

Ladybower
Tor

Ladybower
Wood

2

Ladybower Inn

Priddock
Wood

Stanage End

Ladybower
Resr

Jarvis Clough

Stanage Edge

1

Moscar Moor

S10

86

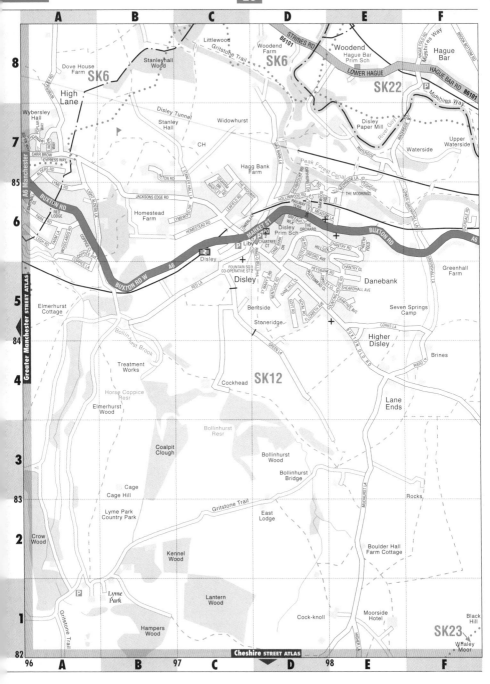

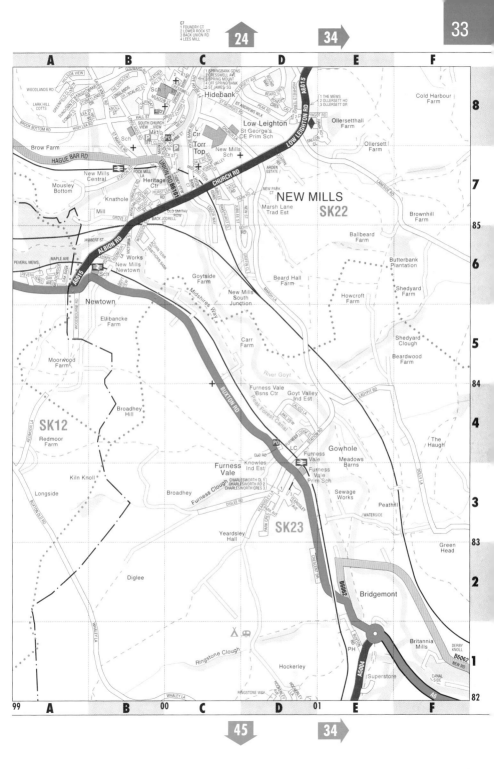

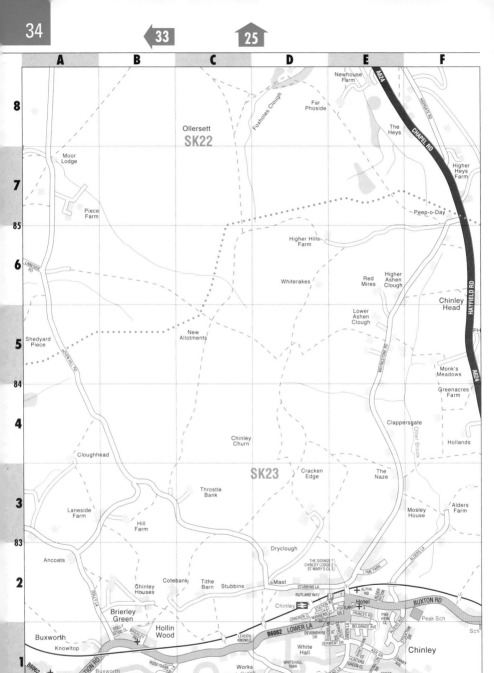

8

7

85

6

5

84

4

3

83

2

1

82

Moor Lodge

Piece Farm

Shedyard Piece

Cloughhead

Laneside Farm

Hill Farm

Ancoats

Chinley Houses

Brierley Green

Hollin Wood

Buxworth

Knowltop

Buxworth Prim Sch

Inn

Ollersett
SK22

Foxholes Clough

Far Phoside

Newhouse Farm

The Heys

Higher Heys Farm

Peep-o-Day

Higher Hills Farm

Whiterakes

Red Mires

Higher Ashen Clough

Chinley Head

Lower Ashen Clough

New Allotments

Monk's Meadows

Greenacres Farm

SK23

Chinley Churn

Clappersgate

Hollands

Cracken Edge

The Naze

Throstle Bank

Dryclough

Mosley House

Alders Farm

Cotebank

Tithe Barn

Stubbins

Mast

THE SIDINGS 1
CHINLEY LODGE 2
ST MARY'S CL 3

STUBBINS LA

RUTLAND WAY

LYME PARK

ALDERS LA

Chinley

Hotel

Alpha Rd

BUXTON RD

Peak Sch

Sch

Dolly Wood Cl

Leaden Knowle

B6062 LOWER LA

Works
Black Brook

White Hall

Whitehall Terr

Inn

Devonshire Dr

Derwent Dr

Belgrade Ave

Forge Terr

Mill

Chinley

B6062

New Rd

Station Rd

A6

Roseybank

Laneside Rd

Pinfold Rd

Maynestone Rd

Hayfield Rd

Chapel Rd

Reigate Rd

A624

A624

Otter Brook

02

03

04

33

46

A B C D E F

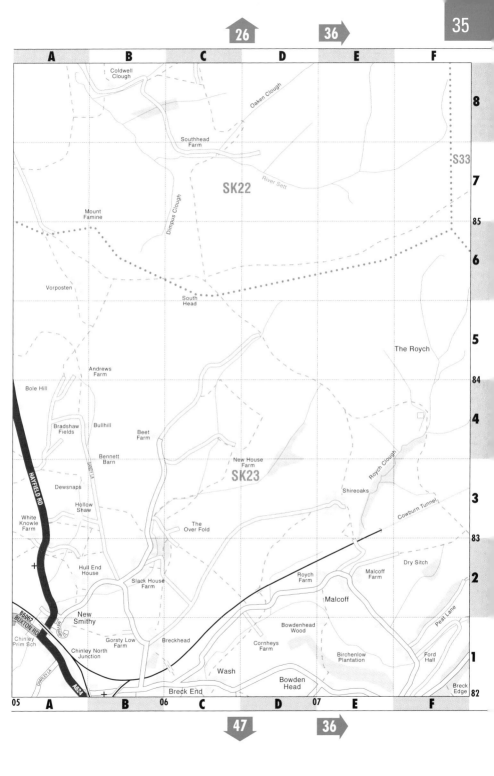

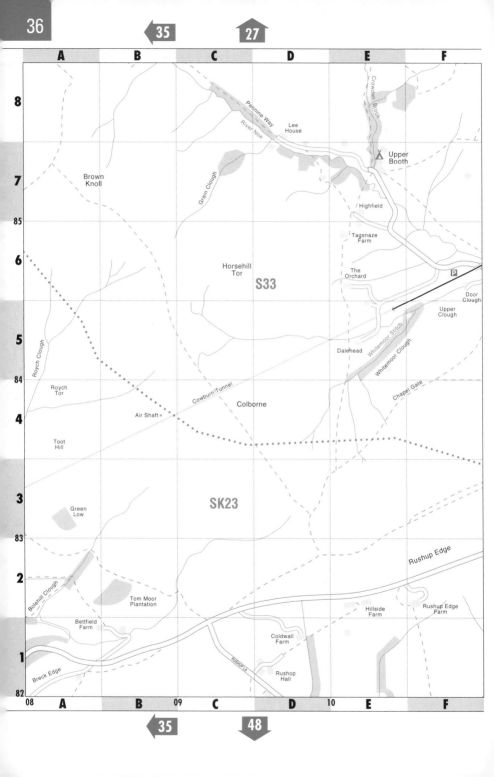

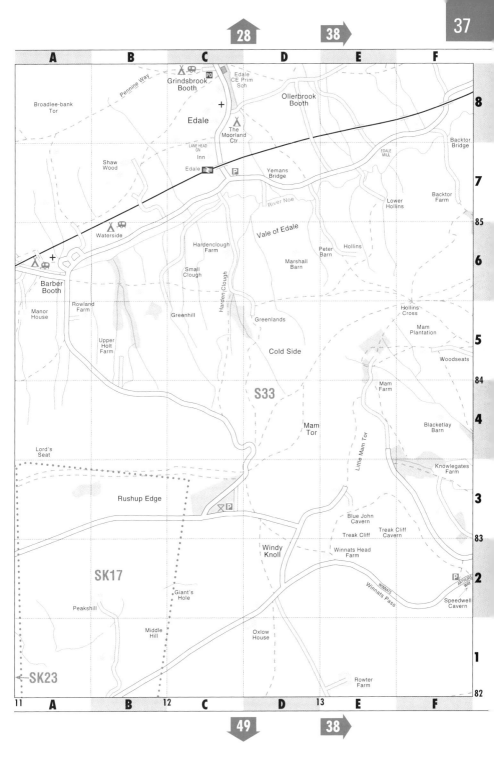

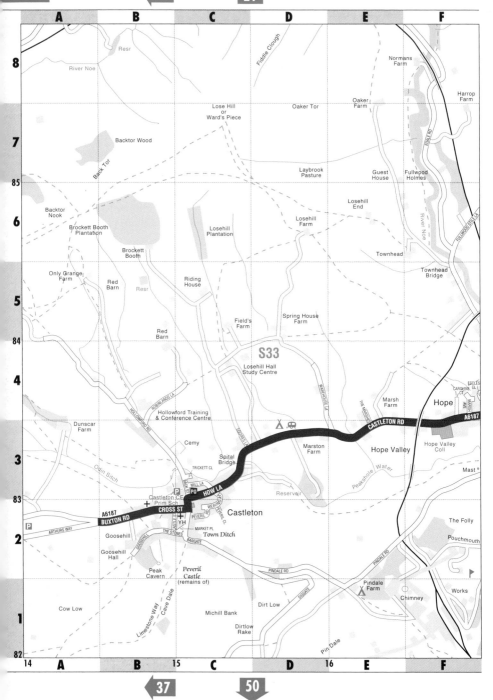

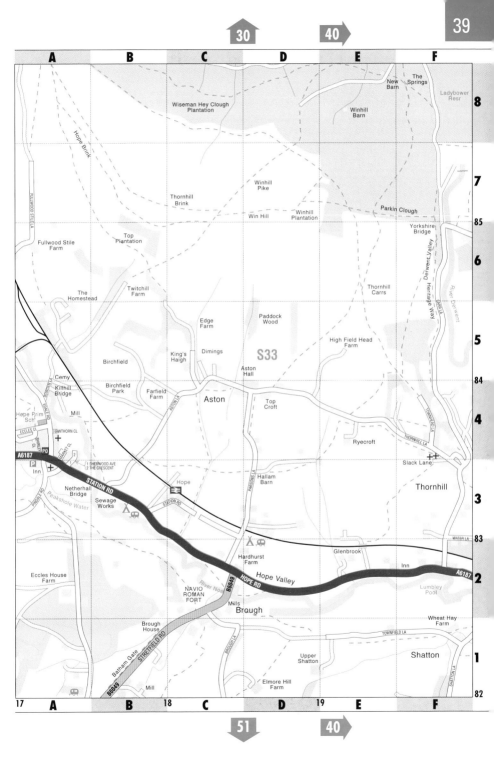

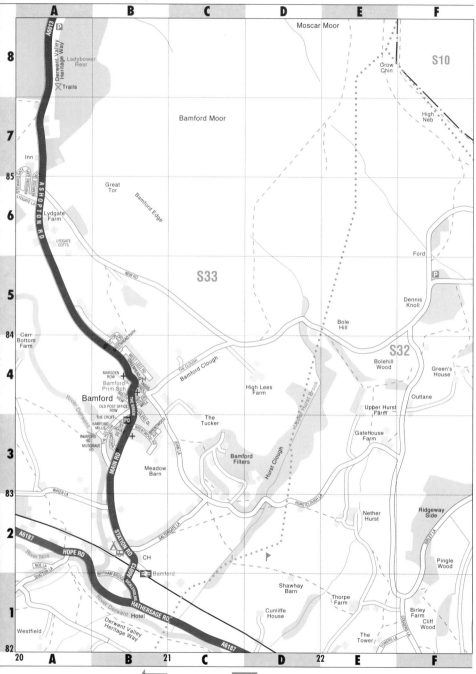

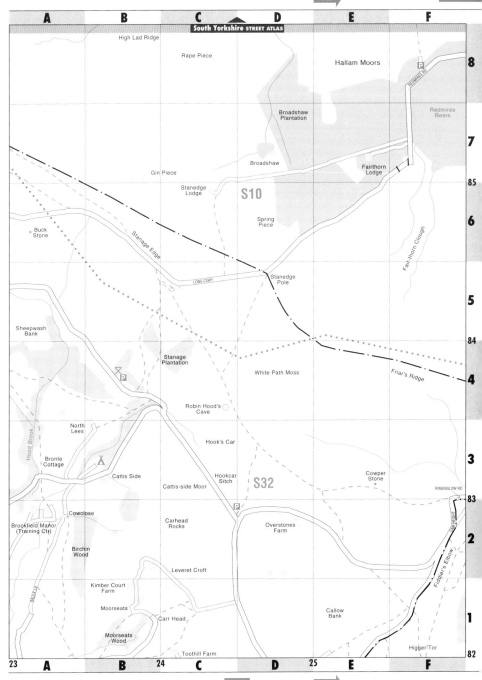

South Yorkshire STREET ATLAS

Map labels:

High Lad Ridge

Rape Piece

Hallam Moors

P

Broadshaw
Plantation

Redmires
Resrs

Gin Piece

Broadshaw

Fairthorn
Lodge

Stanedge
Lodge

S10

Spring
Piece

Buck
Stone

Stanage Edge

Fairthorn Clough

LONG CSWY

Stanedge
Pole

Sheepwash
Bank

Stanage
Plantation

White Path Moss

Friar's Ridge

P

Robin Hood's
Cave

Hook's Car

North
Lees

Hood Brook

Bronte
Cottage

Cattis Side

Hookcar
Sitch

S32

Cowper
Stone

RINGINGLOW RD

Cattis-side Moor

Brookfield Manor
(Training Ctr)

Cowclose

P

Carhead
Rocks

Overstones
Farm

Fiddler's Elbow

Birchin
Wood

Leveret Croft

Kimber Court
Farm

Moorseats

Carr Head

Callow
Bank

BRICK LA

Moorseats
Wood

Higger Tor

Toothill Farm

23   A   B   24   C   D   25   E   F

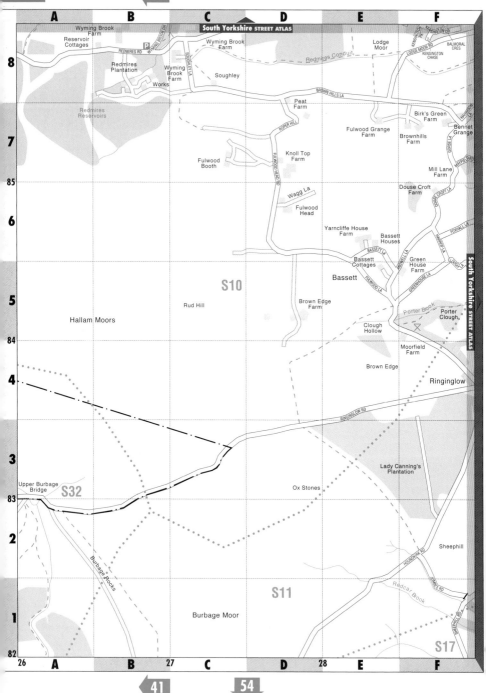

A | B | C | D | E | F

8

Wyming Brook Farm
Reservoir Cottages
REDMIRES RD
Redmires Plantation
Works
Wyming Brook Farm
Wyming Brook Farm
Soughley
Redmires Conduit
Lodge Moor
LODGE MOOR RD
KENSINGTON CHASE
BALMORAL CRES
KENSINGTON DR

7

Redmires Reservoirs
ROPER HILL
BROWN HILLS LA
Peat Farm
Fulwood Grange Farm
Birk's Green Farm
Brownhills Farm
Bennet Grange
MAYFIELD RD

85

FULWOOD HEAD RD
Fulwood Booth
Knoll Top Farm
Mill Lane Farm
Douse Croft Farm
DOUSE CROFT LA

6

Wagg La
Fulwood Head
Yarncliffe House Farm
Bassett Houses
FORNALL LA
HARPER LA

5

S10
Hallam Moors
Rud Hill
Brown Edge Farm
Bassett Cottages
BASSETT LA
Bassett
FULWOOD LA
Green House Farm
GREENHOUSE LA
Porter Brook
Porter Clough

84

Clough Hollow
Moorfield Farm
Brown Edge
Ringinglow

4

RINGINGLOW RD

3

Lady Canning's Plantation

83

Upper Burbage Bridge
S32
Ox Stones

2

BURBAGE ROCKS
Sheephill
HOUNDKIRK RD
Redcar Brook

1

Burbage Moor
S11
S17
SHEEPHILL RD

82

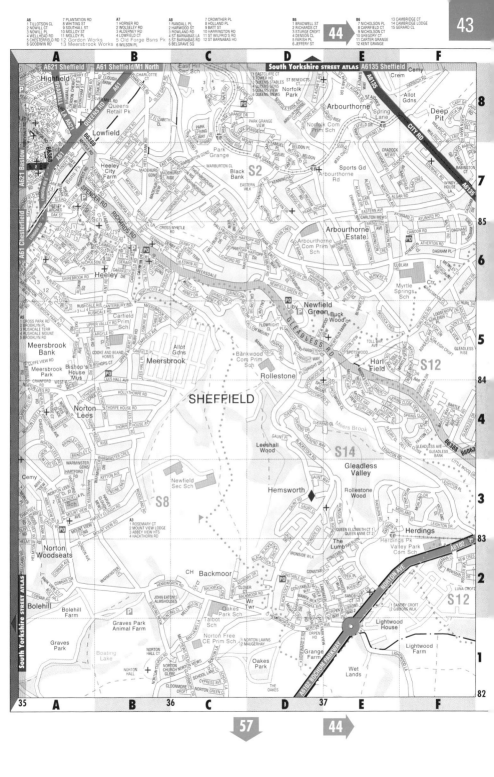

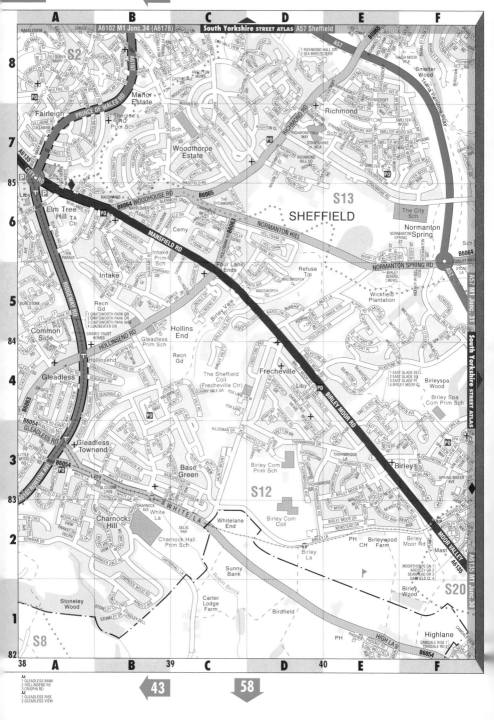

SHEFFIELD

S13

S2

S12

S20

S8

A4
1 GLEADLESS BANK
2 HOLLINSEND RD
3 CRISPIN RD
A3
1 GLEADLESS RISE
2 GLEADLESS VIEW

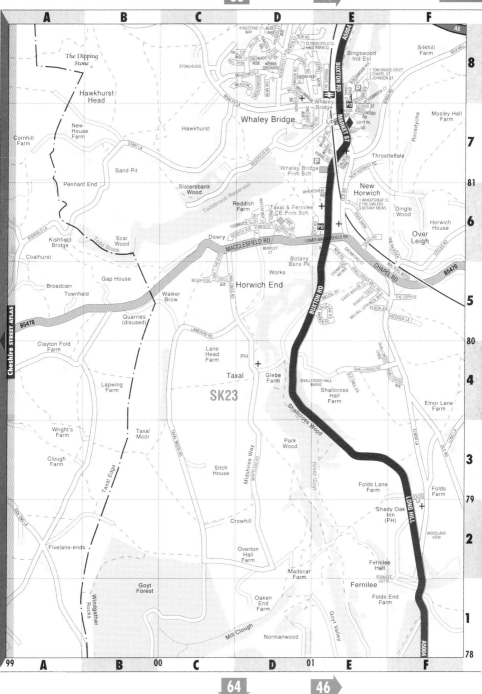

45
34

A · B · C · D · E · F

8

7

81

6

5

80

4

3

79

2

1

78

SILK HILL
A6
LANESEND COTTS
WESTERN LA
Crist
Portobello

Whitehough
ECCLES FARM
A6
Sewage Works

Eccles Fold
Eccles House
Whitehough Head
WHITEBOROUGH HEAD LA
A6
Laneside

Moseley Hall Farm
Eccles Pike
Lidgate
Hallhill Farm
Hallhill

Sunart
Top Eccles Farm
ECCLES RD
Digleach Farm
Lower Courses Farm

Horwich Farm
Ollerenshaw Hall
Hilltop
Lydgate
Higher Crossings

Woodside Farm
Bradshaw Hall Farm
Roeside Farm
Lower Crossings

CHAPEL RD
MELTON LA
Sparkbottom Farm
SK23
B5470

Randal Carr Brook
Canal Feeder
THE PEAKS
MANCHESTER RD
PH
Tunstead Milton
Tomlane
TOM LA
CH
Newfield Farm
PH
MANCHESTER RD
Cockyard
Marsh Hall

Cadster Farm
P
Meveril Farm
Combs Reservoir
Bridgefield

Tunstead Farm
LONG LA
Meveril Brook
COMBS RD
Owlgreave Farm

Ladder Hill
Spire Hollins Farm

Black Edge Plantation
Television Station
Thorney Lee
THE PASTURE
PH
Brook Houses

Long Edge Plantation
OLD RD
Haylee House
Pritchard Green Farm
P
Whitehills

Overhill Farm
LESS RES LA
RIDGE LA
Combs Inf Sch
Combs

Heylee Farm
Rye Flatt Farm
COWLOW LA

02 · A · B · 03 · C · D · 04 · E · F

45
65

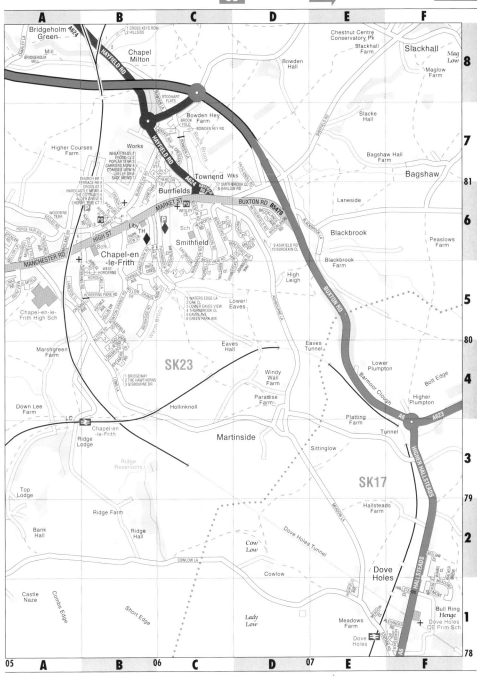

35 48

66 48

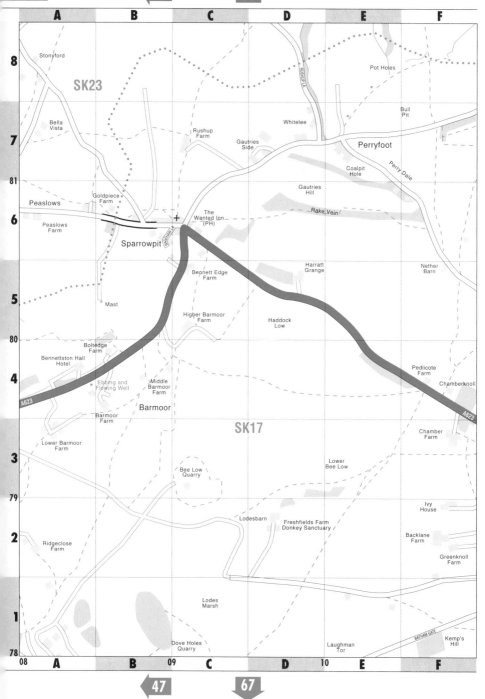

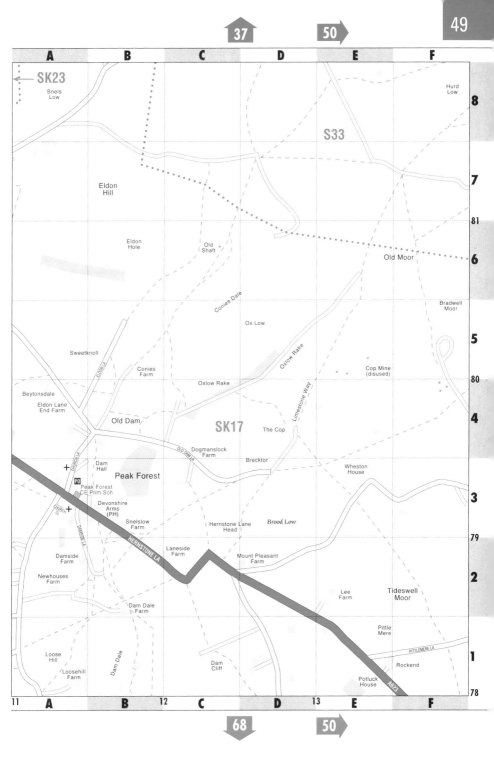

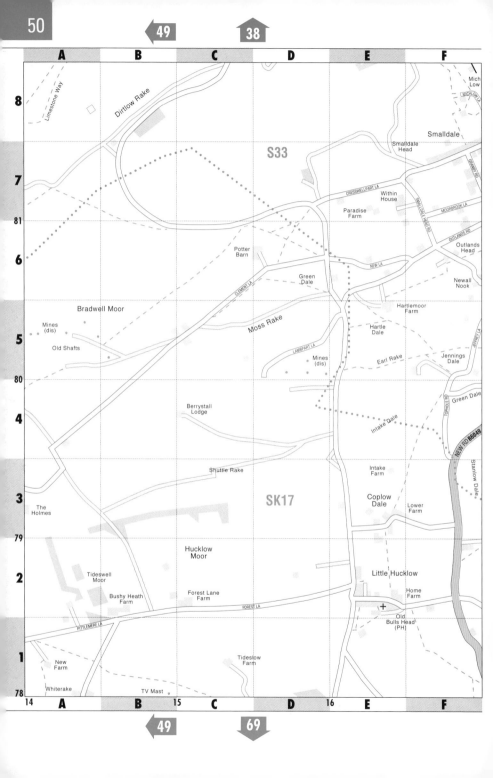

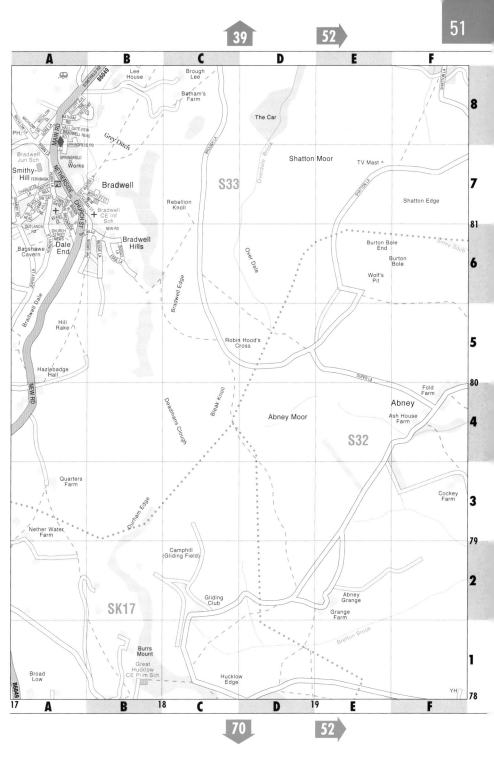

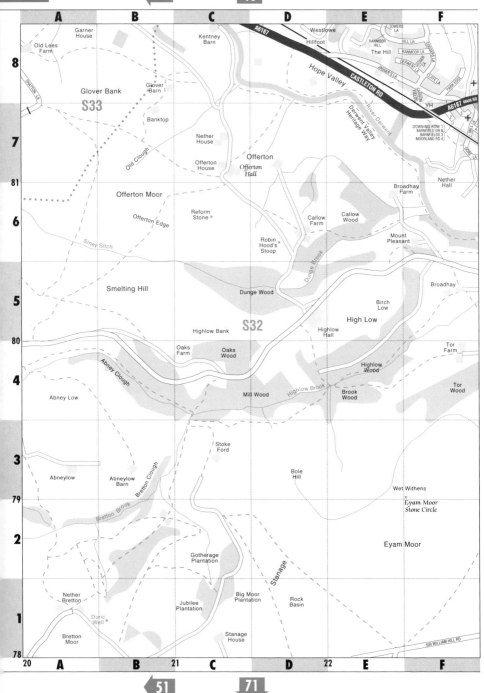

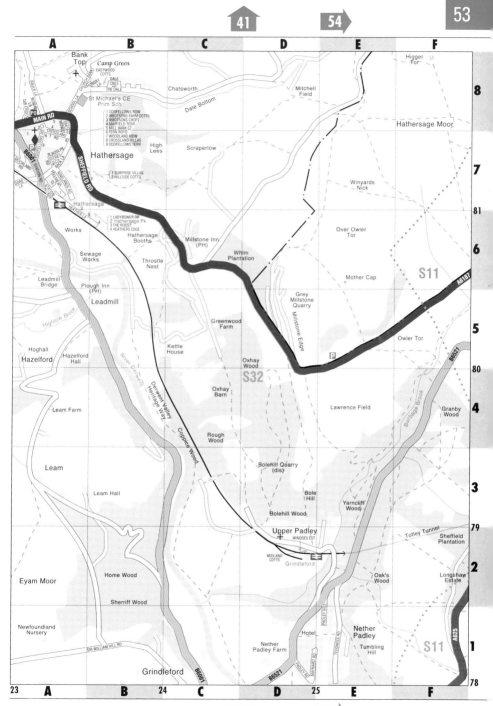

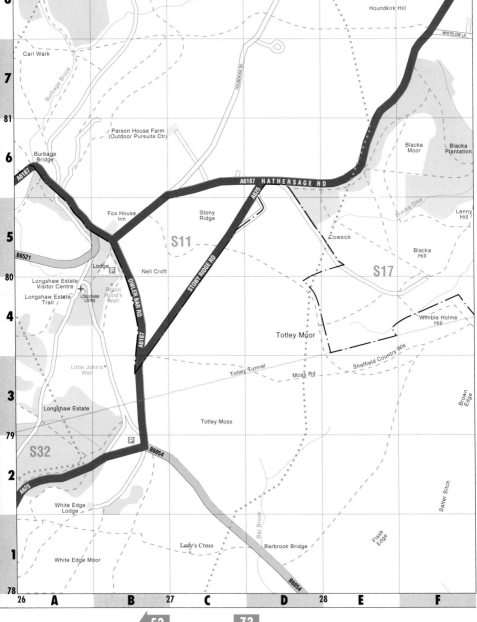

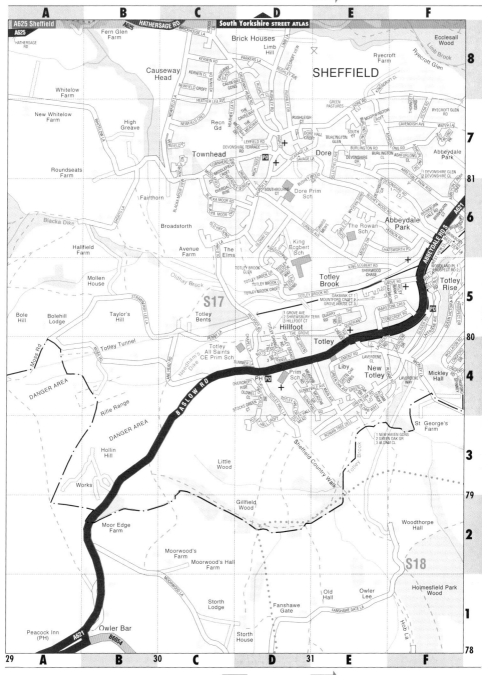

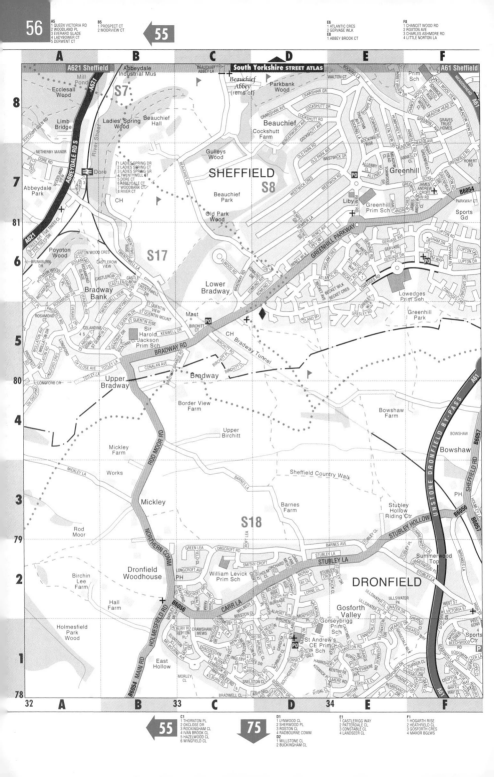

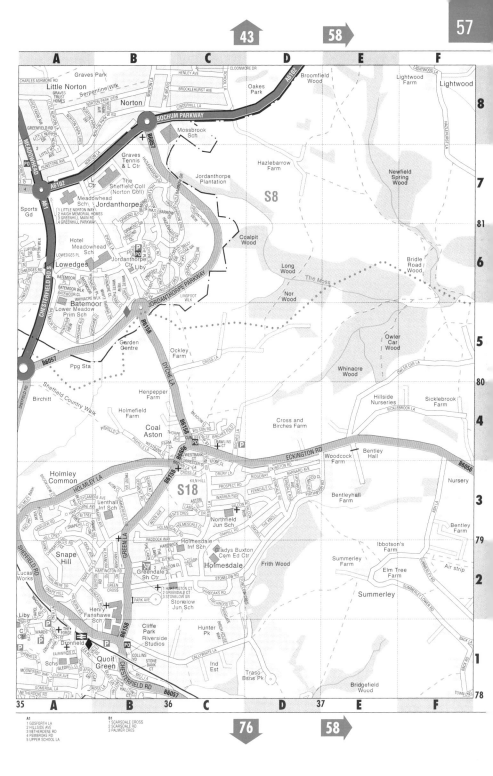

A1
1 GOSFORTH LA
2 HILLSIDE AVE
3 NETHERDENE RD
4 PEMBROKE RD
5 UPPER SCHOOL LA

B1
1 SCARSDALE CROSS
2 SCARSDALE RD
3 PALMER CRES

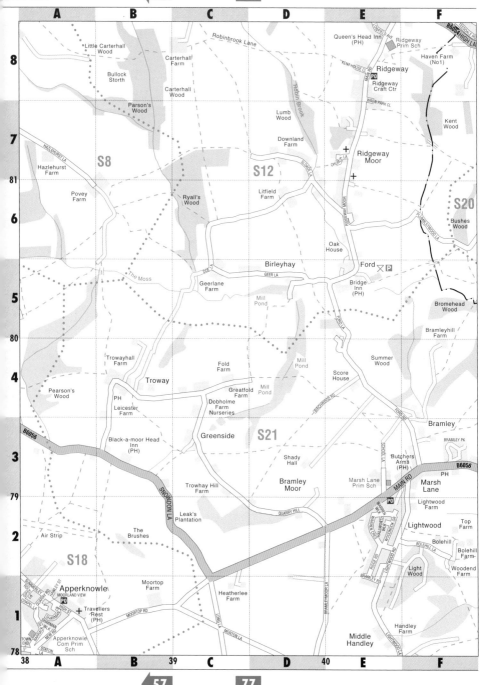

A B C D E F

8

Little Carterhall Wood

Robinbrook Lane

Queen's Head Inn (PH)

Ridgeway Prim Sch

B6054 HIGH LA

Haven Farm (No1)

Carterhall Farm

Ridgeway

Bullock Storth

KENT HOUSE CL

Ridgeway Craft Ctr

Carterhall Wood

WREN PARK CL

Kent Wood

Parson's Wood

Robin Brook

Lumb Wood

7

HAZLEHURST LA

S8

Downland Farm

SLACK LA

Ridgeway Moor

81

Hazlehurst Farm

S12

RIDGEWAY MOOR

S20

Povey Farm

Ryall's Wood

Litfield Farm

CHURCH LA

6

Bushes Wood

PLUMBLEY WOOD LA

Oak House

5

The Moss

DICK LA

Geerlane Farm

GEER LA

Birleyhay

Ford ✈ P

Bridge Inn (PH)

Bromehead Wood

Mill Pond

FORD LA

80

Bramleyhill Farm

Trowayhall Farm

Fold Farm

Mill Pond

Summer Wood

4

Pearson's Wood

Troway

Greatfold Farm

Mill Pond

Score House

BIRCHWOOD RD

FORD RD

Bramley

PH

Leicester Farm

Dobholme Farm Nurseries

BRAMLEY PK

Black-a-moor Head Inn (PH)

Greenside

S21

Butchers Arms (PH)

PH

B6056

3

B6056

Shady Hall

SCHOOL LA

Marsh Lane Prim Sch

MAIN RD

Marsh Lane

79

SNOWDON LA

Trowhay Hill Farm

Bramley Moor

QUARRY HILL

PO

Lightwood Farm

Lightwood

Top Farm

2

Air Strip

The Brushes

Leak's Plantation

BOLEHILL LA

Bolehill

Bolehill Farm

S18

RIDGE RD

Light Wood

Woodend Farm

Apperknowle

PO

MOORLAND VIEW

Moortop Farm

Heatherlee Farm

LONG LA

MORTON LA

BRAMLEY MOOR LA

BRAMLEY RD

LIGHTWOOD LA

1

Travellers Rest (PH)

MOORTOP RD

Handley Farm

78

TOWN END

STATION LA

Apperknowle Com Prim Sch

Middle Handley

38 A B 39 C D 40 E F

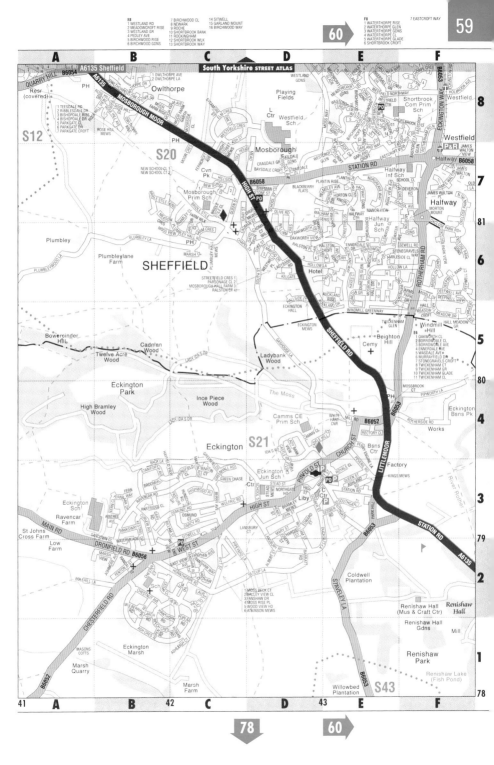

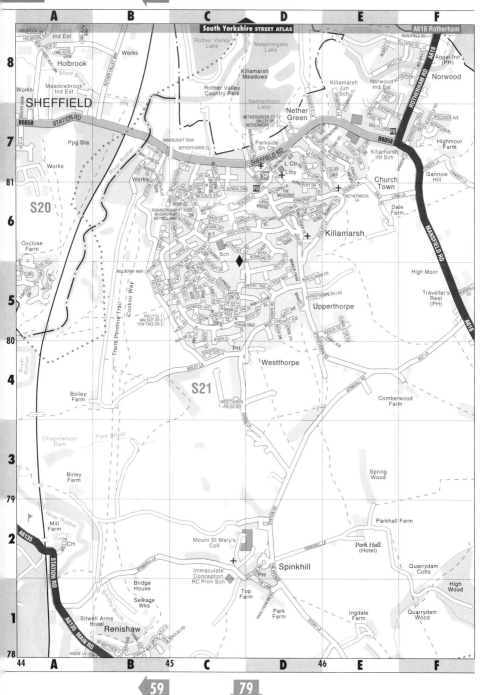

South Yorkshire STREET ATLAS

A618 Rotherham

59

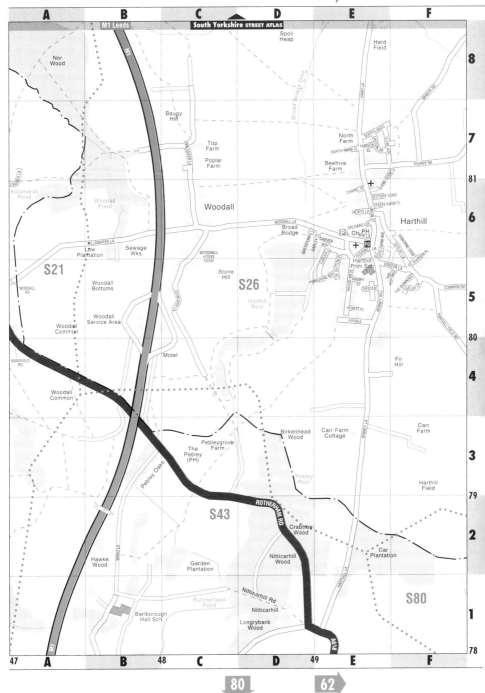

Spoil Heap

Hard Field

8

Nor Wood

Broad Bridge Dike

7

Baugy Hill

North Farm

Hard La

Manor Rd

Top Farm

Northlands

Hudson Cl

Glebe Av

Thorpe Rd

Valdera La

Poplar Farm

North Farm La

Beehive Farm

Chapel Fd

Rectory Gdns

81

Killamarsh Pond

Dirt La

Woodall Pond

Woodall

Street Farm Cl

Jackys La

Harthill

6

Woodall La

Orchard Lee

Broad Bridge

PL Ctr PH

Carver Way

Osborne Croft

Sellie Ct

Killamarsh La

Low Plantation

Sewage Wks

Greystones

Dance Ct

Carver Way

Sutton La

Doghill La

Harthill Prim Sch

Doctor La

The Downings

Gatley Pl

S21

Woodall House Farm

Firgrove Way

Prior Mede

Priory Cl

Winney Hill

De Warren Pl

Common Rd

Woodall Rd

Woodall Bottoms

Stone Hill

S26

Hewitt Pl

Crescent

Firvale

Harthill Field Rd

5

Harthill Resr

80

Woodall Service Area

Woodall Common

Motel

Fir Hill

4

Mansfield Rd

Woodall Common

Birkenhead Wood

Carr Farm Cottage

Winney La

Carr Farm

3

Pebleygrove Farm

The Pebley (PH)

Pebley Resr

Harthill Field

Pebley Oaks

S43

ROTHERHAM RD

79

Crabtree Wood

Car Plantation

2

Ward La

Hawke Wood

Garden Plantation

Nitticarhill Wood

Harthill La

S80

Butcherlawn Pond

Nitticarhill Rd

Nitticarhill

1

Barlborough Hall Sch

Longrybank Wood

A618

78

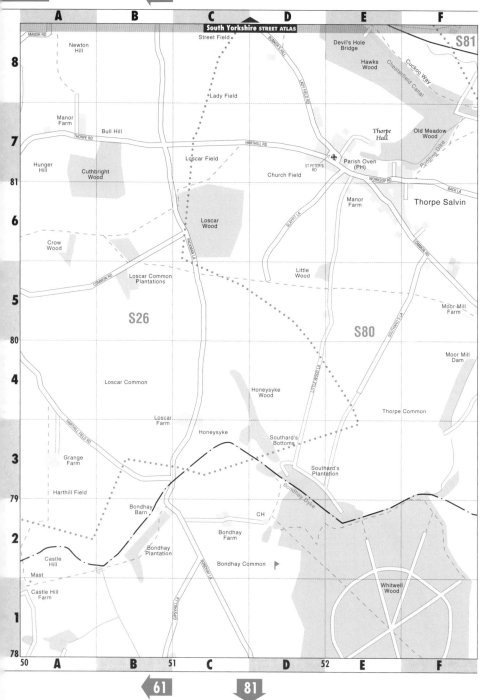

South Yorkshire STREET ATLAS

S81

8

MANOR RD

Newton
Hill

Street Field

Devil's Hole
Bridge

Hawks
Wood

Cuckoo Way

Chesterfield Canal

Lady Field

BURGESS HILL

LADY FIELD RD

7

Manor
Farm

Bull Hill

THORPE RD

HARTHILL RD

Loscar Field

St PETER'S
RD

Thorpe
Hall

Parish Oven
(PH)

Old Meadow
Wood

Pudding Dike

81

Hunger
Hill

Cuthbright
Wood

Church Field

Manor
Farm

WORKSOP RD

BACK LA

Thorpe Salvin

6

Crow
Wood

Loscar
Wood

PACKMAN LA

SLAYPIT LA

COMMON RD

5

Loscar Common
Plantations

COMMON RD

Little
Wood

LITTLE WOOD LA

SOUTHARD LA

Moor Mill
Farm

S26

S80

80

4

Loscar Common

Honeysyke
Wood

Thorpe Common

Moor Mill
Dam

3

HARTHILL FIELD RD

Grange
Farm

Loscar
Farm

Honeysyke

Southard's
Bottoms

Southard's
Plantation

79

Harthill Field

Bondhay
Barn

CH

Bondhay Dyke

2

Bondhay
Plantation

Bondhay
Farm

Bondhay Common

Castle
Hill

Mast

BONDHAY LA

GIPSYHILL LA

Whitwell
Wood

1

Castle Hill
Farm

78

50 **A** **B** 51 **C** **D** 52 **E** **F**

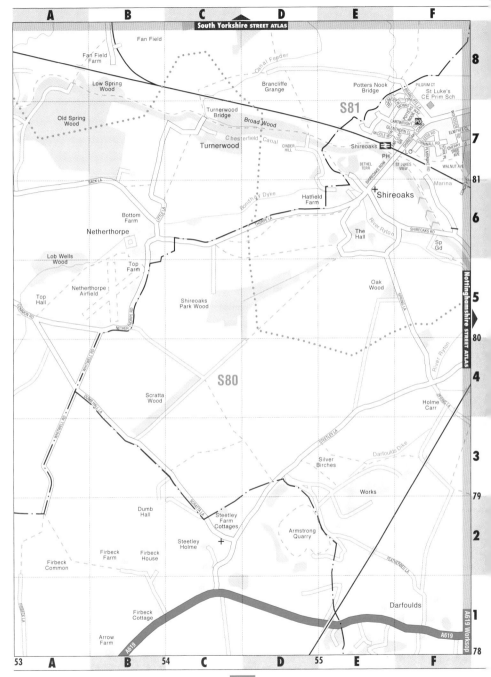

Nottinghamshire STREET ATLAS

A619 Worksop

A 53   **B** 54   **C**   **D** 55   **E**   **F**

8
7
81
6
5
80
4
3
79
2
1
78

Fan Field
Fan Field Farm
Low Spring Wood
Old Spring Wood
Turnerwood Bridge
Broad Wood
Chesterfield Canal
Turnerwood
Brancliffe Grange
Canal Feeder
Potters Nook Bridge
St Luke's CE Prim Sch
PILGRIM CT
S81
CARTWRIGHT
Shireoaks
PH
LO
BETHEL TERR
ST LUKES VIEW
WALNUT AVE
Marina
Shireoaks
BACK LA
LITTLE LA
Bondhay Dyke
Hatfield Farm
CINDER HILL
The Hall
River Ryton
SHIREOAKS RD
Sp Gd
Bottom Farm
Netherthorpe
Lob Wells Wood
Top Farm
Netherthorpe Airfield
Shireoaks Park Wood
Oak Wood
SPRING LA
Top Hall
COMMON RD
NETHER
THORPE RD
WHITWELL RD
River Ryton
S80
Scratta Wood
Holme Carr
SPRING LA
STEETLEY LA
Silver Birches
Darfoulds Dike
RUMBLING LA
Dumb Hall
SCRATTA LA
Steetley Farm Cottages
Works
Armstrong Quarry
Steetley Holme
Firbeck Farm
Firbeck House
Firbeck Common
Darfoulds
FEATHERBED LA
TIBBECK LA
Firbeck Cottage
Arrow Farm
A619

82

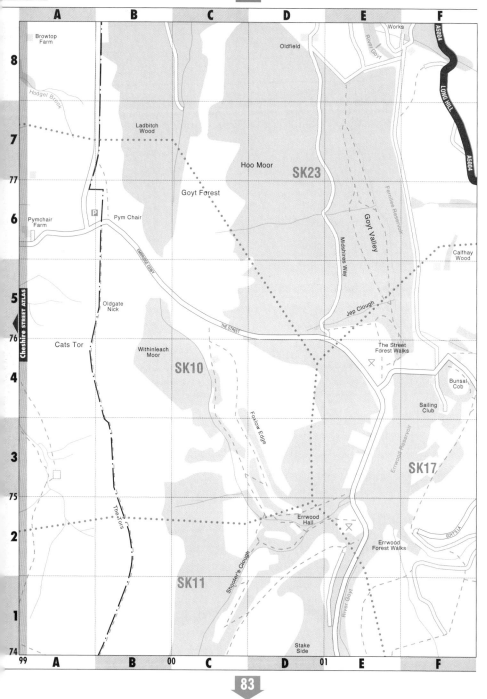

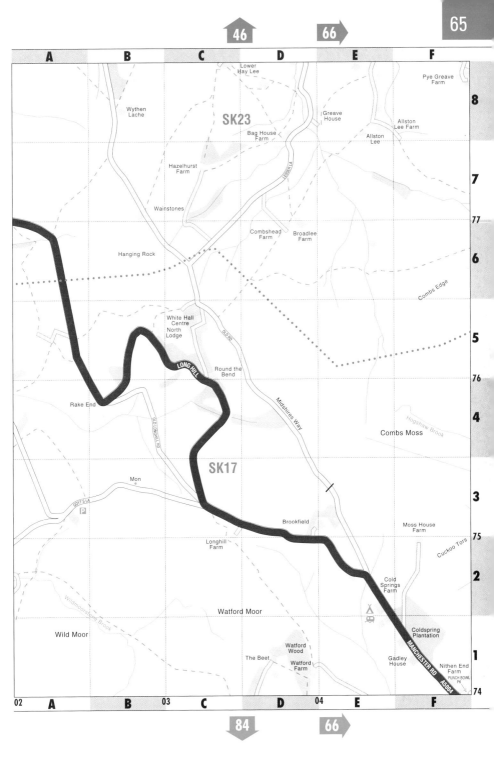

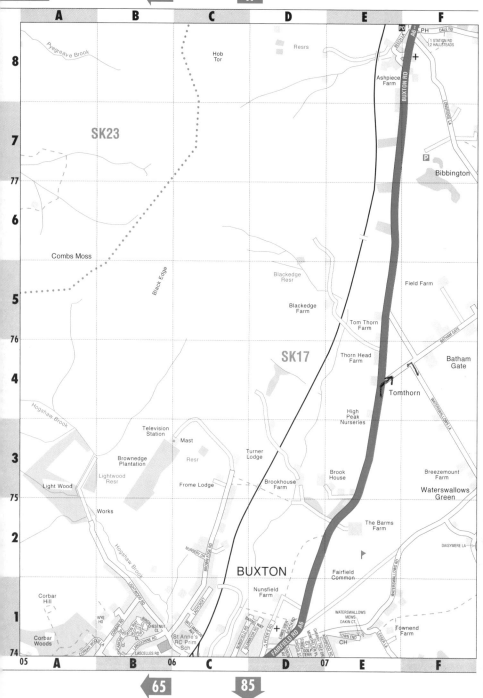

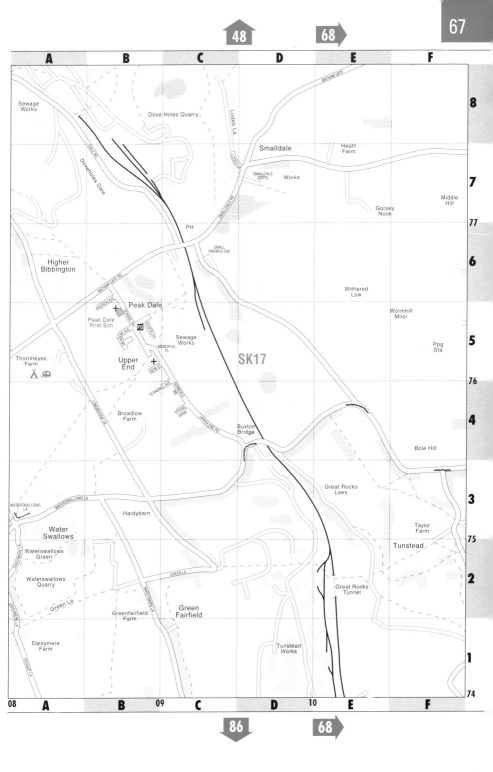

A B C D E F

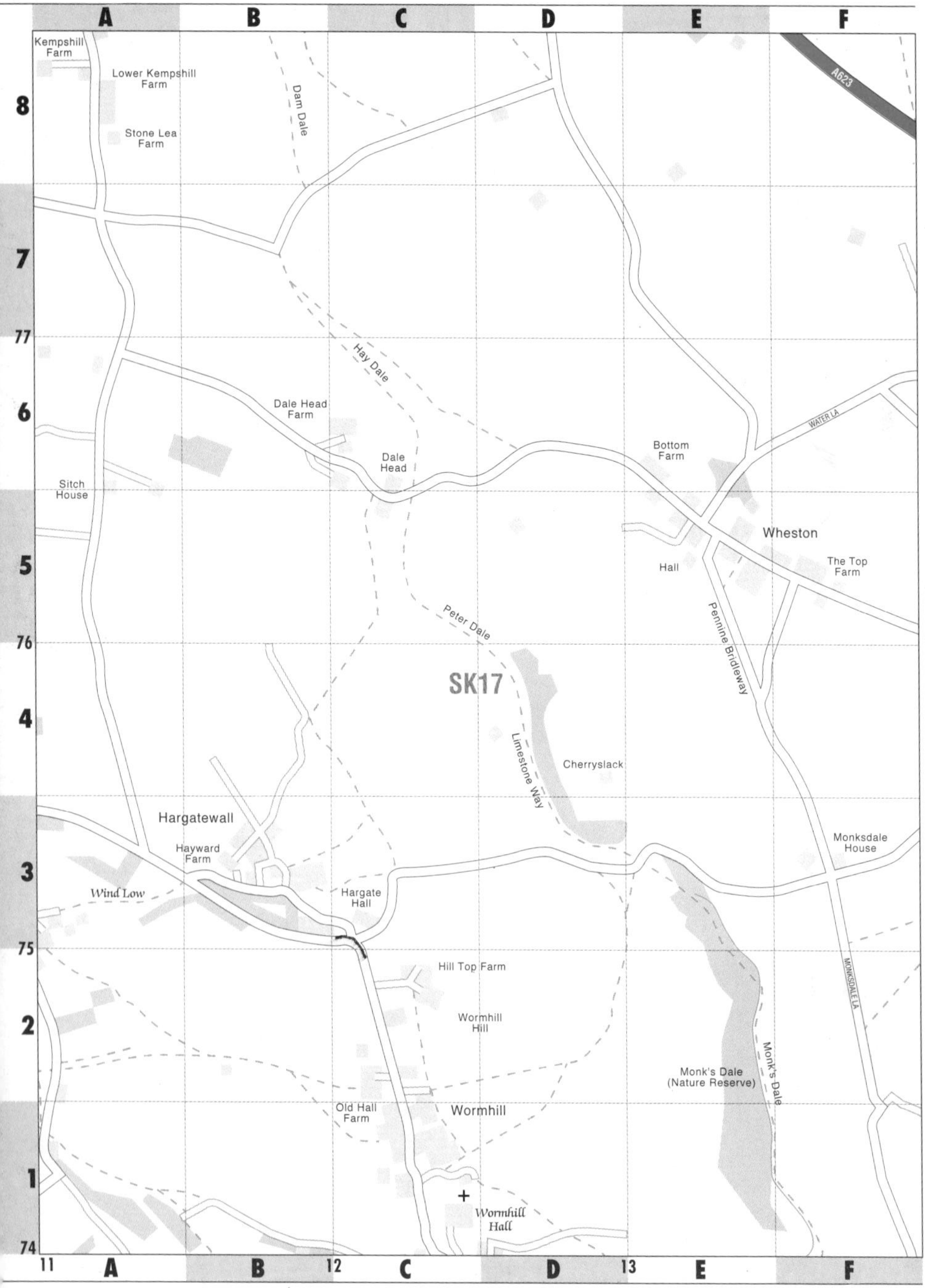

8

Kempshill Farm

Lower Kempshill Farm

Stone Lea Farm

Dam Dale

A623

7

77

Hay Dale

6

Dale Head Farm

Dale Head

Sitch House

Bottom Farm

WATER LA

Wheston

5

Hall

The Top Farm

Peter Dale

Pennine Bridleway

76

SK17

4

Limestone Way

Cherryslack

Hargatewall

Hayward Farm

Monksdale House

3

Wind Low

Hargate Hall

Hill Top Farm

75

Wormhill Hill

MONKSDALE LA

2

Monk's Dale

Monk's Dale (Nature Reserve)

Old Hall Farm

Wormhill

1

+ Wormhill Hall

74

11 A B 12 C D 13 E F

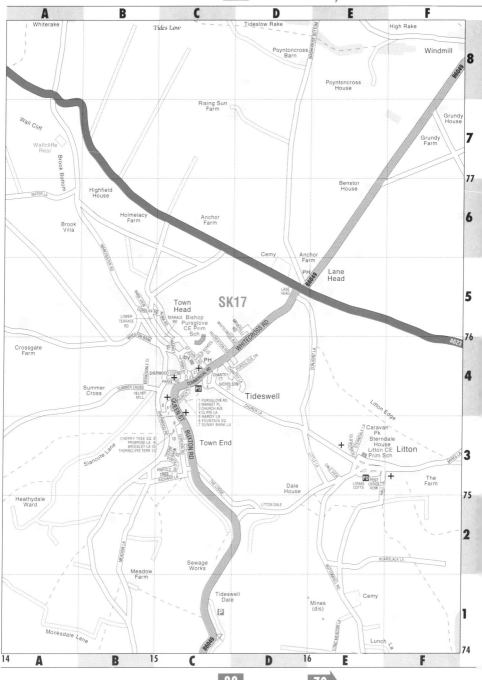

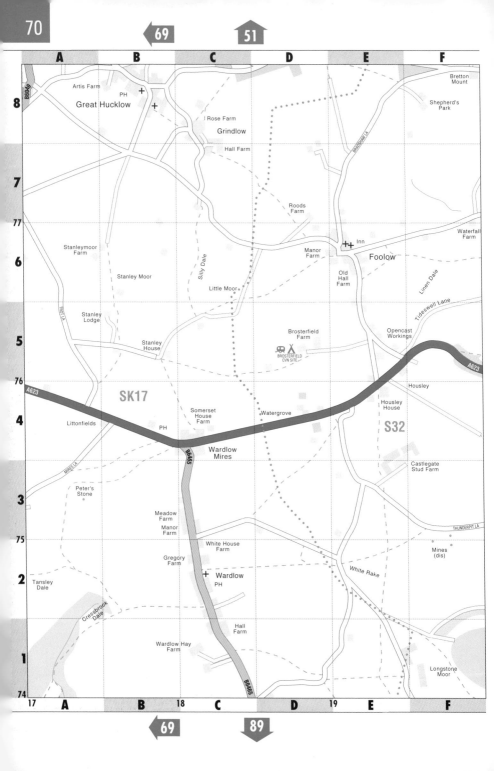

A B C D E F

8

Artis Farm

PH

Great Hucklow

Rose Farm

Grindlow

Bretton Mount

Shepherd's Park

Hall Farm

7

77

Stanleymoor Farm

Roods Farm

Waterfall Farm

BRADSHAW LA

6

Stanley Moor

Silly Dale

Manor Farm

Inn

Foolow

Little Moor

Old Hall Farm

Linen Dale

Stanley Lodge

Tideswell Lane

5

Stanley House

Brosterfield Farm

Opencast Workings

BROSTERFIELD CVN SITE

Housley

76

A623

SK17

Housley House

4

Littonfields

PH

Somerset House Farm

Watergrove

S32

A623

Wardlow Mires

Castlegate Stud Farm

MIRES LA

B6465

3

Peter's Stone

THUNDERPIT LA

Meadow Farm

Manor Farm

75

White House Farm

Mines (dis)

Gregory Farm

White Rake

2

Tansley Dale

Wardlow

PH

Cressbrook Dale

Hall Farm

Longstone Moor

1

Wardlow Hay Farm

B6465

74

17 A 18 B C 18 D 19 E F

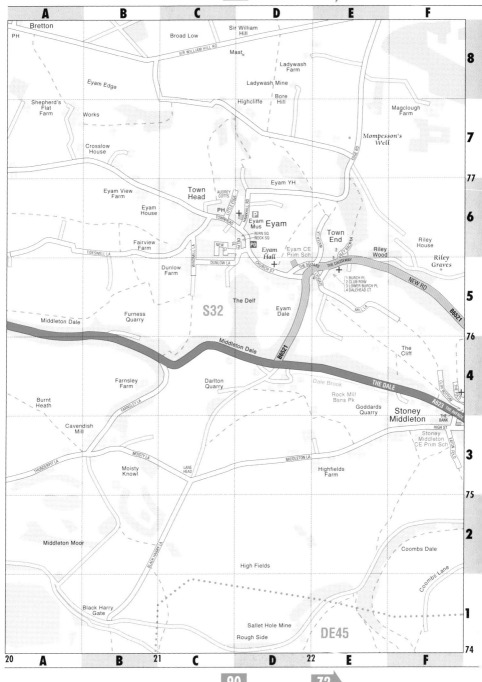

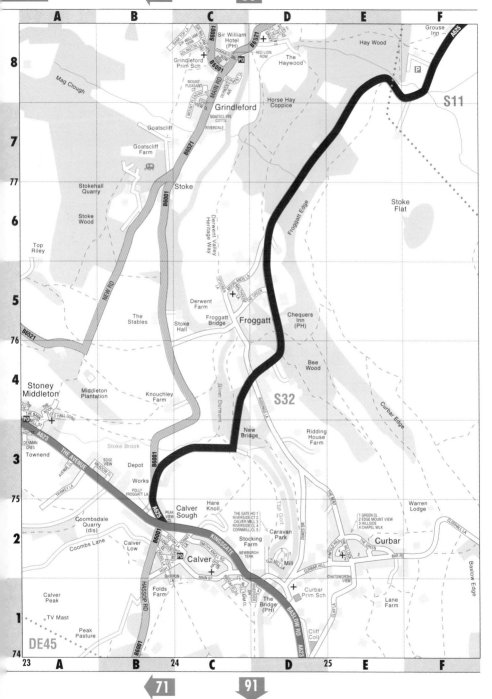

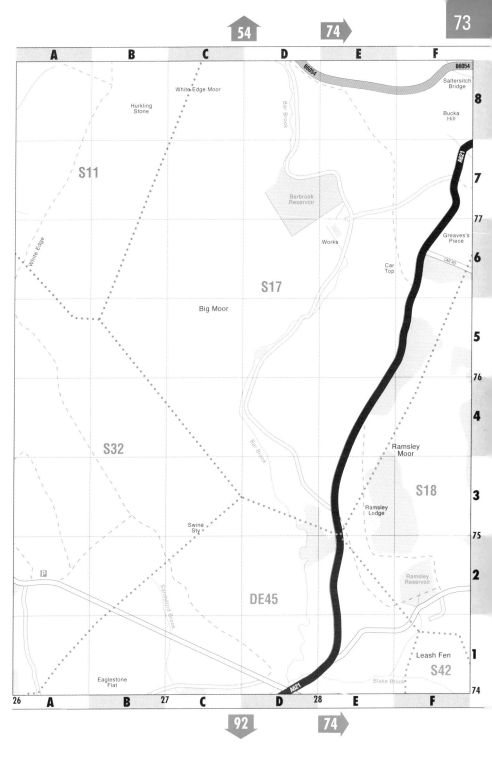

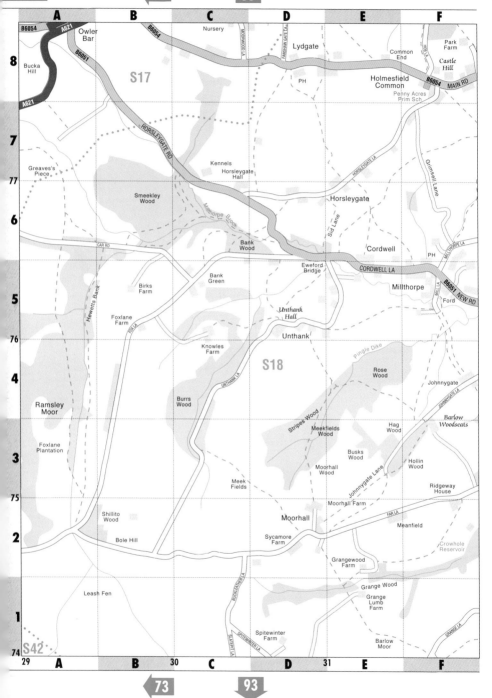

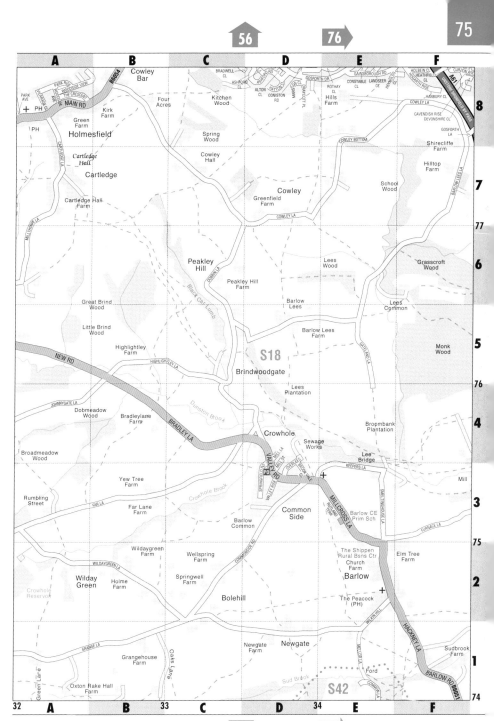

56
76

A **B** **C** **D** **E** **F**

Cowley Bar

PARK AVE
VICARAGE PL
PARK RISE
WOODSIDE VIEW
THE CRESCENT
B6054
Kirk Farm
Four Acres
Kitchen Wood
BRADWELL CL
ASHFORD CL
HATTON CL
ALTON CL
CONISTON RD
FOSTON CL
DRAYCOTT PL
ROSSLYN CL
GOSFORTH DR
ROTHAY CL
Hills Farm
CONSTABLE CL
LANDSEER DE
GAINSBOROUGH RD
HEATHFIELD CL
HOLBEIN CL
MCCARTY RISE
CURZON CL
A61

8

PH
MAIN RD
Green Farm
Holmesfield
Spring Wood
COWLEY BOTTOM
CAVENDISH RISE
DEVONSHIRE CL
HANBURY CL
COWLEY LA
GOSFORTH LA
Shirecliffe Farm

PH
CARTLEDGE LA
Cartledge Hall
Cowley Hall
School Wood
Hilltop Farm

7

Cartledge
MILLTHORPE LA
Cartledge Hall Farm
Cowley
Greenfield Farm
COWLEY LA
BARLOW LEES LA

77

Peakley Hill
Peakley Hill Farm
DOBBIN LA
Lees Wood
Grasscroft Wood

6

Great Brind Wood
Black Car Lumb
Barlow Lees
Lees Common

Little Brind Wood
Barlow Lees Farm
Monk Wood

5

NEW RD
Highlightley Farm
HIGHLIGHTLEY LA
S18
Brindwoodgate
GATELANE LA

76

JOHNNYGATE LA
Dobmeadow Wood
Bradleylane Farm
BRADLEY LA
Dunston Brook
Lees Plantation
Broombank Plantation

4

Broadmeadow Wood
Crowhole
VALLEY RD
Sewage Works
Lee Bridge
KEEPERS LA
Mill

Rumbling Street
Yew Tree Farm
FAR LA
Far Lane Farm
Crowhole Brook
OLD SPRINGS
OVERLEES
BROOK HALL
MILL LA
MILL CFT
MILLCROSS LA
SMELTINGHOUSE LA
Barlow CE Prim Sch
FURNACE LA

3

WILDAYGREEN LA
Wildaygreen Farm
Barlow Common
Common Side
HILL TOP
The Shippen Rural Bsns Ctr
Church Farm
Elm Tree Farm

75

Wilday Green
Holme Farm
Wellspring Farm
COMMONSIDE RD
Springwell Farm
Barlow
The Peacock (PH)

2

Crowhole Reservoir
Bolehill
WILKIN HILL
HACKNEY LA

GRANGE LA
Green Lane
Grangehouse Farm
Oaks Lane
Newgate Farm
Newgate
MELTON LA
COMMON LA
Ford
BARLOW RD B6051
Sudbrook Farm

1

Oxton Rake Hall Farm
Sud Brook
S42

74

A **B** **C** **D** **E** **F**

32   33   34

94
76

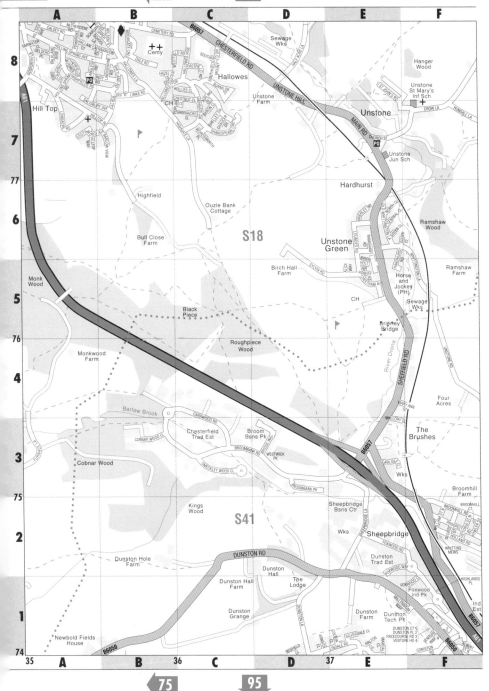

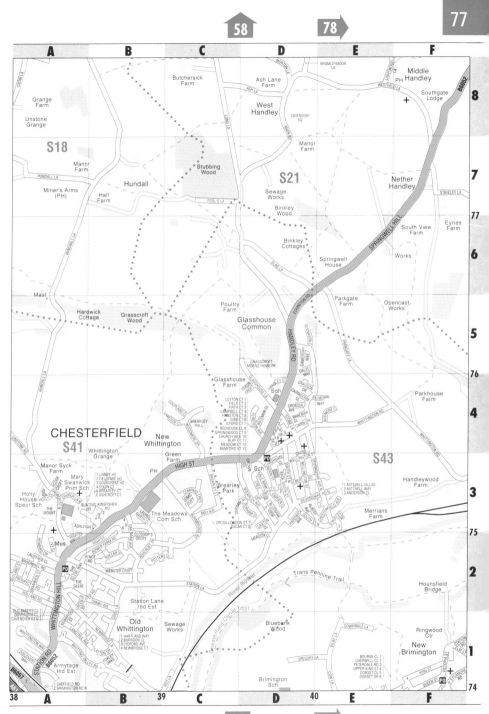

A   B   C   D   E   F

8

BRAMLEYMOOR LA

Middle Handley

MORTON LA

Butchersick Farm

Ash Lane Farm

West Handley

CAVENDISH SQ

Southgate Lodge

Westfield LA

LIGHTWOOD

B6052

Grange Farm

Unstone Grange

S18

Manor Farm

Manor Farm

Nether Handley

7

Hundall LA

Miner's Arms (PH)

Hundall

Hall Farm

POOL'S LA

Stubbing Wood

S21

Sewage Works

Binkley Wood

STAVELEY LA

77

Binkley Cottages

South View Farm

Eyries Farm

6

Mast

Hardwick Cottage

Grasscroft Wood

SLAG LA

Binkley Cottages

Springwell House

SPRINGWELL HILL

Works

ECKINGTON RD

5

Poultry Farm

Glasshouse Common

HANDLEY RD

Parkgate Farm

Opencast Works

Grasscroft Mobile Home Pk

Parkhouse Farm

76

Glasshouse Farm

LEYTON CT 1
FIELD CT 2
FIRTH CT 3
CAMPBELL CT 4
HAWSTON CT 5
GIBB CT 6
ILFORD CT 7
REDHOUSE CL 8
SPRINGWOOD CT 9
CHURCH WLK 10
BLAY CT 11
MEADOW CT 12
BAMFORD ST 13

Sch

CROMDALE AVE

BRAEMAR

CARISBROOKE

BALMORAL WAY

Handleywood Farm

4

CHESTERFIELD

S41

New Whittington

Whittington Grange

Brearley Hall

COUPLANDS

LAKESIDE DR

HIGH ST

Green Farm

PH

Sch

S43

WHITTINGTON RD

Manor Syck Farm

Mary Swanwick Prim Sch

Bunting Kingfisher Ho

1 LINNET HO
2 FIELDFARE HO
3 GOLDCREST HO
4 DIXON CT
5 BREARLEY CT
6 ASHCROFT CT

Brearley Park

Sch

1 MITCHELL VILLAS
2 MITCHELL WAY
3 ANDERSON CL

Merrians Farm

3

Holly House Specl Sch

THE MOUNT

ASHLEIGH

HIGH ST

CHURCH ST

The Meadows Com Sch

MAY AVE

CROSS LONDON ST 1
OSCAR CT 2

DEVONSHIRE RD

75

Mus

LAURENCE CL

BROOMHALL CT

PYNOT RD

ROEGAR CT

BLOSSOM CT

WEBSTER CROFT

POTTERS CL

2

PO

WHITTINGTON HILL

THE SLEBE

DANBY AVE

Station Lane Ind Est

STATION LA

River Rother

Trans Pennine Trail

Hounsfield Bridge

Ringwood Ctr

OLD BAKERY CL 1
DOVERIDGE CL 2
CAVENDISH ST N 3

Old Whittington

Sewage Works

Chesterfield Canal (dis)

Bluebank Wood

COWPINGLE LA

New Brimington

1

STATION RD

B6052

Armytage Ind Est

YOXLEY OAKS

BELL LA

GREGORY LA

LONG LA

KING ST

QUEEN ST

B6057 A61

1 SHEFFIELD RD
2 BRIMINGTON RD N

1 HARTLAND WAY
2 BURSDON CL
3 LYDFORD AVE
4 NEWBRIDGE CT

Brimington Sch

BOURNE CL 1
CHERWELL CL 2
PETERDALE RD 3
UPPER NGN ST 4
DORSET CL 5
DORSET DR 6

PO

74

A   38   B   39   C   D   40   E   F

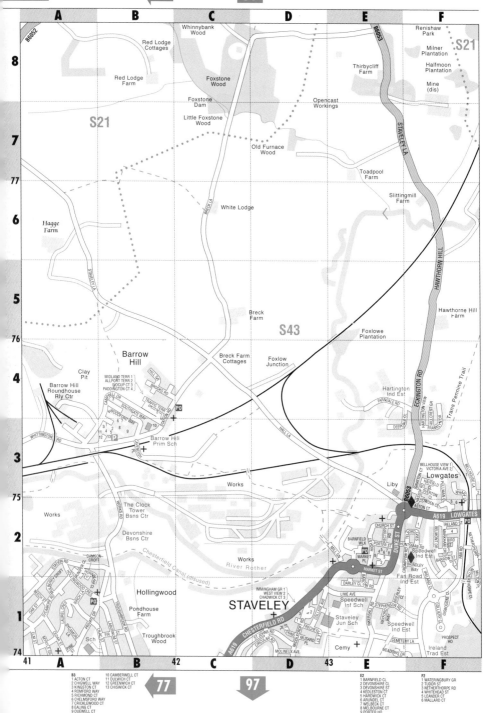

S21

8

7

77

6

5

76

4

3

75

2

1

74

A **B** **C** **D** **E** **F**

Whinnybank Wood

Red Lodge Cottages

Red Lodge Farm

S21

Foxstone Wood

Foxstone Dam

Little Foxstone Wood

S21

Hagge Farm

Old Furnace Wood

White Lodge

Breck Farm

S43

Breck Farm Cottages

Foxlow Junction

Barrow Hill

Clay Pit

Barrow Hill Roundhouse Rly Ctr

MIDLAND TERR 1
ALLPORT TERR 2
SIDCUP CT 3
PADDINGTON CT 4

Barrow Hill Prim Sch

Works

The Clock Tower Bsns Ctr

Works

Devonshire Bsns Ctr

Chesterfield Canal (disused)

Hollingwood

Pondhouse Farm

Troughbrook Wood

Sch

Works

River Rother

STAVELEY

IMMINGHAM GR 1
WEST VIEW 2
CHADWICK CT 3

CHESTERFIELD RD

MOLINEUX AVE

Cemy

Renishaw Park

Milner Plantation

Halfmoon Plantation

Mine (dis)

S21

Thirbycliff Farm

Opencast Workings

Toadpool Farm

Slittingmill Farm

Hawthorne Hill Farm

Hawthorne Hill Farm

Foxlowe Plantation

Trans Pennine Trail

Hartington Ind Est

Lowgates

BELLHOUSE VIEW 1
VICTORIA AVE 2

Liby

A619 LOWGATES

PO

Speedwell Inf Sch

Fan Road Ind Est

Speedwell Ind Est

Staveley Jun Sch

Speedwell Ind Est

CEMETERY LA

Ireland Trad Est

PROSPECT HO

41 **A** **42** **B** **C** **42** **D** **E** **43** **F**

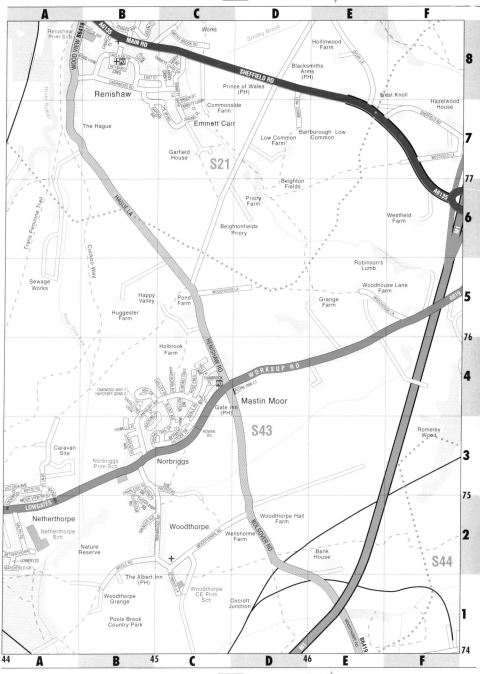

79
61

S80

Barlborough

Longrybank Wood

Coltsworth La

Speetley Plantation

Eastwood Cottage

Eastwood Farm

Whitebrick Moor

WALLS LA

Barlborough Prim Sch

De Rodes Arms (PH)

Speetley Farm

Van Dyk Hotel

A619

WEST FIELD BANK

WEST END

ORCHARD CL

CHURCH VIEW

RUTHYN AVE

Mill Farm

SPEETLEY VIEW

BOURNE MILL CL

CLOWNE RD

HEYWOOD VIEW

A616

Occupation CL

WOODLAND GR

WHITES CROFT VIEW
SPARROWBUSK CL

Hawthorns Farm

PH Hotel

CHESTERFIELD RD

OXCROFT WAY

Networkcentre Barlborough Links

MIDLAND CT

NAPIER GR

WINDERS CNR

WORKSOP RD

HIGH HAZELS RD

Barlborough Common

HIGH WOOD WAY

Cemy

SLAYLEY VIEW

PEAK VIEW

DOURNES ENC

New Barlborough

BARLBOROUGH RD

1 NEW BARLBOROUGH CL
2 HUTCHINGS CRES

Forrest's Plantation

ROTHERHAM RD

Harlesthorpe

HARLESTHORPE LA

Manor Farm

PROSPECT COTTS

CH

HAWTHORN VIEW

WESTLEA

WEST LEA COTTS

WEST LEA

BLACKBERRY CL

Heritage Com Sch

Liby

CRESWELL RD

A616

B6417

NORTH RD

EATON CROFT

RHOADS COTTS

BROOK LA

CLUMBER CL

GRAY ST

CHATSWORTH AVE

MITCHELL ST

DEVONSHIRE WAY

STATION RD

Chesterfield Coll Clowne Campus

Clowne Linear Park

S43

(dis)

Hood Croft Farm

SLAYLEY HILL

CHESTNUT DR

Superstore

ROCKSIDE COTTS

THE GREEN

OWEN GREEN WAY

College VIEW

Clowne Jun & Inf Schs

1 SOUTHWOOD DR
2 DUKERIES CT

CLIFF HILL

HIGH ST

B6418

PH

PESGER ST

CROWN ST

CRAGGS DR

Clowne

Hoodcroft La

Clowne Common

LOW RD

MILKING LA

Stanfree Farm

Chesterfield Coll Clowne Campus

JOHN ST

HIGH LEYS

STERRY CL

RAMPER AVE

Low Common Farm

ROMELEY LA

Sterry House Farm

MANSFIELD RD

CRICKET VIEW

Ringer House

Ringer Villa Farm

Romeley Hall Farm

S44

High Ash Farm

BEST RD

CLOWNE RD

Appletree Inn (PH)

Stanfree Cottage

Congreave House

Border Farm

Grange Farm

MILL LA

B6418

OXCROFT VIEW

EAST AVE

Calow Farm

B6417

47

48

49

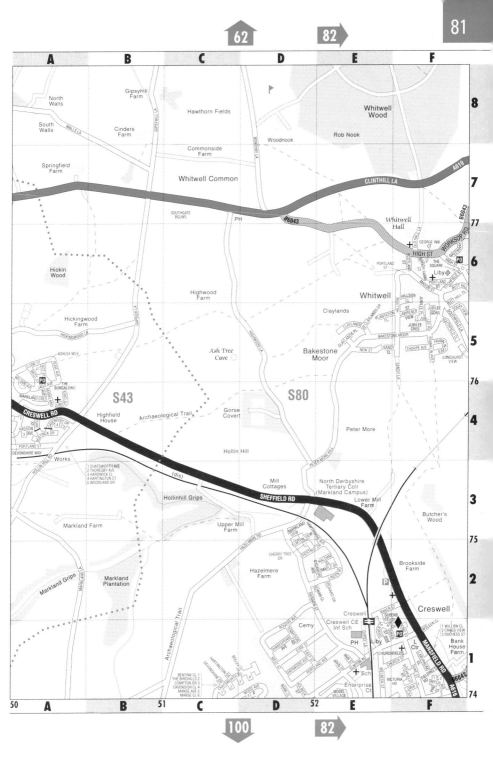

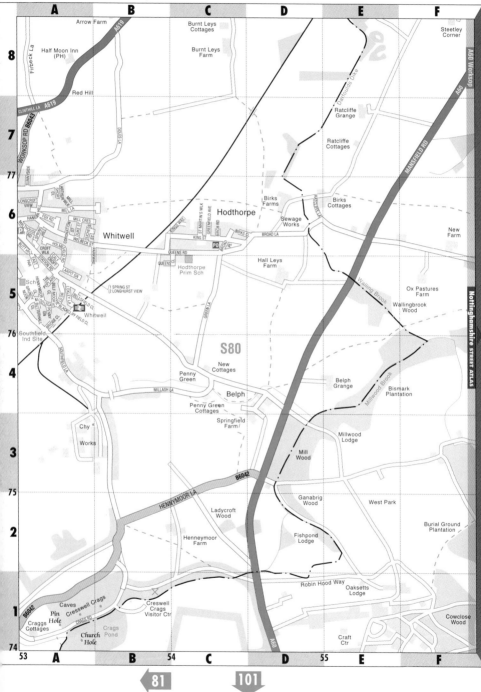

A   B   C   D   E   F

8

Arrow Farm

Burnt Leys
Cottages

Steetley
Corner

Half Moon Inn
(PH)

Burnt Leys
Farm

A60 Workshop

Finbeck La

Red Hill

Danburds Dike

7

CLINTHILL LA   A619

WORKSOP RD B6043

DOLES LA

Ratcliffe
Grange

Ratcliffe
Cottages

MANSFIELD RD

A60

77

SUNNYSIDE

Birks Farms

Birks
Cottages

New
Farm

6

LONGCROFT
VIEW

Hodthorpe

ST MARTIN'S WLK

KINGS WAY

GREENFIELD AVE

BIRCH RD

BIRKS CL

Sewage
Works

RATCLIFFE LA

Whitwell

MILL CRES

KING ST

BROAD LA

Walling Brook

Ox Pastures
Farm

QUEENS RD

PO

Hall Leys
Farm

Wallingbrook
Wood

Hodthorpe
Prim Sch

QUEENS

5

1 SPRING ST
2 LONGHURST VIEW

GREEN LA

S80

Sch

BELLSFIELD CL

Whitwell

New
Cottages

Belph
Grange

Bismark
Plantation

76

Southfield
Ind Site

SOUTHFIELD LA

MILLASH LA

Penny
Green

Belph

Millwood Brook

4

Penny Green
Cottages

Millwood
Lodge

Chy

Springfield
Farm

Mill
Wood

Works

West Park

Burial Ground
Plantation

3

B6042

HENNYMOOR LA

Ladycroft
Wood

Ganabrig
Wood

75

Henneymoor
Farm

Fishpond
Lodge

A60

2

CRAGS RD

Robin Hood Way

Oaksetts
Lodge

Cowclose
Wood

Caves

Cresswell Crags

Creswell
Crags
Visitor Ctr

1

B6042

Pin
Hole

Craggs
Cottages

Crags
Pond

Church
Hole

Craft
Ctr

74

53   A   B   54   C   D   55   E   F

Nottinghamshire STREET ATLAS

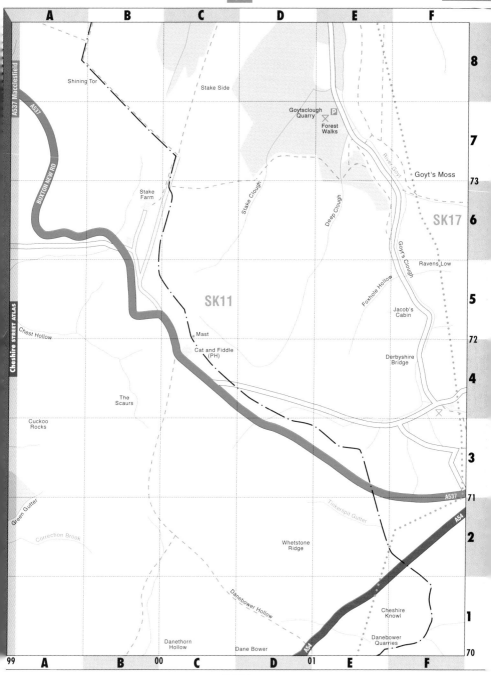

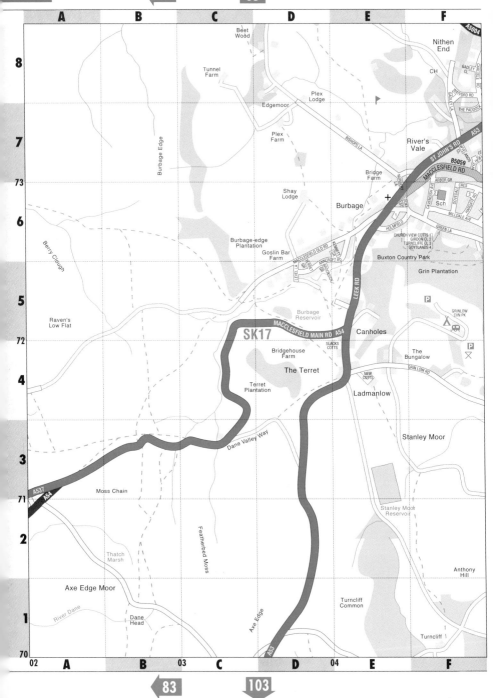

A B C D E F

8

7

73

6

72

5

4

3

71

2

1

70

Beet Wood

Tunnel Farm

Plex Lodge

Edgemoor

Plex Farm

Burbage Edge

Shay Lodge

Burbage

Nithen End

CH

GADLEY CL

WATFORD RD

THE PADDOCK

A5004

River's Vale

ST JOHN'S RD

B5059

MACCLESFIELD RD

ARBOR GR

CRES

Sch

MILLDALE AVE

CHURCH VIEW COTTS 1
GIRDON CL 2
TURNCLIFFE CL 3
GOYTLANDS 4

A53

Bridge Farm

Berry Clough

Burbage-edge Plantation

Goslin Bar Farm

MACCLESFIELD OLD RD

LEVEL LA

KENNEL LA

RAINOW RD

PODMORE RD

LEEK RD

GREEN LA

Buxton Country Park

Grin Plantation

P

GRINLOW CVN PK

Raven's Low Flat

Burbage Reservoir

SK17

MACCLESFIELD MAIN RD   A54

Canholes

SLACKS COTTS

The Bungalow

P

GRIN LOW RD

Bridgehouse Farm

The Terret

NEW COTTS

Ladmanlow

Terret Plantation

Dane Valley Way

Stanley Moor

Moss Chain

A537

A54

Stanley Moor Reservoir

Thatch Marsh

Featherbed Moss

Axe Edge Moor

River Dane

Dane Head

Axe Edge

A53

Turncliff Common

Anthony Hill

Turncliff

02   A   B   03   C   D   04   E   F

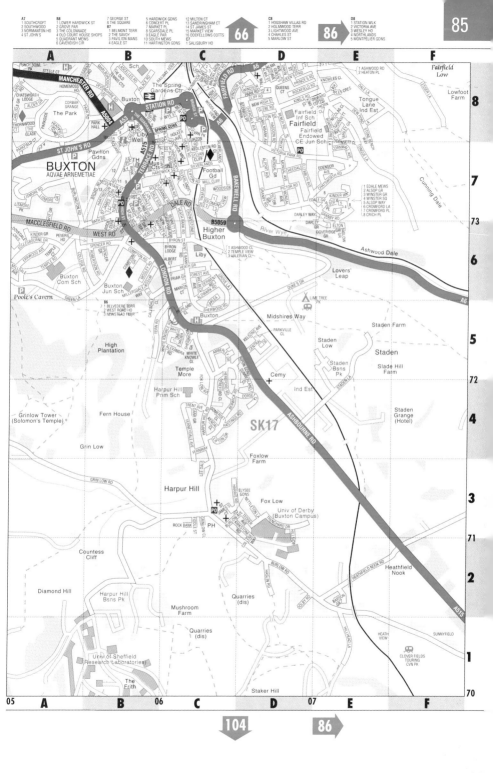

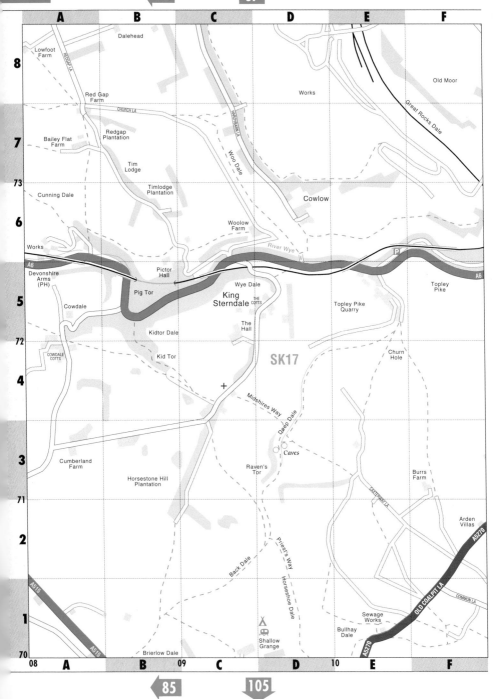

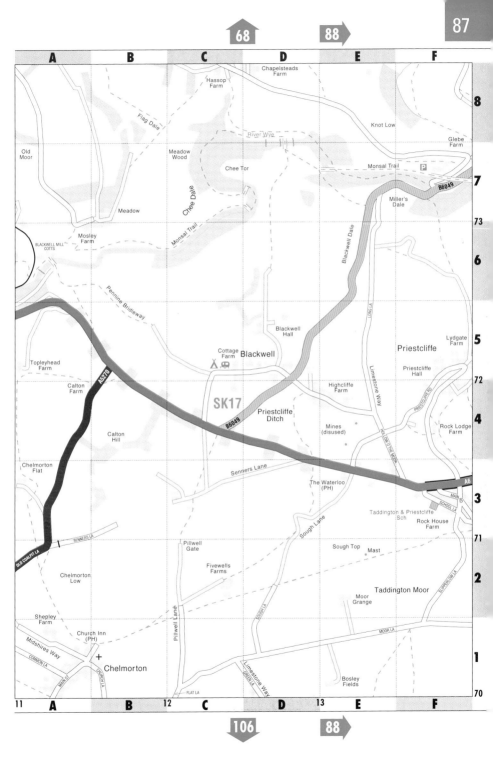

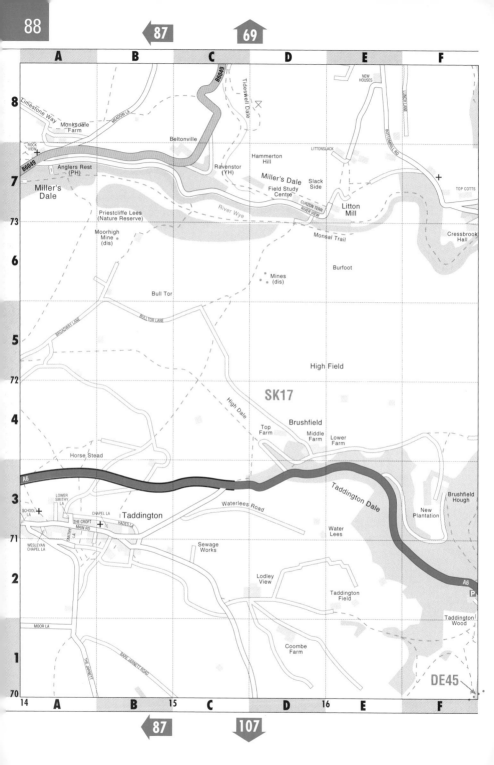

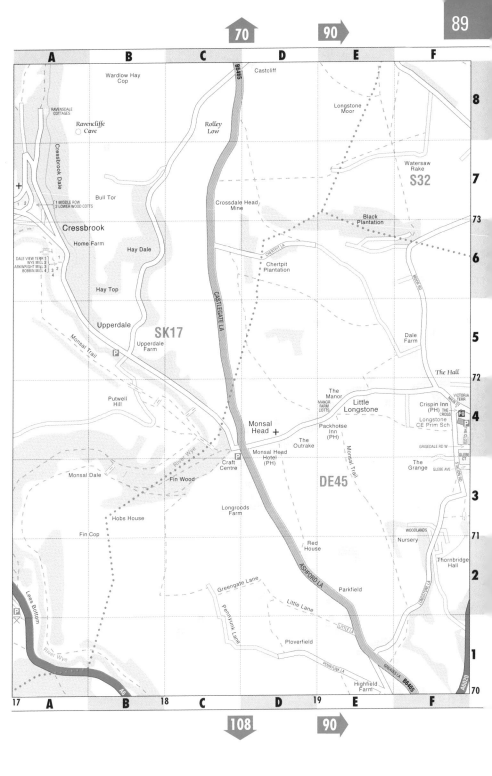

8 — Mines (disused) · Deep Rake · Opencast Workings

Longstone Moor Farm · Opencast Workings · Bleaklow · Opencast Workings

S32 · High Rake · Beacon Rod · Opencast Workings

7 — Longstone Edge · Opencast Workings · Opencast Workings · Hassop Common · B6001

73

6 — Top Farm

Hardrake Lane · Rowland · Torrs Farm · Eyre Arms (PH)

5 — Underedge · Hassop Hall (Hotel) · Home Farm · Hassop · Dog Kennel Wood · Hermitage Pond

72 — BEGGARWAY LA · Standhill Farm · Long Rake Plantation · Bowling Green Wood · LONGREAVE LA

Great Longstone Bsns Pk · The Mires · **Great Longstone** · **DE45** · Hassop Park · Flatts Farm · Birchill Bank Wood

4 — CHURCHDALE RD · TRANS... · MAIN ST · GRISEDALE RD W · ROY H... · LONG... VIEW... · CRISEDALE RD E · GLEBE AVE · MIRES LA

1 SUNNY BANK · 2 SPRING BANK · 3 WESTERN VIEW · 4 THE MEADOWS

Buskey Cottage · Oak Wood · Park Farm · Birchills Farm

3

71 — A6020 · Rowdale House · Toll Bar House

Churchdale Farm · Cracknowl Wood · Monsal Trail · Station Farm · Nether Wood · A619 · B6048

2 — A6020 · HASSOP RD · A6020

1 — Churchdale Hall · Flatt Plantation · Old Hollow Plantation

70 — Cracknowl House · B6001 · BASLOW RD A619

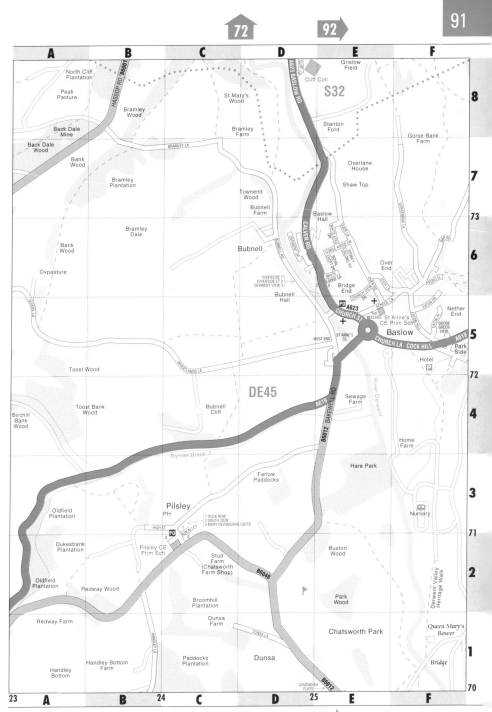

91
73

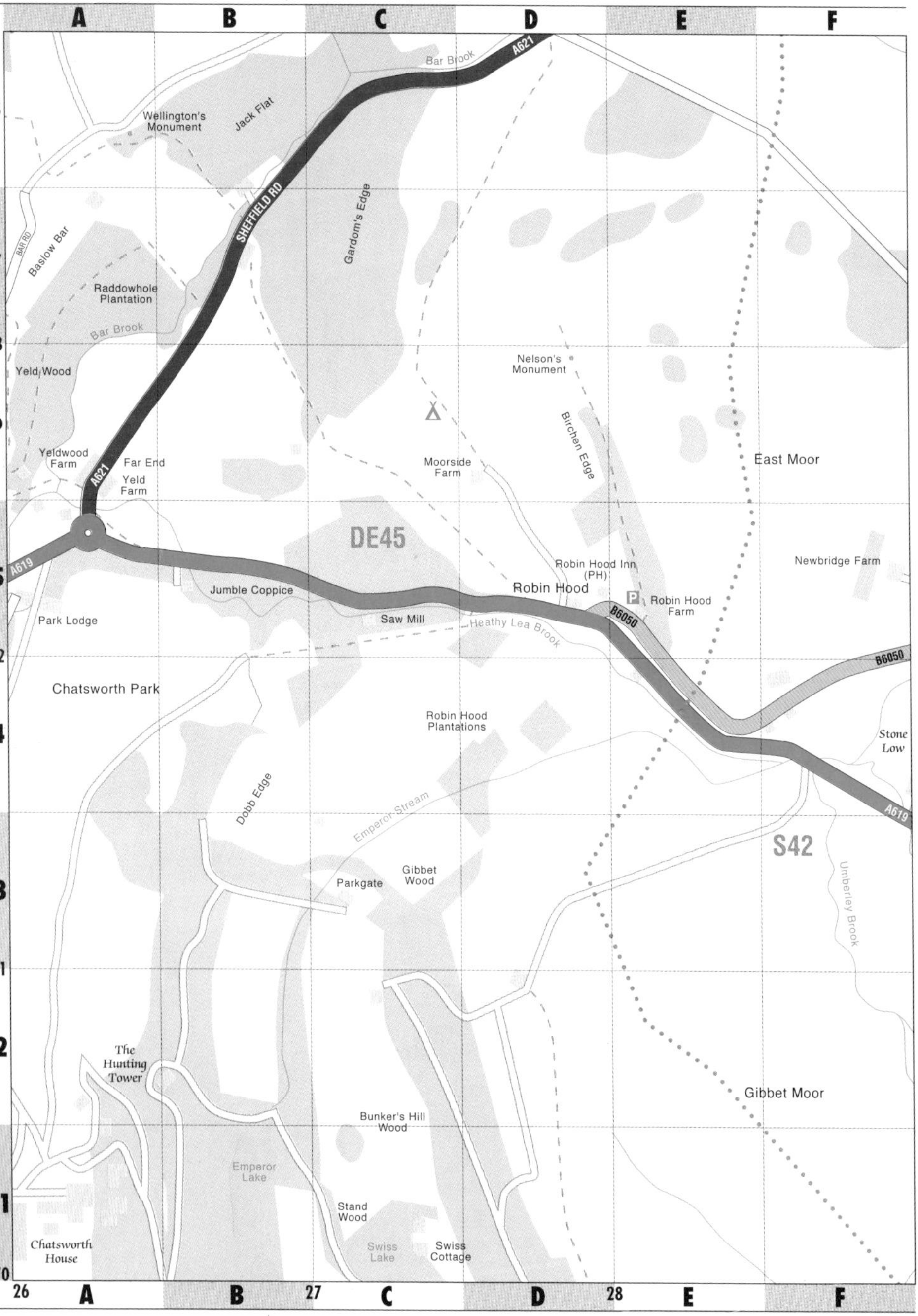

A **B** **C** **D** **E** **F**

Bar Brook

A621

8

Wellington's
Monument

Jack Flat

Gardom's Edge

SHEFFIELD RD

7

Baslow Bar

Raddowhole
Plantation

Bar Brook

Nelson's
Monument

73

Yeld Wood

Birchen Edge

6

Yeldwood
Farm

Far End

A621

Yeld
Farm

Moorside
Farm

East Moor

DE45

Newbridge Farm

A619

5

Robin Hood Inn
(PH)

Park Lodge

Jumble Coppice

Robin Hood

P

Robin Hood
Farm

B6050

Saw Mill

Heathy Lea Brook

B6050

72

Chatsworth Park

Robin Hood
Plantations

Stone
Low

4

Dobb Edge

A619

Emperor Stream

S42

Umberley Brook

3

Parkgate

Gibbet
Wood

71

2

The
Hunting
Tower

Gibbet Moor

Bunker's Hill
Wood

1

Emperor
Lake

Stand
Wood

Chatsworth
House

Swiss
Lake

Swiss
Cottage

70

26 **A** **B** 27 **C** **D** 28 **E** **F**

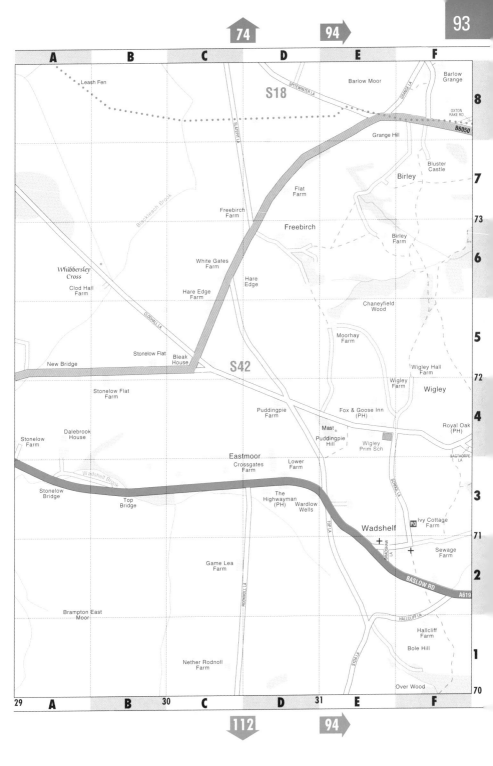

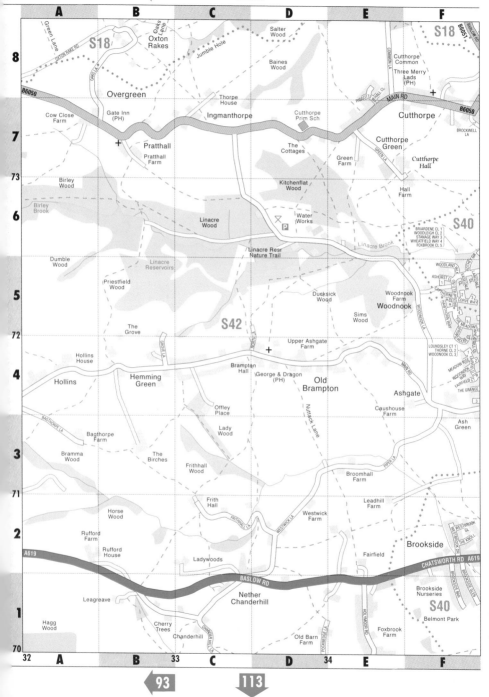

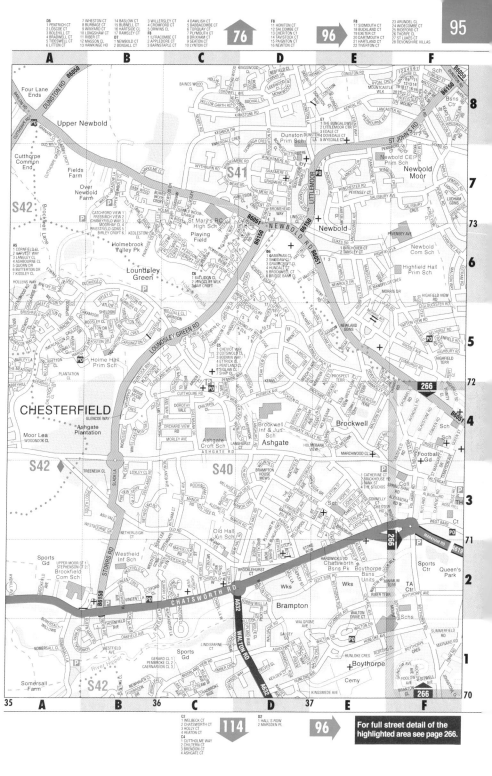

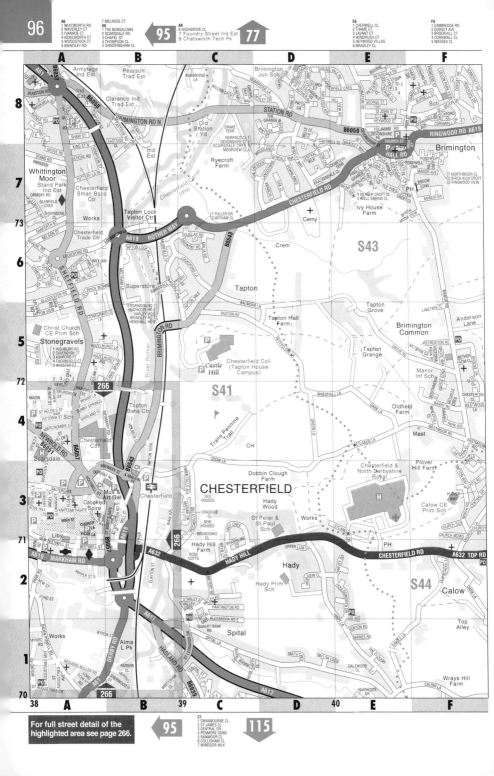

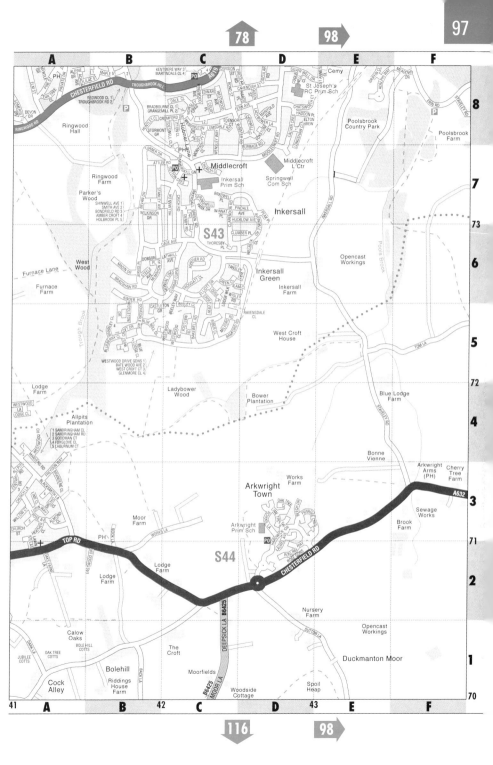

CHESTERFIELD RD
TROUGHBROOK HILL

REDWOOD CL 1
TROUGHBROOK RD 2

Ringwood
Hall

Ringwood
Farm

KENTMERE WAY 3
MARTINDALE CL 4

DIVISION

CAVENDISH ST

SILVER WELL DR
COOKE

Cemy

St Joseph's
RC Prim Sch

Poolsbrook
Country Park

Poolsbrook
Farm

Parker's
Wood

SHINWELL AVE 1
SMITH AVE 2
BONDFIELD RD 3
AMBER CROFT 4
HOLBROOK PL 5

WILKINSON
DR

Middlecroft

Inkersall
Prim Sch

Middlecroft
L Ctr

Springwell
Com Sch

Inkersall

S43

THORESBY

West
Wood

Furnace Lane

Furnace
Farm

DOBSON

LATHKILL
AVE

Inkersall
Green

Inkersall
Farm

Opencast
Workings

RAVENSDALE
CL

West Croft
House

Pools Brook

WESTWOOD DRIVE GDNS 1
BATE WOOD AVE 2
WEST CROFT CT 3
GLENMORE CL 4

Lodge
Farm

WESTWOOD
LA
LODGE CL

Allpits
Plantation

Ladybower
Wood

Bower
Plantation

Blue Lodge
Farm

Trough Brook

1 SANDRINGHAM CL
2 SANDRINGHAM RD
3 GOODMAN CT
4 FOXGLOVE CL
5 LABURNUM CT

Bonne
Vienne

Works
Farm

Arkwright
Arms
(PH)

Cherry
Tree
Farm

A632

Arkwright
Town

Moor
Farm

PH

CHURCH
ST

TOP RD

Lodge
Farm

Lodge
Farm

S44

OAK TREE

Arkwright
Prim Sch

PO

CHESTERFIELD RD

Sewage
Works

Brook
Farm

Nursery
Farm

Opencast
Workings

DEEPSICK LA B6425

MOOR LA

Calow
Oaks

OAK TREE
COTTS

BOLE HILL
COTTS

JUBILEE
COTTS

The
Croft

BACK LA

Moorfields

B6425

Duckmanton Moor

Spoil
Heap

Cock
Alley

Bolehill

Riddings
House
Farm

Woodside
Cottage

8 7 73 6 5 72 4 3 71 2 1 70

41   42   43

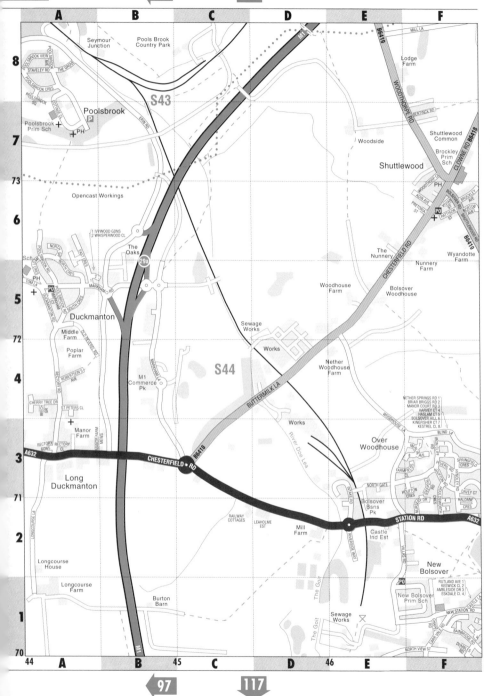

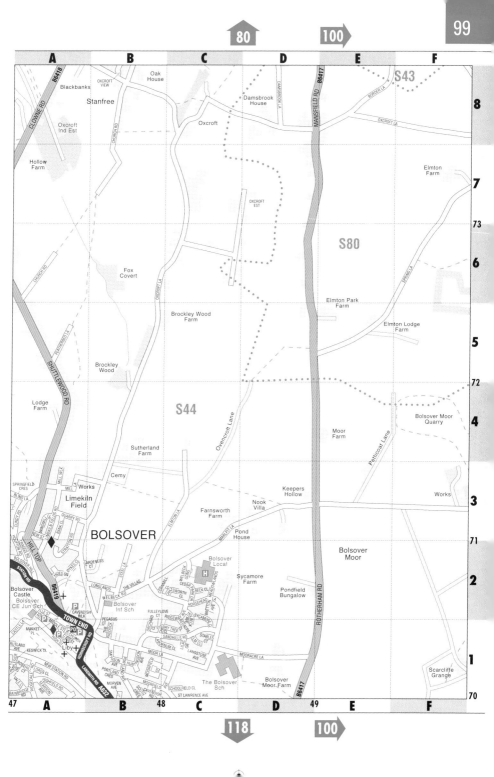

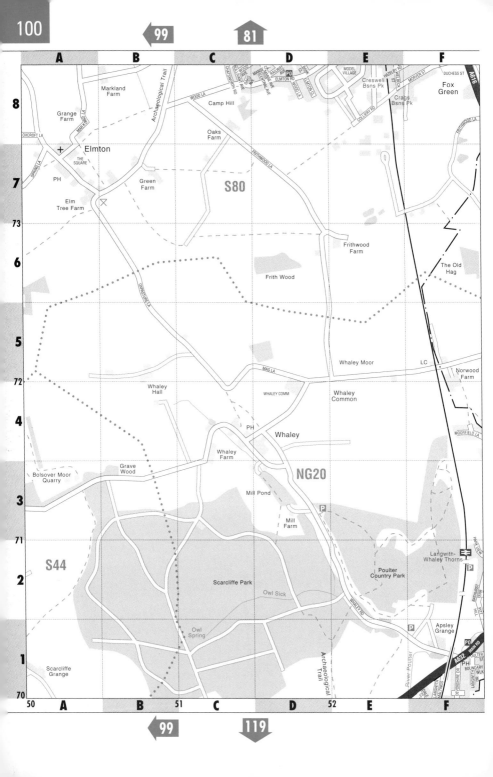

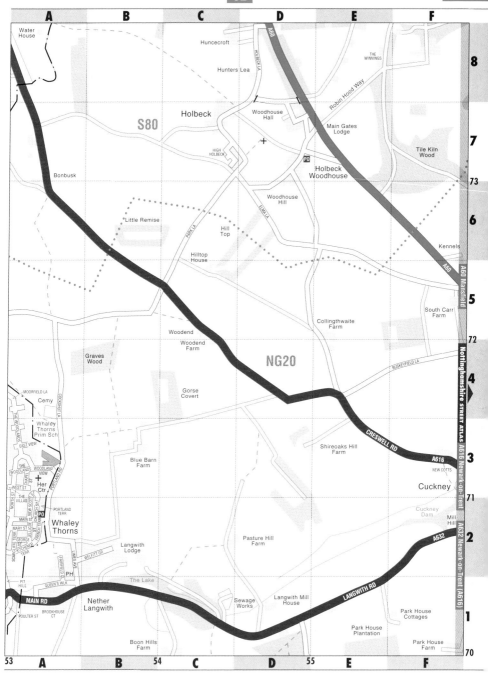

82

Water House

Huncecroft

Hunters Lea

THE WINNINGS

HOLBECK LA

A60

Robin Hood Way

8

Woodhouse Hall

Holbeck

S80

Main Gates Lodge

7

HIGH HOLBECK

PO

Tile Kiln Wood

Bonbusk

Holbeck Woodhouse

73

Woodhouse Hill

ELM LA

Little Remise

PINK LA

Hill Top

6

Hilltop House

Kennels

South Carr Farm

5

Woodend

Collingthwaite Farm

Woodend Farm

72

Graves Wood

NG20

BUSKEYFIELD LA

4

Gorse Covert

MOORFIELD LA

Cemy

Whaley Thorns Prim Sch

COLKSHUT LA

EAST VIEW

Shireoaks Hill Farm

CRESWELL RD

A616

3

NEW COTTS

THE WOODLANDS

WOODLAND VIEW

Her Ctr

Blue Barn Farm

Cuckney

71

PORTLAND TERR

Cuckney Dam

Mill Hill

WEST ST

THE VILLAS

MAIN ST

MARY ST

Whaley Thorns

Langwith Lodge

A632

2

ST GEORGE ST

LIMES AVE

WELLETT DR

Pasture Hill Farm

PIT HILL

QUEEN'S WLK

The Lake

Langwith Mill House

LANGWITH RD

Park House Cottages

MAIN RD

Nether Langwith

Sewage Works

1

BROOKHOUSE CT

POULTER ST

Park House Plantation

Boon Hills Farm

Park House Farm

70

53 54 55

120

A60 Mansfield

Nottinghamshire STREET ATLAS

A616 Newark-on-Trent

A632 Newark-on-Trent (A616)

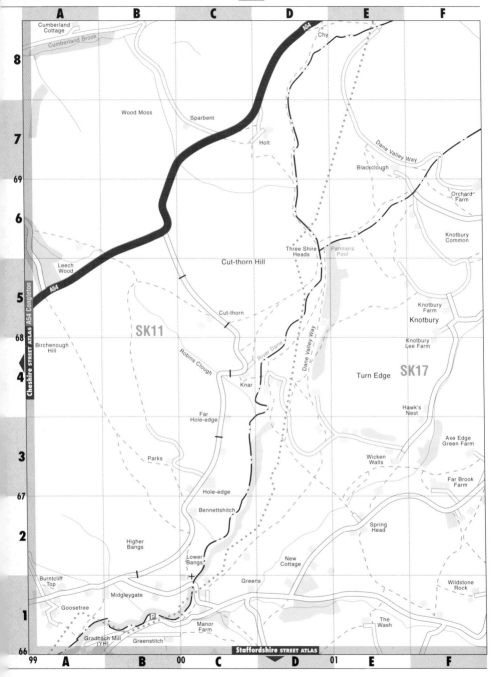

A B C D E F

8

Cumberland
Cottage

Cumberland Brook

Wood Moss

Sparbent

7

Holt

A54

Chy

Dane Valley Way

69

Blackclough

Orchard
Farm

6

Knotbury
Common

Leech
Wood

Three Shire
Heads

Panniers
Pool

Cut-thorn Hill

A54

5

Cut-thorn

Knotbury
Farm

Knotbury

SK11

68

Birchenough
Hill

Robins Clough

River Dane

Dane Valley Way

Knotbury
Lee Farm

SK17

4

Knar

Turn Edge

Hawk's
Nest

Far
Hole-edge

Axe Edge
Green Farm

3

Parks

Wicken
Walls

Far Brook
Farm

Hole-edge

67

Bennettshitch

Spring
Head

2

Higher
Bangs

Lower
Bangs

New
Cottage

Wildstone
Rock

Burntcliff
Top

Greens

Goosetree

Midgleygate

The
Wash

1

Manor
Farm

66

Gradbach Mill
(YH)

Greenstitch

99 A B 00 C D 01 E F

Cheshire STREET ATLAS A54 Congleton

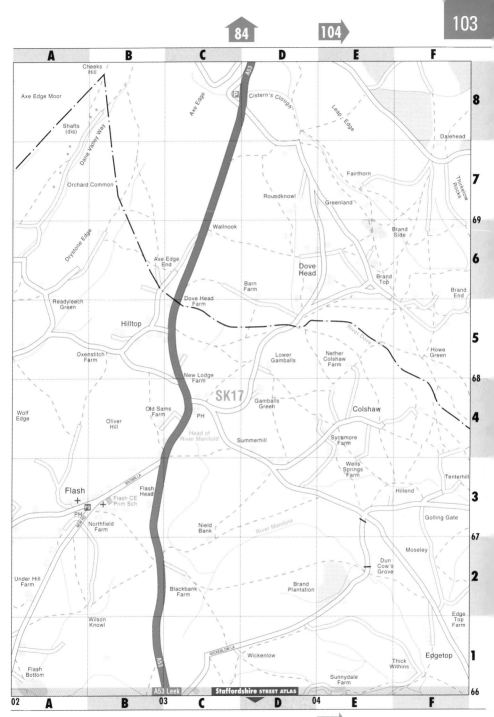

A B C D E F

8

7

69

6

Cheeks Hill

Axe Edge Moor

Shafts (dis)

Dane Valley Way

Orchard Common

Axe Edge

Cistern's Clough

P

A53

Leap Edge

Dalehead

Fairthorn

Roundknowl

Greenland

Thirkelow Rocks

Wallnook

Brand Side

Drystone Edge

Axe Edge End

Dove Head Farm

Barn Farm

Dove Head

Brand Top

Brand End

Readyleech Green

Hilltop

Oxenstitch Farm

New Lodge Farm

Lower Gamballs

Nether Colshaw Farm

River Dove

Howe Green

5

68

SK17

Wolf Edge

Oliver Hill

Old Sams Farm

PH

Head of River Manifold

Gamballs Green

Summerhill

Colshaw

Sycamore Farm

4

Flash

Flash Head

BROWN LA

Wells Springs Farm

Hillend

Tenterhill

Golling Gate

3

67

Flash CE Prim Sch

PO

PH

NEW RD

Northfield Farm

Nield Bank

River Manifold

Moseley

Under Hill Farm

Blackbank Farm

Brand Plantation

Dun Cow's Grove

2

Wilson Knowl

Edge Top Farm

Flash Bottom

A53

WICKENLOW LA

Wickenlow

Sunnydale Farm

Thick Withins

Edgetop

1

66

02 A B 03 C D 04 E F

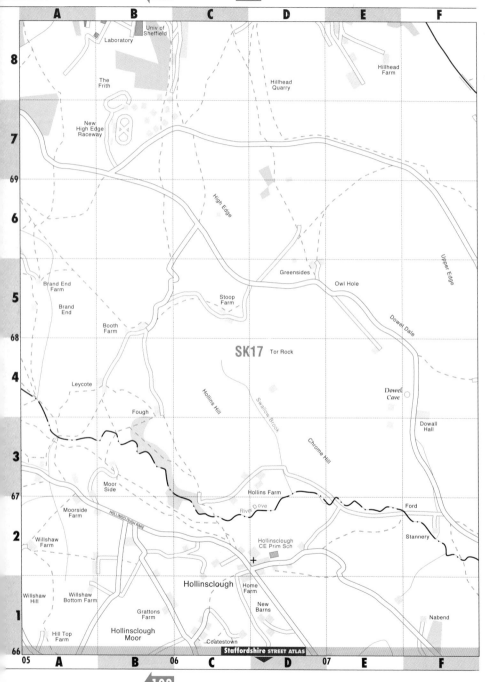

A   B   C   D   E   F

8

Univ of
Sheffield
Laboratory

The
Frith

Hillhead
Quarry

Hillhead
Farm

7

New
High Edge
Raceway

69

6

High Edge

Greensides

Owl Hole

Upper Edge

5

Brand End
Farm

Stoop
Farm

Dowel Dale

Brand
End

68

Booth
Farm

SK17   Tor Rock

4

Leycote

Hollins Hill

Swallow Brook

Dowel
Cave

Fough

Chrome Hill

Dowall
Hall

3

Moor
Side

Hollins Farm

67

Moorside
Farm

HOLLINSCLOUGH RAKE

River Dove

Ford

2

Willshaw
Farm

Hollinsclough
CE Prim Sch

Stannery

Hollinsclough

Home
Farm

1

Willshaw
Hill

Willshaw
Bottom Farm

Grattons
Farm

New
Barns

Nabend

Hill Top
Farm

Hollinsclough
Moor

Coatestown

66

05   A   B   06   C   D   07   E   F

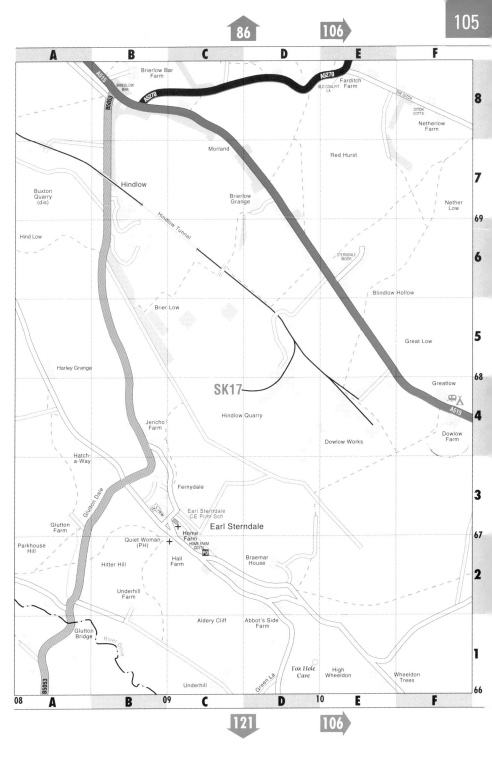

	A	B	C	D	E	F

8

Chelmorton

Townend Farm

LUMSDALE RD

TWAIN ST

CHURCH LA

FLEETA

GREEN LA

WHITFIELD LA

7

The Paddock

Mines (disused)

Town Head

CROSS LA

TAGGS LA

FLAGG LA

69

Town Head Farm

New Buildings Farm

Ash Tree Farm

Limestone Way

PIPERWELL RD

UPPER BLINKLOW LA

NETHER BLINKLOW LA

HIGHSTOOL LA

Midshires Way

6

Flagg

Back o' th' Hill Farm

PASTUREL LA

MAIN RD

Flagg Hall

Hobson Farm

Plough Inn (PH)

5

Blinder House

Mines (disused)

BYROCK LA

SK17

68

4

A515

Hall

Pomeroy

Street House Farm

Street Farm

POMEROY COTTS

Duke of York (PH)

STONEBENCH LA

MOOR LA

3

Flagg Moor Farm

Flagg Moor

Mines (disused)

67

Hutmoor Butts

2

Hurdlow Hall

Hurdlow Grange

Hurdlow Town

Bull-i'-th'-Thorn Hotel

DE45

Mines (disused)

The Whim

1

Cronkston Low

High Peak Trail
Pennine Bridleway

Columbia Cottage

Royal Oak (PH)

A515

B5055

TAGG LA

66

11	A	B	12	C	D	13	E	F

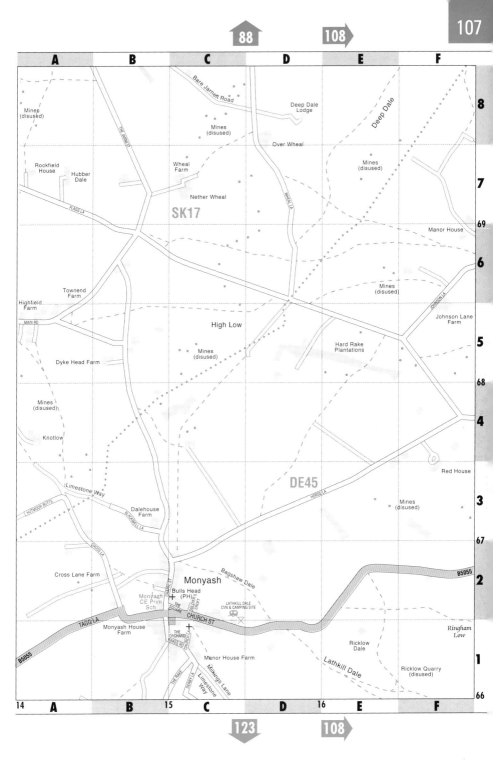

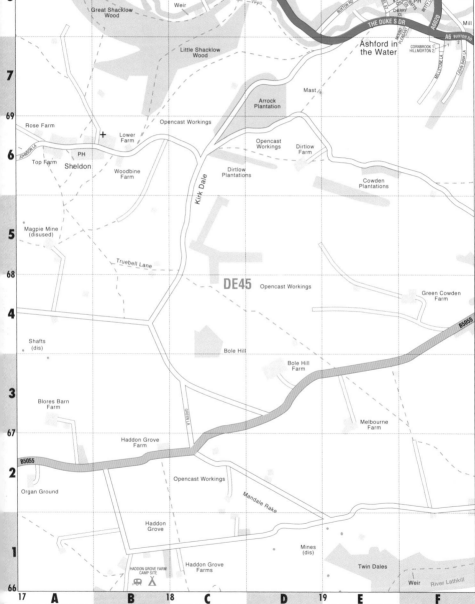

A   B   C   D   E   F

8

7

69

6

5

68

4

67

3

2

66

Great Shacklow Wood

Weir

River Wye

Little Shacklow Wood

Arrock Plantation

Mast

THE DUKE'S DR

Ashford in the Water

Mill

CORNBROOK 1
HILLMORTON 2

Rose Farm

Lower Farm

Opencast Workings

Opencast Workings

Dirtlow Farm

Top Farm

PH

Sheldon

Woodbine Farm

Kirk Dale

Dirtlow Plantations

Cowden Plantations

Magpie Mine (disused)

Truebell Lane

DE45   Opencast Workings

Green Cowden Farm

B5055

Shafts (dis)

Bole Hill

Bole Hill Farm

Blores Barn Farm

GREEN LA

Melbourne Farm

Haddon Grove Farm

B5055

Organ Ground

Opencast Workings

Mandale Rake

Haddon Grove

Haddon Grove Farms

HADDON GROVE FARM CAMP SITE

Mines (dis)

Twin Dales

Weir   River Lathkill

17   A   B   18   C   D   19   E   F

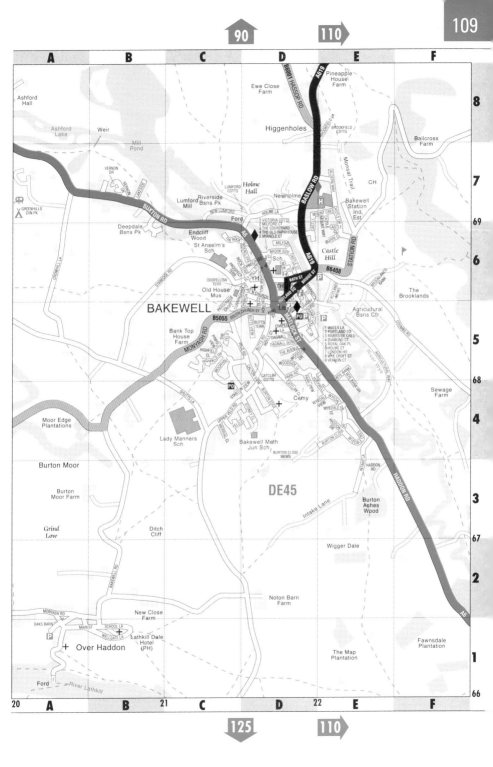

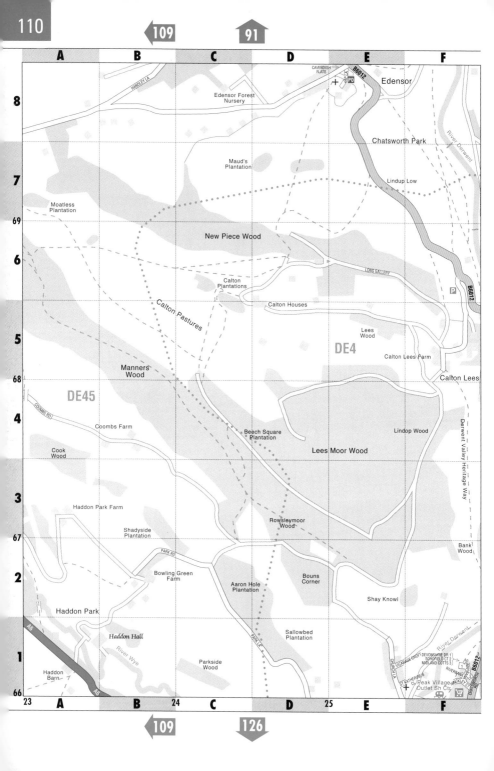

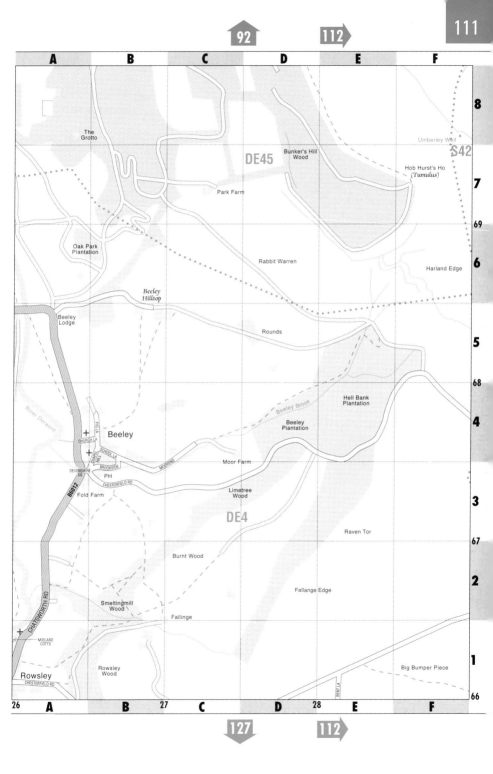

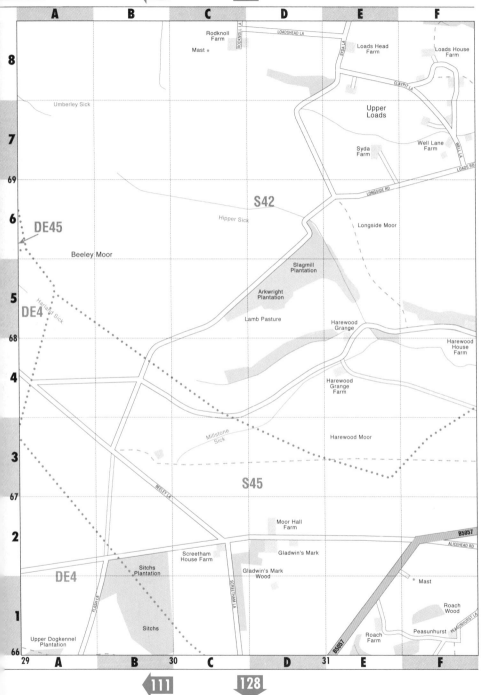

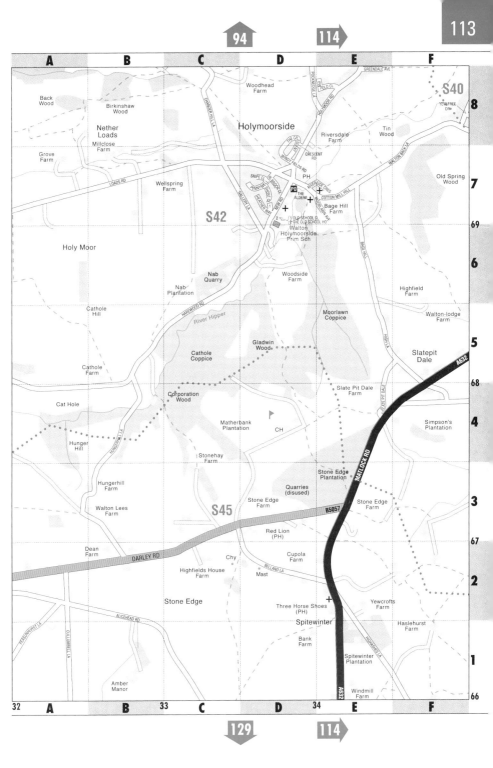

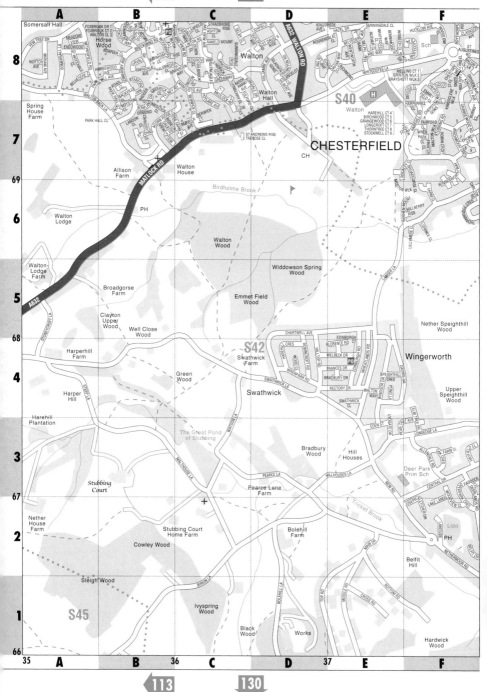

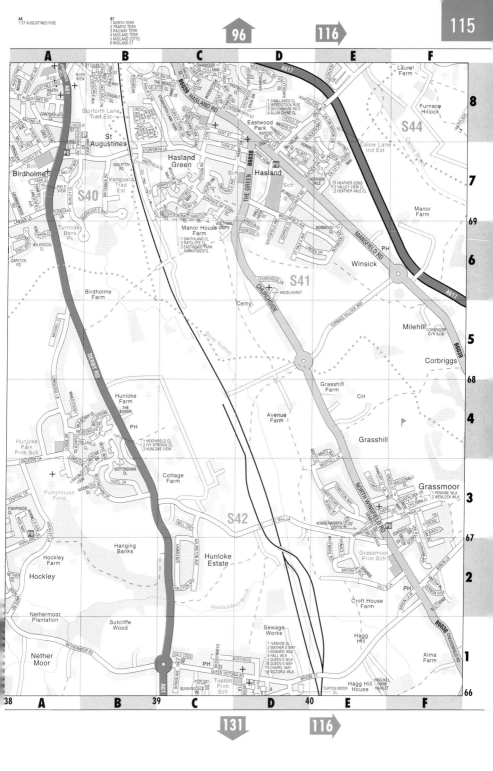

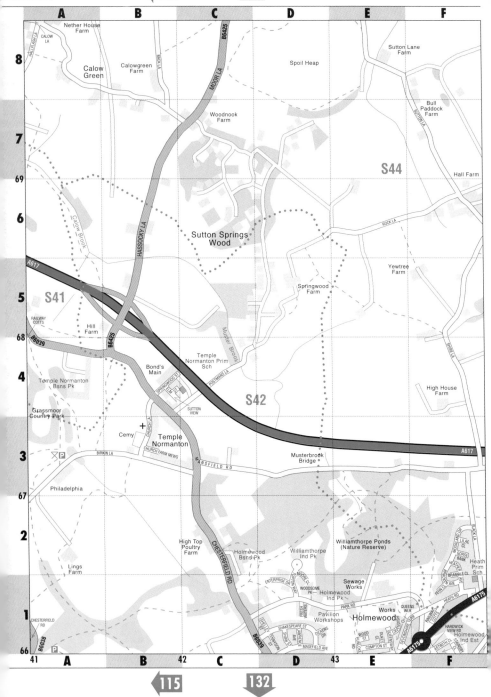

A   B   C   D   E   F

8

Nether House Farm

CALOW LA

HALL PLANT LA

CALOW LA

Calow Green

Calowgreen Farm

BACK LA

Sutton Lane Farm

Spoil Heap

MOOR LA

B6425

Bull Paddock Farm

SUTTER LA

7

Woodnook Farm

69

S44

Hall Farm

6

Calow Brook

HASSOCKY LA

Sutton Springs Wood

ROCK LA

Yewtree Farm

Springwood Farm

SURREY LA

A617

5

S41

Master Brook

68

RAILWAY COTTS

B6039

Hill Farm

B6425

Temple Normanton Prim Sch

POSTMANS LA

SURREY LA

High House Farm

4

Temple Normanton Bsns Pk

Bond's Main

SPRINGWOOD ST

S42

Grassmoor Country Park

SUTTON VIEW

Cemy

Temple Normanton

YY CHURCH

CHURCH FARM MEWS

MANSFIELD RD

Musterbrook Bridge

A617

3

BIRKIN LA

67

Philadelphia

2

High Top Poultry Farm

CHESTERFIELD RD

Holmewood Bsns Pk

ENTERPRISE DR WAY

MOOR CL

Williamthorpe Ind Pk

WOODSOME PK

Williamthorpe Ponds (Nature Reserve)

BLACK LA

LILAC CL

GORSEBROOK RD

HEATH CL

GORSE BANK

Heath Prim Sch

Lings Farm

Holmewood Ind Pk

PARK RD

Sewage Works

LILAC AVE

A6175

1

CHESTERFIELD RD

B6038

SHAKESPEARE ST

DICKENS DR

Pavilion Workshops

Works

Holmewood

QUEENS WLK

HEATH RD

PARKWAY

A6175

HARDWICK VIEW RD

Holmewood Ind Est

66

WOOD ST

DUKES CLOSE

COMPTON ST

KEYWORTH CL

STANLEY

A6175

41   A   B   42   C   D   43   E   F

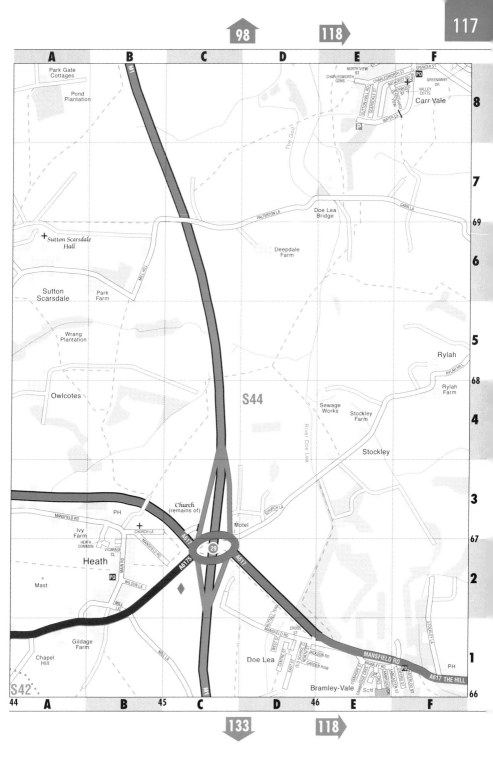

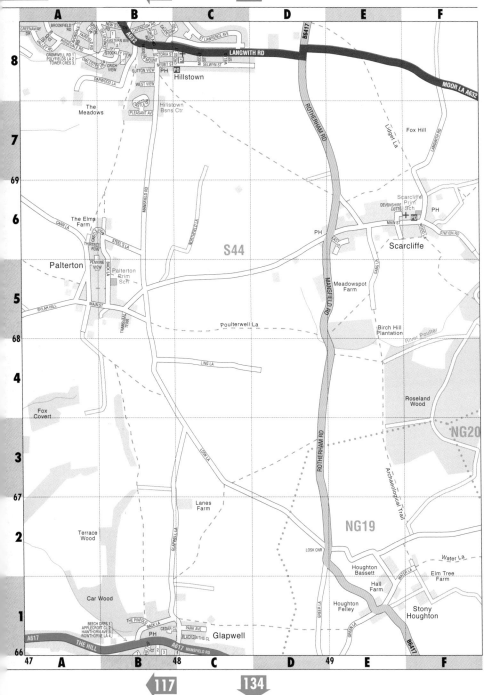

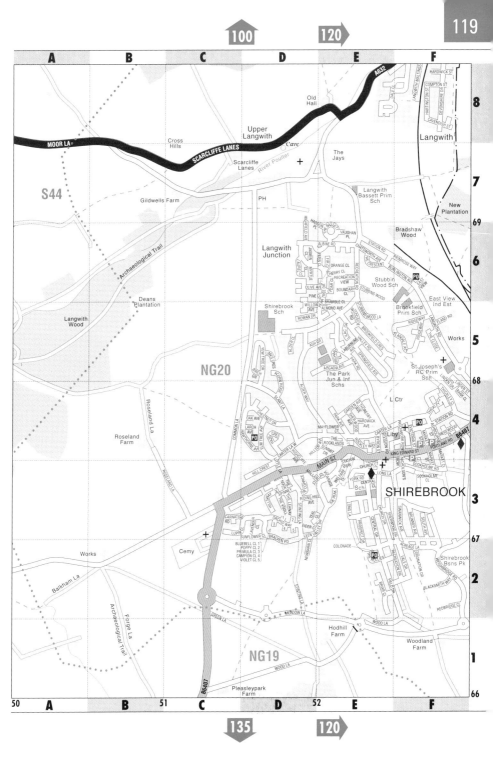

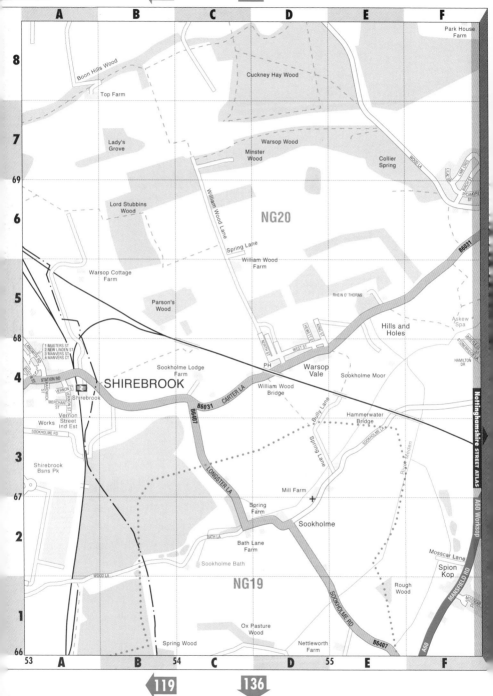

A **B** **C** **D** **E** **F**

8

Boon Hills Wood

Top Farm

Cuckney Hay Wood

Park House Farm

7

Lady's Grove

Warsop Wood

Minster Wood

Collier Spring

69

6

Lord Stubbins Wood

William Wood Lane

Spring Lane

William Wood Farm

NG20

B6031

Warsop Cottage Farm

5

Parson's Wood

RHEIN O' THORNS

Hills and Holes

Askew Spa

68

1 MUSTERS ST
2 NEW LINDEN ST
3 MANVERS ST
4 MANVERS CT

Sookholme Lodge Farm

NORTH ST
WEST ST

HAMILTON DR

4

STATION RD

VERNON ST

SHIREBROOK

Shirebrook

CARTER LA

William Wood Bridge

PH

Warsop Vale

Sookholme Moor

MERCHANT ST

VERNON ST

Works

Vernon Street Ind Est

B6031

B6407

Hammerwater Bridge

Bully Lane

SOOKHOLME RD

Spring Lane

3

Shirebrook Bsns Pk

LONGSTER LA

Mill Farm

River Meden

67

Spring Farm

Sookholme

2

BATH LA

Bath Lane Farm

Mosscar Lane

Spion Kop

WOOD LA

Sookholme Bath

NG19

Rough Wood

MANSFIELD RD

1

SOOKHOLME RD

Ox Pasture Wood

A60

66

Spring Wood

Nettleworth Farm

B6407

53 **A** **B** **54** **C** **D** **55** **E** **F**

Nottinghamshire STREET ATLAS

A60 Worksop

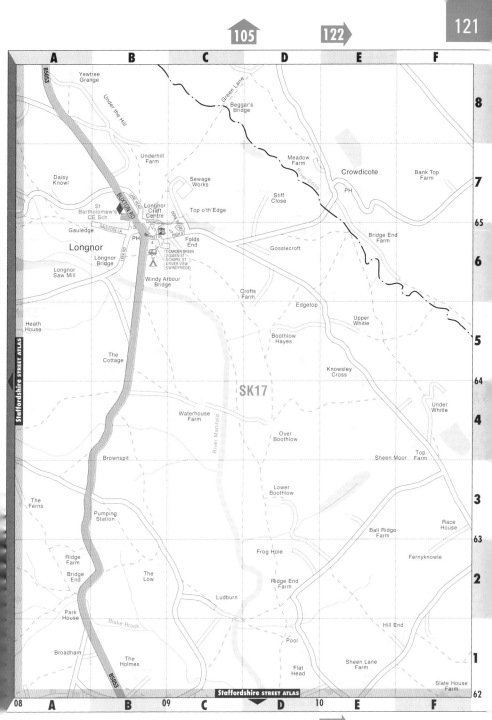

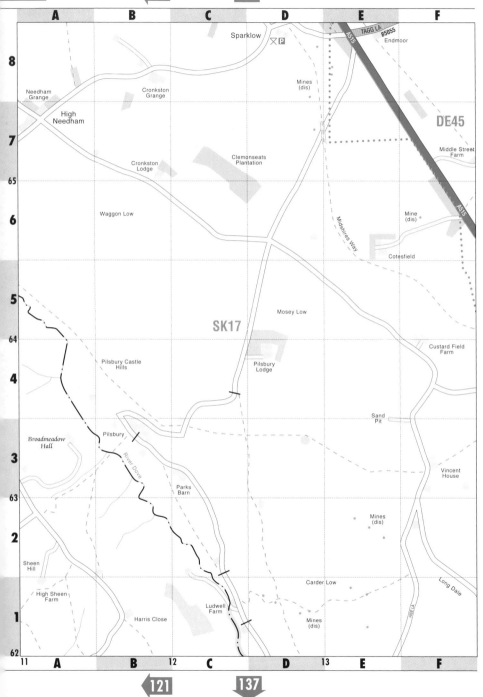

	A	B	C	D	E	F

Sparklow

B5055

TAGG LA

A515

Endmoor

8

Needham Grange

High Needham

Cronkston Grange

Mines (dis)

DE45

7

Cronkston Lodge

Clemonseats Plantation

Middle Street Farm

65

Waggon Low

Midshires Way

Mine (dis)

6

Cotesfield

A515

Mosey Low

5

SK17

64

Pilsbury Castle Hills

Pilsbury Lodge

Custard Field Farm

4

Broadmeadow Hall

Pilsbury

River Dove

Sand Pit

3

Vincent House

63

Parks Barn

Sheen Hill

2

Mines (dis)

High Sheen Farm

Harris Close

Carder Low

Long Dale

NEE LA

1

Ludwell Farm

Mines (dis)

62

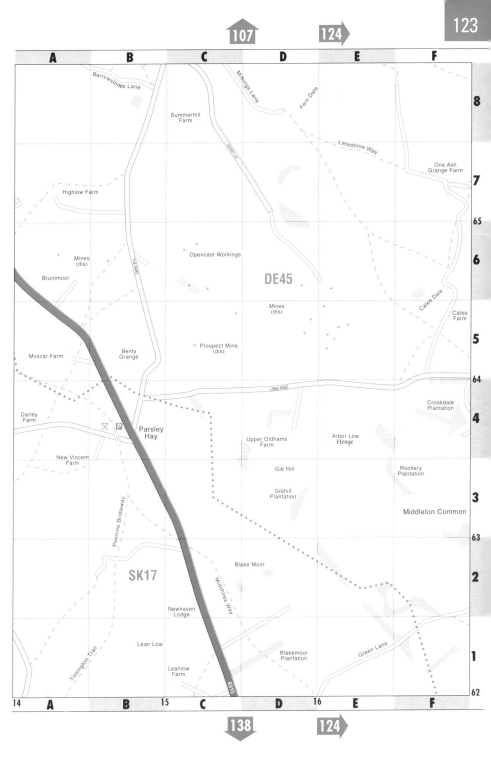

8

Barrowstones Lane

Summerhill
Farm

Milkings Lane

Fern Dale

Limestone Way

One Ash
Grange Farm

7

65

Highlow Farm

DERBY LA

Mines
(dis)

Opencast Workings

DE45

6

Bruntmoor

THE RAKE

Mines
(dis)

Cales Dale

Cales
Farm

Prospect Mine
(dis)

5

Moscar Farm

Benty
Grange

64

LONG RAKE

Crookdale
Plantation

Darley
Farm

P

Parsley
Hay

Upper Oldhams
Farm

Arbor Low
Henge

4

New Vincent
Farm

Gib Hill

Rookery
Plantation

Pennine Bridleway

Gibhill
Plantation

Middleton Common

3

63

SK17

Blake Moor

Middlehires Way

2

Newhaven
Lodge

Lean Low

Tissington Trail

Leanlow
Farm

Blakemoor
Plantation

Green Lane

1

A575

62

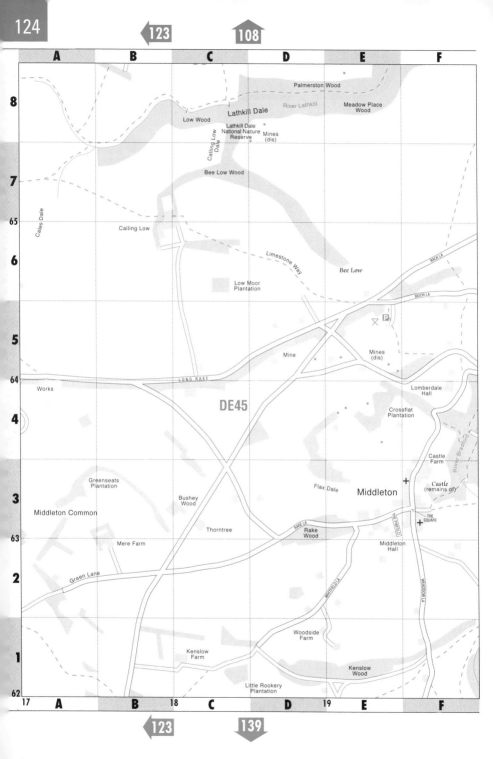

123
108

A **B** **C** **D** **E** **F**

8

Palmerston Wood

River Lathkill

Meadow Place
Wood

Lathkill Dale

Low Wood

Lathkill Dale
National Nature
Reserve

Calling Low Dale

Mines
(dis)

7

Bee Low Wood

Cales Dale

65

Calling Low

Limestone Way

BACK LA

6

Bee Low

Low Moor
Plantation

MOOR LA

P

5

Mine

Mines
(dis)

LONG RAKE

64

Works

Lomberdale
Hall

DE45

Crossflat
Plantation

4

Castle
Farm

River Bradford

Greenseats
Plantation

Flax Dale

Middleton

Castle
(remains of)

3

Bushey
Wood

THE FINFOLD

THE
SQUARE

Middleton Common

Thorntree

RAKE LA

Rake
Wood

Middleton
Hall

63

Mere Farm

WEADOW LA

2

Green Lane

WHITFIELD LA

Woodside
Farm

1

Kenslow
Farm

Kenslow
Wood

Little Rookery
Plantation

62

17 **A** **B** 18 **C** **D** 19 **E** **F**

123
139

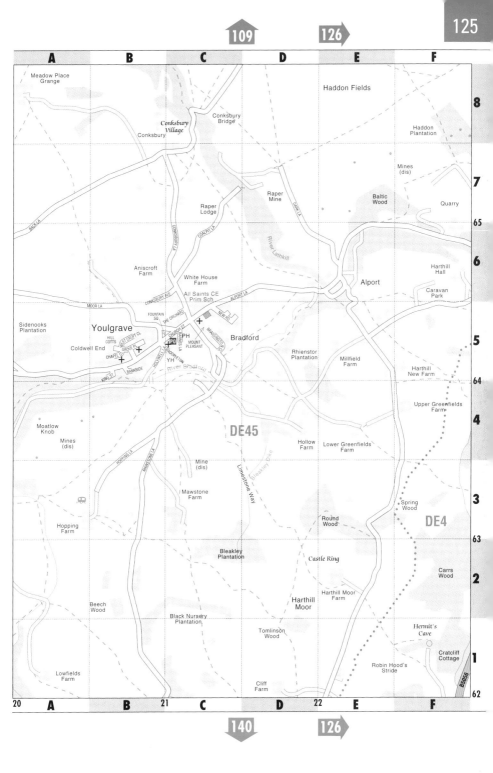

Meadow Place Grange

Haddon Fields

8

Conksbury Bridge

Conksbury Village
Conksbury

Haddon Plantation

Mines (dis)

7

Raper Mine

Baltic Wood

Quarry

65

River Lathkill

Raper Lodge

6

Aniscroft Farm

White House Farm

Harthill Hall

Alport

Caravan Park

BACK LA

CONKSBURY LA

COALPIT LA

TISSAY LA

All Saints CE Prim Sch

MOOR LA

CONKSBURY AVE

ALPORT LA

NEW RD

Sidenooks Plantation

Youlgrave

FOUNTAIN SQ

THE ORCHARD

Bradford

Rhienstor Plantation

Millfield Farm

Harthill New Farm

5

Coldwell End

HILL COTTS

WEST CROFT CL

GROVE PL

PH

CHURCH ST

BROOKLETON

BRASSINGTON LA

MOUNT PLEASANT

CHAPEL LA

KING ST

BANKSIDE

YH

River Bradford

64

Upper Greenfields Farm

DE45

4

Moatlow Knob

Mines (dis)

HOPPING LA

MAWSTONE LA

Mine (dis)

Hollow Farm

Lower Greenfields Farm

3

Mawstone Farm

Limestone Way

Bleakley Dike

Spring Wood

DE4

63

Hopping Farm

Round Wood

Bleakley Plantation

Castle Ring

Carrs Wood

2

Beech Wood

Harthill Moor

Harthill Moor Farm

Black Nursery Plantation

Hermit's Cave

Cratcliff Cottage

1

Tomlinson Wood

Robin Hood's Stride

B5056

Lowfields Farm

Cliff Farm

62

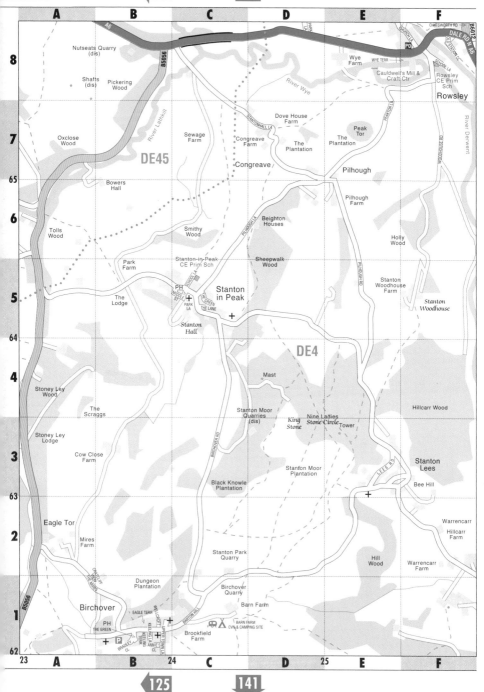

Nutseats Quarry (dis)

Shafts (dis)

Pickering Wood

Oxclose Wood

River Lathkill

B5056

A6

River Wye

Wye Farm

Cauldwell's Mill & Craft Ctr

Rowsley CE Prim Sch

Rowsley

CHATSWORTH RD

DALE RD N A6

B6012

PO

SCHOOL LA

River Derwent

WOODHOUSE RD

Dove House Farm

STANTONHALL LA

Sewage Farm

Congreave Farm

The Plantation

The Plantation

Peak Tor

DE45

Congreave

Pilhough

Bowers Hall

Tolls Wood

Smithy Wood

PILHOUGH LA

Beighton Houses

Pilhough Farm

Holly Wood

Park Farm

The Lodge

Stanton-in-Peak CE Prim Sch

SCHOOL LA

PH

PARK LA

MIDDLE LA

THE GREEN

Stanton in Peak

PARK LA

THE LANE

Sheepwalk Wood

PILHOUGH RD

Stanton Woodhouse Farm

Stanton Woodhouse

Stanton Hall

DE4

Stoney Ley Wood

The Scraggs

Mast

Stanton Moor Quarries (dis)

King Stone

Nine Ladies Stone Circle

Tower

Hillcarr Wood

Stoney Ley Lodge

Cow Close Farm

BIRCHOVER RD

Black Knowle Plantation

Stanton Moor Plantation

Stanton Lees

Bee Hill

LEES RD

Warrencarr

Hillcarr Farm

Eagle Tor

Mires Farm

Stanton Park Quarry

Hill Wood

Warrencarr Farm

B5056

CLOVER CLOSE THE MIRES

Dungeon Plantation

Birchover Quarry

Barn Farm

Birchover

PH

THE GREEN

EAGLE TERR

WELLINGTON

KEELING LA

UPPER TOWN LA

BARTON HILL

Brookfield Farm

Barn Farm CVN & Camping Site

BRAMLEY CL

ANNIE'S CL

23 24 25

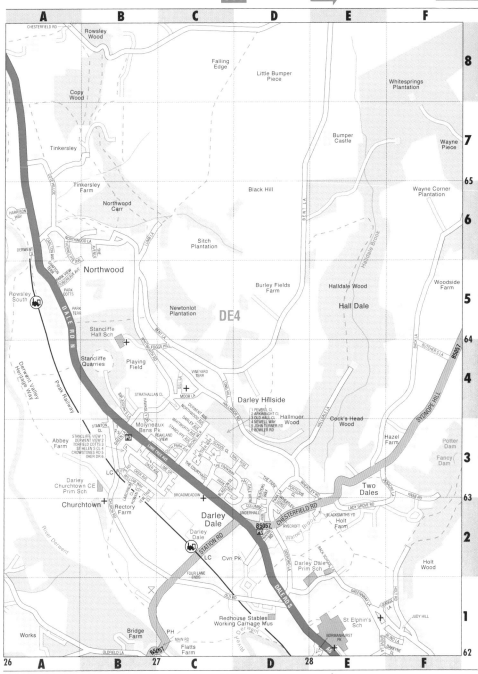

A   B   C   D   E   F

8

Darley Forest Grange

Fishpond Wood

7

FLASH LA

BACK LA

Nine Acre Piece

Darwin Forest Holiday Country Park

Mast

North Brittain

Wilkin House

S45

Hodgelane Brook

SCRETTON LA

B5057

HODGE LA

65

6

Seventy Acre Plantation

Moor House

Shooters-Lea Farm

Burnt Piece

5

Nursery Farm

SYDNOPE HILL

Flash Dam

Upper Moor

JAGGERS LA

Matlock Farm Park

Rushley Lodge

Grouse Cottage Farm

B5057

64

SYDNOPE HALL

DE4

Black Brook

4

The Warren

Sydnope Brook

Farley Moor

Middle Moor

Sydnope Stand

FARLEY LA

3

Clarke's Plantation

63

Tax Farm

2

Matlock Moor

Cuckoostone Grange

CUCKOOSTONE LA

Cuckoostone House

1

Farley Farm

FARLEY HILL

Farley

SANDY LA

Cuckoo Stone

Bottom Farm

62

Cuckoostone Dale

A632

29   A   B   **30**   C   D   **31**   E   F

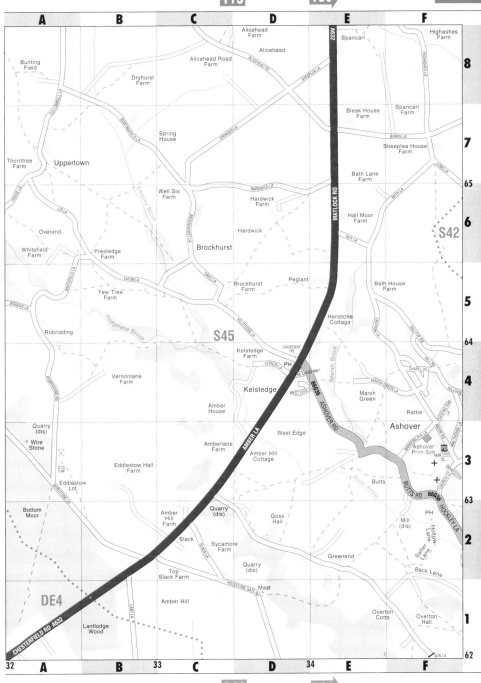

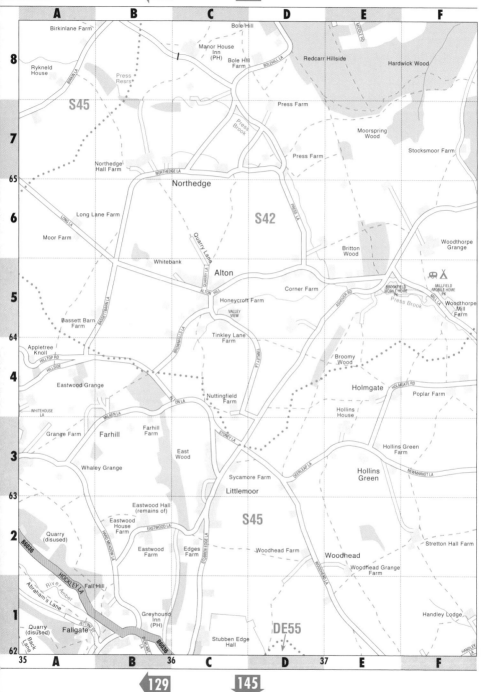

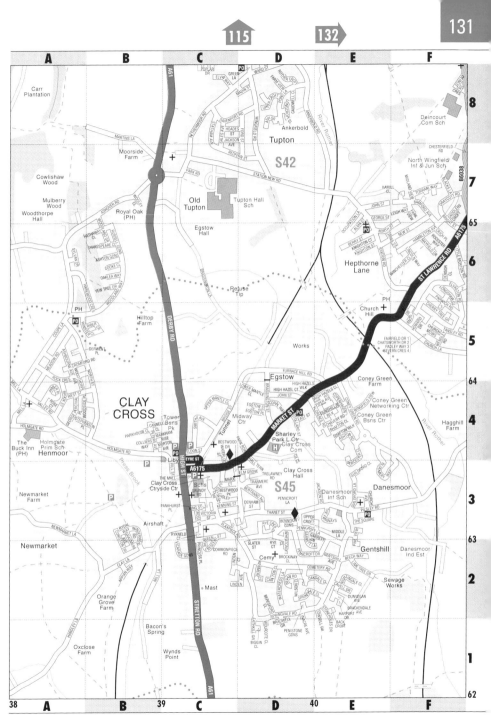

A B C D E F

8

7

65

6

5

64

4

3

63

2

1

62

B6038

Williamthorpe

North Wingfield

Hillyfields

WILLIAMTHORPE RD

Highfields

Cemy

THE GREEN

A6175

S42

HEATH RD

Liby

Common End

S44

Holme Farm

Holmewood Ind Est

HARDWICK VIEW RD

HARDWICK CT

ST ALBANS CL
QUEENSWAY

MASEFIELD AVE

SEARSTON AVE

HALL FARM

CENTRAL ST

RALLEY CL

CHURCHLAND

CRASTON CL

B6039

HUNLOKE RD

HARDWICK

TIBSHELF RD

OUT LA

Stainsby Common

High House Farm

Timber Lane Farm

P

TIMBER LA

BRANCH LA

Park View Farm

Seanor Farm

SEVERN CRES

ELTON RD
LANGLEY RD
CHURCH CL
CHURCH LA

PACKHORSE RD

SEANOR LA

Bridle Path Farm

Broomridding Wood

Headland Farm

Moorhouse Farm

Pear Tree Farm

Locko Lane Farm

Hardstoft Common

Hagg Hill

Parkhouse Green

Park House Farm

Poplar Farm
Park House Prim Sch

VALLEY CL
PENN RD
THE ACRES
ACACIA DR
ACRES RD

Waterloo

LOCKO RD

S45

LOCKO LA

Hall View Cottage Herb Garden

Lower Pilsley

PH

DALE VIEW CL
RUPERT ST

P

GREEN LA

HARDSTOFT RD

DEEP LA

PH

B6039

EVELYN DEVONSHIRE COTTS

GRANBY
BACK LA
OLD HALL CL

Upper Pilsley

Haltgate Farm

HALTGATE LA
LONGDALE RD
PADLEY WOOD RD
GROVE ST
HOUSE ST
BLACK LA
DARK LA

Bushypark Farm

Tenacres

PEAK TREE LA
GREEVES AVE
BRADY ST
MARSH CL
GREENWAY
LADSBURE AVE

ROTHER CL
WARREN CL

Pilsley

STATION RD
SOUTH ST
NEW ST
HOUSE ST
MANOR FARM
MORTON RD

WILLOW CL
BRUNSWICK ST
PROSPECT RD

PH

P

Pilsley Prim Sch

Nether Pilsley

P

DE55

River Rother

41 A B 42 C D 43 E F

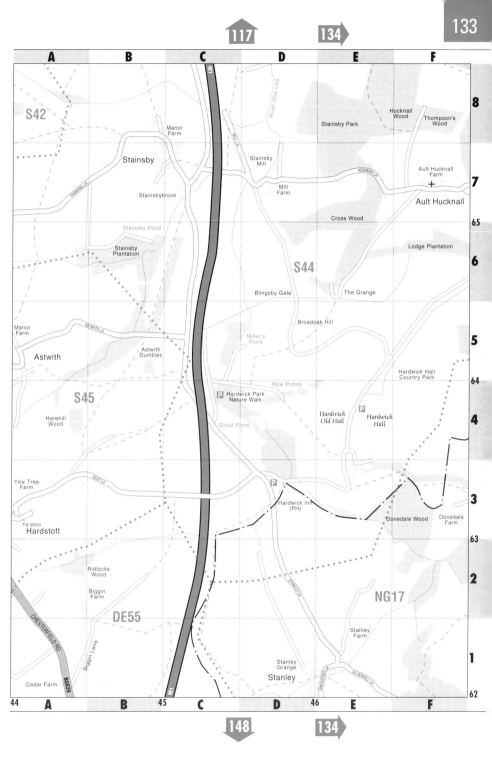

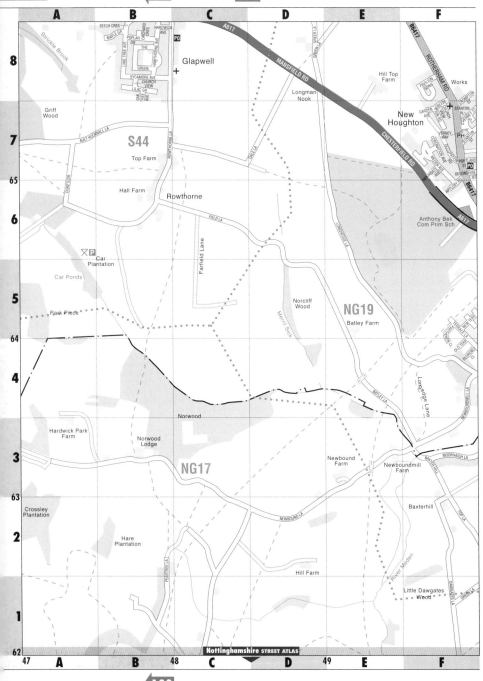

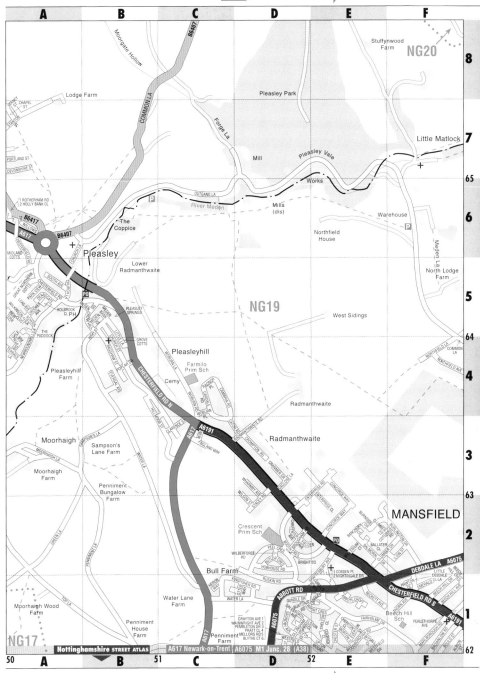

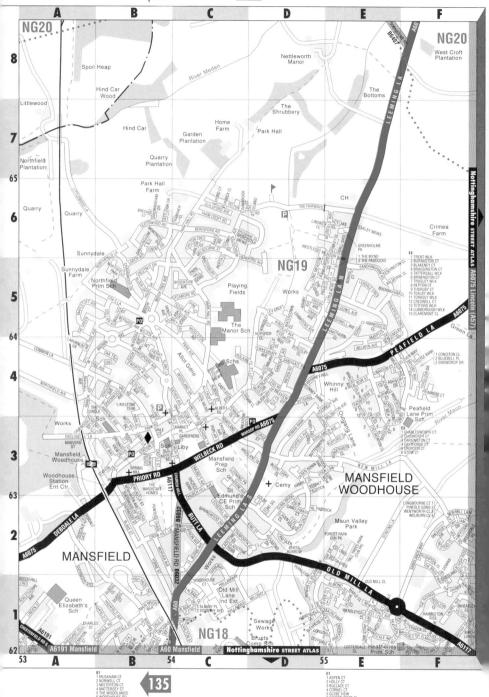

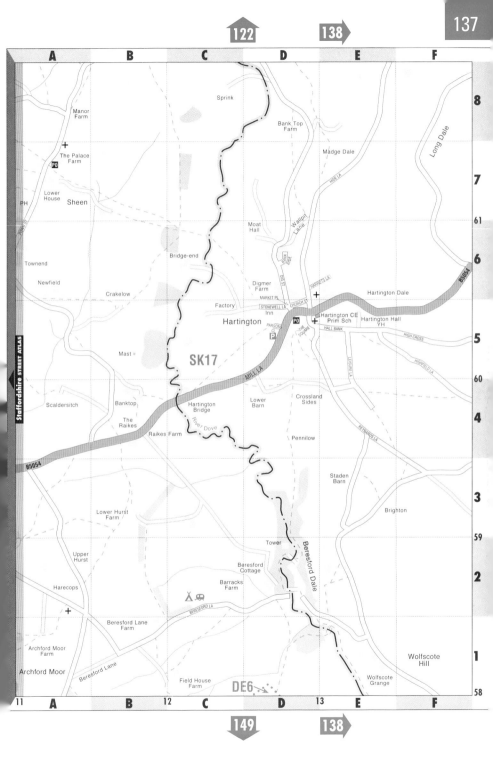

122
138
149
138

Staffordshire STREET ATLAS

Manor Farm

The Palace Farm

PO

PH

Lower House

Sheen

Townend

Newfield

Crakelow

Bridge-end

Sprink

Bank Top Farm

Madge Dale

Long Dale

Moat Hall

Wallpit Lane

Digmer Farm

Factory

Hartington

MARKET PL

STONEWELL LA

Inn

PARSON'S

P

HARPUTS LA

HIDE LA

BURN SIDE

DIG ST

CHURCH ST

HALL BANK

THE SQUARE

PO

Hartington CE Prim Sch

Hartington Dale

Hartington Hall YH

HIGH CROSS

HIGHFIELD LA

LEISURE LA

B5054

Mast

SK17

MILL LA

Hartington Bridge

River Dove

Lower Barn

Crossland Sides

REYNARDS LA

Scaldersitch

Banktop

The Raikes

Raikes Farm

Pennilow

Staden Barn

Brighton

Lower Hurst Farm

Upper Hurst

Harecops

Archford Moor Farm

Archford Moor

Beresford Lane Farm

Beresford Lane

Field House Farm

Barracks Farm

Beresford Cottage

Tower

BERESFORD LA

Beresford Dale

Wolfscote Hill

Wolfscote Grange

DE6

B5054

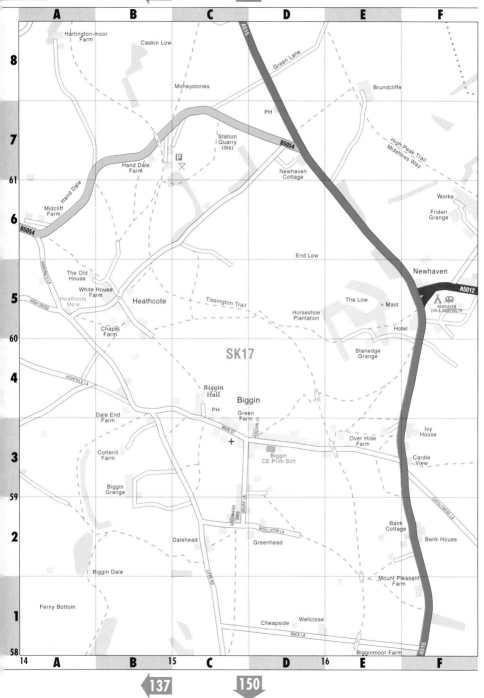

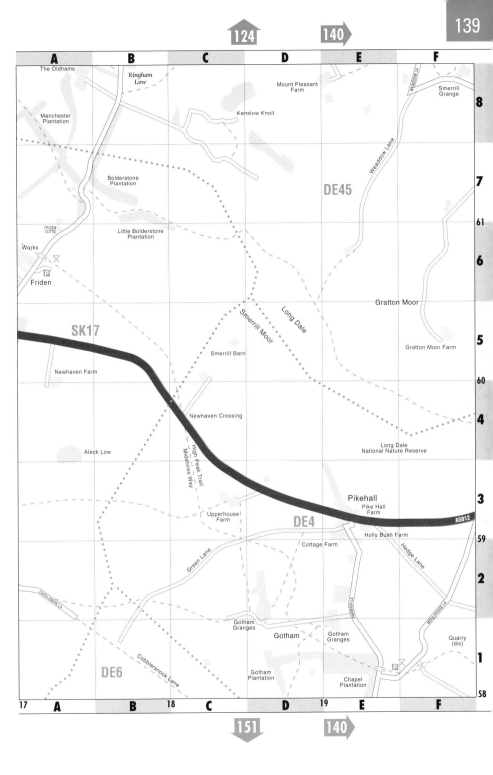

A **B** **C** **D** **E** **F**

The Oldhams

Ringham
Low

Mount Pleasant
Farm

Kenslow Knoll

Smerrill
Grange

8

Manchester
Plantation

WEADLOW LA

Bolderstone
Plantation

DE45

Weadlow Lane

7

FRIDEN
COTTS

Little Bolderstone
Plantation

61

Works

Gratton Moor

6

Friden

Smerrill Moor

Long Dale

Gratton Moor Farm

5

SK17

Smerrill Barn

60

Newhaven Farm

Newhaven Crossing

Long Dale
National Nature Reserve

4

Aleck Low

High Peak Trail
Midshires Way

Pikehall

Pike Hall
Farm

3

A5012

Upperhouse
Farm

DE4

Holly Bush Farm

59

Green Lane

Cottage Farm

Hedge Lane

CARDLEMERE LA

BARWICH LA

MOORLANDS LA

2

Gotham
Granges

Gotham
Granges

Quarry
(dis)

Gotham

Cobblersnook Lane

DE6

Gotham
Plantation

Chapel
Plantation

P

1

58

17 **A** **B** 18 **C** **D** 19 **E** **F**

	A	B	C	D	E	F

8

Fishpond Wood

Gratton Grange Farm

Rock Farm

Dud Wood

Dudwood Farm

B5056

Limestone Way

DUDWOOD LA

Dale End House

Anthony Hill

DE45

7

Dale End

Dale End Farm

GRATTON LA

GREEN LA

Well Street Farm

Woodbine Farm

Bury Cliff Farm

61

Gratton Dale

Oddo House Farm

THE BUNGALOWS

WEST END

Dark Lane

Elton House Farm

PH

PO

Elton CE Prim Sch

GRAVEL CROFT

MAIN ST

BACK LA

EAST END

WINSTER LA

Elton

6

Gratton Moor

Hungerhill Lane

Leadmines Farm

Blake Low

5

MOOR LA

Shafts (dis)

60

Barker Barn

ECCLESBANE LA

4

Elton Common

DE4

Mouldridge Grange

Allsop Barn

Sacheveral Farm

SACHEVERAL LA

Stunstead Lane

3

A5012

MOULDRIDGE LA

Little Wisels Wood

59

2

Astonhill

Grange Barn

A5012

1

Pennine Bridleway
Midshires Way

New Barn

Rockhurst Farm

Greenlow Farm

58

20	A		B	21	C		D	22	E		F

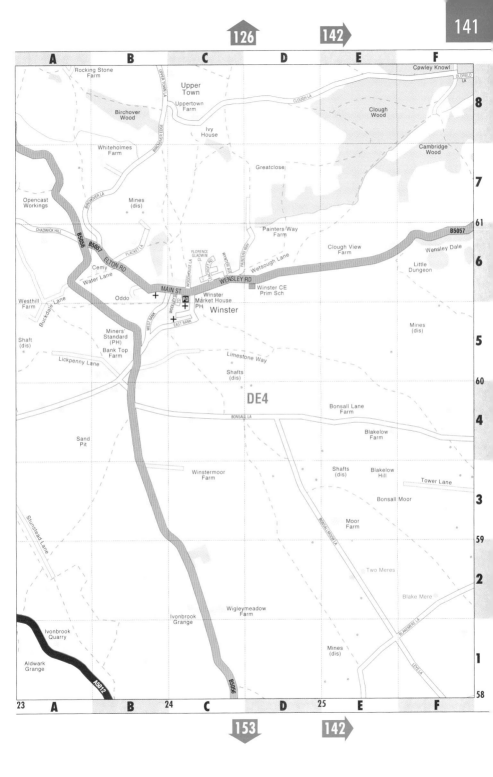

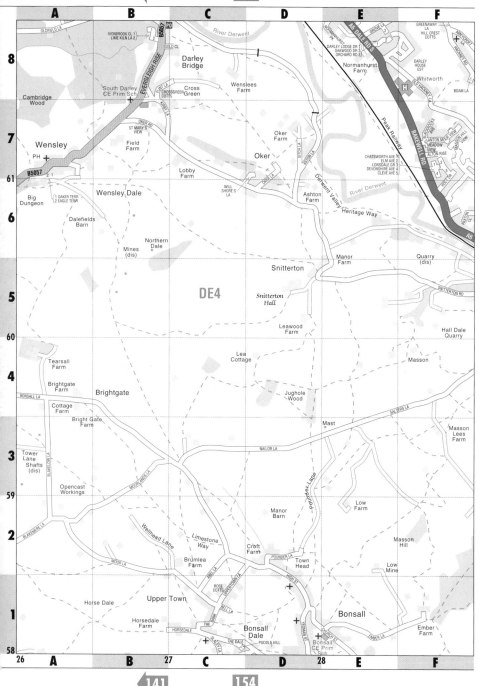

141
127

8

7

61

6

5

60

4

3

59

2

1

58

141
154

A   B   C   D   E   F

26   27   28

OLDFIELD LA

IVONBROOK CL 1
LIME KILN LA 2
GOLD CL

River Derwent

B5057
PO

EVERSLEIGH RISE

Darley
Bridge

South Darley
CE Prim Sch

UNIT LA
KIRK LA
CROSSGREEN
COTTS

Cross
Green

Wenslees
Farm

OKER RD
ST MARY'S
VIEW

Cambridge
Wood

Wensley

PH

B5057

Big
Dungeon

1 OAKER TERR
2 EAGLE TERR

Wensley Dale

Dalefields
Barn

Field
Farm

Lobby
Farm

WILL
SHORE'S
LA

OKER LA

Oker
Farm

Oker

SITCH LA

ASTON LA

Ashton
Farm

Derwent Valley Heritage Way

River Derwent

Mines
(dis)

Northern
Dale

Snitterton

Manor
Farm

Quarry
(dis)

DE4

Snitterton
Hall

Leawood
Farm

SNITTERTON RD

Hall Dale
Quarry

Tearsall
Farm

Brightgate
Farm

Lea
Cottage

Masson

BONSALL LA

Brightgate

Cottage
Farm

Bright Gate
Farm

BLAKELOW LA

Jughole
Wood

Mast

SALTERS LA

Masson
Lees
Farm

Tower
Lane
Shafts
(dis)

Opencast
Workings

MOORLANDS LA

NAILOR LA

POUNDER LANE

Low
Farm

BLAKEMERE LA

Wellhead Lane

Limestone
Way

Brumlea
Farm

Manor
Barn

Croft
Farm

POUNDER LA

Town
Head

Masson
Hill

Low
Mine

MOOR LA

BELL LA

ROSE
COTTS

NEWTON LA

HIGH ST

Horse Dale

Upper Town

Horsedale
Farm

THE BANK

HORSEDALE

BELL LA

THE

Bonsall
Dale

THE DALE

PUDDLE HILL

BLAKE CL LA

FERNEY ST

HIGH ST

DURCH ST

Bonsall
CE Prim
Sch

EMBER LA

Bonsall

Ember
Farm

A6 DALE RD S

NORMANHURST
PK
GROVE

DARLEY LODGE DR 1
OAKWOOD DR 2
ORCHARD RD 3

Normanhurst
Farm

GREENAWAY
LA
HILL CREST
COTTS

AA CLOSE

HACKNEY RD

DARLEY
HOUSE
EST

Whitworth

BOAM CL

H

OLD TICKNEY

Peak Railway

BAKEWELL RD

CHATSWORTH AVE 1
LONSDALE GR 3
DEVONSHIRE AVE 4
CLEVE AVE 5

CANTON MOUNT
ELM AVE 2
MEADOW
VIEW
ALTON RISE

COLOCKS
AVE

MASSEY HILL
VIEW

HOLT DR

PAXTON CL

A6

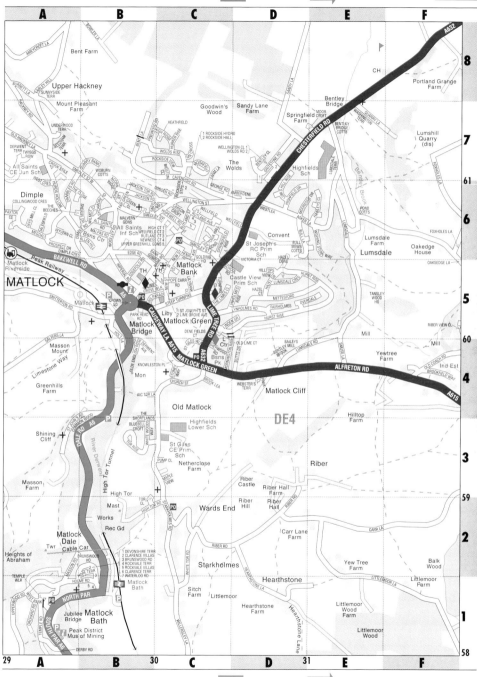

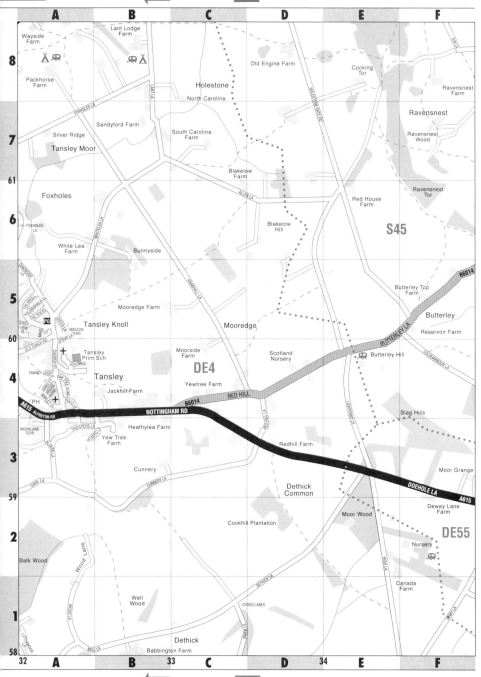

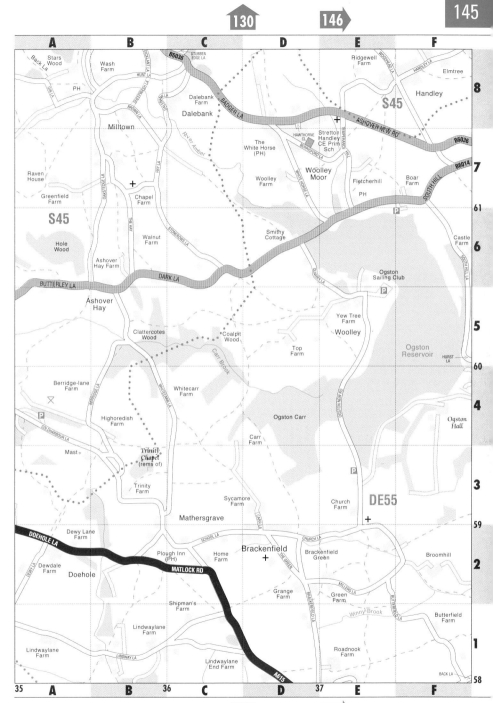

130   146

Stars Wood
Back La
Wash Farm
PH
B6036
STUBBEN EDGE LA
Ridgewell Farm
Elmtree
Handley
S45

Dalebank Farm
Dalebank
BADGER LA
HANDLEY LA

Milltown
River Amber
The White Horse (PH)
HAWTHORNE CL.
Stretton Handley CE Prim Sch
BERRISFORD LA
Ashover New Rd
B6036
B6014

Raven House
Woolley Farm
Woolley Moor
WHITE HORSE LA
Fletcherhill
PH
Boar Farm
SOUTH HILL
7

Greenfield Farm
Chapel Farm
THE HWY
61

S45
Hole Wood
Walnut Farm
STONESONS LA
Smithy Cottage
Ogston Sailing Club
P
Castle Farm
SOUTH HILL
6

Ashover Hay Farm
DARK LA
Yew Tree Farm
P
BUTTERLEY LA
Ashover Hay

Clattercotes Wood
Coalpit Wood
Top Farm
Woolley
5

Carr Brook
Ogston Reservoir
HURST LA
60

Berridge-lane Farm
BERRIDGE LA
WHITCARR LA
Whitecarr Farm
Ogston Carr
Ogston Hall
4

P
COLDHARBOUR LA
Highoredish Farm
Carr Farm

Mast
Trinity Chapel (rems of)
Church Farm
DE55
P
3

Trinity Farm
Sycamore Farm
LARK LA
59

DOEHOLE LA
Dewy Lane Farm
Mathersgrave
Brackenfield
Brackenfield Green
CHURCH LA
Broomhill
2

Dewdale Farm
GIN LA
Doehole
Plough Inn (PH)
SCHOOL LA
Home Farm
THE GREEN
Green Farm
MILLERS LA
BUTTERLEY LA

MATLOCK RD
Grange Farm
BRACKENFIELD LA
Green Farm
Winny Brook
Butterfield Farm

Lindwaylane Farm
Shipman's Farm
Roadnook Farm
1

Lindwaylane Farm
LINDWAY LA
Lindwaylane End Farm
A615
BACK LA
58

157   146

35   36   37

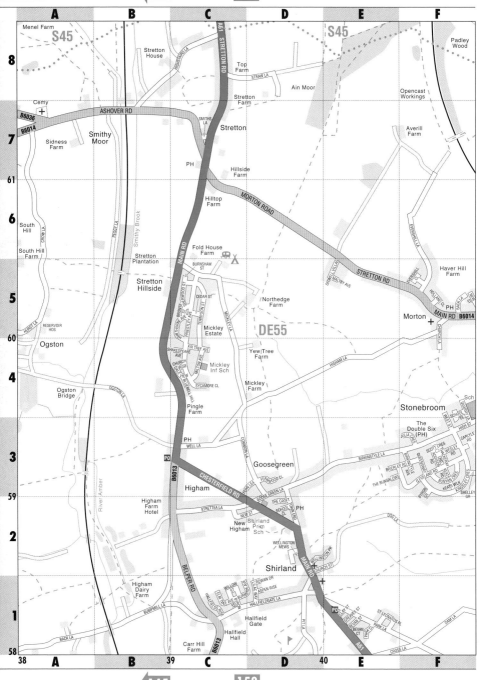

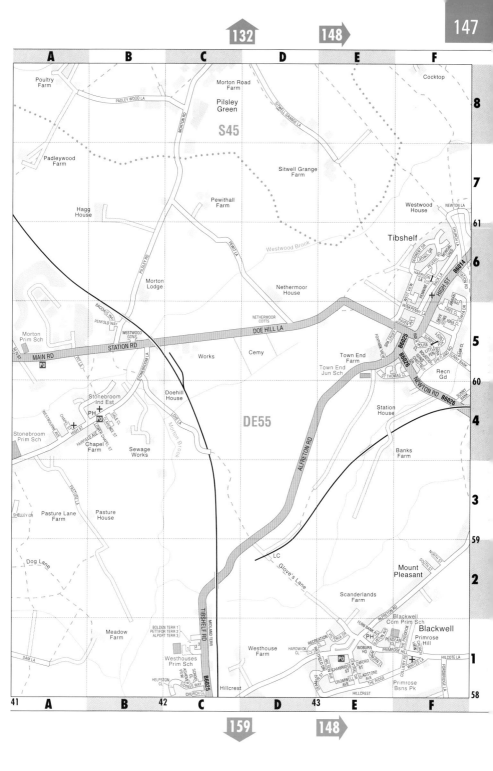

147
133

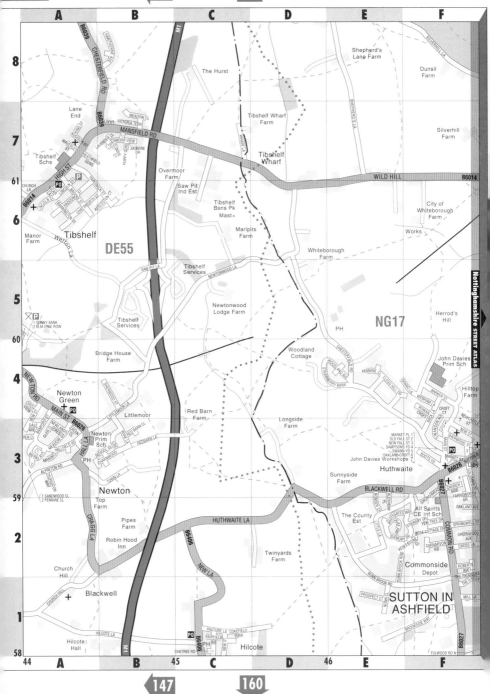

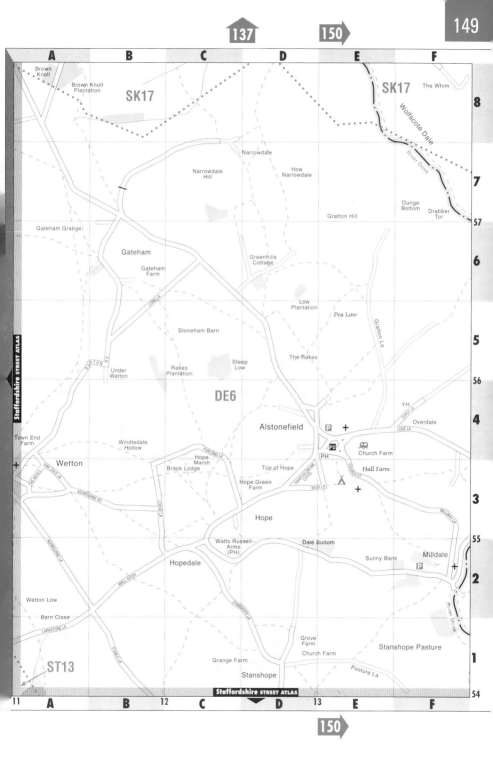

SK17

Brown Knoll

Brown Knoll Plantation

SK17

The Whim

Wolfscote Dale

River Dove

Narrowdale

Narrowdale Hill

How Narrowdale

Dunge Bottom

Drabber Tor

Gratton Hill

Gateham Grange

Gateham

Gateham Farm

Greenhills Cottage

Low Plantation

Pea Low

Gratton La

Stoneham Barn

Under Wetton

Rakes Plantation

Steep Low

The Rakes

DE6

Alstonefield

YH

Overdale

Lode La

Town End Farm

Windledale Hollow

Hope Marsh

Brook Lodge

Top of Hope

Church Farm

Hall Farm

Wetton

Furlong La

Hope Green Farm

Back La

Church St

Hope

Milldale La

Watts Russell Arms (PH)

Dale Bottom

Sunny Bank

Milldale

Hopedale

Wall Ditch

River Dove

Wetton Low

Stanshope La

Barn Close

Larkstone La

Grove Farm

Stanshope Pasture

Grange Farm

Church Farm

Pasture La

ST13

Stanshope

Staffordshire STREET ATLAS

Ashbourne Rd

Longe La

Buxton Rd

Long La

Etter La

149
138

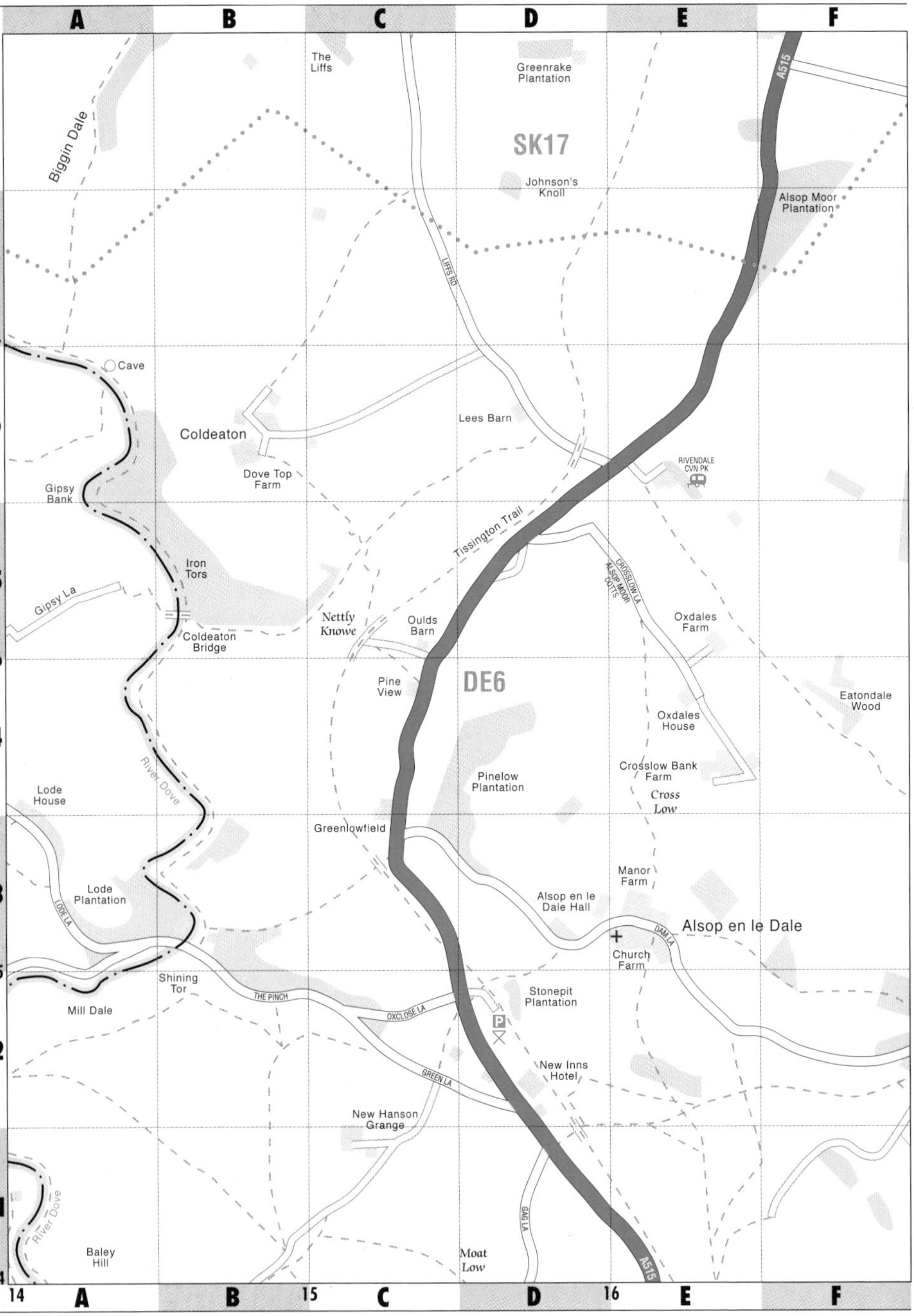

SK17

DE6

8

7

57

6

5

56

4

55

3

2

1

54

A   B   C   D   E   F

Biggin Dale

The Liffs

Greenrake Plantation

Johnson's Knoll

A515

Alsop Moor Plantation

Cave

Coldeaton

Lees Barn

RIVENDALE CVN PK

Gipsy Bank

Dove Top Farm

Iron Tors

Tissington Trail

Gipsy La

Coldeaton Bridge

Nettly Knowe

Oulds Barn

Oxdales Farm

Eatondale Wood

Pine View

Oxdales House

River Dove

Lode House

Pinelow Plantation

Crosslow Bank Farm

Cross Low

Lode Plantation

Greenlowfield

Manor Farm

A515

Alsop en le Dale Hall

Alsop en le Dale

Shining Tor

Church Farm

Mill Dale

THE PINCH

OXCLOSE LA

Stonepit Plantation

New Inns Hotel

GREEN LA

New Hanson Grange

Baley Hill

River Dove

Moat Low

A515

BAG LA

14   A   15   B   C   15   D   16   E   F

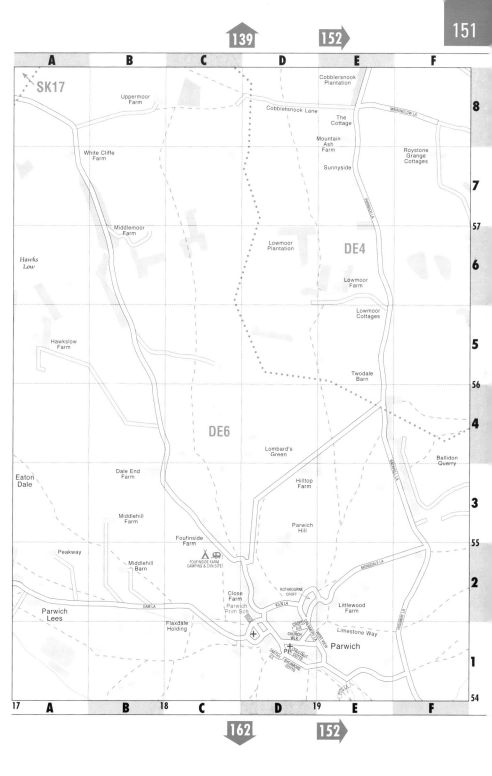

151
140

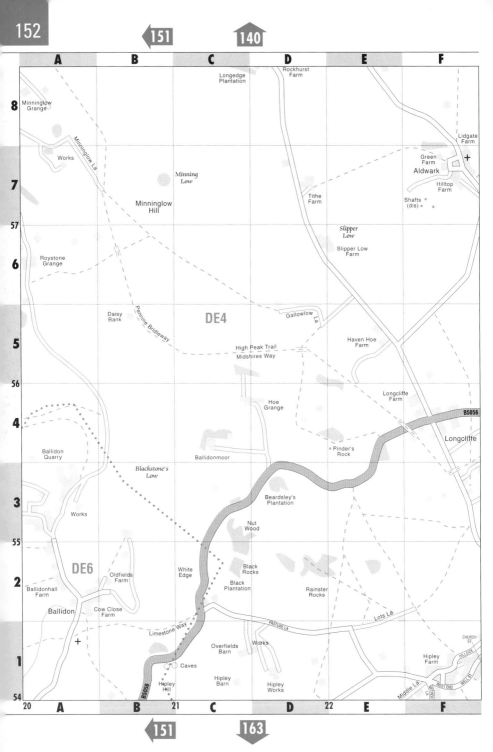

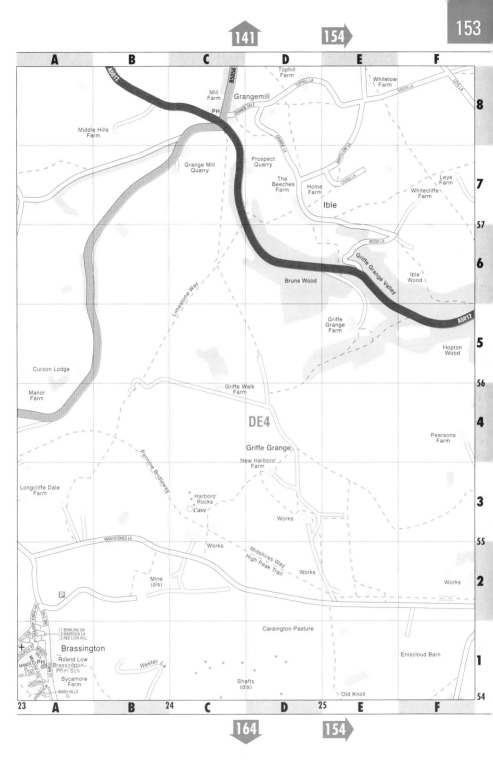

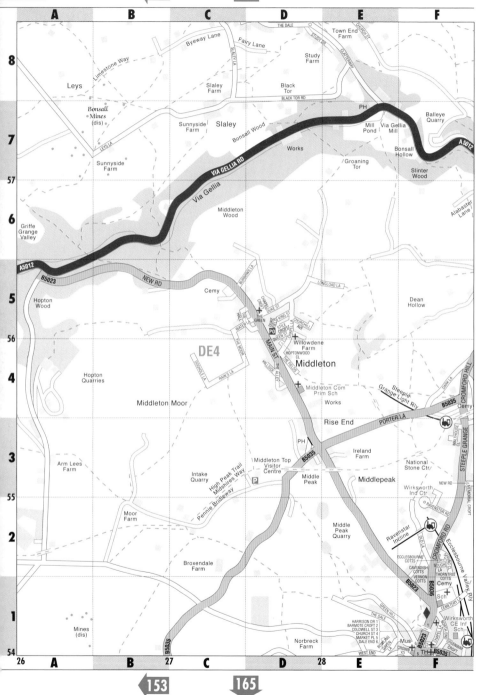

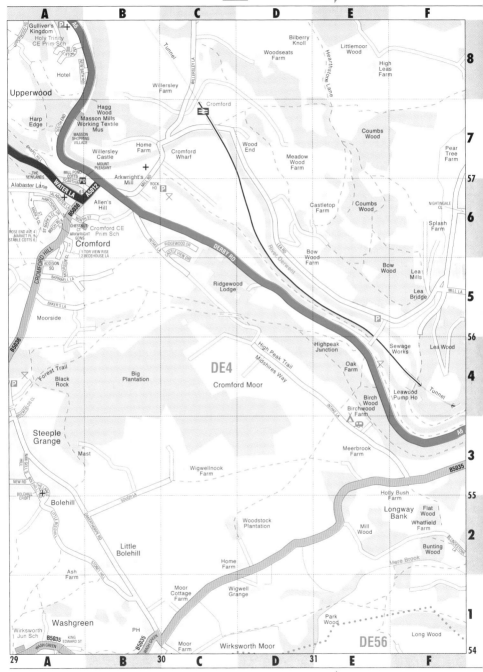

Gulliver's Kingdom
Holy Trinity CE Prim Sch
Hotel
Upperwood
Harp Edge
Hagg Wood
Masson Mills Working Textile Mus
MASSON SHOPPING VILLAGE
Willersley Castle
MOUNT PLEASANT
Home Farm
THE NEWLANDS
MILL POND COTTS
Arkwright's Mill
Alabaster Lane
WATER LA
Allen's Hill
ROCK RD
Cromford CE Prim Sch
CHESTNUT CT
ARKWRIGHT GDNS
Cromford
ROSE END AVE
MARKET PL
STABLE COTTS
2 TOR VIEW RISE
2 BEDEHOUSE LA
CROMFORD HILL
ADDISON SQ
BARNWELL LA
BAKER'S LA
Moorside
B5036
Forest Trail
Black Rock
Big Plantation
DE4
Cromford Moor
Steeple Grange
Mast
NEW RD
BOLEHILL CROFT
Bolehill
Little Bolehill
Ash Farm
SIDNEY HILL
Wirksworth Jun Sch
Washgreen
B5035
KING EDWARD ST
PH
WASH GREEN
B5035
WASH GREEN
Moor Farm
Moor Cottage Farm
Wigwell Grange
Wirksworth Moor
Home Farm
Woodstock Plantation
SOUGH LA
Wigwellnook Farm
High Peak Trail
Midshires Way
Cromford Wharf
Willersley Farm
Tunnel
WILLERSLEY LA
Cromford
Wood End
Woodseats Farm
Bilberry Knoll
Littlemoor Wood
High Leas Farm
Meadow Wood Farm
Coumbs Wood
Castletop Farm
Coumbs Wood
Hearthstone Lane
DERBY RD
RIDGEWOOD DR
Ridgewood Lodge
CASTLE VIEW DR
River Derwent
LEA RD
Bow Wood Farm
Bow Wood
Highpeak Junction
Oak Farm
Birch Wood
Birchwood Farm
INTAKE LA
Leawood Pump Ho
Tunnel
Sewage Works
Lea Wood
Bow Wood
Lea Mills
Lea Bridge
MILL LA
Pear Tree Farm
Splash Farm
NIGHTINGALE CL
A6
Meerbrook Farm
B5035
Holly Bush Farm
Longway Bank
Flat Wood
Whatfield Farm
Mill Wood
Bunting Wood
BUNTING LA
Mere Brook
Park Wood
Long Wood
DE56
Wirksworth Moor

8
7
57
6
5
56
4
3
55
2
1
54

29 30 31
A B C D E F

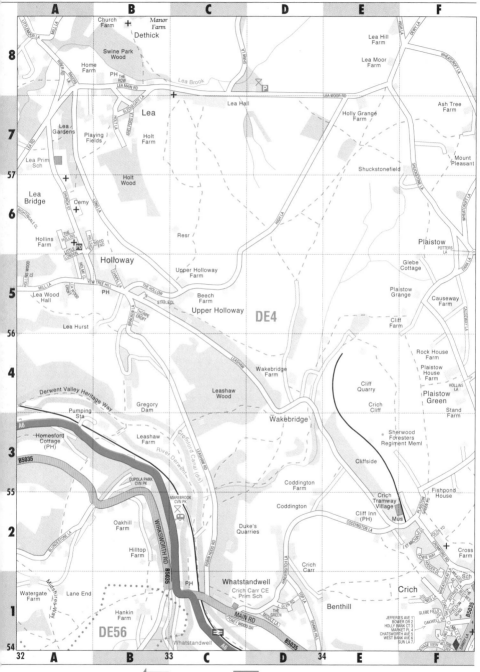

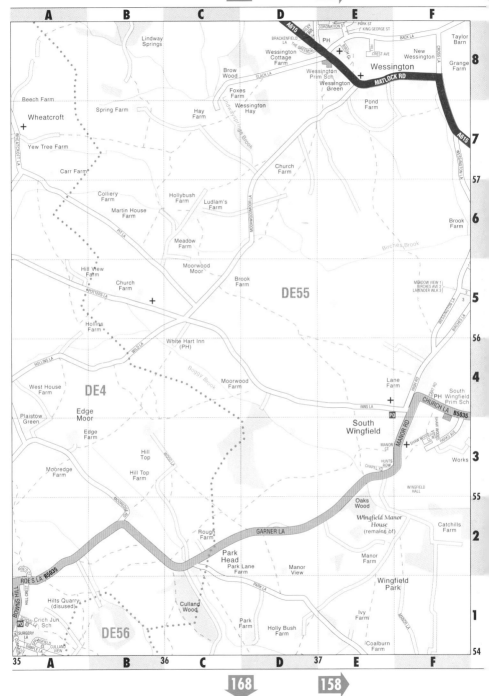

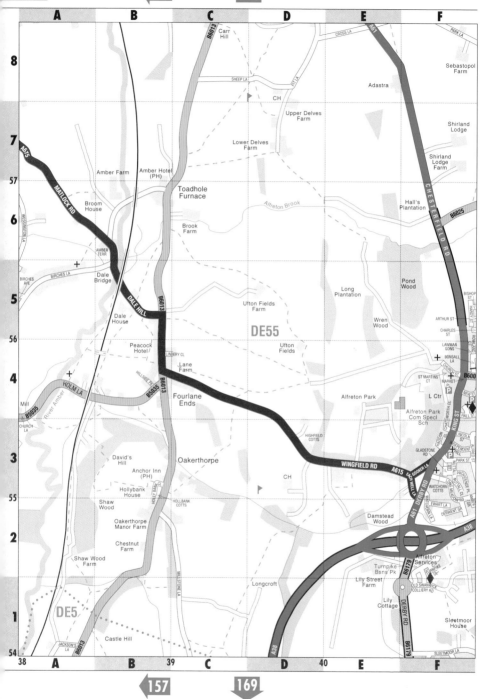

157
146

A   B   C   D   E   F

8

7

57

6

5

56

4

3

55

2

1

54

38   A   B   39   C   D   40   E   F

157
169

Carr Hill
PIT LA
CROSS LA
PARK LA
SHEEP LA
Sebastopol Farm
Adastra
Upper Delves Farm
Shirland Lodge
Lower Delves Farm
Shirland Lodge Farm
Amber Farm
Amber Hotel (PH)
Toadhole Furnace
Alfreton Brook
Hall's Plantation
B6025
Broom House
Brook Farm
MATLOCK RD
WESSINGTON LA
A615
AMBER TERR
Dale Bridge
BIRCHES AVE
BIRCHES LA
Dale House
DALE HILL
B6013
Ufton Fields Farm
Long Plantation
Pond Wood
CHESTERFIELD RD
BISHOP
HARDY ST
ARTHUR ST
Peacock Hotel
Wren Wood
CHARLES ST
LAWMAN GDNS
BONSALL LA
B600
DE55
Ufton Fields
LINBERY CL
Lane Farm
HILLSIDE CL
B6013
B5035
HOLM LA
River Amber
Mill
B5035
CHURCH LA
Fourlane Ends
Ufton Fields
HIGHFIELD COTTS
ST MARTINS CT
MARKET
L Ctr
P
Alfreton Park
Alfreton Park Com Specl Sch
GLADSTONE RD
KING ST
LINCOLN
PARK ST
P
David's Hill
Anchor Inn (PH)
Oakerthorpe
CH
WINGFIELD RD
A615
EASTWELL LA
A61 DERBY RD
Hollybank House
Shaw Wood
HOLLBANK COTTS
HOLLBANK COTTS
WATCHORN COTTS
EWART LA
DERWENT DR
Oakerthorpe Manor Farm
Chestnut Farm
MILLSTONE LA
Damstead Wood
A38
Shaw Wood Farm
Turnpike Bsns' Pk
Alfreton Services
B6179
OLD SWANWICK COLLIERY RD
Longcroft
Lily Street Farm
Lily Cottage
DE5
JACKSON'S LA
B6013
Castle Hill
A38
DERBY RD
B6179
SLEETMOOR LA
Sleetmoor House

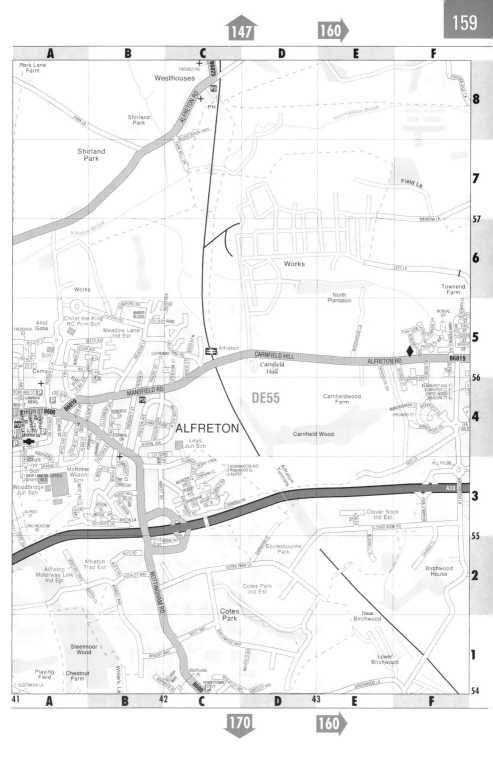

159
148

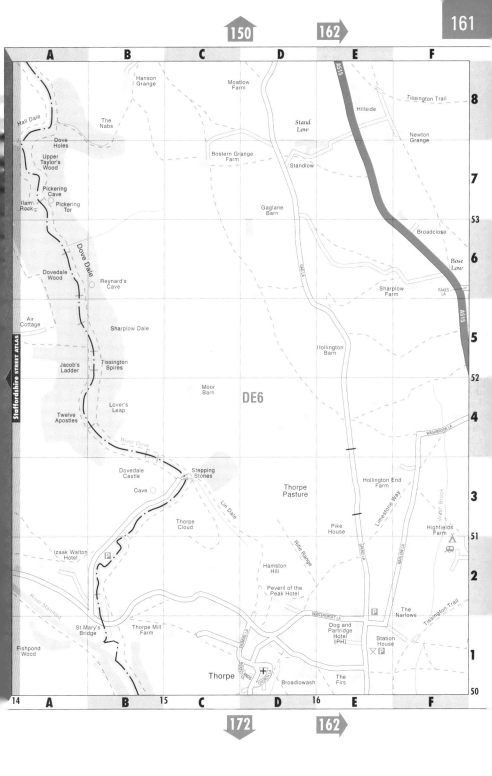

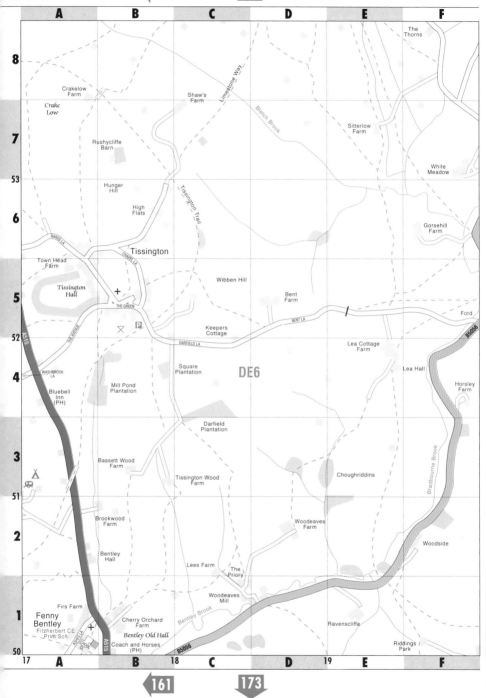

The Thorns

8

Crakelow
Farm

Crake
Low

Shaw's
Farm

Limestone Way

Bletch Brook

Sitterlow
Farm

7

Rushycliffe
Barn

White
Meadow

53

Hunger
Hill

High
Flats

Tissington Trail

6

Gorsehill
Farm

RAKES LA

Tissington

Town Head
Farm

CHAPEL LA

Wibben Hill

Bent
Farm

Ford

B5056

5

Tissington
Hall

THE GREEN

BENT LA

52

THE AVENUE

P

Keepers
Cottage

DARFIELD LA

Lea Cottage
Farm

Lea Hall

A515

Square
Plantation

DE6

Horsley
Farm

4

WASHBROOK
LA

Bluebell
Inn
(PH)

Mill Pond
Plantation

Darfield
Plantation

Bradbourne Brook

Choughriddins

3

Bassett Wood
Farm

Tissington Wood
Farm

51

Brookwood
Farm

Woodeaves
Farm

Woodside

2

Bentley
Hall

Lees Farm

The
Priory

Firs Farm

Fenny
Bentley

Fitzherbert CE
Prim Sch

BENTLEY LA

A515

Cherry Orchard
Farm

Bentley Old Hall

Coach and Horses
(PH)

Woodeaves
Mill

Bentley Brook

B5056

Ravenscliffe

Riddings
Park

1

50

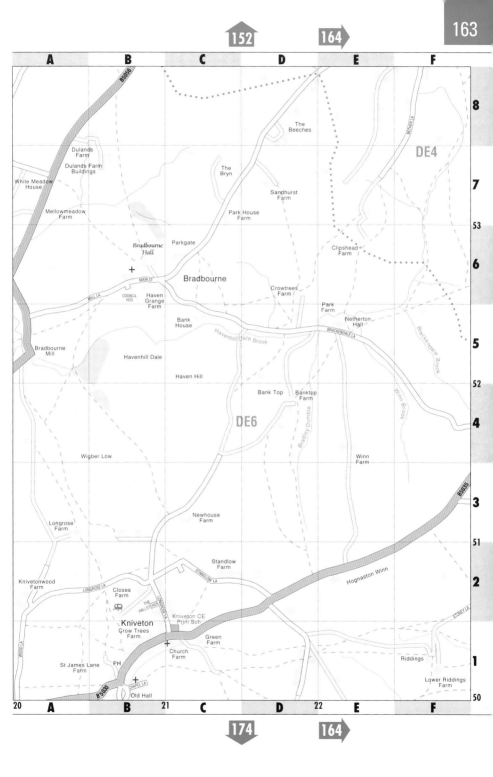

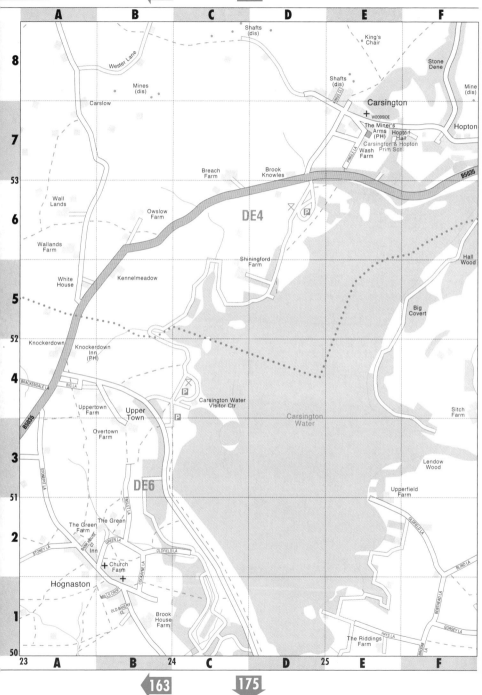

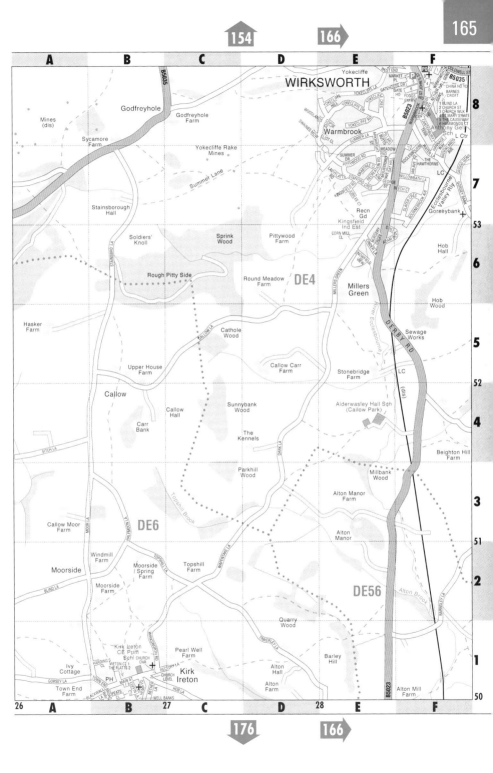

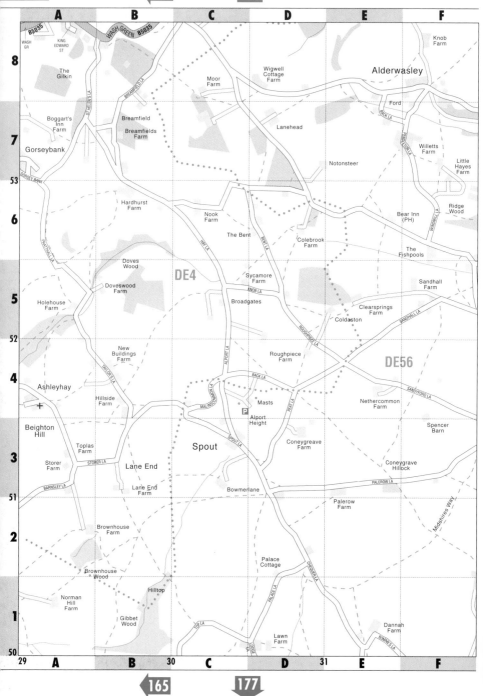

165
155

A B C D E F

8

7

53

6

5

52

4

3

51

2

1

50

29 A B 30 C D 31 E F

165
177

B5035
WASH GR
KING EDWARD ST
The Gilkin
Boggart's Inn Farm
Gorseybank
GORSEL BANK
PINFOLD LA
ST HELEN'S LA
WASH GREEN B5035
Breamfield
Breamfields Farm
BREAMFIELD LA
Moor Farm
Wigwell Cottage Farm
Lanehead
Notonsteer
Alderwasley
Ford
BACK LA
FIRESTONE LA
Knob Farm
Willetts Farm
Little Hayes Farm
Hardhurst Farm
Nook Farm
The Bent
HAY LA
BENT LA
Colebrook Farm
Bear Inn (PH)
WINDMILL LA
Ridge Wood
The Fishpools
DE4
Doves Wood
Doveswood Farm
Sycamore Farm
KNOB LA
Broadgates
Coldaston
Clearsprings Farm
Sandhall Farm
SANDHALL LA
Holehouse Farm
New Buildings Farm
TAYLOR'S LA
ALPORT LA
ROUGHPIECE LA
Roughpiece Farm
DE56
Ashleyhay
Hillside Farm
MALTHOUSE LA
MALENS LA
BACK LA
Masts
Alport Height
PEAT LA
Nethercommon Farm
SANDYFORD LA
Spencer Barn
Beighton Hill
Toplas Farm
Storer Farm
STORER LA
BARNSLEY LA
Lane End
SPOUT LA
Spout
Coneygreave Farm
Coneygrave Hillock
PALEROW LA
Lane End Farm
Bowmerlane
Palerow Farm
Midshires Way
Brownhouse Farm
Brownhouse Wood
Hilltop
Gibbet Wood
Norman Hill Farm
Palace Cottage
PLACE LA
CRESER LA
TOP LA
LODGE LA
Lawn Farm
Dannah Farm
ROMAN LA
P

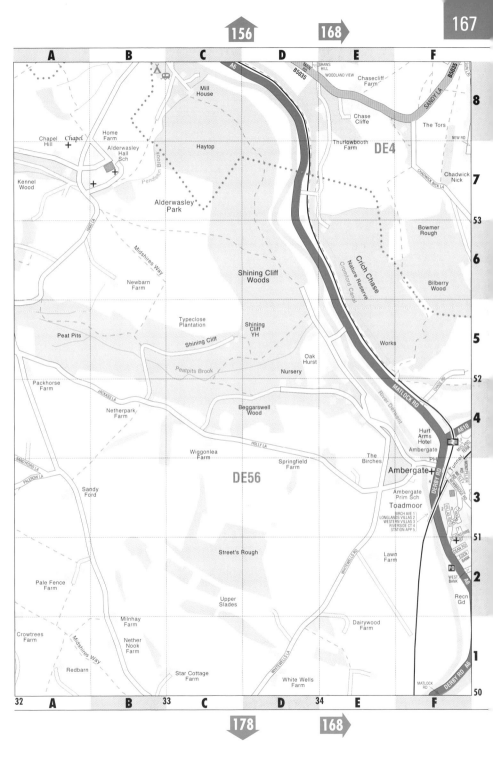

167
157

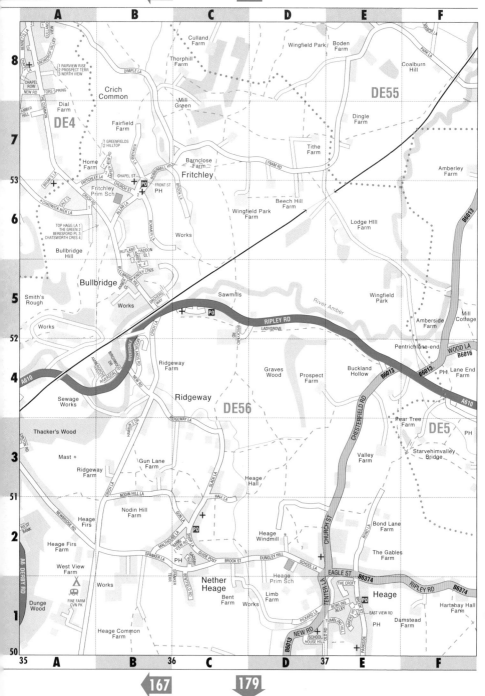

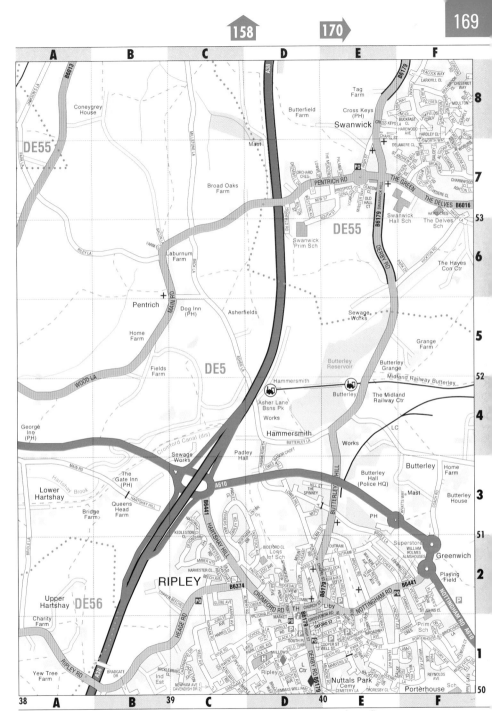

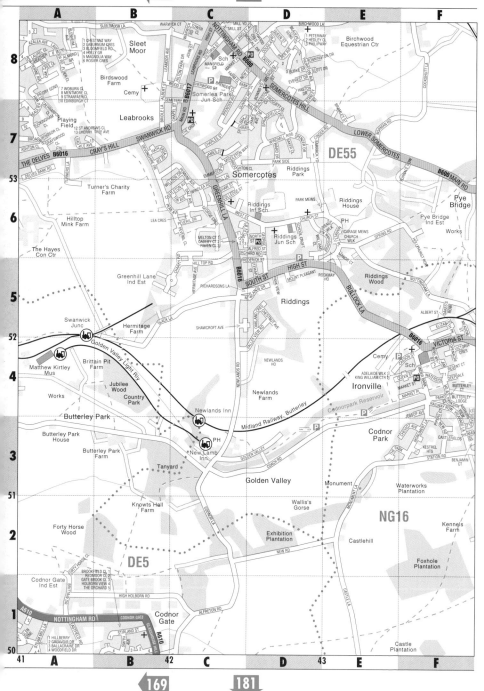

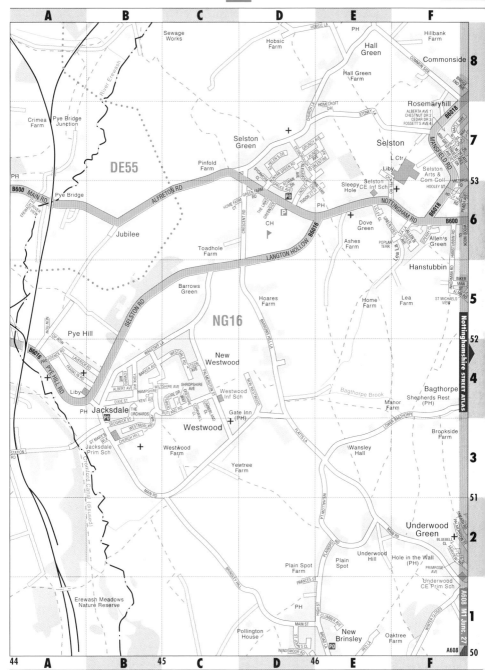

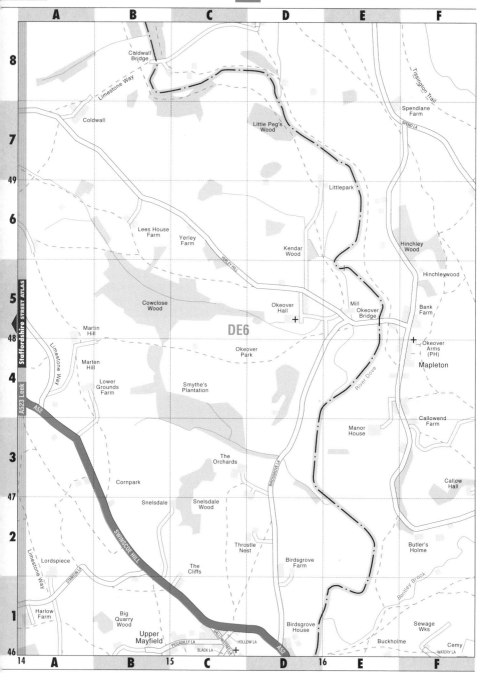

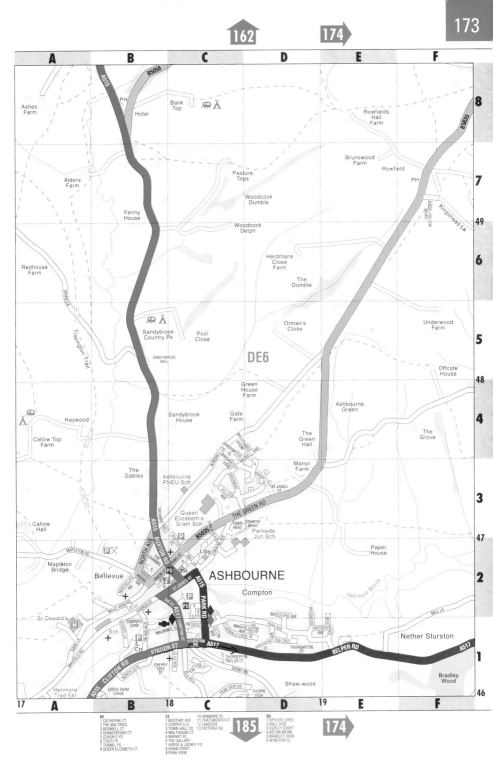

162   174

Ashes Farm

Alders Farm

Rowfields Hall Farm

Brunswood Farm

Rowfield PH

Fenny House

B5056

A515

PH

Hotel

Bank Top Hotel

Kings Hollow Mews

Kingshead La

49

Pasture Tops

Woodcock Dumble

Woodcock Delph

Redhouse Farm

Tissington Trail

Herdmans Close Farm

The Dumble

Underwood Farm

6

Sandybrook Country Pk

Pool Close

Orman's Close

Offcote House

5

SANDYBROOK HALL

DE6

48

Haywood

Green House Farm

Ashbourne Green

Sandybrook House

Gate Farm

The Green Hall

The Grove

4

Callow Top Farm

The Gables

Ashbourne PNEU Sch

Manor Farm

St James Ct

The Green Rd

47

Callow Hall

Queen Elizabeth's Gram Sch

Cokayne Mews Town Head

Parkside Jun Sch

Paper House

3

Mapleton Bridge

Bellevue

A515 BUXTON RD NORTHAVE

Liby

PO

TH

ASHBOURNE

Compton

Henmore Brook

2

St Oswald's H

Sch

PARK RD

A515

PO

Peter St

Beresford Ave

Park Ave

Brookside

Mill La

Nether Sturston

St John's St

Malbon's St

Sturston Rd

A517

Thornley Pl
Taylor Ct

Manifold Ave
Oswald Cres
Owton Cres
Rousseau Ct
Thurgarton Ct

Okeover Ave

Belper Rd

A517

1

Ctr

Station St

Clifton Rd

A515

Cherry Tree Ct

Derby Rd

Peak View Dr

Thorpe View

Shaw-wood

Bradley Wood

46

Henmore Trad Est

Lodge Farm Chase

17   A   18   B   C   18   C   D   19   E   F

185   174

B2
1 CATHERINE CT
2 THE MALTINGS
3 BOSWELL CT
4 SHAKESPEARE CT
5 COXON'S YD
6 TIGER YD
7 TUNNEL YD
8 QUEEN ELIZABETH CT

C2
1 BOOTHBY AVE
2 COOPER S CL
3 TOWN HALL YD
4 MALTHOUSE CT
5 MARKET PL
6 THE GALLERY
7 HORSE & JOCKEY YD
8 SHAW CROFT
9 PARK VIEW
10 HENMORE PL
11 CHATSWORTH CT
12 LAKESIDE
13 VICTORIA SQ

D3
1 OFFCOTE CRES
2 HALL RISE
3 COPLEY CROFT
4 ATLOW BROW
5 BRADLEY VIEW
6 WINDSOR CL

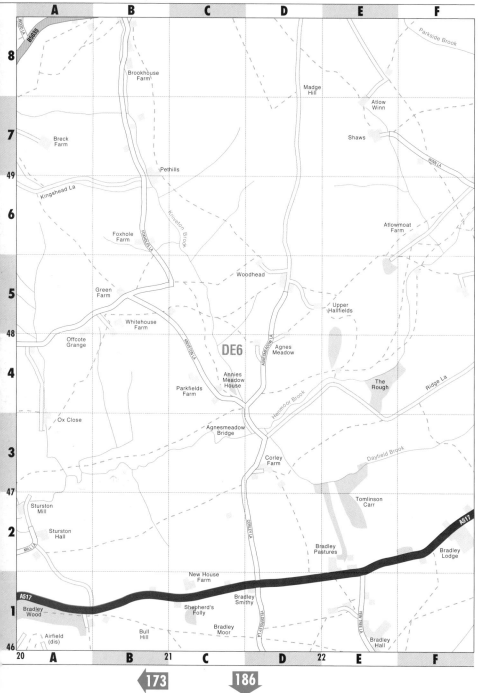

1ST set of crossroads turn left onto biggin lane

Pentagraph Limited   Hammond House   Heapy Street   Macclesfield   Cheshire   SK11 7JB
Tel: 01625 619257   Fax: 01625 424888   ISDN: 01625 501253
Web: www.pentagraph.co.uk   E-mail: sales@pentagraph.co.uk

Pentagraph

TOTAL PRINT SOLUTIONS

Leek, ashbourne,

over 1st roundabout, 2nd roundabout

turn left (pg 185 derbyshire) - A515 Clifton Rd - (pg 173)

- keep straight on A517 Belper Rd keep going

Holland ward - stay on A517 - follow main rd

Holland
Ward

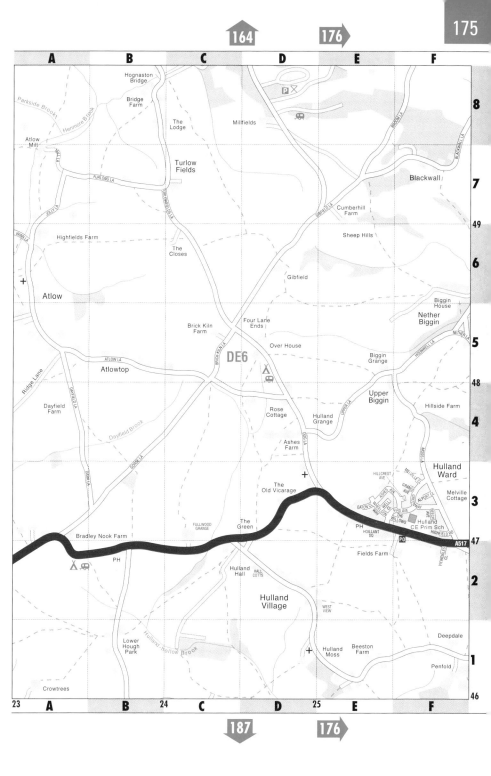

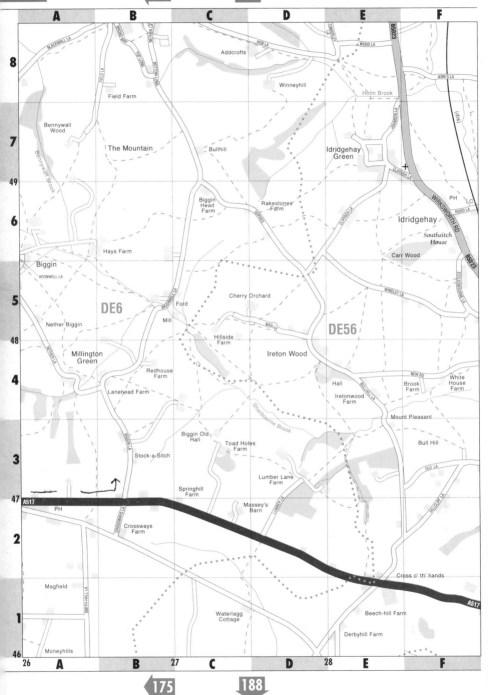

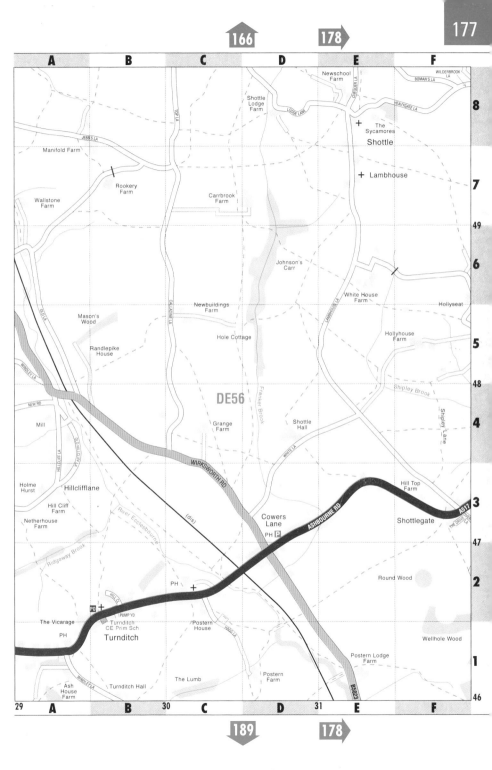

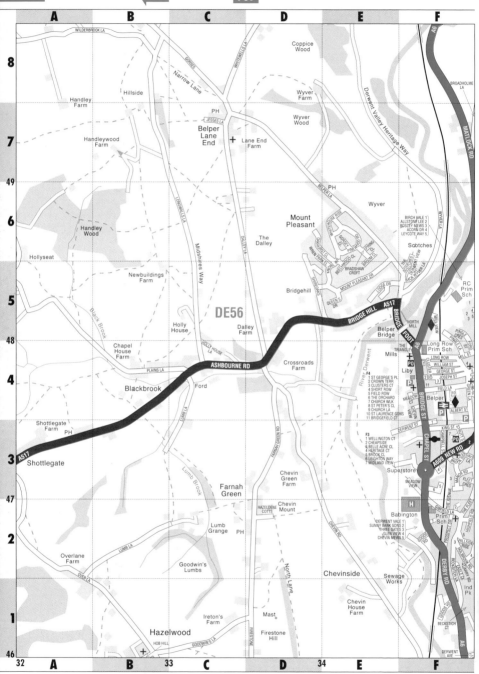

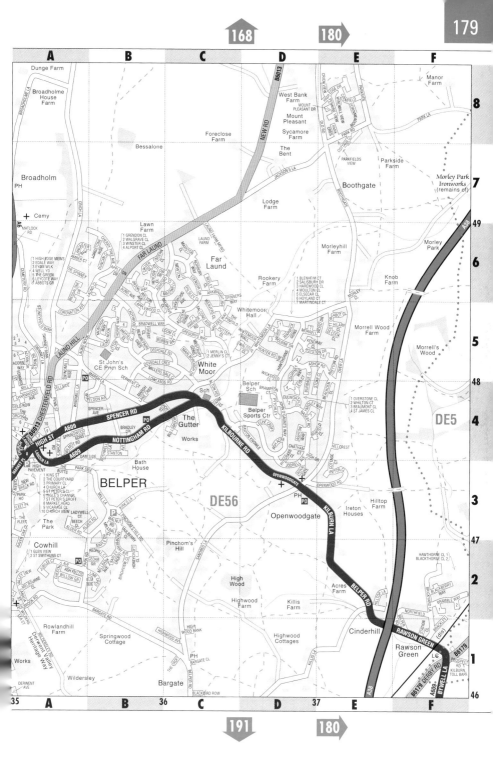

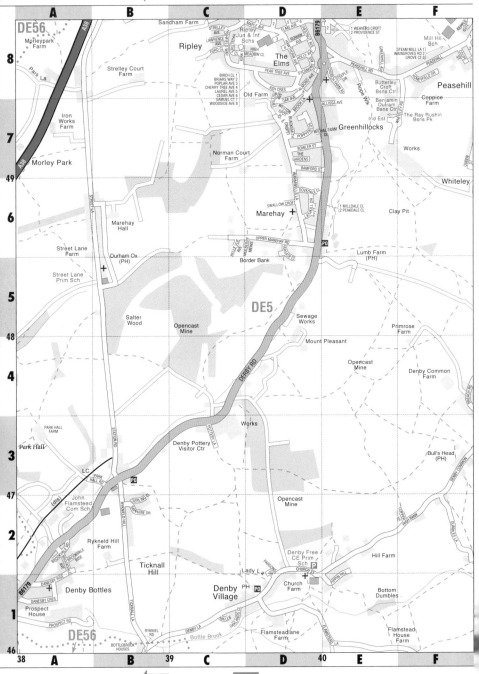

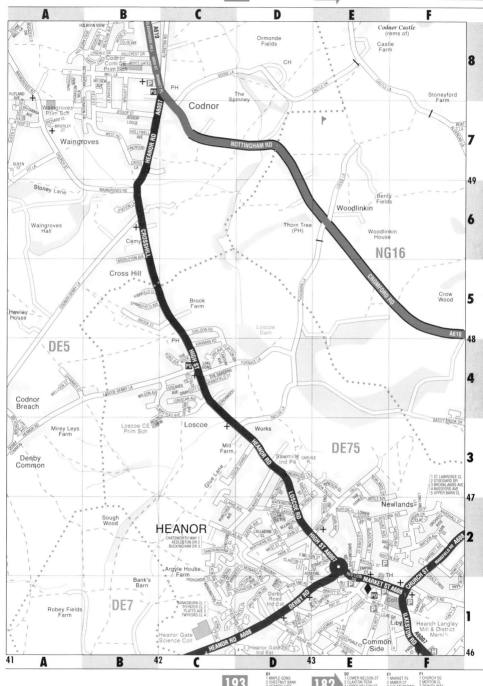

D1
1 MAPLE GDNS
2 CHESTNUT BANK
3 HEANOR GATE
4 HEANOR GATE RD
5 KIRKHAM CL

D2
1 LOWER NELSON ST
2 CLAXTON TERR
3 UPPER NELSON ST
4 HAMPTON CT

E1
1 MARKET PL
2 AMBER CT
3 THE MEADOWS
4 LOCTON AVE

F1
1 CHURCH SQ
2 MERTON CL
3 TRINITY WAY
4 GREYFRIARS CL
5 WESTFIELD AVE
6 ELLA BANK RD

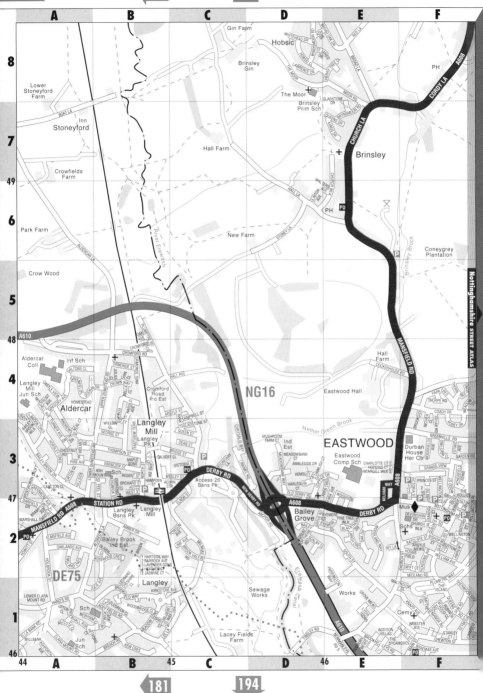

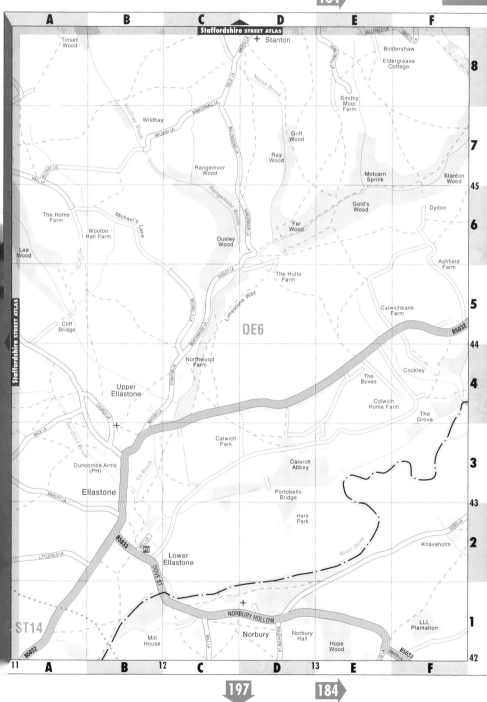

184

Staffordshire STREET ATLAS

Staffordshire STREET ATLAS

| | A | B | C | D | E | F |

Tinsell
Wood

Stanton

Boldershaw

Eldergreave
Cottage

8

Marsh Brook

Smithy
Moor
Farm

Wildhay
Brook

Wildhay

BANKERWALL LA

SALLYFIELD LA

DAGLEY LA

HOWL LA

THWALL LA

7

Griff
Wood

WILDHAY LA

Rangemoor
Wood

Ray
Wood

FEILD LA

WILLSDOWNE LA

MAPPS LA

Motcarn
Sprink

Stanton
Wood

45

WILDHAY LA

Rangemoor Brook

HALL LA

The Home
Farm

Michael's
Lane

Far
Wood

Gold's
Wood

Dydon

6

Wooton
Hall Farm

Ousley
Wood

RANGEMOOR LA

Lee
Wood

Ashfield
Farm

DUSLEY LA

The Hutts
Farm

5

Cliff
Bridge

Limestone Way

MICHAEL ST LA

Calwichbank
Farm

DE6

B5032

44

NORTHWOOD LA

Northwood
Farm

Cockley

The
Boxes

4

Upper
Ellastone

STANTON LA

Colwich
Home Farm

The
Grove

CHURCH LA

WATERY LA

Calwich
Park

BACK LA

Sandford Brook

Duncombe Arms
(PH)

Tit Brook

Calwich
Abbey

3

Ellastone

MARLPIT LA

Portobello
Bridge

SIDES LA

43

Hare
Park

Knaveholm

2

LITTLEFIELD LA

B5033

MILL LA

PO

River Dove

Lower
Ellastone

ST14

DOVE ST

Norbury
Hall

LLL
Plantation

1

B5032

Mill
House

Norbury

NORBURY HOLLOW

MILL LA

Hope
Wood

GREEN LA

B5033

ROUGH LA

42

| 11 | A | B | 12 | C | D | 13 | E | F |

184

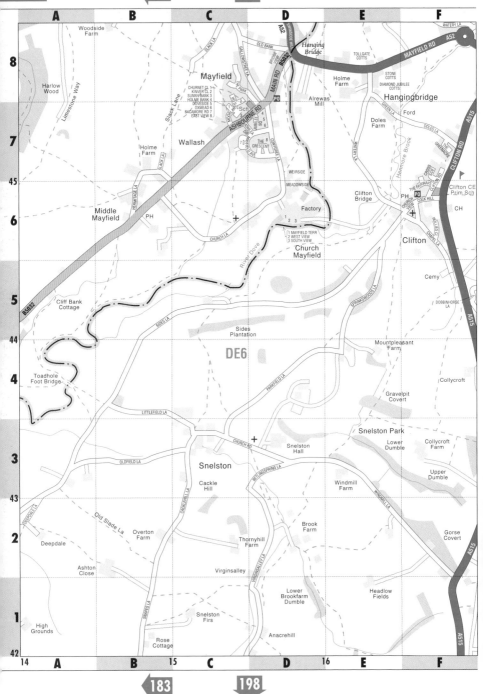

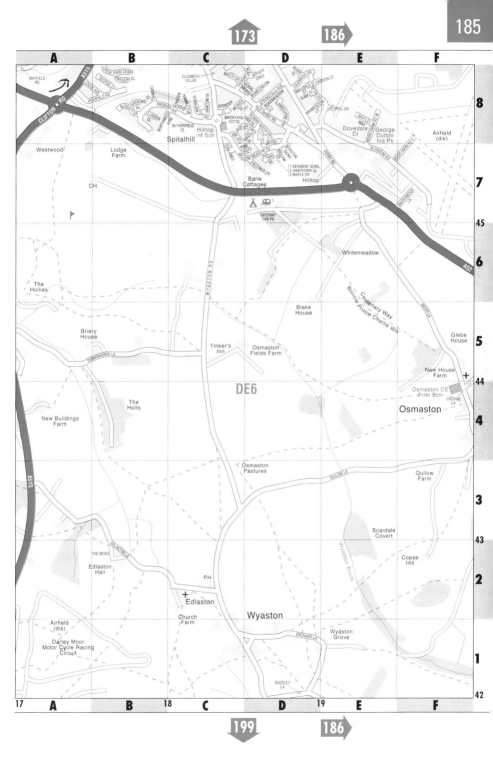

A B C D E F

8

MAYFIELD RD

CLIFTON · RD
A515

COSE FARM CHASE
ORGERY CL
GEORGE ST
LOOK AVE
HIGHFIELD RD
HABORO
PREMIER
DURENT
NORTHINGTON
UMBER
HAMILTON
FORESTON
ELIZABETH VILLAS
BOOTH DR
DUNCOMBE DR
SPENCER
WOFLDC
BUMFORD DR
WRIGHT
GATES
SPRINGFIELD RD
OLD DERBY RD
CHINMEADOW
MILLDALE
MOSS
HADDON CT
LATHKILL DR

Westwood
Lodge Farm
NETHERFIELD CL
Spitalhill
Hilltop Inf Sch
BRICKYARD COTTS
POPLAR DR
CROFT
WILLOW MEADOW RD
COM GDNS
WILLOW CHESTNUT DR
WELLOW
WEYSTON

Dovedale Ct
WHITLEY WAY
George Dutton Ind Pk
Airfield (dis)

7

CH

1 DERWENT GDNS
2 HAWTHORN CL
3 MAPLE DR
Hilltop
Bank Cottages
GATEWAY CVN PK

BLENHEIM RD
MOAT FARM RD
DERBY RD

SNIPEMOOR LA

45

WYASTON RD

Whitemeadow

6
A52

The Hollies

Blake House
Centenary Way
Bonnie Prince Charlie Wlk
MOOR LA

Glebe House

5

Briery House

DOBBINHORSE LA

Tinker's Inn
Osmaston Fields Farm

New House Farm

44

DE6

Osmaston CE Prim Sch
CHURCH LA
Osmaston

4

New Buildings Farm
A515

The Holts

Osmaston Pastures

QUILOW LA

Quilow Farm

3

Scardale Covert

43

EDLASTON LA
THE MEWS
Edlaston Hall

PH

Copse Hill

WYASTON BROOK

2

Airfield (dis)
Darley Moor Motor Cycle Racing Circuit

Edlaston
Church Farm

Wyaston

ORCHARD LA

Wyaston Grove

RODSLEY LA

1

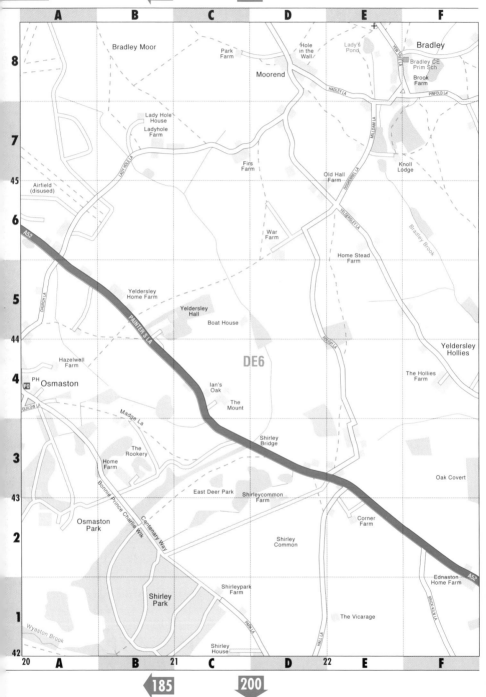

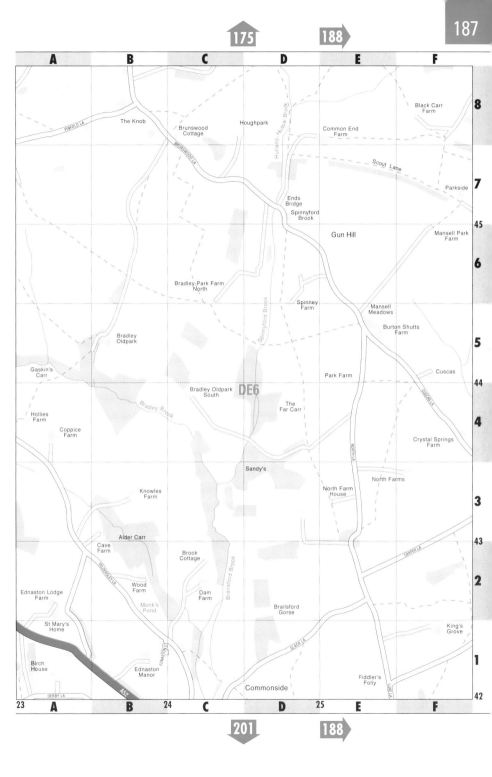

175
188

A   B   C   D   E   F

8

Black Carr
Farm

The Knob

Brunswood
Cottage

Houghpark

Common End
Farm

PINFOLD LA

BRUNSWOOD LA

Hulland Hollow Brook

Scout Lane

Parkside

7

Ends
Bridge

Spinnyford
Brook

45

Gun Hill

Mansell Park
Farm

6

Bradley Park Farm
North

Spinnyford Brook

Spinney
Farm

Mansell
Meadows

Burton Shutts
Farm

Bradley
Oldpark

5

Gaskin's
Carr

Bradley Oldpark
South

DE6

Park Farm

Cuscas

GISGATE LA

44

Hollies
Farm

Bradley Brook

The
Far Carr

Crystal Springs
Farm

4

Coppice
Farm

Sandy's

North Farms

NORTH LA

Knowles
Farm

North Farm
House

3

Alder Carr

43

Cave
Farm

Brook
Cottage

CAMPER LA

FLTCHERS LA

Wood
Farm

Dam
Farm

Brailsford Brook

2

Ednaston Lodge
Farm

Monk's
Pond

Brailsford
Gorse

King's
Grove

EDNASTON LA

St Mary's
Home

SLACK LA

1

Birch
House

A52

Ednaston
Manor

Fiddler's
Folly

LUME LA

DERBY LA

Commonside

42

23   A   B   24   C   D   25   E   F

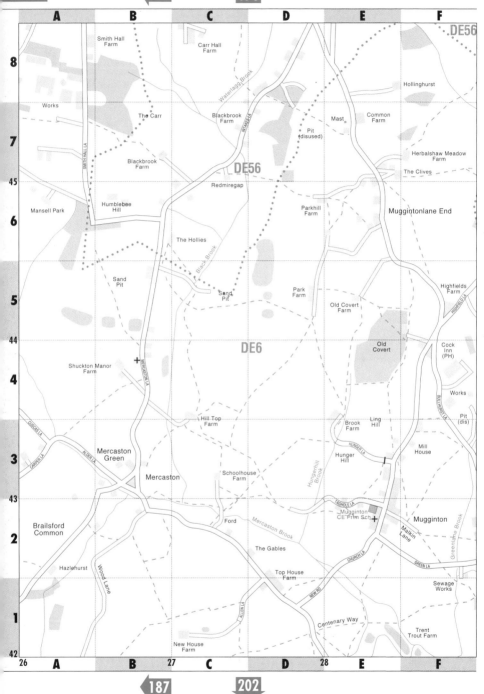

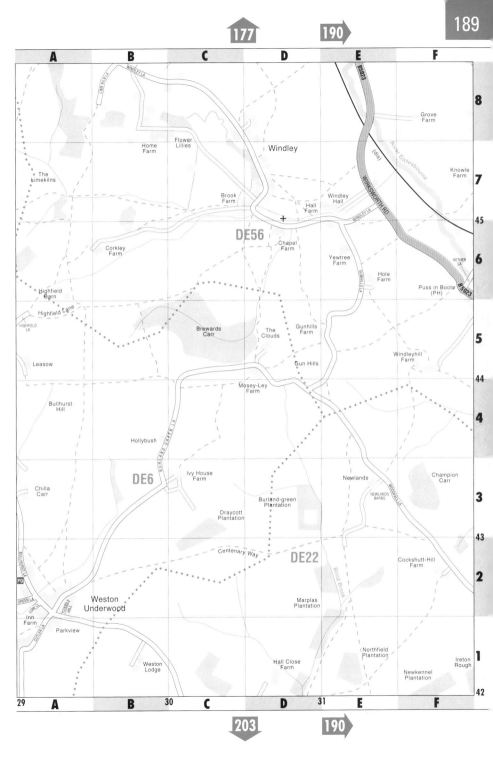

A B C D E F

8

B5023

Grove
Farm

River Ecclesbourne

(dis)

Knowle
Farm

7

The
Limekilns

Home
Farm

Flower
Lillies

Windley

Brook
Farm

Windley
Hall

WIRKSWORTH RD

Windley LA

45

Hall
Farm

+

DE56

Corkley
Farm

Chapel
Farm

Yewtree
Farm

Hole
Farm

NETHER
LA

6

Puss in Boots
(PH)

B5023

Highfield
Barn

Highfield Lane

HIGHFIELD
LA

Brewards
Carr

The
Clouds

Gunhills
Farm

GUNHILLS LA

Windleyhill
Farm

5

Leasow

Gun Hills

44

Bullhurst
Hill

Mosey-Ley
Farm

4

Hollybush

BURLAND GREEN LA

Ivy House
Farm

Newlands

WOODFALL LA

Champion
Carr

3

Chilla
Carr

DE6

Draycott
Plantation

Burland-green
Plantation

NEWLANDS
BARNS

43

BALLHURST LA

GREEN LA

PO

Centenary Way

DE22

Cockshutt-Hill
Farm

2

LOW LA

THIMBLE
HILL

Weston
Underwood

Marplas
Plantation

Blind Brook

Inn
Farm

COTTER LA

Parkview

Northfield
Plantation

Ireton
Rough

1

Weston
Lodge

Hall Close
Farm

Newkennel
Plantation

42

29 A B 30 C D 31 E F

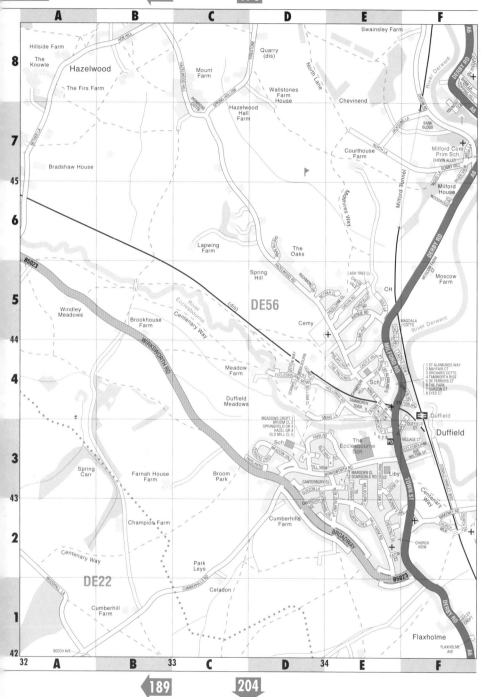

A B C D E F

8

Hillside Farm
The Knowle
Hazelwood
The Firs Farm
Mount Farm
Quarry (dis)
Swainsley Farm

Wallstones Farm House
North Lane
Chevinend
Milford Com Prim Sch
BANK BLDGS
CHEVIN ALLEY
SUNNY HILL

7

Hazelwood Hall Farm
Courthouse Farm
Milford House

Bradshaw House

45

6

Lapwing Farm
The Oaks
Spring Hill
Moscow Farm

River Derwent

DERBY RD

A6

Milford Tunnel

B5023

Windley Meadows
Brookhouse Farm
River Ecclesbourne
Centenary Way
(dis)
DE56
ASH TREE CL
CH
CH

5

44

Cemy
River Derwent
MAGDALA COTTS

WIRKSWORTH RD

Meadow Farm
ECCLESBOURNE
THE PASTURES
Sch
St ALKMUNDS
MILFORD RD
CASTLE HILL
STATION APP

4

1 ST ALKMUNDS WAY
2 MAYFAIR CT
3 ORCHARD COTTS
4 TAMWORTH RISE
5 DE FERRERS CT
6 THE PARK
7 CURZON CT
8 EYES CT

Duffield Meadows
SNAKE LA
TAMWORTH TERR
Duffield
DUFFIELD CT
Duffield

3

Spring Carr
Farnah House Farm
Broom Park
MEADOWS CROFT 1
BROOM CL 2
SPRINGFIELD DR 3
HAZEL GR 4
OLD MILL CL 5
Sch
MEADOW VALE
HILL VIEW
PARK RD
The Ecclesbourne Sch
VILLAGE CT
ECCLESBOURNE
WILTRA GR
Liby
Centenary Way
MAKENEY RD

43

CHAMPION FARM
Canterbury Cl
CURZON LA
CAVENDISH
1 MARSDEN CL
2 SCARSDALE RD
CHURCH VIEW
CHURCH WLK

2

Champion Farm
Cumberhills Farm
BROADWAY
EATON CL
B5023

Centenary Way
DE22
Park Leys
Celadon
Flaxholme
FLAXHOLME AVE

1

Cumberhill Farm
BEECH AVE

42

32 A 33 B C 33 D 34 E F

DERBY RD
A6

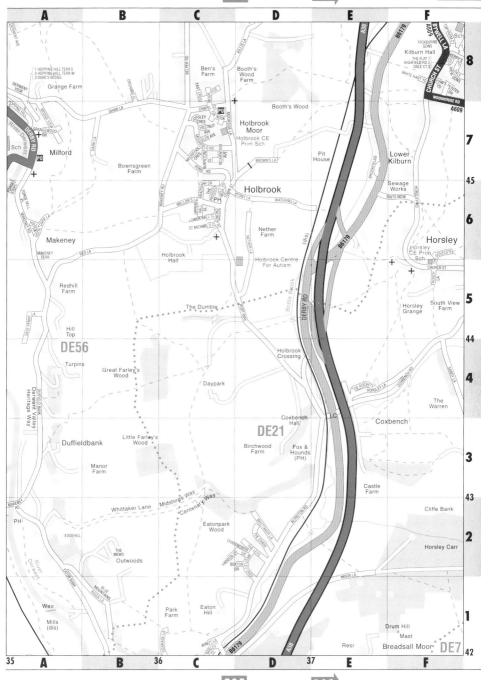

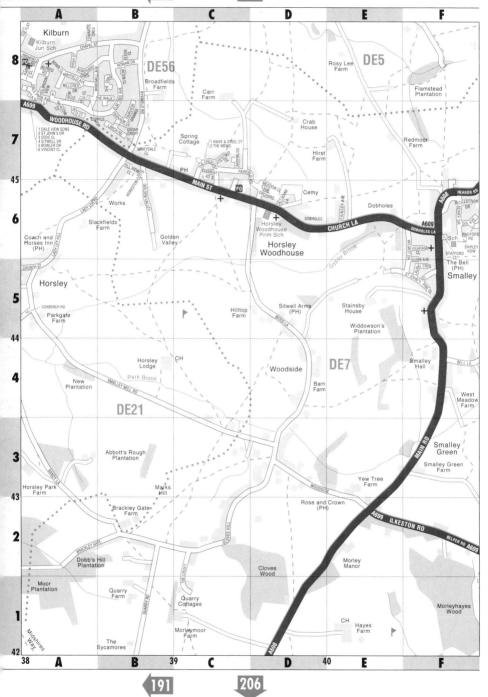

A   B   C   D   E   F

8

Kilburn

Kilburn
Jun Sch

PO

DE56

HIGHFIELD
RD
ALFRED
RD
MAYFIELD
AV
HILLCREST
DR
PARK AV
MEADOW
DR
THE WALK
EDWARDS
CRES
CHAPEL ST
HIGH ST
JOAN ST
ROWAN DR
JOYCE AV
HOLBROOK DR
ROWAN DR
THE OAKS
RYKNELD RD
LIME GR
BRIAR LEA
COPPICE
ABBEYDALE
BIRCH RD
CEDAR
CROFT

Broadfields
Farm

Carr
Farm

Rosy Lee
Farm

DE5

Flamstead
Plantation

A609
WOODHOUSE RD

1 DALE VIEW GDNS
2 ST JOHN'S DR
3 DOVE CL
4 SITWELL DR
5 BOWLER DR
6 VINCENT CL

Spring
Cottage

Crab
House

Redmoor
Farm

7

MAIN ST

PH

1 KNIFE & STEEL CT
2 THE MEWS

LIME GR CRES
CLEMENT
RD
FAIRFIELD

MEADOW CL
THE
ORCHARD
CHESTNUT
LA
CARRFIELDS

Hirst
Farm

45

HILL VIEW
CL
HORSESTON
GOLDEN VALLEY

PO

Cemy

CLANGERY AVE

Dobholes

6

Works

Horsley
Woodhouse
Prim Sch

DOBHOLES

CHURCH LA

Dobholes

A609

DOBHOLES LA

A608
HEANOR RD

Slackfields
Farm

Golden
Valley

Horsley
Woodhouse

WM MTR CL
VICARAGE
CL
GLEBE AVE
ALL CRES

Sch

RICHARDSON
DR
KERRY DR
DIX AV
BRADFORD
RD
SHIPLEY
VIEW

STAFFORD
CL

Coach and
Horses Inn
(PH)

LADY LANE

LIMEY LANE HILL

Gypsey Brook

The Bell
(PH)

ST JOHN'S
PINE CL

Smalley

CHURCH ST

Horsley

COXBENCH RD

Sitwell Arms
(PH)

Stainsby
House

5

Parkgate
Farm

Hilltop
Farm

Widdowson's
Plantation

BELL LA

44

CH

WOOD LA

Woodside

DE7

Smalley
Hall

4

New
Plantation

SMALLEY MILL RD

Horsley
Lodge

Park Brook

Barn
Farm

West
Meadow
Farm

DE21

Abbott's Rough
Plantation

Yew Tree
Farm

MAIN RD

Smalley
Green

3

Smalley Green
Farm

43

Horsley Park
Farm

Marks
Hill

WOODSIDE

Rose and Crown
(PH)

GARDT LA

CLOVES HILL

A609
ILKESTON RD

BELPER RD
A609

2

Brackley Gate
Farm

BRACKLEY GATE

Morley
Manor

Dobb's Hill
Plantation

THE CROFT

Cloves
Wood

Moor
Plantation

QUARRY RD

Quarry
Farm

Quarry
Cottages

A608

CH

Hayes
Farm

Morleyhayes
Wood

1

Morleymoor
Farm

Midshires Way

The
Sycamores

42

38   A   B   39   C   D   40   E   F

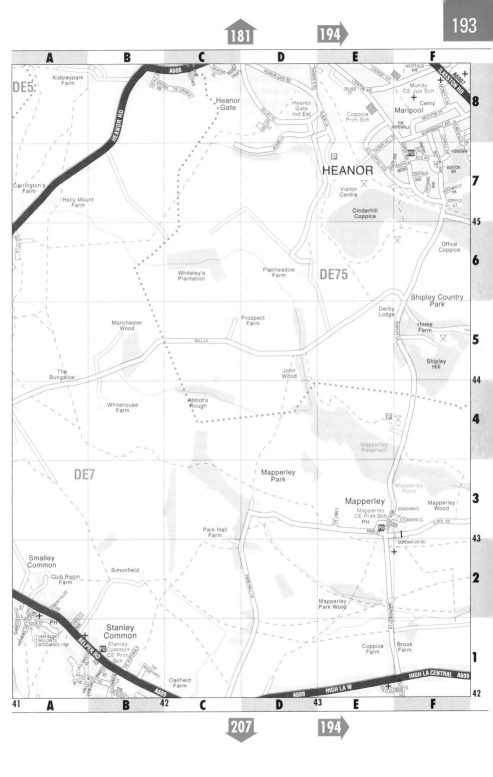

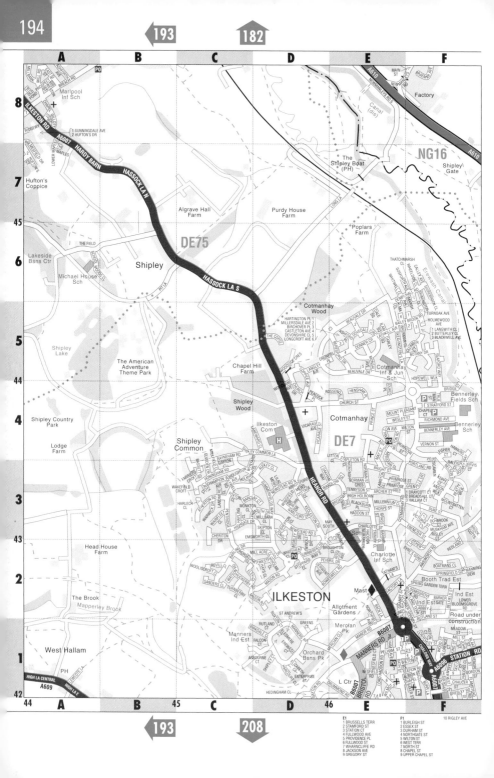

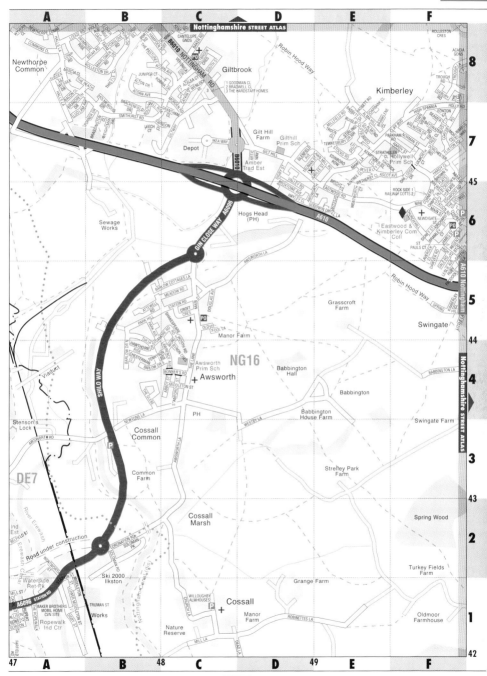

Nottinghamshire STREET ATLAS

8

Newthorpe
Common

Giltbrook

Kimberley

1 GOODMAN CL
2 BRADWELL CL
3 THE HARDSTAFF HOMES

Robin Hood Way

ROLLESTON
CRES

ACACIA
GDNS

TROUGH
RD

7

Gilt Hill
Farm

Gilthill
Prim Sch

IKEA WAY

Depot

Amber
Trad Est

HIGH SPANNIA

45

ROCK SIDE 1
RAILWAY COTTS 2

6

Hogs Head
(PH)

Sewage
Works

GIN CLOSE WAY A6096

Eastwood &
Kimberley Com
Coll

NEWDIGATE
ST

ST
PAULS CT

A610

Robin Hood Way

BARLOW COTTAGES LA

MEADOW RD

STATION RD

CROFT
RD

DOUGLAS AV

Grasscroft
Farm

A610 Nottingham

5

PARK HILL

Manor Farm

Swingate

44

Awsworth
Prim Sch

NG16

Babbington
Hall

BABBINGTON LA

SHILO WAY

Awsworth

MIDDLETON ST

Babbington

Swingate Farm

4

PH

WESTBY LA

Babbington
House Farm

Cossall
Common

Stenson's
Lock

AWSWORTH RD

NEWTON LA

Strelley Park
Farm

3

DE7

Viaduct

Common
Farm

Spring Wood

43

Ind
Est

River Erewash

Road under construction

Erewash Canal

CORONATION RD

SOLOMAN
RD

SOLOMAN
PK

Cossall
Marsh

Turkey Fields
Farm

Grange Farm

2

Ski 2000
Ilkston

Waterside
Ret-Pk

STATION RD

A6096

NOTTINGHAM RD

WILLOUGHBY
ALMSHOUSES

Cossall

Oldmoor
Farmhouse

1

BAKER BROTHERS
MOBIL HOME 1
CVN SITE

TRUMAN ST

Works

Ropeside
Ind Ctr

Manor
Farm

ROBINETTES LA

Nature
Reserve

MILL LA

Nottinghamshire STREET ATLAS

42

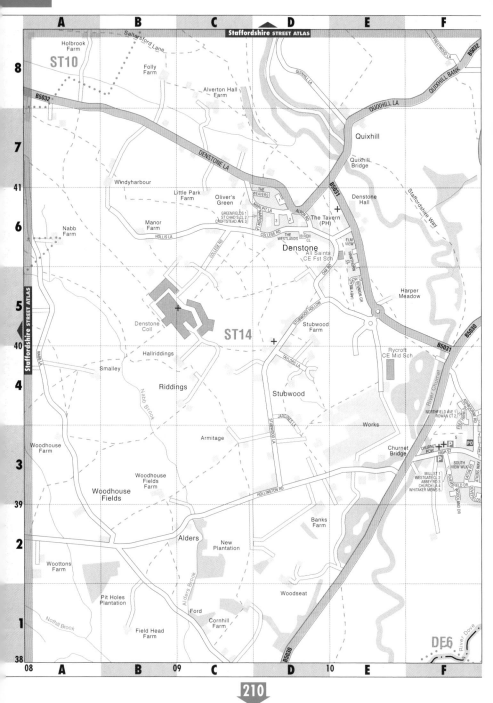

Holbrook Farm

Saltersford Lane

ST10

Folly Farm

Alverton Hall Farm

B5032

Quixhill LA

QUIXHILL LA

QUIXHILL BANK

B5032

PRESTWOOD LA

DENSTONE LA

Quixhill

Quixhill Bridge

Windyharbour

Little Park Farm

Oliver's Green

THE WEAVERS

Denstone Hall

Staffordshire Way

B5031

Manor Farm

HOLLIS LA

MARLPIT LA

GREENFIELDS 1
ST CHAD'S CL 2
CROFTSTEAD AVE 3

COLLEGE RD

THE WESTLANDS

BIRCH CL

ALTON RD

The Tavern (PH)

ELM VIEW

Nabb Farm

Denstone

All Saints CE Fst Sch

HAWTHORN

LADY MEADOW CE

BENNION GR

OAK RD

Harper Meadow

Denstone Coll

ST14

Stubwood Hollow

Stubwood Farm

Rycroft CE Mid Sch

B5031

B5030

Hallriddings

Smalley

TAYLORS LA

River Churnet

Riddings

Stubwood

ASHBOURNE RD

Nabb Brook

JARDINES LA

Works

NORTHFIELD AVE 1
ROWAN CT 2

Woodhouse Farm

STUBWOOD LA

Armitage

CHURNET ROW

HIGH ST

P

PO

Churnet Bridge

P

Woodhouse Fields Farm

HOLLINGTON RD

SOUTH VIEW WLK

MILL ST 1
WESTGATE CL 2
ABBEY RD 3
CHURCH LA 4
WHITAKER MEWS 5

FIELD DR

Woodhouse Fields

Banks Farm

Alders

New Plantation

Woottons Farm

Alders Brook

Woodseat

Pit Holes Plantation

Nothill Brook

Ford

Cornhill Farm

Field Head Farm

B5030

River Dove

DE6

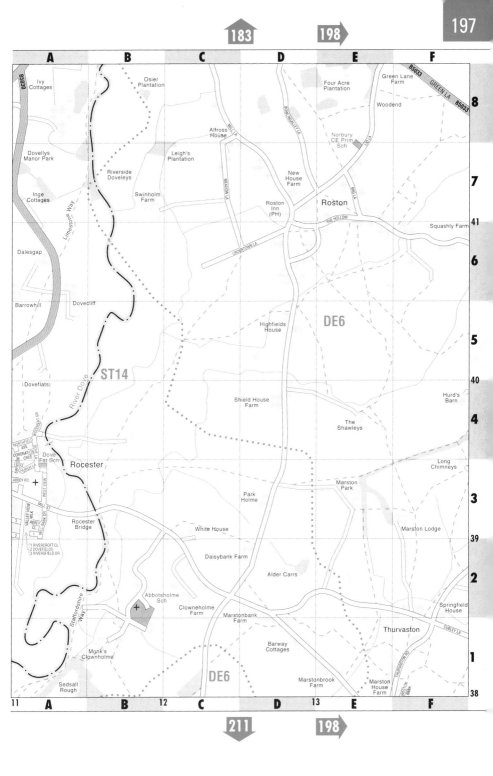

197
184

A B C D E F

8

B5033

Shepherdswood

Chapel House

SNIPES LA

Queen Adelaide Arms (PH)

BROADGALLEY LA

Cindershills Wood

Darley Moor

GREEN LA

7

Common Farm

Snelston Common

COCKSHEAD LA

Old Queen Farm

Flat Covert

B5033

A515

41

John Roe's Covert

Quarry (dis)

Grange Cottage

Top Stydd

6

Birchwood Park

Grange Farm

Roston Common

Manor House

Cubley Brook

Birchwoodmoor

5

DE6

Cubley Wood Farm

Marstoncommon Farm

40

Accession Wood

Wood Hay Farm

HOLLIES LA

4

The Hollies

Side Gate

Broad Lane

Sandhills Farm

Cubley Covert

Sammy's Wood

Whiterley

3

Holme Lea

Cubley Common

39

Cubley Cottage Farm

2

Gorse Covert

Common Farm

Mountpleasant Farm

Rough Grounds

THE ROW

1

Great Cubley

Birch Field Farm

The Spinney

Brookside Farm

DERBY LA

CUBLEY LA

SNIPE LA

Cubley Fields Farm

Howard Arms (PH)

A515

LONG MDW

38

14 A B 15 C D 16 E F

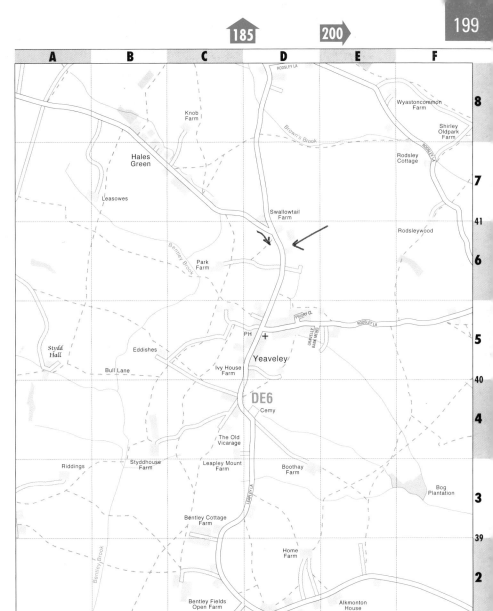

	A	B	C	D	E	F	

8

RODSLEY LA

Wyastoncommon
Farm

Shirley
Oldpark
Farm

Knob
Farm

Brown's Brook

Hales
Green

Rodsley
Cottage

7

Leasowes

41

Swallowtail
Farm

Rodsleywood

Bentley Brook

Park
Farm

6

PRIORY CL

RODSLEY LA

5

PH +

GRAVELLY BANK MEWS

Stydd
Hall

Eddishes

Yeaveley

Bull Lane

Ivy House
Farm

40

DE6

Cemy

4

The Old
Vicarage

Riddings

Styddhouse
Farm

Leapley Mount
Farm

Boothay
Farm

Bog
Plantation

3

Bentley Brook

LEAPLEY LA

Bentley Cottage
Farm

39

Home
Farm

2

Bentley Fields
Open Farm

Alkmonton
House

+

Alkmonton

1

Alkmonton Bottoms

DERBY LA

Bentley Hall

Top House
Farm

38

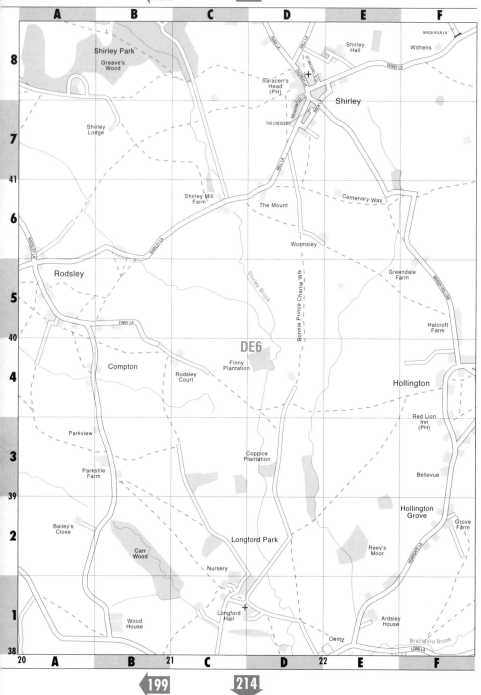

199
186

A **B** **C** **D** **E** **F**

8

Shirley Park

Greave's Wood

BRICK-KILN LA

Shirley Hall

Withens

DERBY LA

PARK LA

DITCH HILL LA

ST MICHAEL STS.

CHURCH LA

Saracen's Head (PH)

Shirley

7

Shirley Lodge

MEADOWBROOK LA

ASH LA

THE CRESCENT

41

Shirley Mill Farm

MILL LA

Centenary Way

6

The Mount

Wormsley

Greendale Farm

MARSH HOLLOW

RODSLEY LA

SHIRLEY LA

Rodsley

Shirley Brook

Bonnie Prince Charlie Wlk

5

Halcroft Farm

FINNY LA

40

Compton

Rodsley Court

Finny Plantation

DE6

Hollington

4

Parkview

Red Lion Inn (PH)

3

Parkstile Farm

Coppice Plantation

Bellevue

39

Hollington Grove

Bailey's Close

Grove Farm

2

Carr Wood

Longford Park

Reev's Moor

HORGATE LA

Nursery

Wood House

Longford Hall

Ardsley House

Cemy

Brailsford Brook

1

Cemy

LONG LA

38

A **B** 21 **C** **D** 22 **E** **F**

20

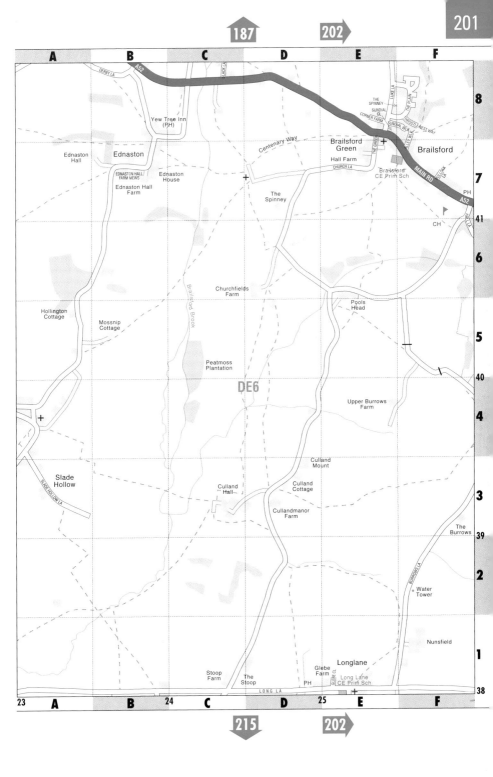

187
202
215
202

A52

DERBY LA

Yew Tree Inn
(P.H)

Ednaston

Ednaston
Hall

EDNASTON HALL
FARM MEWS

Ednaston Hall
Farm

Ednaston
House

SLACK LA

Centenary Way

Brailsford
Green

THE
SPINNEY

SUNDIAL
CL

CORNER FARM

LINES LA

THE PLAIN

THROSTLE NEST WAY

SUNDIAL WLK

Brailsford

MAIN RD

Hall Farm

CHURCH LA

Brailsford
CE Prim Sch

THE GREEN

GLEBE WY

The
Spinney

A52

PH

HALL LA

CH

Hollington
Cottage

Brailsford Brook

Mossnip
Cottage

Churchfields
Farm

Pools
Head

Peatmoss
Plantation

DE6

Upper Burrows
Farm

Slade
Hollow

SLADE HOLLOW LA

Culland
Hall

Culland
Mount

Culland
Cottage

Cullandmanor
Farm

The
Burrows

BURROWS LA

Water
Tower

Nunsfield

Stoop
Farm

The
Stoop

PH

Glebe
Farm

GLEBE CL

Longlane

Long Lane
CE Prim Sch

LONG LA

41

8

7

6

5

40

4

3

39

2

1

38

23

24

25

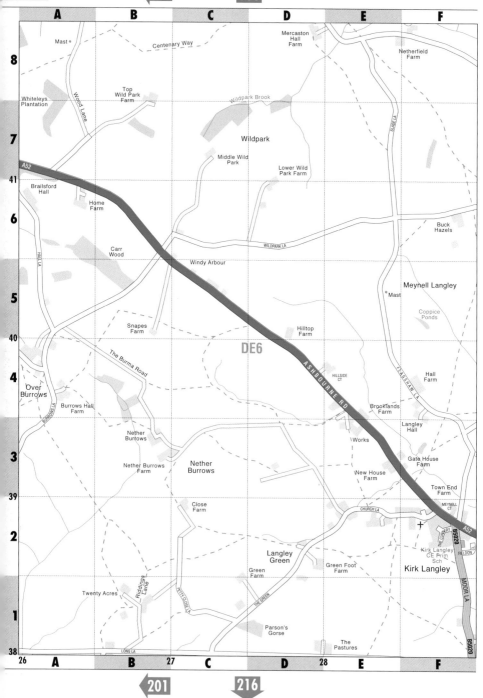

A B C D E F

8

Mast

Centenary Way

Mercaston
Hall
Farm

Netherfield
Farm

Whiteleys
Plantation

Wood Lane

Top
Wild Park
Farm

Wildpark Brook

7

A52

Wildpark

Middle Wild
Park

Lower Wild
Park Farm

SLABE LA

41

Brailsford
Hall

Home
Farm

6

Buck
Hazels

Carr
Wood

WILDPARK LA

HALL LA

Windy Arbour

Meynell Langley

Mast

5

Coppice
Ponds

Snapes
Farm

40

The Burma Road

DE6

Hilltop
Farm

ASHBOURNE RD

FLAGSHAW LA

Hall
Farm

4

Over
Burrows

HILLSIDE
CT

Brooklands
Farm

Langley
Hall

BURROWS LA

Burrows Hall
Farm

Works

Nether
Burtows

Gate House
Farm

3

Nether Burrows
Farm

Nether
Burrows

New House
Farm

Town End
Farm

39

Close
Farm

CHURCH LA

MEYNELL
CT

A52

2

Langley
Green

Green Foot
Farm

THE COVERTS

Kirk Langley
CE Prim
Sch

B5020

FIELDON

RIDDINGS LANE

PETTY CLOSE LA

Green
Farm

Kirk Langley

MOOR LA

1

Twenty Acres

THE GREEN

Parson's
Gorse

38

LONG LA

The
Pastures

B5020

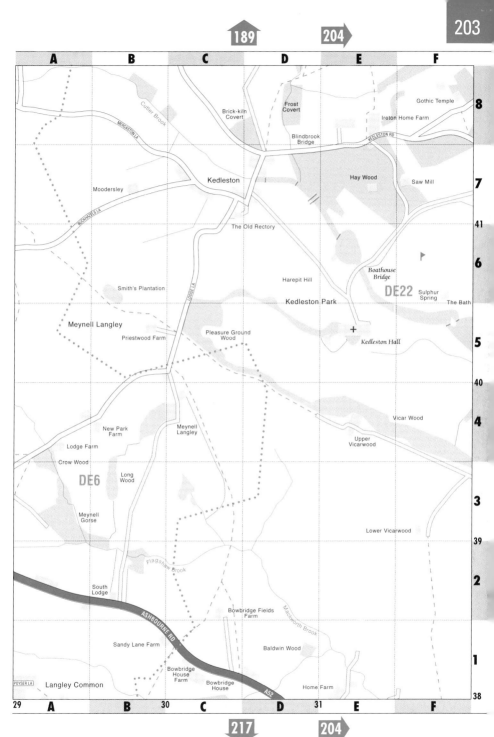

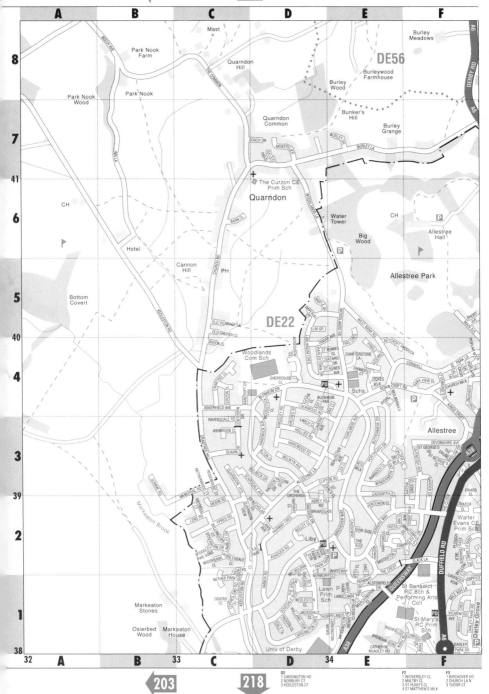

DE56

Burley
Meadows

Mast

Park Nook
Farm

Quarndon
Hill

Burleywood
Farmhouse

Burley
Wood

Park Nook
Wood

Park Nook

Quarndon
Common

Bunker's
Hill

Burley
Grange

CH

The Curzon CE
Prim Sch

Quarndon

Water
Tower

CH

Allestree
Hall

Hotel

Cannon
Hill

Big
Wood

Allestree Park

PH

Bottom
Covert

DE22

OLD VICARAGE LA

OLD CHURCH CL

BROOK CL

Woodlands
Com Sch

Allestree

Woodlands
Com Sch

Askerfield Ave

Ravensdale Rd

Ashbrook Cl

Devonshire Ave

Walter
Evans CE
Prim Sch

The
Orchards

Liby

Markeaton Brook

Markeaton
Stones

Osierbed
Wood

Markeaton
House

Lawn
Prim
Sch

St Benedict
RC Sch &
Performing Arts
Coll

St Mary's
RC Prim
Sch

Univ of Derby

Queensway

Duffield Rd

Darley Grove

203

218

D2
1 CARSINGTON HO
2 NORBURY CT
3 KEDLESTON CT

F2
1 WICKERSLEY CL
2 MALTBY CL
3 ST HUGH'S CL
4 ST MATTHEW'S WLK

F3
1 BIRCHOVER HO
2 CHURCH LA N
3 TUDOR CT

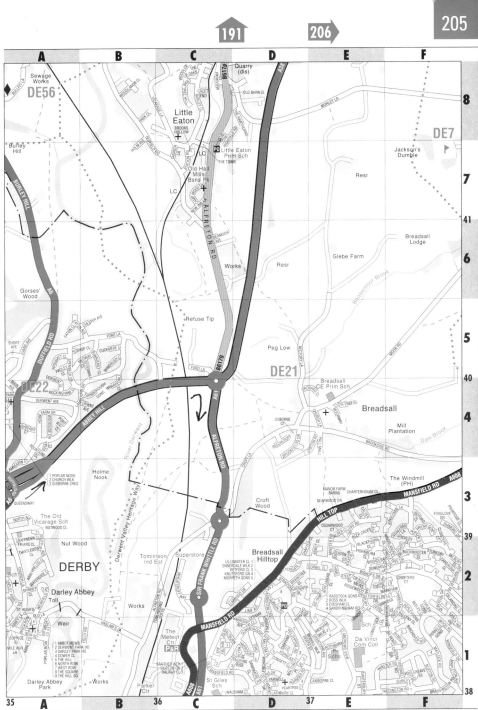

DE56

Sewage
Works

Burley
Hill

Little
Eaton

BROOKS
HOLLOW

Little Eaton
Prim Sch

THE TOWN

Old Hall
Mills
Bsns Pk

DE7

Jackson's
Dumble

Resr

Breadsall
Lodge

Glebe Farm

Works

Resr

Brackenbour Brook

BURLEY HILL

Gorses'
Wood

Refuse Tip

Peg Low

DE21

Breadsall
CE Prim Sch

Breadsall

Short
Ave

DE22

DERBY

Holme
Nook

Mill
Plantation

Dam Brook

1 POPLAR NOOK
2 CHURCH WLK
3 GISBORNE CRES

Queensway

The Old
Vicarage Sch
NUTWOOD CL

Nut Wood

Croft
Wood

The Windmill
(PH)

MANSFIELD RD
A608

HILL TOP

CHARTERHOUSE CL

MANOR FARM
BARNS
NEARWOOD DR

CEDARWOOD

Breadsall
Hilltop

FOXGLOVE CR

Tomlinson
Ind Est

Superstore

Darley Abbey
Toll

1 ABBOT MEWS
2 DERWENT PARK HO
3 DARLEY PARK HO
4 DOWER CL
5 THE HILL
6 NORTH ROW
7 WEST ROW
8 THE SQUARE
9 THE HILL SQ

Weir

Works

Da Vinci
Com Coll

Sch

The
Meteor
Ctr
P&R

MANSFIELD RD

Sch

P.O.

St Giles
Sch

Peartree
Sch

Darley Abbey
Park

Works

Parker
Ctr

A61

A608

WALSHAM CL

TADDINGTON RD

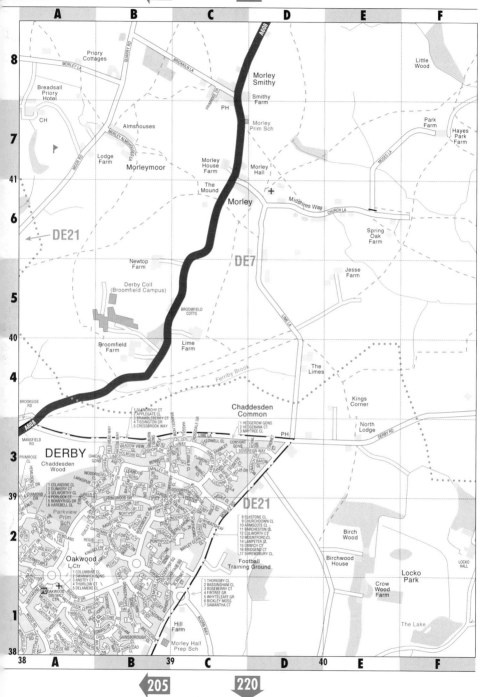

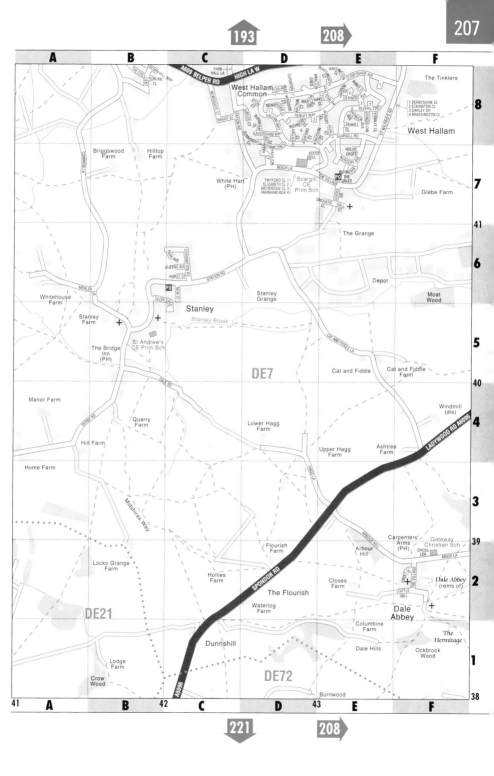

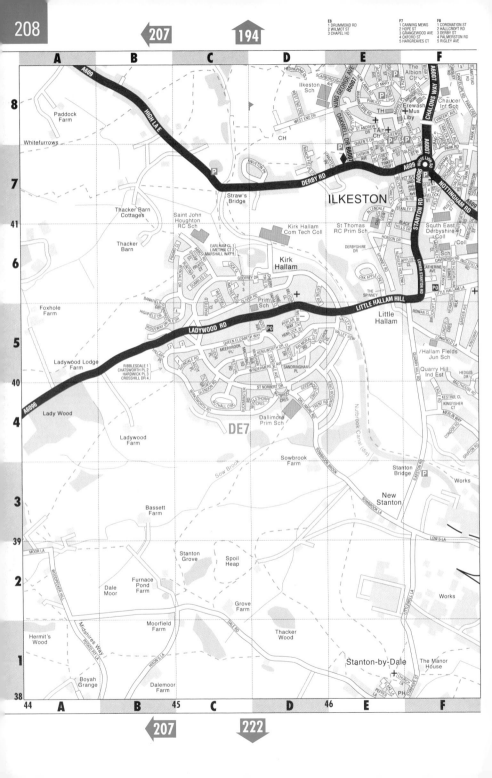

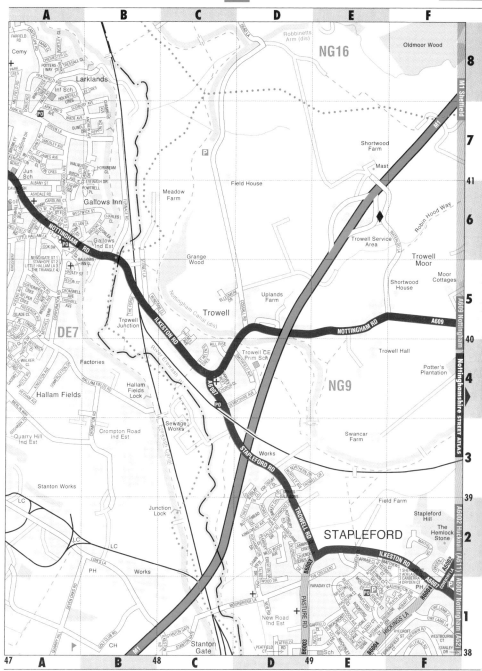

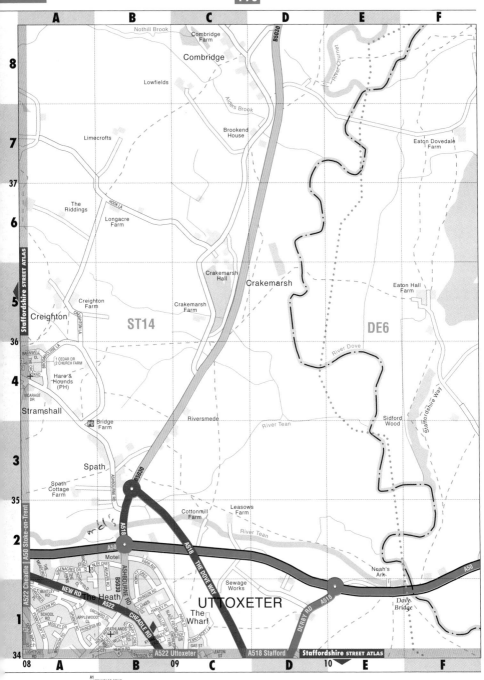

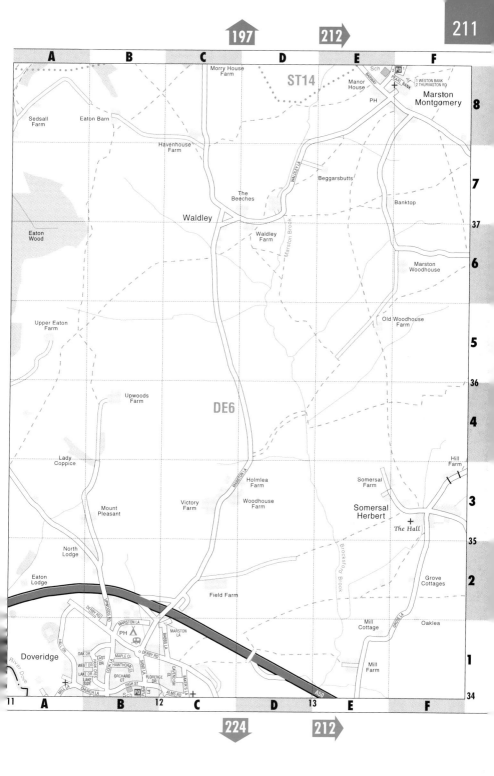

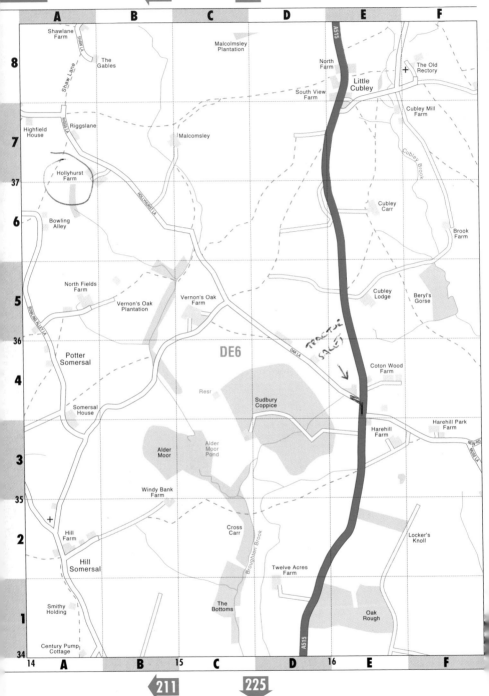

211
198

	A	B	C	D	E	F

8

Shawlane Farm

Shaw Lane

The Gables

Malcolmsley Plantation

North Farm

Little Cubley

The Old Rectory

South View Farm

Cubley Mill Farm

7

Highfield House

Riggslane

Malcomsley

Cubley Brook

37

Hollyhurst Farm

HOLLYHURST LA

6

Bowling Alley

Cubley Carr

Brook Farm

5

North Fields Farm

Vernon's Oak Plantation

Vernon's Oak Farm

Cubley Lodge

Beryl's Gorse

BOWLING ALLEY LA

36

Potter Somersal

DE6

OAK LA

TRACTOR SALES

Coton Wood Farm

4

Resr

Sudbury Coppice

Harehill Farm

Harehill Park Farm

Somersal House

3

Alder Moor

Alder Moor Pond

NEW RD

Windy Bank Farm

35

Hill Farm

Cross Carr

Broughton Brook

Locker's Knoll

2

Hill Somersal

Twelve Acres Farm

1

Smithy Holding

The Bottoms

Oak Rough

34

Century Pump Cottage

A515

14	A	B	15	C	D	16	E	F

211
225

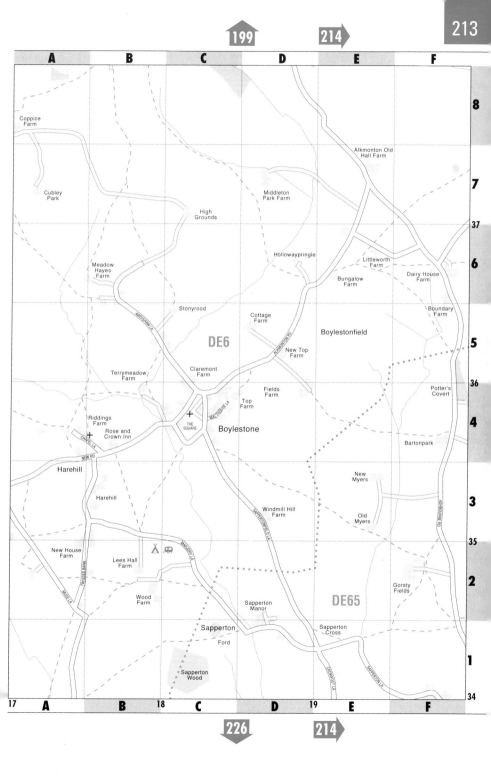

| A | B | C | D | E | F |

8

Coppice
Farm

Alkmonton Old
Hall Farm

7

Cubley
Park

Middleton
Park Farm

37

High
Grounds

Hollowaypringle

Littleworth
Farm

Dairy House
Farm

6

Meadow
Hayes
Farm

Bungalow
Farm

AMBISHAM LA

Stonyrood

Boundary
Farm

DE6

Cottage
Farm

Boylestonfield

5

ALKMONTON RD

New Top
Farm

Potter's
Covert

36

Claremont
Farm

Fields
Farm

Terrymeadow
Farm

MALTHOUSE LA

Top
Farm

4

Riddings
Farm

THE
SQUARE

Boylestone

Bartonpark

CHAPEL LA

Rose and
Crown Inn

NEW RD

Harehill

New
Myers

3

Harehill

Windmill Hill
Farm

Old
Myers

ASHBOURNE RD

SAPPERTON LA

35

New House
Farm

Lees Hall
Farm

Gorsty
Fields

2

MUSE LA

TWOSSE BANK

MANOR LA

Wood
Farm

Sapperton
Manor

DE65

Sapperton

Ford

Sapperton
Cross

1

Sapperton
Wood

CRONKFOOT LA

SAPPERTON LA

34

| 17 | A | B | 18 | C | D | 19 | E | F |

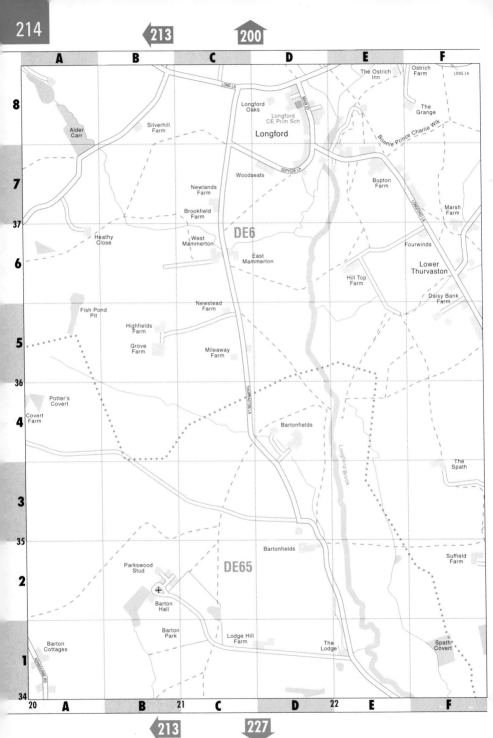

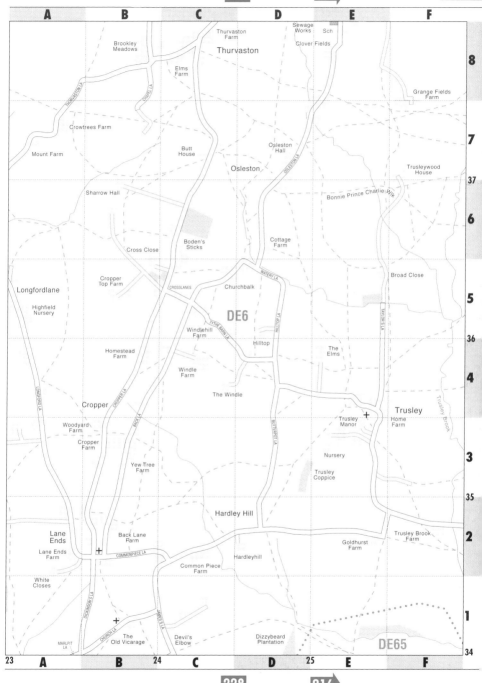

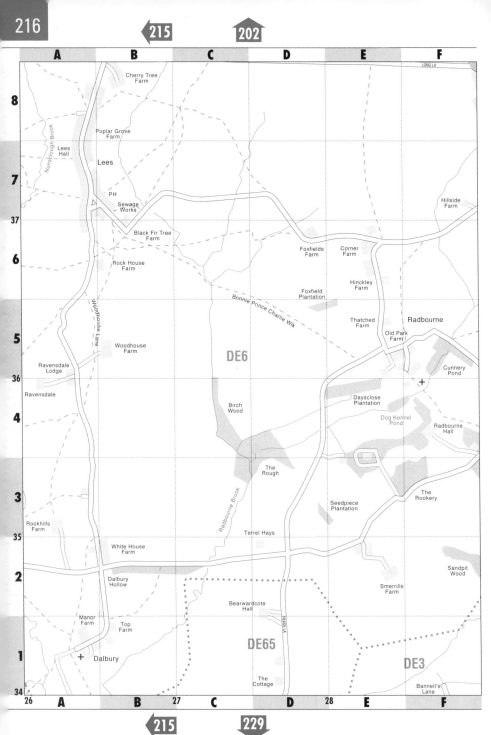

215
202

A **B** **C** **D** **E** **F**

8

LONG LA

Cherry Tree
Farm

Poplar Grove
Farm

Nunsbough Brook

Lees
Hall

Lees

7

Hillside
Farm

PH

Sewage
Works

37

Black Fir Tree
Farm

Foxfields
Farm

Corner
Farm

6

Rock House
Farm

Hinckley
Farm

Foxfield
Plantation

Bonnie Prince Charlie Wlk

Woodhouse Lane

Thatched
Farm

Radbourne

5

Old Park
Farm

Woodhouse
Farm

DE6

Cunnery
Pond

Ravensdale
Lodge

36

Daysclose
Plantation

Ravensdale

Birch
Wood

Dog Kennel
Pond

4

Radbourne
Hall

Radbourne Brook

The
Rough

3

The
Rookery

Rookhills
Farm

Seedpiece
Plantation

35

White House
Farm

Tetrel Hays

Sandpit
Wood

2

Dalbury
Hollow

Smerrills
Farm

Bearwardcote
Hall

HAGE LA

Manor
Farm

Top
Farm

DE65

DE3

1

Dalbury

The
Cottage

Bannell's
Lane

34

26 **A** **B** 27 **C** **D** 28 **E** **F**

215
229

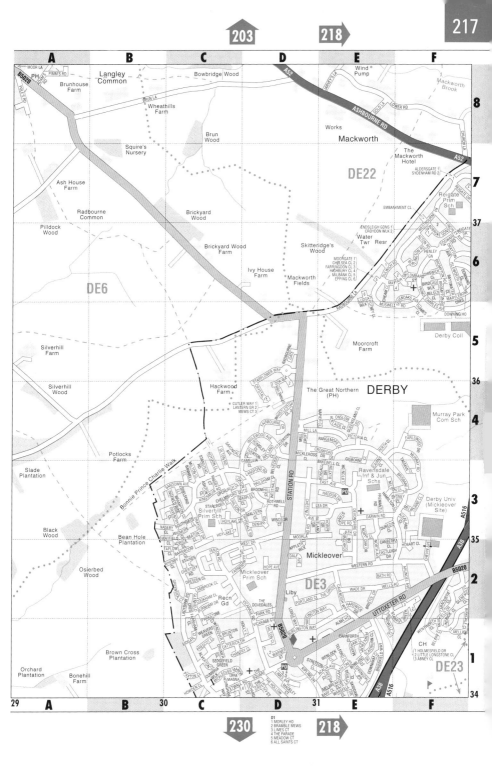

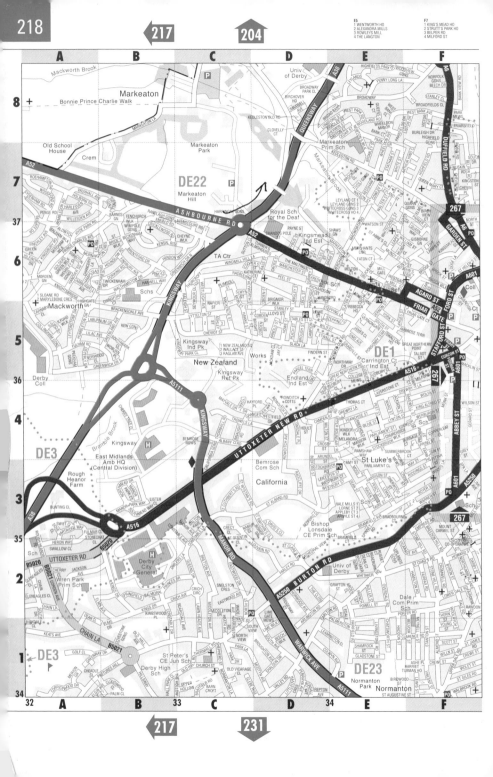

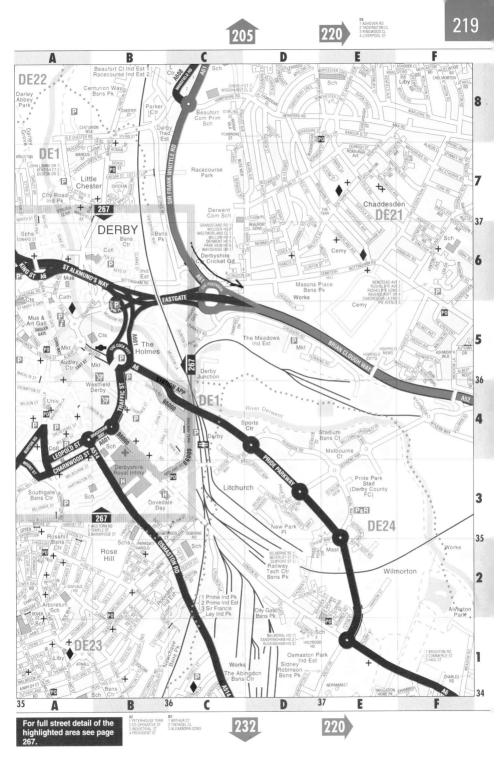

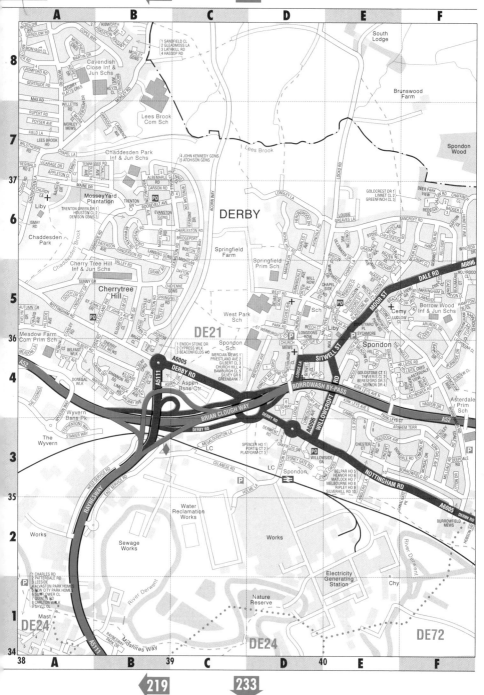

DERBY

DE21

DE24

DE24

DE72

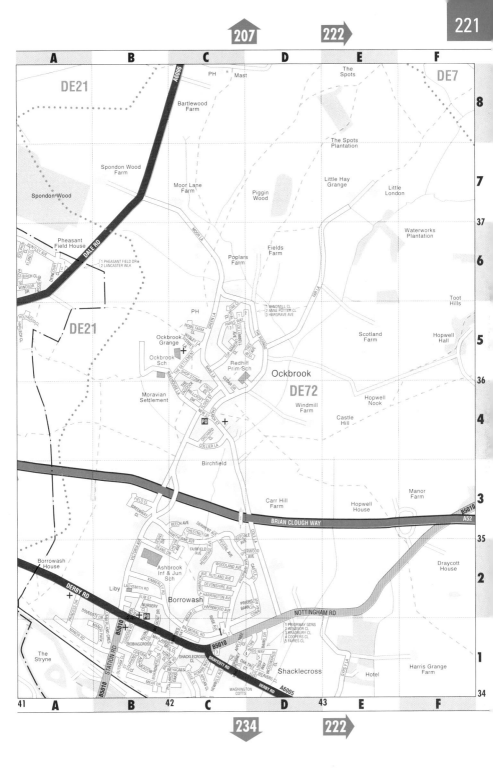

221
208

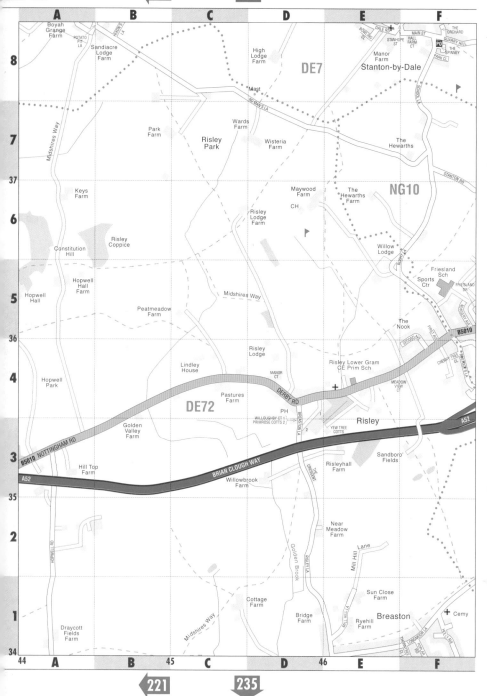

221
235

B5
1 HART LEA
2 HUNTINGDON WLK
3 MOORFIELD CRES

B6
1 KING EDWARD GDNS
2 HOLME LEA

C5
1 WESTMINSTER AVE
2 GRASMERE ST

C6
1 MILL LA
2 BROOKFIELD MEWS
3 ST JAMES'S ST

D7
1 LOWER ORCHARD ST
2 KAYES CT

E5
1 JILL IAIN CT
2 BRUNSWICK DR
3 DALTON CL

E7
1 DALLEY CL
2 UPPER ORCHARD ST
3 CHURCH WLK
4 SPRING CT

E8
1 MACKINLEY AVE
2 CHURCHILL DR
3 WHITELY CL

F8
1 MARSHALL DR
2 LEICESTER HO
3 HILLFIELD RD

209

223

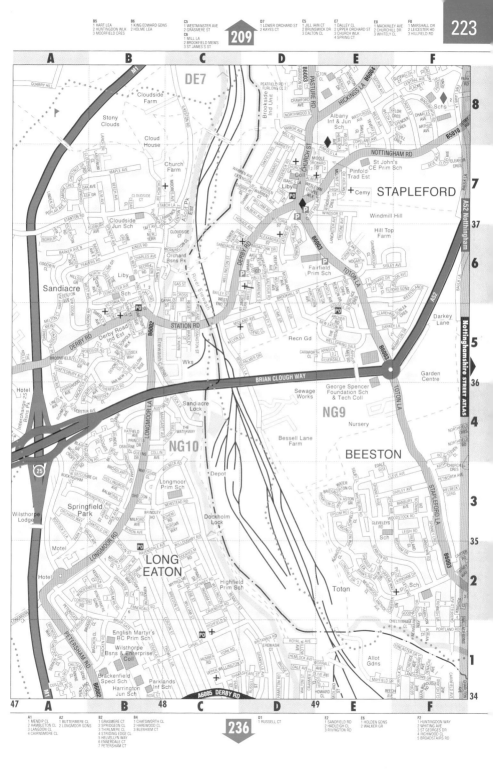

A1
1 MENDIP CL
2 HAMBLETON CL
3 LANGDON CL
4 CAIRNSMORE CL

A2
1 BUTTERMERE CL
2 LONGMOOR GDNS

B2
1 GRASMERE CT
2 SPRIDGEON CL
3 THIRLMERE CL
4 STRIDING EDGE CL
5 HELVELLYN WAY
6 ENNERDALE CT
7 PETERSHAM CT

B4
1 CHATSWORTH CL

C4
3 HAREWOOD CL
4 BLENHEIM CT.

D1
1 RUSSELL CT

E2
1 SANDFIELD RD
2 HADLEIGH CL
3 RIVINGTON RD

E6
1 HOLDEN GDNS
2 WALKER GR

F2
1 HUNTINGDON WAY
2 WHITING AVE
3 ST GEORGES DR
4 INCHWOOD CL
5 BROADSTAIRS RD

236

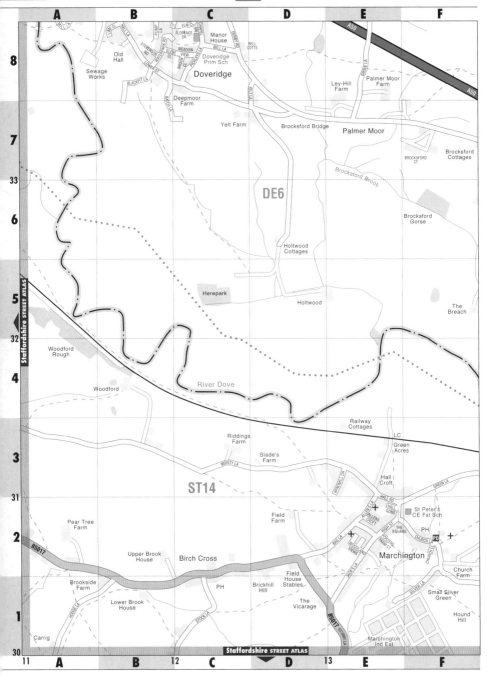

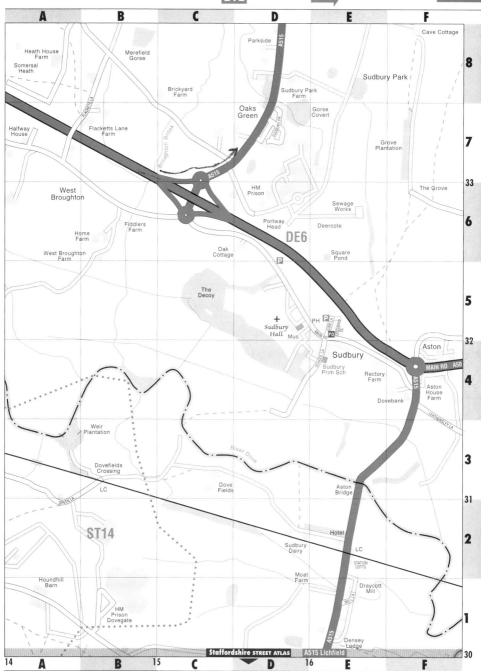

225
213

| | A | B | C | D | E | F |

8

Mackley House

Fox Hole

Sapperton Brook

The Homestead

SAPPERTON LA

7

Dale Brook

MUSE LA

Muselane Farm

Foston Mill Farm

Crowfoot Farm

CROWFOOT LA

Cotefield Farm

MILL LA

WOODHOUSE LA

33

Dalebrook

Ford

Aston Heath

Broomhill Farm

Haylane Farm

Conygree Wood

6

Foston Brook

ASTON LA

Aston Heath Farm

Breach Gorse

BREACH LA

Sailor's Holme

Rough Wood

COPLOW LA

HALL LA

5

DE6

Home Farm

DE65

Lawn House

PINFOLD LA

32

MAIN RD

A50

Foston

UTTOXETER RD

Tomlinson Bsns Pk

4

Maidensley Farm

UTTOXETER RD

HM Detention Centre

WOODLAND DR

UTTOXETER RD

A50

UTTOXETER RD

Dale Brook

Lemon's Holme

Cote House

3

Leathersley Farm

Puddingbag Covert

Roundabout Covert

Fishpond Plantation

The Churchleys

31

LEATHERSLEY LA

WATERY LA

2

BROOK S LA

Sweet Holme

Scropton

Ivy House Farm

1

River Dove

PH

LC

Brookside Farm

SCROPTON RD

MILL LA

Brookhouse Farm

LC

30

River Dove

| 17 | A | | B | 18 | C | | D | 19 | E | | F |

225
238

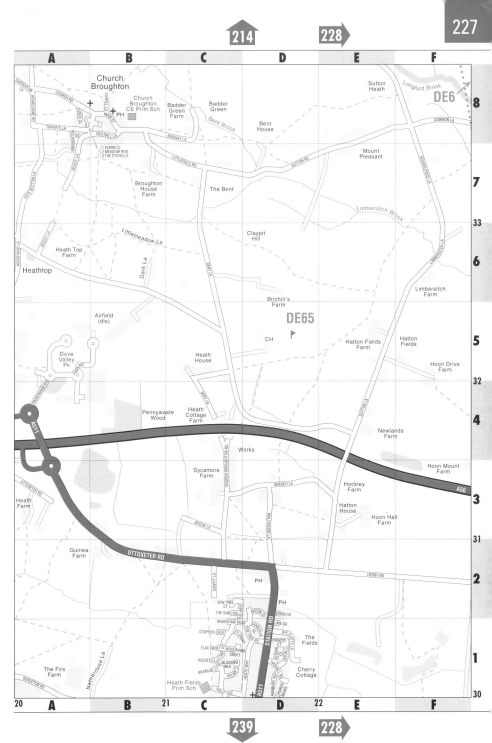

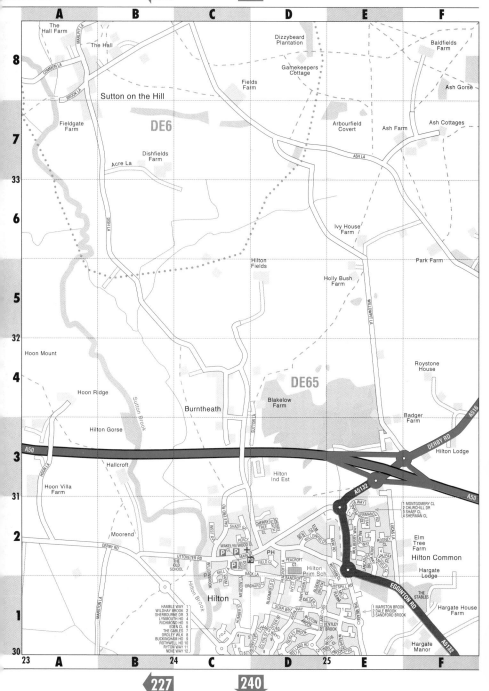

A B C D E F

8

The Hall Farm
The Hall
Dizzybeard Plantation
Baldfields Farm
MAREPIT LA
COMMON LA
Gamekeepers Cottage
Ash Gorse
Sutton on the Hill
BROOK LA
Fields Farm
DE6
Fieldgate Farm
Arbourfield Covert
Ash Farm
Ash Cottages

7

Acre La
Dishfields Farm
ASH LA
DISH LA

33

6

Ivy House Farm
Park Farm
Hilton Fields
Holly Bush Farm
WILLOWPIT LA

5

Hoon Mount
Roystone House

32

Hoon Ridge
Blakelow Farm
DE65
Burntheath
Badger Farm
A516
Hoon Gorse
Sutton Brook
Hilton Gorse
SUTTON LA

4

A50
DERBY RD
Hilton Lodge
Hallcroft
A5132

3

Hoon Villa Farm
Hilton Ind Est
A50

31

1 Montgomery Cl
2 Churchill Dr
3 Shaef Cl
4 Sherman Cl
Moorend
Elm Tree Farm
Hilton Common
DERBY RD
UTTOXETER RD
THE OLD SCHOOL
WAKELYN WOOD CL
PERCY
PEACROFT CT
PH
Hargate Lodge

2

WEST AVE
SHADY GR
CHERRY TREE CL
CHERRY CL
FIELD CL
Hilton Prim Sch
THE STABLES
MILL
BACK LA
ORCHARD
BLOOMFIELD CL
PEACROFT LA
EGGINTON RD
Hargate House Farm
Hilton
HAMBLE WAY 2
WILDHAY BROOK
SHERBOURNE DR 3
LYNMOUTH HO 4
RICHMOND HO 5
EDEN CL 6
THE GABLES 7
ORDLEY WLK 8
BUCKINGHAM HO 9
ROTHWELL HO 10
RYTON WAY 11
NENE WAY 12
Hilton Brook
KIMBER RD
MEADOW LA
SOAR WAY
1 MARSTON BROOK
2 DALE BROOK
3 SANDFORD BROOK
Hargate Manor

1

MARSTON LA
DERBY RD
THE MERSE
A5132

30

23 A B 24 C D 25 E F

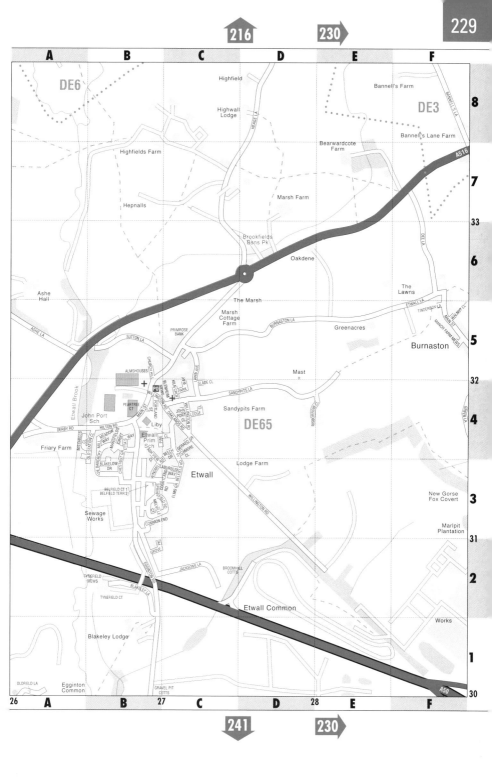

DE6

Highfield

Highwall
Lodge

Bannell's Farm

DE3

Highfields Farm

Bearwardcote
Farm

Bannell's Lane Farm

A516

Hepnalls

Marsh Farm

Brookfields
Bsns Pk

Oakdene

The Lawns

Ashe
Hall

The Marsh

Marsh
Cottage
Farm

Greenacres

ETWALL LA

TINDERBOX LA

WALNUT CL

MANOR FARM MEWS

Burnaston

PRIMROSE
BANK

SUTTON LA

BURNASTON LA

ASHE LA

CHURCH HILL

ALMSHOUSES

Mast

SANDYPITS LA

DE65

PEARTREE
CT

John Port
Sch

Liby

Sandypits Farm

Friary Farm

DERBY RD

Etwall
Prim
Sch

JOHN
PORT
LODGE

GERARD DR

Lodge Farm

New Gorse
Fox Covert

Etwall

WELLINGTON RD

Marlpit
Plantation

BELFIELD CT 1
BELFIELD TERR 2

Sewage
Works

COMMON END

THE
GROVE

JACKSONS LA

BROOMHILL
COTTS

Works

TYNEFIELD
MEWS

BLAKELEY LA

TYNEFIELD CT

Etwall Common

Blakeley Lodge

OLDFIELD LA

Egginton
Common

GRAVEL PIT
COTTS

A50

8
33
7
6
5
32
4
3
31
2
1
30

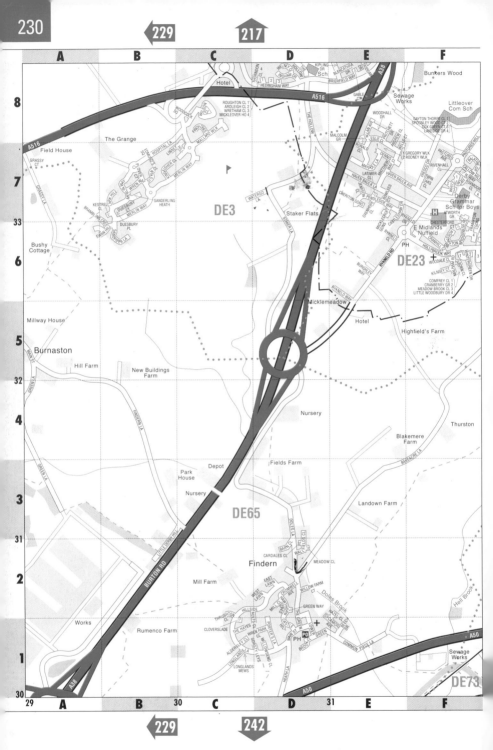

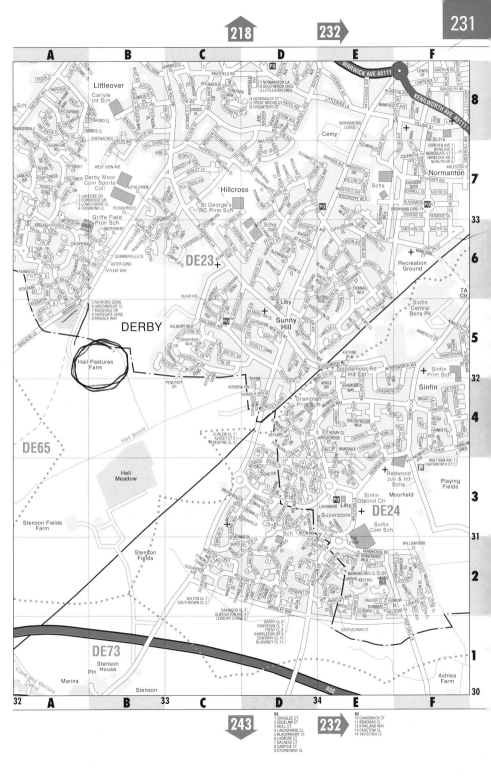

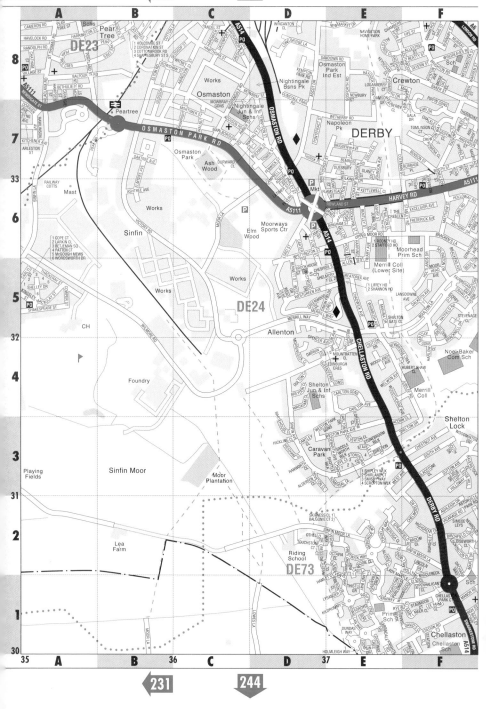

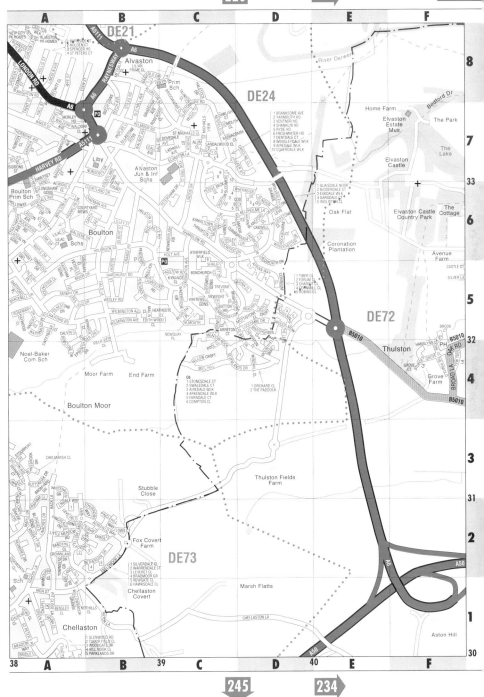

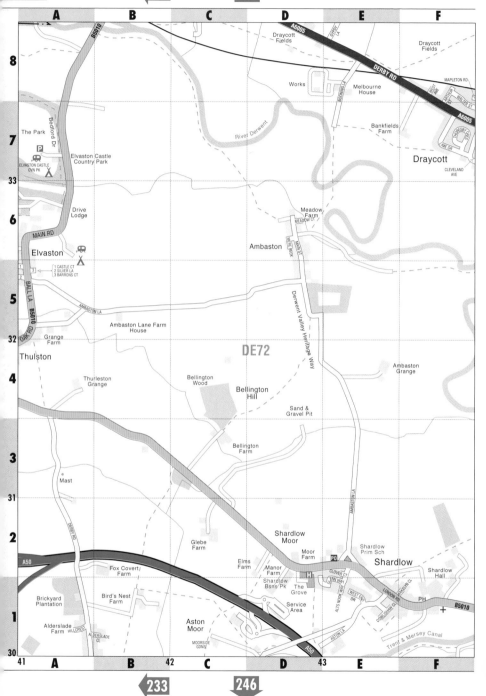

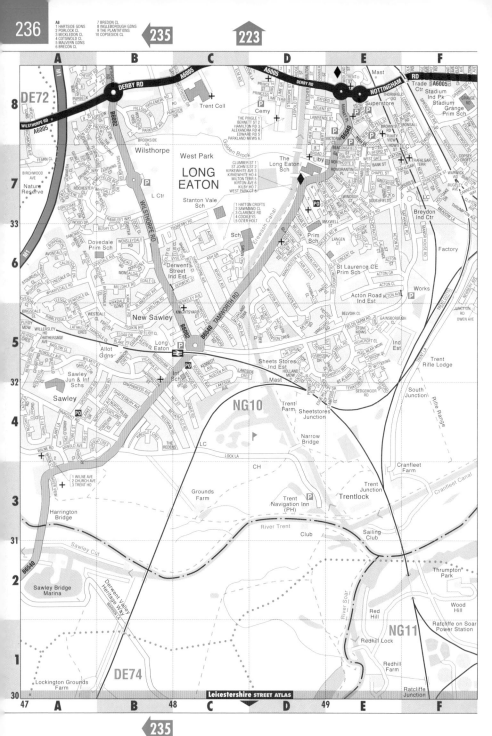

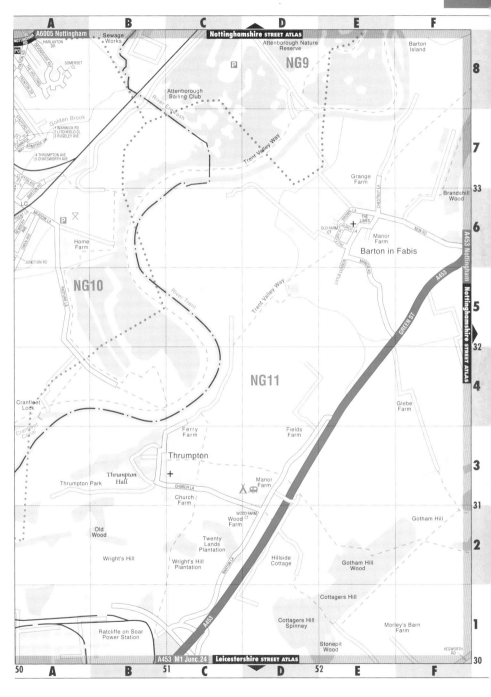

NG9

Barton Island

Attenborough Nature Reserve

Sewage Works

Attenborough Sailing Club

River Erewash

Trent Valley Way

Grange Farm

Brandshill Wood

THE LIMES

OLD FARM CT

Manor Farm

Barton in Fabis

A6005 Nottingham

HARLAXTON DR

SOMERSET CL

1 WARWICK RD
2 LITHFIELD CL
3 RUGELEY AVE

4 THRUMPTON AVE
5 CHATSWORTH AVE

Golden Brook

LC

Home Farm

JUNCTION RD

NG10

River Trent

Trent Valley Way

MEADOW LA

PASTURE LA

A453 Nottingham

NEW RD

GREEN ST

33

6

5

32

4

31

2

1

30

Cranfleet Lock

Cranfleet Canal

NG11

Ferry Farm

Thrumpton

Thrumpton Hall

Thrumpton Park

CHURCH LA

Church Farm

Old Wood

Wright's Hill

Wright's Hill Plantation

Twenty Lands Plantation

Fields Farm

Manor Farm

WOOD FARM CT

Wood Farm

BARTON LA

Hillside Cottage

Glebe Farm

Gotham Hill

Gotham Hill Wood

Cottagers Hill

Cottagers Hill Spinney

Stonepit Wood

Morley's Barn Farm

KEGWORTH RD

Ratcliffe on Soar Power Station

A453

50   A   B   51   C   D   52   E   F

A453 Nottingham

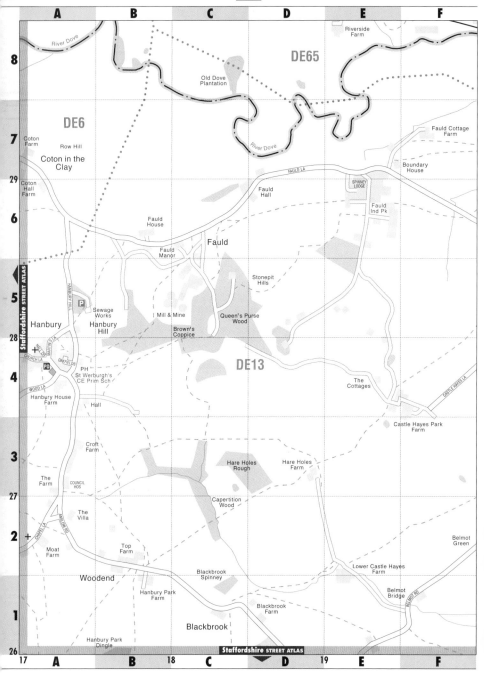

A   **B**   **C**   **D**   **E**   **F**

River Dove

DE65

Riverside Farm

Old Dove Plantation

8

DE6

Coton Farm

Row Hill

Coton in the Clay

7

River Dove

Fauld Cottage Farm

Boundary House

FAULD LA

29

Coton Hall Farm

Fauld Hall

SPINNEY LODGE

Fauld House

Fauld Ind Pk

6

Fauld Manor

Fauld

Stonepit Hills

HANBURY HILL

5

P

Sewage Works

Mill & Mine

Queen's Purse Wood

Hanbury

Hanbury Hill

Brown's Coppice

28

MARTIN ST LA

CHURCH LA

OAKFIELDS

DE13

The Cottages

4

PO

PH
St Werburgh's CE Prim Sch

WOOD LA

Hanbury House Farm

Hall

Castle Hayes Park Farm

CASTLE HAYES LA

Croft Farm

3

The Farm

COUNCIL HOS

Hare Holes Rough

Hare Holes Farm

27

Capertition Wood

HANBURY RD

CHAPEL LA

The Villa

2

Belmot Green

Moat Farm

Top Farm

Lower Castle Hayes Farm

Blackbrook Spinney

Woodend

Hanbury Park Farm

Belmot Bridge

BELMOT RD

Blackbrook Farm

1

Blackbrook

26

Hanbury Park Dingle

17   **A**   **B**   **18**   **C**   **D**   **19**   **E**   **F**

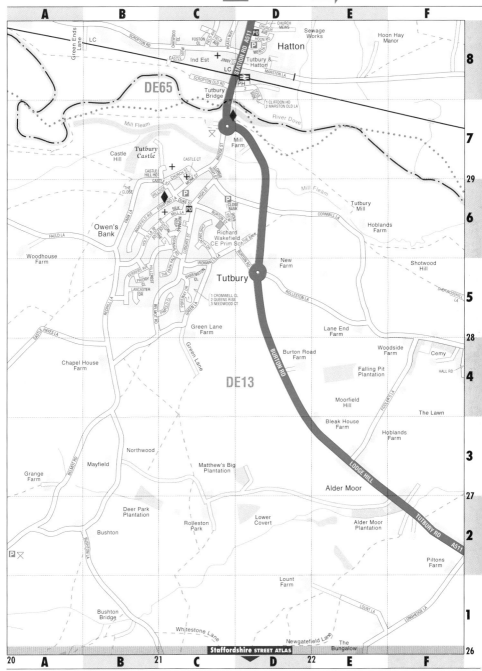

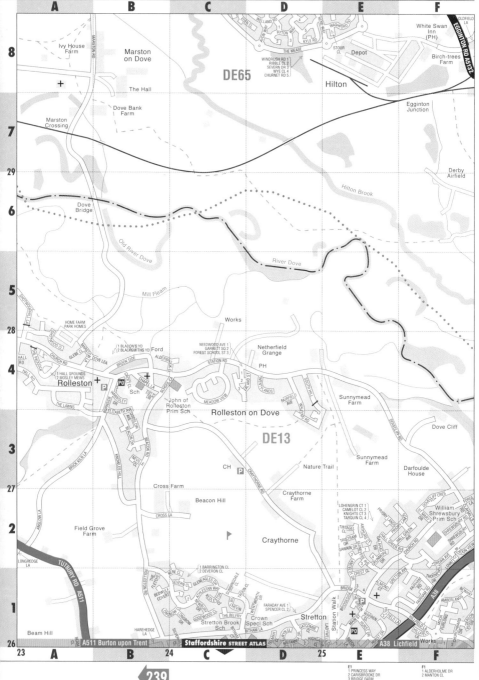

240

8

7

29

6

5

28

4

3

27

2

1

26

A   B   C   D   E   F

23   24   25

Ivy House Farm

Marston on Dove

DE65

White Swan Inn (PH)

Birch-trees Farm

EGINTON RD A5132

OLDFIELD LA

The Hall

Depot

Hilton

Egginton Junction

WINDRUSH RD 1
RIBBLE CL 2
SEVERN DR 3
WYE CL 4
CHURNET RD 5

THE MEASE

STOUR CL

Derby Airfield

Marston Crossing

Dove Bank Farm

Dove Bridge

Hilton Brook

Old River Dove

River Dove

Mill Fleam

Works

Home Farm Park Homes

SOUTHWOOD CL

1 BLADON'S YD
2 BLACKSMITHS YD

Ford

NEEDWOOD AVE 1
GARRETT SQ 2
FOREST SCHOOL ST 3

Netherfield Grange

PH

Sunnymead Farm

Dove Cliff

Rolleston

1 HALL GROUNDS
2 MOSLEY MEWS

HALL RD

THE LAWNS

John of Rolleston Prim Sch

Rolleston on Dove

DE13

Sunnymead Farm

Darfoulde House

CH

Nature Trail

Cross Farm

Beacon Hill

Craythorne Farm

LOHENGRIN CT 1
CAMELOT CL 2
KNIGHTS CT 3
TARQUIN CL 4

William Shrewsbury Prim Sch

Field Grove Farm

CROSS LA

Craythorne

TINTAGEL CL
TRISTRAM
GAWAIN AVE

LONGHEDGE LA

TUTBURY RD A511

1 BARRINGTON CL
2 DEVERON CL

1 FARADAY AVE 1
SPENCER CL 2

Station Walk

Beam Hill

HAREHEDGE LA

Stretton Brook Sch

Crown Speci Sch

Stretton

Works

A511 Burton upon Trent   **Staffordshire STREET ATLAS**   **A38 Lichfield**

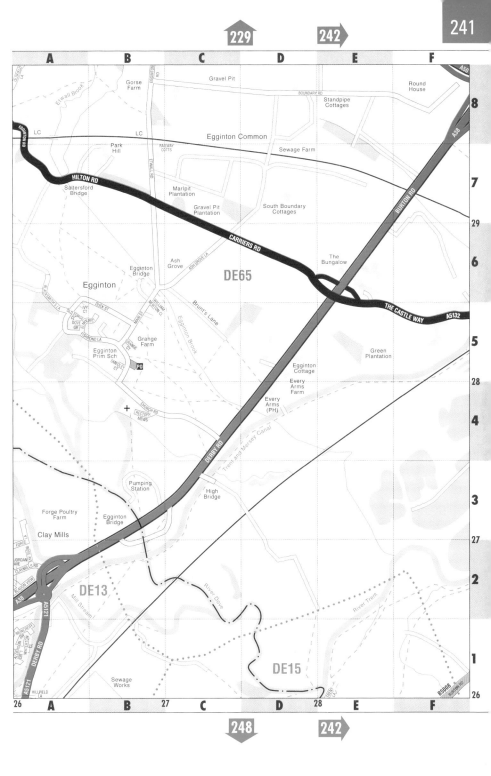

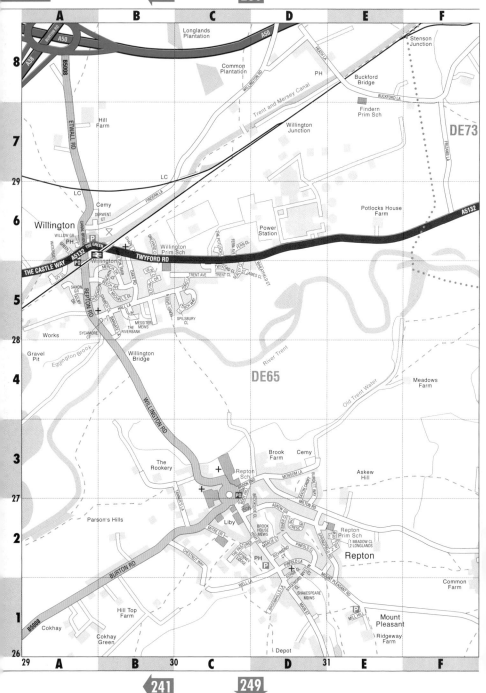

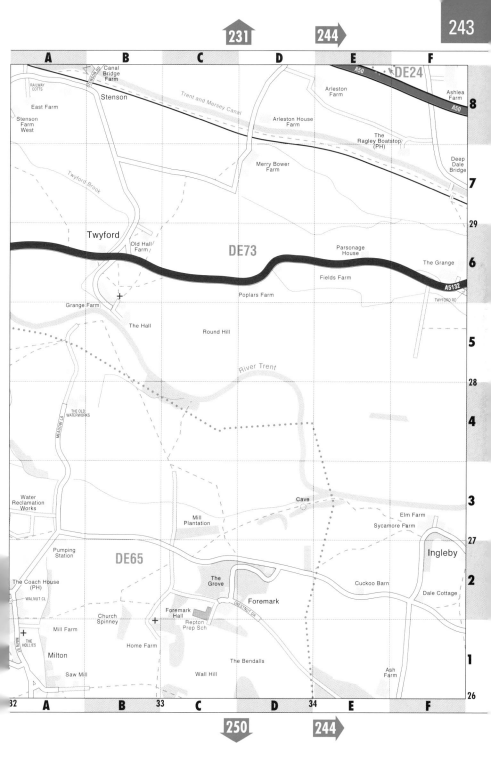

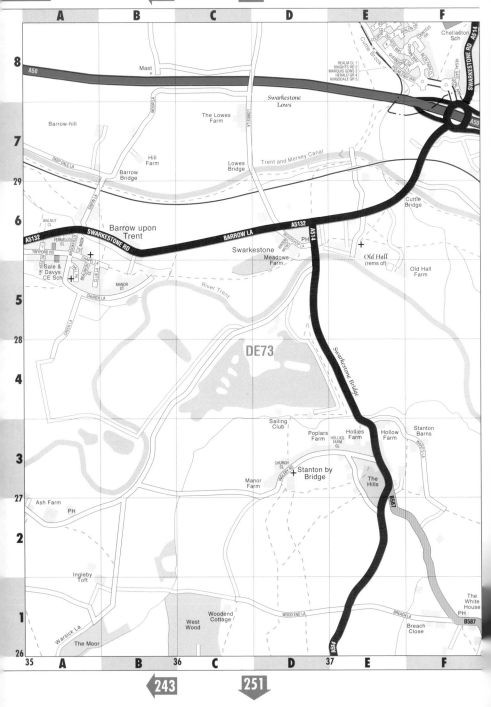

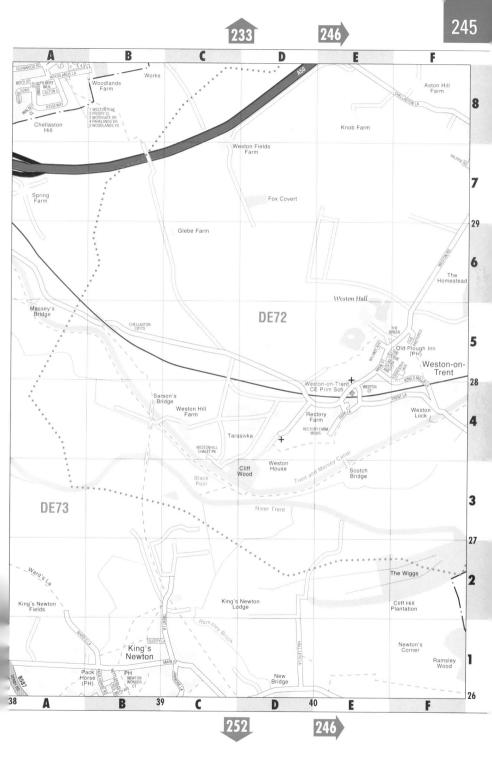

A B C D E F

8

A50

Glenwood Rd
Boyd Gr
Filbert Wlk
Gons
Walsh St
Ridgeway
Second
Aston Cl
Woodlands La
Woodlands Yd

Works

Woodlands Farm

1 WESTON RISE
2 PRIORY CL
3 WOODGATE DR
4 PARKLANDS DR
5 WOODLANDS YD

Aston Hill Farm

CHELLASTON LA

Chellaston Hill

Knob Farm

Weston Fields Farm

VALERIE RD

7

Spring Farm

Fox Covert

29

Glebe Farm

WESTON RD

6

The Homestead

Massey's Bridge

CHELLASTON COTTS

DE72

Weston Hall

THE GREEN
THE PASTURES

Old Plough Inn (PH)

5

Weston-on-Trent

Sarson's Bridge

Weston Hill Farm

WILMOT RD
MAIN ST

Weston-on-Trent CE Prim Sch

WESTON CT

KING'S MILL RD

28

Tarasivka

WESTONHILL CHALET PK

Rectory Farm

PARK LA

TRENT LA

Weston Lock

4

RECTORY FARM MEWS

Black Pool

Cliff Wood

Weston House

Trent and Mersey Canal

Scotch Bridge

DE73

River Trent

3

27

Ward's La

The Wiggs

2

King's Newton Fields

King's Newton Lodge

Ramsley Brook

Cliff Hill Plantation

TRENT LA
SLEEPY LA
WARD'S LA

King's Newton

Newton's Corner

Ramsley Wood

1

B5871
DERBY RD

Pack Horse (PH)

MAIN ST
PACK HORSE LA
NETTLE BANK
SMITH AVE
LAWRENCE LA

PH
NEWTON WONDER CT

New Bridge

HALL LEYS LA

26

38 A B 39 C D 40 E F

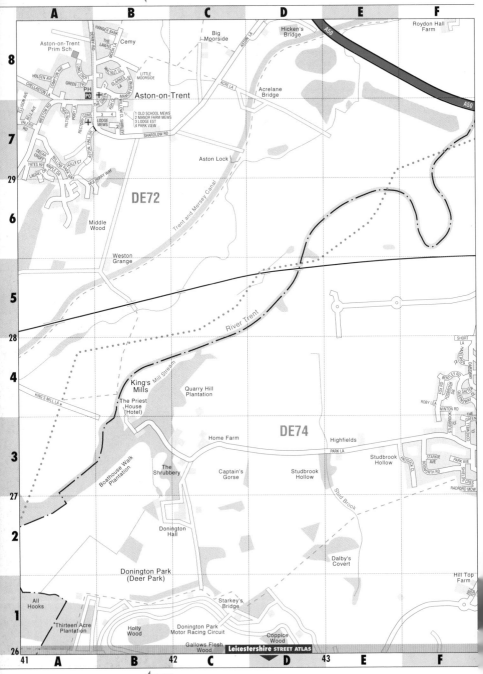

A | B | C | D | E | F

8

Aston-on-Trent Prim Sch

HANGER BANK

DERBY RD

THE LAWNS

Cemy

LONG CROFT

Big Moorside

Little Moorside

ASTOR LA

Hicken's Bridge

A50

Roydon Hall Farm

HOLDEN AVE

GREEN LEYS

WILLOW CT

CLARKES

Aston-on-Trent

ACRE LA

Acrelane Bridge

CHELLASTON LA

ELLISON AVE

VAN BELL AVE

WESTON RD

HELTON'S PL

RECTORY LA

POST LA

PH
PO

GDNS

LODGE MEWS

MANOR

ADELA

MILTON RD

THE SHRUBS

WALTON RD

1 OLD SCHOOL MEWS
2 MANOR FARM MEWS
3 LODGE EST
4 PARK VIEW

7

3 4

SHARDLOW RD

29

CROSS CROFT

YATES AVE

LAUREL DR

APPLE DR

MEADOW

HOLLY CT

HALL HILL RD

MULBERRY WAY

Aston Lock

DE72

6

Middle Wood

Weston Grange

Trent and Mersey Canal

5

River Trent

28

4

King's Mills

KING'S MILL LA

Mill Stream

Quarry Hill Plantation

The Priest House (Hotel)

DE74

SHORT LA

HAZEL RD

BENNS RD

ESK RD

HIGHBROOK DR

SALTER CL

THE GREENWAY

ROBY LEA

MINTON RD

STUDBROOK GDNS

THE GREEN

LIME WOOD

3

Boathouse Walk Plantation

The Shrubbery

Home Farm

Captain's Gorse

PARK LA

Highfields

Studbrook Hollow

Studbrook Hollow

STARKIE AVE

PADDOCK CL

BOSWORTH RD

PARK AVE

SHIELS

CRES

27

RADFORD MDW

Donington Hall

Stud Brook

2

Donington Park (Deer Park)

Dalby's Covert

Hill Top Farm

1

All Hooks

Thirteen Acre Plantation

Holly Wood

Starkey's Bridge

Donington Park Motor Racing Circuit

Coppice Wood

26

Gallows Flesh Wood

41 | A | B | 42 | C | D | 43 | E | F

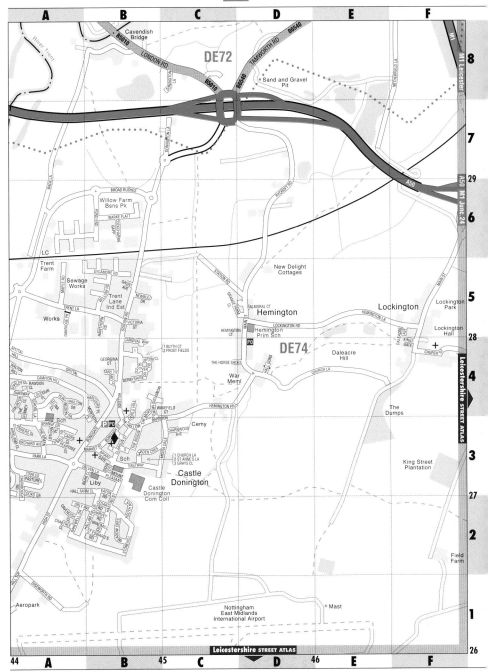

A **B** **C** **D** **E** **F**

River Trent

Cavendish Bridge

B5010

LONDON RD

DONINGTON LA

B5010

B6540

TAMWORTH RD

B6540

DE72

Sand and Gravel Pit

NETHERFIELD LA

M1

M1 Leicester

8

7

A50

A50

M1 Junc. 24

29

6

BROAD RUSHES

Willow Farm Bsns Pk

WARKE FLATT

POND END

COCKSHARME

GAPP

DONINGTON LA

BACK LA

LC

Trent Farm

Sewage Works

MAPLE RD

OLD HILL

SYCAMORE RD

GAGGY AVE

NEWBOLD DR

Trent Lane Ind Est

STATION RD

GRANGE FARM CT

New Delight Cottages

MAIN ST

Lockington

Lockington Park

Lockington Hall

HEMINGTON LA

MAIN ST

5

Works

Trent Farm

TRENT LA

OLD HILLCROFT

VICTORIA ST

BALMORAL CT

Hemington

LOCKINGTON RD

DALEACRE LANE

KINGS GATE

CHURCH

28

SPITTAL HILL

DALTON HILL

CARNIVAL WAY

HEMINGTON CT

HEMINGTON CT

Hemington Prim Sch

PO

DE74

Daleacre Hill

Leicestershire STREET ATLAS

Campion Hill

SPITTAL

Georgina Ct

TANY

UPTON CL

1 BLYTH CT
2 FROST FIELDS

DERBYSHIRE CL

THE HORSE SHOES

HALL GDNS

War Meml

CHURCH LA

The Dumps

4

VALLEY CL

RAWDON

LOUDON

DARSWAY

SCHOOL LA

HUNTINGDON DR

HAULTON DR

HARGATE

MONTFORT

HILSIDE

TRENT ST

DONINGTON

WAKEFIELD CT

BAWDON

HEMINGTON HO

Cemy

CHARNWOOD AVE

King Street Plantation

3

Sch

THE FOLLOW

P PO

MARKET ST

BONDGATE

CHAPELMAKE

Sch

ADEN CRES

MOOR LA

EASTWAY

1 CHURCH LA
2 ST ANNE S LA
3 GRAYS CL

Castle Donington

27

TOWLES PASTURES

MOSS DR

COOKS DR

Liby

PARK LA

ORCHARD AVER

CLOSE

CLEATREE CL

PARK LA

DELVEN LA

HALL FARM CL

MOUNT PLEASANT

EATON CL

Castle Donington Com Coll

2

CAVENDISH DR

CRABTREE RD

ST EDWARDS RD

ORLY AVE

CEDARS RD

HARVEY RD

WINDMILL CL

Field Farm

HILL TOP

HISWORTH RD

Aeropark

Nottingham East Midlands International Airport

Mast

1

Leicestershire STREET ATLAS

26

44 **A** **B** 45 **C** **D** 46 **E** **F**

241

A   B   C   D   E   F

8

DE13

DE65

7

25

DE14

6

5

24

DE15
BURTON UPON TRENT

4

3

23

2

1

22

26   A   **27**   B   C   **28**   D   E   F

255

MEADOW LA
LC
Sewage
Works

A5121 Burton upon Trent

River Trent

NEWTON RD

Castle
Wood

Bladon
Castle

Bladon
Hill

Bladon House
Sch

Bladon
Paddocks

Meadows
Farm

Dale Brook

Burton
Mill

Bladon Farm
Cotts

MILLERSDALE
CL

HANCHURCH
CL

Abbot Beyne
Sch

Abbot Beyne
Sch

Winshill
Inf Sch

Holy
Rosary
RC Prim
Sch

Winshill

Tower
View
Prim
Sch

Water
Tower

TOWER RD

Cemy

ASHBY RD

Brizlincote
Hall Farm

Newton
Park

Home
Wood

Wranglands
Plantation

Victory
Plantation

Bladon
Farm

Bend's
Oak
Jun Sch

Common
Farm

Newton
Solney
CE Inf Sch

Hotel

The Hill
Farm

Newton
Park Farm

Beaconhill
Plantation

REPTON RD

B5008 BURTON RD

Trent
Farm

Grange
Farm

Newton
Solney

Cricket
Gd

Blacksmiths
La

Hamfield La

Grafton
Smallholdings

Nursery

BRETBY LA

Oldicote
Farm

Crem

Stockings
Plantation

CH

Stanhope
Bretby

Geary
House

BRETBY
FAIRWAYS

A511

ASHBY RD E

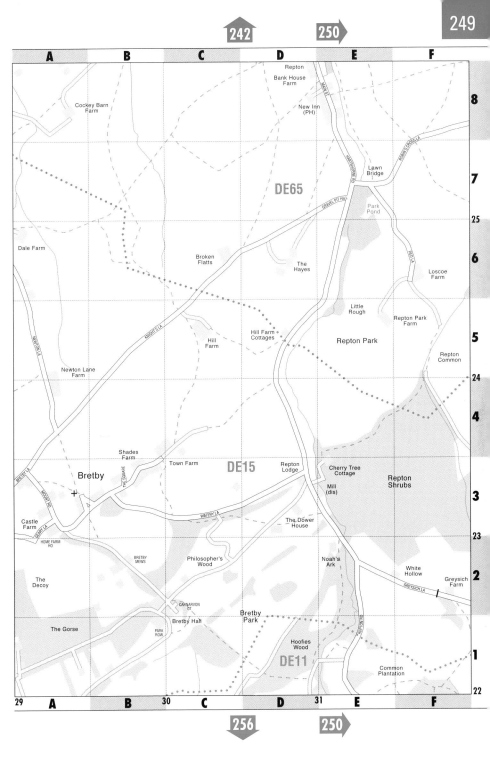

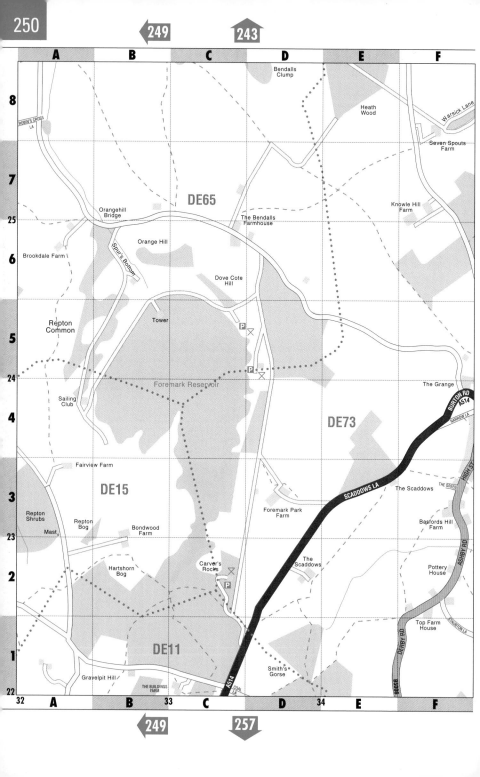

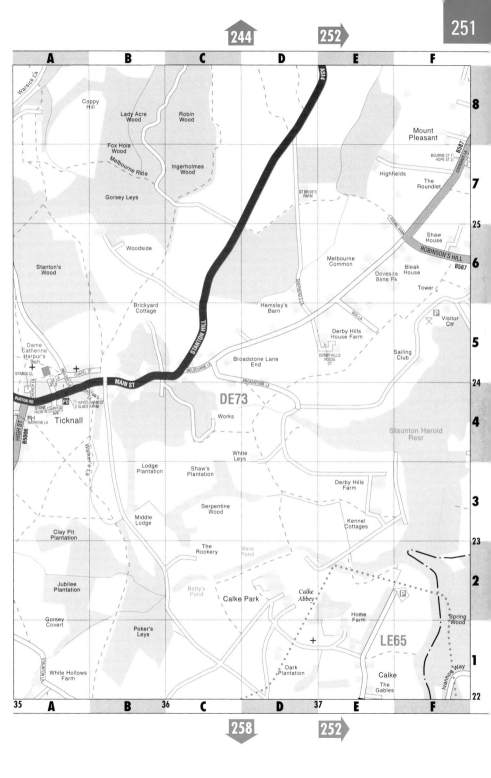

244

252

258

252

35 A B 36 C D 37 E F

A B C D E F

8 7 25 6 5 24 4 3 23 2 1 22

Warsick La

Coppy Hill

Lady Acre Wood

Robin Wood

A514

Mount Pleasant

BOURNE CT 1
HOPE ST 2

B587

Fox Hole Wood

Ingerholmes Wood

Highfields

The Roundlet

Melbourne Ride

ST BRIDE'S FARM

TOWNE BANK

ROBINSON'S HILL

Shaw House

Gorsey Leys

Woodside

Melbourne Common

Bleak House

Dovesite Bsns Pk

B587

Stanton's Wood

Tower

Brickyard Cottage

STANTON HILL

Hemsley's Barn

SHEPHERD'S LA

BOG LA

Derby Hills House Farm

Sailing Club

Visitor Ctr

P

Dame Catherine Harpur's Sch

GRANGE CL

CHAPEL ST

MELBOURNE LA

Broadstone Lane End

DERBY HILLS HOUSE CT

BROADSTONE LA

DE73

MAIN ST

STANTON'S LA

BURTON RD

STONE FRONTS

HARPUR AVE

PD

1 HAYES FARM CT
2 SLADE FARM

Works

HIGH ST

B5006

PH

NARROW LA

Ticknall

Staunton Harold Resr

Walker's La

White Leys

Lodge Plantation

Shaw's Plantation

Derby Hills Farm

Serpentine Wood

Kennel Cottages

Middle Lodge

Clay Pit Plantation

The Rookery

Mere Pond

Betty's Pond

P

Spring Wood

Jubilee Plantation

Calke Park

Calke Abbey

Home Farm

Gorsey Covert

Poker's Leys

+

LE65

Ivanhoe Way

STAUNTON LA

White Hollows Farm

Dark Plantation

Calke

The Gables

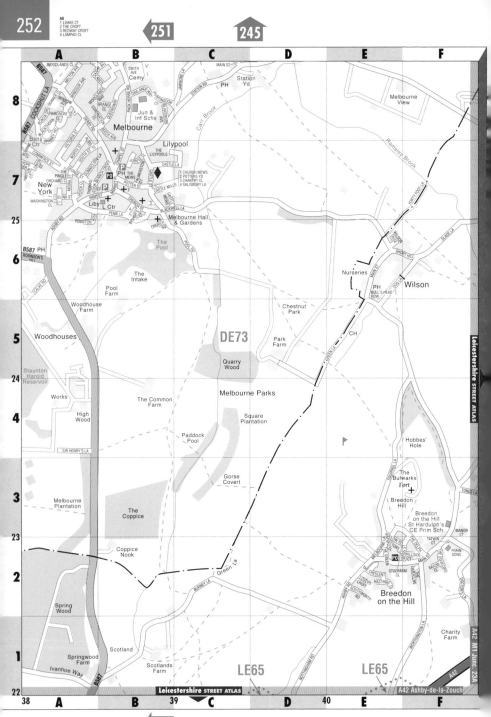

252

All
1 LOAKE CT
2 THE CROFT
3 REDWAY CROFT
4 LAMPAD CL

251

245

DE73

Melbourne

Lilypool

New
York

Woodhouses

Staunton
Harold
Reservoir

Works

High
Wood

Melbourne
Plantation

The
Coppice

Spring
Wood

Springwood
Farm

Ivanhoe Way

Scotland

Scotlands
Farm

The
Pool

The
Intake

Pool
Farm

Woodhouse
Farm

Melbourne Hall
& Gardens

Melbourne Parks

Quarry
Wood

The Common
Farm

Paddock
Pool

Gorse
Covert

Coppice
Nook

Green La

Square
Plantation

Chestnut
Park

Park
Farm

Nurseries

Wilson

Melbourne
View

Hobbes'
Hole

The
Bulwarks
Fort

Breedon
Hill

Breedon
on the Hill
St Hardulph's
CE Prim Sch

MANOR
CT

FRAIN
GDNS

Breedon
on the Hill

Charity
Farm

LE65

LE65

DE73 references:
1 CHURCH MEWS
2 POTTERS YD
3 CHANTRY CL
4 SALISBURY LA

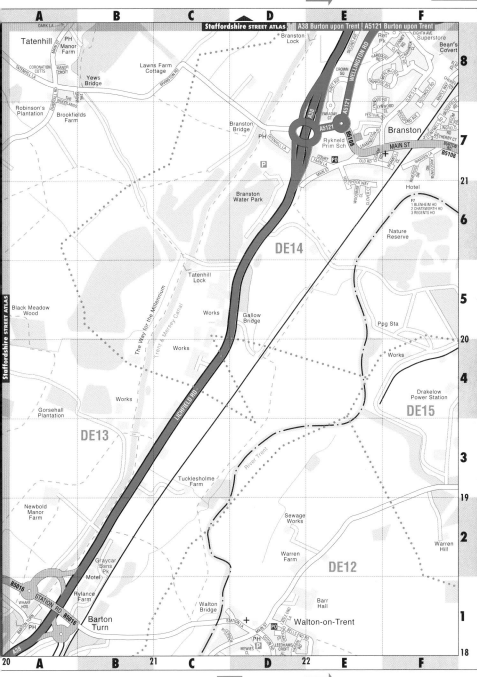

Tatenhill

Manor Farm

Lawns Farm Cottage

Branston Lock

Bean's Covert

Superstore

Yews Bridge

Robinson's Plantation

Brookfields Farm

Branston Bridge

Branston

Rykneld Prim Sch

DE14

Branston Water Park

Hotel

F7
1 BLENHEIM HO
2 CHATSWORTH HO
3 REGENTS HO

Nature Reserve

Black Meadow Wood

Tatenhill Lock

The Way for the Millennium

Works

Gallow Bridge

Ppg Sta

Works

Works

Works

Drakelow Power Station

DE15

Gorsehall Plantation

Works

DE13

Tucklesholme Farm

River Trent

Newbold Manor Farm

Sewage Works

Warren Hill

Warren Farm

DE12

Graycar Bsns Pk

Motel

Rylance Farm

Barr Hall

Barton Turn

Walton Bridge

Walton-on-Trent

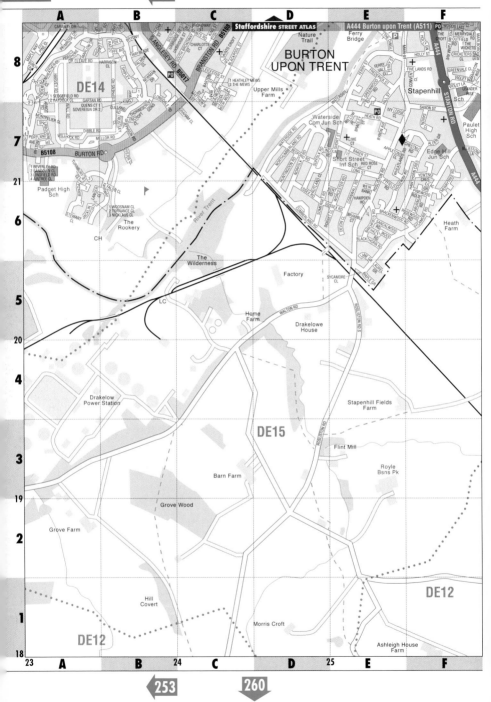

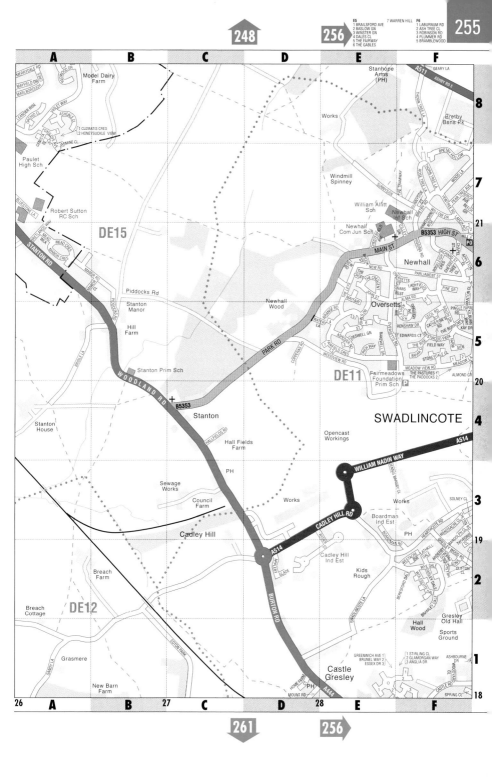

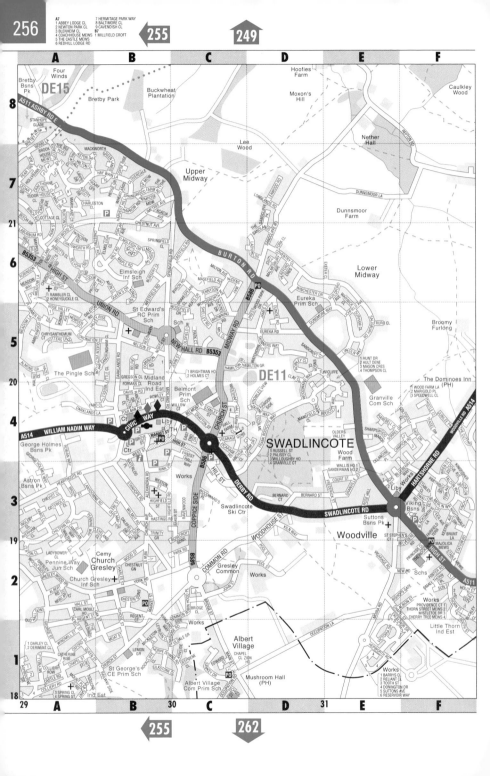

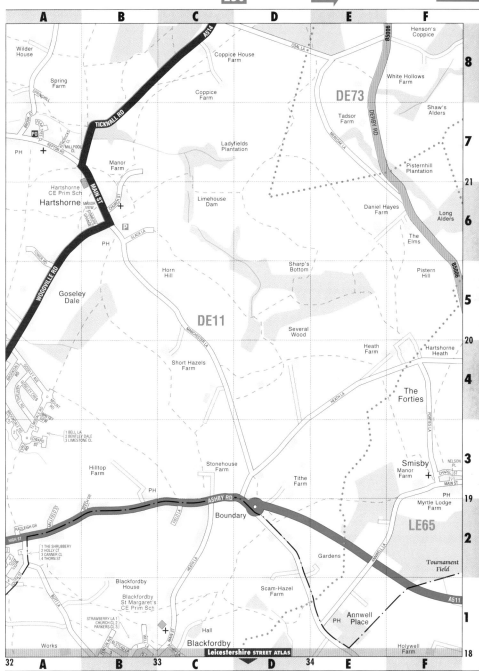

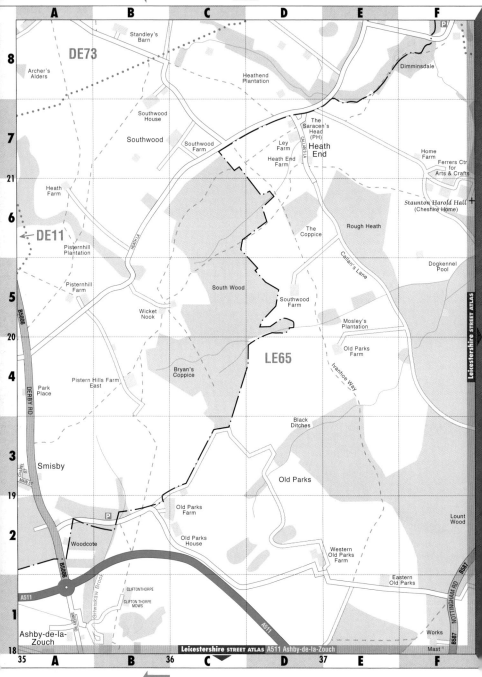

DE73

Standley's Barn

8

Archer's Alders

Heathend Plantation

Dimminsdale

Southwood House

7

Southwood

Southwood Farm

The Saracen's Head (PH)

Heath End

Ley Farm

Home Farm

Ferrers Ctr for Arts & Crafts

21

Heath Farm

Staunton Harold Hall (Cheshire Home)

6

DE11

Pisternhill Plantation

The Coppice

Rough Heath

Pisternhill Farm

Callan's Lane

Dogkennel Pool

5

Wicket Nook

South Wood

Southwood Farm

Mosley's Plantation

20

Old Parks Farm

LE65

B5006

Bryan's Coppice

Ivanhoe Way

4

Pistern Hills Farm East

Park Place

DERBY RD

Black Ditches

3

Smisby

Old Parks

19

Lount Wood

Old Parks Farm

2

Woodcote

Old Parks House

Western Old Parks Farm

NOTTINGHAM RD

B5006

B587

Eastern Old Parks

CLIFTONTHORPE

A511

CLIFTON THORPE MDWS

A511

1

Works

Ashby-de-la-Zouch

Mast

18

35   A   B   36   C   D   37   E   F

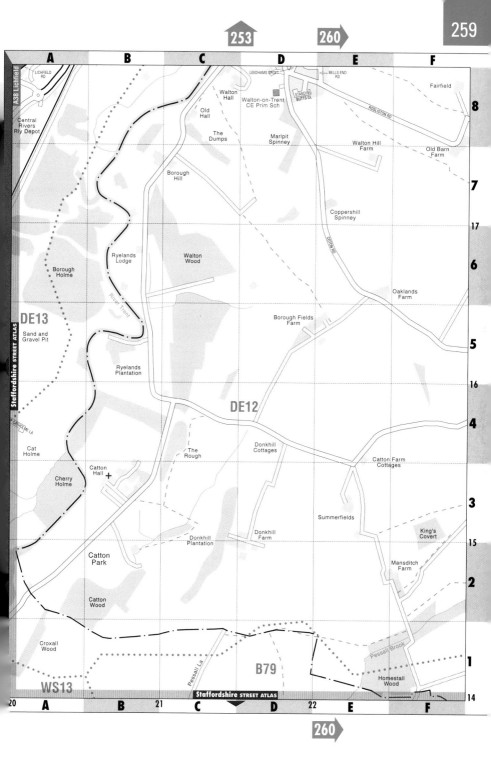

DE15

ROSLISTON RD

Corner
Farm

Nursery

Rosliston
Forestry
Visitor Ctr

Walton Lane
Farm

Fox
Covert

The
Royal Oak
(PH)

Priory
Farm

Caldwell

Calves Croft
Farm

Moonraker

Pegasus
Sch

Manor
Farm

THE CHASE

BURTON RD

Rosliston CE
Prim Sch

PH

PO

Roskiston

Caldwell
Covert

HOLDON CROFT

THE GLEBE

COTTAGE WALK

YEW TREE RD

YEW TREE
GDNS

MAIN ST

NEW ST

CAULDWELL RD

COTON LA

STRAWBERRY LA

LINTON RD

Blakenhall
Farm

Field House
Farm

DE12

Beehive
Farm

COTON RD

Lads Grave

Longfurlong
Farm

P

P

Coton in the
Elms

BURTON RD

Pessall Brook

Overfields
Farm

Church
Farm

PO

GREENACRE
PK

CHURCH CROFT

ELMS RD

GLEBE RD

ST LEDGER LA

CHAPMANS
CROFT

Coton in the
Elms CE Prim
Sch

Queen's Head
Inn (PH)

COALPIT LA

GRANGE LANE LA

COTON LA

CHURCH LA

NEW RD

MILL ST

MILL GREEN CL

Pessall Brook

Malt House
Farm

P

Raddle Farm
Wood

LITTLE LIVERPOOL

Pessall Brook

Church Flatts
Farm

The Crosses

Grafton
House

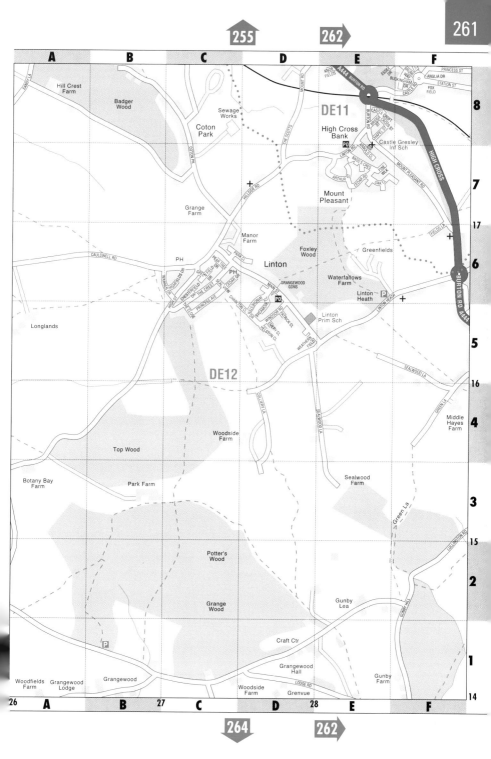

A B C D E F

8

PRINCESS ST
BANK AVE
STATION ST
Gresley Wood
Sch
Littleworth
DE11
Boothorpe

7

Gresley Tunnel
Spoil Heaps and Clay Pits
COPPORTON RD
GOYDEL PL
MEDOWOOD LA
MOIRA RD
RECKWOOD HILL
Gorse La

17

Swainspark
Swainspark Ind Est
RICKMANS CNR CVN SITE
PARK RD

6

Hanging Hill
Hanging Hill Farm

5

A444
BURTON RD
Works
SPRING COTTAGE RD
Spring Cottage
GORSE LA
P
CONKERS HOLM AVE
MARQUIS CT

16

PH
Conkers Discovery Centre
Works
MARQUIS CT
BRITON LODGE CL

4

ALEXANDRA CT
ALEXANDRA
EDWARD ST
ROYAL LA
CORNELIUS ST
WOODLANDS
ST PETERS
ALICE GDNS
WOODLANDS CRES
ROSEDALE VIEW
WOODVILLE RD
STAPLE DENE
SLACKS LA
DE12
HARLEY'S
Overseal Prim Sch
Gorsey Leys
BATH LA
Blencathra
Conkers Waterside Centre
Sarah's Wood
Visitors Ctr
WHITMORE CL
GORSE LA
ASHBY RD
PH
FURNACE LA
PO

3

Overseal
LULLINGTON MEWS
PH
DAISY LA
BEDFORD VIEW
HALLCROFT AVE
MOIRA RD
CARAVAN PK
Gresley Leys
Brooklands Farm
SHORT HEATH RD
Moira
Furnace Lane Ind Est
Moira Furnace Mus
Warren House Farm
Ashby-de-la-Zouch Canal
MEASHAM RD

15

MAIN ST
JACKSON ST
BAILEY
ASHBY LEY
Sewage Works
Grange Farm
Short Heath
Shortheath Farm
DONISTHORPE
PARK RD
POPLAR AVE
SCHOOL ST

2

LULLINGTON RD
ACRESFORD RD
Rookery Farm
Hooborough Brook
FINNEY CL
IVANHOE WAY
P

1

Cadborough Hill
Church Way
Cadborough Farm
Sewage Works
JUBILEE TERR
GREENSIDE CL
SEALS RD
NEW ST
BARKLAM
IVY CL
DAINA
BLUEBELL
BUTTERCUP CL
COWSLIP CL
Donisthorpe Cemy
ASHLAR DR
CHURCH ST

14

29 A B 30 C D 31 E F

Leicestershire STREET ATLAS

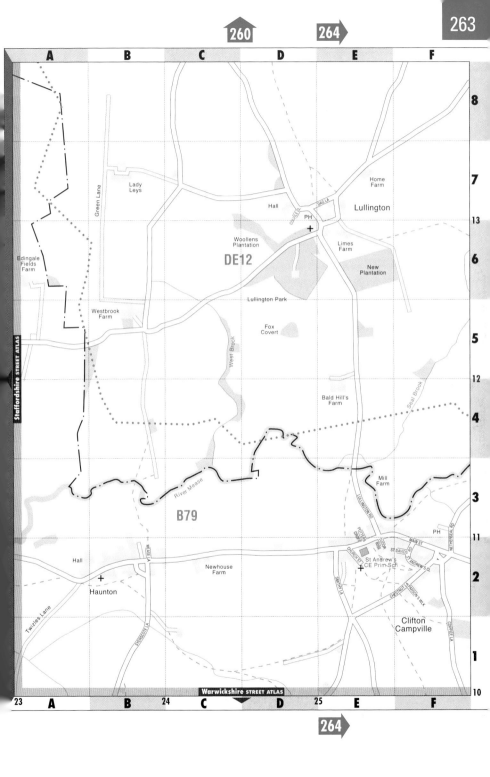

A B C D E F

8

7

Green Lane

Lady
Leys

Home
Farm

Hall

Lullington

PH
+

COLE LA

CMG LA

13

Woollens
Plantation

Limes
Farm

Edingale
Fields
Farm

DE12

New
Plantation

6

Lullington Park

Westbrook
Farm

Fox
Covert

West Brook

5

12

Bald Hill's
Farm

Seal Brook

4

B79

River Mease

Mill
Farm

LULLINGTON RD

3

PH

NETHERSEAL RD

11

POTTERS
CROFT

MAIN ST

TOOT
HILL

ST DAVIDS

ST ANDREW'S CL

Hall

MEASE LA

Newhouse
Farm

CHURCH ST

St Andrew's
CE Prim Sch
+

SMITH LA

BARTONS WLK

2

+

Haunton

Twizles Lane

STREDSALL LA

CHESTNUT LA

Clifton
Campville

COPPICE LA

1

23 A 24 B C 25 D E F 10

Staffordshire STREET ATLAS

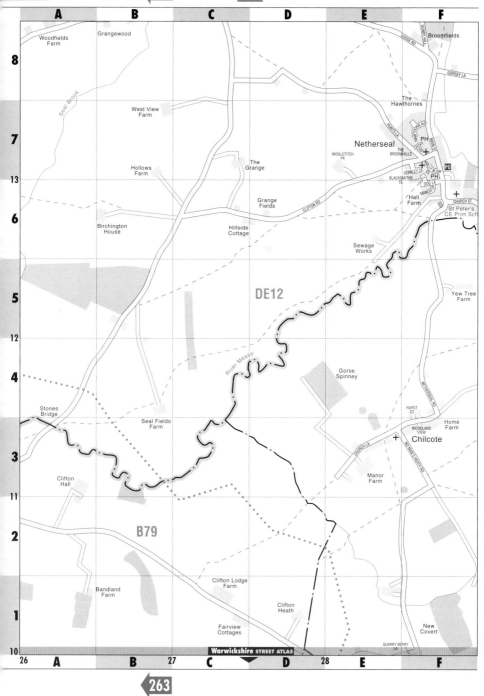

A B C D E F

8

7

13

6

5

12

4

3

11

2

1

10

26 A B 27 C D 28 E F

Woodfields Farm
Grangewood
Seal Brook
West View Farm
Hollows Farm
The Grange
Grange Fields
Birchington House
Hillside Cottage
DE12
Sewage Works
Stones Bridge
Seal Fields Farm
River Mease
Gorse Spinney
Clifton Hall
B79
Bandland Farm
Clifton Lodge Farm
Clifton Heath
Fairview Cottages
Broomfields
The Hawthornes
Netherseal
WOOLSTITCH PK
THE BROOMHILLS
Hall Farm
St Peter's CE Prim Sch
CHURCH ST
Yew Tree Farm
HURST CT
WOODLAND VIEW
Home Farm
CHURCH LA
Chilcote
Manor Farm
New Covert
QUARRY BERRY LA
LODGE RD
GORSEY LA
NETHERSEAL RD

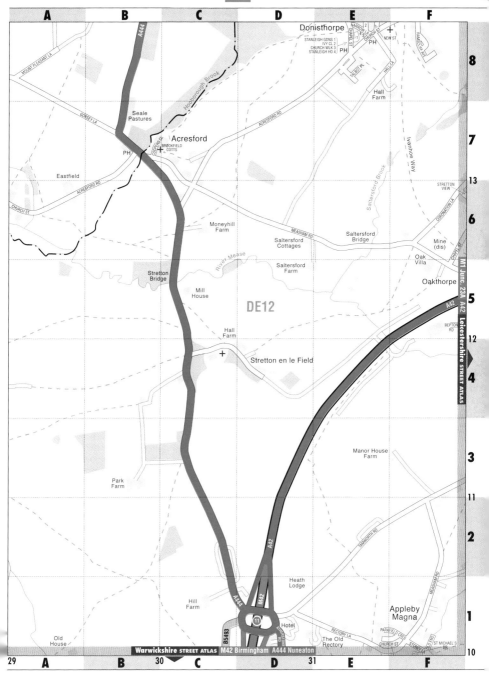

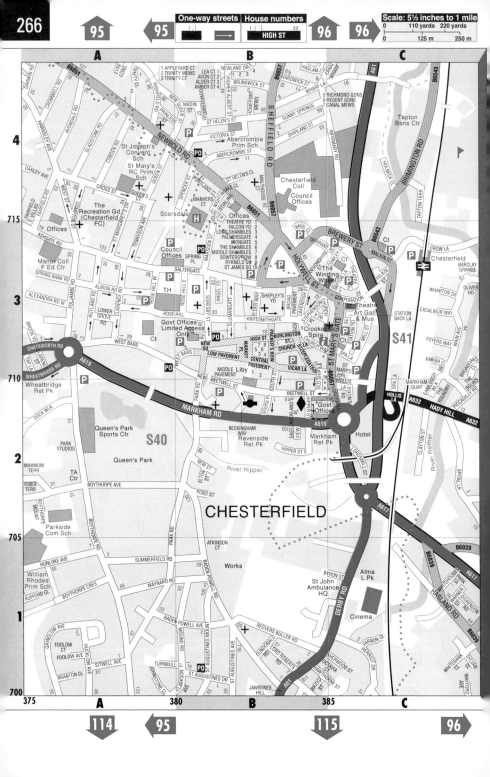

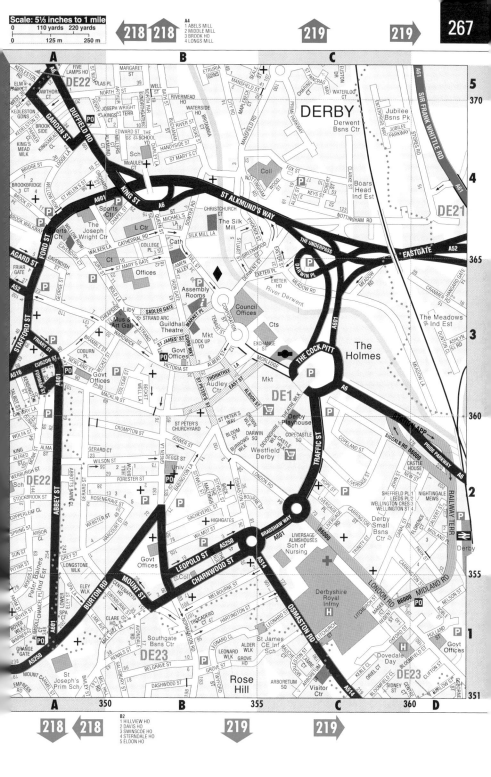

Index

Place name May be abbreviated on the map

Location number Present when a number indicates the place's position in a crowded area of mapping

Locality, town or village Shown when more than one place has the same name

Postcode district District for the indexed place

Page and grid square Page number and grid reference for the standard mapping

Church Rd **6** Beckenham BR2..........**53** C6

Public and commercial buildings are highlighted in magenta   Places of interest are highlighted in blue with a star*

Abbreviations used in the index

Acad	Academy	Comm	Common	Gd	Ground	L	Leisure	Prom	Promenade
App	Approach	Cott	Cottage	Gdn	Garden	La	Lane	Rd	Road
Arc	Arcade	Cres	Crescent	Gn	Green	Liby	Library	Recn	Recreation
Ave	Avenue	Cswy	Causeway	Gr	Grove	Mdw	Meadow	Ret	Retail
Bglw	Bungalow	Ct	Court	H	Hall	Meml	Memorial	Sh	Shopping
Bldg	Building	Ctr	Centre	Ho	House	Mkt	Market	Sq	Square
Bsns, Bus	Business	Ctry	Country	Hospl	Hospital	Mus	Museum	St	Street
Bvd	Boulevard	Cty	County	HQ	Headquarters	Orch	Orchard	Sta	Station
Cath	Cathedral	Dr	Drive	Hts	Heights	Pal	Palace	Terr	Terrace
Cir	Circus	Dro	Drove	Ind	Industrial	Par	Parade	TH	Town Hall
Cl	Close	Ed	Education	Inst	Institute	Pas	Passage	Univ	University
Cnr	Corner	Emb	Embankment	Int	International	Pk	Park	Wk, Wlk	Walk
Coll	College	Est	Estate	Intc	Interchange	Pl	Place	Wr	Water
Com	Community	Ex	Exhibition	Junc	Junction	Prec	Precinct	Yd	Yard

Index of localities, towns and villages

A

Abbeydale Park 55 F6
Abney 51 F4
Acresford 265 C7
Albert Village 256 C1
Aldercar 182 A4
Alders 196 C2
Aldervasley 166 E8
Aldwark 152 F7
Alfreton 159 C4
Alkmonton 199 D1
Allenton 232 D5
Allestree 204 F3
Alsop en le Dale 150 E3
Alstonefield 149 D4
Alton 130 C5
Alvaston 233 B8
Ambaston 234 D6
Ambergate 167 F3
Annwell Place 257 E1
Apperknowle 58 A1
Appleby Magna 265 F1
Arbourthorne 43 E8
Arbourthorne Estate ..43 E6
Arkwright Town 97 D3
Ashbourne 173 C2
Ashby-de-la-Zouch ..258 A1
Ashford in the Water ..108 F7
Ashgate
  Chesterfield 95 D4
  Old Brampton 94 F4
Ashleyhay 166 A4
Ashopton 30 E2
Ashover 129 F3
Ashover Hay 145 B5
Aston
  Hope 39 C4
  Sudbury 225 F4
Aston Heath 226 B6
Aston-on-Trent 246 B8
Astwith 133 A5
Atlow 175 A6
Atlowtop 175 B5
Ault Hucknall 133 F7
Awsworth 195 C4

B

Backmoor 43 C2
Bagshaw 47 F7
Bagthorpe 171 F4
Bailey Grove 182 D2
Bakestone Moor 81 E5
Bakewell 109 C5

Ballidon 152 A2
Bamford 40 B4
Bank Top 53 A8
Bankwood Gate 16 C8
Barber Booth 37 A6
Bargate 179 C1
Barlborough 80 B7
Barlborough Common ..80 B5
Barlow 75 E2
Barrow Hill 78 B4
Barrow upon Trent ..244 B6
Barton in Fabis 237 E6
Barton Turn 253 B1
Baslow 91 F5
Bassett 42 E5
Batemoor 57 A5
Batham Gate 56 C8
Beauclief 56 D8
Beeley 111 B4
Beeston 223 E4
Bellevue 173 B2
Belper 179 B3
Belper Lane End 178 C7
Belph 82 C4
Bibbington 66 F7
Biggin
  Hartington 138 C4
  Hulland Ward 176 A5
Birch Cross 224 C2
Birchover 126 B1
Birch Vale 25 B2
Birdholme 115 A7
Birley 93 F7
Birleyhay 58 D5
Blackbrook
  Belper 178 B4
  Chapel-en-le-Frith ..47 E6
  Tutbury 238 C1
Blackfordby 257 C1
Blackwall 175 F7
Blackwell
  Sutton in Ashfield ..147 F1
  Taddington 87 D5
Bolehill
  Calow 97 B1
  Common Side 75 C2
  Sheffield 43 A2
  Wirksworth 155 A2
Bolsover 99 B3
Bonsall 142 E1
Bonsall Dale 142 D1
Boothgate 179 F2
Boothorpe 262 F8
Borrowash 221 C2
Boulton 233 B6
Boundary 257 C2
Bowden Head 35 D1

Bowshaw 56 F4
Boylestone 213 C4
Boylestonfield 213 E5
Boythorpe 95 E1
Brackenfield 145 D2
Bradbourne 163 C6
Bradley 186 F8
Bradway 56 C5
Bradway Bank 56 A6
Bradwell 51 B7
Bradwell Hills 51 B6
Brailsford 201 F7
Bramley 58 F3
Bramley-Vale 117 E1
Brampton 95 D2
Branston 253 F7
Brassington 153 A1
Breadsall 205 E4
Breadsall Hilltop ..205 D2
Breaston 235 D7
Breck End 35 C1
Breedon on the Hill ..252 E2
Bretby 249 A3
Bretton 71 A8
Brick Houses 55 D8
Bridgefield 17 B7
Bridgeholm Green 47 A8
Bridgemont 33 E2
Brierley Green 34 B2
Brightgate 142 B4
Brimington 96 F7
Brimington Common ..96 F5
Brindwoodgate 75 D5
Brinsley 182 E7
Broadbottom 16 A8
Broadholm 179 A7
Brockhurst 129 C6
Brockwell 95 E4
Brook Bottom 23 F1
Brookfield 9 E3
Brookside 94 F2
Brough 39 D2
Brushfield 88 A7
Bubnell 91 D6
Buildbridge 168 B5
Bull Farm 135 C2
Burbage 84 E6
Burnaston 229 F5
Burntheath 228 C4
Burrfields 47 C6
Burton upon Trent ..254 D8
Butterley
  Ripley 169 F3
  Tansley 144 F5
Buxton 85 A7
Buxworth 34 A1

C

Caldwell 260 E7
California 218 D3
Calke 251 E1
Calow 96 F1
Calow Green 116 A8
Calton Lees 110 F5
Calver 72 C2
Calver Sough 72 C2
Canholes 84 E5
Carr Vale 117 F8
Carsington 164 E7
Cartledge 75 B7
Castle Donington ..247 C3
Castle Gresley 255 E1
Castleton 38 C2
Causeway Head 55 C8
Chaddesden 219 E7
Chapel-en-le-Frith ..47 B6
Chapel Milton 47 B8
Charlestown 17 C6
Charlesworth 16 C6
Chellaston 233 A1
Chelmorton 87 B1
Cherrytree Hill ...220 B5
Chesterfield 266 B2
Chevinside 178 E2
Chew 16 A5
Chilcote 264 F3
Chinley 34 F1
Chinley Head 34 F5
Chisworth 16 B5
Chunal 17 D4
Church Broughton ..227 B8
Church Broughton,
  Heathtop 227 A6
Church Mayfield ...184 D6
Churchtown 127 B2
Church Town 60 E6
Cinderhill 179 E1
Clay Cross 131 B4
Clay Mills 241 A3
Clifton 184 F6
Clifton Campville ..263 F1
Clowne 80 D3
Coal Aston 57 B4
Cock Alley 97 A1
Cockyard 46 E4
Codnor 181 C7
Codnor Breach 181 A4
Codnor Gate 170 B1
Codnor Park 170 E3
Coldeaton 150 B6

Colshaw 103 E4
Combridge 210 C8
Combs 46 E1
Common End 132 F7
Commonside
  Brailsford 187 D1
  Selston 171 F8
  Sutton in Ashfield ..148 F2
Common Side
  Barlow 75 D3
  Heanor 181 E1
Compstall 15 A3
Compton 173 D2
Congreave 126 D7
Coplow Dale 50 E3
Corbriggs 115 F5
Cordwell 74 E6
Cossall 195 C1
Cossall Common 195 B3
Cossall Marsh 195 C2
Cote Green 15 C1
Cotes Park 159 C2
Cotmanhay 194 E4
Coton in the Clay ..238 A7
Coton in the Elms ..260 C4
Coton Park 261 C8
Covers Lane 177 D3
Cowhill 179 A2
Cowley 75 D7
Cowley Bar 75 B8
Coxbench 191 F3
Crakemarsh 210 D5
Craythorne 240 D2
Cressbrook 89 A6
Cresswell 81 F2
Crewton 232 F8
Crich 156 F1
Crich Common 168 B8
Crist 46 B8
Cromford 155 A6
Cropper 215 B4
Cross Hill 181 B5
Crowden 6 E5
Crowdicote 121 E2
Crowhole 75 D4
Cuckney 101 F3
Curbar 72 E2
Cutthorpe 94 F7
Cutthorpe Green 94 E7

D

Dalbury 216 E2
Dale Abbey 207 F3
Dalebank 145 C4

Dale End
- Bradwell 51 A6
- Elton 140 C7

Danebank 32 E5
Danesmoor 131 E3
Darfoulds 63 F1
Darley Abbey 205 A2
Darley Bridge 142 C8
Darley Dale 127 C2
Darley Hillside 127 C4
Deep Pit 43 F8
Denby Bottles 180 A1
Denby Common 181 A3
Denby Village 180 C1
Denstone 196 D6
Derby 267 C4
Derwent 30 C6
Dethick 156 B8
Dimple 143 A6
Disley 32 C5
Doehole 145 A2
Doe Lea 117 D1
Donisthorpe 262 F1
Dore 55 E7
Dove Head 103 D6
Dove Holes 47 E2
Doveridge 211 A1
Draycott 234 F7
Dronfield 56 E2
Duckmanton 98 A5
Duffield 190 F3
Duffieldbank 191 A3
Dunnshill 207 C1

E

Eagle Tor 126 A2
Earl Sterndale 105 C3
Eastmoor 93 D4
Eastwood 182 E3
Eccles Fold 46 C8
Eckington 59 C4
Edale 37 C8
Edale End 29 D2
Edensor 110 E8
Edgetop 103 F1
Edlaston 185 C2
Egginton 241 B6
Egstow 131 D5
Ellastone 183 B3
Elmton 100 A7
Elton 140 E6
Elvaston 234 A6
Emmett Carr 79 C7
Etwall 229 C3
Etwall Common 229 D2
Eyam 71 D6

F

Fairfield 85 D8
Far Laund 179 C6
Farley 128 B1
Farnah Green 178 C3
Fauld 238 C6
Fenny Bentley 162 A1
Fernilee 45 E1
Findern 230 D2
Flagg 106 F6
Flash 103 A3
Flaxholme 190 F1
Foolow 70 E6
Ford 58 E5
Foremark 243 D2
Foston 226 D4
FourLane Ends 158 C4
Fox Green 100 F8
Freebirch 93 D6
Friden 139 A6
Fritchley 168 C7
Froggatt 72 C5
Furness Vale 33 C3

G

Gallows Inn 209 B6
Gamesley 9 D1
Gentshill 131 E2
Giltbrook 195 C8
Glapwell 134 C8
Glasshouse Common 43 E3
Gleadless Valley 43 E3
Glossop 10 B2
Godfreyhole 165 B8
Golden Valley 170 D3
Goosegreen 146 D3
Gorseybank 166 A7
Gorsey Leys 262 C4
Gosforth Valley 56 E2
Gotham 139 D1
Gowhole 33 E4
Grangemill 153 D8
Grasshill 115 E4
Grassmoor 115 C4
Great Cubley 198 F1
Great Hucklow 70 B8
Great Longstone 90 B4
Great Wilne 235 C2
Green Fairfield 67 C2
Greenhill 56 F7
Greenhillocks 180 E7
Greenside 58 C3
Greenwich 169 F2
Griffe Grange 153 D4
Grindleford 72 C7

Grindlow 70 C8
Grindsbrook Booth 37 C8

H

Hadfield 10 B5
Hady 96 D2
Hague Bar 32 E8
Hales Green 199 B7
Halfway 59 F7
Hallam Fields 209 A4
Hallam Moors 41 E8
Hall Green 171 E8
Hallhill 46 F7
Hallowes 76 C8
Hammersmith 169 D4
Hanbury 238 A5
Handley 145 F8
Hangingbridge 184 F8
Hanstubbin 171 F5
Hardhurst 76 E6
Hardley Hill 215 C2
Hardstoft 133 A3
Harehill 213 A3
Hargatewall 68 B3
Harlesthorpe 80 C5
Harpur Hill 85 C3
Harthill 61 F6
Hartington 137 D5
Hartshorne 257 A6
Hasland 115 C7
Hasland Green 115 C7
Hassop 90 F5
Hathersage 53 B7
Hatton 239 D8
Haunton 263 B2
Hayfield 25 C2
Hazelford 53 A5
Hazelwood 190 A8
Heage 168 E1
Heanor 181 C2
Heanor Gate 193 C8
Hearthstone 143 D1
Heath 117 B2
Heathcote 138 B5
Heath End 258 D7
Heathtop 227 A6
Heeley 43 B6
Hemington 247 D5
Hemming Green 94 B4
Hemsworth 43 D3
Henmoor 131 A4
Hepthorne Lane 131 E6
Herdings 43 F3
Hidebank 33 C8
Higgenholes 109 D8
Higham 146 C3
High Cross Bank 261 E8
Higher Bibbington 67 A6
Higher Buxton 85 C6
Higher Chisworth 16 B4
Higher Crossings 46 F6
Higher Dinting 10 A2
Higher Disley 32 E5
Higher Gameslay 16 B8
Highfield 43 A8
Highfields 132 C7
Highgate 25 D1
High Lane 32 A8
High Low 52 E5
Hilcote 148 C1
Hillclifflane 177 A3
Hillcross 231 C7
Hillfoot 55 D5
Hills and Holes 120 E5
Hill Somersal 212 A2
Hillstown 118 C8
Hilltop
- Chapel-en-le-Frith 46 B6
- Flash 103 B5

Hill Top 76 A7
Hillyfields 132 B7
Hilton 228 C1
Hilton Common 228 F2
Hindlow 105 B7
Hobsic 182 D8
Hockley 115 A2
Hodthorpe 82 C6
Hognaston 164 A1
Holbeck 101 C7
Holbeck Woodhouse 101 E7
Holbrook
- Belper 191 D6
- Sheffield 60 A8

Holbrook Moor 191 D7
Holehouse 16 C5
Holestone 144 C8
Hollington 200 F4
Hollingworth 9 C4
Hollins 94 A4
Hollinsclough 104 C1
Hollins Green 130 E3
Hollin Wood 26 A3
Holloway 156 B5
Holme 2 F8
Holmesdale 57 C2
Holmesfield 75 A8
Holmesfield Common 74 E8
Holmewood 116 E1
Holmgate 130 E4
Holmley Common 57 A3
Holymoorside 113 D8
Hope
- Alstonefield 149 D3
- Castleton 38 F4

Hopedale 149 C2
Hopton 164 F7

Horsley 191 F6
Horsleygate 74 E6
Horsley Woodhouse 192 D6
Horwich End 45 D5
Hulland Village 175 D2
Hulland Ward 175 F3
Hundall 77 B7
Hunloke Estate 115 C2
Hurl Field 43 E6
Huthwaite 148 E3

I

Ible 153 E7
Idridgehay 176 F6
Idridgehay Green 176 E7
Ilkeston 208 E2
Ingleby 243 F2
Ingmanthorpe 94 C7
Inkersall 97 D7
Inkersall Green 97 D6
Ireton Wood 176 D4
Ironville 170 E4

J

Jacksdale 171 B4
Jordanthorpe 57 B7
Jubilee 171 B6

K

Kedleston 203 C7
Kelstedge 129 D4
Kilburn 192 A8
Killamarsh 60 E6
Kimberley 195 F8
King's Newton 245 B1
King Sterndale 86 C5
Kirk Hallam 208 D6
Kirk Ireton 165 C1
Kirk Langley 202 F2
Kirkstead 160 D3
Kniveton 163 B1
Knotbury 102 F5

L

Ladmanlow 84 E4
Lambhouse 177 E7
Lane 2 E8
Lane Ends
- Disley 32 E4
- Marple 15 D1
- Sutton on the Hill 215 A2

Lane Head 69 E5
Langley 182 A8
Langley Common 217 B8
Langley Green 202 D2
Langley Mill 182 B3
Langwith 119 F8
Langwith Junction 119 D6
Larklands 209 B8
Lea 156 B7
Lea Bridge 156 A6
Leabrooks 170 B7
Leadmill 53 B5
Leam 53 A3
Lee Head 16 C6
Lees 216 B7
Leys 154 A8
Lightwood
- Eckington 58 F2
- Sheffield 57 F8

Lilypool 252 B7
Limekiln Field 99 A3
Linton 261 D6
Litchurch 219 C3
Little Bolehill 155 B2
Little Chester 219 A4
Little Cubley 212 E8
Little Eaton 205 C8
Little Hallam 208 E5
Little Hayfield 25 B5
Little Hucklow 50 E2
Little Longstone 89 E4
Little Matlock 135 F7
Littlemoor 130 C3
Little Norton 57 A8
Littleover 231 B8
Littleworth 202 D8
Litton 69 E3
Litton Mill 88 E7
Lockington 247 F5
Longcliffe 152 F4
Long Duckmanton 98 A3
Long Eaton 236 C7
Longford 214 D8
Longfordlane 215 A5
Longnor 121 A6
Loscoe 181 C3
Loundsley Green 95 B6
Lowedges 57 A6
Lower Bradway 56 C6
Lower Crossings 46 F4
Lower Dinting 10 B1
Lower Ellastone 183 C2
Lower Hartshay 169 A3
Lower Kilburn 191 F7
Lower Midway 256 E6
Lower Pilsley 132 B3
Lower Thurvaston 214 F6
Lowfield 43 B8
Lowgates 78 F3

Low Leighton 33 D8
Lullington 263 E2
Lumsdale 143 E6
Lydgate 74 D8

M

Mackworth 217 E8
Mackeney 191 A6
Malcoff 35 E2
Mansfield 135 F2
Mansfield Woodhouse 136 E2
Mapleton 172 F4
Mapperley 193 E3
Marchington 224 E2
Marehay 180 D6
Marketon 218 B8
Marlpool 193 E8
Marple 23 A5
Marpleridge 23 A2
Marsh Lane 58 F3
Marston Montgomery 211 F8
Marston on Dove 240 B8
Martinside 47 D3
Mastin Moor 79 D4
Mattersgrave 145 C3
Matlock 143 A5
Matlock Bank 143 C5
Matlock Bath 143 B5
Matlock Bridge 143 B5
Matlock Cliff 143 D4
Matlock Dale 143 A2
Matlock Green 143 C5
Mayfield 184 C8
Meersbrook 43 B5
Meersbrook Bank 43 A5
Melbourne 252 B8
Mellor 23 D5
Mercaston 188 B3
Mercaston Green 188 B3
Mickleover 217 E2
Mickley 56 B3
Middlecroft 97 C7
Middle Handley 77 F8
Middle Mayfield 184 B6
Middlepeak 154 E3
Middleton
- Wirksworth 154 D4
- Youlgrave 124 E3

Milehill 115 F5
Milford 191 A7
Mill Brow 23 E8
Millbank 149 F2
Miller's Dale 88 A2
Millers Green 165 E6
Millington Green 176 A4
Millthorpe 74 F5
Milltown 145 B8
Milton 243 A1
Moira 262 F3
Monsal Head 89 D4
Monyash 107 C2
Mooredge 144 C5
Moorend
- Bradley 186 D8
- Marple 24 A6

Moorhaigh 135 A3
Moorhall 74 D2
Moorside 165 A2
Morley 206 C6
Morton 146 F5
Mosborough 59 D7
Mount Pleasant
- Belper 178 D6
- Blackwell 147 F2
- Castle Gresley 261 E7
- Melbourne 251 F8
- Repton 242 E1

Mudd 9 A2
Mugginton 188 F2
Muggintonlane End 188 E6

N

Nether Biggin 175 F5
Nether Booth 29 A1
Nether Burrows 202 C3
Nether Chanderhill 94 C1
Nether Green 60 D7
Nether Handley 77 F7
Nether Heage 168 C1
Nether Langwith 101 B1
Nether Padley 53 E1
Nether Sturston 173 F1
Netherseal 264 E7
Netherthorpe 79 A2
New Barlborough 80 D5
Newbold 95 E6
Newbold Moor 95 F7
New Bolsover 98 F2
New Brimmington 77 F1
New Brinsley 171 E1
Newfield Green 43 D5
Newgate 75 D1
Newhall 255 F6
Newhaven 138 F5
New Horwich 45 E6
New Houghton 134 F7
Newlands 181 F2
Newmarket 131 A2
New Mills 33 D7
New Sawley 236 B5
New Smithy 35 A1
New Stanton 208 E3

Newthorpe 195 A8
Newthorpe Common 195 A8
Newton 148 B3
Newton Green 148 A4
Newton Solney 248 E8
New Totley 55 E4
Newtown 33 B6
New Westwood 171 C4
New York 252 A7
New Zealand 218 C5
Nithen End 84 F8
Norbriggs 79 C3
Norbury 183 D1
Normanton 231 F7
Northedge 130 C6
North Wingfield 132 B8
Northwood 127 B5
Norton 57 B8
Norton Lees 43 A4
Norton Woodseats 43 A2
Norwood 60 F8
Nuttals Park 169 E1

O

Oakerthorpe 158 C3
Oaks Green 225 D7
Oakthorpe 265 F5
Oakwood 206 A2
Ockbrook 221 D5
Offerton 52 D7
Ogston 146 A4
Oker 142 D7
Old Brampton 94 D4
Old Dam 9 B4
Old Glossop 10 E2
Old Matlock 143 C4
Old Tupton 131 C7
Old Whittington 77 B1
Ollerbrook Booth 37 D8
Openwoodgate 179 D3
Osleston 215 D7
Osmaston
- Ashbourne 185 F4
- Derby 232 C8

Over Burrows 202 A4
Overgreen 94 B8
Over Haddon 109 B1
Over Leigh 45 F6
Overseal 262 A3
Oversetts 255 E5
Over Woodhouse 98 E3
Owen's Bank 239 B6
Owlcotes 117 A4
Owler Bar 55 B1
Owlthorpe 59 C8
Oxton Rakes 94 B8

P

Padfield 10 C5
Palmer Moor 224 E7
Palterton 118 A5
Park Head 157 C2
Parsley Hay 123 B4
Parwich 151 E1
Parwich Lees 151 A2
Peak Dale 67 B5
Peak Forest 49 B3
Peakley Hill 75 C6
Pear Tree 232 B8
Peasehill 180 F8
Pentrich 169 B5
Perryfoot 48 E7
Pikehall 139 E3
Pilhough 126 E7
Pilsley Baslow 93 C3
  Clay Cross 132 D1
Pilsley Green 147 C8
Pinxton 160 C2
Plaistow 156 F6
Plaistow Green 156 F4
Pleasley 135 B6
Pleasleyhill 135 C4
Plumbley 59 B8
Pomeroy 98 A7
Porterhouse 169 F1
Potter Somersal 212 A4
Pratthall 94 B7
Priestcliffe 87 F5
Priestcliffe Ditch 87 D4
Pye Bridge 170 F6
Pye Hill 171 A5

Q

Quarndon 204 D6
Quixhill 196 E7
Quoit Green 57 B1

R

Radbourne 216 F5
Radmanthwaite 135 D3
Ravensnest 144 F7
Rawson Green 179 F1
Renishaw 79 B8
Repton 242 E2
Riber 143 E3
Riddings
- Denstone 196 B4
- Somercotes 170 D5

Ridgeway
- Bullbridge 168 C4
- Sheffield 58 E8

Ridgeway Moor 58 E7
Ringinglow 42 F4
Ripley 169 C2
Rise End 154 E3
Risley 222 E3
River's Vale 84 F7
Robin Hood 92 D5
Rocester 197 A3
Rodsley 200 A5
Rolleston 240 A4
Rollestone 43 D5
Rolleston on Dove 240 C3
Rose Hill 219 B2
Rosemaryhill 171 F7
Rosliston 260 D6
Roston 197 E7
Rowarth 24 E7
Rowland 90 C5
Rowsley 111 A1
Rowthorne 134 C6
Rylah 117 F5

S

St Augustines 115 B7
St Luke's 218 E3
Sandiacre 223 A6
Sapperton 213 C1
Sawley 236 A4
Scarcliffe 118 E6
Scropton 226 E1
Selston 171 E7
Selston Green 171 D7
Shacklecross 221 D1
Shardlow 234 E2
Shatton 39 F1
Sheen 137 A7
Sheepbridge 76 E2
Sheffield 44 D6
Sheldon 108 A6
Shelton Lock 232 F3
Shipley 194 B6
Shipley Common 194 C4
Shirebrook 119 F3
Shireoaks 63 E6
Shirland 146 D2
Shirley 200 E8
Short Heath 262 D2
Shottle 177 E8
Shottlegate 177 F3
Shuttlewood 98 F7
Simmondley 17 A7
Sinfin 231 F4
Slackhall 47 F8
Slaley 154 C7
Sleat Moor 170 B8
Smalldale
  Bradwell 50 E8
  Peak Dale 67 D7
Smalley 192 F5
Smalley Common 193 A2
Smalley Green 192 F3
Smisby 257 F3
Smithfield 47 C6

Smithy-Hill 51 A7
Smithy Moor 146 B7
Snape Hill 57 A2
Snelston 184 C3
Snitterton 142 D5
Somercotes 170 C7
Somersal Herbert 211 E3
Sookholme 120 D2
South Normanton 160 A7
South Wingfield 157 E3
Southwood 258 B7
Sparrowpit 48 B6
Spath 210 A3
Spinkhill 60 D2
Spion Kop 120 F2
Spital 96 C1
Spitalhill 185 C8
Spitewinter 113 D1
Spondon 220 E4
Spout 166 C3
Spring Cottage 262 D5
Springfield Park 223 A3
Staden 85 E5
Stainsby 133 B7
Stanfree 99 B8
Stanhope Bretby 248 F1
Stanley
  Tibshelf 133 D1
  West Hallam 207 C5
Stanley Common 193 B1
Stanshope 149 D1
Stanton
  Mayfield 183 D8
  Swadlincote 255 C4
Stanton by Bridge 244 D3
Stanton-by-Dale 222 E8
Stanton Gate 209 C1
Stanton in Peak 126 C5
Stanton Lees 126 F3
Stapenhill 254 F8
Stapleford 223 C4
Starkholmes 143 C2
Staveley 78 D1
Steeple Grange 155 A3
Stenson 243 B8
Stockley 117 E4
Stoke 72 C6
Stonebroom 146 F4
Stonegravels 96 A5
Stoneyford 182 A7
Stoney Middleton 72 A4
Stony Houghton 118 F1
Stramshall 210 A4
Stretton
  Clay Cross 146 C7
  Rolleston on Dove 240 D1
Stretton en le Field 265 D4
Stretton Hillside 146 B5
Strines 23 C2
Stubwood 196 D4
Sudbury 225 E4
Summerley 57 E2
Sunny Hill 231 D5
Sutton in Ashfield 148 F1
Sutton on the Hill 228 B8

Sutton Springs Wood . . 116 C6
Swadlincote 256 D4
Swainspark 262 B7
Swanwick 169 E8
Swarkestone 244 D6
Swathwick 114 D4
Swingate 195 F5

T

Taddington 88 B3
Tansley 144 B4
Tansley Knoll 144 A5
Tapton 96 C6
Tatenhill 253 A8
Taxal 45 D4
Temple Normanton 116 B3
The Banks 23 E3
The Brushes 76 F3
The Elms 180 D8
The Flourish 207 D2
The Forties 257 F4
The Gutter 179 C4
The Heath 210 A1
The Wharf 210 C1
Thornhill 39 F3
Thornsett 24 F3
Thorpe 161 C1
Thorpe Salvin 62 F6
Thrumpton 237 C3
Thulston 233 F4
Thurvaston
  Longford 215 C8
  Marston Montgomery . . 197 F1
Tibshelf 148 A6
Tibshelf Wharf 148 D7
Ticknall 251 A4
Tideswell 69 D4
Tintwistle 10 B8
Tissington 162 B6
Toadhole Furnance 158 C6
Toadmoor 167 F3
Tomthorn 66 E4
Torr Top 33 C8
Totley 55 E4
Totley Brook 55 E5
Totley Rise 55 F5
Toton 223 E2
Townend 47 C7
Town End
  Eyam 71 E6
  Tideswell 69 C3
Townhead 55 C7
Town Head
  Eyam 71 C6
  Tideswell 69 C5
Trentlock 236 E3
Troway 58 B4
Trowell 209 C5
Trusley 215 F4
Tunstead 67 F2
Tunstead Milton 46 C5
Tupton 131 D8
Turlow Fields 175 C7

Turnditch 177 B1
Tutbury 239 C5
Tutbury, Fauld 238 C6
Two Dales 127 E3
Twyford 243 B6

U

Underwood Green 171 F2
Unstone 76 E7
Unstone Green 76 E6
Unthank 74 D5
Upper Biggin 175 E4
Upper Booth 36 E7
Upper Bradway 56 B5
Upperdale 89 B5
Upper Ellastone 183 B4
Upper End 67 B5
Upper Hackney 143 A8
Upper Hartshay 169 A2
Upper Holloway 156 C5
Upper Langwith 119 D8
Upper Mayfield 172 B1
Upper Midway 256 C7
Upper Newbold 95 A8
Upper Padley 53 D2
Upper Pilsley 132 D2
Upperthorpe 60 E5
Uppertown 129 A7
Upper Town
  Birchover 141 C8
  Bonsall 142 C1
  Hognaston 164 B4
Upperwood 155 A8
Uttoxeter 210 C1

W

Wadshelf 93 E3
Waingroves 181 A7
Wakebridge 156 D3
Waldley 211 C7
Wallash 184 C7
Walton 114 D8
Walton-on-Trent 253 D1
Wardlow 70 C2
Wardlow Mires 70 C4
Wards End 143 C2
Warhill 9 A3
Warmbrook 165 E8
Warsop Vale 120 D4
Wash 35 C1
Washgreen 155 A1
Waterloo 132 C3
Water Swallows 67 A3
Waterswallows Green 66 F3
Wensley 142 A7
Wensley Dale 142 B6
Wessington 157 E8
West Broughton 225 A6
Westfield 59 F8
West Hallam 207 F8
West Hallam Common . . 207 D8

West Handley 77 D8
Westhouses 159 C8
Weston-on-Trent 245 F5
Weston Underwood 189 A2
Westthorpe 60 D4
Westwood 171 C3
Wetton 149 A3
Whaley 100 D4
Whaley Bridge 45 D7
Whaley Thorns 101 A2
Whatstandwell 156 C1
Wheatcroft 157 A7
Wheston 68 F5
Whitehough 46 E8
Whitehough Head 46 E8
Whiteley 180 F6
White Moor 179 C5
Whitfield 17 D8
Whittington Moor 96 A7
Whitwell 81 E6
Wigley 93 F4
Wilday Green 75 A2
Williamthorpe 132 C8
Willington 242 A6
Wilmorton 219 C2
Wilson 252 F6
Wilsthorpe 236 B7
Windley 189 D1
Windmill 69 F8
Wingerworth 114 F4
Winshill 248 B3
Winsick 115 E6
Winster 141 C5
Wirksworth 165 E8
Woodall 61 C6
Woodend
  Disley 32 E8
  Hanbury 238 A1
Woodhead
  Crowden 7 C4
  Littlemoor 130 E2
Woodhouses 252 A5
Woodlinkin 181 E6
Woodnook 94 E5
Woodseats 16 A6
Woodside 192 D4
Woodthorpe 79 C2
Woodville 256 E6
Woolley 145 E5
Woolley Moor 145 D7
Wormhill 68 C1
Wyaston 185 D2

Y

Yeaveley 199 D5
Yeldersley Hollies 186 F4
Youlgreave 125 B5

Index of streets, hospitals, industrial estates, railway stations, schools, shopping centres, universities and places of interest

1st–And **271**

1st Ave DE7 . . . . .208 F7
2nd Ave DE7 . . . . .208 F7
3rd Ave DE7 . . . . .208 F7

A

Abba Cl NG16 . . . . .195 F7
Abbey Brook Ct **1** S8 . . . .56 E8
Abbey Brook Dr S8 . . . . .56 E8
Abbey Ct S14 . . . . .197 A3
Abbey Croft
  Chesterfield S40 . . . . .95 A7
  Renishaw S21 . . . . .79 C8
Abbeydale Cl DE56 . . . . .192 B7
Abbeydale Ct S17 . . . . .56 A7
Abbeydale Industrial Mus*
  S7 . . . . .56 B8
Abbeydale Park Cres S17 .55 F6
Abbeydale Park Rise S17 . .55 F6
Abbeydale Rd S7 . . . . .43 A8
Abbeydale Rd S S17 . . . . . .56 A7
Abbeyfields Cl DE22 . . . .205 A2
Abbey Gdns SK14 . . . . .9 A3
Abbey Hill DE21, DE22 . . .205 B4
Abbeyhill Cl S42 . . . . .95 A4
Abbey Hill Rd DE22 . . . . .204 D2
Abbey La DE22 . . . . .205 A1
Abbey Lodge Cl **1** DE11 256 A7
Abbey Pl S21 . . . . .79 C8
Abbey St
  Derby DE1, DE22 . . . . . . .267 A2
  Ilkeston DE7 . . . . .194 F2
Abbey View Dr S8 . . . . . . .43 A3
Abbey View Hts **3** S8 . . .43 A3
Abbey View Rd S8 . . . . . . .43 A3
Abbey Yd DE22 . . . . .205 A1
Abbot Beyne Sch DE15 . .248 A3
Abbot Cl DE21 . . . . .205 E2
Abbot Mews DE22 . . . . . .205 A1
Abbot Rd DE7 . . . . .208 C6
Abbots Croft NG19 . . . . . .135 E1
Abbotsford Mews DE7 . .194 D3
Abbots Gr DE56 . . . . .179 A5
Abbotsholme Sch S14 . . .197 B2
Abbott St NG16 . . . . .195 C4
Abbott Rd
  Alfreton DE55 . . . . .159 B3
  Mansfield NG19 . . . . .135 D1
Abbotts Barn Cl DE22 . . .267 A2
Abbotts Cl DE11 . . . . .256 A6
Abbotts Rd DE11 . . . . . . .256 A6
Abbott St
  Heanor DE75 . . . . .181 E1
  Long Eaton NG10 . . . . . . .236 D6
Abel La DE4 . . . . .142 C2
Abells DE5 . . . . .180 C1
Abels Mill **1** DE1 . . . . . .267 A4
Abercrombie Prim Sch
  S41 . . . . .266 B4
Abercrombie St S41 . . . . .266 B4
Aberdare Cl DE21 . . . . . . .206 B2
Abingdon Bsns Ctr The
  DE24 . . . . .219 C1
Abingdon St DE24 . . . . . .232 C8
Abney Cl
  Chesterfield S40 . . . . .95 D6
  Derby DE3 . . . . .217 F2
  Sheffield S14 . . . . .43 C6
Abney Dr S14 . . . . .43 C6
Abney Rd S14 . . . . .43 C6
Acacia Ave
  Brimington S43 . . . . .97 A8
  Derby DE3 . . . . .217 E1
  Swadlincote DE11 . . . . . .256 B7
Acacia Cres S21 . . . . .60 B5
Acacia Ct NG19 . . . . .136 E1
Acacia Dr
  Melbourne DE73 . . . . . . .252 A8
  Ripley S45 . . . . .132 B3
Acacia Gdns NG16 . . . . . .195 F8
Access 26 Bsns Pk NG16 182 C3
Acer Cl
  Killamarsh S21 . . . . .60 C5
  Pinxton NG16 . . . . .160 C3
Acer Croft DE21 . . . . .205 E3
Acorn Ave NG16 . . . . .195 C8
Acorn Cl DE24 . . . . .232 E3
Acorn Ctr NG16 . . . . .182 C3
Acorn Dr DE56 . . . . .179 A5
Acorn Ridge
  Chesterfield S40 . . . . . . .114 B7
  Matlock DE4 . . . . .143 B6
  Shirebrook NG20 . . . . . . .119 D5
Acorn Terr SK22 . . . . .33 B6
Acorn Way
  Belper DE56 . . . . .179 A5
  Derby DE21 . . . . .220 C6
Acreage La NG20 . . . . . . .119 F2
Acre Ct **5** SK13 . . . . .17 C7
Acrefield Way DE73 . . . . .233 B2
Acre La DE72 . . . . .246 D7
Acresford Rd
  Donisthorpe DE12 . . . . . .265 D7
  Netherseal DE12 . . . . . . .265 B6
  Overseal DE12 . . . . .262 B2
Acresford View DE12 . . . .262 B3
Acres Rd S45 . . . . .132 B3
Acre St **4** SK13 . . . . .17 C7
Acres The S45 . . . . .132 B4
Acresview Cl DE22 . . . . . .204 D4
Acres View Cl S41 . . . . .95 F7

Acton Ave NG10 . . . . .236 E6
Acton Cl NG10 . . . . .236 E6
Acton Ct **1** S43 . . . . .78 B3
Acton Gr NG10 . . . . .236 E6
Acton Rd
  Derby DE22 . . . . .217 F6
  Long Eaton NG10 . . . . . . .236 E6
Acton Road Ind Est
  NG10 . . . . .236 E6
Acton St NG10 . . . . .236 E6
Adale Rd DE7 . . . . .193 B8
Adam's Rd DE6 . . . . .217 A8
Adam Bede Cres DE4 . . . .165 F6
Adams Cl DE75 . . . . .193 D7
Adams Ct DE7 . . . . .194 E3
Adam St DE7 . . . . .209 A6
Adastral Ave S12 . . . . .44 A2
Adderley Pl SK13 . . . . .9 F1
Adderley Rd SK13 . . . . .9 F1
Addison Dr DE55 . . . . .159 B4
Addison Rd
  Derby DE24 . . . . .232 C7
  Stonebroom DE55 . . . . . .146 F3
Addison Sq DE4 . . . . .155 A5
Addison St DE55 . . . . .148 A7
Addison Villas NG16 . . . . .182 E1
Adelaide Cl
  Derby DE3 . . . . .217 E4
  Stapleford NG9 . . . . .209 F1
Adelaide Cres DE15 . . . . .248 C2
Adelaide Wlk NG16 . . . . .170 F4
Adelphi Cl DE23 . . . . .231 A6
Adelphi Way S43 . . . . .97 E8
Adin Ave S44 . . . . .98 F6
Adler Ct DE1 . . . . .219 B7
Adlington Ave S42 . . . . . .115 C2
Adlington La S32 . . . . .72 C8
Admiral Cl DE75 . . . . .181 D2
Adrian Cl NG9 . . . . .223 F1
Adrian St DE24 . . . . .232 D6
Adwick Cl DE3 . . . . .217 C2
Agard St DE1 . . . . .267 A4
Agnesmeadow La DE6 . .174 D4
Agricultural Bsns Ctr
  DE45 . . . . .109 E5
Agricultural Way DE45 . .109 E5
Aimploy Ct DE23 . . . . . . .219 A1
Ainley Cl DE24 . . . . .232 F7
Ainsworth Dr DE23 . . . . .231 E7
Aintree Ave S21 . . . . .59 B3
Aintree Cl
  Burton u T DE14 . . . . . . .254 A7
  Kimberley NG16 . . . . .195 E7
Airedale Cl NG10 . . . . . . .236 A6
Airedale Wlk **8** DE24 . .233 C6
Akley Bank Cl S17 . . . . . . .55 F5
Alabaster La DE4 . . . . . . .155 A6
Alandale Ave NG20 . . . . .119 F5
Albany Cl NG19 . . . . .136 C1
Albany Dr NG19 . . . . .209 E1
Albany Inf & Jun Schs
  NG9 . . . . .223 E8
Albany Inf Sch NG9 . . . . .209 E1
Albany Pl NG19 . . . . .136 C1
Albany Rd DE22 . . . . .218 C4
Albany St DE7 . . . . .209 A6
Albemarle Rd DE21 . . . . .220 B7
Alberta Ave NG16 . . . . . . .171 F7
Albert Ave
  Chesterfield S43 . . . . .77 D3
  Jacksdale NG16 . . . . .171 B4
  Stapleford NG9 . . . . .223 D7
Albert Cres DE21 . . . . . . .220 B4
Albert Cl SK17 . . . . .85 C6
Albert Rd
  Breaston DE72 . . . . .235 B7
  Chesterfield S43 . . . . .77 D3
  Derby DE21 . . . . .220 A4
  Long Eaton NG10 . . . . . . .236 D8
  Ripley DE5 . . . . .169 C2
  Sandiacre NG10 . . . . .223 B6
  Sheffield, Heeley S8 . . . . . .43 A6
  Swadlincote DE11 . . . . . .256 A2
Albert St N S41 . . . . .76 F1
Albert Sq NG19 . . . . .136 C4
Albert St
  Belper DE56 . . . . .178 F4
  Derby DE1 . . . . .267 B3
  Eastwood NG16 . . . . .182 F3
  Eckington S21 . . . . .59 D2
  Glossop SK13 . . . . .10 A5
  Ilkeston DE7 . . . . .208 E8
  Ironville NG16 . . . . .170 F5
  Mansfield Woodhouse
    NG19 . . . . .136 C4
  Ripley DE5 . . . . .169 E1
  Somercotes DE55 . . . . . .170 B8
  South Normanton DE55 . .160 B6
  Stapleford NG9 . . . . .223 D7
Albert Village Com Prim Sch
  DE11 . . . . .256 C1
Albine Rd NG20 . . . . .119 E6
Albion Ctr The DE7 . . . . .208 F8
Albion Mill SK14 . . . . .9 C5
Albion Rd
  Chesterfield S40 . . . . . . .266 A3
  Long Eaton NG10 . . . . . . .236 F8
  New Mills SK22 . . . . .33 B6
Albion St
  Derby DE1 . . . . .267 B3
  Ilkeston DE7 . . . . .194 F1

Albion St continued
  Mansfield NG19 . . . . .135 F1
  Ripley DE5 . . . . .169 E1
  Woodville DE11 . . . . .256 F2
Albrighton Ave DE24 . . . .231 D2
Aldam Cl S17 . . . . .55 E4
Aldam Croft S17 . . . . .55 E4
Aldam Rd S17 . . . . .55 F4
Aldam Way S17 . . . . .55 E4
Alder Brook SK23 . . . . .45 D8
Alderbrook Cl DE13 . . . . .240 B4
Aldercar Com Language Coll
  NG16 . . . . .182 A4
Aldercar Inf Sch NG16 . . .182 A4
Aldercar La NG16 . . . . . . .182 A6
Alder Cl
  Derby DE21 . . . . .205 E3
  Glossop SK13 . . . . .9 F4
  Mansfield NG19 . . . . .136 E1
  Shirebrook NG20 . . . . . . .119 D5
Alder Com High Sch SK14 15 A8
Alder La DE11 . . . . .266 B4
Alderfen Cl DE24 . . . . . . .232 D3
Alder Gr
  Burton u T DE15 . . . . . . .254 F7
  Buxton SK17 . . . . .85 A8
  Chapel-en-le-F SK23 . . . . .47 A6
Mansfield Woodhouse
  NG19 . . . . .136 B5
Alderholme Dr **1** DE13 .240 F1
Alder La DE6 . . . . .188 A3
Alderley Ct DE21 . . . . . . .206 A2
Alderney Rd **3** S8 . . . . . .43 A7
Aldern Way DE45 . . . . . . .109 E7
Alder Rd DE56 . . . . .179 A3
Alder Rise SK23 . . . . .45 D8
Alders Ave SK23 . . . . .34 E1
Alders Brook DE65 . . . . . .228 D1
Aldersgate
  Derby DE22 . . . . .217 F7
  New Mills SK22 . . . . .33 B8
Alders La
  Chinley SK23 . . . . .34 E2
  Tansley DE4 . . . . .144 A3
Aldersley Cl DE72 . . . . . . .234 B1
Aldersley Cl DE65 . . . . . . .230 C1
Alderson Dr DE13 . . . . . . .240 F1
Alderson Pl S2 . . . . .43 A8
Alderson Rd S2 . . . . .43 A8
Alderson Rd N S2 . . . . .43 A8
Alders Rd SK12 . . . . .32 A7
Alders The S42 . . . . .113 D7
Alderwasley Hall Sch
  DE56 . . . . .167 B7
Alderwasley Hall Sch (Callow
  Park) DE4 . . . . .165 E4
Alder Way NG20 . . . . .119 D4
Alder Wlk DE23 . . . . .267 B1
Aldred's La DE75, NG16 . .182 B2
Aldwark Rd SK17 . . . . .85 C6
Aldwych DE22 . . . . .218 A6
Alexander Ave NG16 . . . .171 D7
Alexander Rd SK17 . . . . . . .47 F1
Alexander Terr NG16 . . . .160 C1
Alexandra Ave NG19 . . . .136 B5
Alexandra Ct
  Burton u T DE15 . . . . . . .248 A3
  Overseal DE12 . . . . .262 B4
Alexandra Gdns **3** DE23 219 B2
Alexandra Mills **2** DE1 .218 E5
Alexandra Rd
  Burton u T DE15 . . . . . . .248 A3
  Buxton SK17 . . . . .85 C5
  Dronfield S18 . . . . .57 B2
  Long Eaton NG10 . . . . . . .236 D8
  Overseal DE12 . . . . .262 B4
  Sheffield S2 . . . . .43 B7
  Swadlincote DE11 . . . . . .256 B3
Alexandra Rd E S41 . . . . . .96 C1
Alexandra Rd W S40 . . . .266 A3
Alexandra St
  Eastwood NG16 . . . . .182 F2
  Stapleford NG9 . . . . .223 D6
Alexandre Cl DE23 . . . . . .231 D6
Alford Cl S40 . . . . .95 C3
Alfred Rd DE56 . . . . .192 A8
Alfred St
  Alfreton DE55 . . . . .158 F3
  Pinxton NG16 . . . . .160 C4
  Somercotes DE55 . . . . . .170 D6
  South Normanton DE55 . .159 F5
Alfreton & Mansfield
  Parkway Sta DE55 . . . . .159 C5
Alfreton Motorway Link Ind
  Est DE55 . . . . .159 A2
Alfreton Park Com Specl Sch
  DE55 . . . . .158 F4
Alfreton Rd
  Blackwell DE55 . . . . .147 E2
  Breadsall DE21 . . . . .205 B2
  Codnor DE5 . . . . .170 C1
  Holbrook DE21 . . . . .191 C8
  Little Eaton DE21 . . . . . .205 C6
  Matlock DE4 . . . . .143 E4
  Pinxton NG16 . . . . .160 C4
  Selston DE55, NG16 . . . . .171 C6
  Tibshelf DE55 . . . . .147 D4
Alfreton Trad Est DE55 . .159 B2
Algar Cl S2 . . . . .43 B7

Algar Cres S2 . . . . .43 F7
Algar Dr S2 . . . . .43 E7
Algar Pl S2 . . . . .43 E7
Algar Rd S2 . . . . .43 E7
Alice's View S42 . . . . .132 A8
Alice Gdns DE12 . . . . .262 B4
Alicehead Rd S45 . . . . . . .113 B2
Alice St DE1 . . . . .267 C4
Alice Way S18 . . . . .76 E5
Alison Cl DE21 . . . . .220 A6
Alkmonton Rd DE6 . . . . . .213 D5
Alkmund Ct DE1 . . . . .267 B4
Allan Ave DE23 . . . . .230 E8
Allandale Rd DE75 . . . . . .181 D2
Allan La DE56 . . . . .168 B6
Allcroft St NG19 . . . . .136 C4
Allendale DE7 . . . . .208 E7
Allendale Rd S42 . . . . . . .114 F3
Allendale Way NG19 . . . .136 E1
Allen Hill DE4 . . . . .143 B6
Allen La
  Ashover DE4 . . . . .144 C6
  Weston Underwood DE6 . .188 C1
Allens Croft S14 . . . . .224 E2
Allen St DE24 . . . . .232 E5
Allenton Com Prim Sch
  DE24 . . . . .232 D5
Allestree Cl DE24 . . . . . . .232 E8
Allestree Dr S18 . . . . .56 C1
Allestree La DE22 . . . . . . .204 D3
Allestree Pk* DE22 . . . . . .204 F5
Allestree St DE24 . . . . . . .232 F8
Alley The DE4 . . . . .154 D4
Alley Wlk DE6 . . . . .201 F7
Allison Ave DE11 . . . . .256 B3
Allison Gdns DE7 . . . . . . .195 A1
Allissa Ave DE5 . . . . .180 E7
Allpits Rd S44 . . . . .96 F3
Allport Terr S43 . . . . .78 B4
All Saints' Rd DE4 . . . . . .143 B6
All Saints CE Fst Sch
  S14 . . . . .196 E6
All Saints CE Jun Sch
  DE4 . . . . .143 A7
All Saints Croft DE14 . . . .254 C8
All Saints Ct **3** DE3 . . . .217 D1
All Saints Inf Sch DE4 . . .143 B6
All Saints RC Prim Sch
  SK13 . . . . .10 D2
All Saints Rd DE14 . . . . . .254 C8
Allsops Pl S41 . . . . .95 F8
Allstone Lee DE56 . . . . . . .178 F5
Alma CE Inf/ 194 E5
Alma Cres S18 . . . . .57 A3
Alma Hill NG16 . . . . .195 E7
Alma Hts DE3 . . . . .217 E1
Alma L Pk* S40 . . . . .266 C1
Alma Rd
  North Wingfield S42 . . . . .132 A8
  Selston NG16 . . . . .171 F5
  Swadlincote DE11 . . . . . .255 F6
  Tideswell SK17 . . . . .69 C5
Alma St W S40 . . . . .95 E2
Alma St
  Alfreton DE55 . . . . .159 A4
  Buxton SK17 . . . . .85 D8
  Derby DE22 . . . . .267 A2
  Melbourne DE73 . . . . . . .252 A7
  North Wingfield S42 . . . . .131 E6
  Ripley DE5 . . . . .169 D3
Almond Ave
  Ripley DE5 . . . . .180 D8
  Shirebrook NG20 . . . . . . .119 E5
Almond Cl
  Calow S44 . . . . .97 A3
  Kimberley NG16 . . . . .195 E7
Almond Cres S43 . . . . .79 C4
Almond Ct DE13 . . . . .240 E1
Almond Dr S21 . . . . .60 C5
Almond Gr
  Swadlincote DE11 . . . . . .256 A5
  Swanwick DE55 . . . . .170 A8
Almond Rise NG19 . . . . . .136 E1
Almond St DE23 . . . . .218 F1
Almshouses
  Etwall DE65 . . . . .229 B5
  Newton Solney DE15 . . . .248 E8
Alms Rd DE6 . . . . .211 C1
Alnwick Dr S12 . . . . .44 C5
Alnwick Rd S12 . . . . .44 B5
Alonso Cl DE73 . . . . .232 E2
Alpha Rd SK23 . . . . .34 E2
Alpine Gr S43 . . . . .97 A8
Alport Ave
  Buxton SK17 . . . . .85 D7
  Sheffield S12 . . . . .44 E5
Alport Cl
  Belper DE56 . . . . .179 B5
  Hulland Ward DE6 . . . . . .175 F3
Alport Dr S12 . . . . .44 E5
Alport Gr
  3 Gamesley SK13 . . . . . . .9 E2
  Sheffield S12 . . . . .44 E5

Alport La
  Spout DE4, DE56 . . . . . . .166 C4
  Youlgreave DE45 . . . . . . .125 C6
Alport Lea **2** SK13 . . . . . . .9 E2
Alport Pl S12 . . . . .44 E4
Alport Rd S12 . . . . .44 E5
Alport Rise S18 . . . . .56 D2
Alport Terr DE55 . . . . .147 C1
Alport Way **1** SK13 . . . . . .9 E2
Alsager Cl DE21 . . . . .206 A1
Alsfeld Way S42 . . . . .33 A8
Alsop Moor Cotts DE6 . .150 E5
Alsop Pl SK17 . . . . .85 E7
Alsop Way SK17 . . . . .85 E7
Alstonefield YH* DE6 . . . .149 F4
Alstonfield Dr DE22 . . . . .204 E1
Alston Rd SK23 . . . . .47 B5
Althorp Cl DE55 . . . . .169 F7
Alton Cl
  Chesterfield S40 . . . . . . .114 B8
  Derby DE22 . . . . .204 D3
  Dronfield S18 . . . . .75 D8
Alton Dr NG16 . . . . .195 B8
Alton Hill S42 . . . . .130 C5
Alton La S45 . . . . .130 C4
Alton Rd
  Belper DE56 . . . . .179 C4
  Denstone ST14 . . . . .196 D6
Alton Rise DE4 . . . . .142 F7
Alts Nook Way DE72 . . . .234 E1
Alum Chine Cl S41 . . . . . .115 C8
Alum Cl DE24 . . . . .233 C7
Alvaston St DE24 . . . . . . .233 A8
Alvaston Jun Sch DE24 . .233 C7
Alvaston Park Homes
  DE24 . . . . .220 A1
Alvaston St DE24 . . . . . . .233 B8
Alvenor St DE7 . . . . .194 F1
Alverton Cl DE3 . . . . .217 C1
Alveston Pk Homes
  DE24 . . . . .233 A8
Alward's Cl DE24 . . . . . . .233 A6
Ambaston La
  Elvaston DE72 . . . . .234 A5
  Shardlow DE72 . . . . .234 E2
Amber Bldgs DE55 . . . . . .159 B5
Amber Cl DE56 . . . . .168 B5
Amber Cres S40 . . . . .95 C1
Amber Croft S43 . . . . .97 C7
Amber Ct
  Belper DE56 . . . . .179 A6
  Chesterfield S41 . . . . . . .266 B4
  2 Heanor DE75 . . . . . . .181 E1
Amberdene DE4 . . . . .143 D6
Amber Dr NG16 . . . . .182 B2
Ambergate Prim Sch
  DE56 . . . . .167 F3
Ambergate Sta DE56 . . . .167 F3
Amber Gr DE55 . . . . .158 F2
Ambergrove DE56 . . . . . . .168 B4
Amber Hill DE4 . . . . .168 A7
Amber Hts DE5 . . . . .169 C2
Amber La S45 . . . . .129 D3
Amberlands DE13 . . . . . . .240 F1
Amberley Cl DE7 . . . . .208 F6
Amberley Dr
  Buxton SK17 . . . . .85 C5
  Derby DE24 . . . . .231 F5
  Ilkeston DE7 . . . . .131 A4
Amber Rd
  Bullbridge DE56 . . . . .168 B6
  Derby DE22 . . . . .204 D1
Amber St DE24 . . . . .232 C7
Amber Terr DE55 . . . . .158 B6
Amber Trad Est NG16 . . . .195 D3
Amber View Rd DE56 . . . .168 B7
Amberwood DE11 . . . . . . .256 A5
Amble Cl
  Chesterfield S41 . . . . .95 C7
  Sheffield S20 . . . . .59 E6
Ambleside Dr
  Bolsover S44 . . . . .98 F1
  Eastwood NG16 . . . . .182 D3
Ambleside Terr DE61 . . . .218 E5
Amen Alley DE1 . . . . .267 B3
American Adventure Theme
  Pk The* DE75 . . . . .194 B5
Amesbury Cl S41 . . . . .95 E7
Amesbury La DE21 . . . . . .205 E2
Ameycroft La DE4 . . . . . . .143 A8
Amilda Ave DE7 . . . . .208 F8
Amy St DE22 . . . . .218 E4
Anastasia Cl DE4 . . . . .47 C6
Anchor Cl DE11 . . . . .256 C4
Anchor Fold SK23 . . . . . . .47 D6
Anchor Rd NG16 . . . . .182 D2
Anchor Row DE7 . . . . .208 F8
Anchor Sq DE45 . . . . .109 D6
Anderby Gdns DE11 . . . . .255 F2
Anderson Cl S43 . . . . .77 E3
Anderson St DE24 . . . . . . .232 E7
Andrew Ave DE7 . . . . .209 B7
Andrew Cl DE23 . . . . .230 E8
Andrews Dr
  Langley Mill NG16 . . . . . .182 A3
  Stanley Common DE7 . . . .193 A1
Andrew St SK6 . . . . .15 A2
Andwell La S10 . . . . .42 F6

Angel Yd S40 . . . .**266** B3
Angerford Ave S8 . . . .**43** A4
Anglers' La DE21 . . . .**220** E3
Anglesey Rd
  Burton u T DE14 . . . .**254** B8
  Dronfield S18 . . . .**76** A8
Anglesey St DE21 . . . .**219** D8
Angleton Ave S2 . . . .**44** C8
Angleton Ave S2 . . . .**44** C8
Angleton Cl S2 . . . .**44** C8
Angleton Gdns S2 . . . .**44** C8
Angleton Gn S2 . . . .**44** C8
Angleton Mews S2 . . . .**44** C8
Anglia Dr DE21 . . . .**255** F1
Ankerbold Rd S42 . . . .**131** D8
Anncroft Rd SK17 . . . .**84** D5
Anne Potter Cl DE72 . . . .**221** D5
Annesley Cl
  Chesterfield S41 . . . .**115** C8
  Sheffield S8 . . . .**56** F7
Annesley Rd S8 . . . .**56** F7
Annie's Cl S41 . . . .**126** B1
Anns Grove Prim Sch S2 . . .**43** A7
Anns Rd S2 . . . .**43** A7
Anns Rd N S2 . . . .**43** B7
Ann St S80 . . . .**81** E1
Annwell La DE11 . . . .**257** E2
Anslow La DE13 . . . .**240** A2
Anslow Rd DE13 . . . .**238** B2
Anson Wlk DE7 . . . .**194** F3
Anstee Rd NG10 . . . .**236** C5
Anstey Ct DE21 . . . .**206** A1
Anthony Bek Com Prim Sch
  NG19 . . . .**134** F6
Anthony Cres DE24 . . . .**232** F6
Anthony Dr DE24 . . . .**232** F6
Anthony Gell Sch DE4 . . . . .**165** F8
Antill St NG9 . . . .**223** D6
Apiary Gate DE74 . . . .**247** B3
Apperknowle Com Prim Sch
  S18 . . . .**58** A1
Appian Cl DE72 . . . .**221** C1
Appian Way
  Clay Cross S45 . . . .**131** B2
  Derby DE24 . . . .**233** D5
Appleby Cl DE7 . . . .**208** F6
Appleby Glade DE11 . . . .**255** D2
Appleby Rd NG19 . . . .**134** F6
Applecroft SK14 . . . .**9** D4
Applecross Ct DE24 . . . .**231** E3
Appledore Ct [2] S41 . . . .**95** F8
Appledore Dr DE21 . . . .**206** B1
Appledown Way DE23 . . . . . .**231** B6
Applegarth Cl S12 . . . .**44** A6
Applegarth Dr S12 . . . .**44** A6
Applegate Cl DE21 . . . .**206** B3
Applemead Cl DE21 . . . .**205** E2
Apple St SK14 . . . .**15** C7
Appleton Cl
  Burton u T DE15 . . . .**254** F2
  Derby DE21 . . . .**220** A7
  Swadlincote DE11 . . . .**255** F3
Appleton Dr
  Belper DE56 . . . .**179** B6
  Glossop SK13 . . . .**17** F8
Appletree Cl DE72 . . . .**221** C1
Appletree Dr S18 . . . .**57** A1
Appletree Rd
  Bolsover S44 . . . .**80** B1
  Hatton DE65 . . . .**227** C1
Apple Tree Rd SK22 . . . .**24** B1
Appletree Wlk DE3 . . . .**217** D2
Applewood Cl
  Belper DE56 . . . .**179** B5
  Uttoxeter ST14 . . . .**210** A1
Appleyard Ct S41 . . . .**266** A4
Arbor Cl DE22 . . . .**267** A2
Arboretum Prim Sch
  DE23 . . . .**219** A2
Arboretum Sq DE23 . . . .**267** C1
Arboretum St DE23 . . . .**267** C1
Arbor Gr SK17 . . . .**84** F7
Arbor Low (Henge)★
  DE45 . . . .**123** E4
Arbour Ch S41 . . . .**115** D6
Arbour Hill DE7 . . . .**207** E3
Arbourthorne Com Prim Sch
  S2 . . . .**43** D8
Arbourthorne Cotts S2 . . . . .**43** D8
Arbourthorne Rd S2 . . . .**43** E6
Arcadia Ave NG20 . . . .**119** E5
Archdale Cl S2 . . . .**44** B8
Archdale Rd S2 . . . .**44** A8
Archer Rd NG9 . . . .**223** E5
Archer St
  Derby DE24 . . . .**219** E2
  Ilkeston DE7 . . . .**194** E3
Arden Cl
  Chesterfield S40 . . . .**95** C5
  Derby DE23 . . . .**218** E2
Arden Est SK22 . . . .**33** A8
Arden St SK22 . . . .**33** C7
Ardleigh Cl DE3 . . . .**230** D8
Ardsley Cl
  Heanor DE75 . . . .**182** A2
  Sheffield S20 . . . .**44** F2
Ardsley Gr S20 . . . .**44** F2
Ardsley Rd S40 . . . .**95** F2
Argyle Cl
  Market Warsop NG20 . . . . .**120** F4
  Sheffield S8 . . . .**43** B5
Argyle Mews NG16 . . . .**182** F2
Argyle Rd S8 . . . .**43** B5

Argyle St
  Derby DE22 . . . .**218** F3
  Langley Mill NG16 . . . .**182** C4
Argyll Cl DE21 . . . .**220** F5
Argyll Rd DE5 . . . .**169** E2
Aria Ct NG9 . . . .**223** D6
Arkendale Wlk [4] DE24 . . . .**233** C6
Arkle Gn DE24 . . . .**231** E4
Arklow Cl S41 . . . .**115** B8
Arkwright's Mill★ DE4 . . . .**155** B7
Arkwright Ave DE56 . . . .**179** C6
Arkwright Cl DE4 . . . .**127** C3
Arkwright Dr SK6 . . . .**23** A6
Arkwright Gdns DE4 . . . .**155** A6
Arkwright Mill SK17 . . . .**90** C2
Arkwright Prim Sch S44 . . . .**97** D3
Arkwright Rd SK6 . . . .**23** A6
Arkwright St
  Derby DE24 . . . .**232** C7
  Wirksworth DE4 . . . .**165** E8
Arleston La DE24 . . . .**231** D2
Arleston St DE23 . . . .**231** F7
Arlington Ave NG19 . . . .**136** E4
Arlington Dr
  Derby DE24 . . . .**232** F6
  Swanwick DE55 . . . .**169** F7
Armeline Rd DE23 . . . .**218** D2
Armitage Dr NG10 . . . .**237** A7
Armscote Cl DE21 . . . .**206** B2
Arms Park Dr S20 . . . .**59** F6
Armytage Ind Est S41 . . . .**77** A1
Arnfield La S43 . . . .**9** F8
Arnhem Terr DE21 . . . .**220** F3
Arnold Ave
  Long Eaton NG10 . . . .**236** A4
  Sheffield S12 . . . .**44** B1
Arnold Cl DE11 . . . .**261** E7
Arnold Cres NG10 . . . .**236** A4
Arnold St DE22 . . . .**218** D5
Arnot Rd DE14 . . . .**254** A7
Arnside NG9 . . . .**223** E5
Arnside Cl
  Chesterfield S41 . . . .**76** D1
  Swadlincote DE11 . . . .**256** C1
Arran Cl
  Derby DE24 . . . .**231** E3
  Stapleford NG9 . . . .**209** E2
Arran Ct DE55 . . . .**147** F6
Arreton Ct DE24 . . . .**233** C5
Arridge Rd DE21 . . . .**219** F6
Arrowscroft Ct SK14 . . . .**9** D5
Arrowscroft Way SK14 . . . .**9** D4
Arthington Blgs S2 . . . .**43** A6
Arthington St S8 . . . .**43** A6
Arthur Ave NG9 . . . .**223** F8
Arthur Ct [1] DE23 . . . .**219** B2
Arthur Hind Cl DE22 . . . .**218** F7
Arthur Mee Rd NG9 . . . .**223** E5
Arthurs Ct DE13 . . . .**240** E2
Arthur Short Cl S80 . . . .**82** A6
Arthur St
  Alfreton DE55 . . . .**159** A5
  Derby DE1 . . . .**267** B5
  Draycott DE72 . . . .**234** F8
  Linton DE11 . . . .**261** E7
  Pinxton NG16 . . . .**160** D3
Arthurs View NG16 . . . .**170** F4
Arthurs Way S33 . . . .**38** A2
Artic Way NG16 . . . .**95** D7
Artisan View S8 . . . .**43** A6
Arun Dale NG19 . . . .**136** D2
Arundel Ave DE3 . . . .**217** F2
Arundel Cl
  [25] Chesterfield S41 . . . . . .**95** F8
  Dronfield S18 . . . .**56** D1
  Sandiacre NG10 . . . .**223** B4
Arundel Ct [6] S43 . . . .**78** C2
Arundel Dr DE21 . . . .**220** F5
Arundel Grange SK13 . . . .**17** A8
Arundel St
  Derby DE22 . . . .**218** D4
  Glossop SK13 . . . .**10** C1
Asbourne Ct DE7 . . . .**194** D1
Ascot Ave NG16 . . . .**195** E7
Ascot Cl
  Burton u T DE15 . . . .**248** A3
  West Hallam DE7 . . . .**207** D7
Ascot Dr DE24 . . . .**232** D8
Ascot Park Est NG10 . . . .**223** C7
Ascot Pl DE7 . . . .**208** C5
Ascott Dr DE11 . . . .**256** A7
Ash Acre DE56 . . . .**179** D4
Ashberry Ct DE22 . . . .**205** A4
Ashbourne Ave S45 . . . .**131** A5
Ashbourne Ct [4] S40 . . . .**95** A5
Ashbourne Ct
  Derby DE22 . . . .**218** E6
  [3] Glossop SK13 . . . .**17** F8
Ashbourne Dr DE11 . . . .**256** A1
Ashbourne La
  Chapel-en-le-F SK23 . . . . . .**47** D5
  Wetton DE6 . . . .**149** A2
Ashbourne PNEU Sch
  DE6 . . . .**173** C3
Ashbourne Rd
  Alstonefield DE6 . . . .**149** B3
  Belper DE56 . . . .**178** C4
  Buxton SK17 . . . .**85** D4
  Church Broughton DE65 . . .**213** F3
  Derby DE22 . . . .**218** C2
  Kirk Langley DE6 . . . .**202** D4
  Mackworth DE22 . . . .**217** A8
  Mayfield DE6 . . . .**184** C7
  Rocester ST14 . . . .**196** F4
  Shottle DE56 . . . .**177** D3
  Uttoxeter ST14 . . . .**210** B1
Ashbourne St NG20 . . . .**119** F4
Ashbrook DE15 . . . .**248** A1

Ashbrook Ave DE72 . . . .**221** C2
Ashbrook Cl DE22 . . . .**204** C3
Ashbrook Inf Sch DE72 . . . . .**221** B2
Ashbrook Jun Sch DE72 . . . .**221** B2
Ashbury Dr S8 . . . .**43** C2
Ashbury La S8 . . . .**43** C2
Ashby Ave NG19 . . . .**136** D5
Ashby La DE11 . . . .**257** C1
Ashby Rd
  Blackfordby DE11, LE65 . . .**257** D2
  Breedon on t H DE73 . . . . .**252** E2
  Burton u T DE15 . . . .**248** B2
  Melbourne DE73 . . . .**252** A6
  Moira DE12 . . . .**262** F4
Ashby Rd E DE15 . . . .**248** E1
Ashby St DE24 . . . .**232** E6
Ash Cl
  Aston-on-T DE72 . . . .**246** B7
  Barlborough S43 . . . .**80** B6
  Derby DE22 . . . .**204** D4
  Killamarsh S21 . . . .**60** C5
  Mottram in L SK14 . . . .**9** A4
  Pinxton NG16 . . . .**160** D2
Ashcombe Gdns DE21 . . . . .**206** B1
Ash Cres
  Eckington S21 . . . .**59** B1
  Mansfield Woodhouse
  NG19 . . . .**136** E2
  Ripley DE5 . . . .**180** D8
Ashcroft Cl DE24 . . . .**232** F7
Ashcroft Ct S41 . . . .**77** B3
Ashcroft Dr S41 . . . .**77** B2
Ash Croft Prim Sch
  DE24 . . . .**231** E2
Ash Ct DE55 . . . .**159** C3
Ashdale Cl DE15 . . . .**255** A8
Ashdale Rd DE7 . . . .**209** A6
Ashdene Gdns DE56 . . . .**179** C5
Ashdown Dr S40 . . . .**95** D1
Ashe La DE65 . . . .**229** A5
Ashe Pl DE23 . . . .**218** F1
Asher La DE5 . . . .**169** C5
Asher Lane Bsns Pk DE5 . . .**169** D4
Ashes Ave DE6 . . . .**175** F3
Ashes La
  Fenny Bentley DE6 . . . .**162** A1
  Glossop SK13 . . . .**10** B2
Ashes The SK13 . . . .**10** B2
Ashfield Ave
  Derby DE23 . . . .**219** E8
  Somercotes DE55 . . . .**159** D1
Ashfield Cl S12 . . . .**43** F4
Ashfield Dr S12 . . . .**43** F4
Ashfield Gr SK6 . . . .**15** B1
Ashfield Rd
  Chapel-en-le-F SK23 . . . .**47** D6
  Chesterfield S41 . . . .**115** D8
  Glossop SK13 . . . .**9** F3
Ash Fields DE56 . . . .**179** A2
Ashford Ave S42 . . . .**132** A7
Ashford Cl S18 . . . .**75** D8
Ashford Ct
  Chesterfield S41 . . . .**96** A5
  West Hallam DE7 . . . .**207** D8
Ashford Gn [2] SK13 . . . .**9** E1
Ashford La DE45 . . . .**89** D2
Ashford Mews SK13 . . . .**9** E1
Ashford Pl DE7 . . . .**194** E5
Ashford Rd DE15 . . . .**75** D8
Ashford Rise DE56 . . . .**179** C6
Ashforth Ave DE75 . . . .**194** A8
Ashfurlong Cl S17 . . . .**55** F7
Ashfurlong Dr S17 . . . .**55** F7
Ashfurlong Pk S17 . . . .**55** F7
Ashfurlong Rd S17 . . . .**55** F7
Ashgate Ave S40 . . . .**95** C3
Ashgate Croft Sch S40 . . . . . .**95** C4
Ashgate Ct [4] S40 . . . .**95** C4
Ashgate Prim Sch DE22 . . . .**218** D6
Ashgate Rd S40 . . . .**95** C4
Ashgate Valley Rd S40 . . . . . .**95** D4
Ash Gr
  Brinsley NG16 . . . .**182** D8
  Chinley SK23 . . . .**34** E1
  Long Eaton NG10 . . . .**236** C6
  Mastin Moor S43 . . . .**79** B4
  Sandiacre NG10 . . . .**223** A7
  Selston NG16 . . . .**171** F7
  Shirebrook NG20 . . . .**119** E5
  Stapleford NG9 . . . .**223** D5
  Tupton S42 . . . .**131** D8
Ashgrove Ct DE21 . . . .**206** B1
Ash Grove La DE65 . . . .**241** C6
Ash La
  Chesterfield S21 . . . .**77** D8
  Sutton on t H DE6, DE65 . .**228** E7
  Unstone S18 . . . .**57** F3
Ashland Rd S21 . . . .**59** E3
Ashlar Dr DE12 . . . .**262** F1
Ashlea Dr DE6 . . . .**184** D7
Ashlea Wlk S43 . . . .**81** A5
Ashleigh Ave
  Glossop SK13 . . . .**10** B2
  Sheffield S12 . . . .**43** F5
  Swadlincote DE11 . . . .**255** F5
Ashleigh Cl S41 . . . .**77** B3
Ashleigh Croft S12 . . . .**43** F5
Ashleigh Ct S21 . . . .**59** C1
Ashleigh Dr
  Chellaston DE73 . . . .**232** F2
  Sheffield S12 . . . .**43** F5
  Sheffield S12 . . . .**43** F5
Ashleigh Rd S43 . . . .**80** B7
Ashley Cl
  Killamarsh S21 . . . .**60** D6
  Overseal DE12 . . . .**262** B3
  Tansley DE4 . . . .**144** A4
Ashley Ct DE15 . . . .**248** A3

Ashley La S21 . . . .**60** D6
Ashley St DE22 . . . .**218** C5
Ashlyn Rd DE21 . . . .**219** C5
Ashmeadow Ct DE6 . . . .**185** D8
Ashmore Ave S21 . . . .**59** B2
Ash Mount Rd NG16 . . . .**182** B3
Ashop Rd DE56 . . . .**179** D5
Ashopton Ave DE23 . . . .**231** F8
Ashopton Dr S33 . . . .**40** B4
Ashopton Rd
  Bamford S33 . . . .**40** A6
  Chesterfield S41 . . . .**95** C6
Ashover Cl DE21 . . . .**219** F8
Ashover New Rd DE55,
  S45 . . . .**145** E8
Ashover Prim Sch S45 . . . . . .**129** F3
Ashover Rd
  Alton S45 . . . .**130** C5
  Ashover S45 . . . .**129** E4
  Brackenfield DE55 . . . .**146** B7
  [1] Derby, Chaddesden
  DE21 . . . .**219** E8
  Derby DE22 . . . .**204** D2
  Staveley S43 . . . .**97** C6
  Swadlincote DE11 . . . .**255** E5
Ashover View DE55 . . . .**147** C1
Ash St
  Buxton SK17 . . . .**85** B6
  Ilkeston DE7 . . . .**194** E4
  Sheffield, Mosborough S20 .**59** C8
Ash Terr SK17 . . . .**85** C8
Ashton Cl
  Chesterfield S40 . . . .**114** C8
  Derby DE3 . . . .**217** C3
  Killamarsh S21 . . . .**60** C6
  Swanwick DE55 . . . .**170** A7
Ashton Gdns
  Clay Cross S42 . . . .**131** B6
  [1] Glossop SK13 . . . .**17** C7
Ashton Rd S45 . . . .**131** E4
Ashton St S43 . . . .**17** C7
Ashton Way DE56 . . . .**179** D4
Ashtree Ave DE24 . . . .**232** B6
Ash Tree Cl
  Breadsall DE21 . . . .**205** E4
  Chesterfield S40 . . . .**95** C3
  Duffield DE56 . . . .**190** E5
Ash Tree Cres NG19 . . . .**136** C5
Ash Tree Rd S43 . . . .**80** E2
Ashurst Cl S40 . . . .**94** F5
Ash Vale S40 . . . .**95** B3
Ashview Cl NG10 . . . .**236** A8
Ash View Cl DE65 . . . .**229** B3
Ashwater Cl DE24 . . . .**231** F2
Ashwell Ave NG19 . . . .**136** E5
Ashwood SK13 . . . .**16** F8
Ashwood Ct
  Buxton SK17 . . . .**85** C7
  Mansfield Woodhouse
  NG19 . . . .**136** C5
Ashwood Rd
  Buxton SK17 . . . .**85** B7
  Disley SK12 . . . .**32** D6
Ashworth Ave
  Burton u T DE15 . . . .**248** C2
  Derby DE21 . . . .**219** F5
Ashworth Dr NG19 . . . .**136** E4
Ashworth La SK14 . . . .**9** A3
Ashworth Wlk DE21 . . . .**219** F5
Askerfield Ave DE22 . . . .**204** C4
Asker La DE4 . . . .**143** D6
Askew Gr DE65 . . . .**242** D2
Asline Rd S2 . . . .**43** A8
Aspen Bsns Ctr DE21 . . . .**220** B4
Aspen Cl
  Buxton SK17 . . . .**66** B1
  Killamarsh S21 . . . .**60** C5
Aspen Ct [1] NG19 . . . .**136** E1
Aspen Dr DE21 . . . .**220** C4
Aspen Rd S21 . . . .**59** B1
Aspen Way SK6 . . . .**32** A5
Aspley Cl S40 . . . .**95** B1
Astcote Cl DE75 . . . .**182** A1
Asterdale Prim Sch
  DE21 . . . .**220** F3
Asterdale View DE21 . . . .**220** F4
Aster Gdns DE23 . . . .**231** B6
Astil St DE15 . . . .**254** F8
Astlow Dr DE56 . . . .**179** B6
Aston Cl
  Chellaston DE73 . . . .**245** A8
  Dronfield S18 . . . .**57** C3
Aston Ct S43 . . . .**78** F2
Aston Dr DE11 . . . .**256** A7
Aston Gn NG9 . . . .**223** E3
Aston Hall Dr DE72 . . . .**246** A6
Aston Hall Hospl DE72 . . . . .**246** A6
Aston La
  Chellaston DE73 . . . .**233** B1
  Hope S33 . . . .**39** C4
  Shardlow DE72 . . . .**234** E1
  Sudbury DE6 . . . .**226** A5
  Wensley DE4 . . . .**142** D7
Aston-on-Trent Prim Sch
  DE72 . . . .**246** A8
Aston Rd DE23 . . . .**231** C5
Aston Rd Ind Pk [8] DE23 . .**231** C5
Astron Bsns Pk DE11 . . . .**256** D6
Astwith Cl S44 . . . .**116** F1
Astwith La S44, S45 . . . .**133** B5
Atchison Gdns DE21 . . . .**220** B7
Atherfield Gdns NG16 . . . . . .**182** F3
Atherfield Wlk DE24 . . . .**233** C5

Atherstone Rd DE12 . . . .**265** D1
Atherton Ave SK14 . . . .**9** A4
Atherton Cl S2 . . . .**43** F6
Atherton Gr SK14 . . . .**9** A4
Atherton Rd
  Ilkeston DE7 . . . .**194** C3
  Sheffield S2 . . . .**43** F6
Athlestan Way DE13 . . . .**240** C1
Athlone Cl DE21 . . . .**219** D8
Athol Cl
  Chesterfield S40 . . . .**114** B8
  Derby DE24 . . . .**231** E4
Atkin Pl S2 . . . .**43** A8
Atkinson Ct S40 . . . .**266** B1
Atkinson Mews S21 . . . .**59** C3
Atkins Way ST14 . . . .**196** F3
Atlantic Cres [8] S8 . . . .**56** E6
Atlantic Dr S8 . . . .**56** E6
Atlantic Way S8 . . . .**56** E6
Atlantic Wlk S8 . . . .**56** E6
Atlow Brow [4] DE6 . . . .**173** D3
Atlow Cl S40 . . . .**95** B5
Atlow La DE6 . . . .**175** A5
Atlow Rd DE21 . . . .**219** E7
Attenborough Nature
  Reserve★ NG9 . . . .**237** D8
Attewell Cl DE7 . . . .**235** B7
Attewell Rd NG16 . . . .**195** B5
Attlebridge Cl DE21 . . . .**219** D8
Attlee Rd S43 . . . .**97** B7
Atwall Ct DE23 . . . .**219** A1
Atworth Gr DE23 . . . .**230** F7
Auburn Cl DE7 . . . .**207** B8
Auckland's Pl S40 . . . .**266** B2
Auckland Cl DE3 . . . .**217** F3
Auckland Dr S20 . . . .**59** E6
Auckland Rise S20 . . . .**59** E6
Auckland Way S20 . . . .**59** E6
Auction Cl DE6 . . . .**173** C2
Auden Cl DE65 . . . .**227** A8
Audens Way DE11 . . . .**256** C6
Audley Cl DE7 . . . .**194** D3
Audley Ctr DE1 . . . .**267** B3
Audrey Cotts S32 . . . .**71** C6
Audrey Cres NG19 . . . .**136** C5
Audrey Dr DE21 . . . .**220** A8
Audrey Rd S13 . . . .**44** C7
Aughton Cl S13 . . . .**44** D7
Aughton Cres S13 . . . .**44** C8
Aughton Dr S13 . . . .**44** C8
Augusta St DE23 . . . .**219** B2
Ault Dene DE11 . . . .**256** E4
Ault Hucknall La S44 . . . .**134** A7
Aults Cl DE65 . . . .**230** C1
Austen Ave
  Derby DE23 . . . .**231** B8
  Long Eaton NG10 . . . .**236** C5
Austins Dr NG10 . . . .**223** B4
Austin Sq DE23 . . . .**231** F7
Austin St NG20 . . . .**120** A4
Autumn Gr DE21 . . . .**219** F5
Avalon Dr DE73 . . . .**244** F8
Avenue 1 S41 . . . .**115** B8
Avenue 2 S41 . . . .**115** B8
Avenue 3 S41 . . . .**115** B8
Avenue 4 S41 . . . .**115** B8
Avenue 5 S41 . . . .**115** B8
Avenue 6 S41 . . . .**115** B8
Avenue 7 S41 . . . .**115** B8
Avenue 8 S41 . . . .**115** B8
Avenue Cl S32 . . . .**72** A3
Avenue Rd
  Chesterfield S41 . . . .**96** A8
  Duffield DE56 . . . .**190** E5
Avenue The
  Bakewell DE45 . . . .**109** D5
  Belper DE56 . . . .**178** F2
  Chapel-en-le-F SK23 . . . .**46** F2
  Derby, Chaddesden DE21 . .**219** F5
  Derby DE1 . . . .**267** B2
  Dronfield S18 . . . .**57** B2
  Glossop SK13 . . . .**10** A4
  Northwood DE4 . . . .**127** B6
  Spinkhill S21 . . . .**60** D2
  Stoney Middleton S32 . . . . .**72** A3
  Tissington DE6 . . . .**162** A5
  Weston-on-T DE72 . . . .**245** E5
Averham Cl
  Derby DE21 . . . .**206** B1
  Swadlincote DE11 . . . .**256** A3
Aviemore Cl S43 . . . .**77** E4
Aviemore Way DE24 . . . .**231** E4
Avis Ave DE75 . . . .**193** F7
Avocet Ct DE24 . . . .**231** D4
Avon Cl
  Derby DE24 . . . .**231** D2
  Dronfield S18 . . . .**57** B3
  Swadlincote DE11 . . . .**256** B6
Avon Ct S41 . . . .**266** B4
Avondale Cl NG10 . . . .**236** A6
Avondale Rd
  Bolsover S44 . . . .**118** A8
  Chesterfield S40 . . . .**266** A4
  Derby DE21 . . . .**267** B1
  Derby, Spondon DE21 . . . . .**220** D6
  Ilkeston DE7 . . . .**208** C5
  Staveley S43 . . . .**97** D4
Avonlea Cl DE7 . . . .**209** B6
Avonmouth Dr DE24 . . . .**232** E8
Avon St DE24 . . . .**232** E8
Avon Way
  Burton u T DE15 . . . .**248** A1
  Hilton DE65 . . . .**228** D1
Awdishaw La DE6 . . . .**213** B5
Awsworth La
  Cossall NG16 . . . .**195** C3
  Kimberley NG16 . . . .**195** D6

Awsworth Prim Sch
NG16 . . . . **195** C4
Awsworth Rd DE7 . . . . **194** F2
Aycliffe Gdns DE24 . . . . . . **232** F4
Aylesbury Ave DE21 . . . . . **219** F7
Aylward Cl S2 . . . . **43** F7
Aylward Rd S2 . . . . **43** F7
Ayncourt Rd S42 . . . . **132** B7
Ayr Cl DE21 . . . . **220** D4
Azalea Ave DE55 . . . . **170** A8
Azalea Cl S18 . . . . **159** E3
Azalea Ct NG16 . . . . **195** C8

B

Babbacombe Cl DE24 . . . . **233** C7
Babbacombe Ct **5** S41 . . . **95** F8
Babbington Cl DE13 . . . . . **239** C5
Babbington La NG16 . . . . . **195** F4
Babbington St DE55 . . . . . **148** A6
Babbs La DE6 . . . . **211** C1
Babington Bsns Coll
DE1 . . . . **267** B1
Babington Cl S2 . . . . **43** F7
Babington Ct S2 . . . . **43** F7
Babington Hospl DE6 . . . . **178** F2
Babington La DE1 . . . . **267** B2
Bacchus Way DE55 . . . . . . **147** B5
Back Bridge St SK22 . . . . . . **24** C1
Back Croft S45 . . . . **131** E2
Backhill La DE6 . . . . **151** F3
Back Jodrell St SK22 . . . . . . **33** B7
Back La
Alderwasley DE56 . . . . . . **166** E7
Alstonefield DE6 . . . . **149** E3
Biggin SK17 . . . . **138** D1
Brackenfield DE55 . . . . . . **146** A1
Calow S44 . . . . **116** B8
Castle Donington DE74 . . **247** A5
Chellaston DE73 . . . . **233** A2
Darley Dale DE4 . . . . **127** F4
Eckington S21 . . . . **59** B3
Ellastone DE6 . . . . **183** A3
Elton DE4 . . . . **140** E6
Glapwell S44 . . . . **118** B1
Glossop SK13 . . . . **16** E6
Hathersage S32 . . . . **53** A7
Hilton DE65 . . . . **228** D2
Ilkeston DE7 . . . . **194** E2
Mottram in L SK14 . . . . **9** A4
Patterton S44 . . . . **118** B5
Pilsley S45 . . . . **132** C2
Ripley DE5 . . . . **169** C6
Shirley DE6 . . . . **200** D7
Spout DE4 . . . . **166** D4
Stonebroom DE55 . . . . . . **146** F5
Sutton in A NG17 . . . . **148** F4
Thorpe Salvin S80 . . . . **63** B6
Tideswell DE55 . . . . **215** B3
Tibshelf DE55 . . . . **147** F6
Unstone S18 . . . . **57** F1
Wessington DE55 . . . . **157** F8
Youlgreave DE45 . . . . **125** A6
Back Mellor Rd SK22 . . . . . **24** C1
Back Moor SK14 . . . . **9** A4
Backmoor Cres S8 . . . . **43** C2
Backmoor Rd S8 . . . . **43** D2
Back Rd S18 . . . . **57** F1
Back School La DE4 . . . . . **127** E2
Back Sitwell St DE1 . . . . . **267** B2
Back South St S43 . . . . **77** D3
Back St S33 . . . . **38** C3
Back Union Rd **3** SK42 . . **33** C7
Back Wyver La DE56 . . . . . **178** F5
Bacon Cl NG16 . . . . **195** A8
Bacon La DE5 . . . . **169** B6
Bacons La S40 . . . . **115** A8
Baden Powell Ave S40 . . . **266** B1
Baden Powell Rd S40 . . . . **266** B2
Badger Cl
Chesterfield S40 . . . . **114** B7
Derby DE21 . . . . **220** F6
Badgerdale DE23 . . . . **231** A7
Badger La S45 . . . . **145** C8
Badgers Way SK13 . . . . **17** B7
Badgery Cl ST14 . . . . **210** A2
Badway La DE65 . . . . **227** C8
Bage Hill S42 . . . . **113** C6
Baggaley Cres NG19 . . . . . **136** B1
Bag La
Marchington ST14 . . . . . . **224** E2
Roston DE6 . . . . **197** E7
Bagot St DE7 . . . . **208** C4
Bagshaw's Rd S12 . . . . **44** B6
Bagshawe Ave SK23 . . . . . . **46** F6
Bagshawe Cavern * S33 . . . **51** A6
Bagshaw Hill DE45 . . . . . . **109** D6
Bagshaw La SK17 . . . . **48** B6
Bagshaw St
Derby DE24 . . . . **232** E8
Pleasley NG19 . . . . **135** B4
Bagthorpe La S42 . . . . **94** A3
Bailey Ave DE12 . . . . **262** A3
Bailey Brook Cres
Aldercar NG16 . . . . **182** A4
Langley Mill NG16 . . . . . . **182** A3
Bailey Brook Dr NG16 . . . . **182** A3
Bailey Brook Ind Est
NG16 . . . . **182** B2
Bailey Brook Rd NE7 . . . . . **194** F5
Bailey Brook Wlk NG16 . . **182** A3
Bailey Dr S21 . . . . **60** E8
Bailey Gr SK17 . . . . **85** E8
Bailey Grove Rd NG16 . . . **182** D2
Baileys Mill DE4 . . . . **143** D4
Bailey St
Derby DE23 . . . . **267** A1

Bailey St continued
Stapleford NG9 . . . . **223** C6
Bainbridge Rd S44 . . . . **98** F1
Bainbridge St DE23 . . . . . **219** A3
Baines Wood Cl S41 . . . . . . **95** C8
Bains Dr DE72 . . . . **221** D1
Bakeacre La DE65 . . . . **230** E3
Bakehouse La DE72 . . . . . . **221** C5
Bakehurst Cl SK22 . . . . **33** C7
Baker's La
Cromford DE4 . . . . **155** A5
Doveridge DE6 . . . . **211** C1
Baker Ave DE75 . . . . **193** F7
Baker Brothers Mobil Home
Cvn Site DE7 . . . . **195** A1
Baker Cl DE55 . . . . **170** D7
Baker Dr S21 . . . . **60** C6
Baker Rd
Eastwood NG16 . . . . **195** C8
Mansfield Woodhouse
NG19 . . . . **136** C6
Bakers Hill DE56 . . . . **168** L1
Bakers La DE4 . . . . **156** A8
Baker St
Burton u T DE15 . . . . **254** E7
Creswell S80 . . . . **81** E2
Derby DE24 . . . . **232** F8
Ilkeston DE7 . . . . **194** F1
Swadlincote DE11 . . . . . . **256** C3
Bakestone Moor S80 . . . . . . **81** F5
Bakewell Bank **30** SK13 . . . **9** D1
Bakewell CE Inf Sch
DE45 . . . . **109** D6
Bakewell Cl
Derby DE3 . . . . **217** E3
46 Gamesley SK13 . . . . . . **9** D1
Bakewell Dr DE74 . . . . **247** A2
Bakewell Fold **37** SK13 . . . . **9** D1
Bakewell Gdns **41** SK13 . . . **9** D1
Bakewell Gn
35 Gamesley SK13 . . . . **9** D1
Swadlincote DE11 . . . . . . **255** E5
Bakewell Gr **48** SK13 . . . . . **9** D1
Bakewell Lea **34** SK13 . . . . . **9** D1
Bakewell Meth Jun Sch
DE45 . . . . **109** D4
Bakewell Mews **36** SK13 . . . **9** D1
Bakewell Rd
Baslow DE45 . . . . **91** E4
Buxton SK17 . . . . **85** C7
Darley Dale DE4 . . . . **142** F7
Long Eaton NG10 . . . . . . **236** E5
Matlock DE4 . . . . **143** A5
Over Haddon DE45 . . . . . **109** B2
Staveley S43 . . . . **97** C5
Bakewell St DE22 . . . . **218** F4
Bakewell Station Ind Est
DE45 . . . . **109** E7
Bakewell Wlk **44** SK13 . . . . . **9** D1
Balaclava Rd DE23 . . . . . . **232** A8
Balfour Rd
Derby DE23 . . . . **232** A8
Stapleford NG9 . . . . **223** D6
Balgonie Ct DE73 . . . . **232** E2
Balham Wlk DE22 . . . . . . **218** A6
Balk The DE13 . . . . **239** D6
Ballacraine Dr DE5 . . . . . . **170** A1
Ballards Way DE72 . . . . . . **221** D1
Ballater Cl
Derby DE24 . . . . **231** E4
Mansfield NG19 . . . . **135** E2
Balleny Cl DE21 . . . . **205** F2
Ball Hill DE55 . . . . **160** C6
Ballidon Cl **1** S41 . . . . **95** C6
Ball La DE72 . . . . **234** A5
Balmoak La S41 . . . . **96** C5
Balmoral Cl
Derby DE23 . . . . **218** B2
Heanor DE75 . . . . **181** C1
Mansfield Woodhouse
NG19 . . . . **136** E5
Sandiacre NG10 . . . . **223** B3
Balmoral Cres
Dronfield S18 . . . . **56** D2
Sheffield S10 . . . . **42** F8
Balmoral Ct DE74 . . . . **247** D5
Balmoral Dr NG19 . . . . . . **135** E2
Balmoral Rd
Borrowash DE72 . . . . **221** C1
Burton u T DE15 . . . . **248** A3
Ilkeston DE7 . . . . **208** D5
Balmoral Way S43 . . . . **77** E4
Baltimore Cl **8** DE11 . . . . **256** A7
Bamburgh Cl DE21 . . . . . . **220** D4
Bamford Ave
Derby DE23 . . . . **231** F8
North Wingfield S42 . . . . **131** F7
Bamford Fold **3** SK13 . . . . . **9** E1
Bamford Gn **4** SK13 . . . . . . **9** E1
Bamford Ho S33 . . . . **40** B3
Bamford La SK13 . . . . **9** E1
Bamford Mews SK13 . . . . . . **9** E1
Bamford Prim Sch S33 . . . . **40** B3
Bamford Rd S43 . . . . **97** C5
Bamford St
Chesterfield S43 . . . . **77** D4
Newton DE55 . . . . **148** A3
Ripley DE5 . . . . **180** D7
Bamford Sta S33 . . . . **40** B1
Banbury Ave NG9 . . . . **223** F3
Banchory Cl NG19 . . . . . . **135** E2
Bancroft Cl DE65 . . . . **228** D1
Bancroft Dr DE22 . . . . **204** C4
Bancroft The DE65 . . . . . . **229** B3
Bangor St DE21 . . . . **219** E8
Bank Bldgs DE56 . . . . **190** F7
Bankbottom SK13 . . . . **10** A5

Bank Cl
Bolsover S44 . . . . **99** A3
Creswell S80 . . . . **100** D8
Shirebrook NG20 . . . . . . **119** F4
Tibshelf DE55 . . . . **147** F5
Bank Ct DE22 . . . . **218** E8
Bankerwall La DE6 . . . . . . **183** C7
Bankfield Dr
Derby DE21 . . . . **220** F4
Ilkeston DE7 . . . . **208** B6
Bankgate SK14 . . . . **16** A8
Bank Gdns DE4 . . . . **143** B6
Bankholmes Cl DE24 . . . . **231** E2
Bank House Ct DE6 . . . . . **164** A2
Bank La S13 . . . . **10** A7
Bank Rd
Chesterfield S41 . . . . **96** A6
Matlock DE4 . . . . **143** C5
Bank Row SK13 . . . . **10** A7
Banksburn Cl DE75 . . . . . **181** C1
Bankside DE45 . . . . **125** B5
Bank Side
Derby DE22 . . . . **204** E2
Hartington SK17 . . . . **137** D6
Bankside Cl SK6 . . . . **15** C1
Bank Rd NG9 . . . . **223** E2
Bank St
Brimington S43 . . . . **96** D8
Broadbottom SK14 . . . . . . **16** A8
Chesterfield S40 . . . . **95** E3
Glossop SK13 . . . . **10** A5
Hadfield SK13 . . . . **10** A5
Hayfield SK22 . . . . **25** D3
Langley Mill NG16 . . . . . . **182** C3
Long Eaton NG10 . . . . . . **236** E7
Somercotes DE55 . . . . . . **170** C8
Swadlincote DE11 . . . . . . **262** A8
Bank Terr SK13 . . . . **10** A5
Bank The
Bonsall DE4 . . . . **142** C1
Glossop SK13 . . . . **17** D8
Hayfield SK22 . . . . **25** B4
Stoney Middleton S32 . . . . **71** F4
Bank Top La S30 . . . . **72** C8
Bank Vale Rd DE4 . . . . **25** C3
Bank View S17 . . . . **69** B5
Bank View Rd
Derby DE22 . . . . **218** F8
Nether Heage DE56 . . . . . **168** C2
Bankwood Cl S14 . . . . **43** D5
Bank Wood Cl S40 . . . . **95** B7
Bankwood Com Prim Sch
S14 . . . . **43** D5
Bankwood Rd S14 . . . . **43** D5
Bannels Ave DE23 . . . . **231** B7
Banton's La DE73 . . . . **251** A4
Banwell Cl DE3 . . . . **217** C3
Barber's La S21 . . . . **60** D7
Barber St S13 . . . . **194** E3
Barber St SK13 . . . . **10** B6
Barbon Cl S40 . . . . **95** E5
Barcheston Cl DE21 . . . . . **206** B2
Barclay Ct DE7 . . . . **194** D3
Barclay Grange S41 . . . . . **266** C3
Bar Croft **3** S40 . . . . **95** C6
Barden Dr DE22 . . . . **204** F3
Bardolph Cl DE11 . . . . **255** F3
Bardsey Ct DE21 . . . . **206** B3
Bare Jarrett Rd SK17 . . . . . **88** B1
Bare La DE72 . . . . **221** C5
Barf Cl DE21 . . . . **217** E1
Bargate S33 . . . . **38** C2
Bargate Cl DE56 . . . . **179** C1
Bargate La DE65 . . . . **242** B5
Bargate Rd DE56 . . . . **179** B1
Barholme Cl S41 . . . . **95** F7
Barker Ave NG16 . . . . **171** B4
Barker Ave N NG10 . . . . . **223** A6
Barker Cl DE7 . . . . **193** B1
Barker Fold S40 . . . . **95** D3
Barker Gate DE7 . . . . **194** F2
Barker La S40 . . . . **95** D3
Barker St NG17 . . . . **148** F4
Barklam Cl DE12 . . . . **262** E1
Barlborough Hall Sch S43 . . **61** B1
Barlborough Prim Sch
SK43 . . . . **80** B7
Barlborough Rd S43 . . . . . . **80** D5
Barley Cft DE73 . . . . **232** F1
Barley Cl DE21 . . . . **205** C8
Barleycorn Cl DE15 . . . . . **248** A1
Barleycorn Cl DE21 . . . . . **206** C2
Barleycroft SK13 . . . . **9** F4
Barley Croft
Belper DE56 . . . . **179** B2
South Normanton DE55 . . **160** B4
Barley Dale Dr NG9 . . . . . **209** D2
Barley La S42 . . . . **95** A5
Barley Mews
Dronfield S18 . . . . **56** B2
Mansfield Woodhouse
NG19 . . . . **136** E6
Barling Dr DE7 . . . . **194** C2
Barlow CE Prim Sch S18 . . **75** E3
Barlow Cottages La
NG16 . . . . **195** C5
Barlow Dr N NG16 . . . . . . **195** B4
Barlow Dr S NG16 . . . . . . **195** B4
Barlow Lees La S18 . . . . . . **75** F7
Barlow Rd
Chapel-en-le-F SK23 . . . . . **47** C6
Cutthorpe S18, S42 . . . . . . **94** F8
Staveley S43 . . . . **79** E1
Barlow St DE1, DE23 . . . . **267** D1
Barlow View S18 . . . . **76** B7
Barlow Wood Dr SK6 . . . . . **23** B3

Barmote Croft DE4 . . . . . . **154** F1
Barms Way SK17 . . . . **66** D1
Barnard Ave S18 . . . . **57** D3
Barnard Rd DE21 . . . . **205** D2
Barn Cl
Castle Donington DE74 . . **247** B3
Chesterfield S41 . . . . **95** D6
Findern DE65 . . . . **230** D2
Glossop SK13 . . . . **17** D7
Quarndon DE22 . . . . **204** C6
Barn Croft DE23 . . . . **218** C1
Barnes Ave S18 . . . . **56** E2
Barnes Croft
Heanor DE75 . . . . **193** C8
Wirksworth DE4 . . . . **165** F8
Barnes Gn DE22 . . . . **218** B7
Barnes La
Dronfield S18 . . . . **56** C3
Youlgreave DE45 . . . . **125** C5
Barnes Rd S41 . . . . **96** E1
Barn Farm Cvn & Camping
Site DE4 . . . . **126** C1
Barnfield Cl
Holmewood S42 . . . . **132** E8
1 Staveley S43 . . . . **78** E2
Barnfield Dr S32 . . . . **52** F7
Barnfield S32 . . . . **52** F7
Barnfield Wlk S43 . . . . **78** E2
Barn Furlong DE45 . . . . **90** A4
Barnham Cl S40 . . . . **114** B8
Barnhill Gr DE23 . . . . **231** A7
Barnsfold Ct S42 . . . . **25** D3
Barnsley La DE4, DE56 . . . **165** F2
Barnstaple Cl DE21 . . . . . **206** A2
Barnstaple Ct **3** S41 . . . . . . **95** F8
Barns The S42 . . . . **115** B4
Barnwell Cl ST14 . . . . **210** A4
Barnwell Rd DE4 . . . . **155** A5
Barnwood Cl DE3 . . . . **217** C2
Baron Cl DE21 . . . . **206** D3
Barrack Rd S18 . . . . **58** A1
Barrack Yd DE55 . . . . **170** D7
Barratt Rd S21 . . . . **59** D2
Bar Rd
Baslow DE45 . . . . **91** F6
Curbar S32 . . . . **72** F2
Barrett St DE24 . . . . **233** A7
Barrie Dr DE24 . . . . **231** F5
Barringer Rd NG19 . . . . . . **136** D1
Barrington Cl DE13 . . . . . **240** C1
Barron's Way DE72 . . . . . . **221** C1
Barrons Ct DE72 . . . . **234** A5
Barroon The DE74 . . . . . . **247** B3
Barrow Hill Prim Sch S43 . . **78** B3
Barrow Hill Roundhouse Rly
Ctr ★ S43 . . . . **78** A4
Barrow La DE73 . . . . **244** C6
Barrows Hill La NG16 . . . . **171** D5
Barrow St S43 . . . . **78** F2
Barry Rd S43 . . . . **78** F2
Barrys Cl DE11 . . . . **256** E1
Barson Gr SK17 . . . . **85** E2
Bartle Ave S12 . . . . **43** F4
Bartle Dr S12 . . . . **43** F4
Bartle La S12 . . . . **43** F4
Bartle Way S12 . . . . **43** F4
Barton Cl DE21 . . . . **220** F6
Barton Cres S40 . . . . **95** E6
Barton Hill DE4 . . . . **126** C1
Barton Knowle DE56 . . . . **179** D4
Barton La NG11 . . . . **237** C2
Barton Rd
Long Eaton NG10 . . . . . . **237** A6
Sheffield S8 . . . . **43** A6
Barton St
Burton u T DE14 . . . . **254** C8
Clowne S43 . . . . **80** F4
Barton Turn DE13 . . . . . . **253** A1
Barway DE6 . . . . **211** E8
Basegreen Ave S12 . . . . **44** B3
Basegreen Cl S12 . . . . **44** C3
Basegreen Cres S12 . . . . . . **44** B3
Basegreen Dr S12 . . . . **44** B3
Basegreen Pl S12 . . . . **44** C3
Basegreen Rd S12 . . . . **44** C3
Basegreen Way S12 . . . . . . **44** C3
Basil Cl S41 . . . . **266** B3
Basildon Cl DE24 . . . . **232** F5
Basingwerke Ct SK22 . . . . . **25** D3
Baslow Cl
22 Gamesley SK13 . . . . **9** E1
Long Eaton NG10 . . . . . . **236** A5
Baslow Dr **14** S40 . . . . **95** D5
Baslow Fold **21** SK13 . . . . . . **9** E1
Baslow Gn
23 Gamesley SK13 . . . . **9** E1
2 Swadlincote DE11 . . . . **255** E5
Baslow Gr SK17 . . . . **85** E6
Baslow Mews SK13 . . . . **9** E1
Baslow Rd
Bakewell DE45 . . . . **109** D7
Curbar S32 . . . . **72** D1
Holymoorside S42 . . . . **94** C1
Sheffield S17 . . . . **55** C4
Baslow Way **24** SK13 . . . . . . **9** E1
Bass's Cres DE11 . . . . **261** E2
Bassettbarn La S42 . . . . . . **130** B5
Bassett Cl
Ilkeston DE7 . . . . **194** C3
Kimberley NG16 . . . . **195** E7
Bassett La S10 . . . . **42** A8
Bassett Rd NG16 . . . . **195** E7
Bassett The NG20 . . . . **119** E6
Bassford Ave DE75 . . . . . . **181** F2
Bassingham Ct DE21 . . . . **206** B1
Bassledene Ct S2 . . . . **44** A8
Bassledene Rd S2 . . . . **44** A8

Bass St DE22 . . . . **218** D6
Batch La DE6 . . . . **224** B7
Bateman Cl S43 . . . . **77** D4
Bateman St DE23 . . . . **219** C3
Batemill Rd SK22 . . . . **24** D2
Bateman St S8 . . . . **57** A6
Batemoor Dr S8 . . . . **57** A6
Batemoor Pl S8 . . . . **57** A5
Batemoor Rd S8 . . . . **57** A5
Batemoor Wlk S8 . . . . **57** A6
Bate Wood Ave S43 . . . . **97** B5
Batham Gate S17 . . . . **48** F1
Batham Gate Rd SK17 . . . . **67** B6
Batham Rd S33 . . . . **51** A8
Bath La
Ashover S45 . . . . **129** F6
Moira DE12 . . . . **262** D4
Shirebrook NG19 . . . . . . **120** C2
Bath Rd
Buxton SK17 . . . . **85** B6
Derby DE3 . . . . **217** D5
Bath St
Bakewell DE45 . . . . **109** D6
Derby DE1 . . . . **267** B5
Ilkeston DE7 . . . . **194** E1
Bathurst Rd S44 . . . . **117** F8
Bathurst Terr NG20 . . . . . **100** F2
Batley La NG19 . . . . **134** E4
Batt St **9** S8 . . . . **43** A8
Baulk La
Beeston NG9 . . . . **223** F7
Hathersage S32 . . . . **53** A8
Baverstock Cl DE73 . . . . . **232** F3
Baxter Hill NG19 . . . . **134** F3
Baxter Sq DE23 . . . . **231** F6
Baycliff Dr S40 . . . . **95** C3
Bay Ct S21 . . . . **60** C5
Bayleaf Cres DE21 . . . . . . **206** B3
Baysdale Croft S20 . . . . **59** D7
Baysdale Dr NG10 . . . . . . **236** A6
Bayswater Cl DE22 . . . . . . **217** F6
Bayswater Rd NG16 . . . . . **195** F7
Bazley Rd S2 . . . . **43** F6
Beackden Cl DE56 . . . . . . **179** E4
Beacomfold SK6 . . . . **15** B3
Beacon Dr DE13 . . . . **240** B3
Beaconfields Ho DE21 . . . **220** B4
Beacon Rd DE13 . . . . **240** B3
Beaconsfield St NG10 . . . . **236** E7
Beam Cl DE13 . . . . **240** A1
Beamwood Cl **32** DE21 . . . **205** F1
Beard Cres S43 . . . . **33** D8
Beardmore Cl DE21 . . . . . **205** F2
Beards Rd DE11 . . . . **256** A6
Bearwood Hill Rd DE15 . . **248** A3
Beatrix Dr SK13 . . . . **9** E3
Beattie St S44 . . . . **232** F8
Beatty Wlk DE7 . . . . **194** F3
Beauchief Abbey La S8 . . . **56** C8
Beauchief Abbey (rems of) *
S8 . . . . **56** C8
Beauchief Dr S17 . . . . **56** C7
Beauchief Gdns DE55 . . . . **170** C8
Beaufit La NG16 . . . . **160** E2
Beaufort Com Prim Sch
DE21 . . . . **219** C8
Beaufort Court Ind Est
DE21 . . . . **219** C8
Beaufort Rd
Burton u T DE15 . . . . **248** B1
Derby DE24 . . . . **231** D2
Beaufort St DE21 . . . . **219** D7
Beaulieu Way DE55 . . . . . **170** A7
Beaumaris Ct DE21 . . . . . **220** F5
Beaumont Cl
Barrow u T DE73 . . . . **244** A5
Belper DE56 . . . . **179** D1
Stapleford NG9 . . . . **209** E1
Beaumont Dr SK17 . . . . **47** F1
Beaumont Wlk DE23 . . . . **231** E6
Beaurepaire Cres DE56 . . **179** B5
Beaureper Ave DE22 . . . . **204** E3
Beauvale Dr DE7 . . . . **194** F5
Becher St DE23 . . . . **219** A1
Beck Cl S44 . . . . **99** C2
Beckenham Way DE22 . . . **218** B6
Becket Ave S8 . . . . **56** D6
Becket Cres S8 . . . . **56** E6
Becket Prim Sch DE22 . . . **218** F4
Becket Rd S8 . . . . **56** E6
Becket St DE1 . . . . **267** A3
Beckett Ave NG19 . . . . . . **135** E1
Becket Well La DE1 . . . . . . **267** B3
Becket Wlk S8 . . . . **56** E6
Beckingham Way S40 . . . . **266** B2
Beckitt Cl DE24 . . . . **233** A8
Becksitch La DE56 . . . . . . **178** F2
Becksitch Ct DE56 . . . . . . **178** F1
Bedehouse La DE4 . . . . . . **155** A6
Bedford Cl DE22 . . . . **218** D3
Bedford Ct NG9 . . . . **209** E1
Bedford Rd DE15 . . . . **254** D7
Bedford St DE22 . . . . **218** D3
Bedgrave Cl S21 . . . . **60** E8
Beech Ave
Alfreton DE55 . . . . **159** B5
Borrowash DE72 . . . . **221** C3
Breaston DE72 . . . . **235** F8
Creswell S80 . . . . **81** F2
Derby DE24 . . . . **233** B7
Glossop SK13 . . . . **17** A8
Hulland Ward DE6 . . . . . . **175** F3
Long Eaton NG10 . . . . . . **223** C1
Melbourne DE73 . . . . **252** B8
New Mills SK22 . . . . **24** D1

Beech Ave continued
Pinxton NG16 . . . . .160 E3
Quarndon DE22 . . . . .204 B8
Ripley DE5 . . . . .169 C2
Sandiacre NG10 . . . . .223 B7
Willington DE65 . . . . .242 B5
Beech Cl
Belper DE56 . . . . .179 A3
Kilburn DE56 . . . . .192 B8
Beech Cres
Eckington S21 . . . . .59 B1
Glapwell S44 . . . . .134 B8
Killamarsh S21 . . . . .60 D5
Mansfield Woodhouse
NG19 . . . . .136 E2
Beechcroft DE21 . . . . .205 D4
Beech Ct
Derby DE21 . . . . .220 D5
Mansfield Woodhouse
NG19 . . . . .136 B5
Wirksworth DE4 . . . . .165 F7
Beechdale Rd
Alfreton DE55 . . . . .159 C3
Mansfield NG19 . . . . .136 F2
Beech Dr
Arkwright Town S44 . . . . .97 D3
Ashbourne DE6 . . . . .185 D8
Derby DE22 . . . . .218 F8
Etwall DE65 . . . . .229 C4
Findern DE65 . . . . .230 E1
Woodville DE11 . . . . .257 B2
Beeches Ave DE21 . . . . .220 D5
Beeches Dr S2 . . . . .43 C8
Beeches The
Baslow DE45 . . . . .91 E5
Crich DE4 . . . . .156 F1
Heanor DE75 . . . . .193 C8
Matlock DE4 . . . . .143 A6
Beechfield Rd SK13 . . . . .9 F3
Beech Gdns DE24 . . . . .233 B7
Beech Gr
Long Duckmanton S44 . . . . . .98 A4
South Normanton DE55 . . . . .160 B5
Swadlincote DE11 . . . . .255 F7
Beech Hill Ave NG19 . . . . . .135 F1
Beech Hill Cres NG19 . . . . .135 F1
Beech Hill Dr NG19 . . . . . . .135 F1
Beech Hill Sch NG19 . . . . .135 F1
Beech La
Burton u T DE13 . . . . .240 E1
Dove Holes SK17 . . . . .66 E8
West Hallam DE7 . . . . .207 D7
Beechley Dr DE21 . . . . .206 B1
Beech Rd SK23 . . . . .45 E7
Beech Rise SK23 . . . . .45 C5
Beech St S43 . . . . .78 A1
Beech Tree Ave NG19 . . . . .136 B5
Beech Tree Dr S43 . . . . .80 F2
Beech Way
Clay Cross S45 . . . . .131 E2
Dronfield S18 . . . . .57 A3
Beech Wlk
Cromford DE4 . . . . .155 A6
Derby DE23 . . . . .218 D1
Beechwood Cl DE56 . . . . . . .178 E5
Beechwood Cres DE23 . . . .231 C8
Beechwood Ct DE23 . . . . . . .219 B3
Beechwood Dr SK6 . . . . .23 A6
Beechwood Park Dr
DE22 . . . . .204 F1
Beechwood Rd S18 . . . . .56 F1
Beehive Rd S40 . . . . .95 D2
Bee Hives The DE11 . . . . . . .256 A7
Beeley Cl
Belper DE56 . . . . .179 C6
Creswell S80 . . . . .81 D1
Derby DE22 . . . . .204 D2
Derby, Oakwood DE21 . . . . .205 F2
North Wingfield S42 . . . . . . .132 A7
Staveley S43 . . . . .97 C6
Beeley La DE4 . . . . .112 B3
Beeley View S40 . . . . .114 B7
Beeley Way S43 . . . . .97 C5
Beelow Cl SK17 . . . . .47 F2
Beeston Cl S18 . . . . .56 C2
Beetwell St S40 . . . . .266 B2
Beggarway La DE45 . . . . .90 B5
Beighton St DE5 . . . . .169 F1
Beldon Cl S2 . . . . .43 D7
Beldon Pl S2 . . . . .43 D7
Beldon Rd S2 . . . . .43 D7
Belfast Wlk DE21 . . . . .220 A4
Belfield Ct
Etwall DE65 . . . . .229 B3
Heanor DE75 . . . . .181 C4
Belfield Gdns NG10 . . . . . . .236 E7
Belfield Rd
Etwall DE65 . . . . .229 C3
Swadlincote DE11 . . . . .256 B5
Belfield St DE7 . . . . .194 F2
Belfield Terr DE65 . . . . .229 B3
Belfit Dr S42 . . . . .114 F2
Belf Moor Cl S80 . . . . .82 A5
Belfry Cl DE3 . . . . .217 F1
Belfry The DE13 . . . . .240 C1
Belgrade Ave SK23 . . . . .34 E1
Belgrave Ct DE56 . . . . .179 C5
Belgrave Sq 6 S2 . . . . .43 A8
Belgrave St DE23 . . . . .267 B1
Belklane Dr S21 . . . . .60 E7
Bella Cl NG16 . . . . .182 B4
Belland La S45 . . . . .113 D2
Bell Ave DE72 . . . . .246 A7

Bell Cotts DE6 . . . . .224 C8
Belle Acre Cl 3 DE56 . . . . . .178 F3
Belle View Rd DE6 . . . . .173 B2
Belle Vue Ave DE5 . . . . .180 C6
Belle Vue Cl S43 . . . . .96 D8
Bellhouse La S43 . . . . .78 F3
Bell House La S43 . . . . .78 F3
Bellhouse View S43 . . . . .78 F3
Bellingham Ct DE22 . . . . . . .204 C2
Bell La
Bonsall DE4 . . . . .142 C1
Doveridge DE6 . . . . .224 C8
Hartshorne DE11 . . . . .257 A3
Heanor DE7, DE75 . . . . .193 C5
Bells End Rd DE12 . . . . .253 D1
Bellsfield Cl S80 . . . . .82 A5
Belmont Ave DE72 . . . . .235 E8
Belmont Dr
Borrowash DE72 . . . . .221 B1
Marple SK6 . . . . .15 B1
Staveley S43 . . . . .78 F2
Belmont Prim Sch DE11 . . .256 C4
Belmont St DE11 . . . . .256 C4
Belmont Terr 1 SK17 . . . . . . .85 B7
Belpar Ho DE21 . . . . .220 E3
Belper La DE56 . . . . .178 E6
Belper Rd
Ashbourne DE6 . . . . .173 E1
3 Derby DE22 . . . . .218 F7
Holbrook DE56 . . . . .191 C8
Kilburn DE56 . . . . .179 E2
Morley DE7 . . . . .192 F2
Shirland DE55 . . . . .146 C2
Stanley Common DE7 . . . . . .193 B1
West Hallam DE7 . . . . .207 C8
Belper St DE56 . . . . .179 D4
Belper Sta DE56 . . . . .178 F4
Belsize Cl DE21 . . . . .217 F6
Belton Cl
Dronfield S18 . . . . .56 C1
Sandiacre NG10 . . . . .223 B4
Belton Dr DE5 . . . . .169 E1
Belvedere Ave S40 . . . . .114 E8
Belvedere Cl
Chesterfield S40 . . . . .114 A8
Derby DE3 . . . . .217 D3
Swanwick DE55 . . . . .169 F7
Belvedere Rd DE11 . . . . .256 F2
Belvedere Terr 4 SK17 . . . . .85 B6
Belvoir Cl
Breaston DE72 . . . . .235 D7
Ilkeston DE7 . . . . .208 D6
Long Eaton NG10 . . . . .236 E5
Belvoir Cres DE11 . . . . .256 A6
Belvoir St DE23 . . . . .218 F1
Belvoir Way DE55 . . . . .159 C1
Bembridge Dr DE24 . . . . . . .233 C5
Bemrose Com Sch DE22 . . .218 D4
Bemrose Gate S33 . . . . .40 A6
Bemrose Mews DE22 . . . . . .218 C4
Bemrose Rd DE24 . . . . .232 E7
Benbow Ave DE73 . . . . .252 A8
Benches La SK6 . . . . .15 E3
Bench Rd SK17 . . . . .85 D8
Bendall Gn DE23 . . . . .231 C5
Bend Oak Dr DE15 . . . . .248 C4
Bend Oak Jun Sch DE15 . . .248 C3
Benjamin Ct NG16 . . . . .170 F3
Benjamin Outram Bsns Ctr
DE5 .180 E7
Benmore Ct DE21 . . . . .206 B3
Benner Ave DE7 . . . . .209 A5
Bennerley Ave DE7 . . . . .194 F4
Bennerley Fields Sch
DE7 .194 F4
Bennetts La DE7 . . . . .168 A8
Bennett St
Buxton SK17 . . . . .85 C6
Derby DE24 . . . . .232 D5
Hollingworth SK14 . . . . .9 D5
Long Eaton NG10 . . . . .223 C2
Sandiacre NG10 . . . . .223 A5
Bennimoor Way S40 . . . . . . .114 E8
Bennington Wlk NG19 . . . . .136 E4
Bennion Gr ST14 . . . . .196 E5
Bennison Gdns S45 . . . . .131 D3
Bensley Cl DE73 . . . . .233 A1
Benson St DE24 . . . . .232 F7
Bentfield Rd S40 . . . . .168 C1
Bentham Rd S40 . . . . .95 E5
Benthead La DE6 . . . . .164 F1
Bentinck Dr S43 . . . . .81 A4
Bentinck Rd S44 . . . . .98 F7
Bentink Cl S80 . . . . .81 C1
Bent La
Church Broughton DE65 . . . .227 C6
Darley Dale DE4 . . . . .127 D6
Matlock DE4 . . . . .143 B7
Spout DE4, DE56 . . . . .166 C6
Staveley S43 . . . . .79 A3
Tissington DE6 . . . . .162 D5
Bentley Bridge Cotts
DE4 .143 E7
Bentley Brook
Hilton DE65 . . . . .228 D1
Matlock DE4 . . . . .143 D4
Bentley Cl
Alfreton DE55 . . . . .159 B3
Matlock DE4 . . . . .143 D7
Bentley Dale DE11 . . . . .256 F3
Bentley Fields Open Farm★
DE6 .199 C2
Bentley Rd
Castle Donington DE74 . . . . .246 F4
Uttoxeter ST14 . . . . .210 A2

Bentley St DE24 . . . . .232 E6
Benton Dr SK6 . . . . .23 C8
Bents Cres S18 . . . . .57 C3
Bentside Rd SK12 . . . . .32 D5
Bents La S18 . . . . .57 C3
Bent The S32 . . . . .72 E3
Beowulf Covert DE13 . . . . . .240 B1
Beresford Ave
Ashbourne DE6 . . . . .173 D2
Chapel-en-le-F SK23 . . . . .47 C6
Beresford Cl S45 . . . . .131 D2
Beresford Dale DE11 . . . . . . .255 F2
Beresford Dr
Derby DE21 . . . . .220 E4
Ilkeston DE7 . . . . .194 E5
Beresford La SK17 . . . . .137 C2
Beresford Pl DE56 . . . . .168 B6
Beresford Rd
Chapel-en-le-F SK23 . . . . .47 C6
Long Eaton NG10 . . . . .236 A5
Mansfield Woodhouse
NG19 . . . . .136 C6
Berkeley Ave NG10 . . . . .236 C6
Berkeley Cl DE23 . . . . .231 D7
Berkley Ct SK23 . . . . .45 D6
Berkshire St DE21 . . . . .219 D8
Berle Ave DE75 . . . . .181 E2
Bermuda Ave DE21 . . . . .205 C6
Bernard Ave NG19 . . . . .136 B5
Bernard Cl S43 . . . . .96 F8
Bernard Ct DE11 . . . . .256 D3
Bernard St
Glossop SK13 . . . . .10 C1
Swadlincote DE11 . . . . .256 D3
Bernard Walker Ct SK6 . . . . .15 B2
Berners Cl S2 . . . . .43 E6
Berners Dr S2 . . . . .43 E6
Berners Pl S2 . . . . .43 E6
Berners Rd S2 . . . . .43 E6
Berridge La S45 . . . . .145 B4
Berrisford La DE55 . . . . .145 D7
Berristow La DE55 . . . . .160 C7
Berry Ave S21 . . . . .59 C3
Berry Gdns DE15 . . . . .248 C4
Berry Hedge La DE15 . . . . . .248 C4
Berry Park Cl DE22 . . . . .204 E3
Berry St S42 . . . . .131 E6
Bertrand Ave S45 . . . . .131 D3
Berwick Ave
Chesterfield S40 . . . . .114 C7
Derby DE21 . . . . .219 C7
Berwick Cl DE24 . . . . .233 B5
Berwick Ct S40 . . . . .114 C7
Berwick Dr DE24 . . . . .231 D3
Berwick Rd SK17 . . . . .85 C4
Berwin Cl NG10 . . . . .223 A1
Berwyn Cl S40 . . . . .95 C5
Besom La S32 . . . . .53 A8
Bessalone Dr DE56 . . . . .179 A6
Bessell La NG9 . . . . .223 D5
Bessie La S33 . . . . .51 B6
Best Ave DE15 . . . . .248 B1
Besthill Cotts SK14 . . . . .16 B8
Besthorpe Cl DE21 . . . . .206 B1
Bestwick Ave DE75 . . . . .182 B1
Bestwick Cl DE7 . . . . .209 A4
Bestwood Dr S45 . . . . .131 D3
Bestwood Pk S45 . . . . .131 C3
Bestwood Rd NG16 . . . . .160 E2
Bethel Terr S81 . . . . .63 E7
Bethulie Rd DE23 . . . . .232 A8
Betjeman Sq DE24 . . . . .232 A5
Betlingspring La DE6 . . . . . .184 D3
Betony Cl S21 . . . . .60 B5
Betony Rd DE15 . . . . .248 C2
Betty La DE45 . . . . .108 F8
Bevan Cl S45 . . . . .146 E1
Bevan Dr S43 . . . . .97 B7
Bevan Rd S45 . . . . .131 D2
Beverley Dr NG16 . . . . .195 E7
Beverley Rd DE14 . . . . .254 A7
Beverleys Rd S8 . . . . .43 A4
Beverley St DE24 . . . . .219 D2
Bewdley Cl DE73 . . . . .233 A3
Bexhill Wlk DE21 . . . . .205 E1
Bexley Cl SK13 . . . . .10 C3
Bicester Ave DE24 . . . . .231 C2
Bickley Moss DE21 . . . . .206 B1
Bideford Cl DE5 . . . . .169 D2
Bideford Ct 2 S41 . . . . .95 F8
Bideford Dr DE23 . . . . .231 D6
Bidston Cl DE4 . . . . .143 C7
Bidworth La SK13 . . . . .9 D1
Biggin CE Prim Sch
SK17 . . . . .138 D3
Biggin Cl S45 . . . . .131 D1
Biggin La DE6 . . . . .176 B3
Bigginmill La DE4 . . . . .176 C5
Biggin The DE74 . . . . .247 B3
Big La DE6 . . . . .164 A4
Bilberry Cl DE21 . . . . .205 F1
Bilby La DE55 . . . . .77 E1
Billam St S21 . . . . .59 B3
Billingsley Ave NG16 . . . . . .160 D3
Bingham St DE24 . . . . .232 E6
Bings Rd SK23 . . . . .45 F8
Bingswood Ave SK23 . . . . . . .45 E8
Bingswood Ind Est SK23 . . .45 E8
Bingswood Rd SK23 . . . . .45 E7
Binscombe La DE21 . . . . . . .205 F3
Birch Ave
Ambergate DE56 . . . . .167 F3
Ilkeston DE7 . . . . .209 A7
Swadlincote DE11 . . . . .256 A7
Birch Cl
Alfreton DE55 . . . . .159 A5

Birch Cl continued
Burton u T DE14 . . . . .254 A8
Buxton SK17 . . . . .66 B1
Denstone ST14 . . . . .196 D6
Derby DE21 . . . . .221 A6
Grassmoor S42 . . . . .115 F3
Killamarsh S21 . . . . .60 C5
Ripley DE5 . . . . .180 D8
Wessington DE55 . . . . .157 E8
Birchen Cl
Chesterfield S40 . . . . .95 D5
Dronfield S18 . . . . .56 D1
Birchen Holme DE55 . . . . . .160 A4
Birches Ave DE55 . . . . .157 F5
Birches Fold S18 . . . . .57 C4
Birches La
Dronfield S18 . . . . .57 C4
South Wingfield DE55 . . . . . .158 A5
Birches Rd DE22 . . . . .204 D4
Birches The SK22 . . . . .25 C2
Birch Farm Ave S8 . . . . .57 A8
Birchfield Cl DE73 . . . . .232 F2
Birchfield Pk DE75 . . . . .193 F7
Birchfield Rd DE15 . . . . .254 E6
Birch Gn SK13 . . . . .10 E1
Birch Gr
Hatton DE65 . . . . .227 D2
Shirebrook NG20 . . . . .119 D5
Birch Hall Cl SK22 . . . . .25 B2
Birch Holt Gr S18 . . . . .76 E5
Birch House Way S18 . . . . . . .57 C1
Birchills The S80 . . . . .81 C1
Birchington Dr DE55 . . . . . . .146 C2
Birchitt Cl S17 . . . . .56 C5
Birchitt Ct S17 . . . . .56 C5
Birchitt Pl S17 . . . . .56 C5
Birchitt Rd S17 . . . . .56 C5
Birchitt View S18 . . . . .57 A3
Birch Kiln Croft S43 . . . . .96 F7
Birch La S43 . . . . .78 A1
Birchlands NG19 . . . . .136 F1
Birchlands Dr S21 . . . . .60 D5
Birchover Cl S41 . . . . .95 E6
Birchover Edge DE4 . . . . . . .141 B8
Birchover Ho
1 Derby, Allestree
DE22 . . . . .204 F3
Derby, Markeaton DE22 . . . .218 D8
Birchover La DE4 . . . . .141 B7
Birchover Pl DE7 . . . . .194 E5
Birchover Rd DE4 . . . . .126 C3
Birchover Rise DE21 . . . . . . .205 F1
Birchover Way DE22 . . . . . . .204 E2
Birch Rd S80 . . . . .82 C6
Birchside Ave SK13 . . . . .10 E2
Birch St NG20 . . . . .120 F6
Birch Vale Ind Est SK22 . . . .25 A2
Birchvale Rd S12 . . . . .44 D3
Birch Vale Terr SK22 . . . . .24 F3
Birchview Cl DE56 . . . . .179 B2
Birch View Ct DE1 . . . . .218 F7
Birchway Gr DE23 . . . . .231 A6
Birchwood DE75 . . . . .181 C4
Birchwood Ave
Derby DE23 . . . . .231 D6
Long Eaton, Breaston
NG10 . . . . .236 A7
Long Eaton, New Sawley
NG10 . . . . .236 C5
Birchwood Cl
7 Sheffield S20 . . . . .59 E8
South Normanton DE55 . . . . .160 A4
Birchwood Cres
Chesterfield S40 . . . . .114 F7
Somercotes DE55 . . . . .170 D8
Birchwood Croft S20 . . . . . . .59 E8
Birchwood Ct S40 . . . . .114 F7
Birchwood Dr DE56 . . . . .168 B4
Birchwood Gdns 6 S20 . . . . .59 E8
Birchwood Gr DE21 . . . . .59 E8
Birchwood La DE55 . . . . .170 A8
Birchwood Rd
Alfreton DE55 . . . . .159 C3
Eckington S21 . . . . .58 D4
Birchwood Rise 5 S20 . . . . . .59 E8
Birchwood View
Ashbourne DE6 . . . . .173 C3
Sheffield S20 . . . . .59 E8
Birchwood Way
18 Sheffield S20 . . . . .59 D8
Somercotes DE55 . . . . .159 C1
Bircumshaw's Rd DE75 . . . .181 E2
Birdcage Wlk DE22 . . . . .217 F6
Birdcroft La DE7 . . . . .208 F5
Birdholme Cres S40 . . . . . . .115 A7
Birdholme Inf Sch S40 . . . . .115 A7
Birding St NG19 . . . . .136 B1
Birdsgrove La
Ashbourne DE6 . . . . .172 D3
Mayfield DE6 . . . . .172 D4
Bird St S43 . . . . .78 F2
Birdwood St DE23 . . . . .218 F1
Birkdale Ave DE14 . . . . .254 A6
Birkdale Cl
Derby DE3 . . . . .218 A2
Ilkeston DE7 . . . . .194 D1
Birkdale Dr S40 . . . . .114 D8
Birk Hill Inf Sch S21 . . . . .59 C2
Birkin Av S42 . . . . .115 C1
Birkin La
Grassmoor S42 . . . . .115 C1
Holymoorside S42 . . . . .116 A3
Wingerworth S40, S42 . . . . . .114 C1
Birkin La W S42 . . . . .115 F2
Birkinstyle La DE55 . . . . .146 E3
Birkinstyle Rd DE55 . . . . . . .146 E3
Birkland Ave NG19 . . . . .136 B3
Birks Cl S80 . . . . .82 D6

Birley Brook Dr S40 . . . . .95 B7
Birley Com Coll S12 . . . . .44 E3
Birley Com Prim Sch S12 . .44 D3
Birley Croft S41 . . . . .95 B7
Birley La
Bamford S32 . . . . .40 F2
Sheffield S12 . . . . .44 D2
Birley Moor Ave S12 . . . . . . .44 E3
Birley Moor Cl S12 . . . . .44 E3
Birley Moor Cres S12 . . . . . .44 E2
Birley Moor Dr S12 . . . . .44 E2
Birley Moor Pl S12 . . . . .44 E2
Birley Moor Rd S12 . . . . .44 E4
Birley Moor Way S12 . . . . . .44 E2
Birley School Mews S13 . . .44 E5
Birley Spa Com Prim Sch
S12 . . . . .44 E4
Birley Spa La S12 . . . . .44 F3
Birley St NG9 . . . . .223 D5
Birley Vale Ave S12 . . . . .44 C5
Birley Vale Cl S12 . . . . .44 C4
Birstall Cl S41 . . . . .95 C7
Biscay Ct DE21 . . . . .206 C2
Bishop's Ct DE73 . . . . .252 A7
Bishop's Dr DE21 . . . . .205 E2
Bishop's Gn DE22 . . . . .218 D3
Bishop's House Mus★ S8 . .43 A4
Bishopdale Cl NG10 . . . . . . .236 A6
Bishopdale Dr S20 . . . . .59 A8
Bishopdale Rise S20 . . . . .59 A8
Bishop Lonsdale CE Prim Sch
DE22 . . . . .218 E3
Bishop Pastures Rd S8 . . . . .43 A5
Bishops Ct
Melbourne DE73 . . . . .252 B7
Sheffield S8 . . . . .43 B5
Bishops Gate DE11 . . . . .256 E2
Bishops La SK17 . . . . .84 E7
Bishop St
Alfreton DE55 . . . . .159 A5
Eastwood NG16 . . . . .182 F2
Bisham Dr NG9 . . . . .223 F2
Bitham Ct DE13 . . . . .240 C1
Bitham La DE13 . . . . .240 D1
Blaby Cl DE23 . . . . .231 E6
Blacka Moor Cres S17 . . . . . .55 C6
Blacka Moor Rd S17 . . . . .55 C6
Blacka Moor View S17 . . . . .55 C6
Blackberry Cl S40 . . . . .80 D4
Blackberry Flats S20 . . . . .59 E7
Blackberry Way DE56 . . . . . .179 F2
Blackbird Row DE56 . . . . . . .179 C1
Blackbrook La SK23 . . . . .47 E6
Blackburn Pl DE7 . . . . .194 E3
Blackdown Ave S40 . . . . .95 B5
Blackfordby St Margaret's CE
Prim Sch DE11 . . . . .257 C1
Black Harry La S32 . . . . .71 B2
Black Hills Dr DE7 . . . . .208 F6
Blackmore St DE23 . . . . .231 F7
Blackmount Ct 5 DE24 . . . .231 D3
Blackpit La DE6 . . . . .224 B8
Blackpool St DE14 . . . . .254 C8
Black Rock★ DE4 . . . . .155 A4
Blackrocks Ave DE4 . . . . . . .142 F7
Blackshaw Clough SK13 . . . .10 E3
Blackshaw Rd SK13 . . . . .10 E2
Blacks La S42 . . . . .131 F7
Blacksmith's La
Egginton DE65 . . . . .241 A6
Newton Solney DE15 . . . . . . .248 E8
Woodville DE11 . . . . .256 F3
Blacksmith Croft DE5 . . . . .180 D7
Blacksmith La S44 . . . . .97 A3
Blacksmiths Cl
Glapwell S44 . . . . .118 C1
Nethersael DE12 . . . . .264 F7
Blacksmiths Yd
Darley Dale DE4 . . . . .127 E2
Rolleston DE13 . . . . .240 B4
Blacksmith Way NG20 . . . . .119 F2
Blackstock Cl S14 . . . . .43 D2
Blackstock Cres S14 . . . . . . .43 D2
Blackstock Dr S14 . . . . .43 D2
Blackstock Rd S14 . . . . .43 D4
Blackstone Cl DE55 . . . . . . .170 D7
Blackthorn Cl
Chesterfield S41 . . . . .115 D8
Derby DE21 . . . . .205 E2
Melbourne DE73 . . . . .252 A8
Blackthorn Dr NG16 . . . . . . .182 E2
Blackthorne Cl DE55 . . . . . . .159 B5
Blackthorn Rd DE15 . . . . . . .254 E6
Black Tor Rd DE4 . . . . .154 D8
Blackwall La DE4 . . . . .176 A8
Blackwell Ave DE7 . . . . .194 F5
Blackwell Com Prim Sch
DE55 . . . . .147 F1
Blackwell La
Melbourne DE73 . . . . .252 A7
Monyash DE45 . . . . .107 B3
Blackwell Mill Cotts SK17 . .87 A6
Blackwell Rd NG17 . . . . .148 E8
Bladon House Sch DE15 . . .248 B6
Bladon St DE15 . . . . .248 C4
Bladon View DE13 . . . . .241 A2
Blagdon Cl DE4 . . . . .127 C3
Blagreaves Ave DE23 . . . . . .231 C5
Blagreaves La DE23 . . . . .231 C6
Blair Gr NG10 . . . . .223 B3
Blair Ho DE23 . . . . .231 C5
Blakebrook Dr DE73 . . . . . . .233 A3
Blake Ct NG10 . . . . .236 B5
Blakeley La DE65 . . . . .229 B2
Blakelow Dr DE65 . . . . .229 B3
Blakelow La DE4 . . . . .142 A3
Blakemere La DE4 . . . . .141 F1

Blakemore Ave DE73 . . . . 252 B8
Blakeney Ct
  Derby DE21 . . . . 206 C1
  3 Mansfield Woodhouse
  NG19 . . . . 136 E4
Blake Rd NG9 . . . . 223 E6
Blake St
  Ilkeston DE7 . . . . 194 F1
  Mansfield Woodhouse
  NG19 . . . . 136 B2
Blanch Croft DE73 . . . . . . 252 B7
Blandford Ave NG10 . . . . 236 B6
Blandford Cl DE24 . . . . . . 233 D6
Blandford Dr S41 . . . . 95 E7
Blankney Cl DE24 . . . . 231 D2
Blay Ct S41 . . . . 77 D4
Bleaklow Wlk 25 SK13 . . . 9 E3
Blencathra Dr DE3 . . . . . . 230 E8
Blenheim Ave DE55 . . . . . 170 A8
Blenheim Cl
  Burton u T DE15 . . . . 248 C3
  4 Glossop SK13 . . . . 10 A5
  Mansfield NG19 . . . . 136 D1
  3 Swadlincote DE11 . . . 256 A7
Blenheim Ct DE56 . . . . . . 179 D5
Blenheim Dr DE22 . . . . . . 204 D4
Blenheim Ho 1 DE14 . . . . 253 F7
Blenheim Mews DE65 . . . 229 C4
Blenheim Par DE22 . . . . . . 204 D4
Blenheim Pl NG17 . . . . . . 148 E3
Blenheim Rd DE6 . . . . 185 E7
Blenhiem Ct 3 NG10 . . . . 223 B4
Blind La
  Bolsover S44 . . . . 98 F3
  Breaston DE72 . . . . 235 D8
  Darley Dale DE4 . . . . 127 F1
  Kirk Ireton DE6 . . . . 165 A2
  Wirksworth DE4 . . . . 165 F8
Blisworth Way DE55 . . . . 169 F8
Blithe Cl DE65 . . . . 228 E1
Blithfield Gdns DE73 . . . . 233 A2
Bloomery Way S45 . . . . . . 131 E3
Bloomfield Cl
  Derby DE1 . . . . 267 C1
  Hilton DE65 . . . . 228 D1
Bloomfield Rd DE55 . . . . . 170 A8
Bloomfield St DE1 . . . . . . 267 D1
Bloomsgrove Rd DE7 . . . . 194 F2
Bloom St DE1 . . . . 267 B2
Blore Cl DE6 . . . . 185 D8
Blossom Cres S12 . . . . 44 B3
Blossom Wlk DE65 . . . . . . 227 C1
Bluebank View S43 . . . . . . 77 D3
Bluebell Cl
  Barlborough S43 . . . . 80 B6
  Derby DE21 . . . . 231 D2
  Donisthorpe DE12 . . . . . . 262 E1
  Hayfield SK22 . . . . 25 C3
  Shirebrook NG20 . . . . 119 D3
  Somercotes DE55 . . . . . . 159 E2
  Underwood Green NG16 . . 171 F2
Blue Bell Cl S43 . . . . 97 B5
Bluebell Croft DE4 . . . . . . 143 B3
Bluebell Hill DE55 . . . . . . 146 C4
Bluebell Pl NG19 . . . . 136 F4
Bluebell Way DE75 . . . . . . 182 B1
Blueberry Cl S43 . . . . 97 C4
Blueberry Way DE11 . . . . 256 F3
Bluebird Ct DE24 . . . . 231 D4
Blue Cedars Dr DE15 . . . . 248 D2
Blue John Cavern* S33 . . 37 E3
Blue Lodge Cl S43 . . . . . . 97 B5
Blue Mountains DE56 . . . . 191 B1
Bluestone La DE11 . . . . . . 255 A7
Blundestone La DE4 . . . . . 156 A2
Blunt Ave S44 . . . . 79 C4
Blunt St DE7 . . . . 193 A2
Blyth Cl
  Chesterfield S40 . . . . 114 B8
  Mansfield NG19 . . . . 135 D1
Blyth Ct DE74 . . . . 247 B4
Blythe Ct NG19 . . . . 135 D1
Blyth Pl DE21 . . . . 205 D1
Boam La DE4 . . . . 142 F8
Boardman Ind Est DE11 . . 253 B2
Boardman Rd DE11 . . . . . . 255 E2
Boarfold La SK13, SK14 . . 15 E5
Boars Head Ind Est DE1 . 267 C4
Boarslack La SK17 . . . . 69 F2
Boarstones La SK17 . . . . . . 85 E8
Boat La NG16 . . . . 182 A7
Boatmans Cl DE7 . . . . 194 F2
Bobbin Mill SK17 . . . . 89 A6
Bobbinmill Hill DE56 . . . . 168 B7
Bobbin Mill La S40 . . . . . . 95 D2
Bobbin Way DE56 . . . . 179 C5
Bochum Parkway S8 . . . . . 57 C8
Bocking La S8 . . . . 56 E8
Bocking Rise S8 . . . . 56 E8
Boden St DE23 . . . . 219 B2
Bodmin Cl DE24 . . . . 231 D3
Bodmin Way 3 S40 . . . . . . 95 C5
Boggard La SK13 . . . . 16 C6
Bogguard Rd SK6 . . . . 24 A4
Boggy La
  Bradwell S33 . . . . 51 B6
  Church Broughton DE65 . . 227 A7
  Church Broughton, Heathtop
  DE65 . . . . 227 A6
Bog La DE72 . . . . 251 E5
Bohem Rd NG10 . . . . 223 C3
Boiley La S21 . . . . 60 C4
Boland Rd S8 . . . . 56 D5
Bolden Terr DE55 . . . . 147 C1
Bold La DE1 . . . . 267 B3
Bole Hill S8 . . . . 43 A2
Bole Hill Cotts S44 . . . . . . 97 A1
Bolehill Croft DE4 . . . . . . 155 A3

Bolehill Ct 3 S40 . . . . 95 D5
Bolehill La
  Eckington S21 . . . . 58 F2
  Northedge S42 . . . . 130 C7
  Wingerworth S42 . . . . . . 114 D1
Bolehill Rd DE4 . . . . 155 A3
Bolsover Bsns Pk S44 . . . 98 E2
Bolsover Castle* S44 . . . . 99 A2
Bolsover CE Jun Sch S44 . 99 A2
Bolsover Cl DE5 . . . . 169 E1
Bolsover Hill S44 . . . . 99 A2
Bolsover Inf Sch S44 . . . . 99 B2
Bolsover Local Hospl S44 . 99 C2
Bolsover Rd
  Mastin Moor S43 . . . . 79 D2
  Shuttlewood S44 . . . . 98 F6
Bolsover Sch The S44 . . . . 99 C1
Bolton St DE55 . . . . 169 D7
Boman's La DE56 . . . . 177 F8
Bonchurch Cl DE24 . . . . . 233 C6
Bondfield Rd S43 . . . . 97 C7
Bondgate DE74 . . . . 247 B3
Bondhay La S80 . . . . 62 C2
Bond La DE56 . . . . 168 E2
Bond St S43 . . . . 97 C8
Bonington Rise SK6 . . . . . 23 B8
Bonner's Rd NG16 . . . . . . 195 C4
Bonnington Dr DE55 . . . . 170 D8
Bonnyrigg Dr DE21 . . . . . 206 A2
Bonsall Ave DE23 . . . . 231 D8
Bonsall Bank SK13 . . . . . . 9 E2
Bonsall CE Prim Sch
  DE4 . . . . 142 E1
Bonsall Cl SK13 . . . . 9 E2
Bonsall Ct
  2 Chesterfield S41 . . . . . 95 D7
  Long Eaton NG10 . . . . . . 236 F8
Bonsall Dr
  Derby DE3 . . . . 217 D3
  Somercotes DE55 . . . . . . 170 D8
Bonsall Fold SK13 . . . . 9 E2
Bonsall La
  Alfreton DE55 . . . . 158 F4
  Winster DE4 . . . . 141 C4
Bonsallmoor La DE4 . . . . 141 E3
Bonsall St NG10 . . . . 236 E8
Bonser Cres NG17 . . . . . . 148 E2
Booth's Ct 1 SK13 . . . . . . 10 D1
Booth Ave NG19 . . . . 135 A5
Boothby Ave 1 DE6 . . . . . 173 C2
Booth Cres NG19 . . . . 135 D2
Booth Dr DE6 . . . . 185 C8
Boothgate DE56 . . . . 179 E2
Boot Hill DE65 . . . . 242 C3
Booth St
  Derby DE24 . . . . 232 F7
  Hollingworth SK14 . . . . . . 9 C5
  Mansfield Woodhouse
  NG19 . . . . 136 B3
  Ripley DE5 . . . . 169 E2
Booth Trad Est NE7 . . . . . 194 F2
Boots Yd NG17 . . . . 148 F3
Border Cl S43 . . . . 80 F3
Border Cres DE24 . . . . 233 B5
Border La S80 . . . . 80 F2
Borlace Cres NG9 . . . . 223 E6
Borough St DE74 . . . . 247 B3
Borrowash By-pass
  DE72 . . . . 221 C3
Borrowash Rd DE21 . . . . . 220 F4
Borrowdale Ave 3 S20 . . . 59 E6
Borrowdale Cl 2 S20 . . . . 59 E6
Borrowdale Dr
  Long Eaton NG10 . . . . . . 236 A6
  Sheffield S20 . . . . 59 E6
Borrowdale Rd S20 . . . . . . 59 E6
Borrowfield Rd DE21 . . . . 220 F3
Borrowfields DE72 . . . . . . 221 B1
Borrow Wood Inf Sch
  DE21 . . . . 220 F5
Borrow Wood Jun Sch
  DE21 . . . . 220 F5
Boscastle Rd DE24 . . . . . . 233 B6
Boscawen Ct NE7 . . . . 194 F4
Boscowan Ct DE7 . . . . 194 F4
Bosley Mews DE56 . . . . . . 178 F5
Bostock's La
  Long Eaton NG10 . . . . . . 223 A3
  Risley NG10, DE72 . . . . . . 222 F4
Bostock Rd SK14 . . . . 16 A8
Boston Cl DE21 . . . . 220 C6
Boswell Ct 3 DE6 . . . . 173 B2
Boswell Sq DE23 . . . . 231 F7
Bosworth Ave DE23 . . . . . 231 E6
Bosworth Rd DE11 . . . . . . 246 F3
Bosworth Way NG10 . . . . 236 E5
Botany Bsns Pk SK23 . . . . 45 D6
Botany Dr DE7 . . . . 194 F5
Botany Mews SK23 . . . . . . 45 E6
Bothe Cl NG10 . . . . 236 C6
Bottlebrook Houses DE5 . 180 B1
Bottomhill Rd SK17 . . . . . 69 E1
Bottom Lons DE6 . . . . 176 B8
Bottom Rd S42 . . . . 114 E1
Boughton Dr DE55 . . . . . . 169 F8
Boughton La S43 . . . . 80 D4
Bould St NG19 . . . . 135 F1
Boulevard The SK14 . . . . . 9 D4
Boulton Cl S40 . . . . 95 A5
Boulton Dr DE24 . . . . 233 A6
Boulton La
  Derby, Allenton DE24 . . . . 232 F5
  Derby DE24 . . . . 219 A1
Boulton Prim Sch DE24 . . 233 A6
Boundary Cl
  Shirebrook NG20 . . . . 119 C6
  Staveley S43 . . . . 79 A3
Boundary Gdns DE55 . . . . 147 F5

Boundary La NG16 . . . . . . 182 C3
Boundary Rd
  Derby DE22 . . . . 218 E4
  Egginton DE65 . . . . 241 D8
Boundary Wlk NG20 . . . . 100 F1
Bournebrook Ave DE4 . . . 165 F7
Bourne Cl
  Brimington S43 . . . . 96 E8
  Tutbury DE13 . . . . 239 B6
Bourne Dr NG16 . . . . 182 B3
Bourne Mill Cl S43 . . . . . . 80 B6
Bourne Sq DE72 . . . . 235 E7
Bourne St DE1 . . . . 267 B2
Bourne Way DE11 . . . . . . 256 D4
Bowbank Cl DE23 . . . . 231 A6
Bowbridge Ave DE23 . . . . 231 C5
Bowden Cl SK22 . . . . 25 C3
Bowden Cres S22 . . . . 33 D8
Bowden Hey Rd SK23 . . . . 47 C7
Bowden La
  Chapel-en-le-F SK23 . . . . 47 C7
  Hope S33 . . . . 39 A4
Bowden Rd SK13 . . . . 10 C3
Bowdon Ave S43 . . . . 80 A6
Bower Dr DE14 . . . . 254 C5
Bower Farm Rd S41 . . . . . 77 B2
Bower St DE24 . . . . 232 F8
Boweswell Rd DE7 . . . . . . 194 E2
Bowland Cl DE3 . . . . 217 E1
Bowland Dr S40 . . . . 114 B7
Bowland Rd SK13 . . . . 17 A8
Bowlees Ct DE23 . . . . 230 E7
Bowler Dr DE56 . . . . 192 A7
Bowler La
  Darley Dale DE4 . . . . 143 B8
  Matlock DE4 . . . . 143 B8
Bowler Rd DE4 . . . . 127 C3
Bowler St DE5 . . . . 180 D7
Bowling Alley DE56 . . . . . 168 E1
Bowlingalley La DE56 . . . 197 D8
Bowling Alley La DE6 . . . . 212 A5
Bowling Cl DE7 . . . . 222 E8
Bowling Gn DE4 . . . . 153 A1
Bowling Green La DE4 . . . 154 E1
Bowman Cl S12 . . . . 43 F2
Bowmer La DE56 . . . . 168 B6
Bowmer Rd DE24 . . . . 219 E1
Bown Cl DE56 . . . . 192 A8
Bowness Cl
  Chesterfield S41 . . . . 95 D7
  Sheffield S18 . . . . 56 E1
Bowness Rd S41 . . . . 95 D7
Bowns Hill DE4 . . . . 157 A1
Bowns Yd DE55 . . . . 170 D8
Bowshaw S18 . . . . 56 F4
Bowshaw Ave S8 . . . . 57 A5
Bowshaw Cl S8 . . . . 57 A5
Bowshaw View S8 . . . . 57 A5
Bow St NG19 . . . . 136 E4
Box Cl DE11 . . . . 256 A3
Boxmoor Cl DE23 . . . . 230 F7
Boyd Gr DE73 . . . . 245 A8
Boyer St DE22 . . . . 267 A1
Boyer Wlk DE22 . . . . 267 A1
Boylestone Rd DE23 . . . . . 231 C5
Boythorpe Ave S40 . . . . . 266 A4
Boythorpe Bsns Units S40 95 E2
Boythorpe Cres S40 . . . . . 266 A3
Boythorpe Mount S40 . . . 266 A2
Boythorpe Rd S40 . . . . . . 266 A2
Boythorpe Rise S40 . . . . . 95 C2
Brabyns Brow SK6 . . . . . . 23 A7
Bracken's La DE24 . . . . . . 232 F6
Bracken Ave S44 . . . . 116 F1
Bracken Cl
  Hollingworth SK14 . . . . . . 9 D6
  Long Eaton NG10 . . . . . . 223 B1
  Marple SK6 . . . . 23 C7
Brackendale Ave S45 . . . . 131 E2
Brackendale Cl S43 . . . . . . 96 D7
Brackendale La DE56 . . . . 163 E5
Brackendale Rd DE55 . . . . 169 F8
Brackenfield Ave NG16 . . 195 B7
Brackenfield Dr NG16 . . . 195 B7
Brackenfield Gr S12 . . . . . 44 E5
Brackenfield La
  Brackenfield DE55 . . . . . . 145 D1
  Wessington DE55 . . . . . . 157 D8
Brackenfield Specl Sch
  NG10 . . . . 223 B1
Brackenfield Inf Sch
  DE22 . . . . 218 B6
Brackendale Jun Sch
  DE22 . . . . 218 B6
Brackens La S43 . . . . 80 B6
Bracken Way S13 . . . . 177 E7
Brackenwood Rd DE55 . . 254 E6
Brackley S45 . . . . 131 F6
Brackley Dr DE21 . . . . 220 E5
Brackley Gate DE7 . . . . . . 192 A2
Brackmills Cl 7 NG19 . . . 136 E1
Bracknell Dr DE24 . . . . . . 232 F5
Bradbourne Cl S43 . . . . . . 97 C8
Bradbourne Ct DE22 . . . . 218 E3
Bradbury Cl
  Borrowash DE72 . . . . 221 C1
  Chesterfield S40 . . . . 95 E3
Bradbury Dr S42 . . . . 114 E4
Bradbury St S43 . . . . 43 A6
Braddon Ave NG9 . . . . . . 209 E1
Bradgate Cl NG10 . . . . . . 223 B4
Bradgate Croft S41 . . . . . . 115 C7

Bradgate Ct DE23 . . . . 231 E6
Bradgate Dr DE5 . . . . 169 B1
Brading Cl DE24 . . . . 233 D5
Bradley CE Prim Sch
  DE6 . . . . 186 F8
Bradley Cl
  Birchover DE4 . . . . 126 B1
  6 Brimington S43 . . . . . . 96 E8
Bradley Dr DE56 . . . . 179 B4
Bradley La S18 . . . . 75 C4
Bradley St
  Burton u T DE15 . . . . 254 E7
  Derby DE22 . . . . 218 E8
  Sandiacre NG10 . . . . 223 C5
Bradley View 5 DE6 . . . . . 173 D3
Bradley Way S43 . . . . 96 E7
Bradmoor Gr DE73 . . . . . . 232 E7
Bradshaw Ave DE55 . . . . . 170 E6
Bradshaw Cres SK6 . . . . . 23 A2
Bradshaw Croft DE56 . . . . 178 E6
Bradshaw Dr DE56 . . . . . . 191 C6
Bradshaw La
  Old Brampton S42 . . . . . . 93 E2
  Stoney Middleton S32 . . . 70 E8
Bradshaw Mdw DE65 . . . . 227 C1
Bradshaw Rd
  Marple SK6 . . . . 23 A7
  Staveley S43 . . . . 97 B6
Bradshaw Way NG10 . . . . 236 B5
Bradway Cl S17 . . . . 56 B5
Bradway Dr S17 . . . . 56 B5
Bradway Grange Rd S17 . 56 C5
Bradway Rd
  Sheffield, Bradway S17 . . 56 B5
  Sheffield, Lower Bradway
  S17 . . . . 56 C6
Bradwell CE Inf Sch S33 . 51 B7
Bradwell Cl
  Derby DE3 . . . . 217 E1
  Dronfield S18 . . . . 56 C1
  Eastwood NG16 . . . . 195 C8
Bradwell Cl 4 S40 . . . . 95 D5
Bradwell Fold 10 SK13 . . . 9 E1
Bradwell Gr S45 . . . . 131 D2
Bradwell Head Rd S33 . . . 51 A8
Bradwell Jun Sch S33 . . . 51 A7
Bradwell Lea 12 SK13 . . . . 9 E1
Bradwell Pl S43 . . . . 97 C7
Bradwell St 1 S2 . . . . 43 B6
Bradwell Terr 11 SK13 . . . 9 E1
Bradwell Way DE56 . . . . . 179 B5
Braeburn Ct S42 . . . . 218 E2
Braefield Cl DE7 . . . . 208 C5
Braemar Ave NG16 . . . . . . 182 F1
Braemar Cl
  Chesterfield S43 . . . . 77 D4
  11 Derby DE24 . . . . 231 D3
Brafield Cl DE56 . . . . 179 D4
Brailsford Ave
  4 Gamesley SK13 . . . . . . 9 E2
  3 Swadlincote DE11 . . . 255 E5
Brailsford CE Prim Sch
  DE6 . . . . 201 E7
Brailsford Cl 7 SK13 . . . . . 9 E2
Brailsford Gdns 8 SK13 . . 9 E2
Brailsford Gn 5 SK13 . . . . 9 E2
Brailsford Mews 6 SK13 . . 9 E2
Brailsford Rd DE21 . . . . . . 219 F8
Braintree Cl DE21 . . . . 205 D2
Braithwell Cl DE22 . . . . . . 204 F2
Bramah Edge Ct SK13 . . . 9 F7
Bramall Ct S2 . . . . 43 A8
Bramall La S2 . . . . 43 A8
Bramble Bank SK13 . . . . . 17 E8
Brambleberry Ct DE21 . . . 206 B3
Bramble Cl
  Holmewood S44 . . . . 116 F1
  Long Eaton NG10 . . . . . . 223 B2
  Shirebrook NG20 . . . . 119 E6
  South Normanton DE55 . . 160 B6
Bramble Ct DE15 . . . . 254 E6
Bramble Mews 2 DE4 . . . 217 D1
Bramble St DE1 . . . . 267 A3
Bramble Way
  Kilburn DE56 . . . . 179 F2
  South Normanton DE55 . . 159 F3
Bramblewick Dr DE23 . . . 231 A6
Bramblewood 5 DE11 . . . 255 F6
Brambling Cres DE3 . . . . . 230 B6
Brambling Cl S41 . . . . 96 C2
Bramell Cl DE14 . . . . 253 F7
Bramfield Ave DE22 . . . . . 218 E4
Bramfield Ct DE22 . . . . . . 218 E4
Bramham Rd SK6 . . . . 23 A4
Bramley Ave S13 . . . . 44 F8
Bramley Cl
  Derby DE21 . . . . 206 C3
  Sheffield S20 . . . . 59 C7
  Staveley S43 . . . . 97 B5
Bramley Ct
  Hatton DE65 . . . . 227 C1
  Kimberley NG16 . . . . 195 F6
Bramley Dale DE11 . . . . . 255 F2
Bramley Hall Rd S13 . . . . 44 F8
Bramley La
  Baslow DE45 . . . . 91 C7
  Sheffield S13 . . . . 44 F8
Bramley Mews S21 . . . . . . 59 D3
Bramleymoor La S21 . . . . 58 E1
Bramley Park Cl S13 . . . . . 44 F8
Bramley Pk S21 . . . . 58 F3
Bramley Rd
  Bramley-Vale S44 . . . . . . 117 E1
  Eckington S21 . . . . 58 E1
Bramley St DE55 . . . . 170 E6

Bramley Vale Prim Sch
  S44 . . . . 117 E1
Bramlyn Cl S43 . . . . 80 D5
Bramlyn Ct S43 . . . . 80 D5
Brampton Ave DE75 . . . . . 182 A2
Brampton Cl DE3 . . . . 217 C3
Brampton Ct
  Belper DE56 . . . . 179 C2
  Chesterfield S40 . . . . 95 C2
Brampton Dr NG9 . . . . 223 F5
Brampton House Mews
  S40 . . . . 95 D3
Brampton Prim Sch S40 . . 95 D3
Bramshill Rise S40 . . . . . . 95 D1
Branch La S45 . . . . 132 F5
Brancliffe La S81 . . . . 63 F8
Brandelhow Cl DE21 . . . . 206 C3
Brandene Cl S44 . . . . 97 A3
Brandreth Dr NG16 . . . . . 195 A8
Branklene Cl NG16 . . . . . . 195 E7
Branksome Ave DE24 . . . . 233 C6
Branksome Chine Ave
  S41 . . . . 115 C8
Bransdale Ave NG19 . . . . 136 E1
Bransdale Cl NG10 . . . . . . 236 B6
Branston Rd
  Burton u T DE14 . . . . 254 C8
  Tatenhill DE13, DE14 . . . 253 C8
Branton Cl S40 . . . . 266 A1
Brassington Cl
  Eastwood NG16 . . . . 195 B7
  West Hallam DE7 . . . . 207 E8
  Youlgreave DE45 . . . . 125 C5
Brassington Cres SK13 . . . 9 D1
Brassington Ct 4 NG16 . . 195 B7
Brassington La S42, S45 . . 131 C6
Brassington Prim Sch
  DE4 . . . . 153 A1
Brassington Rd DE21 . . . . 205 F1
Brassington St S45 . . . . . . 131 D4
Braybrook Cl DE55 . . . . . . 169 F8
Brayfield Ave DE23 . . . . . 231 D8
Brayfield Rd DE23 . . . . . . 231 D8
Breach La
  Barrow u T DE73 . . . . 244 E1
  Hatton DE65 . . . . 227 D3
  Scropton DE65 . . . . 226 C5
Breach Rd
  Denby DE5 . . . . 181 A4
  Heanor DE75 . . . . 194 A8
Breadsall CE Prim Sch
  DE21 . . . . 205 E4
Breadsall Cl DE11 . . . . . . 256 A7
Breadsall Ct DE21 . . . . . . 194 F3
Breadsall Hill Top Inf Sch
  DE21 . . . . 205 E1
Breadsall Hill Top Jun Sch
  DE21 . . . . 205 E1
Breamfield La DE4 . . . . . . 166 B8
Brearley Ave S43 . . . . 77 D3
Brearley Ct S41 . . . . 77 B3
Brearley Hall S41 . . . . 77 C4
Brearley St S41 . . . . 77 C3
Breaston Ind Est DE72 . . 235 C7
Breaston La DE72 . . . . 222 D3
Brechin Cl NG19 . . . . 136 B6
Breckbank NG19 . . . . 136 E1
Breck La S21, S43 . . . . 78 C6
Breckland Rd S40, S42 . . . 114 B8
Brecknock Dr NG10 . . . . . 236 A7
Brecon Cl
  Chesterfield S40 . . . . 95 C5
  Derby DE21 . . . . 220 E6
  6 Long Eaton NG10 . . . . 236 A8
Bredon Cl 7 NG10 . . . . . . 236 A8
Breedon Ave DE23 . . . . . . 231 D6
Breedon Hill Rd DE23 . . . 218 F3
Breedon on the Hill St
  Hardulph's CE Prim Sch
  DE73 . . . . 252 F3
Breedon St NG10 . . . . 223 C2
Brendan Gdns DE22 . . . . . 204 E1
Brenden Ave NG16 . . . . . . 170 C7
Brenden Cl DE55 . . . . 170 C8
Brendon Ave S40 . . . . 95 C4
Brendon Cl SK13 . . . . 17 A8
Brendon Ct 3 S40 . . . . 95 C4
Brendon Dr NG16 . . . . 195 F7
Brendon Way NG10 . . . . . 223 A8
Brent Cl S40 . . . . 95 D5
Brentford Dr DE22 . . . . . . 218 B6
Brentnall Cl NG10 . . . . . . 236 B7
Brentwood Ave S33 . . . . . 40 B3
Brentwood Rd DE23 . . . . . 40 B3
Bren Way DE65 . . . . 228 E2
Bretby Bsns Pk DE15 . . . . 255 F8
Bretby Fairways DE15 . . . 248 F2
Bretby Hollow DE11 . . . . . 255 F7
Bretby Hts DE15 . . . . 256 A8
Bretby La
  Bretby DE15 . . . . 248 E3
  Burton u T DE15 . . . . 248 D2
Bretby Rd
  Chesterfield S40 . . . . 95 A6
  Swadlincote DE11 . . . . . . 255 F7
Bretby Sq DE23 . . . . 231 C5
Bretby Views Way DE15 . . 257 A4
Bretby Wood DE15 . . . . . . 255 A6
Bretton Ave
  Bolsover S44 . . . . 99 C2
  Derby DE23 . . . . 218 C2
Bretton Cl S40 . . . . 95 A5
Bretton Gr S12 . . . . 44 D3
Bretton Rd DE56 . . . . 179 C5

Brewery St
Chesterfield S41 .... 266 C3
Kimberley NG16 .... 195 F6
Breydon Cl DE24 .... 232 D4
Breydon Ind Ctr NG10 .. 236 F7
Brian Clough Way
Derby DE21 .... 220 C4
Risley DE72 .... 222 C3
Stapleford NG9 .... 223 D5
Briar's La DE4 .... 168 A7
Briar Ave NG10 .... 223 A3
Briar Briggs Rd S44 ..... 98 F2
Briar Cl
Alfreton DE55 .... 159 C3
Borrowash DE72 .... 221 C2
Chesterfield S41 .... 95 E5
Derby DE21 .... 220 B5
Shirebrook NG20 .... 119 E2
Swadlincote DE11 .... 255 F5
Briardene Cl S40 .... 94 F5
Briarfield Ave S12 ...... 44 A3
Briarfield Cres S12 ..... 44 A2
Briarfield Rd S12 .... 44 A3
Briar Gate NG10 .... 223 B1
Briargrove Rd SK22 ..... 24 C4
Briar Lea Cl DE24 ...... 231 F4
Briar Rd NG16 .... 195 B8
Briars Cl S21 .... 60 D5
Briarsgate DE22 .... 204 D2
Briars Way DE5 .... 180 D8
Briar View S43 .... 96 E7
Briarwood Cres SK6 .... 23 A3
Briarwood Way DE23 ... 231 C6
Brickbridge Rd S40 ..... 23 A5
Brickfields Cl DE4 ...... 155 A4
Brickfield St SK13 ...... 10 B5
Brickhouse La S17 ...... 55 C8
Brickhouse Yd S40 ...... 95 E3
Brickkiln La DE7 .... 206 C8
Brick-kiln La
Braisford DE6 .... 186 F1
Hulland Ward DE6 ...... 175 C5
Brick Kiln La DE13 ..... 240 A3
Brick Row DE22 .... 205 A1
Brick St DE1 .... 218 E6
Brickyard Cotts DE6 .... 185 D8
Brickyard La
Kilburn DE56 .... 179 F2
Ripley DE5 .... 169 F1
South Normanton DE55 .. 160 A6
Brickyard Rd DE56 ..... 168 C5
Brickyard The DE7 ...... 193 B1
Bricky Cl S43 .... 80 D5
Bridge Bank Cl S40 ..... 95 D6
Bridge Cl
Swadlincote DE11 .... 256 C2
Whitwell S80 .... 82 A5
Bridge End Rd NG16 .... 171 F8
Bridge Farm S DE13 ... 240 E1
Bridgefield 4 SK13 ..... 17 B8
Bridge Field DE72 ...... 235 C7
Bridgefield Cl 11 DE56 .. 178 F4
Bridge Foot DE56 .... 178 F5
Bridge Hill DE56 .... 178 E5
Bridgeholm Mill SK23 ... 47 A8
Bridgend Cl NG9 .... 223 D5
Bridgend Ct DE21 ...... 206 C2
Bridgeness Rd DE23 .... 230 F6
Bridgeport Rd DE21 .... 220 C6
Bridgeside DE13 .... 240 E1
Bridge St
Bakewell DE45 .... 109 D6
Belper DE56 .... 178 F4
Bradwell S33 .... 51 A7
Burton u t, Stretton DE13 . 240 E1
Buxton SK17 .... 85 C8
Chesterfield S40 .... 266 B1
Clay Cross S45 .... 131 C3
Derby DE1 .... 267 A4
Ilkeston DE7 .... 194 F4
Killamarsh S21 .... 60 D6
Langley Mill NG16 ...... 182 C3
Linton DE11 .... 261 E8
New Mills SK22 .... 24 C1
Pilsley S45 .... 132 C2
Sandiacre NG10 .... 223 C5
Swadlincote DE11 ...... 256 C2
Tupton S42 .... 115 D1
Tutbury DE13 .... 239 C7
Whaley Bridge SK23 .... 45 E7
Bridle La
Ripley, Greenwich DE5 .. 169 E2
Ripley, Lower Hartshay DE5,
DE56 .... 169 A2
Somercotes DE55 .... 170 B7
Swadlincote DE11 ...... 255 A5
Bridle Rd
Bolsover S44 .... 80 B1
Staveley S43 .... 79 B2
Bridle Stile S20 .... 59 C7
Bridle Stile Cl S20 ..... 59 C7
Bridle Stile Gdns S20 ... 59 B7
Bridleway SK22 .... 24 D1
Bridleway The NG19 .... 136 F1

Brierfield Way DE3 ..... 230 E8
Brierley Cl S43 .... 78 E1
Brierley Pk S23 .... 34 B1
Brierley Rd
Stonebroom DE55 ...... 146 F3
Unstone Green S18 ..... 76 E6
Brierlow Bar SK17 ..... 105 B8
Brigden Ave DE24 ...... 232 E2
Brigg Inf Sch The DE5 .. 160 B6
Brighstone Cl DE24 .... 233 C5
Brightman Ho DE11 .... 256 B5
Bright Mdw S20 .... 60 A5
Brighton Rd DE24 ...... 232 F8
Bright Sq NG19 .... 135 D2
Bright St
Derby DE22 .... 218 D5
Ilkeston DE7 .... 194 E3
Kimberley NG16 .... 195 E6
North Wingfield S42 .... 131 F6
South Normanton DE55 .. 159 F5
Brigmor Wlk DE22 ..... 218 C5
Brimington Cl NE7 ..... 194 F6
Brimington 6 NG19 ... 136 E4
Brimington Jun Sch S43 . 96 D8
Brimington Rd N4 ..... 96 B8
Brimmesfield Cl S2 .... 43 F7
Brimmesfield Dr S2 .... 43 E8
Brimmesfield Rd S2 .... 43 E7
Brincliffe Cl S40 .... 95 B1
Brindle Way DE23 ...... 231 A5
Brindley Cl S8 .... 43 A4
Brindley Cres S8 .... 43 A4
Brindley Ct S21 .... 60 C6
Brindley Ho
Chesterfield S41 .... 96 B6
Long Eaton NG10 ...... 223 B3
Brindley Rd S41 .... 96 A6
Brindley Way S43 ...... 78 F2
Brindley Wlk DE24 ..... 231 E2
Brinkburn Cl S17 ...... 55 F6
Brinkburn Ct S17 ...... 55 F6
Brinkburn Dr S17 ...... 55 F6
Brinkburn Vale Rd S17 .. 55 F6
Brinsley Hill NG16 ..... 171 C2
Brinsley Prim Sch NG16 . 182 D8
Brisbane Cl NG19 ...... 136 C6
Brisbane Dr NG9 .... 209 F1
Brisbane Rd DE3 .... 217 F3
Briset Cl DE24 .... 231 E2
Bristol Dr DE3 .... 217 E2
Bristol Rd DE7 .... 194 E1
Britannia Ave DE5 ..... 181 A7
Britannia Ct DE1 .... 267 B4
Britannia Dr DE13 ..... 240 D1
Britannia Rd
Chesterfield S40 .... 115 B7
Long Eaton NG10 ...... 223 D1
Briton Lodge Cl DE12 .. 262 F4
Brittain Dr DE5 .... 170 A1
Brittain Pit Farm* DE5 . 170 A4
Brixham Ct S41 .... 95 F8
Brizlincote La DE15 .... 248 D1
Broad Bank DE22 ..... 218 E8
Broadbottom CE Prim Sch
SK14 .... 15 F8
Broadbottom Rd SK14 .. 9 A3
Broadbottom Sta SK14 .. 16 A8
Broadfield Rd S2 ...... 43 A7
Broadfields Cl DE22 .... 218 F8
Broadgorse Cl S40 ..... 114 F7
Broadhey View SK22 ... 24 B1
Broadholme La DE56 ... 179 A8
Broad La
Brinsley NG16 .... 182 E8
Stapleford NG9 .... 223 D6
Broadoaks Cl S41 ...... 266 C3
Broad Pavement S40 ... 266 B3
Broad Pl S80 .... 82 C6
Broad Rushes DE74 .... 247 B6
Broad St DE11 .... 256 C3
Broadstairs Rd 5 NG9 . 223 F2
Broadstone Cl DE21 ... 206 A1
Broadstone La DE73 ... 251 D4
Broadway
Derby DE22 .... 218 E8
Duffield DE56 .... 190 E2
Heanor DE75 .... 181 E1
Ilkeston DE7 .... 194 E3
Ripley DE5 .... 169 F1
Swanwick DE55 .... 169 F7
Broadway Ave DE6 .... 176 B8
Broadway La SK17 .... 88 A5
Broadway Park Cl DE22 218 E8
Broadway St DE14 .... 254 C8
Broad Wlk
Buxton SK17 .... 85 B7
Darley Dale DE4 ...... 127 C3
Brockhall Rise DE75 ... 182 A1
Brockhill Cl 3 S43 .... 96 F8
Brockholes S13 .... 16 F8
Brockhurst La S45 .... 129 C6
Brocklehurst Ave S8 ... 57 C8
Brocklehurst Ct S40 ... 95 D2

Brocklehurst Piece S40 . 95 D1
Brockley DE21 .... 220 E5
Brockley Ave S44 ...... 98 F6
Brockley La SK17 ..... 69 C3
Brockley Prim Sch S44 .. 98 F7
Brocksford Ct DE6 .... 224 F7
Brockway Cl S45 ...... 131 D2
Brockwell Cl 5 S41 .... 95 D6
Brockwell Inf & Jun Sch
S40 .... 95 D4
Brockwell La
Chesterfield S40 .... 95 E4
Cutthorpe S42 .... 94 F7
Brockwell Pl S40 ...... 95 E4
Brockwell Terr S40 .... 95 E4
Brockwell The DE55 ... 160 B4
Brodie Cl DE73 .... 232 E2
Bromehead Way S41 ... 95 D7
Bromley Ct DE7 .... 209 A7
Bromley St DE22 ...... 218 E7
Brompton Rd DE22 .... 217 F6
Bromyard Dr DE73 .... 233 A3
Bronte Cl NG10 .... 236 A7
Bronte Pl DE23 .... 231 B8
Bronte St DE55 .... 146 C5
Brook Ave DE55 ...... 159 B3
Brookbank Ave S40 ... 95 D4
Brookbank Rd S43 .... 80 F4
Brook Bottom Rd SK22 . 33 A8
Brookbridge Ct DE1 ... 267 A4
Brook Cl
Alfreton DE55 .... 159 B3
5 Belper DE56 .... 178 F3
Doveridge DE6 .... 224 C8
Fhdern DE65 .... 230 D1
Hatton DE65 .... 227 D2
Holymoorside S42 ..... 113 D7
Long Eaton NG10 ..... 236 E5
Quarndon DE22 ...... 204 C4
Brook Cotts DE7 ...... 194 F3
Brook Ct
Elvaston DE72 .... 233 F4
Heanor NG16 .... 182 B2
Brookdale Ave SK6 .... 23 A4
Brookdale Dr DE23 ... 231 A5
Brookdale Rd DE11 ... 257 A4
Brooke Dr S43 .... 96 F5
Brook End DE65 ...... 242 D3
Brooke St
Ilkeston DE7 .... 209 B6
Sandiacre NG10 .... 223 B5
Tibshelf DE55 .... 148 A6
Brookfield Ave
Chesterfield S40 .... 95 A2
Derby, Chaddesden DE21 . 220 B8
Denby Village DE5 ..... 180 A2
Brookfield Cl DE55 .... 170 B1
Brookfield Com Sch S40 . 95 A2
Brookfield Cotts
Acresford DE12 .... 265 C7
Bakewell DE45 .... 109 E8
Brookfield Cres NG20 .. 119 E5
Brookfield Ind Est SK13 . 9 E8
Brookfield La DE45 ... 109 E8
Brookfield Mews 2
NG10 .... 223 B5
Brookfield Mobile Home Pk
S42 .... 130 F5
Brookfield Park Ind Est
DE4 .... 143 F4
Brookfield Prim Sch
Derby DE3 .... 230 D8
Shirebrook NG20 ...... 119 F5
Brookfield Rd S44 .... 118 A8
Brookfields
Calver S32 .... 72 C1
Horsley DE56 .... 191 E7
Brookfields Bsns Pk
DE65 .... 229 D6
Brookfields Dr DE21 .. 205 D4
Brookfield Way
Heanor DE75 .... 182 B1
Tansley DE4 .... 143 F4
Brook Fold SK23 ...... 47 C7
Brookhill S43 .... 80 F4
Brookhill Ave NG16 .. 160 D4
Brookhill Ind Est NG16 . 160 E3
Brookhill La NG16 .... 160 E5
Brookhill Leys Rd NG16 . 182 E1
Brookhill Rd NG16 ... 160 D2
Brookhill St NG9 ..... 223 D6
Brook Ho B DE1 ...... 267 A4
Brookhouse Ct
Hayfield SK22 .... 25 D3
Whaley Thorns NG20 .. 101 A1
Brook House Mews
Repton DE65 .... 242 D2
Swadlincote DE11 ..... 256 A7
Brookhouse St DE24 .. 232 D5
Brook La
Alfreton DE55 .... 159 B3
Clowne S43 .... 80 F4
Crich DE56 .... 168 C6
Hatton DE65 .... 227 C3
Ripley DE5 .... 180 D7
Sutton on t H DE6 .... 228 A8
Brooklands SK17 ...... 85 C8
Brooklands Ave
Chapel-en-le-F SK23 .. 47 D6
Derby DE7 .... 181 F7
Wirksworth DE4 .... 165 F7
Brooklands Bank DE45 . 109 E6
Brooklands Dr
Derby DE23 .... 231 C8
Glossop SK13 .... 17 B7

Brooklands Prim Sch
NG10 .... 236 D6
Brooklands Rd SK23 .. 47 D6
Brookleton DE45 ...... 125 C5
Brooklyn Dr S40 ...... 95 D4
Brooklyn Pl 2 S8 ..... 43 A5
Brooklyn Rd S8 .... 43 A5
Brook Mbr SK13 ...... 10 E1
Brook Rd
Borrowash DE72 ...... 221 B1
Elvaston DE72 .... 233 F4
Sheffield S8 .... 43 A5
Brooks Hollow DE1 ... 205 C7
Brookside
Ashbourne DE6 .... 173 D1
Beeley DE4 .... 111 B3
Bradwell S33 .... 51 A7
Burton u T DE15 ...... 248 B5
Derby DE1 .... 267 A4
Eastwood NG16 .... 182 F4
Glossop SK13 .... 17 B8
New Mills SK22 .... 24 C7
Whaley Bridge SK23 ... 34 A1
Brook Side
Bakewell DE45 .... 109 D6
Belper DE56 .... 178 F3
Rolleston DE13 .... 240 B4
Brookside Ave NG19 .. 136 C6
Brookside Bar S40 ..... 94 F1
Brookside Cl
Derby DE21 .... 218 E7
Glossop SK13 .... 9 F4
Long Eaton NG10 ..... 236 B8
Repton DE65 .... 242 D2
Brookside Glen S40 ... 94 F1
Brookside Gr SK17 .... 84 D5
Brookside Ind Unit NG9 . 223 D8
Brookside Rd
Breadsall DE21 .... 205 E4
Chapel-en-le-F SK23 ... 47 B5
Brookside Way NG17 .. 148 F1
Brooks Rd S43 .... 78 B4
Brook St
Clay Cross S45 .... 131 A4
Derby DE1 .... 267 A4
Glossop SK13 .... 10 C1
Hartshorne DE11 ..... 257 A7
Heage DE56 .... 168 E1
Heanor DE75 .... 181 B5
Nether Heage DE56 ... 168 C2
Renishaw S21 .... 79 C8
Swadlincote DE11 .... 256 A6
DE11 .... 255 E6
Brookvale Ave
Codnor DE5 .... 181 B8
Denby Village DE5 .... 180 A2
Brookvale Rd DE5 ..... 180 A2
Brook Vale Rd NG16 .. 182 C2
Brookvale Rise S18 ... 57 A3
Brookview Ct S18 ..... 57 A3
Brook Walkway DE1 .. 267 A4
Brook Yd S40 .... 266 A3
Broom's La DE6 ...... 226 B2
Broom Ave
Pilsley S45 .... 132 C2
Swanwick DE55 .... 169 F7
Broombank Pk S41 ... 76 D3
Broombank Rd S41 ... 76 C3
Broom Bsns Pk S41 ... 76 D3
Broom Cl
Belper DE56 .... 178 E6
Chellaston DE73 ...... 232 F2
Chesterfield S41 .... 95 D7
Derby, Sinfin DE73 .... 231 E2
Derby DE21 .... 220 F4
Broom Dr S42 .... 115 E2
Broome Acre DE55 ... 160 C4
Broomfield Ave S41 ... 115 D7
Broomfield Cl NG10 .. 223 A5
Broomfield Cotts DE65 . 206 C5
Broomfield Ave DE7 .. 209 A6
Broomhill Cl
Derby DE3 .... 217 D3
Eckington S21 .... 59 B3
Broomhill Cotts DE65 . 229 C2
Broomhill Ct S41 ..... 76 F2
Broomhill Rd S41 .... 76 F2
Broomhills La DE65 ... 242 D1
Broomhills The DE12 .. 264 F7
Broom La DE6 .... 175 E7
Broomscroft SK13 .... 10 A6
Brosscroft Village SK13 . 10 A6
Brosterfield Cvn Site S32 . 71 D7
Brougham Ave NG19 .. 135 D2
Brough La S33 .... 51 C7
Brough Rd DE15 ..... 248 C3
Brough St DE22 ...... 218 D5
Broughton Ave DE23 .. 218 D1
Broughton Cl
Church Broughton DE65 . 227 A8
Ilkeston DE7 .... 194 A8
Somercotes DE55 ..... 170 C7
Broughton Rd S41 .... 95 D7
Brown Ave NG19 ..... 136 B4
Brown Cres S20 ...... 59 F7
Brown Edge Rd SK17 .. 66 C2
Brownhill La HD9 ..... 3 B8

Brownhills La S42 .... 130 C4
Brown Hills La S10 ... 42 E8
Browning Cir DE23.... 231 F1
Browning Rd DE11 ... 256 C5
Browning St DE23 .... 231 F7
Brown La
Ashover S45 .... 145 B8
Baslow In F NG11 ..... 237 E6
Dronfield S18 .... 57 C3
Flash SK17 .... 103 B3
Brownlow Rd NG19 ... 135 F1
Browstowe Ave NG16 . 195 D6
Broxtowe Coll Arthur Mee
Ctr (Coll of F Ed) The
.... 223 D7
Brunel Parkway DE24 . 219 D3
Brunel Way
Castle Gresley DE11 ... 255 E1
Church Gresley DE11 .. 261 F8
Brun La DE6, DE22 .... 217 B8
Brunnen The DE55 ... 160 B4
Brunner Ave NG20 ... 119 F3
Brunswick Dr 2 NG9 . 223 E5
Brunswick St
Chesterfield S41 ...... 266 B4
Derby DE23 .... 231 F8
Pilsley S45 .... 132 C1
Brunswood Cl DE21 ... 220 E5
Brunswood Ho DE4 ... 143 B2
Brunswood La DE6 ... 187 C4
Brunswood Rd DE4 ... 143 B1
Brunt La DE11 .... 256 F5
Brunton Cl DE23 ..... 217 C1
Brunts Comp Sch NG19 . 136 C1
Brushes S45 .... 4 A3
Brushes Rd S15 .... 4 A3
Brushfield Gr S12 ..... 44 D4
Brushfield Rd S40 .... 94 F5
Brussells Terr 1 DE7 . 194 E1
Bryant La DE55 ...... 160 A5
Bryn Lea S41 .... 96 C2
Brynsmoor Rd NG16 .. 182 E7
Bryony DE14 .... 254 B8
Bryony Cl
Derby DE21 .... 206 A1
Killamarsh S21 .... 60 B1
Bryony Way NG19 .... 136 F4
Bubnell Ct 15 S40 .... 95 D5
Bubnell Rd DE45 ..... 91 D6
Buchanan St DE1 ..... 267 B4
Buchan St DE24 ...... 232 D7
Buckden Cl S40 ...... 95 D4
Buckfast Ct DE55 .... 169 E8
Buckford La DE65, DE73.. 242 E8
Buckhazels La DE6, DE22 . 203 B7
Buckingham Ave DE21 . 219 D8
Buckingham Cl
2 Dronfield S18 ..... 56 D2
Mansfield Woodhouse
NG19 .... 136 E5
Swanwick DE55 .... 170 A7
Buckingham Ct
Burton u T DE15 ...... 248 C3
Sandiacre NG10 ...... 223 A3
Buckingham Dr
Church Gresley DE11 .. 261 F8
Heanor DE75 .... 181 C2
Buckingham Ho NG16 . 228 D1
Buckingham Rd NG10 . 223 A4
Buckland Cl DE11 .... 218 E6
Buckland Ct 18 S41 .. 95 F8
Buckland Gr SK14 .... 15 A8
Buckleather La S18 ... 74 C1
Buckley Cl DE11 ..... 256 F2
Buckminster Cl DE21... 205 F2
Buckminster Rd DE7 .. 208 C4
Buck Wood View S14 .. 43 D5
Bull's Head Row DE22 . 252 E6
Bullace Ct 3 NG19 ... 136 E1
Bullbridge Hill DE56 .. 168 B5
Buller St
Derby DE23 .... 218 D2
Ilkeston DE7 .... 209 A6
Bullhill La DE56 ...... 176 E3
Bullhurst La DE6 ..... 188 F6
Bulling La DE4 .... 156 F1
Bullivant Ave S80 .... 100 C8
Bull La DE4 .... 143 D6
Bull Mews Cotts DE4 . 143 C5
Bullock Cl NG19 ..... 136 B5
Bullock La
Braisford DE6 .... 201 F7
Ironville NG16, DE55... 170 E5
Bullpit La DE56 ...... 205 A8
Bullsmoor DE56 ...... 179 C4
Bulltor La SK17 .... 88 B5
Bumpmill La DE55 ... 146 B1
Bun Alley DE45 .... 91 C3
Bungalows The
Chesterfield, Brampton
S40 .... 95 D3
Chesterfield, Hady S41 . 266 C2
11 Chesterfield, Newbold
S41 .... 95 A8
1 Chesterfield, Whittington
Moor S41 .... 96 A8
Clowne S43 .... 81 A4
Elton DE4 .... 140 D6
Killamarsh S21 .... 60 C6
New Mills SK22 .... 24 D1
Sheepbridge S41 ...... 76 F4
Bunkers Hill S80 ..... 82 D2
Bunkers Hill S21 ..... 60 E6
Buntingbank Cl DE55 . 159 F4
Bunting Cl
Chesterfield S42 ...... 95 B1
Derby DE23 .... 218 A3
Ilkeston DE7 .... 208 C6

Bunting Cl *continued*
 Sheffield S8 . . . .**43** B2
Buntingfield La S45. . . . . **129** B7
Bunting Ho S41. . . . .**77** A3
Bunting Nook S8 . . . .**43** B1
Bunyan Gres DE55 . . . .**146** F3
Bunyan Green Rd NG16 . **171** D7
Burbage Bank SK13. . . . .**9** E2
Burbage Cl
 Belper DE56. . . . .**179** D5
 Dronfield S18. . . . .**56** D2
Burbage Ct **8** S40. . . . .**95** D5
Burbage Gr
 Gamesley SK13 . . . .**9** E2
 Sheffield S12 . . . .**44** D5
Burbage Pl DE24. . . . .**232** F7
Burbage Prim Sch SK17. . .**84** F6
Burbage Rd S43 . . . .**97** D8
Burbage Way SK13. . . . .**9** E2
Burch Pl S32 . . . .**71** E6
Burcot Cl DE7 . . . .**207** E8
Burdekin Cl S43 . . . .**47** C6
Burdett Way DE65 . . . .**242** D3
Burdock Cl DE21 . . . .**205** E2
Burgess Cl S41 . . . .**115** D7
Burghley Cl DE73 . . . .**232** F2
Burghley Way DE23 . . . . . .**230** E6
Burke Dr DE55 . . . .**170** D8
Burkitt Dr S43 . . . .**79** B3
Burland Green La DE6 . . .**189** B4
Burleigh Cres DE55 . . . . . .**169** F8
Burleigh Dr DE22 . . . .**218** F8
Burleigh St **8** S47 . . . .**194** F1
Burley Bank La HD9 . . . .**2** E7
Burley Cl S40. . . . .**115** A7
Burley Dr DE22 . . . .**204** E7
Burley Hill DE22 . . . .**205** A7
Burley La DE22 . . . .**204** E7
Burlington Ave NG20. . . . .**119** F6
Burlington Cl
 Breaston DE72. . . . .**235** D8
 Sheffield S17 . . . .**55** E7
Burlington Dr NG19. . . . . .**135** F2
Burlington Glen S17 . . . . . .**55** E7
Burlington Gr S17 . . . .**55** E7
Burlington Rd
 Buxton SK17 . . . .**85** A7
 Derby DE22 . . . .**217** F6
 Sheffield S17 . . . .**55** E7
Burlington St S40. . . . .**266** B3
Burlington Way DE3 . . . . . .**217** D1
Burlow Ave SK17 . . . .**85** C3
Burlow Rd SK17 . . . .**85** D2
Burnaby St DE24 . . . .**232** F8
Burnage Ct DE22 . . . .**218** F4
Burnaston Cl S18. . . . .**56** C1
Burnaston Ct **2** NG19. . . .**136** E4
Burnaston La DE65 . . . .**229** D5
Burnbridge Rd S41. . . . .**77** C3
Burncroft DE7 . . . .**207** E7
Burnell St S43 . . . .**96** F8
Burnett La DE4 . . . .**143** A8
Burney La DE73. . . . .**252** C2
Burnham Cl DE7 . . . .**207** D8
Burnham Dr DE24 . . . .**217** C2
Burns Ave NG19 . . . .**136** C2
Burns Cl
 Chesterfield S40 . . . .**114** F7
 Derby DE23 . . . .**231** B8
Burns Dr
 Dronfield S18. . . . .**76** C8
 Grassmoor S42 . . . .**115** E3
Burnshaw St DE55 . . . .**146** C5
Burnside
 Glossop SK13. . . . .**9** F4
 Rolleston DE13 . . . .**240** B4
Burnside Ave
 Chapel-en-le-F SK23 . . . . .**47** C7
 Sheffield S8 . . . .**43** A5
 Shirland DE55 . . . .**146** D1
Burnside Cl DE24 . . . .**231** D3
Burnside Ct DE24 . . . .**233** A8
Burnside Dr
 Derby DE21. . . . .**220** F4
 Mansfield NG19. . . . .**135** E2
Burnside St DE24 . . . .**233** A8
Burns St
 Heanor DE75 . . . .**181** D2
 Ilkeston DE7 . . . .**208** E8
Burnt House Rd DE75 . . . .**181** D1
Burnt Oaks Cl NG19. . . . . .**136** D3
Burns Wood Croft S41 . . . .**95** B7
Burnwells Rd SK23. . . . .**47** B6
Burr La DE7 . . . .**194** F1
Burrowfield Mews DE21. .**220** F2
Burrows La
 Brailsford DE6 . . . .**201** F2
 Middleton DE4. . . . .**154** D5
Burrows The DE11 . . . .**255** F5
Burrows Wlk DE11 . . . .**267** B2
Bursar Way NG10. . . . .**223** C3
Bursdon Cl S41. . . . .**77** A1
Burton Close Dr DE45. . . .**109** E4
Burton Close Mews
 DE45 . . . .**109** D4
Burton Edge DE45 . . . .**109** D4
Burton Rd
 Burton u T DE14. . . . .**254** B7
 Castle Gresley DE11 . . . . .**255** D2
 Coton in t E DE12 . . . .**260** D3
 Derby DE23 . . . .**218** C1
 Findern DE65 . . . .**230** D4
 Overseal DE12. . . . .**262** A4
 Repton DE15, DE65 . . . . .**242** B2
 Rosliston DE12 . . . .**260** C6
 Swadlincote DE11 . . . .**256** D6
 Ticknall DE73. . . . .**250** F4

Burton Rd *continued*
 Tutbury DE13 . . . .**239** D4
 Willington DE65. . . . .**241** F7
Burton St
 Heanor DE75 . . . .**181** E2
 Tutbury DE13 . . . .**239** C6
Burwell Cl SK13 . . . .**17** A8
Burwell Ct NG19 . . . .**136** E4
Buscott Dr DE6 . . . .**185** B8
Bushey Wood Gr S17 . . . . .**55** D7
Bushey Wood Rd S17 . . . . .**55** E6
Bushton La DE13 . . . .**239** B2
Bushy Cl NG10. . . . .**236** B6
Buskeyfield La NG20 . . . . .**101** F4
Butcher's La DE4 . . . .**127** F4
Bute St SK13 . . . .**10** E3
Bute Wlk DE21. . . . .**219** C7
Butler Cres NG19 . . . .**135** D2
Butler Way S21. . . . .**60** C6
Buttercup Ave DE12 . . . . .**262** E1
Buttercup Cl SK13 . . . .**17** E8
Butterfield Cres DE55 . . .**169** F7
Butterfield La DE55 . . . . . .**145** E1
Butterhall Cl S80 . . . .**82** A5
Butterley Cl NE7 . . . .**194** F6
Butterley Croft Bsns Ctr
 DE5 . . . .**180** E8
Butterley Ct NG16. . . . . . .**170** F4
Butterley Hill DE55. . . . . .**169** E3
Butterley La
 Ashover DE4, S45 . . . .**144** E5
 Ripley DE5. . . . .**169** D4
Butterley Lo NG16 . . . . . .**170** F4
Butterley Sta DE5. . . . .**169** E4
Buttermead Ct NG9 . . . . .**209** D2
Buttermere Cl
 Chesterfield S41 . . . .**95** D7
 1 Long Eaton NG10. . .**223** A2
Buttermere Ct NG19 . . . .**136** D3
Buttermere Dr
 Derby DE22. . . . .**204** E3
 Dronfield S18. . . . .**56** E1
Buttermilk La DE4 . . . .**98** D4
Butterpot La DE6 . . . .**215** D3
Butterton Cl DE7 . . . .**209** A7
Butterton Dr **6** S40 . . . . .**95** A5
Butterwick Cl
 Derby DE23 . . . .**231** E5
 Forest Town NG19 . . . . . .**136** F1
Butt Hill S80 . . . .**81** F6
Butt Hill Cl S80. . . . .**81** F6
Butt La
 Blackfordby DE11 . . . .**257** A1
 Mansfield Woodhouse
 NG19. . . . .**136** C2
Buttonoak Dr DE73 . . . . . .**233** A3
Butts Cl DE7 . . . .**209** A4
Butts Dr DE4 . . . .**143** D4
Butts Hill S17 . . . .**55** D4
Butts Rd
 Ashover S45 . . . .**129** F3
 Bakewell DE45. . . . .**109** D5
 Darley Dale DE4 . . . .**127** B3
Butt St NG10 . . . .**223** B5
Butts Terr DE45 . . . .**109** D5
Butts The DE56 . . . .**179** A3
Butts View DE45 . . . .**109** D5
Buxton Ave DE75 . . . .**193** F7
Buxton Cl
 17 Gamesley SK13 . . . .**9** E2
 Swadlincote DE11 . . . .**256** A7
Buxton Com Sch SK17 . . . .**85** A6
Buxton Ct DE7. . . . .**194** D1
Buxton Ctry Pk* SK17 . . . .**84** E6
Buxton Dr
 Derby DE3. . . . .**217** E3
 Little Eaton DE21 . . . .**191** D2
Buxton Gn DE75 . . . .**193** F7
Buxton Hospl SK17 . . . .**85** C5
Buxton Inf Sch SK17 . . . . . .**85** C7
Buxton Jun Sch SK17 . . . . .**85** B6
Buxton Mews SK13 . . . .**9** E2
Buxton Mus & Art Gal*
 SK17 . . . .**85** B7
Buxton New Rd SK11 . . . . . .**83** A6
Buxton Old Rd SK12 . . . . . .**32** E4
Buxton Rd
 Alstonefield DE6 . . . .**149** B5
 Ashbourne DE6 . . . .**173** B2
 Ashford in t W DE45 . . . . .**108** E8
 Bakewell DE45. . . . .**109** B7
 Castleton S33 . . . .**38** B2
 Chapel-en-le-F SK17, SK23 . .**47** C6
 Chinley SK23 . . . .**34** F2
 Derby DE21. . . . .**219** F8
 Dove Holes SK17. . . . .**66** F8
 High Lane SK12. . . . .**32** A6
 Horwich End, New Horwich
 SK23. . . . .**45** E6
 Longnor SK17 . . . .**121** B7
 Mansfield NG19 . . . .**135** D1
 New Mills SK22, SK23 . . . .**33** C4
 Tideswell SK17 . . . .**69** C3
 Whaley Bridge SK23 . . . . .**33** E1
Buxton Rd W SK12. . . . .**32** B5
Buxton Terr SK14 . . . .**9** D5
Buxton Wlk S12 . . . .**44** D5
Buxworth Prim Sch SK23. .**34** A1
Byfield Cl DE21 . . . .**206** B2
Byng Ave DE23 . . . .**231** F7
Byron Ave
 Alfreton DE55 . . . .**159** B4
 Burton u T DE15. . . . .**254** E7
 Long Eaton NG10. . . . . . .**223** B3
 Mansfield Woodhouse
 NG19. . . . .**136** C2

Byron Cl
 Dronfield S18. . . . .**76** C7
 Grassmoor S42 . . . .**115** E3
Byron Cres NG16. . . . .**195** C4
Byron Gr DE55 . . . .**146** F3
Byron Lo SK17 . . . .**85** C6
Byron Rd
 Chesterfield S40 . . . .**115** A8
 Swadlincote DE11 . . . .**256** C6
Byron St
 Buxton SK17 . . . .**85** C6
 Chesterfield S40 . . . .**266** C1
 Derby DE23 . . . .**218** F2
 Ilkeston DE7 . . . .**194** F1
 Shirebrook NG20 . . . .**119** E4
 Shirland DE55 . . . .**146** C1
Bywell La DE56 . . . .**179** F1

C

Cabot Cl DE56. . . . .**179** E5
Cacklehill La DE6 . . . .**184** C2
Cadeby Ct DE55 . . . .**170** C6
Cadgwith Dr DE22 . . . . . .**204** E3
Cadley Hill Ind Est DE11. .**255** E2
Cadley Hill Rd DE11. . . . . .**255** E3
Cadman Ct S20 . . . .**59** D6
Cadman Rd S12 . . . .**44** C6
Cadman St S20 . . . .**59** D6
Cadwell Cl DE24 . . . .**233** D6
Caerhays Ct DE24 . . . .**231** D3
Caernarfon Cl DE55 . . . . .**170** A7
Caernarvon Cl
 Derby DE21. . . . .**205** C1
Caernarvon Rd S18 . . . .**76** B8
Caesar St DE1 . . . .**219** B7
Cairn Dr S43 . . . .**77** D4
Cairngorm Cl S43. . . . .**77** D4
Cairngorm Dr DE24 . . . . .**231** D3
Cairns Cl
 Burton u T DE15. . . . .**248** C3
 Derby DE3 . . . .**217** E3
Cairnsmore Cl **4** NG10 . .**223** A1
Caldene Terr SK23 . . . .**45** E7
Calder Cl
 Derby DE22 . . . .**204** E3
 Hilton DE65. . . . .**228** D1
Calderdale Dr NG10. . . . . .**236** A6
Caldermill Dr DE21 . . . . . .**206** A2
Caldey Rd S18 . . . .**76** A8
Caldwell DE7 . . . .**194** D1
Cale Rd SK22. . . . .**33** D8
Calesdale Cl SK17 . . . .**85** B5
Calf Croft S80 . . . .**82** A5
Calgary Cres DE15. . . . . . .**248** D3
Calico Cres SK15 . . . .**4** A6
Calico La SK23 . . . .**34** E4
California Gdns DE22 . . . .**218** C4
California La DE43 . . . .**80** A7
Calke Abbey* LE65 . . . . . .**251** D2
Calke Ave NG17. . . . .**148** E2
Calke Rd DE73 . . . .**252** A6
Calke Rise DE5 . . . .**169** F1
Calladine Cl DE75. . . . .**181** D2
Calladine La
 Horsley Woodhouse DE7 . .**192** D6
 Shottle DE56 . . . .**177** C5
Callan's La DE65 . . . .**258** D7
Calley Ave NE7 . . . .**194** F6
Callow Dr S14 . . . .**43** D5
Callow Hill Way DE23 . . . .**231** A7
Callow La DE4, DE6. . . . . .**165** C5
Callow Mount S14 . . . .**43** D5
Callow Pl S14 . . . .**43** D5
Callow Rd S14. . . . .**43** D5
Callywhite La S18. . . . .**57** C1
Calow Brook Dr S41 . . . . .**115** E8
Calow CE Prim Sch S44 . . . .**96** F3
Calow Gn S44 . . . .**9** E2
Calow Gn SK13 . . . .**9** E2
Calow La
 Calow S41, S44 . . . .**96** F1
 Chesterfield S41 . . . .**115** E8
Calow Lane Ind Est S41 . .**115** E8
Calstock Cl S40. . . . .**95** A4
Calton View DE45 . . . .**109** D5
Calver Ave S42 . . . .**132** A7
Calver Bank **8** S40 . . . .**9** D2
Calver Cl
 Belper DE56. . . . .**179** B6
 Derby DE21 . . . .**205** B3
 10 Gamesley SK13 . . . .**9** E2
Calver Cres S43 . . . .**97** D8
Calver Fold **6** SK13. . . . . . .**9** D2
Calver Mews SK13 . . . .**9** E2
Calver Mill S32 . . . .**72** D2
Calver Pl **7** SK13. . . . .**9** D2
Calver Rd DE45 . . . .**91** D6
Calvert Cl NG16. . . . .**182** B3
Calverton Cl DE24 . . . . . .**232** E3
Calvert St DE1 . . . .**267** D2
Calvin Cl DE24. . . . .**233** A5
Camberwell Ave DE22. . . .**218** A6
Camberwell Ct **10** S48 . . .**78** B3
Cambrian Cl DE21 . . . .**205** E1
Cambrian Cl **1** S40. . . . . . .**95** D6
Cambrian Way DE11 . . . . .**256** A3
Cambria Rd NG19 . . . .**135** C4
Cambridge Cres
 Bramley-Vale S44 . . . .**117** E1
 Stapleford NG9 . . . .**209** D2
Cambridge Ct **13** S8 . . . . .**43** B6
Cambridge Lo S8 . . . .**43** B6
Cambridge Rd
 1 Brimington S43 . . . . . .**96** F8

Cambridge Rd *continued*
 Sheffield S8. . . . .**43** B6
Cambridge St
 Blackwell DE55 . . . .**147** E1
 Derby, Rose Hill DE23 . . . .**219** B2
 Derby, Spondon DE21 . . . .**220** E3
Camdale Rise S12 . . . .**44** F1
Camdale View S12 . . . .**44** F1
Camden St DE22 . . . .**218** D4
Camellia Cl DE3 . . . .**217** D3
Camelot Cl DE13 . . . .**240** E2
Cameron Cl DE15 . . . .**248** B1
Cameron Rd DE23 . . . .**231** F8
Camerory Way S43 . . . .**77** D5
Cam Height S32 . . . .**41** F2
Camlough Wlk S41 . . . . . .**266** C2
 Camms CE Prim Sch S21 . .**59** D4
Camms Ct S21 . . . .**59** D4
Campbell Ct S43. . . . .**77** D4
Campbell Dr S43 . . . .**78** B4
Campbell St
 Belper DE56. . . . .**178** F3
 Derby DE24 . . . .**232** D7
 Langley Mill NG16 . . . . . .**182** C4
Campion Cl S21 . . . .**60** C6
Campion Hill DE74. . . . . . .**247** A4
Campion Rd DE11. . . . .**256** F4
Campsie Ct **8** DE24 . . . . .**231** D3
Camp St DE1 . . . .**219** B7
Camp Wood Cl DE21 . . . .**205** C7
Canada St DE56 . . . .**179** A2
Canal Bank DE72 . . . .**235** A1
Canal Bridge
 Killamarsh S21 . . . .**60** D6
 Willington DE65. . . . .**242** A6
Canalgate Pk DE21 . . . . . .**220** F3
Canal Mews S41 . . . .**266** B4
Canalside S21 . . . .**60** B1
Canal Side SK23 . . . .**33** F1
Canal St
 Derby DE1 . . . .**267** C2
 Ilkeston DE7 . . . .**195** A1
 Long Eaton NG10 . . . .**223** C1
 Marple SK6 . . . .**23** A6
 Sandiacre NG10 . . . .**223** C6
 Whaley Bridge SK23 . . . . .**45** E8
Canal Wharf S41 . . . .**96** B5
Canberra Cl
 Derby DE3 . . . .**217** E2
 Stapleford NG9 . . . .**209** F1
Candlemass Ct NG19 . . . .**136** D2
Cannell Cl S45. . . . .**131** B4
Canner Cl DE11. . . . .**257** A2
Canning Mews **1** DE7 . .**208** F7
Cannock Way NG10 . . . . . .**237** A7
Cannon Fields S32. . . . .**52** F8
Cannon St SK14 . . . .**9** C5
Canon's Wlk DE22 . . . .**204** F2
Canterbury Cl
 Chesterfield S40 . . . .**115** A8
 Duffield DE56. . . . .**190** E3
 Mansfield Woodhouse
 NG19. . . . .**136** C5
Canterbury Rd
 Burton u T DE15. . . . .**248** C3
 Sheffield S8 . . . .**43** B6
 Wirksworth DE4 . . . .**165** F8
Canterbury St DE21 . . . . .**219** E8
Canterbury Terr DE4 . . . . .**165** F8
Cantley Cl DE24 . . . .**232** D3
Cantley Rd DE55 . . . .**170** C6
Cantrell Cl S43 . . . .**96** D8
Capel Rise S43 . . . .**96** D8
Capthorne Cl S40 . . . .**94** F5
Caraway Dr DE14 . . . .**254** A8
Cardale Rd NG19 . . . .**135** C4
Cardales Cl DE65 . . . .**230** D2
Cardean Cl DE1 . . . .**219** B7
Carder Gn SK17. . . . .**121** B6
Cardigan St DE21 . . . .**219** D7
Cardinal Cl **1** DE21. . . . . .**205** F2
Cardlemere La S45 . . . .**138** F2
Cardona Cl DE21 . . . .**205** F2
Cardwell Ave S13. . . . .**44** F7
Cardwell Dr S13 . . . .**44** F7
Carfield Ave S8 . . . .**43** B5
Carfield La S8 . . . .**43** B5
Carfield Pl S8 . . . .**43** B5
Carfield Prim Sch S8 . . . . . .**43** B5
Carisbrooke Dr **2** DE13 .**240** E1
Carisbrooke Gdns NG16. .**195** C2
Carlin Cl DE72 . . . .**235** E8
Carlin St S13 . . . .**44** E6
Carlisle Ave DE23 . . . .**231** B8
Carlisle Cl S41 . . . .**76** E3
Carlisle Gr SK17 . . . .**85** E3
Carlisle Rd SK17 . . . .**84** F8
Carl Moult Ho DE11 . . . . .**256** A2
Carlton Ave
 Derby DE24 . . . .**232** E4
 Northwood DE4 . . . .**127** A6
Carlton Cl
 Clay Cross S45 . . . .**131** D2
 Heanor DE75 . . . .**182** A3
 Sheffield S20 . . . .**59** C6
Carlton Dr DE24 . . . .**232** E4
Carlton Gdns DE24. . . . . .**232** E4
Carlton Rd
 Chesterfield S40 . . . .**115** A4
 Derby DE23 . . . .**218** F2
 Long Eaton NG10. . . . . . .**236** B5
Carlton St NG19 . . . .**136** C1

Carlton Wlk
 Derby DE24. . . . .**220** A1
 Derby DE24 . . . .**233** A8
Carlyle Inf Sch DE23 . . . . .**231** B8
Carlyle Pl DE75 . . . .**181** D3
Carlyle Rd DE55 . . . .**146** F3
Carlyle St
 Derby DE24. . . . .**231** F5
 Heanor DE75 . . . .**181** D3
Carlyon Gdns S40. . . . .**114** F8
Carnaby Cl DE22 . . . .**218** A5
Carnarvon Ct DE15. . . . . .**249** C2
Carnarvon Rd NG17. . . . . .**148** F2
Carnegie St DE23 . . . .**232** A8
Carnfield Hall* DE55. . . . .**159** D5
Carnfield Hill DE55 . . . . . .**159** D5
Carnforth Cl
 Derby DE24 . . . .**217** E1
 Stapleford NG9 . . . .**223** D5
Carnival Way DE74 . . . . . .**247** B4
Carnoustie Ave S40 . . . . .**114** C8
Carnoustie Cl DE3 . . . . . .**217** F2
Carol Cres DE21 . . . .**219** F5
Caroline Cl DE24. . . . .**233** D7
Caroline Ct
 Hope S33 . . . .**38** F4
 Ilkeston DE7 . . . .**209** A6
Carpenter Ave
 Mansfield NG19 . . . .**135** D2
 Mastin Moor S43 . . . .**79** B3
Carpenter Croft S12 . . . . . .**44** C6
Carpenter Croft S12 . . . . . .**44** C6
Carpenter Gdns S12. . . . . .**44** C6
Carpenter Mews S12. . . . . .**44** C6
Carper La DE6 . . . .**187** F2
Carradale Gr DE73 . . . . . .**232** E1
Carr Bank S13 . . . .**17** E8
Carr Brook Cl SK23 . . . .**45** E5
Carr Brow SK6 . . . .**32** A7
Carr Cl DE55 . . . .**160** A7
Car Rd S18 . . . .**74** B6
Carfield Ave
 Beeston NG9 . . . .**223** F2
 Long Eaton NG10. . . . . . .**223** F1
Carfield Cl **8** S48 . . . .**43** B6
Carfield Dr S8 . . . .**43** B6
Carfield La S8 . . . .**43** B6
Carfield Rd S8 . . . .**43** B6
Carfields DE7 . . . .**192** C7
Carfield St S8 . . . .**43** B6
Carrhouse La SK14. . . . .**9** C4
Carriage Dr The SK13 . . . . .**9** F5
Carriers Mdw SK23 . . . .**47** B7
Carriers Rd DE55 . . . .**160** E3
Carrington Ct Ind Est
 DE1 . . . .**218** E5
Carrington St DE1 . . . .**267** C2
Carr La
 Brackenfield DE55. . . . . . .**145** D3
 Dronfield S18. . . . .**56** C2
 Matlock DE4 . . . .**143** E2
 Scarcliffe S44 . . . .**117** F7
 South Normanton DE55 . .**160** A7
 Thornhill S33 . . . .**39** F5
Carr Lane Mews S18. . . . . .**56** D2
Carrock Ave DE75. . . . . . .**182** B1
Carron Cl DE24 . . . .**231** E4
Carrs Cl DE74. . . . .**247** A3
Carr Vale Rd S44. . . . .**98** F1
Carrwood Rd
 Chesterfield S41 . . . .**76** C4
 Renishaw S21 . . . .**79** C2
Carsington Cl S40 . . . .**95** B5
Carsington Cres DE22 . . .**204** D1
Carsington Ct **1** DE22. . .**204** D2
Carsington Ho **1** DE22. .**204** D2
Carsington & Hopton Prim
 Sch DE4 . . . .**164** E7
Carsington Mews DE22. . .**204** E1
Carsington Water Visitor
 Ctr* DE6 . . . .**164** C4
Carson Croft DE4 . . . .**143** C6
Carson Mount S12 . . . .**44** B3
Carson Rd DE21. . . . .**220** B6
Carter Cl NG10 . . . .**236** B6
Carter Grange **11** S8 . . . . .**43** B6
Carterhall La S12 . . . .**44** C2
Carterhall Rd S12. . . . .**44** B2
Carter La
 Shirebrook NG20. . . . .**119** C4
 Warsop Vale NG20. . . . . .**120** C4
Carter La E DE55 . . . .**160** C6
Carter La W
 Shirebrook NG20 . . . .**119** D4
 South Normanton DE55 . .**160** C5
Carter Pl S8 . . . .**43** B6
Carter St DE24 . . . .**232** D6
Cartledge La S18 . . . .**75** A7
Cartmel Cl S18 . . . .**56** E1
Cartmel Cres S41 . . . .**95** E8
Cart Rd DE55 . . . .**157** F4
Cartworth Moor Rd HD9 . . .**3** E8
Cartwright La DE55 . . . . . .**160** E7
Cartwright St S81 . . . .**63** F7
Car Vale Dr S13 . . . .**44** C8
Car Vale View S13 . . . .**44** C8
Carver Cl S26 . . . .**61** E6
Carver Way S26 . . . .**61** E6
Cary Gr S2 . . . .**43** F8

Cary Rd
Eckington S21 . . . . .59 B3
Sheffield S2 . . . . .44 A8
Cascade Gr DE23 . . . . . .231 A7
Casson Ave DE24 . . . . . .233 A6
Casson Dr S26 . . . . .61 E7
Casson St NG16 . . . . .170 F4
Castings Rd DE12 . . . . . .262 C2
Castlebeck Ave S2 . . . . . .44 C8
Castlebeck Dr S2 . . . . . . .44 C8
Castle Cl
Bakewell DE45 . . . . .109 E6
Borrowash DE72 . . . . .221 D2
Castlecraig Ct DE24 . . . . .231 E7
Castle Croft
Derby DE24 . . . . .233 D5
Linton DE11 . . . . .261 E8
Castle Ct
Elvaston DE72 . . . . .234 A5
Glossop SK13. . . . . .10 A4
Tutbury DE13 . . . . .239 C7
Castledale Croft S2 . . . . . .44 B8
Castledale Gr S2 . . . . .44 C8
Castledale Pl S2 . . . . .44 B8
Castle Donington Com Coll
DE74 . . . . .247 B3
Castle Dr
Bakewell DE45. . . . . .109 E7
Codnor NG16 . . . . .181 E8
Somercotes DE55 . . . . . . .170 D8
Castle Edge Rd SK22 . . . . .24 B2
Castle Hayes La DE13 . . .239 A5
Castlefields Main Ctr
DE1 . . . . .267 C2
Castle Gn S44 . . . . .118 B7
Castle Gresley Inf Sch
DE11 . . . . .261 E7
Castle Hayes La DE13 . . .239 A5
Castle Hill
Castle Donington DE74 . . .247 B4
Duffield DE56. . . . . .190 E4
Eckington S21 . . . . .59 D4
Findern DE65 . . . . .230 D1
Glossop SK13. . . . . .10 E2
Castle Hill Cl S21 . . . . .59 D4
Castle Hill Dr DE13 . . . . .239 B7
Castle Ho DE1 . . . . .267 D2
Castle Ind Est S44 . . . . . . .98 E2
Castle La
Bolsover S44 . . . . .99 A1
Ironville NG16 . . . . .170 E1
Melbourne DE73 . . . . .252 A7
Castleland Way DE73 . . . .232 E2
Castle Mews
Mansfield Woodhouse
NG19. . . . . .136 B3
Melbourne DE73 . . . . .252 B7
Castle Mews The S
DE11 . . . . .256 A7
Castle Mills DE73 . . . . . .252 B7
Castle Mount Cres DE45 .109 D7
Castle Mount Way DE45. .109 C7
Castle Orch DE56 . . . . . .190 E4
Castle Rd DE11 . . . . .255 F1
Castlerigg Way ■ S18 . . . .56 E1
Castle Row S17 . . . . .56 B6
Castlerow Dr S17 . . . . . . .56 B6
Castlerow View S17 . . . . . .56 B6
Castleshaw Dr DE23 . . . . .230 E7
Castle St
Bakewell DE45. . . . . .109 D6
Bolsover S44 . . . . .99 A2
Castleton S33 . . . . .38 B2
Glossop SK13. . . . . .10 A4
Mansfield Woodhouse
NG19. . . . . .136 B3
Melbourne DE73 . . . . .252 B7
Tutbury DE13 . . . . .239 C6
Castleton Ave
Derby DE23 . . . . .231 F8
Ilkeston DE7 . . . . .194 E5
Somercotes DE55 . . . . . . .170 C6
Castleton Bank ⑳ SK13 . . .9 E1
Castleton CE Prim Sch
S33. . . . . .38 C2
Castleton Cl NG19 . . . . . .136 C4
Castleton Cres SK13 . . . . . .9 E1
Castleton Gn ⑳ SK13 . . . . .9 E1
Castleton Gr
Gamesley SK13 . . . . .9 E1
Staveley S43 . . . . .97 B5
Castleton Rd
Hathersage S32. . . . . .52 E8
Hope S33 . . . . .38 E3
Castleton Terr ⑳ SK13 . . . .9 E1
Castleton YH ⭑ S33. . . . . . .38 C2
Castle View
Aldercar NG16. . . . . .182 A4
Duffield DE56. . . . . .190 E4
Eckington S21 . . . . .59 D3
Hatton DE65 . . . . .239 C7
Palterton S44. . . . . .118 B6
Castle View Dr DE4 . . . . .155 C6
Castle View Prim Sch
DE4 . . . . .143 D5
Castle Way The DE65. . . .241 F5
Castle Wlk DE1 . . . . .267 C4
Catchford View S40 . . . . . .95 B7
Catcliff DE7 . . . . .194 C4
Catcliff Cotts DE45. . . . . .109 D5
Cat & Fiddle La DE7 . . . .207 E5
Cathedral Rd DE1 . . . . . .267 B4
Cathedral View DE22 . . . .218 D2

Catherine Ave
Ilkeston DE7 . . . . .208 F6
Mansfield Woodhouse
NG19. . . . . .136 C3
Catherine Ct
Alfreton DE55 . . . . .159 C5
■ Ashbourne DE6 . . . . . . .173 B2
Chesterfield S40 . . . . .95 E3
Catherine McAuley Ho
DE22 . . . . .204 E1
Catherine Rise DE11 . . . .256 A1
Catherine St
Alfreton DE55 . . . . .159 C4
Chesterfield S40 . . . . .95 E3
Derby DE23 . . . . .219 B2
Cath of All Saints, Derby ⭑
DE1 . . . . .267 B4
Catholme La DE12 . . . . . .259 A4
Catkin Dr NG16. . . . . .195 C8
Cat La S2, S8 . . . . .43 C5
Cator Rd NG19. . . . . .135 D3
Catterick Dr DE3 . . . . . . .217 C1
Catterwood Dr SK6 . . . . . .15 B2
Catton La DE12 . . . . .260 B5
Cauldwell's Mill & Craft Ctr ⭑
DE4 . . . . .126 F8
Cauldwell Cl S42 . . . . . . .131 D8
Cauldon Dr S40. . . . . .95 A5
Cauldwell Rd DE12. . . . . .261 B6
Causeway DE22 . . . . .204 E2
Causeway Gdns S17 . . . . . .55 D8
Causeway Glade S17 . . . . . .55 C8
Causeway Head Rd S17. . . .55 D8
Causeway Ho S45. . . . . . .129 D4
Causeway La
Crich DE4. . . . . .156 F5
Matlock DE4 . . . . .143 C5
Causeway The
Ashover S45 . . . . .129 A4
Eyam S32. . . . . .71 E5
Sheffield S17 . . . . .55 D7
Wirksworth DE4 . . . . .165 F8
Cavan Dr DE21. . . . . .220 B4
Cavell Dr S45 . . . . .131 E2
Cavendish Ave
Buxton SK17 . . . . .84 F6
Derby DE22 . . . . .204 F3
Sheffield, Abbeydale Park
S17 . . . . .55 F7
Cavendish Cir ⑥ SK17 . . . .85 B8
Cavendish Cl
Castle Donington DE74 . . .247 A2
Creswell S80 . . . . .81 D1
Doveridge DE6. . . . . .211 C1
Duffield DE56. . . . . .190 D2
Holmewood S42. . . . . .116 E1
Shardlow DE72 . . . . .235 B2
■ Swadlincote DE11 . . . . .256 A7
Cavendish Close Inf Sch
DE21 . . . . .220 A8
Cavendish Close Jun Sch
DE21 . . . . .220 B8
Cavendish Cotts DE4 . . . .154 F2
Cavendish Cres NG9 . . . .209 D2
Cavendish Ct
Chesterfield S41 . . . . .96 A5
Derby DE1 . . . . .267 A4
Shardlow DE72 . . . . .235 A1
Cavendish Dr
Ashbourne DE6 . . . . .185 D8
Clowne S43 . . . . .81 A4
Ripley DE5 . . . . .169 C1
Cavendish Flats
Edensor DE45. . . . . .110 E8
Pilsley DE45. . . . . .91 E1
Cavendish Hospl The ⭑
SK17. . . . . .85 A8
Cavendish Jun Sch S41 . . .95 F8
Cavendish Pl S43 . . . . .78 B3
Cavendish Rd
Bolsover S44 . . . . .99 B1
Ilkeston DE7 . . . . .208 F6
Long Eaton NG10. . . . . . . .223 C2
Matlock DE4 . . . . .143 C7
Cavendish Rise S18 . . . . . .75 F8
Cavendish St N S41. . . . . . .77 A2
Cavendish Sq S21 . . . . .77 D8
Cavendish St
Chesterfield S40 . . . . .266 B3
Derby DE1 . . . . .267 A3
Langwith NG20 . . . . .119 F8
Mansfield Woodhouse
NG19. . . . . .136 A3
Staveley S43 . . . . .97 D8
Cavendish Way DE3 . . . . .217 C2
Cavendish Wlk S44 . . . . . . .99 A2
Caversfield Cl DE23 . . . . .231 A8
Caversham Way DE7 . . . .207 D8
Cavill Rd S8 . . . . .43 A3
Cawdor Rd S2 . . . . .43 F6
Caxterway La SK17. . . . . . .86 E3
Caxton Cl S43 . . . . .77 D3
Caxton St
Derby DE23 . . . . .231 F6
Derby, Normanton DE23 . .231 E7
Caythorpe Ct ④ NG19. . . .136 E3
Ceal The SK6 . . . . .15 B2
Cecil Ave S18. . . . . .57 A2
Cecil Rd
Dronfield S18. . . . . .57 A2
Swadlincote DE11 . . . . . . .255 F5
Cecil St DE22 . . . . .218 D6
Cedar Ave
Alfreton DE55 . . . . .159 A5
Chesterfield S40 . . . . .95 D5
Long Eaton NG10. . . . . . . .236 C5

Cedar Ave *continued*
Mansfield Woodhouse
NG19. . . . . .136 C5
Ripley DE5 . . . . .169 D1
Cedar Cl
Ashbourne DE6 . . . . .185 D7
Duffield DE56. . . . . .190 D4
Eckington S21 . . . . .59 B2
Glapwell S44 . . . . .118 B1
Glossop SK13. . . . . .10 B2
Killamarsh S21 . . . . .60 C5
Sandiacre NG10. . . . . .223 B7
Shirebrook NG20 . . . . .119 E6
Cedar Croft
Aston-on-T DE7 . . . . .246 A7
Ockbrook DE72 . . . . .221 C4
Cedar Dr
Ockbrook DE72 . . . . .221 C4
Selston NG16. . . . . .171 F7
Uttoxeter ST14 . . . . .210 A4
Cedar Gr
Belper DE56. . . . . .179 B2
Linton DE12 . . . . .261 C6
South Normanton DE55. . .160 B4
Swadlincote DE11 . . . . . . .256 A7
Cedar Park Dr S44 . . . . . . .99 C2
Cedar Pk DE7 . . . . .208 E7
Cedar Rd
Castle Donington DE74 . . .247 B2
Linton DE11 . . . . .261 E7
Cedar St
Brimington S43 . . . . .78 A1
Derby DE22 . . . . .218 E8
Shirland DE55 . . . . .146 C5
Cedarwood Ct DE21 . . . . .205 E2
Celandine Cl
Burton u T DE15. . . . . .248 C2
Derby DE21 . . . . .206 A2
Celandine Ct S17 . . . . .56 A5
Celandine Gdns S17 . . . . . .56 A5
Celandine Pl DE11 . . . . . .256 E4
Celanese Rd DE21 . . . . . .220 C3
Cemetery Hill DE21 . . . . .219 E6
Cemetery La
Ripley DE5 . . . . .169 E1
Staveley S43 . . . . .78 E1
Wirksworth DE4 . . . . .154 F1
Cemetery Rd
Belper DE56. . . . . .179 B3
Chesterfield S41 . . . . .96 C2
Clay Cross S45 . . . . .131 E2
Dronfield S18. . . . . .76 B8
Glossop SK13. . . . . .10 C4
Somercotes DE55 . . . . . . .170 C7
Stapleford NG9 . . . . .223 E7
Cemetery Terr S41. . . . . . .96 E7
Centenary Ho DE1 . . . . . .267 B1
Central Ave
Borrowash DE72 . . . . .221 B1
Chesterfield S40 . . . . .95 E2
Creswell S80 . . . . .100 D8
Sandiacre NG10. . . . . .223 B6
South Normanton DE55. . .160 B5
Stapleford NG9 . . . . .223 F8
Central Dr
Shirebrook NG20 . . . . .119 E3
Unstone Green S18 . . . . . . .76 C6
Central Dr
Blackwell DE55 . . . . .147 E1
Buxton SK17 . . . . .85 D5
Calow S44 . . . . .96 F3
■ Chesterfield S41. . . . . . . .96 C1
Shirebrook NG20 . . . . .119 E3
Wingerworth S42 . . . . .114 F3
Central Pavement S40 . . .266 B3
Central Rd DE55 . . . . .159 A4
Central St
Chesterfield S41 . . . . .96 C1
Holmewood S42. . . . . .132 E8
Central Store ⑥ SK13. . . . .10 C1
Central Wlk S43 . . . . .96 D7
Centre Ct DE1 . . . . .267 C1
Centre St S44 . . . . .117 D1
Centro Pl DE24 . . . . .219 D3
Centrum East Ret Pk
DE14 . . . . .253 F8
Centurion Way Bsns Pk
DE21 . . . . .219 B8
Chaddesden Cl S18 . . . . . . .56 C1
Chaddesden La DE21. . . . .220 A6
Chaddesden Lane End
DE21 . . . . .219 F6
Chaddesden Park Inf Sch
DE21 . . . . .220 B6
Chaddesden Park Jun Sch
DE21 . . . . .220 B7
Chaddesden Park Rd
DE21 . . . . .219 F7
Chadfield Rd DE56. . . . . . .190 E5
Chadwick Ave DE24 . . . . .232 E5
Chadwick Ct S43 . . . . .78 D1
Chadwick Hill DE4 . . . . . .141 A6
Chadwick Nick La
Crich DE4. . . . . .167 F7
Fritchley DE4 . . . . .168 A6
Chadwick St SK13 . . . . . . .17 B8
Chaffinch Cl DE21 . . . . . .220 F6
Chain La DE24 . . . . .218 A2
Chalfont Sq DE21 . . . . . . .206 B2
Chalkley Cl DE24. . . . . . . .232 F7
Challands Cl S41 . . . . .115 C8
Challands Way S41 . . . . . .115 C8
Challis Ave DE21 . . . . .220 B7
Challoner Gn S20 . . . . .59 E8
Challoner Way S20 . . . . . . .59 E8
Chalons Cl DE7 . . . . .194 F1
Chalons Way DE7 . . . . . . .208 F8

Chambers Ave DE7 . . . . . .209 B7
Chambers Ct SK14 . . . . .9 A3
Chambers St DE24 . . . . . .219 F1
Champion Ave DE7 . . . . . .194 C3
Champion Hill DE56. . . . . .190 E4
Chancel Pl DE22 . . . . .267 A1
Chancel La DE22 . . . . .218 A6
Chancet Wood Cl S8 . . . . . .56 F8
Chancet Wood Dr S8 . . . . .56 F8
Chancet Wood Rd ■ S8 . .56 F8
Chancet Wood Rise S8. . . .56 F8
Chancet Wood View S8 . . .56 F8
Chander Hill La S42 . . . . .113 C8
Chandlers Ford DE21 . . . .205 F2
Chandos Cres S21 . . . . .60 D6
Chandos Pole St S42 . . . . .218 D6
Chandres Ct DE22 . . . . . . .218 A6
Chaneyfield Way S40 . . . . .95 B7
Channel The DE6 . . . . .173 B2
Chantrey Ave S41 . . . . .96 A6
Chantrey Rd S8. . . . . .43 A3
Chantry Cl
Derby DE21 . . . . .217 C1
Disley SK12 . . . . .32 E5
Long Eaton NG10. . . . . . . .236 A4
Melbourne DE73 . . . . .252 A7
Chantry Ct S17 . . . . .69 C4
Chantry La SK17 . . . . .69 D4
Chantry Rd SK12. . . . . .32 E5
Chapel Brow
Broadbottom SK13 . . . . . . .16 E6
Glossop SK13. . . . . .10 A7
Chapel Cl
Clowne S43 . . . . .80 E4
Moira DE11 . . . . .256 C1
Willington DE65. . . . . .242 B6
Youlgreave DE45 . . . . .125 B5
Chapel Croft
Elton DE4 . . . . .140 E6
Middleton DE4 . . . . .154 D5
Chapel Ct DE7 . . . . .194 F4
Chapel-en-le-Frith CE Prim
Sch SK23 . . . . .47 C6
Chapel-en-le-Frith High Sch
SK23. . . . . .47 A5
Chapel-en-le-Frith Sta
SK23. . . . . .47 B3
Chapel Gn DE6 . . . . .224 C8
Chapel Hill
Ashover S45 . . . . .129 F4
Beeley DE4 . . . . .111 B4
Cromford DE4 . . . . .155 A7
Chapel Ho ■ DE7 . . . . . . .208 E8
Chapel Houses SK6. . . . . . .23 A5
Chapel Inf Sch SK23 . . . . . .47 B4
Chapel La
Apperknowle S18. . . . . .58 A1
Bakewell DE45. . . . . .109 D5
Barrow u T DE73 . . . . .244 A6
Boylestone DE6 . . . . .213 B4
Chellaston DE73 . . . . .233 A1
Church Broughton DE65 . .227 B8
Clifton DE6. . . . . .184 F6
Crich DE4. . . . . .168 A8
Derby, Chaddesden DE21 . .220 A7
Derby, Spondon DE21 . . . .220 E5
Glossop SK13. . . . . .9 F5
Hanbury DE13 . . . . .238 A2
Holloway DE4 . . . . .156 B5
Kniveton DE6. . . . . .163 B1
Middleton DE4 . . . . .154 D5
Rolleston DE13 . . . . .240 B4
Sheffield, Hillfoot S17 . . . . .55 D4
Taddington SK17 . . . . .88 B3
Thurvaston DE6. . . . . .215 B8
Tissington DE6. . . . . .162 B6
Wirksworth DE4 . . . . .154 F1
Chapel La E S41 . . . . .115 D7
Chapel La W S40 . . . . .95 C2
Chapel Lofts SK13 . . . . . . .10 B5
Chapel Pl NG16 . . . . .195 F6
Chapel Rd
Bolsover S44 . . . . .98 F1
Grassmoor S42 . . . . .115 F3
Hayfield SK22 . . . . .25 D2
Horwich End SK23. . . . . . . .45 E5
Selston NG16. . . . . .171 E6
Chapel Row
Borrowash DE72 . . . . .221 B2
Crich DE4. . . . . .168 A4
Chapel Side DE21 . . . . . . .219 E6
Chapel St
Alfreton DE55 . . . . .159 A4
Belper DE56. . . . . .178 F3
Brimington S43 . . . . .96 F8
Buxton SK17 . . . . .85 B7
■ Chesterfield S41. . . . . . . .96 A8
Coton in t E DE12 . . . . . . .260 D3
Derby DE1 . . . . .267 B4
Derby, Spondon DE21 . . . .220 E5
Donisthorpe DE12 . . . . . . .265 E8
Donisthorpe, Oakthorpe
DE12. . . . . .265 F6
Duffield DE56. . . . . .190 F3
Eastwood NG16. . . . . .182 F1
Fritchley DE56 . . . . .168 B6
Glossop SK13. . . . . .10 C1
Hayfield SK22 . . . . .25 D2
Heanor DE75 . . . . .194 A8
Holbrook DE56. . . . . .191 C7
■ Ilkeston DE7. . . . . .194 F1
Kilburn DE56. . . . . .192 A8
Kimberley NG16. . . . . .195 F6
Linton DE11 . . . . .261 E8
Long Eaton NG10. . . . . . . .236 F2
Longnor SK17 . . . . .121 B6
Melbourne DE73 . . . . .252 B7

Chapel St *continued*
Monyash DE45. . . . . .107 A2
New Houghton NG19. . . . .135 A2
New Mills, Rowarth SK22 . .24 E7
New Mills SK22 . . . . .33 B7
Ripley DE5 . . . . .169 D2
Sheffield S20 . . . . .59 C6
Smisby LE65 . . . . .257 F3
Somercotes DE55 . . . . . . .170 C7
Stonebroom DE55 . . . . . . .147 A4
Swadlincote, Church Gresley
DE11. . . . . .256 A1
Swadlincote, Newhall
DE11. . . . . .255 F6
Swanwick DE55. . . . . .169 E8
Ticknall DE73 . . . . .251 A5
Whaley Bridge SK23 . . . . . .45 E8
Whaley Thorns NG20 . . . .101 A3
Woodville DE11 . . . . .256 F2
Chapel Way S42 . . . . .115 D1
Chapel Wlk
Alfreton DE55 . . . . .159 A4
Staveley S43 . . . . .72 E2
Chapel Yd
Dronfield S18. . . . . .57 A2
Harthill S26 . . . . .61 E6
South Wingfield DE55 . . . .157 E3
Chapman Ave DE24 . . . . . .233 B6
Chapman La S42. . . . . .115 F3
Chapmans Croft DE12. . . .260 D3
Chapter Cl DE21. . . . . .205 D2
Chardin Ave SK6. . . . . .23 C8
Charing Cl DE24 . . . . .267 C5
Charingworth Rd DE21. . .206 B2
Chariot Ct DE24. . . . . .233 D5
Charity Rd DE55. . . . . .170 C5
Charlbury Cl DE23 . . . . . .231 A8
Charles Ashmore Rd S8 . . .57 A4
Charles Ave
Derby DE21 . . . . .220 D6
Sandiacre NG10. . . . . .223 B6
Stapleford NG9 . . . . .223 F8
Charles Cl DE7 . . . . .209 B6
Charles Rd DE24 . . . . .220 A1
Charles St
Alfreton DE55 . . . . .159 A5
④ Buxton SK17. . . . . .85 C8
Chesterfield S40 . . . . .95 E3
Glossop SK13. . . . . .10 C1
Long Eaton NG10. . . . . . . .236 D6
Mansfield NG19 . . . . .136 A1
Somercotes DE55 . . . . . . .170 C7
Swadlincote DE11 . . . . . . .256 B2
Charleston Cl DE11 . . . . . .256 A7
Charleston Dr DE22 . . . . . .204 D4
Charlestown Rd SK13 . . . . .17 C7
Charlestown SK13 . . . . .17 D6
Charlesworth Cl SK23 . . . . .33 D3
Charlesworth Cres SK23 . .33 D3
Charlesworth Ct ■
NG19 . . . . .136 E3
Charlesworth Gdns S44 . .117 E8
Charlesworth Prim Sch
SK13. . . . . .16 C6
Charlesworth Rd SK23 . . . .33 D3
Charlesworth St S44 . . . . .117 E8
Charley La SK23 . . . . .47 A8
Charlotte Ct
Burton u T DE14. . . . . .254 C8
Eastwood NG16. . . . . .182 F3
Sheffield S2 . . . . .43 B8
Charlotte Inf Sch DE7 . . .194 E2
Charlotte La S33. . . . . .51 A7
Charlotte Rd S2 . . . . .43 B8
Charlotte St
Derby DE23 . . . . .219 A2
Ilkeston DE7 . . . . .194 E3
Charlton Ave NG10. . . . . . .223 F1
Charlton Cl DE12 . . . . .261 D5
Charnock Ave S12 . . . . .44 B3
Charnock Cres S12 . . . . . . .44 A3
Charnock Dale Rd S12 . . . .44 B3
Charnock Dr S12 . . . . .44 A3
Charnock Gr S12 . . . . .44 B2
Charnock Hall Prim Sch
S12. . . . . .44 A2
Charnock Hall Rd S12. . . . .44 A2
Charnock View Rd S12 . . . .44 B1
Charnock Wood Rd S12. . . .44 B1
Charnwood Ave
Belper DE56. . . . . .179 A4
Borrowash DE72 . . . . .221 D2
Castle Donington DE74 . . .247 C3
Derby DE23 . . . . .231 D5
Long Eaton NG10. . . . . . . .236 B4
Sandiacre NG10. . . . . .223 A4
Charnwood Cl DE55. . . . . .148 B3
Charnwood Cres DE55 . . .148 C7
Charnwood Dr NG19 . . . . .136 A3
Charnwood Gr NG19 . . . . .136 B3
Charnwood St DE1. . . . . . .267 B2
Charterhouse Cl DE21 . . . .205 F1
Charter Pk DE7. . . . . .208 E2
Charterstone La DE22 . . . .204 E4
Chartwell Ave S42 . . . . . . .114 D5
Chartwell Dr DE21 . . . . . .219 C6
Chase Cl DE7 . . . . .233 B4
Chasecliff Cl S40 . . . . .95 D6
Chase Rd DE56 . . . . .167 F4
Chase The
Derby DE24 . . . . .231 F7
Kilburn DE56 . . . . .192 B4
Little Eaton DE21 . . . . .191 D6
Rosliston DE12 . . . . .260 C6
Chase View DE4 . . . . .156 F7
Chatfield Cl DE15 . . . . . . .248 C5

Chatham Ave DE55 . . . . 159 C3
Chatham Ct DE56 . . . . 179 D4
Chatham St DE23 . . . . 232 A8
Chatsworth Ave
 Chesterfield S40 . . . . 95 B2
 Clowne S43 . . . . 80 F4
 Crich DE4 . . . . 156 F1
 Darley Dale DE4 . . . . 142 F7
 Long Eaton NG10 . . . . 237 A6
 Shirebrook NG20 . . . . 119 E6
Chatsworth Bsns Pk S40 . 95 E2
Chatsworth Cl
 Alfreton DE55 . . . . 158 F3
 Bolsover S44 . . . . 99 C2
 1 Sandiacre NG10 . . . . 223 B4
Chatsworth Cres
 Bullbridge DE56 . . . . 168 B5
 Derby DE22 . . . . 204 F3
Chatsworth Ct
 11 Ashbourne DE6 . . . . 173 C2
 2 Chesterfield S40 . . . . 95 C2
 Derby DE24 . . . . 231 F4
 Staveley S43 . . . . 97 D8
 West Hallam DE7 . . . . 207 E8
Chatsworth Dr
 Derby DE3 . . . . 217 E3
 Little Eaton DE21 . . . . 191 D2
 North Wingfield S42 . . . . 131 F6
 Tutbury DE13 . . . . 239 C6
Chatsworth Farm Shop*
 DE45 . . . . 91 C2
Chatsworth Ho
 Baslow DE45 . . . . 92 A1
 2 Branston DE14 . . . . 253 F7
Chatsworth Lo SK17 . . . . 85 A8
Chatsworth Park Ave S12 . 44 A5
Chatsworth Park Dr S12 . 44 A5
Chatsworth Park Gr S12 . 44 A5
Chatsworth Park Rd S12 . 44 A5
Chatsworth Park Rise
 S12 . . . . 44 A5
Chatsworth Pl
 Dronfield S18 . . . . 56 D2
 Ilkeston DE7 . . . . 208 B5
Chatsworth Rd
 Buxton SK17 . . . . 85 E7
 Chesterfield S40 . . . . 95 C2
 Creswell S80 . . . . 81 C1
 Rowsley DE4 . . . . 111 A2
 Sheffield S17 . . . . 55 F6
 Swadlincote DE11 . . . . 256 A6
Chatsworth St
 Derby DE23 . . . . 218 E1
 Tibshelf DE55 . . . . 148 A6
Chatsworth Tech Pk **8**
 S41 . . . . 96 A8
Chatsworth View S32 . . . . 72 E1
Chatsworth Way DE75 . . . 181 C2
Chatteris Dr DE21 . . . . 205 D1
Chatterton La
 Marple SK6 . . . . 24 A8
 Mellor SK6 . . . . 24 B8
Chaucer Dr S18 . . . . 76 C7
Chaucer Inf Sch DE7 . . . 208 F8
Chaucer Jun Sch DE7 . . . 194 F1
Chaucer Rd S41 . . . . 95 F8
Chaucer St DE7 . . . . 194 F1
Chaucer Terr DE23 . . . . 231 F7
Chavery Rd S45 . . . . 131 E4
Cheadle Cl DE21 . . . . 218 B1
Cheadle Rd ST14 . . . . 210 B1
Cheam Cl DE22 . . . . 217 E6
Cheapside
 2 Belper DE56 . . . . 178 F3
 Derby DE1 . . . . 267 B3
Chedworth Dr DE24 . . . . 233 D6
Cheedale SK17 . . . . 85 D7
Cheedale Ave S40 . . . . 95 D6
Cheedale Cl
 Burton u T DE15 . . . . 248 B5
 Chesterfield S40 . . . . 95 D6
Cheetham Ave S18 . . . . 76 E5
Chellaston Cotts DE72 . 245 B5
Chellaston Inf Sch DE73. 233 A2
Chellaston Jun Sch
 DE73 . . . . 232 F1
Chellaston La
 Aston-on-T DE72, DE73 . . . 233 D1
 Aston-on-Trent DE72 . . . 245 F8
Chellaston Park Ct DE73 . 232 F1
Chellaston Rd DE24 . . . . 232 E4
Chellaston Sch DE73 . . . 232 E1
Chelmarsh Cl DE73 . . . . 233 A3
Chelmorton Cl NG19 . 136 E3
Chelmorton Pl DE21 . . . . 219 F8
Chelmsford Cl DE3 . . . . 217 C3
Chelmsford Way **6** S43 . 78 B3
Chelsea Cl DE22 . . . . 217 F6
Cheltenham Cl NG9 . . . . 223 F2
Chelwood Rd DE73 . . . . 232 F2
Chepstow Cl S40 . . . . 25 C3
Chepstow Gdns S40 . 114 F8
Chequer La DE56 . . . . 166 D2
Chequers La DE21 . . . . 219 D6
Chequers Rd DE21 . . . . 219 D5
Cheribough Rd DE74 . . . 247 A3
Cheriton Cl NG19 . . . . 135 E1
Cheriton Ct **15** S41 . . . . 95 F8
Cheriton Dr DE7 . . . . 194 C3
Cheriton Gdns DE23 . . . . 230 E7
Cherry Bank Rd S8 . . . . 43 A3
Cherrybrook Dr DE21 . 206 B3
Cherry Cl
 Ashford in t W DE45 . . . 108 F8
 Breaston DE72 . . . . 235 E8
 Shirebrook NG20 . . . . 119 E6

Cherry Cl continued
 South Normanton DE55 . . . 160 B7
Cherry Ct DE14 . . . . 253 F6
Cherrydale Ct DE23 . 231 A6
Cherry Garth DE65 . . . . 228 D2
Cherry Leys DE15 . . . . 248 C4
Cherry St **S** S2 . . . . 43 A8
Cherry St S2 . . . . 43 A8
Cherry Tree Ave
 Belper DE56 . . . . 179 B6
 Ripley DE5 . . . . 180 D8
 Shireoaks S81 . . . . 63 F7
 Swanwick DE55 . . . . 170 A7
Cherry Tree Cl
 Bolsover S44 . . . . 99 C1
 Brinsley NG16 . . . . 182 E8
 Clowne S43 . . . . 80 E3
 Derby DE22 . . . . 218 B4
 Hilton DE65 . . . . 228 D2
 Ilkeston DE7 . . . . 208 D6
 Mansfield Woodhouse
  NG19 . . . . 136 B4
 Risley DE72 . . . . 222 F4
 Swadlincote DE11 . . . . 255 F6
Cherry Tree Ct
 Ashbourne DE6 . . . . 173 B1
 Chapel-en-le-F SK23 . . . . 47 A6
Cherry Tree Dr
 Buxton SK17 . . . . 66 D1
 Creswell S80 . . . . 81 D2
 Killamarsh S21 . . . . 60 D8
 Long Duckmanton S44 . . . 98 A4
Cherry Tree Gr
 Mastin Moor S43 . . . . 79 C3
 North Wingfield S42 . . . . 131 F5
Cherry Tree Hill Inf Sch
 DE21 . . . . 220 B5
Cherry Tree Hill Jun Sch
 DE21 . . . . 220 B5
Cherry Tree Mews
 Derby DE21 . . . . 220 B4
 Woodville DE11 . . . . 256 F2
Cherrytree Rd DE15 . . . 254 F6
Cherry Tree Sq SK17 . . . . 69 C3
Chertpit La SK17, DE45 . 89 D6
Chertsey Cl S40 . . . . 114 F8
Chertsey Ct DE7 . . . . 207 D8
Chertsey Rd DE3 . . . . 217 C2
Cherwell Cl **1** S40 . . . . 95 B1
Chesapeake Rd DE21 . . . 220 B6
Chesham Cl
 Glossop SK13 . . . . 10 B5
 Hadfield SK13 . . . . 10 B5
Cheshire St DE24 . . . . 232 E5
Cheshire Way NG16 . . . . 171 C4
Chess Burrow NG16 . . . 136 D2
Chessel Cl S8 . . . . 43 A4
Chessel Cl S8 . . . . 205 B5
Chester Cl
 Derby, Little Chester
  DE21 . . . . 219 B8
 Derby, Spondon DE21 . 220 E3
 Eckington S21 . . . . 59 B2
Chesterfield Art Gall & Mus*
 S41 . . . . 266 C3
Chesterfield Ave
 Chesterfield S43 . . . . 77 E3
 Long Eaton NG10 . . . . 236 F7
 Swadlincote DE11 . . . . 255 E6
Chesterfield Coll S41 . 266 B4
Chesterfield Coll Clowne
 Campus
 Clowne S43 . . . . 80 D3
 Clowne S43 . . . . 80 D4
Chesterfield Coll (Tapton
 House Campus) S41 . . . . 96 C5
Chesterfield Dr DE12 . 261 C6
Chesterfield & North
 Derbyshire Royal Hospl
 S44 . . . . 96 A3
Chesterfield Rd
 Alfreton DE55 . . . . 158 F5
 Barlborough S43 . . . . 80 A5
 Beeley DE4 . . . . 111 B3
 Belper DE56 . . . . 179 A4
 Brimington, Middlecroft S41. 97 B8
 Brimington, Tapton S41,
  S43 . . . . 96 D7
 Calow S41, S44 . . . . 96 C5
 Darley Dale DE4 . . . . 127 D2
 Dronfield S18 . . . . 57 B1
 Eckington S21 . . . . 59 B2
 Grassmoor S42 . . . . 115 F1
 Heage DE56 . . . . 168 E3
 Holmewood S42 . . . . 116 C2
 Long Duckmanton S44 . . . 98 C3
 Matlock DE4 . . . . 143 C7
 New Houghton NG19 . . . 134 F7
 North Wingfield S42 . . . 132 A8
 Pilsley DE55, S45 . . . . 133 A1
 Pleasley NG19 . . . . 135 A6
 Rowsley DE4 . . . . 111 A1
 6 Sheffield S8 . . . . 43 A6
 Shirland DE55 . . . . 146 C3
 Shuttlewood S44 . . . . 98 E5
 Sutton in A NG17 . . . . 148 E4
Chesterfield Rd N NG19 . 135 D3
Chesterfield Rd S S8 . . . 57 A6
Chesterfield Small Bsns Ctr
 S41 . . . . 96 A7
Chesterfield Sta S41 . . . 266 C3
Chesterfield Trade Ctr
 S41 . . . . 96 B6
Chesterfield Trad Est S41 . 76 C3
Chesterford Ct DE23 . 230 F6
Chester Gdns DE11 . . . 256 B2
Chester Gn NG9 . . . . 223 F2
Chester Green Rd DE1 . 219 A7

Chester Ho S40 . . . . 95 E3
Chesterman Cl NG16 . . . 195 B4
Chester St
 Chesterfield S40 . . . . 95 E3
 Mansfield NG19 . . . . 135 E1
Chesterton Ave DE23 . . . 231 E7
Chesterton Cl S43 . . . . 96 F4
Chesterton Rd DE21 . 220 E6
Chestnut Ave
 Belper DE56 . . . . 179 A2
 Chellaston DE73 . . . . 232 F3
 Derby DE3 . . . . 217 D3
 Derby, Rose Hill DE23 . 219 A2
 Eckington S21 . . . . 59 B2
 Holbrook DE56 . . . . 191 C7
 Killamarsh S21 . . . . 60 C5
 Ripley DE5 . . . . 180 D8
 Somercotes DE55 . . . . 170 D5
 Swadlincote DE11 . . . . 256 A6
Chestnut Bank **2** DE75 . 181 D1
Chestnut Centre
 Conservatory Pk* SK23 . 47 E8
Chestnut Cl
 Buxton SK17 . . . . 66 B1
 Dronfield S18 . . . . 76 C8
 Duffield DE56 . . . . 190 E2
 Horsley Woodhouse DE7 . 192 C7
 New Mills SK22 . . . . 24 C1
Chestnut Cotts DE6 . . . . 151 D1
Chestnut Ct
 Cromford DE4 . . . . 155 A6
 Pinxton NG16 . . . . 160 E3
Chestnut Dr
 Ashbourne DE6 . . . . 185 D7
 Clowne S43 . . . . 80 D4
 Creswell S80 . . . . 81 D2
 Repton DE65 . . . . 243 D2
 Selston NG16 . . . . 171 F7
 Shirebrook NG20 . . . . 119 D4
 South Normanton DE55 . . . 160 B4
Chestnut Gr
 Borrowash DE72 . . . . 221 C3
 Etwall DE65 . . . . 229 B3
 Mansfield Woodhouse
  NG19 . . . . 136 B5
 Sandiacre NG10 . . . . 223 A7
 Tibshelf DE55 . . . . 147 F5
Chestnut La
 Barton in F NG11 . . . . 237 E6
 Clifton Campville B79 . 263 F2
Chestnut Rd
 Burton u T DE15 . . . . 254 F7
 Langley Mill NG16 . . . . 182 A3
Chestnuts The NG10 . . . 236 A8
Chestnut Way
 Repton DE65 . . . . 242 C2
 Swanwick DE55 . . . . 170 A8
Clevely Ct DE21 . . . . 219 D8
Cheverton Cl DE24 . . . . 233 D5
Chevin Alley DE56 . . . . 190 F7
Chevin Ave
 Borrowash DE72 . . . . 221 C2
 Derby DE3 . . . . 217 F2
Chevin Bank DE56 . . . . 190 D6
Chevin Mews DE56 . . . . 178 F2
Chevin Pl DE1 . . . . 218 F7
Chevin Rd
 Belper, Chevinside DE56 . 178 E2
 Belper, Milford DE56 . . . . 190 F8
 Derby DE1 . . . . 218 F7
 Duffield DE56 . . . . 190 E5
Chevin The DE13 . . . . 240 C1
Chevin Vale DE56 . . . . 190 E5
Chevin View DE56 . . . . 178 F4
Chevin Cl
 Cheviot Ave NG16 . . . . 170 F3
 Cheviot Cl DE11 . . . . 256 A3
 Cheviot Rd NG10 . . . . 223 A1
 Cheviot St DE22 . . . . 218 C5
 Cheviot Way **1** S40 . . . . 95 C5
Chew Rd OL3 . . . . 5 C8
Chewton St NG16 . . . . 182 F1
Cheyenne Gdns DE21 . 220 C5
Cheyne Wlk DE22 . . . . 218 C6
Chichester Cl DE7 . . . . 209 A8
Chichester Ct DE21 . . . . 205 E2
China House Yd DE4 . . . 165 F8
Chine The DE55 . . . . 160 B3
Chingford Ct DE22 . . . . 218 B6
Chilton Cl **1** NG16 . 136 C6
Chinley Prim Sch SK23. 35 A1
Chinley Rd DE21 . . . . 206 A1
Chinley Sta SK23 . . . . 34 D2
Chippinghouse Rd S2 . . . 43 A7
Chiswick Cl DE22 . . . . 217 F6
Chiswick Ct **13** S43 . . . . 78 B3
Chisworth Ct **2** NG16. 136 E3
Chiverton Cl S18 . . . . 57 A2
Chorlton Terr ST14 . . . . 210 E1
Christ Church CE Prim Sch
 S41 . . . . 96 A5
Christchurch Ct DE1 . . . 267 B4
Christ the King RC Prim Sch
 DE55 . . . . 159 A5
Chrysalis Way NG16 . . . 182 D3
Chrysanthemum Ct
 DE11 . . . . 256 A5

Chunal La SK13 . . . . 17 D5
Chunal Lane Flats SK13 . 17 C6
Church All DE45 . . . . 109 D5
Church Alley DE45 . . . . 109 D5
Church Ave
 Buxton SK17 . . . . 67 B5
 Clay Cross S45 . . . . 131 E3
 Hatton DE65 . . . . 239 D8
 Long Eaton NG10 . . . . 236 A4
 Swadlincote DE11 . . . . 256 B3
 Tideswell SK17 . . . . 69 C4
Church Bank S32 . . . . 53 A8
Church Bk SK23 . . . . 45 D7
Church Broughton CE Prim
 Sch DE65 . . . . 227 B8
Church Broughton Rd
 DE65 . . . . 227 C3
Church Brow
 Chapel-en-le-F SK23 . . . . 47 B6
 Mottram in LK S14 . . . . 9 A3
Church Cl
 Barrow u T DE73 . . . . 244 C3
 Blackfordby DE11 . . . . 257 B1
 Blackwell DE55 . . . . 147 C1
 Burton u T DE15 . . . . 248 B3
 Chellaston DE73 . . . . 233 A1
 Clowne S43 . . . . 80 F3
 Glossop SK13 . . . . 10 E2
 Marchington ST14 . . . . 224 F2
 North Wingfield S45 . . . . 132 A5
 Peak Forest SK17 . . . . 49 A3
 Renishaw S21 . . . . 79 B4
 Staveley S43 . . . . 97 C7
 Trowell NG9 . . . . 209 C4
 Willington DE65 . . . . 242 B5
 Wingerworth S42 . . . . 115 A4
Church Cnr DE6 . . . . 165 B1
Church Cres NG9 . . . . 223 F3
Church Croft
 Coton in t E DE12 . . . . 260 C3
 Ripley DE5 . . . . 169 D2
Church Ct NG20 . . . . 119 E3
Churchdale Ave NG9 . . . 209 E1
Churchdale Mews S12 . 44 D4
Churchdale Rd S12 . . . . 44 D4
Churchdown Cl DE21 . . . 206 B2
Church Dr
 Duffield DE56 . . . . 190 F2
 Ilkeston DE7 . . . . 194 D4
 Sandiacre NG10 . . . . 223 B7
 Shirebrook NG20 . . . . 119 E3
Church Farm ST14 . . . . 210 A4
Church Farm Mews S42. 116 B3
Church Farm Rd DE5 . 180 E8
Churchfields S80 . . . . 81 E1
Church Fold SK13 . . . . 16 C7
Church Gdns NG19 . . . . 136 C3
Church Gresley Inf Sch
 DE11 . . . . 256 B2
Church Hill
 Derby DE21 . . . . 220 D4
 Etwall DE65 . . . . 229 B5
 Jacksdale NG16 . . . . 171 B3
 Kimberley NG16 . . . . 195 F6
 Mansfield Woodhouse
  NG19 . . . . 136 C3
 Selston NG16 . . . . 148 A1
Church Hill Ave NG19 . 136 C3
Church Hill St DE15 . . . . 248 B3
Churchill Ave DE4 . . . . 154 D5
Churchill Cl DE72 . . . . 235 D8
Churchill Dr
 Hilton DE65 . . . . 228 E2
 2 Stapleford NG9 . . . . 223 E8
Church La
 Bakewell DE45 . . . . 109 D6
 Barrow u T DE73 . . . . 244 A5
 Barton in F NG11 . . . . 237 E6
 Baslow DE45 . . . . 91 E5
 Beeley DE4 . . . . 111 A4
 Belper DE56 . . . . 179 A4
 Brackenfield DE55 . . . . 145 D2
 Brailsford DE6 . . . . 201 E7
 Breadsall DE21 . . . . 205 E4
 Brinsley NG16 . . . . 182 E7
 Buxton SK17 . . . . 86 B7
 Caldwell DE12 . . . . 260 E7
 Calow S44 . . . . 97 A3
 Castle Donington DE74 . 247 B3
 Chapel-en-le-F SK23 . . . . 47 B6
 Chelmorton SK17 . . . . 106 B8
 Chesterfield S40 . . . . 266 B3
 Chilcote DE12 . . . . 264 E3
 Clowne S43 . . . . 80 F3
 Cossall NG16 . . . . 195 C1
 Derby, Chaddesden DE21 . 220 A6
 Derby, Darley Abbey DE22. 205 A2
 Doveridge DE6 . . . . 211 B1
 Eckington S12 . . . . 58 E7
 Ellastone DE6 . . . . 183 B4
 Great Longstone DE45 . . . 90 A4
 Hanbury DE13 . . . . 238 A4
 Heath S44 . . . . 117 B3
 Heath, Stockley S44 . . . . 117 D3
 Hemington DE74 . . . . 247 E4
 Holmewood S42 . . . . 116 B3
 Horsley Woodhouse DE7 . 192 C6
 Killamarsh S21 . . . . 60 E6
 Kirk Langley DE6 . . . . 202 E3
 Mackworth DE22 . . . . 217 F7
 Marchington ST14 . . . . 224 F2
 Marple SK6 . . . . 23 A5
 Mayfield DE6 . . . . 184 C6
 Monyash DE45 . . . . 107 C1
 Morley DE7 . . . . 206 E6
 New Mills SK22 . . . . 33 C8
 Newton Solney DE15 . . . 248 D8

Church La continued
 North Wingfield S42 . . . . 131 F5
 Osmaston DE6 . . . . 186 A5
 Peak Forest SK17 . . . . 49 A3
 Pleasley NG19 . . . . 135 A5
 Rocester ST14 . . . . 197 A3
 Rowsley DE4 . . . . 110 E1
 Selston NG16 . . . . 171 D7
 Sheffield, Townhead S17 . . . 55 D6
 Shirley DE6 . . . . 200 D8
 South Wingfield DE55 . 157 F4
 Stanton-by-D DE7 . . . . 208 F1
 Stapleford NG9 . . . . 223 D7
 Stonebroom DE55 . . . . 146 F5
 Sutton on t H DE6 . . . . 215 B1
 Thorpe DE6 . . . . 161 D1
 Thrumpton NG11 . . . . 237 C3
 Tibshelf DE55 . . . . 147 F6
 Ticknall DE73 . . . . 251 A4
 Tideswell SK17 . . . . 69 D4
 Weston Underwood DE6 . 188 E2
Church La N
 Chesterfield S41 . . . . 77 A3
 2 Derby DE22 . . . . 204 F3
Churchland Ave S42 . . . 132 D8
Church Level DE6 . . . . 165 B1
Church Mdws
 Calow S44 . . . . 96 F3
 North Wingfield S42 . . . . 131 F5
Churchmead NG17 . . . . 148 F3
Church Mews
 Derby DE21 . . . . 220 D4
 Hatton DE65 . . . . 227 D1
 Killamarsh S21 . . . . 60 C7
 Melbourne DE73 . . . . 252 B7
 Sheffield S20 . . . . 59 D7
Church Rd
 Branston DE14 . . . . 253 E7
 Burton u T DE13 . . . . 240 F7
 Church Broughton DE65 . 227 A8
 Darley Dale DE4 . . . . 127 B2
 Egginton DE65 . . . . 241 B4
 Hollingworth SK14 . . . . 9 D4
 Marple SK6 . . . . 23 C7
 New Mills SK22 . . . . 33 C7
 Quarndon DE22 . . . . 204 C5
 Rolleston DE13 . . . . 240 A4
 Shuttlewood S44 . . . . 99 A6
 Shuttlewood, Stanfree S44 . 99 B8
 Snelston DE6 . . . . 184 C3
 Swadlincote DE11 . . . . 256 A6
Church Rise DE55 . . . . 146 C4
Church St E NG16 . . . . 160 D3
Church St N S41 . . . . 77 A3
Church St S
 Chesterfield S40 . . . . 115 A7
 Glossop SK13 . . . . 10 E2
Church St W
 Chesterfield S40 . . . . 95 C2
 Pinxton NG16 . . . . 160 D3
Churchside
 Grassmoor S41 . . . . 115 D5
 Willington DE65 . . . . 242 A5
Church Side
 Calow S44 . . . . 96 F3
 Sutton in A NG17 . . . . 148 F3
Churchside La S41 . . . . 115 D4
Churchside Wlk DE22 . 218 E4
Church Sq
 1 Heanor DE75 . . . . 181 F1
 Melbourne DE73 . . . . 252 B6
Church St
 Alfreton DE55 . . . . 158 F4
 Alstonefield DE6 . . . . 149 E3
 Appleby Magna DE12 . . . 265 F1
 Ashbourne DE6 . . . . 173 B2
 Ashford in t W DE45 . . . 108 F8
 Ashover S45 . . . . 129 F3
 Barlborough S43 . . . . 80 B7
 Baslow DE45 . . . . 91 E5
 Belper DE56 . . . . 179 A3
 Bolsover S44 . . . . 99 A1
 Bonsall DE4 . . . . 142 E1
 Bradwell S33 . . . . 51 A7
 Brassington DE4 . . . . 153 A1
 Brimington S43 . . . . 96 E8
 Buxton SK17 . . . . 85 B6
 Calow S44 . . . . 96 F3
 Clifton Campville B79 . 263 E2
 Clowne S43 . . . . 80 E3
 Coton in t E DE12 . . . . 260 C3
 Creswell S80 . . . . 81 F1
 Denby Village DE5 . . . . 180 D1
 Derby DE23 . . . . 218 C1
 Derby, Rose Hill DE23 . 219 A2
 Derby, Spondon DE21 . 220 D5
 Donisthorpe DE12 . . . . 262 F1
 Dronfield S18 . . . . 57 A1
 Eastwood NG16 . . . . 182 F2
 Eckington S21 . . . . 59 E4
 Eyam S32 . . . . 71 D5
 Fritchley DE56 . . . . 168 B6
 Glossop SK13 . . . . 10 D2
 Hadfield SK13 . . . . 10 A4
 Hartington SK17 . . . . 137 D5
 Hatherton DE11 . . . . 257 B6
 Hayfield SK22 . . . . 25 D2
 Heage DE56 . . . . 168 E2
 Holbrook DE56 . . . . 191 C6
 Holloway DE4 . . . . 156 A6
 Horsley DE21 . . . . 191 F5
 Ilkeston DE7 . . . . 194 E4
 Kilburn DE56 . . . . 191 F8
 Lockington DE74 . . . . 247 F4

Church St continued
Longnor SK17 . . . . .121 B6
Mansfield Woodhouse
  NG19 . . . . .136 C3
Marple SK6 . . . . .23 A5
Matlock DE4 . . . . .143 C4
Melbourne DE73 . . . . .252 B7
Monyash DE45 . . . . .107 C2
Nethersel DE12 . . . . .264 F6
Ockbrook DE72 . . . . .221 C4
Pilsley S45 . . . . .132 C1
Pleasley NG19 . . . . .135 B4
Ripley DE5 . . . . .169 D2
Ripley, Waingroves DE5 . .181 A7
Sandiacre NG10 . . . . .223 B7
Shirland DE55 . . . . .146 D2
Somercotes DE55 . . . . . . .170 D6
South Normanton DE55 . .160 A6
Stapleford NG9 . . . . .223 D7
Staveley S43 . . . . .78 E2
Swadlincote DE11 . . . . . . .256 E1
Swadlincote, Lower Midway
  DE11 . . . . .256 C4
Swadlincote, Newhall
  DE11 . . . . .256 C4
Tansley DE4 . . . . .144 A4
Tideswell SK17 . . . . .69 C4
Tintwistle SK13 . . . . .10 A7
Tutbury DE13 . . . . .239 C7
Unstone S18 . . . . .76 E7
Whaley Thorns NG20 . . . .101 A2
Wirksworth DE4 . . . . .165 F8
Youlgreave DE45 . . . . .125 C5
Church Street Mews S33 . .51 A2
Church Terr SK13 . . . . .10 D2
Church View
Barlborough S43 . . . . .80 A7
Belper DE56 . . . . .179 A4
Blackwell DE55 . . . . .147 F1
Breaston DE72 . . . . .235 D7
Chesterfield S40 . . . . .95 C2
Clifton DE6 . . . . .184 F6
Clowne S43 . . . . .80 F3
Duffield DE56 . . . . .190 E2
Glapwell S44 . . . . .134 B8
Heanor DE75 . . . . .181 B4
Ilkeston DE7 . . . . .208 E7
Killamarsh S21 . . . . .60 E7
Mottram in L SK14 . . . . .9 A3
New Houghton NG19 . . . .134 F7
New Mills SK22 . . . . .33 C8
Church View Cotts SK17 . . .84 E6
Church View Dr DE45 . . . . . .91 E6
Churchward Dr DE13 . . . . .240 F1
Church Way S40 . . . . .266 B3
Church Wlk
Brinsley NG16 . . . . .182 E6
Chesterfield, Glasshouse
  Common S43 . . . . .77 D4
Chesterfield S40 . . . . .266 B3
Derby DE22 . . . . .204 F4
Donisthorpe DE12 . . . . . . .265 E8
Duffield DE56 . . . . .190 F2
Eastwood NG16 . . . . .182 F2
Glossop SK13 . . . . .10 D2
Parwich DE6 . . . . .151 D1
Somercotes DE55 . . . . . . .170 E6
5 Stapleford NG9 . . . . . . .223 E7
Wirksworth DE4 . . . . .165 F8
Church View Cl
  S41 . . . . .96 B8
Clarence Rd
Chesterfield S40 . . . . .266 A3
Derby DE23 . . . . .218 F1
Long Eaton NG10 . . . . . . .236 C6

Clarence St
Chesterfield S40 . . . . .266 A3
Pleasley NG19 . . . . .135 C3
Stonebroom DE55 . . . . . . .147 B4
Clarence Terr DE4 . . . . . . .143 A1
Clarence Villas DE4 . . . . .143 B2
Clarendon Rd S43 . . . . .97 C7
Clarke Ave DE75 . . . . .181 C2
Clarke Dr NG10 . . . . .236 A4
Clarkes Cl ST14 . . . . .210 B1
Clarkes La DE72 . . . . .246 B8
Clarke St DE1 . . . . .267 C4
Clarkson Ave S40 . . . . .266 B1
Clatterway DE4 . . . . .154 E8
Claverhouse Rd DE15 . . . .248 A2
Claxton St DE75 . . . . .181 D1
Claxton Terr 2 DE75 . . . .181 D2
Clay's La DE14 . . . . .253 F8
Clay Cl DE11 . . . . .256 D5
Clay Cross Com Hospl
  S45 . . . . .131 D4
Clay Cross Countryside Ctr★
  S45 . . . . .131 C3
Clay Cross Inf & Jun Sch
  S45 . . . . .131 C3
Claye St NG10 . . . . .236 E7
Clay La
Clay Cross S45 . . . . .131 B2
Heanor DE75 . . . . .181 F2
Claylands Cl SK14 . . . . .9 C4
Claylands Gr S80 . . . . .81 E5
Claylands Pl S80 . . . . .81 E5
Claylands Rd S80 . . . . .81 E5
Claymar Dr DE11 . . . . .256 A7
Claymills Rd DE13 . . . . . . .241 A2
Claypit La S42 . . . . .112 F8
Clay Pit Way S43 . . . . .80 C6
Clay St E DE15 . . . . .248 A1
Clay St
Burton u T DE15 . . . . .248 A1
Draycott DE72 . . . . .235 A7
Shirland DE55 . . . . .146 E1
Clayton Gr DE75 . . . . .181 C4
Clayton St S41 . . . . .266 C2
Cleave Rd DE14 . . . . .254 A8
Clegg Hill Dr NG17 . . . . . .148 E4
Clematis Cres DE15 . . . . . .255 A8
Clement La SK17 . . . . .50 C6
Clement Rd
Horsley Woodhouse DE7 . .192 C7
Marple SK6 . . . . .23 C7
Cleva Ave
Beeston NG9 . . . . .223 F3
Darley Dale DE4 . . . . .142 F7
Cleveland Ave
Derby DE21 . . . . .220 B5
Draycott DE72 . . . . .235 A7
Long Eaton NG10 . . . . . . .223 F1
Cleveland Cl DE11 . . . . . . .256 B3
Cleveland Ct DE15 . . . . . . .248 B3
Cleveland Rd DE55 . . . . . .146 F3
Cleveland Way S40 . . . . .95 C5
Cleveleys Rd NG9 . . . . .223 E3
Clewley Rd DE14 . . . . .253 F8
Cliffash La DE56 . . . . .176 E6
Cliff Bottom S32 . . . . .71 F4
Cliff Bvd NG16 . . . . .195 F7
Cliff Coll S32 . . . . .91 D8
Cliffdon Ho DE65 . . . . .239 D8
Cliffefield Rd S8 . . . . .43 A5
Cliffe Field Rd S8 . . . . .43 A5
Cliffe Hill Ave NG9 . . . . . . .223 D7
Cliffe La
Hathersage S32 . . . . .52 F8
Tideswell SK17 . . . . .69 C4
Cliffe Rd SK13 . . . . .17 D8
Cliffe View Rd S8 . . . . .43 A5
Cliff Hill S43 . . . . .80 D3
Cliff La
Curbar S32 . . . . .72 E1
Elton DE45 . . . . .140 D8
Kirby-in-A NG16 . . . . .160 F4
Cliff Nook DE55 . . . . .160 B4
Clifford Cl
Chesterfield S40 . . . . .95 B2
Long Eaton NG10 . . . . . . .236 A4
Clifford St
Derby DE24 . . . . .219 D2
Long Eaton NG10 . . . . . . .236 E7
Cliff Rd SK17 . . . . .85 D8
Clifton Ave
Barlborough S43 . . . . .80 A7
Long Eaton NG10 . . . . . . .237 A7
Clifton CE Prim Sch DE6 .184 F6
Clifton Cl
Overseal DE12 . . . . .262 A3
Swadlincote DE11 . . . . . . .256 A2
Clifton Dr
Buxton SK17 . . . . .85 C4
Derby DE1 . . . . .217 E3
Clifton Rd
Ashbourne DE6 . . . . .185 A8
Buxton SK17 . . . . .85 C7
Derby DE22 . . . . .204 D3
Matlock Bath DE4 . . . . . . .155 A8
Nethersel DE12 . . . . .264 D6
Clifton St
Chesterfield S40 . . . . .95 E3
Derby DE1 . . . . .267 D1
Cliftonthorpe LE65 . . . . . .258 B1
Clifton Thorpe Mdws
  LE65 . . . . .258 B1
Clifton Way DE15 . . . . .248 B2
Clinthill La S80 . . . . .81 E7
Clinton Ave NG16 . . . . .182 D6
Clinton St DE21 . . . . .219 D6
Clipstone Gdns DE21 . . . . .206 B2
Clive Ho DE11 . . . . .256 C3

Clock Tower Bsns Ctr The
  S43 . . . . .78 B2
Clodhall La
Curbar S32 . . . . .72 F2
Old Brampton S42 . . . . .93 B5
Cloisters Ct DE21 . . . . .205 F2
Cloonmore Croft S8 . . . . . . .43 C1
Cloonmore Dr S8 . . . . .43 C1
Close Bank DE13 . . . . .239 C6
Close The
Derby, Allestree DE22 . . . .204 F2
Derby, Normanton Park
  DE23 . . . . .218 D2
Great Longstone DE45 . . . .89 F4
Linton DE12 . . . . .261 C5
Marple SK6 . . . . .23 B3
Matlock DE4 . . . . .143 B6
Moira DE11 . . . . .262 D8
Shirebrook NG20 . . . . .119 F5
Tutbury DE13 . . . . .239 B6
Cloud Ave NG9 . . . . .223 F7
Cloudside Ct NG10 . . . . . .223 B7
Cloudside Jun Sch NG10 .223 B7
Cloudside Rd NG10 . . . . . .223 B7
Cloudwood Cl DE23 . . . . . .218 B1
Clough Ave SK6 . . . . .23 C6
Clough Bank S2 . . . . .43 B8
Clough Field Cl SK23 . . . . . .45 D8
Clough La
Hayfield SK22 . . . . .25 C5
Sheffield S10 . . . . .42 F5
Wensley DE4 . . . . .141 D8
Clough Mill SK22 . . . . .25 C5
Cloughside SK12 . . . . .32 E6
Clough Side SK6 . . . . .23 C7
Clough St SK17 . . . . .85 B7
Clough The
Bamford S33 . . . . .40 C4
Chesterfield S41 . . . . .96 E1
Clovelly Ct DE22 . . . . .218 D8
Clover Cl DE21 . . . . .220 F5
Clover Ct
Branston DE14 . . . . .253 E6
Shardlow DE72 . . . . .234 E2
Sheffield S8 . . . . .43 C2
Tibshelf DE55 . . . . .148 B7
Cloverdale DE11 . . . . .256 B7
Cloverdale Dr DE24 . . . . . .231 F2
Clover Fields Touring Cvn Pk
  SK17 . . . . .85 F1
Clover Nook Ind Est
  DE55 . . . . .159 E3
Clover Nook Rd DE55 . . . .159 E3
Clover Rise NG16 . . . . .195 B8
Cloversdale DE65 . . . . .230 C1
Clover Way NG19 . . . . .136 F4
Cloves Hill DE7 . . . . .192 C2
Clowne Jun & Inf Schs
  S43 . . . . .80 E3
Clowne Rd
Barlborough S43 . . . . .80 C6
Shuttlewood S44 . . . . .99 A8
Club La DE73 . . . . .244 A5
Clubmill Terr S40 . . . . .95 E4
Club Row S32 . . . . .71 E6
Clumber Ave NG16 . . . . . .171 E1
Clumber Cl
Ashbourne DE6 . . . . .185 B8
Clowne S43 . . . . .80 F4
3 Ripley DE5 . . . . .169 E1
Clumber Ct
Ilkeston DE7 . . . . .194 F5
Mansfield NG19 . . . . .135 E2
Clumber Pl S43 . . . . .97 C6
Clumber St NG10 . . . . .236 D7
Clun Ct NG19 . . . . .136 D2
Clune St S43 . . . . .81 A5
Cluster Rd DE56 . . . . .178 F4
Clusters Ct 3 DE56 . . . . .178 F4
Clyde St DE65 . . . . .228 D1
Coach Dr
Eastwood NG16 . . . . .182 F4
Quarndon DE22 . . . . .204 D7
Coach Rd
Hollingworth SK14 . . . . .9 D3
Ironville DE55 . . . . .170 D3
Ripley DE5 . . . . .169 F3
Shireoaks S81 . . . . .63 F6
Coach Way DE65 . . . . .242 C5
Coachways DE7 . . . . .193 F3
Coal La DE11, DE12 . . . . . .257 D8
Coalpit La
Coton in t E DE12 . . . . . . .260 E3
Youlgreave DE45 . . . . .125 C6
Coarses View SK23 . . . . . . .47 C7
Coasthill DE4 . . . . .156 F1
Coatsby Rd NG16 . . . . .195 F7
Cobden Pl NG19 . . . . .135 E2
Cobden Rd
Chesterfield S40 . . . . .266 A4
Matlock DE4 . . . . .143 C6
Cobden St
Derby DE22 . . . . .218 D5
Long Eaton NG10 . . . . . . .236 E7
Ripley DE5 . . . . .169 D2
Cobham Cl DE24 . . . . .231 D3
Cobnar Ave S8 . . . . .43 A2
Cobnar Dr
Chesterfield S41 . . . . .95 D8
Sheffield S8 . . . . .43 A2
Cobnar Rd S8 . . . . .43 A2
Cobnar Wood Cl S18 . . . . . .76 B3
Cobthorn Dr DE22 . . . . . . .204 C3
Coburn Pl DE1 . . . . .267 A3
Cock Ayne Cl NG10 . . . . . .223 B3

Cockayne La DE6 . . . . .164 B2
Cockayne St N DE24 . . . . . .232 E6
Cockayne St S DE24 . . . . . .232 E6
Cock Brow SK14 . . . . .15 C7
Cockcharme Gapp DE74 . .247 B6
Cockerhouse Rd NG16 . . .182 E4
Cock Hill
Baslow DE45 . . . . .91 F5
Clifton DE6 . . . . .184 F6
Cockleys NG10 . . . . .236 C6
Cock Pitt The DE1 . . . . . . .267 C3
Cockshead La DE6 . . . . . . .198 D7
Cockshut La
Melbourne DE73 . . . . .251 F7
Whaley Thorns NG20 . . . .101 A4
Cockshut Lane Bsns Ctr
  DE73 . . . . .252 A7
Cockshutt Ave S8 . . . . .56 D8
Cockshutt Dr S8 . . . . .56 D8
Cockshutt La DE55 . . . . . . .170 F8
Cockshutt Rd S8 . . . . .56 D8
Cod Beck Cl DE24 . . . . . . .233 D6
Coddington La DE4 . . . . . .156 E2
Codnor CE Prim Sch
  DE5 . . . . .181 B8
Codnor-Denby La DE5 . . .181 A5
Codnor Gate DE5 . . . . .170 B1
Codnor Gate Ind Est
  DE5 . . . . .170 A1
Codnor La DE5 . . . . .170 C2
Coffin La DE6 . . . . .165 B1
Coggers La S32 . . . . .52 F8
Coisley Hill S13 . . . . .44 F6
Cokayne Ave DE6 . . . . .173 C2
Cokayne Mews DE6 . . . . . .173 C3
Cokefield Terr DE55 . . . . . .148 C1
Coke St DE22 . . . . .218 D5
Coldharbour La S45 . . . . . .145 A4
Cold Side S33 . . . . .14 F3
Coldstream Wlk DE24 . . . .231 E4
Coldwell St DE4 . . . . .165 F8
Cole La DE7 . . . . .221 D3
Coleman St DE24 . . . . .232 E7
Coleraine Cl DE21 . . . . .220 B4
Coleridge St
Derby, Littleover DE23 . . .231 E6
Derby, Normanton DE23 . .231 F7
Colin Ave DE5 . . . . .181 B8
Colin St DE55 . . . . .159 A4
Colledge St DE55 . . . . .170 C6
College Ave S43 . . . . .78 D1
College Mews DE1 . . . . . . .218 E5
College Rd
Buxton SK17 . . . . .85 A6
Denstone ST14 . . . . .196 C6
Spinkhill S21 . . . . .60 D2
College St NG10 . . . . .223 C2
College View S43 . . . . .80 E3
College Way SK17 . . . . .85 D2
Collier Ave NG19 . . . . .136 B5
Collier La DE72 . . . . .221 C4
Collier St SK13 . . . . .17 C8
Colliers Trek S43 . . . . .80 C5
Colliers Way S45 . . . . .131 B4
Colliery Cl S43 . . . . .78 F1
Colliery La DE12 . . . . .261 D4
Colliery Rd
Blackwell DE55 . . . . .147 F1
Creswell S80 . . . . .100 E8
Swadlincote DE11 . . . . . . .256 A1
Colliery Row
Alfreton DE55 . . . . .159 B5
Pinxton NG16 . . . . .160 D2
Swadlincote DE11 . . . . . . .256 A1
Collin Ave NG10 . . . . .223 B4
Collingham Gdns DE22 . . .218 A5
Collingham Rd NG19 . . . . .135 D1
Collingwood Cres DE4 . . . .143 A6
Collingwood Rd NG10 . . . .236 E6
Collins Ave DE55 . . . . .160 A7
Collins Yd S18 . . . . .57 B1
Collis Cl DE24 . . . . .232 E7
Collishaw Cl 6 S41 . . . . . . .96 C1
Columbell Ave DE72 . . . . . .221 C5
Colne Cl NG19 . . . . .136 D2
Colombo St DE24 . . . . .232 E6
Colonade NG20 . . . . .119 E2
Colonnade The 3 SK17 . . .85 B8
Colonsay Cl NG19 . . . . .209 D3
Colton Cl S41 . . . . .76 E1
Coltsfoot Cl DE11 . . . . .256 F4
Coltsfoot Dr DE24 . . . . . . .231 F2
Coltsworth La S43 . . . . .80 E8
Columbell Way DE4 . . . . . .127 C2
Columbia St NG17 . . . . . . .148 F3
Columbine Cl DE21 . . . . . .206 A1
Colver Rd S2 . . . . .43 A8
Colvile Cl DE12 . . . . .263 D7
Colvile St DE22 . . . . .218 D6
Colwell Dr DE24 . . . . .233 D5
Colwick Cl NG19 . . . . .135 E1
Colwyn Ave DE23 . . . . .218 D1
Colyear St DE1 . . . . .267 B3
Combs Bank 55 SK13 . . . . . .9 D2
Combs Fold 51 SK13 . . . . . .9 D2
Combs Gdns 4 SK13 . . . . . .9 D2
Combs Gr 40 SK13 . . . . .9 D2
Combs Inf Sch SK23 . . . . . .46 E1
Combs Lea 1 SK13 . . . . .9 D1
Combs Mews 45 SK13 . . . . .9 D2
Combs Rd SK23 . . . . .46 F3
Combs Terr 5 SK13 . . . . . . .9 D2
Combs Way 42 SK13 . . . . . .9 D2
Comfrey Cl DE23 . . . . .230 F6
Commerce St
Derby DE24 . . . . .232 F8
Melbourne DE73 . . . . .252 A7

Commercial Rd SK17 . . . . . .69 C4
Commercial Row S32 . . . . . .72 C8
Common End DE65 . . . . . . .229 B3
Common La
Chelmorton SK17 . . . . .87 A1
Cutthorpe S42 . . . . .94 E8
Mansfield Woodhouse
  NG19 . . . . .136 A4
Shirebrook NG20 . . . . .119 C4
Shirland DE55 . . . . .146 C3
Stanley DE7 . . . . .207 A7
Sutton on t H DE6 . . . . . . .228 A8
Commonpiece La DE6 . . . .215 B2
Common Piece La DE65 . .230 E1
Commonpiece Rd S45 . . . .131 C3
Common Rd
Harhill S26 . . . . .62 B5
Sutton in A NG17 . . . . . . .148 F2
Swadlincote DE11 . . . . . . .256 C2
Thorpe Salvin S80 . . . . .62 F6
Commons Cl NG16 . . . . . . .195 A8
Common Side
Selston NG16 . . . . .171 F8
Swadlincote DE11 . . . . . . .256 C2
Commonside Rd S18 . . . . . .75 D2
Common The
Crich DE4 . . . . .168 A7
Quarndon DE22 . . . . .204 C8
South Normanton DE55 . .160 A5
Common Wood DE4 . . . . . .143 B6
Compass Cres S41 . . . . .77 C3
Compstall Mills Ests SK6 . .15 B2
Compstall Rd
Compstall SK6 . . . . .15 A3
Marple SK6 . . . . .15 A3
Compton Ave DE72 . . . . . .246 A8
Compton Dr S80 . . . . .81 D1
Compton Gr SK17 . . . . .85 B6
Compton Rd SK17 . . . . .85 B6
Compton St
Ashbourne DE6 . . . . .173 C2
Chesterfield S40 . . . . .266 A4
Holmewood S42 . . . . .116 E1
Langwith NG20 . . . . .119 F8
Conalan Ave S17 . . . . .56 B5
Concert Pl 8 SK17 . . . . . . .85 B7
Concorde Way NG19 . . . . .135 E2
Condliff Rd SK17 . . . . .69 B5
Conduit Rd DE7 . . . . .208 F4
Conduit St S44 . . . . .118 B8
Conduit St
Glossop SK13 . . . . .9 F7
Tintwistle SK13 . . . . .9 F7
Coney Green Bsns Ctr
  S45 . . . . .131 E4
Coney Green Networking Ctr
  S45 . . . . .131 E4
Coney Green Rd S45 . . . . . .131 E4
Coniston Ave DE21 . . . . . . .220 E6
Coniston Cl NG19 . . . . .136 F4
Coniston Cres DE21 . . . . . .205 D2
Coniston Dr
Clay Cross S45 . . . . .131 D2
Ilkeston DE7 . . . . .208 D5
Coniston Rd
Chesterfield S41 . . . . .95 E8
Dronfield S18 . . . . .56 E1
Long Eaton NG10 . . . . . . .223 A2
Coniston Way S41 . . . . .95 E8
Conjoint La SK17 . . . . .69 E4
Conkers Discovery Ctr★
  DE12 . . . . .262 D5
Conkers Waterside Ctr★
  DE12 . . . . .262 D4
Conksbury Ave DE45 . . . . .125 C6
Conksbury La DE45 . . . . . .125 C6
Connaught Ct DE55 . . . . . .159 B3
Connaught Rd DE22 . . . . . .218 C4
Connelly Ct S40 . . . . .95 E3
Consett Cl DE21 . . . . .205 D1
Consort Gdns DE21 . . . . . .206 C3
Constable Ave DE23 . . . . . .218 C2
Constable Cl
3 Dronfield S18 . . . . .56 E1
Sheffield S14 . . . . .43 E2
Constable Dr
Derby DE23 . . . . .218 B1
Marple SK6 . . . . .23 B8
Sheffield S14 . . . . .43 D2
Constable La DE23 . . . . . . .218 C2
Constable Pl S14 . . . . .43 E2
Constable Rd S14 . . . . .43 D2
Constable Way S14 . . . . . . .43 D2
Convent Cl DE15 . . . . .254 F8
Conway Ave DE72 . . . . .221 D2
Conway Rd NG10 . . . . .236 F8
Conway St NG10 . . . . .236 F8
Conygree La DE6 . . . . .184 D7
Cook Cl DE56 . . . . .179 E5
Cook Dr DE7 . . . . .209 A6
Cooke & Beard Homes S8 .43 B5
Cooke Cl
Clay Cross S42 . . . . .131 B6
Long Eaton NG10 . . . . . . .236 B7
Cookfield DE56 . . . . .179 E8
Cookham Cl DE3 . . . . .217 C2
Cook La DE6 . . . . .211 B1
Cooks Dr DE74 . . . . .247 A3
Coole Well Cl S43 . . . . .97 D8
Coombes La S13 . . . . .16 C5
Coombes View SK14 . . . . . .15 F8
Coombs Rd DE45 . . . . .109 F5
Cooper's Cl 2 DE6 . . . . . . .173 C2
Co-operative St
Derby DE23 . . . . .218 F2
Disley SK12 . . . . .32 D6
Long Eaton NG10 . . . . . . .236 E6

Coopers Cl
Acresford DE12 . . . . .265 B7
Borrowash DE72 . . . . .221 D1
Coopers Croft DE65. . . . . . .227 C1
Coopers Gdns DE6. . . . . . . .173 B1
Cooper St
Derby DE22 . . . . .218 D6
Glossop SK13. . . . . .10 B1
Ripley DE5. . . . . .169 D1
Copecastle Sq DE1 . . . . . . .267 C2
Cope Ct DE24. . . . . .232 A5
Copeland Ave NG9. . . . . . . .223 E8
Copeland St DE1. . . . . .267 C2
Copenhagen Rd S45. . . . . .131 E4
Copestake Cl NG10 . . . . . . .236 A7
Copes Way
Derby DE21 . . . . .220 A8
Uttoxeter ST14 . . . . .210 A1
Copley Croft 3 DE6 . . . . . . .173 D3
Coplow La DE65 . . . . .226 D5
Copperas Rd DE11. . . . . . . .255 D5
Copper Beech Dr SK13. . . . . .9 E1
Copper Beeches DE5 . . . . . .169 C2
Copperleaf Cl DE22 . . . . . .267 A2
Copper Yd DE5 . . . . .180 F2
Coppice Ave
High Lane SK12. . . . . .32 A6
Ilkeston DE7 . . . . .194 D5
Coppice Cl
Chesterfield S41 . . . . .115 D6
Derby DE22 . . . . .204 F1
High Lane SK12. . . . . .32 A6
Kilburn DE56 . . . . .192 A7
Coppice Dr DE75. . . . . .193 F7
Coppice Dr
Eastwood NG16. . . . . .182 D3
Heanor DE75 . . . . .193 F7
Coppice End Rd DE22. . . . . .204 C1
Coppice La
Clifton Campville B79 . . . .263 F1
High Lane SK12. . . . . .32 A5
Coppice Mews DE75 . . . . . .193 F7
Coppice Prim Sch DE75 . . .193 E8
Coppice Side DE11. . . . . . .256 C3
Coppice The
Horwich End SK23. . . . . .45 F5
Shirebrook NG20. . . . . . . .119 D3
Coppice View DE55 . . . . . .160 A4
Coppicewood Dr DE23 . . . .218 A1
Copse Cl DE4. . . . . .165 E8
Copse Gr DE23 . . . . .231 A7
Copse Rise DE11. . . . . .256 B7
Copseside Cl 10 NG10 . . . .236 A6
Copse The
Ilkeston DE7 . . . . .194 D5
Marple SK6 . . . . .23 C8
Copsewood DE55 . . . . .160 A4
Copsey Croft Ct NG10 . . . .236 F7
Copthorne Com Inf Sch
DE55 . . . . .159 A5
Copthurst Rd HD9 . . . . .3 E7
Coral Way S45. . . . . .131 D4
Corbar Grange SK17 . . . . . . .85 A8
Corbar Rd SK17. . . . . .66 B1
Corbar Woods La SK17. . . . .66 A1
Corbel Cl DE21 . . . . .205 D2
Corbridge Gr DE23. . . . . . . .231 A7
Corbriggs Cvn Site S42. . . .115 F5
Corby Cl DE24 . . . . .232 E5
Cordelia Way DE72. . . . . . .232 E2
Corden Ave DE3 . . . . .218 A2
Corden St DE23. . . . . .219 A2
Cordville Cl DE21. . . . . . . .220 B5
Cordwell Ave S41. . . . . .95 C8
Cordwell Cl
Castle Donington DE74 . . .246 F3
Staveley S43 . . . . .97 D8
Cordwell La S18. . . . . .74 E5
Cordy La
Brinsley NG16. . . . . .182 F8
Selston NG16. . . . . .182 F8
Corfe Cl DE23 . . . . .231 D6
Corfield Ave DE75 . . . . . . .193 F7
Corfield CE Inf Sch
DE75 . . . . .181 D1
Coriander Gdns DE23 . . . .231 D4
Corinium Cl DE24. . . . . . . .233 D5
Corker Rd S12. . . . . .44 A6
Corks La SK12. . . . . .32 E5
Corley La DE4 . . . . .174 D2
Cornbrook DE45. . . . . .108 F7
Corn Cl DE55 . . . . .160 B6
Cornel Ct 4 NG19 . . . . . . .136 E1
Corner Farm DE6. . . . . .201 E8
Cornfield Ave DE55 . . . . . .146 A8
Cornfield Cl 8 S42 . . . . . . .95 A5
Cornfield Rd NG16. . . . . . .195 E7
Cornflower Dr DE21. . . . . .206 B3
Cornhill DE22. . . . . .204 F4
Cornhill CI DE56. . . . . .190 D4
Cornhill Dr DE55. . . . . .159 B4
Cornmill Cl
Bolsover S44 . . . . .99 B2
Calver S32. . . . . .72 C1
Derby DE7. . . . . .233 D5
Corn Mill Cl DE4. . . . . .165 C6
Cornmill Ho SK13. . . . . .10 D1
Cornmill La DE13 . . . . .239 E6
Corn Mkt DE1 . . . . .267 B3
Corn St SK13. . . . . .10 C1
Cornwall Ave
Brimington S43 . . . . .96 F8
Buxton SK17 . . . . .85 E7
Cornwall Cl
 4 Brimington S43 . . . . . . .96 F8
Westwood NG16. . . . . .171 C4
Cornwall Dr
Brimington S43 . . . . .96 F8

Cornwall Dr continued
Grassmoor S42 . . . . .115 F3
Cornwallis Cl NG10 . . . . . .236 D6
Cornwall Rd
Burton u T DE15. . . . . .254 E6
Derby DE21 . . . . .219 D6
Shireoaks S81. . . . . .63 F7
Coronation Ave
Derby DE4. . . . . .179 A5
Ilkeston DE7. . . . . .233 C5
New Houghton NG19. . . . .134 F7
Sandiacre NG10. . . . . .223 A7
Coronation Cl DE73 . . . . . .268 B2
Coronation Cotts DE13. . . .253 A8
Coronation Cres ST14 . . . .197 A4
Coronation Dr
Shirebrook NG20. . . . . . . .119 F2
South Normanton DE55. . .160 B5
Coronation La DE12. . . . . . .265 F6
Coronation Rd
Brimington S43 . . . . .96 E8
Cossall DE7, NG16. . . . . . .195 A2
Mapperley DE7 . . . . .193 F3
Stanley DE7. . . . . .207 C6
Coronation St
Derby DE23 . . . . .232 B8
 1 Ilkeston DE7 . . . . .208 F8
Overseal DE12. . . . . .262 A4
Swadlincote DE11 . . . . . . .256 A5
Whitwell S80 . . . . .82 A6
Coronet Ct DE21 . . . . .206 D3
Corporation Rd DE7 . . . . . .209 A5
Corporation St
Chesterfield S41 . . . . .266 C3
Derby DE1 . . . . .267 B3
Corve Way S40 . . . . .94 F5
Cossall Rd NG9 . . . . .209 D5
Cote Bottom La DE65 . . . . .227 A7
Cote Green La SK6. . . . . . . .15 B1
Cote Green Rd SK6 . . . . . . .15 C1
Cote Hilloc DE4. . . . . .127 A6
Cote La SK22 . . . . .25 D3
Cotes Park Ind Est DE55 . .159 D2
Cotes Park La DE55. . . . . . .159 E2
Cotgrave Rd NG19. . . . . . . .135 F2
Cotman Dr SK6. . . . . .23 C8
Cotmanhay Inf & Jun Sch
DE7 . . . . .194 E5
Cotmanhay Rd DE7 . . . . . .194 F3
Coton Cl NG19. . . . . .136 E4
Coton in the Elms CE Prim
Sch DE12 . . . . .260 D3
Coton La
Coton in t E DE12 . . . . .260 F3
Rosliston DE12 . . . . .260 D5
Coton Pk DE12 . . . . .255 C1
Coton Rd DE12 . . . . .259 E6
Cotswold Cl
 2 Chesterfield S40 . . . . . . .95 C5
Derby DE23 . . . . .231 C8
Glossop SK13. . . . . .17 A8
 4 Long Eaton NG10 . . . . .236 B8
Swadlincote DE11. . . . . . . .256 A3
Cotswold Dr S42. . . . . .115 E3
Cotswold Rd DE14 . . . . . . .253 F8
Cottage Cl
Heage DE56. . . . . .179 E8
Ilkeston DE7 . . . . .194 D3
Poolsbrook S43 . . . . .98 A7
Swadlincote DE11. . . . . . . .256 A7
Cottage Gdn DE56 . . . . . . .179 E3
Cottage Garden La DE75 . .181 D2
Cottage La SK13 . . . . .9 E2
Cottages The DE23. . . . . . . .47 B6
Cottam Cres SK6 . . . . .23 B7
Cottam Dr S43. . . . . .80 C6
Cotterdale Cl NG19 . . . . . .136 E1
Cotterhill La S43 . . . . .96 E7
Cottesmore Cl DE15. . . . . .248 A1
Cottesmore Rd DE15 . . . . .248 A1
Cottisford Cl DE23 . . . . . . .232 B8
Cottonbrook Rd DE23 . . . .232 B8
Cotton La DE24 . . . . .219 C1
Cotton Mill Hill S42. . . . . . .113 C7
Cotton St S44 . . . . .99 A1
Cotts The SK17 . . . . .86 D5
Council Hos
Bradbourne DE6 . . . . .163 B6
Hanbury DE13 . . . . .238 A3
Countess Gr DE53. . . . . . .244 F8
Counting House Rd SK12 . .32 E5
Countisbury Dr DE21. . . . .206 A2
County Est The NG17. . . . .148 E2
Coupe La S42, S45 . . . . . . .131 A5
Coupe St DE5 . . . . .180 F8
Coupland Cl S41 . . . . .77 C4
Coupland Pl DE55 . . . . . . .159 C1
Court Farm La DE14 . . . . . .253 E7
Court La DE45 . . . . .108 E8
Courtland Dr DE24 . . . . . . .233 B6
Courtland Gdns DE24 . . . .233 B6
Courtland Rd DE65. . . . . . .229 C3
Courtney Way DE56 . . . . . .179 D5
Court Pl S43 . . . . .97 C8
Court St DE11 . . . . .256 E3
Court The DE24 . . . . .233 B6
Court View S43 . . . . .80 E3
Courtway Cres DE73 . . . . . .244 E8
Courtyard Mews DE24. . . . .233 A6
Courtyard Pl DE21. . . . . . . .220 C5
Courtyard The
Bakewell DE45. . . . . .109 D6
Belper DE56. . . . . .179 A4
Darley Dale DE4 . . . . .127 C3
Hollingworth SK14. . . . . .9 D3
Coventry Cl DE11. . . . . . . .256 D6
Coventry La NG9 . . . . .209 F2
Coverdale Wlk DE24 . . . . .233 C7

Covert Pl DE11 . . . . .262 C8
Covert The DE21. . . . . .220 E4
Cowbrook Ave SK13. . . . . . .10 F1
Cowburn Dr SK13. . . . . .10 F1
Cowburn Dr SK22. . . . . .24 C1
Cowdale Cotts SK17 . . . . . . .86 A4
Cowdray Cl DE24 . . . . .231 D2
Cowham Cl DE55 . . . . .159 C3
Cow La S43 . . . . .77 E1
Cowley Bottom S18. . . . . . . .75 E8
Cowley Cl S41 . . . . .266 C3
Cowley Gdns S20 . . . . .59 E8
Cowley La S18. . . . . .75 D7
Cowley St DE22 . . . . .218 E7
Cowlishaw Cl DE73 . . . . . .234 E1
Cowlow La SK17, SK23. . . . .47 C2
Cowper Rd NG16 . . . . .195 A8
Cowper St DE24 . . . . .232 A5
Cowpingle La S43 . . . . .77 E1
Cowsell Dr S45. . . . . .131 E2
Cowsley Rd DE21 . . . . .219 D7
Cowslip Cl DE12 . . . . .262 E1
Cowslip Mdw DE72 . . . . . .235 A7
Cox's La NG19 . . . . .136 B5
Coxbench Rd DE21 . . . . . . .191 F4
Cox Green Ct DE23 . . . . . . .231 A7
Coxon's Yd 4 DE6 . . . . . . .173 B2
Coxon St DE21. . . . . .220 E5
Crabtree Ave SK12 . . . . .32 E5
Crabtree Cl
Castle Donington DE74 . . .247 A2
Derby DE23 . . . . .204 C4
Wirksworth DE4 . . . . .165 E7
Crabtree Ct SK12 . . . . .32 D6
Crabtree Hill DE22 . . . . . . .204 C3
Crab Tree Hill DE21. . . . . . .205 C8
Cracken Cl SK23. . . . . .34 D2
Craddock Ave DE21. . . . . . .220 E3
Cradock Mews S2 . . . . .43 E7
Cradock Rd S2 . . . . .43 F7
Crafty Flats La DE12. . . . . .260 F3
Cragdale Gr S20. . . . . .59 D7
Crag La DE55 . . . . .148 A2
Craggon Dr S43 . . . . .77 D4
Craggs Dr S43. . . . . .80 E3
Craggs Rd S44. . . . . .99 A2
Craglands Gr S40. . . . . .95 A5
Cragside Cl S41 . . . . .96 C3
Cragside S80. . . . . .82 A1
Crags View S80. . . . . .81 F1
Crag Dr SK23 . . . . .45 F6
Craiglee Ct 4 DE24 . . . . . .231 D3
Craig St NG10 . . . . .236 E7
Cranberry Gr DE23 . . . . . . .230 F6
Cranborne Rd S41 . . . . .95 E7
Cranbourne Cl NG9 . . . . . .209 D2
Cranbrook Cl NG10 . . . . . .136 C6
Cranfleet Way NG10 . . . . . .236 B7
Cranhill Cl DE23 . . . . .230 F6
Cranleigh Rd S43 . . . . .79 B3
Cranmer Gr NG19 . . . . .136 D3
Cranmer Rd DE21. . . . . . . .267 D3
Cranmer St
Ilkeston DE7 . . . . .194 F1
Long Eaton NG10. . . . . . . .223 D1
Cratcliff View DE4 . . . . . . .126 A1
Craven Rd S41. . . . . .95 F5
Crawford Ave DE24 . . . . . . .232 A5
Crawford Rd S8 . . . . .43 A4
Crawley Rd DE24 . . . . .232 F5
Crawshaw Ave S8 . . . . .56 D8
Crawshaw Gr S8. . . . . .56 D8
Crawshaw Mews S18 . . . . .56 C1
Cray's Hill DE55 . . . . .170 B7
Crayford Rd DE24. . . . . . . .233 A5
Craythorne Cl DE11. . . . . . .256 A7
Craythorne Rd DE13 . . . . . .240 D3
Creamery La DE6 . . . . .151 D1
Crecy Cl DE22 . . . . .218 C3
Creighton La ST14 . . . . . . .210 A5
Crescent S26 . . . . .61 E5
Crescent Dr SK23. . . . . .33 D2
Crescent Prim Sch
NG19 . . . . .135 D2
Crescent Rd
Ashover S42 . . . . .113 D7
Selston NG16. . . . . .171 D6
Crescent Row SK22 . . . . . . .25 A2
Crescent The
Alfreton DE55 . . . . .159 B3
Barlborough S43 . . . . .80 C6
Bradwell S33 . . . . .51 A8
Breaston DE72. . . . . .235 C7
Breedon on t H DE73. . . . .252 F2
Brimington S43 . . . . .96 C7
Buxton SK17 . . . . .85 B8
Chapel-en-le-F SK23 . . . . . .47 C7
Clay Cross S45 . . . . .131 C2
Derby, Boulton DE24 . . . . .232 E6
Derby, Chaddesden DE21 . .219 F5
Holmesfield S18 . . . . .75 A8
Holymoorside S42 . . . . . . .113 D8
Horsley Woodhouse DE7 . .192 C7
Mayfield DE6 . . . . .184 D7
New Mills SK22 . . . . .33 B8
Repton DE65. . . . . .242 D2
Risley DE72 . . . . .222 D3
Sheffield S17 . . . . .55 E5
Shirebrook NG20. . . . . . . .119 E6
Stanley DE7. . . . . .207 B8
Stapleford NG9 . . . . .209 E2
Swadlincote DE11. . . . . . . .255 E6
Cressbrook Ave S42. . . . . . .132 B7
Cressbrook Way DE21. . . . .206 B3
Cressida Ct DE73 . . . . .232 D2

Cresswell Ave SK22 . . . . . . .33 C1
Cresswellpart La S33 . . . . . .50 E7
Cresswell St SK22 . . . . .33 C8
Cressy Rd DE55. . . . . .159 A4
Cresta Gr DE21 . . . . .205 F1
Crest Cl DE13. . . . . .240 E1
Crest The
Derby DE22 . . . . .204 E1
Linton DE12 . . . . .261 C6
Creswell Bsns Pk S80. . . . .100 E8
Creswell CE Inf Sch S80 . . .81 E1
Creswell Crags Visitor Ctr*
S80. . . . . .82 B1
Creswell Ct 12 NG19 . . . . .136 E4
Creswell Jun Sch S80. . . . . .81 E1
Creswell Rd
Clowne S43 . . . . .80 F4
Cuckney NG20 . . . . .101 E3
Creswell Sta S80 . . . . .81 E1
Creswick Cl S40 . . . . .114 B8
Crewe St DE23. . . . . .218 F1
Crewton Way DE24. . . . . . .232 F7
Crich Ave DE23 . . . . .218 C2
Crich Carr CE Prim Sch
DE4 . . . . .156 C1
Crich CE Inf Sch DE4 . . . . .156 F1
Crich Cir DE23. . . . . .218 C2
Crich Jun Sch DE4. . . . . . . .157 A1
Crich La
Belper DE56. . . . . .178 A7
Ridgeway DE56 . . . . .168 B3
Crich Pl
Buxton SK17 . . . . .85 E7
North Wingfield S42 . . . . . .131 F6
Crich Rd
Fritchley DE56. . . . . .168 A6
Staveley S43 . . . . .97 C7
Crich Tramway Village*
DE4 . . . . .156 C2
Crich View
Bolsover S44 . . . . .118 B8
Newton DE55. . . . . .148 A4
Crich Way DE11. . . . . .255 E5
Cricket Cl DE15. . . . . .248 E8
Cricketers Cl DE15. . . . . . .254 F8
Cricketers Ct DE23. . . . . . .231 D8
Cricket View S43. . . . . .80 E2
Cricklewood Ct 7 S43. . . . .78 B3
Cricklewood Rd DE22 . . . . .218 B6
Cringle Mews DE21. . . . . . .205 E2
Cripton La S45 . . . . .129 E5
Crispin Cl S12 . . . . .44 A4
Crispin Dr S12 . . . . .44 A4
Crispin Gdns S12. . . . . .44 A4
Crispin Rd 8 S12. . . . . .44 A4
Critch's Flats NG16 . . . . . . .195 F6
Critchley St DE7 . . . . .194 F1
Croft Ave DE6 . . . . .151 D1
Croft Cl
Dale Abbey DE7. . . . . .207 F2
Derby DE21 . . . . .220 F5
Nethersesal DE12 . . . . . . .264 F7
Ockbrook DE72 . . . . .221 C4
Pinxton NG16. . . . . .160 C3
Rolleston DE13 . . . . .240 B4
Croft Cres NG16 . . . . .195 C5
Croft Ct NG17 . . . . .148 F4
Croft End DE21 . . . . .205 C8
Crofters Cl S21 . . . . .60 C4
Crofters Ct DE21 . . . . .205 E2
Croft Gr ST14. . . . . .210 C1
Croft Inf Sch DE55 . . . . . . .159 A3
Croft La DE21. . . . . .205 D3
Croft Lea S18. . . . . .56 C2
Croft Manor SK13. . . . . .10 E1
Crofton Cl S18. . . . . .56 F1
Crofton Rise S18 . . . . .56 F1
Croft Rd
Great Longstone DE45. . . . .90 A4
Sheffield, Intake S12. . . . . .44 B5
Croftstead Ave ST14 . . . . .196 D6
Crofts The S32. . . . . .53 A8
Croft View
Clowne S43 . . . . .80 F3
Staveley S43 . . . . .97 C6
Croft Wlk S80 . . . . .82 A6
Cromarty Cl DE24. . . . . . . .231 E4
Cromarty Rise S18. . . . . . . .56 D2
Cromdale Ave S43 . . . . .77 D4
Cromer Cl DE3 . . . . .217 C1
Cromford Bank 21 SK13. . . .9 D2
Cromford CE Prim Sch
DE4 . . . . .155 B6
Cromford Cl
 4 Chesterfield S41 . . . . . . .95 D7
Horwich End SK23. . . . . . . .45 E6

Cromford Dr
Derby DE3 . . . . .217 E4
Staveley S43 . . . . .97 C8
Cromford Fold 23 SK13. . . . .9 D2
Cromford Gn 20 SK13 . . . . . .9 D2
Cromford Gr 18 SK13 . . . . . .9 D2
Cromford Hill DE4 . . . . . . .155 A5
Cromford La SK17 . . . . .85 E7
Cromford Lea 16 SK13 . . . . .9 D2
Cromford Mews SK23. . . . . .45 E5
Cromford Pl
Buxton SK17 . . . . .85 E7
 22 Gamesley SK13 . . . . .9 D2
Cromford Rd
Aldercar NG16. . . . . .182 B4
Clay Cross S45 . . . . .131 A5
Crich DE4. . . . . .156 F2
Derby DE21 . . . . .220 A8
Heanor NG16. . . . . .181 E5
Ripley DE5. . . . . .169 C2
Wirksworth DE4 . . . . .154 F1
Cromford Road Ind Est
NG16. . . . . .182 A8
Cromford Sta DE4 . . . . . . .155 C7
Cromford Way 17 SK13. . . . .9 D2
Cromford Wharf* DE4 . . . .155 C7
Crompton Rd
Ilkeston DE7 . . . . .209 B4
Mansfield NG19. . . . . .135 D3
Staveley S43 . . . . .78 F2
Crompton Road Ind Est
DE7 . . . . .209 B3
Crompton St
Derby DE1 . . . . .267 B2
New Houghton NG19. . . . .134 F8
Cromwell Ave
Blackwell DE55 . . . . .147 E1
Chapel-en-le-F SK23 . . . . . .47 A5
Findern DE65. . . . . .230 D2
Ilkeston DE7 . . . . .209 A5
Cromwell Cl DE13 . . . . . . .239 C5
Cromwell Dr DE55 . . . . . . .169 D7
Cromwell Rd
Bolsover S44 . . . . .118 B8
Chesterfield S40 . . . . .266 A4
Derby DE23 . . . . .218 F2
Cromwell Spire NG16 . . . .195 C8
Crooked Spire (St Mary & All
Saints Church)* S40 . . . .266 B3
Crookes Ave
Mansfield Woodhouse
NG19. . . . . .136 C3
Pleasley NG19. . . . . .135 A5
Crook Stile DE4. . . . . .143 A7
Cropper La DE6. . . . . .215 B4
Cropston Cl S41 . . . . .115 C7
Cropton Cl DE24 . . . . .233 C6
Crosby St DE22 . . . . .218 D4
Cross Chantrey Rd S8 . . . . .43 A3
Cross Cl DE23 . . . . .231 C8
Cross Cliffe SK13 . . . . .17 E8
Crossdale Gr DE21 . . . . . . .206 C3
Crossfield Gr SK6. . . . . .15 B1
Crossgate La S13 . . . . .9 F7
Crossgreen Cotts DE4. . . . .142 B8
Crosshill DE5. . . . . .181 B6
Crosshill Dr DE7 . . . . .208 C5
Crossings Ave SK23. . . . . . .47 A6
Crossings Mdw SK23 . . . . . .47 A6
Cross Keys La DE55 . . . . . .169 F7
Cross Keys Row SK23 . . . . . .47 B8
Cross La
Calver S32. . . . . .72 B2
Codnor DE5 . . . . .181 B7
Dronfield, Coal Aston S18 . .57 C3
Dronfield, Quoit Green S18 . .57 B1
Dronfield S18. . . . . .57 C5
Flagg SK17. . . . . .106 F3
Ible DE4. . . . . .153 C7
Monyash DE45. . . . . .107 B2
Rolleston DE13 . . . . .240 B2
Sheffield S17 . . . . .55 C8
Shirland DE55. . . . . .158 E8
Sutton in A NG17 . . . . . . .148 F2
Wessington DE55 . . . . . . .157 F8
Crossland Pl S12. . . . . .44 A4
Crossland Rd S12 . . . . .44 A4
Crossland Rd S32. . . . . .53 A7
Crosslands Cl SK13 . . . . . . .17 D8
Crossland Villas S32 . . . . . .53 A7
Cross Lanes DE6 . . . . .215 C5
Cross Lea DE7 . . . . .207 F2
Crossley St DE5 . . . . .169 E2
Cross London St S43. . . . . . .77 D3
Crosslow La DE6. . . . . .150 E5
Cross Myrtle Rd S2 . . . . . . .43 A5
Cross Park Rd 1 S8 . . . . . . .43 A5
Cross Rd S14 . . . . .210 B1
Cross Rise S18. . . . . .57 E8
Cross Side DE6 . . . . .184 F7
Cross St
Bolsover S44 . . . . .118 C8
Bramley-Vale S44 . . . . . . .117 D1
Breedon on t H DE73. . . . .252 F2
 8 Broadbottom SK14. . . . . .16 A8
Buxton SK17 . . . . .85 D8
Castleton S33 . . . . .38 B2
Chapel-en-le-F SK23 . . . . . .47 B6
Chesterfield S40 . . . . .266 A4
Clay Cross S45 . . . . .131 C3
Derby DE22 . . . . .218 D6
Glossop SK13. . . . . .10 C1

Cross continued
Grassmoor S42 ....115 F3
Hadfield SK13 ....10 A5
Hollingworth SK14..........9 D4
Killamarsh S21 ....60 F7
Linton DE11................261 E8
Long Eaton NG10........236 E8
Mansfield Woodhouse
NG19......................136 B2
New Mills SK22.............33 C8
North Wingfield S42......131 C6
Sandiacre NG10.............223 C6
Cross The
1 Glossop SK13..............10 A5
Great Longstone DE45....89 F4
Crossways La DE6 ....176 B2
Cross Wellington St S43 ..77 D3
Crow Croft Rd S45 ....132 C2
Crowcroft Way NG10....223 B2
Crowden Dr SK13..........10 B5
Crowden YH* SK13..........6 E3
Crowestones SK17 ....85 C6
Crowfoot La DE65........226 E8
Crow Hill NG19 ....135 B5
Crowhill La DE45 ....109 A6
Crow Hill La NG19 ......136 B2
Crow La
Brackenfield DE55.......146 A6
Chesterfield S41.........96 C3
Unstone S18 ....76 F7
Crown Cl
Chesterfield S43..........77 D3
Long Eaton NG10........236 A7
Crown Hill Way DE7....207 B8
Crownland Dr DE7 ......233 A2
Crown Mews DE22 ......218 E3
Crown Rd S41 ....96 A5
Crown Specl Sch DE13 ..240 C1
Crown Sq
Branston DE14............253 E8
Mattock DE4 ....143 B5
Crown St
Clowne S43 ....80 E3
Derby DE22 ....218 E3
Duffield DE56.............190 E4
Crown Terr **2** DE56......178 F4
Crown Way
Aldercar NG16............182 B4
Chellaston DE73..........244 F8
Crown Wlk DE1............267 B2
Crown Yd DE4 ....154 F1
Crowshaw St DE24......232 B8
Crowstones Rd DE4......127 B3
Crowther Pl **7** S7 ....43 A8
Croxton Ct **5** NG19......136 E3
Croydon Wlk DE21......217 F6
Cruck Cl S18 ....56 E2
Crystal Cl DE3 ....217 D4
Cubley La DE6 ....198 B1
Cuckmere Cl DE24......205 B5
Cuckoostone La DE4....128 F2
Cuillin Cl NG10 ....223 A1
Cullabine Ct S2............44 A7
Cullabine Rd S2...........44 A7
Culland Rd DE14..........254 B7
Culland View DE4........168 A8
Cullen Ave DE6 ....173 C1
Cullumbell La S45 ......129 A7
Culworth Ct DE56........179 D4
Culworth Ct DE21........206 B2
Cumberhills Rd DE22,
DE56......................190 C1
Cumberland Ave DE21 ..219 E6
Cumberland Cl
Buxton SK17 ....85 D4
Westwood NG16.........171 C4
Cumberland Cres DE72..221 B2
Cumberland Rd DE15 ..254 D6
Cumbria Wlk DE3........217 C1
Cummings St DE23 ....219 A2
Cundy Rd S44 ....99 A3
Cunliffe St S18 ....57 C4
Cunnery La DE4............144 B3
Cunnery The DE6 ....202 F2
Cunningham Pl DE45 ..109 D6
Cupola Park Cvn Pk DE4.156 B3
Curbar Cl S42 ....132 A7
Curbar Curve S42.........97 C6
Curbar Hill S32 ....72 D2
Curbar Prim Sch S32 ....72 D1
Curborough Dr DE24....233 D6
Curlew Ave S21............59 B3
Curlew Cl DE24 ....231 D4
Curlew Way SK13 ....16 F8
Curtis Gr SK13..............10 A5
Curzon Ave S18 ....75 F8
Curzon CE Prim Sch The
DE22 ....204 D6
Curzon Cl
Derby DE22 ....204 C4
Killamarsh S21............60 D6
Curzon Ct DE56..........190 E3
Curzon La
Derby DE24 ....233 A8
Duffield DE56.............190 D3
Curzon Rd
Buxton SK17 ....85 C7
Derby DE21................219 F7
Curzon St
Derby DE1 ....267 A3
Long Eaton NG10........223 B2
Curzon Terr SK17 ....88 D7
Cuscas La DE6............187 F4
Cut La DE1, DE21 ....219 B7
Cutler La S21 ....60 B7
Cutler La DE6 ....189 A1
Cutler Way DE21 ....217 D4
Cuttholme Cl S40..........95 B4
Cuttholme Rd S40........95 C4
Cuttholme Way **1** S40..95 C4
Cutthorpe Grange S40 ..95 A7
Cutthorpe Prim Sch S42 ..94 D7
Cutthorpe Rd S40..........95 A8
Cutting The DE11........256 F4
Cuttlebrook Cl DE23....231 E6
Cyclamen Cl DE14........254 A8
Cygnet Fold NG19........136 C4
Cypress Ave S8............43 C1
Cypress Cl S21 ....60 C5
Cypress Way SK6 ....32 A7
Cypress Wlk DE21........220 B5
Cypruss Rd S8..............43 A5
Cyril Ave NG9..............223 D7**

D

Dade Ave S43 ....97 C6
Dag La DE12................263 E7
Dagnall Gdns DE45 ....109 D5
Dagnall Terr DE45........109 D5
Dagnam Ct S2..............43 F6
Dagnam Cres S2 ....43 F6
Dagnam Dr S2 ....43 F7
Dagnam Pl S2 ....43 F6
Dagnam Rd S2 ....33 C7
Dahlia Ave DE55........160 B7
Dahlia Dr DE21 ....206 C3
Dairy House Rd DE23 ..219 B1
Daisy Cl DE12 ....262 E1
Daisy Farm Rd NG16....195 B8
Daisy La DE22 ....262 B3
Daisymere La SK17 ....67 A2
Dakeyne Cl DE4 ....127 F1
Dakin Ave SK17............85 D8
Dakin Cl SK17 ....66 E1
Dalbury Rd S18 ....56 C1
Dalbury Wlk DE23......231 C5
Daleacre Ave DE74......247 F5
Dale Ave
Long Eaton NG10........223 D1
Newton DE55 ....148 A3
Somercotes DE55 ......170 C6
Dale Bank Cres S43........77 D3
Dalebank La S45..........145 B8
Dale Brook DE65........228 E1
Dalebrook Rd DE15 ....248 B5
Dale Cl
Breaston DE72............235 D8
Fritchley DE56............168 A6
Langwith NG20 ....119 E8
Staveley S43 ....97 C8
Stonebroom DE55........147 B4
Whaley Thorns NG20....100 F1
Dale Com Prim Sch
DE55 ....218 F1
Dale Cres
Hathersage S32............53 B8
Tupton S42................115 C1
Dale Ct DE56 ....191 F8
Dale End
Brassington DE4 ....153 A1
Wirksworth DE4 ....154 F1
Dale End Rd DE65........228 C2
Dalefield Dr DE11........256 A3
Dalehead Cl S32............71 E5
Dale Hill DE55............158 B5
Dale La
Buxton SK17 ....85 E8
Glapwell S44 ....134 D7
Dale Park Ave DE56......192 A8
Dale Rd
Beeston NG9..............223 F3
Buxton, Higher Buxton
SK17.......................85 C7
Buxton, Peak Dale SK17 ..67 B7
Derby, Alvaston DE24 ..233 B7
Derby, Normanton DE23..218 F2
Dronfield S18................76 B8
Killamarsh S21............60 E6
Kimberley NG16..........195 F6
Matlock Bath DE4 ......143 B3
New Mills SK22 ....33 C7
Stanley DE7................207 C4
Stanton-by-D DE7 ......208 C1
Tupton S42................115 C1
Dale Rd N DE4............127 A5
Dale Rd S DE4 ....127 D1
Dales Cl **4** DE11........255 E5
Dalesfield DE4 ....143 B5
Dalesgate Cl DE23......231 C5
Daleside DE15 ....248 B1
Dale Side SK17............85 B7
Dale St
Ilkeston DE7 ....208 F7
Mansfield NG19..........136 B1
Dales The DE7............207 E7
Dale Terr SK17............85 B6
Dale The
Bonsall DE4 ....142 D1
Hathersage S32............53 B8
Stoney Middleton S32 ..71 E4
Wirksworth DE4 ....154 E1
Dale View
Earl Sterndale SK17 ....105 A3
Ilkeston DE7 ....208 E7
Litton SK17 ....69 E3
Mottram in L SK14........9 A3
Shirland DE55............146 C4
Dale View Cl S45..........132 B3
Dale View Gdns DE56....191 F8
Dale View Rd S45..........132 B4

Dale View Terr SK17........89 A6
Dalewood Cl
Chesterfield S41............96 E1
South Normanton DE55 ..160 A3
Dalkeith Ave DE24........232 F5
Dalley Cl **1** NG9..........223 E7
Dalley La DE56 ....178 C6
Dallimore Prim Sch DE7 ..208 D4
Dallimore Rd DE7........208 D4
Dalness Ct **8** DE24......231 D3
Dalston Rd DE11..........256 A5
Dalton Ave
Burton u T DE15..........248 B1
Derby DE22 ....218 C3
Dalton Cl **3** NG9..........223 E5
Daltons La NG16..........182 A4
Dalvey Way S43 ....77 D5
Dame Catherine Harpur's
Sch DE73 ....251 A5
Dam La
Alsop en la D DE6........150 E3
Shirland DE55............146 F1
Damon Cl S45............132 C1
Damon Dr S43..............96 F8
Damsbrook Dr S43........80 E3
Damsbrook La
Bolsover S80 ....99 D8
Clowne S43 ....80 D1
Dam Side DE6............179 A4
Damside La SK17..........49 A3
Damson Croft S43 ....78 A2
Damson Gr DE24........232 E8
Damson Way S42........115 E3
Dane Ave S41 ....77 B2
Dane Bank Dr SK12 ......32 D6
Danebridge Cres DE21 ..206 A1
Dane Gr SK17..............85 C4
Dane Hill Cl SK12..........32 D5
Danesby Cres DE5 ......180 A1
Danesby Rise DE5........180 A1
Danesmoor Ind Est S45 ..131 F2
Danesmoor Inf Sch S45 ..131 E3
Danesway SK23............47 B6
Daniel Mews NG10......223 A5
Dannah Cres DE5........169 F1
Dannah St DE5............169 F2
Darby St DE23 ....218 F2
Darcy Rd S21..............59 C3
Daresbury Cl S2............43 D6
Daresbury Dr S2 ....43 D6
Daresbury Pl S2 ....43 D6
Daresbury Rd S2 ....43 D6
Daresbury View S2........43 D6
Darfield Ave S20..........44 F2
Darfield Cl S20 ....44 F2
Darfield Dr DE75..........182 A2
Darfield La DE6............162 C4
Darkey La NG9............223 E5
Dark La
Ashbourne DE6 ....173 A1
Ashover DE55 ....145 C6
Bradley DE6................175 B3
Calow S44 ....96 F7
Chesterfield S44..........96 E4
Crich DE4..................156 F5
Cromford DE4............154 F4
Holbrook DE56............191 B7
North Wingfield S42......132 B7
Pilsley S45................132 B8
Tatenhill DE13 ....253 A8
Wirksworth DE4, DE65 ..165 D3
Youlgreave DE45 ....125 D7
Darklands La DE11......256 A4
Darklands Rd DE11 ......256 B5
Darley Abbey Dr DE22..204 F2
Darley Abbey Pk DE22 ..205 A1
Darley Ave
Beeston NG9..............223 F3
Darley Dale DE4 ....127 C3
North Wingfield S42......132 B7
Darley Churchtown CE Prim
Sch DE4 ....127 B3
Darley Cl
Burton u T DE15..........248 C1
Harthill S26 ....61 E6
Staveley S43 ....78 E1
Swadlincote DE11........255 F6
Darley Dale Rd DE11 ....255 A7
Darley Dale Prim Sch
DE4 ....127 E2
Darley Dale Sta * DE4 ..127 C2
Darley Dr
Long Eaton NG10........236 A5
Ripley DE5.................169 C3
West Hallam DE7........207 E8
Darley Gr
Buxton SK17 ....85 D6
Derby DE1 ....219 A4
Darley La DE1 ....267 B4
Darley Lodge Dr DE4....127 C3
Darley House Est DE4 ..142 E8
Darley Park Cl DE22 ....204 F1
Darley Park Ho DE22....205 A1
Darley Park Rd DE22....204 F1
Darley Rd S45 ....113 B2
Darley Sq DE7 ....194 E5
Darley St DE22 ....205 A1
Darley Way
Buxton SK17 ....85 E7
North Wingfield S42......132 B7
Darnley Dr S42 ....44 A8
Darsway DE74............246 F4
Dartford Ph DE24........233 A5
Dartmouth Ct **20** S41....95 F8
Dartnall Cl SK12............32 A6
Darwent Rd S41............96 C6**

Darwin Ave
Buxton SK17 ....85 C7
Chesterfield S40 ....95 E5
Derby DE24 ....232 D4
Ilkeston DE7 ....208 F7
Darwin Cl DE15............248 C1
Darwin Pl DE1............267 C3
Darwin Rd
Chesterfield S40 ....266 A4
Derby DE3 ....217 E3
Long Eaton NG10........236 B5
Darwin Sq DE1............267 B2
Darwood La S44..........118 B8
Dashwood St DE23......267 B1
Datchet Cl DE23 ....231 A8
Daveham Ave SK17........85 C6
Davenport Rd
Derby DE24 ....232 C8
Tupton S42................131 C8
Daventry Ct DE23 ....217 C3
Davey Ct S44................98 F3
Davian Way S40..........114 E8
David's Cl DE73............232 F1
Davids Dr S42............114 E4
Da Vinci Com Coll DE21..205 E1
Davis Ho **2** DE21 ....267 B2
Davis Rd DE11............256 B4
Dawber La S21 ....60 F7
Dawgates La NG17, NG19 .134 F2
Dawkins Rd DE21........262 C1
Dawlish Ct
4 Chesterfield S41 ......95 F8
Derby DE24 ....233 C7
Eastwood NG16..........182 D3
Dawn View NG9 ....209 D2
Dawsmere Cl DE21 ......217 C1
Dawver Rd NG16..........195 F6
Dayfield La DE6 ....175 A4
Day Gr SK14................9 A3
Daylesford Cl DE23 ......231 A8
Days La DE21..............178 F3
Days Mill Cl DE4 ....143 A6
Dayton Cl DE21 ....220 C5
Dayton Ct DE22..........218 E8
Deacon Cl
Derby DE21................205 E2
Swanwick DE55..........169 E7
Dead La NG16............195 D1
Deadman's La DE24......219 D2
Deamon St DE55..........147 E1
Dean Cl DE23 ....218 A2
Dean Ct DE23 ....218 E2
Deanhead Dr DE21........44 F2
Dean Rd DE56 ....167 F2
Deans Dr DE72............221 B2
Deansgate NG19 ....135 A5
Dean St
Derby DE22 ....218 E3
Langley Mill NG16 ......182 C3
Debdale La NG19 ....136 A2
Debden Cl S40............114 C8
Deben Down S40..........136 D3
Deborah Dr DE21 ....220 F4
Dee Cl DE24..............231 E3
Dee La DE65..............229 F6
Deepdale NG16............170 F4
Deepdale Ave
Borrowash DE72 ....221 C3
Stapleford NG9 ....223 D6
Deepdale Bsns Pk DE45..109 B6
Deepdale Cl
Burton u T DE15..........248 B5
Staveley S43 ....78 E3
Deepdale Ct DE55........181 E1
Deepdale La DE6 ....184 A2
Deep Dale La
Barrow u T DE73..........244 A7
Derby DE23, DE73......231 F1
Deepdale Rd
Belper DE56................179 B5
Bolsover S44 ....98 F3
Derby DE21................220 F3
Long Eaton NG10........236 E1
Mansfield NG19..........136 E1
Deepdene Cl DE11 ......256 C1
Dee La S44, S45..........133 B3
Deepsick La S44..........97 C1
Deepwell Ave S20 ....59 F6
Deepwell Bank S20 ......59 F6
Deepwell Ct S20 ....59 F6
Deepwell View S20........59 F6
Deerlands Rd
Chesterfield S40 ....95 B3
Wingerworth S42 ....114 F2
Deerleap La S42..........130 D3
Deerpark Cres S42 ......114 F3
Deer Park Prim Sch S42.114 F3
Deer Park View DE21....220 F6
De Ferrers Ct DE56 ......190 E3
Degge St DE1 ....267 B2
Deincourt Cl DE21 ......221 A6
Deincourt Com Sch S42.131 F8
Deincourt Cres S42......131 F8
Delamere Cl
Breaston DE72............235 D8
Derby DE21................206 A1
Swanwick DE55..........169 F7
Delf St S2..................43 E7
Delhi Cl DE15..............248 C3
Dell The S40................95 B3
Delph Bank S40 ....114 E8
Delph Cl S32 ....71 D6
Delph The DE73..........252 F2
Delven La DE74..........247 B3
Delves Bank Rd DE55....170 A7
Delves Cl S40..............95 D1
Delves Dr DE75..........193 E8**

Delves Rd
Heanor DE75..............193 D8
Killamarsh S21............60 C6
Delves Sch The DE55....169 F7
Delves The DE7 ....169 F7
Denacre Ave NG10......223 F1
Denacre La DE4............127 F3
Denarth Ave DE24........232 F3
Denbigh St DE21..........219 E7
Denby Comm DE5 ......180 F3
Denby Free CE Prim Sch
DE5 ....180 D1
Denby Hall Rd NE7......194 F6
Denby La DE5, DE56......180 C1
Denby Pottery Visitor Ctr*
DE5 ....180 E1
Dene Fields Ct DE4 ......143 C5
Denfield Cl S43 ....15 B1
Denham St S45............131 D3
Denison Gdns DE21......220 B6
Denman Cres S32..........72 A3
Denmark Rd S2............43 B6
Dennis Barsby Cl DE11..255 E3
Dennis Cl DE23 ....36 E2
Dennor Dr NG19..........136 E5
Denson Cl **4** S2............43 B6
Denstone Coll ST14......196 B5
Denstone Dr DE24 ......233 A4
Denstone La ST14 ....196 C7
Dentdale Ct DE24........233 C7
Dent La S12................44 F2
Denton Ave NG10........223 A6
Denton Cl DE56 ....136 C1
Denton Cl NG19 ....136 C1
Denton Way DE55........169 F7
Denver Ct NG9............209 E1
Denver Rd DE3............217 D3
Depedale Ave DE7........208 D5
Depot St DE23............219 A2
Derby Ass Rm * DE1......267 B3
Derby City General Hospl
DE23 ....218 A5
Derby Coll DE22 ....218 A5
Derby Coll (Broomfield
Campus) DE7............206 B5
Derby Gram Sch for Boys
DE23 ....230 F7
Derby High Sch DE23....218 B1
Derby Hills House Ct
DE73 ....251 E5
Derby Industrial Mus*
DE1........................267 B3
Derby Knoll SK23..........33 F1
Derby La
Brailsford DE6............201 B8
Derby DE23................231 F8
Great Cubley DE6........198 F1
Monyash DE45............123 C7
Shirley DE6................200 E8
Derby Moor Com Sports Coll
DE23 ....231 B7
Derby Mus & Art Gallery*
DE1........................267 B3
Derby Pl S2................43 C6
Derby Rd
Alfreton DE55............158 F3
Ambergate DE56..........167 F3
Ashbourne DE6 ....185 E7
Aston-on-T DE72........234 A2
Borrowash DE21, DE72 ..221 A2
Burton u T DE13..........241 A1
Chellaston DE73 ....232 F2
Clay Cross S45, S42......131 C5
Cromford DE4 ....155 C6
Dale Abbey DE7, DE21..206 C3
Draycott, Spondon DE21 ..220 C3
Doveridge DE6............211 B1
Draycott DE72............209 F6
Duffield DE56..............190 F6
Duffield, Flaxholme DE56..190 F1
Eastwood NG16..........182 E2
Etwall DE65................229 C4
Hatton DE65..............227 E2
Heanor DE75..............181 D1
Hilton DE65................228 F3
Horsley DE21, DE56......191 D5
Ilkeston DE7 ....208 D7
Kilburn DE56..............179 F1
Langley Mill NG16 ......182 C1
Long Eaton NG10........236 B8
Marston on D DE65......228 B2
Melbourne DE73 ....252 A8
New Mills SK22 ....30 C1
Ripley DE5.................180 C3
Risley DE72................222 D4
Sandiacre NG10..........223 A5
Smisby LE65 ....258 A4
Stanley DE7................208 A5
Stapleford NG9 ....208 D5
Swadlincote DE11........256 C3
Swanwick DE55, DE55..169 E5
Ticknall DE11, DE73......251 A4
Uttoxeter ST14 ....210 D1
Wingerworth S42 ....115 A6
Wirksworth DE4 ....165 E6
Derby Road Ind Est
Heanor DE75..............181 D1
Sandiacre NG10..........223 B5
Derbyshire Ave
Trowell NG9................209 D4
West Hallam DE7........207 E8
Derbyshire Ct DE7........182 D1
Derbyshire Cty Cricket Gd
DE21 ....219 C6
Derbyshire Dr
Castle Donington DE74 ..247 B4
Ilkeston DE7 ....208 E6**

Derbyshire Dr continued
Westwood NG16 . . . . 171 C4
Derbyshire La S8 . . . . 43 A3
Derbyshire Level SK13 . . . 17 F6
Derbyshire Royal Infmy
DE1 . . . . 267 C1
Derby Small Bsns Ctr
DE22 . . . . 267 C2
Derby, Pear Tree DE23 . . .219 B1
Derby St
Glossop SK13 . . . . 17 C8
3 Ilkeston DE7 . . . . 208 F8
Sheffield S2 . . . . 43 C6
Derby Sta DE1 . . . . 219 C4
Derby Terr S2 . . . . 43 C6
Derby Trad Est DE21 . . . .219 B8
Derby Univ (Mickleover Site)
DE3 . . . . 217 F3
Derrington Leys DE4 . . . . 233 D6
Derventio Cl DE1 . . . . . . 219 A7
Derwent Ave
Belper DE56 . . . . 179 A1
Borrowash DE72 . . . . . . 221 C3
Darley Dale DE4 . . . . . . 127 C4
Derby DE72 . . . . 205 A4
Grindleford S32 . . . . 72 C8
Ilkeston DE7 . . . . 194 D2
West Hallam DE7 . . . . . . 207 E8
Derwent Bsns Ctr DE1 . . 267 C4
Derwent Cl
Derby DE22 . . . . 205 A4
Dronfield S18 . . . . 57 B3
Glossop SK13 . . . . 17 F8
Grindleford S32 . . . . 72 C8
Swadlincote DE11 . . . . . 256 A1
Derwent Com Sch DE21 . 219 C7
Derwent Cres S41 . . . . . . 95 D7
Derwent Ct
Belper DE56 . . . . 179 B4
5 Sheffield S17 . . . . 56 A5
Willington DE65 . . . . 242 B6
Derwent Dr
Baslow DE45 . . . . 91 D6
Chinley SK23 . . . . 34 E1
Derby DE24 . . . . 231 D2
Tibshelf DE55 . . . . 147 F6
Derwent Gdns DE6 . . . . . 185 D8
Derwent Gr DE55 . . . . . . 158 F2
Derwent Ho DE21 . . . . . . 219 C6
Derwent La
Derwent S33 . . . . 30 B7
Hathersage S32 . . . . 52 F8
Northwood DE4 . . . . 127 A6
Derwent Par DE1,DE24 . .219 E3
Derwent Park Ho DE22 . .205 A1
Derwent Pl S45 . . . . 131 A5
Derwent Rd
Burton u T DE15 . . . . . . 248 A2
Buxton SK17 . . . . 85 C6
Derby DE21 . . . . 220 D3
Dronfield S18 . . . . 57 B3
Ripley DE5 . . . . 169 C1
Derwent Rise DE21 . . . . 220 F4
Derwentside Ind Pk
DE56 . . . . 178 F1
Derwent Sq SK23 . . . . . . 34 E1
Derwent St
Belper DE56 . . . . 178 F3
Derby DE1 . . . . 267 C4
Draycott DE72 . . . . 235 A7
Long Eaton NG10 . . . . . . 236 C6
Derwent Street Ind Est
NG10 . . . . 236 C6
Derwent Terr DE4 . . . . . . 143 A2
Derwent Vale DE56 . . . . . 178 F2
Derwent View
Baslow DE45 . . . . 91 E6
Belper, Milford DE56 . . . 191 A8
Belper, Mount Pleasant
DE56 . . . . 178 F5
Darley Dale DE4 . . . . . . 127 B3
Mastin Moor S43 . . . . . . 79 C3
Desborough Rd Ho DE10 . 171 D7
De Sutton Pl S26 . . . . . . 61 E5
Dethick La DE4 . . . . 144 D1
Dethick Way S42 . . . . . . 132 B7
Devas Gdns DE21 . . . . . . 220 D5
Deveron Cl DE13 . . . . . . 240 C1
Deveron Rd S20 . . . . 59 F7
Devizes Cl S40 . . . . 114 F8
Devon Cl
Burton u T DE15 . . . . . . 254 E6
Grassmoor S42 . . . . 115 F2
Sandiacre NG10 . . . . . . 223 B5
Devon Dr S43 . . . . 96 F8
Devonish Royal Hospl The
SK17 . . . . 85 B8
Devon Park View S43 . . . 96 F8
Devonshire Ave
Borrowash DE72 . . . . . . 221 C2
Darley Dale DE4 . . . . . . 142 F7
Derby DE24 . . . . 204 F3
Long Eaton NG10 . . . . . . 237 A8
Ripley DE5 . . . . 169 C2
Devonshire Ave E S41 . . . 115 C8
Devonshire Ave N S43 . . .77 E3
Devonshire Bsns Ctr S43 . 78 B2
Devonshire Cl
Chesterfield S41 . . . . . . 95 F8
Dronfield S18 . . . . 75 F8
Ilkeston DE7 . . . . 194 E5
Sheffield S17 . . . . 55 F6
2 Staveley S43 . . . . 78 E2
Devonshire Cotts S44 . . . 118 E6
Devonshire Ct S43 . . . . . 96 D7
Devonshire Dr
Chinley SK23 . . . . 34 E2
Creswell S80 . . . . 81 C1

Devonshire Dr continued
Derby DE3 . . . . 217 E3
Duffield DE56 . . . . 190 D2
Eastwood NG16 . . . . 182 F2
Langwith NG20 . . . . 119 F8
Rowsley DE4 . . . . 110 F1
Sheffield S17 . . . . 55 E7
Somercotes DE55 . . . . . 170 B7
Stapleford NG9 . . . . 209 D2
Devonshire Glen S17 . . . . 55 F6
Devonshire Gr S17 . . . . . 55 E6
Devonshire Pk S43 . . . . . 96 E8
Devonshire Rd
Buxton SK17 . . . . 85 B8
Sheffield S17 . . . . 55 F6
Devonshire Rd E S41 . . . 115 C8
Devonshire Rd N S43 . . . .77 D3
Devonshire Sq DE4 . . . . . 111 A3
Devonshire St
Ambergate DE56 . . . . . . 167 F3
Brimington S43 . . . . 96 E8
Chesterfield S41 . . . . . . 266 B3
New Houghton NG19 . . . 135 A7
3 Staveley S43 . . . . 78 E2
Devonshire Terr
Holmewood S42 . . . . . . 116 E1
Matlock Bath DE4 . . . . . 143 A2
Devonshire Terrace Rd
S17 . . . . 55 D7
Devonshire Villas **20** S41 . 95 F8
Devonshire Way S41 . . . . 81 A4
Devonshire Wlk DE1 . . . . 267 C2
De Warren Pl S26 . . . . . . 61 F5
Dewchurch Dr DE23 . . . . 231 E5
Dewint Ave S41 . . . . 23 B8
Dew Pond La SK17 . . . . . 85 E8
Dewsnap La SK14 . . . . . . 9 A6
Dewy La DE4,DE55 . . . . . 144 F1
Dexter St DE23 . . . . 219 C2
D H Lawrence Mus*
NG16 . . . . 182 F3
Dialstone S33 . . . . 51 A7
Diamond Cl DE45 . . . . . . 109 D5
Diamond Dr DE21 . . . . . . 205 F3
Diamond Jubilee Cotts
DE6 . . . . 184 E8
Dibble Rd DE14 . . . . 254 A7
Dickens Dr
Holmewood S42 . . . . . . 116 D1
Swadlincote DE11 . . . . . 256 C5
Dickenson Rd S41 . . . . . 266 C1
Dickens Sq DE23 . . . . . . 231 F7
Dickinson's La DE6 . . . . . 215 B1
Dickinson St DE24 . . . . . 219 D2
Dicklant La S45 . . . . 145 B8
Didcot Cl S40 . . . . 114 F8
Didsbury Terr SK22 . . . . . 25 E2
Digby St
Cossall DE7 . . . . 195 A1
Kimberley NG16 . . . . . . 195 D7
Diglands Ave SK22 . . . . . 24 D1
Diglands Cl SK22 . . . . . . 24 D1
Diglee Rd SK23 . . . . 33 C3
Digmire La DE6 . . . . 161 D1
Dig St
Ashbourne DE6 . . . . 173 B2
Hartington SK17 . . . . . . 137 D6
Dimple Cres DE4 . . . . . . 143 B5
Dimple La DE56 . . . . 168 B8
Dimple Rd DE4 . . . . 143 A6
Dimple Road Bsns Ctr
DE4 . . . . 143 B6
Dingle Cl SK13 . . . . 17 A8
Dingle La S41,S44 . . . . . . 96 E1
Dingle The DE15 . . . . . . 254 E8
Dingley Cl NG19 . . . . 136 E5
Dinmore Grange DE11 . . 257 B6
Dinting CE Prim Sch
SK13 . . . . 10 A1
Dinting La S13 . . . . 10 A1
Dinting Lane Trad Est
SK13 . . . . 10 A1
Dinting Lodge Ind Est SK13 . 9 F2
Dinting Rd SK13 . . . . 10 B2
Dinting Sta SK13 . . . . . . 10 A2
Dinting Vale SK13 . . . . . . 10 A1
Dinting Vale Bsns Pk SK13 . 9 F2
Discovery Way S41 . . . . . 77 A1
Diseworth Cl DE73 . . . . . 232 F2
Diseworth Rd DE74 . . . . . 247 A1
Dish La DE6, DE65 . . . . . 228 B6
Dishwell La S26 . . . . 61 E6
Disley Prim Sch SK12 . . . 32 D6
Disley Sta SK12 . . . . 32 C6
Disraeli Cres DE7 . . . . . . 208 F8
Ditch Cotts SK17 . . . . . . 105 F8
Ditch The SK17 . . . . 105 F8
Division Rd NG19 . . . . . . 119 C4
Division St S43 . . . . 97 C8
Dix Ave DE7 . . . . 192 F6
Dixie St NG16 . . . . 171 B4
Dixon's Rd S41 . . . . 266 C2
Dixon Croft S43 . . . . 77 D4
Dixon Ct S41 . . . . 77 B3
Dobbinhorse La DE6 . . . . 185 B5
Dobbin La S18 . . . . 75 C6
Dobbs St S21 . . . . 60 C6
Dobholes DE7 . . . . 192 D6
Dobholes La DE7 . . . . . . 192 F6
Dobson Pl S43 . . . . 97 B6
Dockholm Rd NG10 . . . . 223 C2
Dock Wlk S40 . . . . 266 A2
Doctor's La DE73 . . . . . . 252 F2
Doctor La S26 . . . . 61 F7
Dodburn Ct DE24 . . . . . . 231 D4
Dodslow Ave DE13 . . . . . 240 B3
Doe Hill La DE55 . . . . . . 147 D5

Doehole La
Ashover DE4, DE55 . . . . . 144 F3
Brackenfield DE55 . . . . . 145 A2
Doe La S12 . . . . 58 C5
Doghole La DE4 . . . . 154 C4
Dogkennel La DE6 . . . . . 186 E7
Dog La
Hulland Ward DE6 . . . . . 175 D4
Netherseal DE12 . . . . . 264 F6
Stonebroom DE55 . . . . . 146 E2
Wilson DE73 . . . . 252 E6
Dolby Rd SK17 . . . . 85 D2
Doles La
Clifton DE6 . . . . 184 F7
Findern DE65 . . . . 230 D3
Whitwell S80 . . . . 82 B7
Dolly La
Chinley SK23 . . . . 34 A2
Furness Vale SK23 . . . . . 33 F3
Dolly Wood Cl SK23 . . . . 34 B1
Dolphin Cl DE21 . . . . . . 221 A6
Domain Dr DE73 . . . . . . 232 E1
Dominion Rd DE11 . . . . . 256 B5
Dominoe Gr S12 . . . . 44 D5
Donald Hawley Way
DE6 . . . . 190 F3
Doncaster Ave NG10 . . . 223 B6
Doncaster Gr NG10 . . . . 223 F1
Donegal Wlk DE21 . . . . . 220 A4
Donington Cl DE23 . . . . . 231 E5
Donington Dr
Derby DE23 . . . . 231 E5
Woodville DE11 . . . . 256 F3
Donington La DE72, DE74 . 247 C7
Donisthorpe La DE12 . . . 262 E2
Donkey La S32 . . . . 72 C2
Donner Cres DE7 . . . . . . 194 E5
Dorchester Ave DE21 . . . 219 F7
Dorchester Rd NG16 . . . 195 F7
Dore Cl S17 . . . . 56 A7
Dore Cl S17 . . . . 56 A7
Dore Hall Croft S17 . . . . 55 D7
Dore La S32 . . . . 53 A7
Dore Prim Sch S17 . . . . . 55 D6
Dore Rd S17 . . . . 55 E8
Dore Sta S17 . . . . 56 A7
Doris Rd DE7 . . . . 209 A7
Dorking Rd DE22 . . . . . . 218 B6
Dormy Cl NG19 . . . . 136 E5
Dorothy Ave
Mansfield Woodhouse
NG19 . . . . 136 C1
Sandiacre NG10 . . . . . . 223 B5
Dorothy Dr NG19 . . . . . . 136 F1
Dorothy Vale S40 . . . . . . 95 C4
Dorrien Ave DE23 . . . . . . 232 A7
Dorset Ave **2** S43 . . . . . . 96 F8
Dorset Cl
Brimington S43 . . . . 77 F1
Burton u T DE15 . . . . . . 254 E6
Buxton SK17 . . . . 85 D4
Dorset Dr S43 . . . . 96 F8
Dorset St DE21 . . . . 219 D6
Dorterry Cres DE7 . . . . . 209 A5
Douglas Ave
Awsworth NG16 . . . . . . 195 C5
Heanor DE75 . . . . 181 C2
Douglas Rd
Chesterfield S41 . . . . . . 96 C6
Long Eaton NG10 . . . . . . 223 B1
Somercotes DE55 . . . . . 170 D8
Douglas St DE23 . . . . . . 219 B2
Douse Croft La S10 . . . . . 42 F6
Dove Bk SK6 . . . . 23 F6
Dove Cl
Derby DE3 . . . . 218 A3
Kilburn DE56 . . . . 192 A8
Woodville DE11 . . . . 256 F3
Dovecliff Cres DE13 . . . . 240 F2
Dovecliff Rd DE13 . . . . . 240 E3
Dovecote DE74 . . . . 247 B3
Dovecote Dr DE72 . . . . . 221 B2
Dovecotes S45 . . . . 129 F3
Dovecote The
Borrowash on T DE73 . . . 252 F2
Horsley DE21 . . . . 191 F6
Dovedale Ave
Ashbourne DE6 . . . . 173 D1
Derby DE24 . . . . 233 C7
Long Eaton NG10 . . . . . . 236 D8
Staveley S43 . . . . 97 B5
Dovedale Circ DE7 . . . . . 194 E5
Dovedale Cres
Belper DE56 . . . . 179 B5
Buxton SK17 . . . . 84 F6
Dovedale Ct
Ashbourne DE6 . . . . 185 E8
4 Chesterfield S41 . . . . . 95 E7
1 Glossop SK13 . . . . 10 F1
Long Eaton NG10 . . . . . . 236 B6
Dovedale Day Hospl
DE1 . . . . 267 C1
Dovedale Prim Sch
NG10 . . . . 236 B6
Dovedale Rd DE21 . . . . . 220 F3
Dovedale Rise DE22 . . . . 204 D1
Dovedales The DE3 . . . . . 217 D2
Dovefields ST14 . . . . 196 F3
Dove Fst Sch ST14 . . . . . 197 A3
Dove Gr DE65 . . . . 241 A5
Dove Holes CE Prim Sch
SK17 . . . . 47 L5
Dove Holes Sta SK17 . . . 47 L5
Dove House Gn DE6 . . . . 173 B2

Dove La
Long Eaton NG10 . . . . . . 236 C8
Rocester ST14 . . . . 197 A4
Dove Lea DE13 . . . . 240 B4
Dover Ct DE23 . . . . 219 A2
Dover Rd DE5 . . . . 169 C1
Dove Ridge SK17 . . . . . . 121 C6
Doveridge Cl S41 . . . . . . 77 A2
Doveridge Gr DE7 . . . . . . 85 E6
Doveridge Prim Sch
Doveridge DE6 . . . . 211 A1
Doveridge, Manor House
DE6 . . . . 224 C8
Doveridge Rd DE15 . . . . 248 B1
Doveridge Wlk DE23 . . . 231 C5
Dove Rise DE65 . . . . 228 C2
Dover St
Creswell S80 . . . . 81 E1
Derby DE23 . . . . 219 A1
Doveside
Doveside DE6 . . . . 184 D7
Dove Side DE65 . . . . 239 D8
Dovesite Bsns Pk DE73 . . 251 E6
Dove St DE23 . . . . 183 B2
Dove Valley Pk DE65 . . . 227 A5
Dove View DE13 . . . . . . 239 C6
Dove Way The ST14 . . . . 210 C2
Dovewood Cl DE23 . . . . . 231 A7
Dowcarr La S26 . . . . 61 C5
Dowdeswell St S41 . . . . . 266 B4
Dower Cl DE22 . . . . 205 A1
Dowie Way DE4 . . . . 156 F2
Downham Cl DE3 . . . . . . 217 C1
Downing Cl DE22 . . . . . . 217 F6
Downing Ho DE22 . . . . . 217 F6
Downing Rd
Derby DE21 . . . . 219 D5
Sheffield S8 . . . . 56 E8
Downing Row S32 . . . . . . 52 F8
Downings The S26 . . . . . 61 F5
Downlands S43 . . . . 96 F8
Downlee Cl SK23 . . . . . . 46 F5
Downmeadow DE56 . . . . 179 E8
Downs The NG19 . . . . . . 136 F1
Drabbles Rd DE4 . . . . . . 143 A6
Drage St DE1 . . . . 219 B7
Drake Terr S43 . . . . 96 C8
Draycott Cl DE75 . . . . . . 181 C4
Draycott Com Prim Sch
DE72 . . . . 235 A7
Draycott Ct DE7 . . . . 194 F3
Draycott Dr DE3 . . . . 217 C3
Draycott Mills DE72 . . . . 235 A7
Draycott Pl S18 . . . . 75 D8
Draycott Rd
Borrowash DE72 . . . . . . 221 C1
Breaston DE72 . . . . 235 C7
Long Eaton NG10 . . . . . . 236 A4
North Wingfield S42 . . . . 131 F7
Drayton Ave
Derby DE22 . . . . 217 F6
Mansfield NG19 . . . . . . 135 D1
Drayton St DE11 . . . . . . 256 C4
Dresden Cl DE3 . . . . 217 C2
Drewry Ct DE1 . . . . 218 F5
Drewry La DE22 . . . . 218 F4
Dreyfus Cl DE21 . . . . 220 F5
Drive The DE56 . . . . 177 F3
Dronfield Inf Sch S18 . . . 57 A1
Dronfield Jun Sch S18 . . . 57 A1
Dronfield Pl DE7 . . . . 194 E5
Dronfield Rd S21 . . . . . . 59 B2
Dronfield Sta S18 . . . . . . 57 A1
Drovers Way
Ashbourne DE6 . . . . 173 B3
Bullbridge DE56 . . . . . . 168 B5
Drovers Wlk **3** SK13 . . . . 10 C1
Drummond Rd DE7 . . . . . 194 E1
Drummond Way DE73 . . . 232 E2
Drum The DE22 . . . . 204 F3
Drury Ave DE21 . . . . 220 D4
Drury La
Biggin SK17 . . . . 138 C2
Dronfield S18 . . . . 57 C3
Sheffield S17 . . . . 55 D7
Dryden Ave S40 . . . . 115 A8
Dryden Cl NG9 . . . . 209 E1
Dryden St DE23 . . . . 231 F7
Dryhurst Dr SK12 . . . . . . 32 D6
Dryhurst La SK12 . . . . . . 32 C6
Drysdale Rd DE3 . . . . . . 217 D3
Duchess St
Creswell S80 . . . . 81 F1
Whitwell S80 . . . . 82 A4
Duchess Way DE73 . . . . . 244 E8
Duckmanton Prim Sch
S44 . . . . 98 A5
Duckmanton Rd S44 . . . . 98 A5
Duck Row DE45 . . . . 91 C3
Ducksett La S21 . . . . 59 E2
Duck St DE65 . . . . 241 B5
Dudwood La DE4 . . . . . . 140 F7
Duesbury Cl DE24 . . . . . 232 E7
Duesbury Ct DE3 . . . . . . 230 B7
Duesbury Pl DE3 . . . . . . 230 B7
Duesbury The DE55 . . . . 160 B4
Duewell Ct **9** S43 . . . . . . 78 B3
Duffield Bank DE56 . . . . 191 A4
Duffield Cl NG10 . . . . . . 236 A5
Duffield Ct DE56 . . . . . . 190 E4
Duffield Rd DE21 . . . . . . 205 A5
Duffield Sta DE56 . . . . . 190 F4
Duke's Bldgs DE56 . . . . . 191 A7
Duke's Dr
Buxton SK17 . . . . 85 C5
Glapwell S44 . . . . 134 A7
Duke's Dr The DE45 . . . . 108 E8

Duke Field DE4 . . . . 154 D5
Duke of Norfolk CE Prim Sch
SK13 . . . . 10 D1
Duke of Norfolk CE Prim Sch
(Annexe) SK13 . . . . 10 E2
Dukeries Ct S43 . . . . 80 F3
Dukeries La DE21 . . . . . . 206 B2
Dukes Cl S42 . . . . 116 E1
Dukes Dr
Chesterfield S41 . . . . . . 95 E6
Curbar S32 . . . . 72 D2
Dukes Fold SK13 . . . . . . 17 B7
Dukes Pl DE7 . . . . 194 E4
Dukes St SK13 . . . . 17 C8
Duke St
Buxton SK17 . . . . 84 E6
Chesterfield S41 . . . . . . 96 A8
Clowne S43 . . . . 81 A4
Creswell S80 . . . . 81 F1
Derby DE1 . . . . 267 B4
Ilkeston DE7 . . . . 194 F3
Middleton DE4 . . . . 154 D5
Sheffield S20 . . . . 59 D6
South Normanton DE55 . 160 B6
Staveley S43 . . . . 78 E2
Tutbury DE13 . . . . 239 C6
Whitwell S80 . . . . 82 A6
Duluth Ave DE21 . . . . . . 220 A7
Dulverton Ave DE24 . . . . 231 C2
Dulwich Ct **10** S43 . . . . . 78 B3
Dulwich Cl DE22 . . . . . . 217 E6
Dumb Hall La S80 . . . . . . 63 B4
Dumbles Cl DE5 . . . . 180 F2
Dumbles La DE5 . . . . 180 F2
Dumbles Rd S44 . . . . 98 F1
Dumbleton Rd S21 . . . . . 60 E5
Dumble Wood Grange
S41 . . . . 95 C7
Dunbar Cl DE24 . . . . 231 E2
Duncan Cl DE56 . . . . 179 B6
Duncan Rd DE23 . . . . . . 231 F8
Duncombe Dr DE6 . . . . . 185 C8
Dundas Way DE73 . . . . . 232 E1
Dundee Dr NG19 . . . . . . 136 B6
Dundee Rd DE11 . . . . . . 256 D5
Dundonald Rd S40 . . . . . 266 B1
Dunedin Cl DE3 . . . . 217 E3
Dunedin Cres DE15 . . . . 248 C2
Dunedin Glen S20 . . . . . . 59 E6
Dunedin Gr S20 . . . . 59 E6
Dungley Hill DE56 . . . . . 168 D2
Dungreave Ave DE4 . . . . 127 A5
Dunkery Ct DE21 . . . . . . 206 A1
Dunkirk DE22 . . . . 267 A2
Dunlow La S32 . . . . 71 C5
Dunn Brigg NG19 . . . . . . 136 D2
Dunn Dr NG10 . . . . 236 B7
Dunne La SK13 . . . . 10 E2
Dunnicliffe La DE73 . . . . 252 A7
Dunnsmoor La DE11 . . . . 256 F7
Dunoon Cl DE24 . . . . 231 E3
Dunsa La DE45 . . . . 91 D1
Dunsford Rd DE55 . . . . . 159 B5
Dunshill Wlk S45 . . . . . . 131 E4
Dunsil Cl NG19 . . . . 136 B1
Dunsil Dr DE23 . . . . 231 D5
Dunsil Rd
7 Mansfield NG19 . . . . . 136 B1
Pinxton NG16 . . . . 160 D2
Dunsmore Dr DE21 . . . . . 205 F2
Dunsmore Way DE11 . . . 256 D5
Dunstall Brook DE15 . . . . 248 A1
Dunstall Park Rd DE24 . . 232 D8
Dunstall Rd DE13 . . . . . . 253 A7
Dunston Cl NG10 . . . . . . 236 E7
Dunston Ct S41 . . . . 76 F1
Dunston La S41 . . . . 76 F1
Dunston Prim Sch S41 . . 95 D8
Dunston Rd S41 . . . . 76 D2
Dunston Tech Pk S41 . . . 76 E1
Dunston Trad Est S41 . . . 76 C2
Dunton Cl DE21 . . . . 220 B5
Dunvegan Ave S45 . . . . . 131 E2
Dunvegan Cl DE24 . . . . . 231 D2
Duper La S32 . . . . 51 E5
Durban Cl DE15 . . . . 248 C3
Durban House Her Ctr*
NG16 . . . . 182 F3
Durham Ave
Chesterfield S43 . . . . . . 77 D3
Derby DE21 . . . . 219 E6
Grassmoor S42 . . . . 115 F2
Durham Cl
Chesterfield S43 . . . . . . 77 D3
Mansfield Woodhouse
NG19 . . . . 136 D4
Swadlincote DE11 . . . . . 256 E5
Durham St **8** DE7 . . . . . . 194 F1
Durley Chine Dr S41 . . . . 115 C8
Durley Cl DE24 . . . . 233 C7
Durlstone Cl S12 . . . . 44 A5
Durlstone Cres S12 . . . . . 44 A5
Durlstone Dr S12 . . . . . . 44 A5
Durlstone Gr S12 . . . . . . 44 A5
Durrant Rd S41 . . . . 266 B3
Durvale Ct S17 . . . . 55 C6
Durward Cl DE24 . . . . . . 232 C7
Dyche Cl S8 . . . . 57 B6
Dyche La S8, S18 . . . . . . 57 B5
Dyche Pl S8 . . . . 57 B6
Dyche Rd S8 . . . . 57 B6
Dye House La SK22 . . . . . 33 C8
Dykes Cl S44 . . . . 99 A2

Dyke Vale Rd S12 . . . . .44 F5
Dymond Gr S42 . . . . .115 F3
Dystelegh Rd SK12 . . . . .32 D6

E

Each Well La DE55 . . . . .158 F3
Eagle Cl DE56 . . . . .178 F2
Eagle Ctr DE1 . . . . .267 C2
Eagle Hts DE15 . . . . .248 D3
Eagle Par **9** SK17 . . . . .85 B7
Eagle Rd DE7 . . . . .208 F4
Eagle St
  4 Buxton SK17 . . . . .85 B7
  Heage DE56 . . . . .168 E2
Eagle Terr
  Birchover DE4 . . . . .126 B1
  Wensley DE4 . . . . .142 A7
Ealand St DE13 . . . . .240 D4
Ealing Cl DE22 . . . . .218 B6
Ealing Ct **3** S43 . . . . .78 B3
Eardley Cl DE21 . . . . .220 B5
Earlham Cl DE7 . . . . .208 C6
Earls Cres DE21 . . . . .206 B3
Earl Sterndale CE Prim Sch
  SK17 . . . . .105 C3
Earlsway **5** SK13 . . . . .17 B8
Earlswood Cl DE72 . . . . .235 D8
Earlswood Dr DE23 . . . . .217 F4
Earnshaw St SK14 . . . . .9 D4
Easedale Cl S40 . . . . .94 F5
East Ave
  Derby DE3 . . . . .217 E3
  Stanfree S44 . . . . .80 B1
East Bank DE4 . . . . .141 C5
East Bank Pl S2 . . . . .43 D6
East Bank Rd S2 . . . . .43 D6
East Bank Way S2 . . . . .43 D6
Eastbrae Rd DE23 . . . . .231 D7
Eastbrook Cl SK23 . . . . .47 C6
East Cl DE22 . . . . .204 E2
Eastcliffe Ct S2 . . . . .43 C8
East Cres
  Holbrook DE56 . . . . .191 C8
  Long Duckmanton S44 . . . . . . .98 A6
East Croft Ave DE23 . . . . . . .231 D5
Eastcroft Cl S20 . . . . .59 F8
Eastcroft Dr S20 . . . . .59 F8
Eastcroft Glen S20 . . . . .59 F8
Eastcroft View S20 . . . . .59 F7
Eastcroft Way **7** S20 . . . . . . .59 F8
East Dr DE6 . . . . .211 B1
East End DE4 . . . . .140 F7
East End Dr DE11 . . . . .256 C4
Eastern Ave
  Boisover S44 . . . . .118 B8
  Sheffield S2 . . . . .43 E7
Eastern Cres S2 . . . . .43 D6
Eastern Dr S2 . . . . .43 D7
Eastern Wlk S2 . . . . .43 D7
Eastfield Dr DE55 . . . . .160 A5
Eastfield Rd
  Dronfield S18 . . . . .76 C8
  Ripley DE5 . . . . .170 A1
  Swadlincote DE11 . . . . .256 C6
Eastgate DE1, DE21 . . . . . . .267 D4
East Glade Ave S12 . . . . .44 E3
East Glade Cl S12 . . . . .44 E3
East Glade Cres S12 . . . . .44 E4
East Glade Dell S12 . . . . .44 E3
East Glade Pl S12 . . . . .44 E3
East Glade Rd S12 . . . . .44 E4
East Glade Sq S12 . . . . .44 E3
East Glade Way S12 . . . . .44 E4
East Hill Sec Sch S2 . . . . .43 C8
East Lawn DE65 . . . . .230 D2
Eastleigh Ct S41 . . . . .115 D8
Eastleigh Dr
  Derby DE3 . . . . .217 E2
  Mansfield Woodhouse
    NG19 . . . . .136 B6
East Midlands Designer
  Outlet DE55 . . . . .160 E6
East Midlands International
  Airport DE74 . . . . .247 C1
Eastmoor Rd S43 . . . . .96 F4
East Nelson St DE75 . . . . . . .181 D2
East Par S80 . . . . .82 A5
East Rd S2 . . . . .43 B7
East Service Rd DE21 . . . . . . .220 B3
Eastside Cl S41 . . . . .96 B8
Eastside Rd S41 . . . . .96 B8
East St
  Bramley-Vale S44 . . . . .117 D1
  Burton u T DE15 . . . . .248 C3
  Clay Cross S45 . . . . .131 D4
  Clowne S43 . . . . .81 A5
  Creswell S80 . . . . .81 D1
  Derby DE1 . . . . .267 B3
  Heanor DE75 . . . . .194 A8
  Ilkeston DE7 . . . . .208 F8
  Long Eaton NG10 . . . . .236 F8
  Renishaw S21 . . . . .79 B8
  Scarcliffe S44 . . . . .118 E6
East Vale SK6 . . . . .23 A5
East View
  Chesterfield S40 . . . . .266 B2
  Mayfield DE6 . . . . .184 D7
  Shirebrook NG20 . . . . .119 F6
  Whaley Thorns NG20 . . . . . .101 A3
East View Ave S21 . . . . .59 C2
East View Ind Est NG20 . . . . .119 F6

East View Rd DE56 . . . . .168 E1
Eastview Terr NG16 . . . . .182 B3
Eastway DE74 . . . . .247 B3
Eastwood Ave DE23 . . . . . . .218 C2
Eastwood Cl S41 . . . . .115 D8
Eastwood Comp Sch
  NG16 . . . . .182 E3
Eastwood Cotts S32 . . . . .53 B8
Eastwood Dr
  Calow S44 . . . . .97 B2
  Derby DE23 . . . . .218 C2
Eastwood Jun & Inf Schs
  NG16 . . . . .182 F2
Eastwood & Kimberley Com
  Coll NG16 . . . . .195 F6
Eastwood La S45 . . . . .130 B2
Eastwood Park Appartments
  S41 . . . . .115 D8
Eastwood Park Dr S41 . . . . . .115 D8
Eastwood Rd NG16 . . . . .195 E6
Eather Ave NG19 . . . . .136 C4
Eaton Ave
  Derby DE22 . . . . .205 B5
  Ilkeston DE7 . . . . .208 D6
Eaton Bank DE56 . . . . .191 A1
Eaton Cl
  Derby DE22 . . . . .205 A5
  Hatton DE65 . . . . .227 D1
  Hulland Ward DE6 . . . . .175 E3
Eaton Ct
  Derby DE1 . . . . .218 E6
  Duffield DE56 . . . . .190 E2
Eaton Dr DE45 . . . . .91 F5
Eaton Fold S32 . . . . .71 E7
Eaton Grange Dr NG10 . . . . .236 A8
Eaton Hill DE45 . . . . .91 F5
Eaton La S45 . . . . .129 B5
Eaton Pl DE45 . . . . .91 F5
Eaton Rd
  Castle Donington DE74 . . . . .247 B3
  Rocester ST14 . . . . .196 F3
Eaton's Rd NG9 . . . . .223 D6
Eaton St ST14 . . . . .210 C1
Eaves Ave SK23 . . . . .47 C5
Eaves Knoll Rd SK22 . . . . .33 B8
Ebenezer St
  Glossop SK13 . . . . .17 D7
  Ilkeston DE7 . . . . .194 F3
  Langley Mill NG16 . . . . .182 B3
Ecclesbourne Ave DE56 . . . . .190 F3
Ecclesbourne Cl
  Duffield DE56 . . . . .190 E3
  Wirksworth DE4 . . . . .165 F7
Ecclesbourne Cotts DE4 . . . . .154 F2
Ecclesbourne Dr SK17 . . . . . . .85 A6
Ecclesbourne La DE56 . . . . . .176 F5
Ecclesbourne Mdws
  DE56 . . . . .190 D4
Ecclesbourne Pk DE55 . . . . . .159 D2
Ecclesbourne Sch The
  DE56 . . . . .190 E3
Ecclesbourne Valley Rly*
  DE4 . . . . .154 F2
Eccles Cl
  Hope S33 . . . . .39 A4
  Whaley Bridge SK23 . . . . . . .45 D8
Eccles Fold SK23 . . . . .47 A6
Eccles Rd
  Chapel-en-le-F, Higher
    Crossings SK23 . . . . .47 A6
  Chapel-en-le-F, Hilltop SK23 . .46 C7
Eccles Terr SK23 . . . . .46 D8
Eckington Bsns Pk 59 F4
Eckington Cl DE7 . . . . .207 E8
Eckington Hall 59 D5
Eckington Jun Sch S21 . . . . . .59 D3
Eckington Mews S20 . . . . . . .59 D5
Eckington Rd
  Chesterfield S43 . . . . .77 D5
  Dronfield S18 . . . . .57 D4
  Sheffield S20 . . . . .59 F8
  Staveley S43 . . . . .78 F4
Eckington Sch S21 . . . . .59 A3
Eckington Way S20 . . . . .59 F8
Edale Ave
  Derby, Alvaston DE24 . . . . . .233 B7
  Derby DE23 . . . . .218 E2
  Derby, Mickleover DE3 . . . . .217 D2
Edale Bank SK13 . . . . .9 E2
Edale Cl
  Derby DE22 . . . . .204 D1
  Gamesley SK13 . . . . .9 E2
  Long Eaton NG10 . . . . .236 B6
Edale Cres SK13 . . . . .9 E1
Edale Ct **3** S41 . . . . .95 E7
Edale Dr
  Derby DE21 . . . . .220 F3
  South Normanton DE55 . . . . .160 B7
Edale Fold SK13 . . . . .9 E2
Edale Gr SK17 . . . . .85 E7
Edale Mews SK17 . . . . .85 E7
Edale Mill S33 . . . . .37 E7
Edale Rd
  Hayfield SK22 . . . . .26 A2
  Hope S33 . . . . .38 F7
  Mastin Moor S43 . . . . .79 C4
Edale Rise NG9 . . . . .223 E3
Edale Sq DE7 . . . . .194 E5
Edale Sta S33 . . . . .37 C7
Edale Way DE56 . . . . .179 B3
Edale YH* S33 . . . . .29 A2
Eden Bank DE56 . . . . .167 F2
Eden Cl DE65 . . . . .240 C8
Edenhall Rd S2 . . . . .43 F7
Eden Low NG19 . . . . .136 E3
Eden Rd DE21 . . . . .220 B4
Edensor Ave SK17 . . . . .85 E7

Edensor Cl S42 . . . . .131 F6
Edensor Ct S43 . . . . .97 C8
Edensor Dr DE56 . . . . .179 C6
Edensor Sq DE22 . . . . .218 F4
Eden St
  Derby DE24 . . . . .233 A8
  Wingerworth S42 . . . . .114 E3
Edes Farm Dr ST14 . . . . .196 F4
Edgbaston Ct DE23 . . . . .231 C8
Edgecote Dr DE11 . . . . .256 A7
Edgefold Rd DE4 . . . . .143 B5
Edgehill DE56 . . . . .191 A2
Edge Hill DE73 . . . . .232 F3
Edge Hill Ct NG10 . . . . .236 D4
Edgehill Gr NG19 . . . . .136 C2
Edge Hill Jun Sch DE15 . . . . .254 F7
Edge La S33 . . . . .51 B6
Edgelaw Ct **2** DE24 . . . . . . .231 D3
Edge Mount View S32 . . . . . . .72 E2
Edge Rd
  Eyam S32 . . . . .71 E7
  Matlock DE4 . . . . .143 B6
Edge View S32 . . . . .72 B3
Edge View Cl S32 . . . . .72 E2
Edge View Dr S32 . . . . .90 A4
Edgware Rd DE22 . . . . .217 F6
Edgwood Rd NG16 . . . . .195 F6
Edinboro Row NG16 . . . . . . .195 E7
Edinburgh Cres DE24 . . . . . . .232 E4
Edinburgh Ct
  Chesterfield S42 . . . . .114 E4
  Swanwick DE55 . . . . .170 A7
Edinburgh Rd
  Chesterfield S41 . . . . .95 F5
  Wingerworth S42 . . . . .114 E4
Edith Wood Cl DE24 . . . . . . .233 B5
Edlaston La DE6 . . . . .185 B2
Edmonton Pl DE15 . . . . .248 D2
Edmund's Sq DE23 . . . . .230 B7
Edmund Ave S17 . . . . .56 D6
Edmund Cl S17 . . . . .56 D6
Edmund Dr S17 . . . . .56 D6
Edmund Rd
  Derby DE22 . . . . .220 F3
  Sheffield S2 . . . . .43 B8
Edmund St S41 . . . . .95 F8
Ednaston Ave DE23 . . . . .231 D5
Ednaston Hall Farm Mews
  DE6 . . . . .201 B7
Edward Ave
  Derby DE21 . . . . .220 A5
  Jacksdale NG16 . . . . .171 B4
Edward Rd DE74 . . . . .247 B3
Edwards Cres DE56 . . . . .192 A8
Edward St
  Aldercar NG16 . . . . .182 B4
  Belper DE56 . . . . .179 A4
  Derby DE1 . . . . .267 B4
  Eckington S21 . . . . .59 D3
  Glossop SK13 . . . . .10 C1
  Hartshorne DE11 . . . . .257 A3
  Marple SK6 . . . . .15 B1
  Moira DE11 . . . . .256 C1
  Overseal DE12 . . . . .262 A4
  Stapleford NG9 . . . . .223 D7
  Staveley S43 . . . . .97 C8
Edward Wlk S42 . . . . .115 D7
Edwin Ave S40 . . . . .114 D8
Edwin Rd S2 . . . . .43 C6
Edwinstowe Rd DE11 . . . . . . .206 B1
Egerton Dr NG9 . . . . .209 D2
Egerton Rd S18 . . . . .57 B2
Eggesford Rd DE24 . . . . .231 D2
Eggington Rd DE65 . . . . .240 F8
Egginton Prim Sch DE65 . . . . .241 B5
Egginton Rd DE65 . . . . .229 B7
Egmanton Cl DE21 . . . . .206 B1
Egreaves Ave DE75 . . . . .181 C4
Egstow Pl S45 . . . . .131 D4
Egstow St S45 . . . . .131 D4
Ehlinger Ave SK13 . . . . .10 A5
Eider Cl NG20 . . . . .119 D3
Eighth Ave DE14 . . . . .253 F8
Eland Cl DE21 . . . . .221 A6
Eland Rd NG20 . . . . .119 F5
Elder Cl DE55 . . . . .170 A8
Elder Ct S21 . . . . .60 C5
Elder Way S40 . . . . .266 B3
Eldon Cl SK23 . . . . .47 C6
Eldon Ho **5** DE1 . . . . .267 B2
Eldon La SK17 . . . . .49 B5
Eldon St
  Burton u T DE15 . . . . .248 B3
  Clay Cross S45 . . . . .131 C4
Eleanor Ave DE7 . . . . .209 A5
Eleanor Cres NG9 . . . . .223 F7
Elesmere Ct DE7 . . . . .194 D1
Eley Cl DE7 . . . . .194 C2
Eley Wlk DE1 . . . . .267 A1
Elgar Dr NG10 . . . . .236 B5
Elgin Ave DE23 . . . . .218 A1
Elgin Cl S40 . . . . .114 C7
Eliot Cl
  Calow S44 . . . . .96 F5
  Long Eaton NG10 . . . . .236 B5
  Wirksworth DE4 . . . . .165 E8
Eliot Dr DE7 . . . . .208 D5
Eliot Rd DE23 . . . . .231 B8
Elizabeth Ave
  Buxton SK17 . . . . .85 D7
  Disley SK12 . . . . .32 D5
  Rolleston DE13 . . . . .240 A8
Elizabeth Cl
  Derby DE21 . . . . .220 B5
  West Hallam DE7 . . . . .207 D8
Elizabeth Ct
  Burton u T DE15 . . . . .248 C3
  Ilkeston DE7 . . . . .194 D1

Elizabeth Pk NG16 . . . . .170 F5
Elizabeth Villas DE6 . . . . .185 C8
Elkstone Cl DE21 . . . . .206 B2
Elkstone Rd S40 . . . . .95 A5
Ella Bank Rd DE75 . . . . .182 A5
Ellastone Gdns DE24 . . . . . . .233 B7
Ellendale Rd DE21 . . . . .220 B7
Ellerslie Gr NG10 . . . . .223 A5
Ellesmere Ave
  Alfreton DE55 . . . . .159 B4
  Derby DE24 . . . . .219 D1
Ellesmere Dr NG9 . . . . .209 D5
Ellesmere Rd NG19 . . . . .136 F1
Elliott Ave S33 . . . . .51 A8
Elliott Dr S43 . . . . .97 C6
Ellis Cl NG10 . . . . .236 C6
Ellison Ave DE72 . . . . .246 A7
Ellison Cl S14 . . . . .9 D5
Ellisons Rd S21 . . . . .60 C5
Ellison St SK13 . . . . .10 D1
Elma La S80 . . . . .101 D6
Elm Ave
  Belper DE56 . . . . .179 B2
  Darley Dale DE4 . . . . .142 F7
  Long Eaton NG10 . . . . .236 C8
  Sandiacre NG10 . . . . .223 B7
Elm Cl
  Bolsover S44 . . . . .99 C1
  Branston DE14 . . . . .253 F8
  Chesterfield S41 . . . . .95 F8
  Doveridge DE6 . . . . .224 C8
  Killamarsh S21 . . . . .60 C5
  Mottram in L SK14 . . . . .9 A4
  Pinxton NG16 . . . . .160 D3
Elm Cres S20 . . . . .59 C8
Elm Dr
  Hilton DE65 . . . . .228 D2
  Killamarsh S21 . . . . .60 C5
Elmfield SK23 . . . . .47 A5
Elm Gr
  Clay Cross S45 . . . . .131 D3
  Derby, Cherrytree Hill
    DE21 . . . . .220 B5
  Derby DE22 . . . . .204 D5
  Glossop SK13 . . . . .10 C2
Elmhurst DE65 . . . . .241 A5
Elmhurst Ave DE55 . . . . .160 A4
Elmhurst Cl DE55 . . . . .160 A4
Elmhurst Rd NG19 . . . . .136 E1
Elm Lodge Farm Cl S41 . . . . . .95 F7
Elm Park Ct DE1 . . . . .267 A5
Elm Rd
  Eckington S21 . . . . .59 C2
  Pilsley S45 . . . . .132 C1
Elms Ave
  Alfreton DE55 . . . . .159 A4
  Derby DE23 . . . . .218 B6
  Ripley DE5 . . . . .180 D8
Elms Cl DE55 . . . . .159 A4
Elmsdale Rd DE11 . . . . .257 A4
Elms Dr DE23 . . . . .218 B1
Elms Farm Way DE23 . . . . . . .231 A8
Elms Gr DE65 . . . . .229 C3
Elmslea Ave DE12 . . . . .260 D3
Elmsleigh Cl DE11 . . . . .256 B6
Elmsleigh Dr DE11 . . . . .256 B6
Elmsleigh Gr DE11 . . . . .256 B6
Elmsleigh Inf Sch DE11 . . . . .256 B6
Elms Rd
  Burton u T DE15 . . . . .248 A1
  Coton in t E DE12 . . . . .260 D3
Elms St DE1 . . . . .218 F7
Elm St
  Borrowash DE72 . . . . .221 B2
  Brimington S43 . . . . .97 A8
  Holmewood S42 . . . . .116 B4
Elms The NG16 . . . . .195 F7
Elmton Cl
  Clowne S80 . . . . .80 F3
  Creswell S80 . . . . .100 D8
Elmton Rd S80 . . . . .81 E1
Elmton View S80 . . . . .81 D2
Elmtree Ave
  Derby DE24 . . . . .232 B7
  Selston NG16 . . . . .171 F7
Elm Tree Ave
  Kilburn DE56 . . . . .192 B7
  Mansfield Woodhouse
    NG19 . . . . .136 A4
  Shirebrook NG20 . . . . .119 D4
  Shirland DE55 . . . . .146 C1
Elm Tree Cl
  Clifton DE6 . . . . .184 F8
Elm Tree Cres S18 . . . . .57 A3
Elm Tree Dr S42 . . . . .114 F4
Elm Tree Ho S12 . . . . .44 A6
Elm Tree Row DE55 . . . . .148 A5
Elm View ST14 . . . . .196 E6
Elm Wlk S45 . . . . .132 C1
Elmwood Dr
  Alfreton DE55 . . . . .159 C3
  Derby DE21 . . . . .205 D2
  Sheffield S20 . . . . .59 D6
Elnor Ave SK23 . . . . .45 E5
Elnor La SK23 . . . . .45 F4
Elnor St NG16 . . . . .182 C3
Elsecar Cl DE56 . . . . .179 D5
Elstead La DE11 . . . . .257 B1
Elston Cl NG19 . . . . .135 D1
Elston Dr S12 . . . . .44 B4
Elstree Rd S12 . . . . .44 B4
Elton Bank **6** SK13 . . . . .9 D1
Elton CE Prim Sch DE4 . . . . . .140 E6
Elton Cl
  8 Gamesley SK13 . . . . .9 D1
  North Wingfield S42 . . . . . . .132 A5
  Stapleford NG9 . . . . .223 D8

Elton Gr SK17 . . . . .85 E6
Elton La S42 . . . . .9 D1
Elton Pl **7** SK13 . . . . .9 D1
Elton Rd
  Derby DE24 . . . . .232 B8
  Winster DE4 . . . . .141 B6
Elton St S40 . . . . .266 B2
Elton View S43 . . . . .97 D8
Elvaston Castle* DE7 . . . . . . .233 F7
Elvaston Castle Ctry Pk*
  DE21 . . . . .233 F6
Elvaston Castle Cvn Pk
  DE72 . . . . .234 A7
Elvaston Cl S18 . . . . .56 B1
Elvaston Dr NG10 . . . . .236 A4
Elvaston Estate Mus*
  DE72 . . . . .233 F7
Elvaston La DE24 . . . . .233 C7
Elvaston Rd S42 . . . . .131 F6
Elvaston St DE72 . . . . .235 B7
Elveden Dr DE7 . . . . .194 C3
Elvin Way S42 . . . . .131 C8
Elwood Rd S17 . . . . .56 C6
Elwyn Cl DE13 . . . . .240 D1
Ely Cl
  Mansfield Woodhouse
    NG19 . . . . .136 D4
  Swadlincote DE11 . . . . .256 D6
Elyn Ave S42 . . . . .132 B7
Elysee Gdns SK17 . . . . .85 C3
Embankment Cl DE22 . . . . . .217 F7
Ember La DE4 . . . . .142 E1
Embridge Cswy SK10 . . . . . . .64 B5
Emerald Cl
  Derby DE21 . . . . .206 A2
  Mansfield NG19 . . . . .135 F1
Emerson Sq DE23 . . . . .231 F6
Emery Cl DE12 . . . . .261 D5
Emmas Williams Ct DE55 . . . .169 D1
Emmerson Rd DE55 . . . . .170 C7
Emmet Field Cl S40 . . . . .114 F8
Emmett Carr Cl S21 . . . . .79 C7
Emmett Carr Dr S21 . . . . .79 C8
Emmett Carr La S21 . . . . .79 C8
Empire Ct DE75 . . . . .181 E2
Empire Rd DE15 . . . . .248 D3
Empress Rd DE23 . . . . .267 A1
Emsworth Cl DE7 . . . . .194 D3
Endland Ind Est DE11 . . . . . . .218 D5
Endowood Rd S40 . . . . .114 A8
Endsleigh Gdns DE22 . . . . . . .217 F6
End The DE15 . . . . .248 E8
Enfield Cl DE65 . . . . .228 E2
Enfield Rd
  Chesterfield S41 . . . . .96 A5
  Derby DE22 . . . . .218 B6
England Cres DE75 . . . . .182 A2
English Martyrs RC Prim Sch
  NG10 . . . . .223 B1
Ennerdale Ave **4** S20 . . . . . . .59 E6
Ennerdale Cl S18 . . . . .56 E1
Ennerdale Cres S41 . . . . .95 C8
Ennerdale Ct **6** NG10 . . . . .223 B2
Ennerdale Rd NG10 . . . . .223 B2
Ennerdale Wlk DE21 . . . . . . .205 D2
Ennis Cl DE21 . . . . .220 C7
Enoch Stone Dr DE21 . . . . . . .220 E4
Enslet La DE6 . . . . .164 B2
Ensor Cl DE11 . . . . .256 D5
Enterprise Cl NG19 . . . . .135 E2
Enterprise Ct
  Creswell S80 . . . . .81 E1
  Ilkeston DE7 . . . . .194 D1
Enterprise Par S42 . . . . .116 D1
Enterprise Rd NG19 . . . . .135 E3
Enterprise Way DE21 . . . . . . .267 C4
Epping Cl DE22 . . . . .217 E6
Epsom Cl DE14 . . . . .253 F7
Epsom Rd NG9 . . . . .223 E3
Epworth Dr DE24 . . . . .233 A4
Epworth Ho DE15 . . . . .248 D3
Erdington Way NG9 . . . . .223 E3
Eric Ave
  Ilkeston DE7 . . . . .194 D1
  Long Eaton NG10 . . . . .223 D1
Erewash Ct DE21 . . . . .220 F6
Erewash Dr DE7 . . . . .209 B6
Erewash Gr NG9 . . . . .223 F2
Erewash Mus* NG16 . . . . . . .208 F8
Erewash Rd NG16 . . . . .160 E2
Erewash Sq DE7 . . . . .209 A6
Erica Dr DE55 . . . . .160 B7
Erin Rd S43, S44 . . . . .98 B7
Ernest Hall Way DE11 . . . . . . .256 C4
Ernocroft La SK6 . . . . .15 E2
Ernocroft Rd SK6 . . . . .15 B1
Erringham View S2 . . . . .43 E6
Errington Ave S2 . . . . .43 E6
Errington Cl S2 . . . . .43 E6
Errington Cres S2 . . . . .43 E6
Errington Rd
  Chesterfield S40 . . . . .114 D8
  Sheffield S2 . . . . .43 E6
Errington Way S2 . . . . .43 E7
Errwood Ave S17 . . . . .85 A6
Errwood Forest Walks*
  SK17 . . . . .64 E2
Erskine Cres S2 . . . . .43 C7
Erskine Rd S2 . . . . .43 C7
Erskine St S2 . . . . .43 B6
Erskine View S2 . . . . .43 C6
Escolme Cl DE11 . . . . .256 D4
Eskdale Cl
  Bolsover S44 . . . . .98 F1
  Dronfield S18 . . . . .56 E1
  Long Eaton NG10 . . . . .236 B5
Eskdale Wlk DE24 . . . . .233 D6

Essendine Cres S8 . . . . 43 B3
Essex Dr DE11 . . . . 255 E1
Essex Rd DE15 . . . . 254 D6
Essex St
  Derby DE21 . . . . 219 D6
  2 Ilkeston DE7 . . . . 194 F1
Estwic Ave NG16 . . . . 182 F3
Etchells The DE65 . . . . 227 A8
Etherow Brow 6 SK14 . . . . 16 A8
Etherow Ctry Pk* SK6 . . 15 C3
Etherow Ctry Pk Visitor Ctr*
  SK6 . . . . 15 B2
Etherow Ind Est SK13 . . . 9 E5
Etherow Way SK13 . . . . 9 E5
Eton Cl DE7 . . . . 207 D8
Eton St DE24 . . . . 219 E1
Etruria Gdns DE1 . . . . 267 B5
Etta's Way DE65 . . . . 229 B4
Ettrick Cl 4 S40 . . . . 95 C5
Ettrick Dr DE24 . . . . 231 E2
Etwall Cl S40 . . . . 95 A6
Etwall La DE65 . . . . 229 F5
Etwall Prim Sch DE65 . 229 B4
Etwall Rd
  Derby DE3 . . . . 217 C1
  Eggington DE65 . . . . 241 B7
  Willington DE65 . . . . 242 A7
Etwall St DE22 . . . . 218 C5
Eureka Prim Sch DE11 . . 256 D5
Eureka Rd DE11 . . . . 256 D5
Euston Dr DE1 . . . . 219 B7
Evans Ave DE22 . . . . 205 A5
Evans Cl S33 . . . . 51 A7
Evanston Gdns DE21 . . . 220 B6
Evelyn Devonshire Cotts
  S45 . . . . 132 F2
Evelyn Gr DE21 . . . . 220 A5
Everard Ave S17 . . . . 56 A5
Everard Dr S17 . . . . 56 A5
Everard Glade 3 S17 . . . 56 A5
Everest Dr DE55 . . . . 170 D8
Everett Cl S41 . . . . 96 E7
Evergreen Cl DE24 . . . . 206 A3
Evershill Cl DE55 . . . . 146 F5
Evershill La DE55 . . . . 146 F6
Eversleigh Rise DE4 . . 142 B8
Everton St NG19 . . . . 135 E1
Evesham Ave SK13 . . . . . 10 A5
Evesham Cl DE21 . . . . . . 205 E1
Ewart La DE55 . . . . 138 E3
Ewe Dale La DE6 . . . . . . 149 A3
Ewe Lamb Cl NG9 . . . . . . 209 F1
Ewe Lamb La NG9 . . . . . . 209 F1
Excalibur Way S41 . . . . 266 C3
Excelsior Ave DE24 . . . 232 F6
Excelsior Dr DE11 . . . . 256 E2
Exchange St DE1 . . . . . . 267 B3
Eye Fold NG19 . . . . 119 D6
Exeter Cl DE11 . . . . 256 E6
Exeter Ct 1 S41 . . . . 95 F8
Exeter Ho DE1 . . . . 267 C3
Exeter Pl DE1 . . . . 267 C3
Exeter St DE1 . . . . 267 C4
Exford Ct NG19 . . . . 136 C6
Exlowmere La DE4 . . . . . 140 F5
Export Dr NG17 . . . . 160 F8
Eyam CE Prim Sch S32 . . 71 D5
Eyam Cl
  Burton u T DE15 . . . . 248 B2
  15 Gamesley SK13 . . . . . 9 D2
  North Wingfield S42 . 132 A8
Eyam Fold 20 SK13 . . . . . 9 D2
Eyam Gdns 17 SK13 . . . . . 9 D2
Eyam Gn 16 SK13 . . . . 9 D2
Eyam Gr 14 SK13 . . . . 9 D2
Eyam Hall* S32 . . . . 71 B5
Eyam La SK13 . . . . 9 E2
Eyam Lea SK13 . . . . 9 E2
Eyam Mews SK13 . . . . 9 E2
Eyam Moor Stone Circ*
  S32 . . . . 52 F3
Eyam Mus* S32 . . . . 71 D6
Eyam Wlk DE56 . . . . 179 A5
Eyam YH* S32 . . . . 71 D6
Eyes Ct DE56 . . . . 190 E3
Eyre's Gdns DE7 . . . . . . 194 F2
Eyre St E S41 . . . . 115 C8
Eyre St
  Clay Cross S45 . . . . 131 C3
  Creswell S80 . . . . 81 D1
Eyrie The
  Burton u T DE15 . . . . 248 C3
  Derby DE24 . . . . 231 E3

F

Fabis Cl DE11 . . . . 256 A3
Fabric View S42 . . . . . . 132 D8
Factory La DE7 . . . . 194 E2
Factory St S40 . . . . 95 D2
Fairbourne Dr DE3 . . . . 217 D4
Fairburn Croft Cres S43 . 80 B6
Faircroft Ave NG10 . . . 223 B5
Fairdene DE23 . . . . 218 F2
Faires Cl DE72 . . . . 221 D1
Faire St DE22 . . . . 218 E3
Fairfax Dr S2 . . . . 44 B8
Fairfax Rd
  Derby DE23 . . . . 218 F2
  Sheffield S2 . . . . 44 B8
Fairfax Rise S2 . . . . 44 B8
Fairfield Ave
  Borrowash DE72 . . . . 221 C3
  Hilcote DE55 . . . . 148 C1
  Rolleston DE13 . . . . 240 D4
  Stonebroom DE55 . . . 147 B4

Fairfield Cl
  Brimington S43 . . . . . . 96 D8
  Whaley Thorns NG20 . 101 A2
Fairfield Cres
  Long Eaton NG10 . . . . 236 B4
  Swadlincote DE11 . . . 255 E5
Fairfield Ct S42 . . . . 94 F4
Fairfield Dr S42 . . . . 94 F4
Fairfield Endowed CE Jun
  Sch SK17 . . . . 85 E7
Fairfield Inf Sch SK17 . . 85 E8
Fairfield Prim Sch NG9 . 223 D6
Fairfield Rd
  Bolsover S44 . . . . 118 A8
  Buxton SK17 . . . . 85 C8
  Chesterfield S40 . . . 266 A4
  Derby DE23 . . . . 218 E1
  Horsley Woodhouse DE7 . 192 C7
Fairfield Terr DE11 . . 256 F3
Fairfield Villas S40 . . 266 A4
Fairford Cl S40 . . . . . . 114 F7
Fairford Gdns DE23 . . . 231 A6
Fairham Rd DE13 . . . . . . 240 F1
Fairholme Dr NG19 . . . . 135 E1
Fairholmes DE4 . . . . 143 D5
Fairisle Cl DE21 . . . . . . 206 C3
Fairlawns DE56 . . . . 190 D3
Fair Lea Cl NG10 . . . . . . 236 D6
Fairleigh S2 . . . . 44 A8
Fairmeadows Foundation
  Prim Sch DE11 . . . . . 255 E5
Fair View S40 . . . . 95 E4
Fairview Ave NG16 . . . . 171 F2
Fairview Cl
  Derby DE23 . . . . 231 A8
  Kilburn DE56 . . . . . . 192 B7
Fairview Grange DE56 . 192 B7
Fairview Rd S18 . . . . 57 A3
Fairview Rise DE4 . . . . 168 A8
Fairway DE14 . . . . 254 B6
Fairway Cl DE22 . . . . . . 204 D2
Fairway Cres DE22 . . . . 204 D2
Fairways Cl SK13 . . . . . . 10 F1
Fairways The
  Clay Cross S45 . . . . 131 E3
  Clifton DE6 . . . . 184 F6
  Mansfield Woodhouse
  NG19 . . . . 136 D6
Fairway The 5 DE11 . . . 255 E5
Fairwinds Cl S18 . . . . . . 57 A1
Fairwood Dr DE24 . . . . . 233 D6
Fairy Bank Cres SK22 . . 25 D3
Fairy Bank Rd SK22 . . . . 25 D3
Falaise Way DE65 . . . . . 228 E2
Falcon Cl S42 . . . . 94 F3
Falcon Ct DE7 . . . . 194 D1
Falcon Rd S18 . . . . 57 C3
Falcon Rise S18 . . . . 57 D3
Falcons Rise DE56 . . . . 179 C5
Falcon Way
  Derby DE24 . . . . 231 E2
  Woodville DE11 . . . . . 256 F1
Falcon Yd S40 . . . . 266 B3
Faldo Ct DE14 . . . . 254 B6
Falkland Rise S18 . . . . . . 76 A8
Fallowfield Rd S43 . . . . 77 D3
Fallow Rd DE21 . . . . . . 220 F6
Fall Rd DE75 . . . . 181 E3
Falmouth Rd DE24 . . . . 233 C5
Fal Paddock S42 . . . . . . 136 D2
Fanny Ave S21 . . . . 60 E5
Fan Rd S43 . . . . 78 F1
Fan Road Ind Est S43 . . 78 F2
Fanshaw Ave S21 . . . . . . 59 C2
Fanshaw Bank S18 . . . . . 57 A1
Fanshaw Cl S21 . . . . 59 C2
Fanshaw Dr S21 . . . . 59 C2
Fanshawe Gate La S17,
  S18 . . . . 55 E1
Fanshaw Rd
  Dronfield S18 . . . . 57 A1
  Eckington S21 . . . . 59 C2
Fanshaw Way S21 . . . . . . 59 C2
Faraday Ave DE13 . . . . . 240 D1
Faraday Ct
  Branston DE14 . . . . . 253 E7
  Stapleford NG9 . . . . . 209 E1
Far Clay Gr S81 . . . . 63 F7
Far Croft DE72 . . . . 235 D8
Far Cross DE4 . . . . 143 C7
Farfield Rd DE7 . . . . . . 209 A8
Far Dale DE4 . . . . 143 B6
Far Hill S33 . . . . 51 A7
Farish Pl 8 S2 . . . . 43 B6
Far La
  Barlow S18 . . . . 75 B3
  Ockbrook DE72 . . . . . 221 D6
Far Laund DE56 . . . . . . 179 B6
Farley Hill DE4 . . . . . . 143 A8
Farley La DE4 . . . . 128 B3
Farley Rd DE23 . . . . . . 218 D2
Farm Cl
  Belper DE56 . . . . 179 C4
  Chesterfield S40 . . . 114 F6
  Dronfield S18 . . . . 57 B4
  Hilton DE65 . . . . 228 C1
  Ilkeston DE7 . . . . 209 A8
  Kilburn DE56 . . . . . . 192 A8
  Long Eaton NG10 . . . . 236 E5
  Ripley DE5 . . . . 169 B6
  Sheffield S12 . . . . 44 A6
  Somercotes DE55 . . . 170 C8
Farm Cres S20 . . . . 59 C6
Farm Croft Rd NG19 . . 136 C6
Farm Dr DE24 . . . . 233 A5
Farmfields Cl S44 . . . . . . 98 E3
Farmhouse Rd DE24 . . . 231 E2
Farmilo Cres NG19 . . . 135 E1

Farmilo Prim Sch NG19 . 135 C4
Farm La
  High Lane SK12 . . . . . . 32 A6
  Matlock DE4 . . . . 143 C7
  Newton Solney DE15 . 248 E1
Farmlands La DE23 . . . . 231 B6
Farm Side DE11 . . . . . . 255 F5
Farm St DE22 . . . . 267 A1
Farmstead Cl S14 . . . . . . 43 D5
Farm View S42 . . . . 131 D8
Farmway NG19 . . . . 136 C2
Farn Wlk S20 . . . . 59 C7
Farnah Green Rd DE56 . 178 D3
Farnborough Gdns DE22 . 205 B4
Farncombe La DE21 . . . 205 F3
Farndale Ave S40 . . . . . 114 B8
Farndale Cl NG10 . . . . . 236 A5
Farndale Ct 5 DE24 . . . 233 C6
Farndale Rd S43 . . . . 78 E4
Fardon Dr NG9 . . . . 223 F3
Far New Cl NG10 . . . . . 223 B5
Farnworth Rd DE3 . . . . 217 D2
Farnham Wlk DE7 . . . . . 207 D8
Farningham Cl DE7 . . . 220 F5
Farnon Cl S40 . . . . 266 C1
Farnsley La S32 . . . . 71 B4
Farnsworth Gr NG17 . . 148 F3
Farnsworth St S41 . . . . 115 C8
Farnway DE22 . . . . 204 E1
Farrendale Cl NG19 . . . 136 D1
Farrier Gdns DE24 . . . . 231 A7
Farriers Croft DE7 . . . 194 C3
Farringdon Cl DE22 . . 217 F6
Farrington Way NG16 . 182 E1
Farthing Cl NG10 . . . . . 236 B7
Farwater Cl S18 . . . . 76 A8
Farwater La S18 . . . . 57 A1
Far Woodseats La SK13 . 15 F5
Fauld Ind Pk DE13 . . . . 238 E6
Fauld La
  Tutbury DE13 . . . . . . 239 A6
  Tutbury, Fauld DE13 . 238 D7
Fauvel Pl SK13 . . . . 10 C1
Fauvel Rd SK13 . . . . 10 C2
Faversham Cl DE24 . . . 232 F5
Fawn Cl S42 . . . . 114 F3
Fay Gdns SK13 . . . . 9 E4
Faywood Dr SK6 . . . . 23 A6
Fearn Ave DE5 . . . . 169 E1
Fearn Cl
  Church Broughton DE65 . 227 B8
  Long Eaton DE72 . . . . 236 A7
Featherbed La
  Bolsover S44 . . . . 99 A5
  Darfoulds S80 . . . . 63 F2
Felkin St S41 . . . . 266 C3
Fellbrigg Rd S2 . . . . 43 D7
Fellow Lands Way DE73 . 233 A2
Fellside
  Belper DE56 . . . . 179 A4
  Derby DE21 . . . . 220 F6
Fellview Cl S32 . . . . 53 A7
Felton Ave NG19 . . . . . 136 C6
Fenchurch Wlk DE22 . . 218 B7
Fen Cl DE55 . . . . 148 A3
Fenland Way S40 . . . . . 114 B8
Fennel St DE45 . . . . . . 108 E8
Fenton Ave DE11 . . . . . 257 B1
Fenton Rd DE3 . . . . 217 C2
Fenton St S21 . . . . 59 B2
Fenwick St DE24 . . . . . 232 D7
Ferguson Ave NG19 . . . 136 B4
Fern Ave
  Staveley S43 . . . . 97 D8
  Willington DE65 . . . . 242 C6
Fernbank S33 . . . . 51 A7
Fern Bank Ave DE55 . . 147 E1
Fernbank Dr S21 . . . . . . 59 B3
Fern Cl
  Eckington S21 . . . . 59 B3
  Holmewood S44 . . . . . 116 F1
  Shirebrook NG20 . . . 119 E6
  Willington DE65 . . . . 242 C6
Ferncroft Ave S20 . . . . . 59 C7
Ferndale Ave SK17 . . . . . 67 C4
Ferndale Cl S18 . . . . 57 D3
Ferndale Rd
  Buxton SK17 . . . . 67 C4
  Dronfield S18 . . . . 57 D3
Ferndene Dr NG10 . . . . 236 A7
Fernello Cl S43 . . . . 78 E4
Ferneydale Ave SK17 . . . 85 C4
Fernhill SK6 . . . . 23 B6
Fernhill Cl SK13 . . . . . . 10 D3
Fernhill Ct DE73 . . . . . 233 A3
Fernilee Cl
  New Mills SK22 . . . . . . 24 C1
  West Hallam DE7 . . . . 207 E8
Fernilee Cotts SK23 . . . 45 E1
Fernilee Gdns DE21 . . . 205 F1
Fern Lea
  Hollingworth SK14 . . . 9 D6
  Shirland DE55 . . . . . . 146 D3
Fernlea Cl SK13 . . . . 9 E4
Fernleigh Rise NG19 . . 136 D1
Fern Rd SK17 . . . . 85 B5
Fern Royd S32 . . . . 54 F7
Fern Sq S32 . . . . 71 D6
Fernway SK17 . . . . 85 C4
Fern Way S21 . . . . 59 B3
Fernwood SK6 . . . . 23 C7
Fernwood Cl
  Chesterfield S41 . . . 115 C7
  Derby DE23 . . . . 231 D8
  Shirland DE55 . . . . . . 146 D3

First Ave
  Branston DE14 . . . . . 253 E7
  Risley NG10 . . . . 222 F5
Firs The DE6 . . . . 173 C1
Firth Ct S43 . . . . 77 D4
Firthwood Ave S18 . . . . . 57 D3
Firthwood Cl S18 . . . . . . 57 D3
Firthwood Rd S18 . . . . . 57 D3
Fir Tree Ave DE55 . . . 146 C4
Fir Tree Dr DE73 . . . . 244 A6
Firtree Gr DE21 . . . . . . 206 B2
Firvale S26 . . . . 61 E5
Firvale Rd S40 . . . . . . 114 B8
Fisher Cl
  Chesterfield S40 . . . 114 F7
  Repton DE65 . . . . 242 D2
Fisher Ct DE7 . . . . 194 F4
Fisher La DE56 . . . . . . 190 E4
Fishers Bridge SK22 . . . 25 D2
Fisher St DE24 . . . . . . 232 E6
Fishpond La
  Egginton DE65 . . . . . 241 A5
  Tutbury DE13 . . . . . . 239 C6
Fishponds Cl S42 . . . . 115 A3
Fishponds Rd S13 . . . . 44 C7
Fishponds Rd W S13 . . 44 C7
Fiskerton Way DE21 . . 206 B1
Fitzalan St SK13 . . . . . . 10 C1
Fitzherbert CE Prim Sch
  DE6 . . . . 162 A1
Fitzhubert Rd
  Sheffield S2 . . . . 44 A7
  Sheffield S2 . . . . 44 A8
Fitzroy Rd S2 . . . . 43 B6
Fitzwilliam Dr NG19 . . 136 F2
Five Lamps Ct DE1 . . . 218 F6
Five Lamps Ho DE1 . . . 267 A5
Five Lamps Rd DE15 . . 254 F8
Five Trees Ave S17 . . . . 56 A6
Five Trees Cl S17 . . . . . 56 A6
Five Trees Dr S17 . . . . . 56 A6
Flackets La DE6 . . . . . . 225 B7
Flagg La SK17 . . . . 106 F7
Flagshaw La DE6 . . . . . . 202 F4
Flake La DE7 . . . . 208 E1
Flamstead Ave DE75 . . 181 C4
Flamstead La DE55 . . . 180 E1
Flamstead Rd DE7 . . . . 194 F1
Flamstead St DE24 . . . 232 E6
Flamsteed Cres S41 . . . 96 A6
Flash CE Prim Sch SK17 . 103 B3
Flash La DE4 . . . . 128 A7
Fiat La SK17 . . . . 106 B8
Flat The DE56 . . . . 191 F8
Flatts The DE6 . . . . 171 D3
Flatts The DE6 . . . . 165 B1
Flax Croft DE65 . . . . . . 227 C1
Flaxholme Ave DE56 . . 190 F1
Flaxpiece Rd S45 . . . . 131 D3
Fleet Cres DE56 . . . . . . 179 E3
Fleet Pk DE56 . . . . 179 A3
Fleet St DE23 . . . . 219 A2
Fleet The DE56 . . . . . . 178 F2
Fletcher's Row DE5 . . 169 F2
Fletcher Ave S18 . . . . . . 57 A1
Fletcher St
  Heanor DE75 . . . . 181 E2
  Long Eaton NG10 . . . 236 D8
  Ripley DE5 . . . . 169 E2
Fletches The DE13 . . . 240 E1
Fleury Cl S14 . . . . 43 E4
Fleury Cres S14 . . . . . . 43 E4
Fleury Pl S14 . . . . 43 E4
Fleury Rd S14 . . . . 43 E4
Fleury Rise S14 . . . . . . 43 E4
Flint Ave NG19 . . . . . . 136 F1
Flint La DE4 . . . . 142 B8
Flintson Ave S43 . . . . . . 77 D4
Flint St DE24 . . . . 232 D6
Flixton Rd NG16 . . . . . 195 F7
Flood St DE72 . . . . 221 C4
Florence Ave NG10 . . . 223 F1
Florence Cl
  Chesterfield S40 . . . 114 F6
  Pleasley NG19 . . . . . 134 F4
Florence Ct
  Derby DE1 . . . . 267 D2
  Ilkeston DE7 . . . . 194 F1
Florence Dr DE24 . . . . 224 C8
Florence Gladwin Cl
  DE4 . . . . 141 C6
Florence Rd
  Clay Cross S45 . . . . 131 E4
  Wingerworth S42 . . . 114 E4
Florence Way SK14 . . . . 9 D5
Florin Gdns NG10 . . . . 236 B7
Flowery Leys La DE55 . 159 C3
Floyd St DE24 . . . . 80 F5
Foggs Entry DE4 . . . . . 165 F8
Foggs Hill DE4 . . . . . . 127 C4
Folds La SK23 . . . . 45 E3
Folds Yd DE4 . . . . 156 F2
Fold The S32 . . . . 71 A6
Foljambe Ave S40 . . . . 114 D8
Foljambe Rd
  Brimington S43 . . . . . . 96 E8
  Chesterfield S41 . . . . 96 A8
Folkestone Dr DE24 . . 233 A5
Folly Rd DE22 . . . . 205 B1
Fontwell Rd DE14 . . . . 253 F7
Foolow Ave S40 . . . . . . 266 A1
Foolow Ct S40 . . . . 266 A1
Forbes Cl NG10 . . . . . . 236 E5
Ford Ave DE75 . . . . 181 C4
Fordbridge La DE55 . . 160 A7

Ford Cl
Dronfield S18. . . . . .56 F1
Ripley DE5 . . . . .180 C8
Ford Ct SK14. . . . . .9 A4
Ford La
Breadsall DE21 . . . . . . .205 C5
Derby DE22 . . . . .205 B5
Eckington S12, S21 . . . . .58 E5
Willington DE65. . . . . . .242 C5
Ford Rd S21. . . . . .58 E4
Ford St
Belper DE56. . . . . .178 F4
Burton u T DE15. . . . . . .254 E7
Derby DE1 . . . . .267 A4
Tupton S42. . . . . .131 D8
Ford Way SK14 . . . . .9 A4
Fordwells Ct DE28 . . . . . .231 A8
Fordyce Cl DE73. . . . . . . .232 E1
Foremark Ave DE23 . . . . .231 E8
Forest Ave SK17 . . . . .85 C6
Forest Cl DE56. . . . . .179 B5
Forest Ct S43. . . . . .80 B6
Forest Dr S45 . . . . .132 C2
Foresters Rd DE5 . . . . . .169 C2
Forest La SK17 . . . . .50 C2
Forest Lea DE12 . . . . . . .262 E4
Forest Park Cvn Pk
NG19. . . . . .136 E2
Forest School St DE13 . . .240 C4
Forest View DE12 . . . . . .262 B4
Forge Cl DE65 . . . . .242 D2
Forge La
Burton u T DE13. . . . . . .241 A2
Killamarsh S21 . . . . .60 B7
Forge Mill Pl DE56. . . . . .191 A6
Forge Rd S23. . . . . .45 E7
Forge Stps DE56. . . . . . .191 A6
Forge Terr SK23 . . . . .34 E1
Forge The
Dronfield S18. . . . . .57 A1
Trowell NG9. . . . . .209 B5
Forman Cl DE11 . . . . . . .256 B4
Forman St DE1, DE22 . . .267 A3
Forrester's La S18 . . . . . .57 C4
Forrester Ave DE72 . . . . .245 F5
Forshaw Cl DE6 . . . . . . .185 C8
Forth Ave S18 . . . . .56 D2
Forties La DE65 . . . . .257 F3
Forty Foot La DE73 . . . . .252 F7
Forty Horse Cl DE5 . . . . .170 A2
Forum Cl DE24 . . . . .233 D5
Fosbrook Dr DE24 . . . . . .246 F4
Fosbrooke Dr NG10 . . . . .236 D5
Fosse Cl DE72 . . . . .221 C1
Fossett's Ave NG16 . . . . .171 F7
Foster Rd DE11 . . . . .256 F2
Foston Cl DE65 . . . . .239 C8
Foston Dr S40 . . . . .95 B5
Foufinside Farm Camping &
Cvn Site DE6 . . . . .151 C2
Foundry Ct ■ SK22 . . . . .33 C7
Foundry La DE56 . . . . . . .190 F8
Foundry St S41 . . . . .96 A8
Foundry Street Ind Est ⊠
S41. . . . . .96 A8
Foundry The S41. . . . . . .266 C2
Fountains Cl DE22 . . . . . .205 A4
Fountain Sq
Disley SK12 . . . . .32 D6
Tideswell SK17 . . . . .69 C4
Youlgreave DE45. . . . . . .125 B5
Fountain St S41 . . . . .85 B7
Four Lane Ends
Darley Dale DE4 . . . . . . .127 C1
Swadlincote DE11 . . . . . .256 A6
Four Lanes SK14. . . . . .9 A4
Fowler Ave DE21 . . . . . . .220 D4
Fowler St
Chesterfield S41 . . . . . . .76 F2
Derby DE22 . . . . .218 E6
Draycott DE72 . . . . .235 B7
Foxbrook Cl
Chesterfield S42 . . . . . . .94 F5
Derby DE23 . . . . .231 A8
Foxbrook Ct S40. . . . . . .114 B8
Foxbrook Dr S40. . . . . . .114 B8
Fox Cl
Burton u T DE14. . . . . . .254 B8
Derby DE24 . . . . .231 D2
Long Eaton NG10 . . . . . .236 D5
Foxcote Way S40 . . . . . .114 B8
Fox Croft DE55 . . . . .147 F5
Foxcroft Chase S21. . . . . .60 C6
Foxcroft Dr S21 . . . . .60 C5
Foxcroft Gr S21. . . . . .60 C6
Foxdale Ave S12. . . . . .44 B5
Foxdell Way DE73 . . . . . .233 A2
Foxes Wlk DE22 . . . . . . .204 E4
Foxes Yd SK17 . . . . .66 D1
Fox Field DE11 . . . . .261 F8
Foxfields Dr DE21. . . . . . .205 E2
Foxglove Ave
Burton u T DE15. . . . . . .255 A8
Donisthorpe DE12 . . . . . .262 E1
Foxglove Cl S44 . . . . .97 A3
Foxglove Dr DE21 . . . . . .206 A3
Foxglove Gr NG19. . . . . . .136 C3
Foxglove Rd NG16 . . . . . .195 B8
Foxhall La S10. . . . . .42 F6
Foxholes La
Kniveton DE6 . . . . .174 B6
Tansley DE4 . . . . .144 A7
Fox La
Holmesfield S18 . . . . . . .74 B5

Fox La continued
Sheffield, Base Green S12. . .44 C3
Sheffield, Lower Bradway
S17. . . . . .56 D6
Foxlands Ave DE22. . . . . .204 F2
Fox Lane Ct S12 . . . . .44 C4
Fox Lane View S12. . . . . .44 C4
Foxlea SK3 . . . . .16 F8
Foxley Ct DE21 . . . . .206 A2
Foxley Oaks S41. . . . . . . .77 B1
Fox Low Ave SK17 . . . . . .85 C4
Foxpark View DE55. . . . . .147 E5
Fox Rd
Castle Donington DE74 . . .246 F4
Whitwell S80 . . . . .82 A6
Fox St DE1. . . . . .267 C4
Foxstone Cl S43 . . . . .97 D8
Foxton Cl DE7 . . . . .194 C3
Foxwood Ave S12 . . . . . . .44 B6
Foxwood Cl
Chesterfield S41 . . . . . . .115 D6
Chesterfield, Sheepbridge
S41. . . . . .76 F2
Foxwood Dr S12 . . . . .44 B6
Foxwood Gr S12 . . . . .44 B5
Foxwood Ind Pk S41. . . . . .76 F1
Foxwood Rd
Chesterfield S41 . . . . . . .76 F2
Sheffield S12. . . . . .44 B6
Foxwood Way S41 . . . . . . .76 E2
Foyers Way S41 . . . . . . .266 C3
Foyle Ave DE21 . . . . .220 E4
Frain Gdns DE73 . . . . . . .252 F2
Framingham Pl S2 . . . . . . .43 D7
Framlingham Rd S2 . . . . . .43 D7
Frampton Gdns DE23 . . . .230 F6
Frances Dr S42 . . . . .114 E4
Frances St NG16. . . . . . . .171 D1
Franchise St DE22 . . . . . .218 E4
Francis Cl S43. . . . . .96 D7
Francis St DE21. . . . . . . .219 D6
Frank Bodicote Way
DE11. . . . . .256 D4
Franklin Ave S80 . . . . .81 F5
Franklin Cl DE15. . . . . . . .248 B1
Franklin Cres S80. . . . . . . .81 F5
Franklin Rd NG16 . . . . . .171 A4
Franklyn Dr
Derby DE24 . . . . .233 A6
Staveley S43 . . . . .78 F3
Franklyn Rd S40 . . . . .95 E4
Frazer Cl DE21. . . . . .220 E6
Frecheville St S43 . . . . . . .78 D1
Frederic Ave DE75 . . . . . .193 F7
Frederick Ave
Derby DE24 . . . . .232 F6
Ilkeston DE7 . . . . .209 A5
Frederick Gent Sch
DE55 . . . . .160 B5
Frederick Harrison Inf Sch
NG9. . . . . .223 F8
Frederick Rd NG9. . . . . . .223 D7
Frederick St
Alfreton DE55 . . . . .159 A5
Burton u T DE15. . . . . . .254 E8
Derby DE22 . . . . .218 D6
Grassmoor S42 . . . . .115 E3
Long Eaton NG10. . . . . . .236 F7
Somercotes DE55 . . . . . .170 D5
Woodville DE11 . . . . .256 E3
Freebirch View S40. . . . . . .95 B7
Freeby Ave NG19 . . . . . . .136 D5
Freehold St DE22 . . . . . . .218 E4
Freeland Cl NG9 . . . . .223 F3
Freeman Ave DE23 . . . . . .231 E6
Freesia Cl DE21. . . . . .217 E1
Freeston St SK13 . . . . .17 C8
Fremantle Rd DE7 . . . . . .217 E3
French La DE21. . . . . .191 F5
French St
Derby DE21 . . . . .218 E2
Ilkeston DE7 . . . . .209 A6
French Terr NG20 . . . . . . .101 A2
Fresco Dr DE21 . . . . .230 F7
Fresh Ct SK13 . . . . .16 F7
Freshfield Cl SK6. . . . . . . .15 B1
Freshfields Farm Donkey
Sanctuary* SK17. . . . . . .48 D2
Freshwater Ho DE24 . . . . .233 C7
Freshwaters S42. . . . . . . .116 D1
Fretson Cl S2. . . . . .44 A8
Fretson Gn S2 . . . . .44 A8
Fretson Rd S2 . . . . .44 A8
Fretson Rd S S2 . . . . .44 A8
Freydon Way S44 . . . . . . .97 A3
Friar Gate DE1. . . . . .218 F5
Friar Gate Ct DE1. . . . . . .218 F5
Friar Gate House Sch
DE1. . . . . .218 E6
Friar Gr SK17 . . . . .85 C6
Friars Ct DE22. . . . . .205 A2
Friars Ct DE7 . . . . .208 C6
Friarsfield DE22 . . . . .218 F8
Friar St NG10 . . . . .236 D7
Friary Ave DE24 . . . . .232 E6
Friary Croft DE11 . . . . . . .256 A7
Friary St DE1 . . . . .267 A3
Friden Cotts SK17 . . . . . . .139 A6
Friesland Dr NG10 . . . . . .222 F5
Friesland Sch NG10 . . . . . .222 F5
Friezeland DE6 . . . . .26 B6
Frisby Ave NG10 . . . . .236 E6
Fritchley CE Prim Sch
DE56 . . . . .168 B6
Fritchley Cl DE21 . . . . . . .206 A1
Fritchley La DE56 . . . . . . .168 A7
Frith Cl S42 . . . . .94 B5
Frithhall La S42. . . . . .94 C2

Frith Knoll Rd SK23 . . . . . .47 D7
Frith Rd S12. . . . . .44 B5
Frith View SK23. . . . . .47 A5
Frithwood Dr S18. . . . . . . .57 C2
Frithwood La
Creswell S80 . . . . .100 F8
Elmton S80 . . . . .100 D7
Frizams La DE73 . . . . .242 F7
Froggatt Cl
Derby DE22 . . . . .205 A5
Staveley S43 . . . . .97 C6
Froggatt Cl DE55 . . . . . . .170 D7
Front St DE56 . . . . .168 B6
Frood Cl SK23 . . . . .47 C7
Frost Ave NG16 . . . . .182 A4
Frost Fields DE74 . . . . . . .247 B4
Fryar Rd NG16. . . . . .182 F4
Fulbrook Rd DE23 . . . . . .231 A8
Fulford S40. . . . . .114 C8
Fulham Rd DE22 . . . . . . .218 A5
Fuller Dr S41. . . . . .96 C6
Fulleylove Ct S44 . . . . . . .99 B1
Full St DE1 . . . . .267 B3
Fullwood Ave ◢ DE7 . . . .194 E1
Fullwood Grange DE6 . . . .175 C3
Fullwood St ◢ DE7 . . . . .194 E1
Fullwood Stile La S33. . . . .38 F6
Fulmar Cl DE3 . . . . .218 A3
Fulwood Dr NG10 . . . . . . .236 A7
Fulwood Head Rd S10 . . . .42 D7
Fulwood Ind Est NG17 . . .160 F8
Fulwood La S10, S11. . . . . .42 E5
Fulwood Rd N NG17 . . . . .148 F1
Fulwood Rd S NG17. . . . . .160 F8
Furlong Cl NG9 . . . . .223 D8
Furlong La
Alstonefield DE6 . . . . . . .149 C4
Atlow DE6 . . . . .175 B7
Furnace Cl S42 . . . . .115 E2
Furnace Hillock Way
S41. . . . . .115 E5
Furnace La
Barlow S18 . . . . .75 F3
Heanor DE75 . . . . .181 D4
Moira DE12 . . . . .262 E3
Furnace Lane Ind Est
DE12. . . . . .262 E3
Furnace Rd DE7 . . . . .209 B6
Furnace Row DE55. . . . . .170 F7
Furnall Ave DE45. . . . . . . .90 A3
Furness Cl ◢ SK13 . . . . . . .17 F8
Furness Lodge Cl SK23. . . .33 D4
Furness Vale Bsns Ctr
SK23. . . . . .33 D4
Furness Vale Prim Sch
SK23. . . . . .33 D3
Furness Vale Sta SK23. . . . .33 D4
Furniss Ave S17 . . . . .55 D6
Furniss Mews S17. . . . . . .55 E6
Furrows Cl DE21 . . . . . . .206 C3
Fyfield Rd DE15. . . . . . . .254 E6
Fylde Cl NG9 . . . . .223 F2

G

Gable Ct DE55 . . . . .230 E8
Gables Cl S42 . . . . .132 D8
Gables The
Hilton DE65 . . . . .228 D1
◻ Swadlincote DE11 . . . .255 E5
Gadley Cl SK17 . . . . .84 F8
Gadley La SK17 . . . . .84 F8
Gadsby Cl DE7. . . . . .209 A4
Gadsby Rise DE56. . . . . . .168 C2
Gag La DE6. . . . . .161 D6
Gainsborough Ave SK6. . . .23 B1
Gainsborough Cl
Derby DE21 . . . . .206 B1
Long Eaton NG10. . . . . . .236 E5
Stapleford NG9 . . . . .223 B6
Gainsborough Rd S18. . . . .75 E8
Gainsborough Way DE15. .248 B3
Gairloch Cl DE24 . . . . . . .231 D2
Gala Dr DE24 . . . . .232 F7
Galahad Dr DE13 . . . . . . .240 E2
Gallery La S42 . . . . .113 D7
Gallery The ◻ DE6. . . . . .173 C2
Gallows Ind Est DE7 . . . . .209 B6
Gallows Inn Cl DE7 . . . . .209 A5
Gallowstree La DE6 . . . . .184 C8
Galway Ave DE21 . . . . . . .220 B4
Gamesley Com Prim Sch
SK13. . . . . .9 E2
Gander La S43. . . . . .80 B5
Gang La S44. . . . . .118 E5
Gannow Cl S21. . . . . .60 F7
Gapsick La S43, S80. . . . . .81 B5
Garden Ave
Ilkeston DE7 . . . . .208 F5
New Houghton NG19. . . . .134 F7
Renishaw S21 . . . . .79 B7
Shirebrook NG20. . . . . . .119 E4
Garden Cl S43 . . . . .77 D3
Garden Cres
Castle Donington DE74 . . .247 B3
South Normanton DE55. . .159 F4
Gardeners Ct
Bolsover S44. . . . . .99 A2
Mansfield Woodhouse
NG19. . . . . .136 C3
Garden Rd NG16. . . . . . . .182 F3
Garden Row S44. . . . . . . .117 D1
Garden St
◻ Broadbottom SK14. . . . .16 A8
Derby DE1 . . . . .267 A4

Gardens The
Heanor DE75 . . . . .181 C4
Ripley DE5 . . . . .180 D7
Gardner Pl ST14 . . . . .210 A1
Gardom Cl S18 . . . . .56 D1
Garfield Ave DE72 . . . . . .235 A7
Garfield Cl
Derby DE23 . . . . .231 C6
Stapleford NG9 . . . . .209 E1
Garland Cl S20. . . . . .59 E7
Garland Croft S20 . . . . . . .59 E7
Garland Mount ◢ S20 . . . .59 E8
Garland Way S20. . . . . . . .59 E7
Garner La DE4, DE55. . . . .157 D2
Garnett Ave DE75 . . . . . . .181 F2
Garnham Cl DE55. . . . . . .159 D2
Garrett Cl S45. . . . . .131 E3
Garrett La S45. . . . . .131 D2
Garrett Sq DE13 . . . . . . .240 C4
Garrick St DE24 . . . . .233 A7
Garry Cl DE24 . . . . .231 D2
Garsdale Ct DE24. . . . . . .233 D6
Gartan Rd DE14. . . . . . . .254 A8
Garth Ave ◢ DE7 . . . . . . .194 E4
Garthorpe Ct ◢ DE21. . . .205 F2
Garth Rd SK6. . . . . .23 A6
Garth Way S18 . . . . .56 F1
Gartrice Gdns S20 . . . . . . .60 A5
Gartrice Gr S20. . . . . .60 A5
Gary Cl DE21 . . . . .231 D5
Gascoigne Dr DE21 . . . . . .220 D4
Gashouse La S20, S21 . . . .59 D5
Gaskell Ave DE23 . . . . . . .231 E7
Gasny Ave DE74 . . . . .247 B5
Gas St
Hollingworth SK14. . . . . . .9 D5
Sandiacre NG10. . . . . . . .223 C6
Uttoxeter ST14 . . . . .210 C1
Gatcombe Cl
Burton u T DE13. . . . . . .240 D1
Derby DE21 . . . . .206 B2
Gatcombe Gr NG10 . . . . . .223 A3
Gate Brook Cl DE55. . . . . .170 B1
Gatefield Cl S41. . . . . .95 C7
Gate Ho DE4 . . . . .165 F8
Gate Ho The S32. . . . . . . .72 D2
Gatehouse Dr DE4 . . . . . .165 F8
Gateland La S18 . . . . .75 E5
Gateway Christian Sch
DE7. . . . . .207 F2
Gateway Cvn Pk DE6. . . . .185 D7
Gauledge La SK17 . . . . . . .121 B6
Gaunt Cl
Killamarsh S21 . . . . .60 C6
Sheffield S14 . . . . .43 D3
Gaunt Dr S14 . . . . .43 D3
Gaunt Pl S14 . . . . .43 D3
Gaunt Rd S14 . . . . .43 D3
Gaunt Way S14 . . . . .43 D3
Gawain Gr DE13 . . . . .240 E2
Gawsworth Cl SK13 . . . . . .10 A5
Gayton Ave DE23 . . . . . . .231 D6
Gayton Com Jun Sch
DE23 . . . . .231 D6
Gayton Thorpe Cl DE23. . .230 F7
Geary La DE15. . . . . .248 F2
Geer La S32 . . . . .58 D5
Gelderd Pl S18 . . . . .76 A8
Gema Cl DE24 . . . . .205 A4
Genista Cl DE15 . . . . .255 A8
Gentshill Ave S45. . . . . . . .131 E2
George Ave NG10 . . . . . . .223 F1
George Cres DE55 . . . . . . .170 C6
George Dutton Ind Pk
DE6 . . . . .185 E8
George Holmes Bsns Pk
DE11 . . . . .256 A4
George Holmes Way
DE11 . . . . .256 A4
George Inn Ct S80. . . . . . .81 F6
George Percival Pl S45 . . .131 A4
George Rd DE4 . . . . .143 C6
George Spencer Foundation
Sch & Tech Coll NG9 . . .223 E5
George St
Alfreton DE55 . . . . .159 A4
Ashbourne DE6 . . . . . . .185 B8
Belper DE56. . . . . .178 F4
◪ Buxton SK17. . . . . .85 B8
Chesterfield S41 . . . . . . .76 F2
Compstall SK6. . . . . .15 B2
Derby DE1 . . . . .267 A3
Glossop SK13. . . . . .17 C8
Langley Mill NG16. . . . . .182 B3
Mansfield Woodhouse
NG19. . . . . .136 C3
Melbourne DE73 . . . . . . .252 A7
North Wingfield S42 . . . . .131 E7
Somercotes DE55 . . . . . .160 C4
Somercotes, Riddings
DE55. . . . . .170 D6
South Normanton DE55. . .159 F5
Swadlincote DE11 . . . . . .256 A1
Whaley Bridge SK23 . . . . .45 E7
Whaley Thorns NG20. . . . .101 A2
Georgina Ct DE74. . . . . . .247 B4
Gerard Cl
Chesterfield S40 . . . . . . .95 C1
Derby DE21 . . . . .220 B4
◪ Sheffield S8 . . . . .43 B6
Gerard Ct DE1 . . . . .267 A2
Gerard St
Derby DE1 . . . . .267 A2

Gerard St continued
Sheffield S8 . . . . .43 B6
Gertrude Rd
Derby DE21 . . . . .220 A8
Draycott DE72 . . . . .235 A7
Gervase Ave S8. . . . . .56 E6
Gervase Dr S8. . . . . .56 E6
Gervase Pl S8 . . . . .56 E6
Gervase Rd S8. . . . . .56 E6
Gervase Wlk ◨ S8. . . . . . .56 E6
Ghyll Cl DE24. . . . . .220 A1
Gibb Ct S43 . . . . .77 D4
Gibb La
Marple SK6 . . . . .23 E5
Sudbury DE6 . . . . .225 E5
Gibbons Ave NG9 . . . . . . .223 D6
Gibbons Dr S14. . . . . .43 E2
Gibbons Way S14. . . . . . . .43 E2
Gibbons Wlk S14 . . . . .43 E2
Gibb St NG10. . . . . .236 E7
Gibfield La
Belper DE56. . . . . .178 F2
Kirk Ireton DE6. . . . . . . .175 F7
Gifford Rd S8 . . . . .43 A7
Gilbert Ave S40. . . . . .114 D8
Gilbert Cl DE21. . . . . .220 D4
Gilbert Cres DE56 . . . . . . .190 E2
Gilbert Heathcote Inf Sch
S41. . . . . .96 A8
Gilbert St DE24 . . . . .233 D6
Gilderdale Way DE21. . . . .206 B3
Gill's La S42. . . . . .115 C2
Gillamoor Ct DE24 . . . . . .233 D6
Gilleyfield Ave S17 . . . . . . .55 E7
Gilliver Gdns DE72 . . . . . .235 A7
Gill La DE4 . . . . .127 C4
Gillott St DE75. . . . . .194 A8
Gilltbrook Cres NG16 . . . .195 C8
Gilt Hill NG16. . . . . .195 D7
Gilthill Prim Sch NG16 . . .195 C7
Giltway NG16. . . . . .195 C7
Gimson Cl DE7 . . . . .194 C3
Gin Close Way NG16 . . . . .195 C6
Gin La S45 . . . . .144 F8
Gipsyhill La S80 . . . . .81 B8
Gipsy La
Alstonefield DE6 . . . . . . .149 F4
Apperknowle S18. . . . . . .58 A1
Chesterfield S41 . . . . . . .77 B1
Gird La SK6 . . . . .15 C1
Girdon Cl SK17 . . . . .84 F6
Gisborne Cl DE3 . . . . .217 E3
Gisborne Cres DE22 . . . . .204 F4
Gisborne Gn DE1 . . . . . . .218 E6
Gisbourne Cl S43 . . . . .78 F1
Gisbourne Dr SK23 . . . . . . .47 B5
Glade Cl S40 . . . . .95 E5
Glade Croft S12 . . . . .44 A4
Glade Lea S12 . . . . .44 A4
Glade The
Buxton SK17 . . . . .85 A8
Chesterfield S40 . . . . . . .95 D3
Gladstone Ave
Blackwell DE55 . . . . .147 C1
Heanor DE75 . . . . .181 F2
Gladstone Cl
Chellaston DE73 . . . . . . .232 F3
Glossop SK13 . . . . .17 C8
Gladstone Dr NG16 . . . . . .182 E7
Gladstone Rd
Alfreton DE55 . . . . .158 F3
Chesterfield S40 . . . . . . .266 A4
Derby DE21 . . . . .220 E5
Gladstone St W DE7 . . . . .208 F7
Gladstone St
Derby DE23 . . . . .218 E1
Glossop SK13. . . . . .17 C8
Hadfield SK13 . . . . .10 A4
Heanor DE75 . . . . .181 E2
Langley Mill NG16 . . . . . .182 C3
Long Eaton NG10. . . . . . .236 D6
Mansfield Woodhouse
NG19. . . . . .136 C2
South Normanton DE55. . .160 B6
Somercotes DE55 . . . . . .170 C6
Gladwin Gdns S40 . . . . . . .114 D8
Gladys Buxton Com Ed Ctr
S18. . . . . .57 C2
Glaisdale Nook DE24. . . . .233 D6
Glamis Cl DE21 . . . . .206 B2
Glamorgan Way DE11 . . . .255 F1
Glapwell La S44 . . . . .118 B2
Glasshouse Hill DE5 . . . . .181 B8
Glasshouse La S41 . . . . . . .76 F2
Glastonbury Cl NG19. . . . .136 D4
Glastonbury Rd DE24 . . . .233 C7
Glaven Cl NG19. . . . . .136 D2
Gleadless Ave S12 . . . . . . .44 A4
Gleadless Bank S12. . . . . . .43 F4
Gleadless Comm S12 . . . . .44 A5
Gleadless Ct S2 . . . . .43 B6
Gleadless Dr S12 . . . . .43 F4
Gleadless Mount S12 . . . . .44 A4
Gleadless Prim Sch S12 . . .44 A5
Gleadless Rd S12, S14, S2. .43 D5
Gleadless Rise
◻ Sheffield, Gleadless
Townend S12 . . . . .44 A3
Sheffield S12. . . . . .43 F5
Gleadless View
◻ Sheffield, Gleadless
Townend S12 . . . . .44 A3
Sheffield S12. . . . . .43 F5
Gleadsmoss La DE21 . . . . .206 A1
Glebe Ave
Great Longstone DE45. . . .90 A3
Harthill S26 . . . . .61 E7
Pinxton NG16 . . . . .160 D3

Glebe Ave continued
Ripley DE5 . . . . 169 C2
Smalley DE7 . . . . 192 F6
Glebe Cl
Coton in t E DE12 . . . . 260 C3
Doveridge DE6 . . . . 224 B8
Holmewood S42 . . . . 132 D8
Rolleston DE13 . . . . 240 A4
South Normanton DE55 . . 160 A5
Thurvaston DE6 . . . . 201 E1
Glebe Cres
Ilkeston DE7 . . . . 209 A7
Stanley DE7 . . . . 207 B6
Glebe Farm Cl S26 . . . . 61 E7
Glebe Field Cl DE4 . . . . . . 156 F1
Glebe Gdns S42 . . . . 131 F5
Glebe Jun Sch DE55 . . . . . 160 A5
Glebe Rd SK17 . . . . 85 D8
Glebe Rise DE23 . . . . 218 D1
Glebe St DE11 . . . . 256 B3
Glebe The
Awsworth NG16 . . . . 195 B4
Chesterfield S41 . . . . 77 A2
Rosliston DE12 . . . . 260 C6
Glebe View
Barlborough S43 . . . . 80 B6
5 Forest Town NG19 . . 136 E1
Glebe Way The S41 . . . . 77 A2
Gledhill Cl S18 . . . . 57 A1
Glen Ave DE56 . . . . 191 C7
Glenavon Cl S43 . . . . 77 D5
Glenbrook Hill SK13 . . . . . . 10 C2
Glen Cl DE55 . . . . 148 A3
Glencoe Way S40 . . . . 95 B4
Glencroft Cl DE14 . . . . 254 B7
Glencroft Dr DE24 . . . . 231 D3
Glendale Dr DE21 . . . . 220 F5
Glendevon Way DE73 . . . . 232 E2
Glendon Rd
Derby DE24 . . . . 231 D3
Ilkeston DE7 . . . . 208 C4
Glendon St DE7 . . . . 193 A1
Gleneagles Cl
Chesterfield S40 . . . . 114 C8
Derby DE3 . . . . 217 F2
Gleneagles Dr DE13 . . . . . 240 C1
Glenfield Ave NG16 . . . . . . 195 D7
Glenfield Cres
Chesterfield S41 . . . . 96 A7
Derby DE3 . . . . 217 C2
Glenfield Rd NG10 . . . . 236 D5
Glengarry Way DE24 . . . . . 231 E4
Glenholme Dr S13 . . . . 44 E7
Glenholme Pl S13 . . . . 44 F7
Glenholme Rd S13 . . . . 44 F7
Glenholme Way S13 . . . . . . 44 F7
Glenmoor Rd SK17 . . . . 66 D1
Glenmore Cl S43 . . . . 97 B5
Glenmore Croft S12 . . . . . . 44 C6
Glenmore Dr DE24 . . . . . . 231 D3
Glenmore Dr DE24 . . . . . . 231 D3
Glenmoy Cl DE23 . . . . 231 D7
Glenn Way DE72 . . . . 234 E1
Glenorchy Ct DE21 . . . . . . 206 B3
Glen Park Cl DE73 . . . . 244 F8
Glen Rd DE4 . . . . 156 D1
Glenthorn Cl S81 . . . . 63 F7
Glenthorne Cl S40 . . . . 95 C2
Glen Vale S18 . . . . 56 D1
Glen View DE56 . . . . 178 F2
Glen View Rd S8 . . . . 56 F8
Glen Vine DE5 . . . . 170 A1
Glenwood Rd D7 . . . . 245 A8
Glinton Ave DE55 . . . . 147 E1
Glossop's Croft S41 . . . . 77 B2
Glossopbrook Bsns Pk
SK13 . . . . 10 C1
Glossop Brook Rd SK13 . . . 10 B1
Glossop Central Sta SK13 . 10 C1
Glossopdale Com Coll
SK13 . . . . 10 C2
Glossopdale Com Coll
(Annexe) SK13 . . . . 10 A4
Glossop Heritage Ctr*
SK13 . . . . 10 C1
Glossop Rd
Broadbottom SK13 . . . . 16 D7
Gamesley SK13 . . . . 9 E1
Hayfield SK22 . . . . 25 C6
Marple SK6 . . . . 15 D3
Glossop St DE24 . . . . 232 B8
Gloster St DE24 . . . . 219 C2
Gloucester Ave
Chesterfield S41 . . . . 95 F5
Sandiacre NG10 . . . . 223 A4
Gloucester Rd S41 . . . . 95 F5
Gloucester Way
Burton u T DE15 . . . . 248 B1
4 Glossop SK13 . . . . 17 F8
Glover Rd
Castle Donington DE74 . . 247 B4
Sheffield, Highfield S8 . . . . 43 A7
Sheffield, Totley Rise S17 . 55 F5
Gloves La DE55 . . . . 147 D2
Glumangate S40 . . . . 266 B3
Goathland Rd DE24 . . . . . 231 D2
Goatscliffe Cotts S32 . . . . . 72 C7
Goddard La
Glossop SK13 . . . . 10 A6
New Mills SK22 . . . . 24 E7
Goddard Rd SK13 . . . . 10 A6
Godfrey Dr DE7 . . . . 208 D6
Godfrey St DE7 . . . . 181 E1
Godkin Dr NG16 . . . . 182 A4
Godward Rd SK22 . . . . 33 B8
Gold Cl DE4 . . . . 142 B8
Goldcrest Dr DE21 . . . . . . 220 F6
Goldcrest Ho S41 . . . . 77 B3

Golden Valley
Horsley Woodhouse DE7 . . 192 B6
Somercotes DE55 . . . . 170 D3
Golden Valley Light Rly*
DE5 . . . . 170 B4
Golders Green Wlk DE22 218 A6
Goldhill DE4 . . . . 144 A4
Golding Ho DE4 . . . . 143 C6
Gold La DE22 . . . . 217 E8
Goldstone Ct DE21 . . . . . . 220 E4
Golf Cl DE23 . . . . 218 A1
Golf Club Rd DE7 . . . . 209 B1
Golf La DE56 . . . . 190 E5
Golf Terr SK17 . . . . 66 D1
Gomersal La S18 . . . . 57 A1
Goodale St DE23 . . . . 219 A1
Goodman Cl NG16 . . . . . . 195 C8
Goodman Ct S44 . . . . 97 A3
Goodrington Rd DE21 . . . 206 C3
Goodsmoor Rd DE23,
DE24 . . . . 231 E5
Goodsmoor Rd Ind Est
DE24 . . . . 231 E5
Goods Rd DE56 . . . . 178 F2
Goods Yd DE56 . . . . 178 F1
Goodvin's La DE56 . . . . . . 178 C1
Goodwin Cl NG10 . . . . 223 A6
Goodwin Dr NG16 . . . . . . 195 C6
Goodwin Rd **6** S8 . . . . . 43 A6
Goodwood Cl DE24 . . . . . . 240 C1
Goodwood Cres DE7 . . . . 208 D4
Goodwood Dr
Beeston NG9 . . . . 223 F2
Derby DE23 . . . . 231 C6
Gooker La DE55 . . . . 158 F3
Goole Ave DE7 . . . . 208 D5
Goose Green La DE55 . . . . 146 D3
Goose Green View DE45 . . . 91 F5
Goosehill S33 . . . . 38 B2
Goose La S26 . . . . 181 C8
Gordon Ave S8 . . . . 43 A2
Gordon Cres DE55 . . . . . . 160 B4
Gordondale Rd NG19 . . . . 136 B1
Gordon Rd
Borrowash DE72 . . . . 221 B1
Derby DE23 . . . . 218 F3
Swanwick DE55 . . . . 169 F8
Tideswell SK17 . . . . 69 C3
Gordon St DE7 . . . . 195 A1
Gordon Works **12** S2 . . 43 A6
Gore La S33 . . . . 51 A8
Gorman Cl S41 . . . . 96 A8
Gorse Bank S44 . . . . 116 F2
Gorsebank La DE45 . . . . . . 91 F7
Gorse Cl
Derby DE23 . . . . 231 B6
Eastwood NG16 . . . . 195 B8
Long Eaton NG10 . . . . 223 B2
Gorse Dr S21 . . . . 60 D5
Gorshill Gr DE23 . . . . 231 A7
Gorse La
Bradley DE6 . . . . 175 B3
Moira DE12 . . . . 262 E6
Sheffield S10 . . . . 42 F7
Gorse Ridge Dr DE45 . . . . . 91 F6
Gorses
Alderwasley DE56 . . . . 178 C8
Idridgehay DE6 . . . . 176 D5
Gorse Valley Rd S41 . . . . . 115 F7
Gorse Valley Way S41 . . . 115 F7
Gorse Way SK13 . . . . 17 F7
Gorsey Bank DE4 . . . . 165 F7
Gorsey Brigg S18 . . . . 56 D1
Gorseybrigg Prim Sch
S18 . . . . 56 D1
Gorsey Brow SK14 . . . . 9 A1
Gorsey Cl DE56 . . . . 178 E6
Gorsey Intakes SK14 . . . . . 16 A8
Gorsey La
Kirk Ireton DE6 . . . . 165 A1
Nethersedge DE12 . . . . . . 265 A7
Gorsty Leys DE65 . . . . 230 D1
Gosber Rd S21 . . . . 59 E3
Gosber St S21 . . . . 59 D3
Goseley Ave DE11 . . . . 257 A4
Goseley Cres DE11 . . . . . . 257 A4
Gosforth Ave NE7 . . . . 194 E6
Gosforth Cl **3** S18 . . . . . 56 F1
Gosforth Dr S18 . . . . 75 D8
Gosforth Gn S18 . . . . 56 F1
Gosforth La S18 . . . . 56 F1
Gosforth Rd DE24 . . . . 232 E8
Goshawk Rd DE7 . . . . 209 A3
Gower Cres S40 . . . . 95 C5
Gower St DE1 . . . . 267 B2
Goyt's La SK17 . . . . 65 A3
Goyt Forest Walks* SK11 . 83 E7
Goytlands SK17 . . . . 84 F6
Goyt Pl SK23 . . . . 45 E7
Goyt Rd
Disley SK12 . . . . 32 D5
Horwich End SK23 . . . . 45 E6
New Mills SK22 . . . . 33 D6
Goyt Side Rd S40 . . . . 95 E2
Goyt Valley Ind Est SK23 . . 33 D4
Goyt View DE4 . . . . 33 B6
Grace Cres DE75 . . . . 181 D1
Gradbach Mill (YH)*
SK17 . . . . 102 A1
Grafton Cl DE21 . . . . 233 A2
Grafton Rd DE15 . . . . 248 B1
Grafton St DE23 . . . . 218 E2
Grafton Terr DE4 . . . . 127 A5
Graham Cl DE14 . . . . 254 C7
Graham St SK12 . . . . 32 C6
Graham St DE7 . . . . 208 F7
Grammer St DE5 . . . . 181 A4

Grampian Cres S40 . . . . 95 B4
Grampian Prim Sch
DE24 . . . . 231 D4
Grampian Way
Derby DE24 . . . . 231 E4
Long Eaton NG10 . . . . 236 A8
Granary Cl S40 . . . . 95 A8
Granby Ave SK23 . . . . 34 E1
Granby Cl S45 . . . . 132 C2
Granby Croft DE45 . . . . . . 109 D5
Granby Jun Sch DE7 . . . . 194 E3
Granby Rd
Bakewell DE45 . . . . 109 D5
Bradwell S33 . . . . 50 F7
Buxton SK17 . . . . 85 D7
Granby St DE7 . . . . 194 E2
Grandfield St DE75 . . . . . . 181 C4
Grandstand Rd DE21 . . . . 219 C6
Grange Ave
Breaston DE72 . . . . 235 D8
Chapel-en-le-F SK23 . . . . . 47 B5
Derby DE23 . . . . 231 E7
Dronfield S18 . . . . 56 E1
Hulland Ward DE6 . . . . . . 175 F3
Grange Cl
Melbourne DE73 . . . . 252 B8
Somercotes DE55 . . . . 159 F2
Ticknall DE73 . . . . 251 A4
Grange Ct DE65 . . . . 241 B5
Grange Dale DE4 . . . . 153 C8
Grange Dr
Castle Donington DE74 . . 247 A3
Long Eaton NG10 . . . . 236 F8
Grange Farm Cl DE14 . . . 247 D5
Grange Gate DE22 . . . . . . 267 A1
Grange La
Barlow S18 . . . . 75 B1
Darley Dale DE4 . . . . 127 F1
Ible DE4 . . . . 153 D7
Grangemill Pl S43 . . . . 97 C8
Grangeover Way DE22 . . . 218 D4
Grange Park Ave
Calow S43 . . . . 96 F4
Chapel-en-le-F SK23 . . . . . 47 B5
Grange Park Rd SK23 . . . . . 47 B5
Grange Pk NG10 . . . . 236 F8
Grange Prim Sch NG10 . . 236 F8
Grange Rd
Buxton SK17 . . . . 85 C7
Derby DE24 . . . . 233 B6
Long Eaton NG10 . . . . 236 D5
Pilsley S45 . . . . 132 C2
Swadlincote DE11 . . . . 255 E5
Uttoxeter ST14 . . . . 210 A1
Grange Rd S DE14 . . . . 15 A8
Grange St
Alfreton DE55 . . . . 159 A3
Derby DE23 . . . . 219 B2
Grange The
Dinnington S43 . . . . 96 D8
Chesterfield S42 . . . . 94 F4
Smalley DE75 . . . . 193 C8
South Normanton DE55 . . 160 A4
Grange View NG16 . . . . . . 182 F3
Grange Wlk S42 . . . . 115 E2
Grangewood Ave **3** DE7 . 208 F7
Grangewood Cl S40 . . . . . . 114 F7
Grangewood Dr DE56 . . . 191 A7
Grangewood Gdns DE21 . . 206 B2
Grangewood Rd S40 . . . . . 114 F7
Gransden Way S40 . . . . . . 114 C8
Grant Ave DE21 . . . . 220 B5
Grantham Ave DE21 . . . . . 205 E1
Grantham Cl NG16 . . . . . . 195 C7
Granville Ave NG10 . . . . . . 223 D1
Granville Cl
Chesterfield S41 . . . . 115 D8
Duffield DE56 . . . . 190 E3
Hatton DE65 . . . . 227 D1
Granville Com Sch DE11 . 256 E4
Granville Ct DE11 . . . . 256 C4
Granville St
Derby DE11 . . . . 218 E5
Woodville DE11 . . . . 256 E3
Graphite Way
Glossop SK13 . . . . 9 F6
Hollingworth SK13 . . . . 9 F6
Grasmere Ave
Clay Cross S45 . . . . 131 B3
Derby DE21 . . . . 220 E6
Grasmere Cl
Burton u T DE15 . . . . 248 B1
11 Dronfield S18 . . . . . . 56 F1
Grasmere Cres DE24 . . . . 231 E4
Grasmere Ct **1** NG10 . . 223 B2
Grasmere Rd
Dronfield S18 . . . . 56 D1
Long Eaton NG10 . . . . 223 B2
Grasmere St **2** NG10 . . 223 C5
Grasscroft **3** S40 . . . . . . 95 D6
Grasscroft Mobile Home Pk
S43 . . . . 77 D5
Grassdale View S12 . . . . . . 44 F3
Grassmoor Ct S12 . . . . 43 F5
Grassmoor Cres SK13 . . . . . 9 E3
Grassmoor Cntry Pk* S42,
S41 . . . . 116 A4
Grassmoor Prim Sch
S42 . . . . 115 F2
Grass St DE7 . . . . 194 E3
Grassthorpe Cl DE21 . . . . 206 B1
Grassthorpe Rd S12 . . . . . . 44 B4
Grassy Ct S43 . . . . 78 F3
Grassy La DE65 . . . . 230 A7
Gratton Ct S43 . . . . 78 F3
Gratton La DE45 . . . . 140 C7
Gravelly Bank Mews
DE6 . . . . 199 D5

Gravel Pit Cotts DE65 . . . 229 B1
Gravel Pit Hill DE65 . . . . . 249 E7
Gravel Pit La DE21 . . . . . . 220 E4
Graves Park Animal Farm*
S8 . . . . 43 B1
Graves Tennis & L Ctr S8 . 57 B7
Graves Trust Homes
Sheffield, Common Side
S12 . . . . 44 A5
Sheffield, Greenhill S8 . . . . 56 F8
Sheffield, Little Norton S8 . 57 A8
Graycar Bsns Pk DE13 . . . 253 B2
Gray Fallow DE55 . . . . 160 B4
Grayling St DE23 . . . . 219 B2
Grays Cl DE74 . . . . 247 B3
Grayshott Wlk S40 . . . . . . 114 F8
Gray St
Clowne S43 . . . . 80 F4
Sheffield, Mosborough S20 . 59 C7
Grayston Cl S40 . . . . 23 B7
Grayswood Cl DE55 . . . . . 170 A7
Great Common Cl S43 . . . . 80 B6
Great Croft S18 . . . . 56 D2
Great Hucklow Prim Sch
SK17 . . . . 51 B1
Great Longstone Bsns Pk
DE45 . . . . 90 A4
Great Northern Cotts
NG19 . . . . 135 A5
Great Northern Point
DE22 . . . . 218 F4
Great Northern Rd
Derby DE1 . . . . 218 F5
Eastwood NG16 . . . . 182 D2
Greatorex Ave DE24 . . . . . 232 E5
Greaves La DE45 . . . . 108 F8
Greaves St
Ripley DE5 . . . . 169 E2
Shirland DE55 . . . . 146 E1
Greave Way S43 . . . . 96 C8
Greenacre Ave DE75 . . . . 182 A3
Greenacre Pk DE12 . . . . . . 260 C3
Greenacres DE23 . . . . 231 B8
Greenacres Cl S18 . . . . 76 C7
Greenacres Dr
South Normanton DE55 . . 160 B6
Uttoxeter ST14 . . . . 210 A2
Greenacre The DE6 . . . . . . 184 F7
Green Ave DE73 . . . . 233 A1
Greenaway Dr S44 . . . . . . 118 A8
Greenaway La DE4 . . . . . . 127 E1
Greenbank
Derby DE21 . . . . 220 D4
Hollingworth SK13 . . . . 9 F5
Greenbank Dr S40 . . . . 95 C4
Greenbank Rd SK6 . . . . 15 B1
Greenburn Cl DE23 . . . . . 231 C6
Green Chase S21 . . . . 59 C3
Green Cl
Curbar S32 . . . . 72 E2
Matlock DE4 . . . . 143 B6
Newton DE55 . . . . 148 A3
Renishaw S21 . . . . 79 B8
Staveley S43 . . . . 97 C6
Unstone Green S18 . . . . 76 E6
Willington DE65 . . . . 242 A6
Green Cres NG16 . . . . 171 E6
Green Cross S18 . . . . 57 B2
Greendale Ave S42 . . . . . . 113 E8
Greendale Ct S18 . . . . 57 B2
Greendale Sh Ctr S18 . . . . 57 B2
Greendale The DE55 . . . . . 157 D8
Green Farm Cl S40 . . . . 95 C6
Green Farm Rd NG16 . . . . 171 D6
Greenfield Ave S80 . . . . 82 C6
Greenfield Cl
New Mills SK22 . . . . 33 A8
Sheffield S8 . . . . 56 F7
Greenfield Dr
Linton DE12 . . . . 261 C6
Sheffield S8 . . . . 56 F7
Greenfield Ho SK13 . . . . . . 10 A6
Greenfield Rd S8 . . . . 56 F7
Greenfields
Aldercar NG16 . . . . 182 A4
Denstone ST14 . . . . 196 D6
Eckington S21 . . . . 59 C3
Fritchley DE56 . . . . 168 B7
Greenfields Ave DE23 . . . 231 B8
Greenfinch Cl DE21 . . . . . 220 F6
Greengate Cl S40 . . . . 95 C2
Green Glen S40 . . . . 95 C2
Greenhall Rd S21 . . . . 59 C3
Greenhead S33 . . . . 40 B4
Greenhead Cres SK17 . . . . 138 C2
Greenhead Pk S33 . . . . 40 B4
Green Hill DE4 . . . . 154 E1
Greenhill Ave
Ripley DE5 . . . . 180 E8
Sheffield S8 . . . . 56 F8
Greenhill La DE55 . . . . 170 D6
Greenhill Lane Ind Est
DE55 . . . . 170 B5
Greenhill Main Rd
Sheffield S8 . . . . 56 F7
Sheffield S8 . . . . 56 F7
Greenhill Parkway S8 . . . . . 56 D6
Greenhill Prim Sch S8 . . . . 56 F8
Greenhills Cvn Pk DE45 . . 109 A7
Greenhills Rd NG16 . . . . . 182 F3
Greenhill Wlk SK12 . . . . . . 32 D6
Greenholme Pk NG19 . . . . 136 E6
Green Inf Sch The DE55 . . 160 A6
Green La
Alsop en le D DE6 . . . . 150 C2

Green La continued
Bakewell DE45 . . . . 108 C3
Barrow u T DE73 . . . . 244 A5
Belper DE56 . . . . 178 F4
Bonsall DE4 . . . . 153 F8
Burnaston DE65 . . . . 230 A4
Buxton SK17 . . . . 85 A6
Buxton, Water Swallows
SK17 . . . . 67 C2
Chelmorton SK17 . . . . 106 D8
Chesterfield S41 . . . . 96 D4
Chinley SK23 . . . . 34 E2
Clifton DE6 . . . . 184 E7
Compstall SK14 . . . . 15 B8
Creswell S80 . . . . 82 C5
Cutthorpe S42 . . . . 94 E7
Darley Dale DE4 . . . . 127 B3
Derby, Alvaston DE24 . . . . 233 C8
Derby DE1 . . . . 267 B2
Disley SK12 . . . . 32 D4
Dronfield S18 . . . . 56 E1
Glossop, Brookfield SK13 . . 9 F4
Glossop SK13 . . . . 16 F8
Hognaston DE6 . . . . 164 B2
Hollingworth SK14 . . . . 9 D6
Ilkeston DE7 . . . . 209 A7
Killamarsh S21 . . . . 60 C3
Mansfield NG19 . . . . 135 A2
Marchington ST14 . . . . . . 225 A2
Ockbrook DE72 . . . . 221 C5
Overseal DE12 . . . . 261 F4
Pilsley S45 . . . . 132 C3
Pleasley S44 . . . . 134 D8
Roston DE6 . . . . 197 F8
Shirebrook NG19, NG20 . . 119 C2
Tansley DE4 . . . . 144 A5
Tupton S42 . . . . 115 D1
Tutbury DE13 . . . . 239 C5
Weston Underwood DE6 . . 188 F2
Wilson DE73 . . . . 252 E5
Greenland Ave DE22 . . . . . 218 B5
Greenland Cl S41 . . . . 132 A7
Green Lands S41 . . . . 256 B7
Green Lea S18 . . . . 56 C2
Green Leas DE72 . . . . 246 A8
Greenmount Cl DE21 . . . . 231 A6
Green Oak Ave S17 . . . . 55 E4
Green Oak Cres S17 . . . . . . 55 E4
Green Oak Dr S17 . . . . 55 E4
Green Oak Gr S17 . . . . 55 E4
Green Oak Rd S17 . . . . 55 E4
Green Park Ave SK23 . . . . . 47 C6
Green Pastures S17 . . . . 55 E7
Green Pk DE56 . . . . 218 A6
Green Rd The DE6 . . . . 173 C3
Greens Ct DE7 . . . . 194 D1
Greenset La S41 . . . . 32 F5
Greenside NG16 . . . . 171 D6
Greenside Ave S41 . . . . 96 A7
Greenside Cl
Barlborough S43 . . . . 80 C4
Donisthorpe DE12 . . . . 262 E1
Long Eaton NG10 . . . . 236 E7
Greenside Ct S18 . . . . 217 C2
Greens La NG16 . . . . 195 F6
Greenside Cl DE15 . . . . . . 248 C3
Greensquare Rd NG16 . . . 160 E2
Green St
Barton in F NG11 . . . . 237 F5
Chesterfield S41 . . . . 77 A2
Green The
Alfreton DE55 . . . . 159 B3
Aston-on-T DE72 . . . . 246 B8
Bamford S33 . . . . 40 B4
Barlow S18 . . . . 179 A5
Birchover DE4 . . . . 126 B6
Brackenfield DE55 . . . . 145 D2
Bradwell S33 . . . . 51 B6
Brailsford DE6 . . . . 201 E4
Breedon on t h DE73 . . . . . 252 E2
Burton u T DE13 . . . . 240 E1
Castle Donington DE74 . . 247 A3
Chesterfield S41 . . . . 115 D7
Clowne S43 . . . . 80 C4
Crich DE4 . . . . 156 D1
Curbar S32 . . . . 72 E2
Derby DE22 . . . . 204 D1
Derby, Mickleover DE3 . . . 217 D1
Draycott DE72 . . . . 235 A7
Findern DE65 . . . . 230 D1
Fritchley DE56 . . . . 168 B6
Froggatt S32 . . . . 72 C5
Glapwell S44 . . . . 134 B8
Glossop SK13 . . . . 17 A7
Hardstoft S45 . . . . 133 A3
Kirk Langley DE6 . . . . 202 C1
Mansfield Woodhouse
NG19 . . . . 136 A5
Marple SK6 . . . . 23 A3
Netherseal DE12 . . . . 264 F6
North Wingfield S42 . . . . . 132 A7
Sheffield S17 . . . . 55 D4
Stanton in Peak DE4 . . . . . 126 C5
Sutton in A NG17 . . . . 148 F1
Swanwick DE55 . . . . 169 E7
Ticknall DE73 . . . . 250 F3
Tissington DE6 . . . . 162 B5
Weston-on-T DE72 . . . . . . 245 F5
Wingerworth S42 . . . . 242 A6
Greenvale Cl DE15 . . . . . . 254 F8
Greenview DE4 . . . . 153 A1
Greenville Croft DE73 . . . 232 E1
Green Water Mdw SK14 . . . 9 C5
Greenway
Ashbourne DE6 . . . . 173 C3

Greenway continued
Brassington DE4 . . . . 153 A1
Burton u T DE15 . . . . 248 A4
Hulland Ward DE6 . . . . . . 175 F3
Whitwell S80 . . . . 81 F6
Wingerworth S42 . . . . . . 115 C2
Green Way DE65 . . . . 230 D2
Greenway Cl DE72 . . . . . 221 B3
Greenway Croft DE4 . . . . 154 F1
Greenway Dr DE23 . . . . . 218 A1
Greenways S40 . . . . 114 C8
Greenway The
Derby DE72 . . . . 233 D5
Sandiacre NG10 . . . . 223 B6
Sheffield S8 . . . . 56 F8
Greenwich Ave DE11 . . . . 255 C1
Greenwich Ct **12** S43 . . . . . 78 B3
Greenwich Dr N DE22 . . 218 C6
Greenwich Dr S DE22 . . 218 B5
Greenwood Ave
Derby DE21 . . . . 219 F8
Ilkeston DE7 . . . . 209 A7
Mansfield Woodhouse
NG19 . . . . 136 B4
Sutton in A NG17 . . . . . . 148 F2
Greenwood Cl DE24 . . . . 232 D5
Greenwood Ct DE1 . . . . . 267 A4
Greenwood Rd DE15 . . . . 254 E8
Greer La S44 . . . . 118 D1
Gregg Ave DE55 . . . . 181 F2
Greggs Ave SK23 . . . . 46 F5
Gregory Ave
Aldercar NG16 . . . . 182 A4
Breaston DE72 . . . . 235 D8
Gregory Cl
Brimington S43 . . . . 96 D8
Stapleford NG9 . . . . 223 F8
Gregory Ct **10** S8 . . . . 43 B6
Gregory La S43 . . . . 77 D1
Gregory Rd S8 . . . . 43 A6
Gregory St DE7 . . . . 208 E8
Gregorys Way DE56 . . . . 179 C5
Gregory Wlk DE23 . . . . . 230 E7
Gregson Cl DE11 . . . . 256 B5
Grendon Cl DE56 . . . . . . 179 B6
Grenfell Ave DE23 . . . . . 231 E6
Grenville Dr
Ilkeston DE7 . . . . 194 F3
Stapleford NG9 . . . . 223 E8
Grenvoir Dr DE5 . . . . 170 A1
Gresham Rd DE24 . . . . . 232 C8
Gresley Rd
Ilkeston DE7 . . . . 194 F1
Sheffield S8 . . . . 56 E5
Gresley Wlk S8 . . . . 56 E5
Gresley Woodlands
DE11 . . . . 256 A2
Gresley Wood Rd
Swadlincote DE11 . . . . . 255 F2
Woodville DE11 . . . . 256 A2
Gretton Ave DE13 . . . . . 240 E1
Gretton Rd SK17 . . . . 85 D8
Greyfriars Cl **4** DE75 . . 181 F1
Greysich La DE65 . . . . . . 249 F2
Grey St DE22 . . . . 267 A2
Greystones Ct S26 . . . . . . 61 D6
Griffe Field Prim Sch
DE23 . . . . 231 A6
Griffin Cl
Derby DE24 . . . . 232 F7
New Mills SK22 . . . . 33 D6
Staveley S43 . . . . 97 E8
Griffon Rd DE7 . . . . 208 D7
Griggs Gdns DE4 . . . . . . 165 F7
Grimshaw Ave DE24 . . . 233 B7
Grindleford Gdns **15** SK13 . 9 E2
Grindleford Gr **13** SK13 . . . 9 E2
Grindleford Lea **14** SK13 . . 9 E2
Grindleford Prim Sch S32 72 C8
Grindleford Sta S32 . . . . . 53 D2
Grindleford Wlk **16** SK13 . . 9 E2
Grindlow Ave S40 . . . . . . 266 A1
Grindlow Cl S14 . . . . 43 C6
Grindlow Dr S14 . . . . 43 C6
Grindlow Rd DE21 . . . . . . 220 A8
Grindon Cl S40 . . . . 95 C5
Grindslow Ave DE7 . . . . . 207 E8
Grinlow Cl SK17 . . . . 85 C3
Grinlow Cvn Pk SK17 . . . . 84 F5
Grin Low Rd SK17 . . . . 85 B3
Gritton Wlk S40 . . . . 114 F8
Grisedale Rd E DE45 . . . . . 90 A4
Grisedale Rd W DE45 . . . . 90 A4
Grisedale Wlk S18 . . . . 56 E1
Gritstone Rd DE4 . . . . . . 143 D7
Grizedale Cl DE15 . . . . . 248 B1
Groombridge Cres DE23 231 A6
Groome Ave DE75 . . . . . . 181 C4
Grosvenor Ave
Breaston DE72 . . . . 235 F8
Long Eaton NG10 . . . . . . 236 A4
Grosvenor Dr DE23 . . . . 231 A6
Grosvenor Rd
Eastwood NG16 . . . . 182 F2
Marple SK6 . . . . 23 A7
Ripley DE5 . . . . 169 D2
Grosvenor St DE24 . . . . . 232 C8
Grove Ave S17 . . . . 55 D5
Grovebury Dr DE23 . . . . 231 C5
Grove Cl DE72 . . . . 233 F4
Grove Cotts NG19 . . . . . 135 B4
Grove Ct
Elvaston DE72 . . . . 233 F4
Ripley DE5 . . . . 180 F8
Grove Farm Cl S43 . . . . . . 96 E7

Grove Gdns S43 . . . . 96 F5
Grove Ho DE23 . . . . 267 B1
Grove Hospl The DE72 . . 234 D1
Grove House Ct S17 . . . . . 55 E5
Grove La
Buxton SK17 . . . . 85 C6
Darley Dale DE4 . . . . 127 E1
Old Brampton S42 . . . . . . 94 B4
Somersal Herbert DE6 . . 211 F2
Grove Mews NG16 . . . . . 182 E1
Grove Par **2** SK17 . . . . 85 B8
Grove Pk DE65 . . . . 229 B2
Grove Pl DE45 . . . . 125 B5
Grove Rd
Calow S43 . . . . 96 C5
Chesterfield S41 . . . . . . 115 C8
Sheffield, Totley Brook S17 55 F5
Groves Nook DE73 . . . . . 232 E1
Grove St
Chesterfield S41 . . . . . . 115 C8
Derby DE23 . . . . 267 B1
Mansfield Woodhouse
NG19 . . . . 136 B3
New Mills SK22 . . . . 33 B7
Swadlincote DE11 . . . . . 256 B4
Grove The
Breaston DE72 . . . . 235 F8
Derby DE3 . . . . 217 E2
Glossop SK13 . . . . 9 F4
Poolsbrook S43 . . . . 98 A8
Sheffield, Hillfoot S17 . . . . 55 D5
Tatenhill DE13 . . . . 253 A8
Grove Way
Calow S43 . . . . 96 F5
Mansfield Woodhouse
NG19 . . . . 136 B3
Grundy Ave NG16 . . . . . . 171 D7
Grundy Nook S80 . . . . 82 A5
Grundy Rd S41 . . . . 131 C3
Grunmore Dr DE13 . . . . . 240 E2
Guernsey Rd S2 . . . . 43 A7
Guide Post DE56 . . . . . . 168 C2
Guildford Ave
Chesterfield S40 . . . . . . 114 D8
Mansfield Woodhouse
NG19 . . . . 136 C6
Sheffield S8 . . . . 43 D8
Swadlincote DE11 . . . . . 256 E6
Guildford Cl S41 . . . . 131 E3
Guildford La S45 . . . . 131 E3
Guildford Rise S8 . . . . 43 E8
Guildford View S2 . . . . . . 43 E7
Guildhall Dr NG16 . . . . . 160 F2
Guildhall Theatre* DE1 . 267 B3
Guinea Cl NG10 . . . . 236 A7
Guinevere Ave DE73 . . . 232 E1
Gulliver's Kingdom*
DE4 . . . . 155 A8
Gunby Hill DE12 . . . . 261 F2
Gunhills La DE56 . . . . . . 189 E6
Gun La DE56 . . . . 168 C2
Gun Rd SK6 . . . . 16 C2
Gurney Ave DE23 . . . . . . 231 D6
Gutersloh Ct NG9 . . . . . 223 F8
Guy Cl NG9 . . . . 223 E6
Gypsy La
Creswell S80 . . . . 81 E1
Draycott DE72 . . . . 221 E1

H

Hackney La S18 . . . . 75 F1
Hackney Rd DE4 . . . . . . 143 A7
Hackthorn Rd **4** S8 . . . . . 43 A3
Haddon Ave S43 . . . . 81 A4
Haddon Cl
Alfreton DE55 . . . . 158 F3
Bullbridge DE56 . . . . . . 168 B6
Chesterfield S40 . . . . 95 C1
Derby DE22 . . . . 204 D3
Dronfield S18 . . . . 57 B2
Heanor DE75 . . . . 181 C2
West Hallam DE7 . . . . . . 207 E8
Haddon Ct DE6 . . . . 185 D8
Haddon Dr
Bakewell DE45 . . . . 109 E4
Derby DE22 . . . . 204 D3
Derby, Mickleover DE3 . . 217 E3
Derby, Spondon DE21 . . 220 F4
Little Eaton DE21 . . . . . . 191 C2
Haddon Gn **51** SK12 . . . . 9 E2
Haddon Hall* DE45 . . . . 110 B1
Haddon Ho DE45 . . . . . . 109 E3
Haddon Lea S43 . . . . 9 D2
Haddon Mews **30** SK13 . . . 9 E2
Haddon Nurseries DE7 . 194 E3
Haddon Pl
Shirebrook NG20 . . . . . . 119 E6
Staveley S43 . . . . 97 D8
Haddon Rd
Bakewell DE45 . . . . 109 F3
Buxton SK17 . . . . 85 D8
North Wingfield S42 . . . 132 A8
Haddon St
Derby DE23 . . . . 218 E1
Ilkeston DE7 . . . . 194 E3
Tibshelf DE55 . . . . 148 A6
Haddon Way NG10 . . . . . 235 F4
Hade La SK17 . . . . 106 E7
Hades La SK17 . . . . 88 B3
Hadfield Ind Est SK13 . . . . 9 F6
Hadfield Inf Sch SK13 . . . . 9 F5
Hadfield Pl SK13 . . . . 17 C8
Hadfield Rd
Glossop SK13 . . . . 9 F4

Hadfield Rd continued
Hadfield SK13 . . . . 10 A5
Hadfields Ave SK14 . . . . . . 9 D5
Hadfield Sq **1** SK13 . . . . . 17 C8
Hadfield St SK13 . . . . 17 C8
Hadfield Sta SK13 . . . . 9 F4
Hadleigh Cl **22** NG9 . . . . . 223 E2
Hadley La DE6 . . . . 186 E8
Hadley St DE7 . . . . 209 A5
Hadstock Cl NG10 . . . . . 223 B4
Hady Cres S41 . . . . 96 C3
Hady Hill S41 . . . . 96 C2
Hady La S41 . . . . 96 E1
Hady Prim Sch S41 . . . . . 96 D2
Hag Bank La SK12 . . . . . . 32 D7
Hagg La
Dale Abbey DE7 . . . . 207 D4
Turnditch DE56 . . . . 177 C1
Hague Ave S21 . . . . 79 B8
Hague Bar Prim Sch SK22 32 E8
Hague Bar Rd SK22 . . . . . 33 A7
Hague Fold Rd SK22 . . . . . 32 F8
Hague La S21, S43 . . . . . . 79 B6
Hague Rd SK14 . . . . 16 A8
Hague St SK13 . . . . 17 D7
Haig Hill Farm Hamlet
S42 . . . . 115 E1
Haigh Meml Homes S8 . . 57 A7
Haigh Moor Rd S13 . . . . . 44 F8
Haigh Moor Wlk S13 . . . . 44 F8
Haig St DE22 . . . . 232 F8
Hailsham Cl DE23 . . . . . 217 D3
Haines Cl DE24 . . . . 231 E2
Halcyon App S42 . . . . . . 115 C2
Halcyon Cl S12 . . . . 44 F3
Haldane Cl S80 . . . . 81 E2
Haldane Cres S44 . . . . 98 F2
Halesworth Cl S40 . . . . . 114 B8
Half Acre La S18 . . . . 76 D8
Half Croft S43 . . . . 96 F7
Halfmoon La DE6 . . . . . . 165 B3
Halfway Ctr S20 . . . . 59 E7
Halfway Dr S20 . . . . 59 E7
Halfway Gdns S20 . . . . . . 59 E7
Halfway Inf Sch S20 . . . . 59 E7
Halfway Jun Sch S20 . . . . 59 E6
Halifax Cl
Derby DE21 . . . . 205 C1
Hilton DE65 . . . . 228 E2
Hall's Ct SK13 . . . . 10 C1
Hall's Row **1** S40 . . . . 95 D2
Hallam Ct
Dronfield S18 . . . . 76 A8
Ilkeston DE7 . . . . 194 F3
Hallam Fields DE74 . . . . 247 B2
Hallam Fields Jun Sch
DE7 . . . . 208 F5
Hallam Fields Rd DE7 . . 209 B4
Hallamway NG19 . . . . . . 136 C1
Hallam Way DE7 . . . . . . 207 D8
Hall Bank
Buxton SK17 . . . . 85 B7
Hartington SK17 . . . . 137 E5
Hall Cl
Cutthorpe S42 . . . . 94 E8
Dronfield S18 . . . . 56 C2
Mottram in L SK14 . . . . . . 9 A5
Hall Cotts DE6 . . . . 175 D2
Hallcroft Ave DE7 . . . . . 208 D7
Hallcroft Rd **2** DE7 . . . . 208 F8
Hall Ct DE7 . . . . 207 E7
Halldale La DE4 . . . . 127 E3
Hall Dale View DE4 . . . . 127 D3
Hall Dr
Doveridge DE6 . . . . 211 A1
Hanbury DE13 . . . . 238 A4
Mottram in L SK14 . . . . . . 9 A5
Sandiacre NG10 . . . . 223 B6
Hall Dyke DE21 . . . . 220 D5
Hall End La DE45 . . . . . . 108 F8
Hall Farm S42 . . . . 132 D8
Hall Farm Cl
Castle Donington DE74 . 247 B3
Chesterfield S41 . . . . . . 115 D7
Swadlincote DE11 . . . . . 256 C4
Whaley Bridge SK23 . . . . 45 D8
Hall Farm Ct DE7 . . . . . . 222 F8
Hall Farm Gdns S42 . . . 132 D8
Hall Farm Rd
Duffield DE56 . . . . 190 E2
Swadlincote DE11 . . . . . 256 C4
Hall Grounds
Hemington DE74 . . . . . . 247 D4
Marchington ST14 . . . . . 224 E2
Hall Green Ave DE13 . . . 240 F2
Hall Grounds DE11 . . . . 240 A4
Hallington Dr DE75 . . . . 181 D1
Hall La
Ashbourne DE6 . . . . 173 C2
Brailsford DE6 . . . . 201 F8
Brinsley NG16 . . . . 182 D6
Donisthorpe DE12 . . . . . 265 E8
Doveridge DE6 . . . . 224 B8
Litton SK17 . . . . 69 E3
Mayfield DE6 . . . . 183 A7
Nether Heage DE56 . . . . 168 C3
Newton DE55 . . . . 148 A3
Shirley DE6 . . . . 200 D8

Hall La continued
Staveley S43 . . . . 78 D3
Willington DE65 . . . . . . 242 B5
Hall Leys La DE73 . . . . . 245 D1
Hall Meadow Croft S20 . . 59 F5
Hall Meadow Dr S20 . . . . 59 F5
Hall Meadow Gr S20 . . . . 59 F5
Hall Meadow Rd SK13 . . . 10 D2
Hallmoor Rd DE14 . . . . . 127 C4
Hallowes Ct S18 . . . . 57 B1
Hallowes Dr S18 . . . . 76 B8
Hallowes La S18 . . . . 76 B8
Hallowes Rise S18 . . . . . . 76 C8
Hall Park Cl DE23 . . . . . . 218 B1
Hall Pk DE73 . . . . 244 A5
Hall Rd
Aldercar NG16 . . . . 182 C4
Brimington S43 . . . . 96 E7
Marchington ST14 . . . . . 224 E2
Rolleston DE13 . . . . 239 F4
Hall Rise
2 Ashbourne DE6 . . . . . 173 D3
Darley Dale DE4 . . . . 127 D3
Hallside Ct S20 . . . . 59 D6
Halls La NG16 . . . . 195 A8
Halls Rd NG9 . . . . 223 D6
Hall St
Alfreton DE55 . . . . 159 A4
Derby DE24 . . . . 233 A7
New Mills SK22 . . . . 33 B8
Swadlincote DE11 . . . . . 256 A2
Hallsteads Cl SK17 . . . . . . 47 F1
Hallsteads The DE6 . . . . 163 B2
Hall Terr S41 . . . . 131 D3
Hall The
Glossop SK13 . . . . 17 A7
Middleton DE4 . . . . 154 D5
Hall View S41 . . . . 95 E6
Hall View Cottage Herb
Gdn * S45 . . . . 132 E3
Hall Wlk S42 . . . . 115 D1
Hallworth Wlk S12 . . . . . 58 E2
Hallyburton Cl S2 . . . . . . 43 C6
Hallyburton Dr S2 . . . . . . 43 C6
Hallyburton Rd S2 . . . . . . 43 C6
Halstead Cl NG19 . . . . . . 136 F2
Halstock Dr DE24 . . . . . 233 C8
Halton Cl S41 . . . . 76 E1
Hamble Cl NG19 . . . . . . 136 D3
Hambledon Cl S40 . . . . . . 95 C5
Hambledon Dr DE24 . . . 231 D2
Hambleton Ave S42 . . . . 131 F6
Hambleton Cl
Ashbourne DE6 . . . . 185 C8
2 Long Eaton NG10 . . . 223 A1
Hambleton Rise NG19 . . 136 F1
Hamble Way DE65 . . . . . 228 C1
Hamblin Cres DE24 . . . . 231 F4
Hamil Cl S42 . . . . 131 F6
Hamilton Cl
Beeston NG9 . . . . 223 F2
Derby DE3 . . . . 217 F3
Hamilton Dr
Market Warsop NG20 . . . 120 F4
Swadlincote DE11 . . . . . 256 C5
Hamilton Rd
Burton u T DE15 . . . . . . 248 A2
Derby DE23 . . . . 218 F2
Long Eaton NG10 . . . . . . 223 D1
Hamilton Terr DE65 . . . . 242 B6
Hamlet Ct DE73 . . . . 232 E1
Hamlet La DE55 . . . . . . 160 A5
Hamlet The
Heanor DE75 . . . . 181 E3
South Normanton DE55 . 160 A4
Hammer Leys DE55 . . . . 160 C4
Hammersmith DE5 . . . . . 169 D4
Hammersmith Sta* DE5 169 D4
Hammonds Ct DE4 . . . . . 165 F8
Hampden Ho DE55 . . . . 254 C6
Hampden St
Derby DE23 . . . . 232 A8
Eastwood NG16 . . . . 195 B8
Langley Mill NG16 . . . . . 182 B3
Hampshire Cl SK13 . . . . . 17 E8
Hampshire Ct NG16 . . . . 171 B4
Hampshire Dr NG10 . . . . 223 B5
Hampshire Rd DE21 . . . . 219 C8
Hampstead Dr DE22 . . . 218 A6
Hampton Cl
Beeston NG9 . . . . 223 F3
Derby DE21 . . . . 220 F5
West Hallam DE7 . . . . . . 207 D8
Hampton Ct **4** DE75 . . . 181 D2
Hampton St S41 . . . . 115 D7
Hanbury Ave DE65 . . . . . 227 D1
Hanbury Cl
Chesterfield S40 . . . . 95 A5
Dronfield S18 . . . . 56 F1
Hanbury Hill DE13 . . . . . 238 A5
Hanbury Rd DE21 . . . . . 219 F6
Hanchurch Cl DE15 . . . . 248 A4
Handby Cl S41 . . . . 115 D7
Handby St S41 . . . . 115 D8
Handel Mews DE6 . . . . . 185 D8
Handel St DE23 . . . . 232 C8
Handford Cl DE22 . . . . . 218 D6
Handford St DE22 . . . . . 218 D5
Handley Cl S43 . . . . 77 D4
Handley La
Ashover S45 . . . . 145 F8
Clay Cross S45 . . . . 131 A1
Pilsley DE45 . . . . 91 B1

Handley Rd S43 . . . . 77 D5
Handsacre Cl DE11 . . . . 255 F3
Handyside St DE1 . . . . . . 267 B4
Hangar Hill S80 . . . . 82 A6
Hanger Bank DE22 . . . . . 246 B8
Hanley Cl SK12 . . . . 32 D5
Hannage Way DE4 . . . . . 165 F7
Hanover Sq DE22 . . . . . . 218 A6
Hansard Gate DE21 . . . . 267 D3
Hanslynn DE72 . . . . 233 F4
Hanston Ct S43 . . . . 77 D4
Hanstubbin Rd NG16 . . . 171 F6
Hanwell Way DE22 . . . . 218 B6
Harbin Rd DE12 . . . . 253 D1
Harby Ave DE55 . . . . . . 185 B8
Harby Ave NG19 . . . . . . 136 D5
Harcourt Cl
Chesterfield S41 . . . . . . 115 C7
Ilkeston DE7 . . . . 194 D1
Harcourt Pl DE74 . . . . . 247 B4
Harcourt Rd DE14 . . . . . 253 F8
Harcourt St DE11 . . . . . . 267 B2
Hardacre Cl DE73 . . . . . 252 A8
Hardcastle Mews SK23 . . 47 B6
Hardhurst Rd
Derby DE24 . . . . 233 B5
Unstone Green S18 . . . . . 76 E6
Hardie Ave DE55 . . . . . . 160 A6
Hardie Pl S43 . . . . 97 D8
Hardie St S21 . . . . 59 D3
Harding's Cl DE6 . . . . . . 165 B1
Harding's La SK17 . . . . . 138 A5
Hard La S26 . . . . 61 E8
Hard Meadow La S45 . . . 130 B2
Hardstaff Homes The
Eastwood NG16 . . . . 195 C8
Mansfield Woodhouse
NG19 . . . . 136 B3
Hardstoft Rd S45 . . . . . . 132 E2
Hardwick's Yd S40 . . . . . . 95 E2
Hardwick Ave
Chesterfield S41 . . . . 77 D3
Derby DE22 . . . . 204 D3
Glapwell S44 . . . . 134 B8
Shirebrook NG20 . . . . . . 119 E4
West Hallam DE7 . . . . . . 207 E8
Hardwick Cl
Blackwell DE55 . . . . 147 E5
Clowne S43 . . . . 81 A4
Dronfield S18 . . . . 57 C2
Holmewood S42 . . . . . . 132 E8
Ripley DE5 . . . . 169 C3
Hardwick Ct
Holmewood S42 . . . . . . 132 E8
Long Eaton NG10 . . . . . . 235 F4
5 Staveley S43 . . . . 78 E2
Hardwick Dr
Arkwright Town S44 . . . . . 97 D3
Derby DE3 . . . . 217 E2
Hardwick Gdns **5** SK17 . 85 B7
Hardwick Hall* S44 . . . . 133 C4
Hardwick Hall Ctry Pk* S44 . . . . 133 F5
Hardwick La S45 . . . . . . 129 D6
Hardwick Mount SK17 . . . 85 C7
Hardwick Old Hall* S44 . 133 E4
Hardwick Park Nature Wlk*
S44 . . . . 133 C4
Hardwick Pl DE7 . . . . . . 208 C5
Hardwick Prim Sch
DE23 . . . . 219 A1
Hardwick Sq E SK17 . . . . 85 C7
Hardwick Sq N SK17 . . . . 85 B7
Hardwick Sq S SK17 . . . . 85 B7
Hardwick Sq W SK17 . . . 85 B7
Hardwick St
Buxton SK17 . . . . 85 B8
Chesterfield S41 . . . . . . 266 B4
Derby DE24 . . . . 232 C8
Langwith NG20 . . . . 119 F8
Shirebrook NG20 . . . . . . 120 A4
Tibshelf DE55 . . . . 147 F5
Hardwick View Rd S42 . . 132 F8
Hardy Barn DE75 . . . . . . 194 A7
Hardybarn La SK17 . . . . . 67 B2
Hardy Cl
Kimberley NG16 . . . . . . 195 F7
Long Eaton NG10 . . . . . . 236 D5
Hardy Cres DE5 . . . . 181 B8
Hardy La SK17 . . . . 69 C4
Hardy St
Alfreton DE55 . . . . 158 F5
Kimberley NG16 . . . . . . 195 F7
Harebell Cl
Derby DE21 . . . . 206 A3
Swadlincote DE11 . . . . . 256 E4
Harehedge La DE13 . . . . 240 B1
Harehill Cres S42 . . . . . . 114 D4
Harehill Rd S40 . . . . 114 C7
Harepit Cl DE24 . . . . 233 A5
Harewood Ave S44 . . . . . 16 A8
Harewood Ave DE55 . . . 169 B8
Harewood Cl
Belper DE56 . . . . 179 D5
2 Sandiacre NG10 . . . . 223 B4
Harewood Cres S42 . . . . 131 B6
Harewood Rd
Derby DE23 . . . . 204 D3
Holymoorside S42 . . . . . 113 C5
Hargate Hill La SK13 . . . . 16 E7
Hargate Rd
Burton u T DE15 . . . . . . 248 C1
Buxton SK17 . . . . 84 F6
Hargrave Ave DE72 . . . . 221 C5
Hargreaves Cl DE23 . . . 231 A6

Hargreaves Ct **6** DE7 . . . . .208 F7
Harlaxton Dr NG10 . . . . . . .237 A8
Harlech Cl
　Derby DE21 . . . . .221 A5
　Ilkeston DE7 . . . . .194 C3
Harlequin Ct NG16 . . . . . .182 D3
Harlesden Ave DE22 . . . . .218 A7
Harlesthorpe Ave S43 . . . .80 F5
Harlesthorpe La S43 . . . . .80 E5
Harley's Ct DE12 . . . . .262 C4
Harlow Cl
　Derby DE24 . . . . .232 F4
　Mansfield Woodhouse
　NG19 . . . . .136 C6
Harold Ave NG16 . . . . .182 B4
Harold Ct DE23 . . . . .219 B2
Harperhill Cl S40 . . . . .114 F7
Harpole Cl DE55 . . . . .169 F8
Harport Dr S45 . . . . .131 E2
Harpswell Cl DE22 . . . . . . .204 E2
Harpur Ave
　Derby DE23 . . . . .231 B8
　Ticknall DE73 . . . . .151 A4
Harpur Crewe Cotts DE6 149 D3
Harpur Hill Bsns Pk SK17 .85 B2
Harpur Hill Prim Sch
　SK17 . . . . .85 C2
Harpur Hill Rd SK17 . . . . .85 C4
Harrier Rd DE56 . . . . .179 C5
Harrier Way DE24 . . . . . . .231 E3
Harriet St DE23 . . . . .219 A3
Harriett St NG9 . . . . .223 E7
Harriet Tubman Ho
　DE23 . . . . .218 F1
Harrimans Dr DE7 . . . . . . .235 F8
Harringay Gdns DE22 . . . .218 C6
Harrington Ave DE72 . . . . .221 C2
Harrington Jun Sch
　NG10 . . . . .223 B1
Harrington Rd
　Derby DE23 . . . . .218 C1
　10 Sheffield S2 . . . . . . .43 A8
Harrington St
　Derby, Allenton DE24 . . . .232 E6
　Derby, Normanton DE23 .232 A8
　Draycott DE72 . . . . .235 B7
　Long Eaton NG10 . . . . . .236 B5
Harris Ave DE5 . . . . .169 C2
Harris Cl DE5 . . . . .169 C1
Harrison Ct DE14 . . . . .254 B8
Harrison Dr DE4 . . . . .154 F1
Harrison La
　Sheffield S10 . . . . .42 F7
　Tibshelf DE55 . . . . .147 F6
Harrison Rd NG9 . . . . .223 D8
Harrison St DE22 . . . . .218 C3
Harrison Way DE4 . . . . . . .127 A6
Hart Ave NG10 . . . . .223 A6
Hart Rd SK17 . . . . .85 C3
Harrogate Cres DE21 . . . . .205 D1
Harrop La S10 . . . . .42 F6
Harrots La SK17 . . . . .137 D6
Harrow Dr
　Burton u T DE14 . . . . . . .254 C8
　Ilkeston DE7 . . . . .209 A4
Harrow Rd DE11 . . . . .256 B7
Harrow St DE24 . . . . .219 E2
Hart Ave NG10 . . . . .223 A6
Hartfield Cl S41 . . . . .115 B7
Hartford Cl S8 . . . . .43 A3
Hartford Rd S8 . . . . .43 A3
Harthill Field Rd S26 . . . . .62 A3
Harthill La S43 . . . . .61 E1
Harthill Prim Sch S26 . . . .61 E1
Harthill Rd
　Sheffield S13 . . . . .44 B7
　Thorpe Salvin S80 . . . . . .62 D7
Hartington CE Prim Sch
　SK17 . . . . .137 D5
Hartington Cl DE7 . . . . . . .207 E8
Hartington Ct
　Clowne S43 . . . . .81 A4
　Dronfield S18 . . . . .57 B2
Hartington Dr
　Chinley SK23 . . . . .34 E1
　Creswell S80 . . . . .81 C1
Hartington Gdns **11** SK17 .85 B7
Hartington Hall YH*
　SK17 . . . . .137 E5
Hartington Ind Est S43 . . .78 E4
Hartington Pl DE7 . . . . . . .194 E5
Hartington Rd
　Buxton SK17 . . . . .85 B7
　Chesterfield S41 . . . . . . .96 C2
　Dronfield S18 . . . . .57 B2
Hartington St
　Derby DE1, DE23 . . . . . .267 B1
　Langwith NG20 . . . . .119 F8
Hartington View S43 . . . . .78 F4
Hartington Way DE3 . . . . .217 D2
Hartland Ct **2** S41 . . . . . . .95 F8
Hartland Dr DE23 . . . . . . .231 E6
Hartland Way S42 . . . . . . .77 A1
Hart Lea **11** NG10 . . . . . . .223 B5
Hartley St S2 . . . . .43 A7
Hartopp Ave S2 . . . . .43 C6
Hartopp Cl S2 . . . . .43 C6
Hartopp Dr S2 . . . . .43 C6
Hartopp Rd S2 . . . . .43 D6
Hartshay Hill DE5 . . . . . . .166 D6
Hartshill Rd DE11 . . . . . . .257 A4
Hartshorne CE Prim Sch
　DE11 . . . . .257 B6
Hartshorne Rd
　Derby DE23 . . . . .231 C5
　Repton DE65 . . . . .249 E7
　Woodville DE11 . . . . .256 F3
Hartside Cl **16** S40 . . . . . .95 D5

Hartside Gdns **1** NG10 . . .236 A8
Hartside Way DE75 . . . . . .182 B1
Hartwood Dr NG9 . . . . . . .209 D1
Harvester Cl DE55 . . . . . . .169 C2
Harvest Hill DE11 . . . . . . .256 B7
Harvest Way
　2 Chesterfield S42 . . . .95 A5
　Derby DE21 . . . . .206 C3
Harvey Clough Mews S8 . .43 B3
Harvey Clough Rd S8 . . . .43 B3
Harvey Croft NG9 . . . . . . .209 C4
Harvey Ct S44 . . . . .98 F2
Harvey Pl ST14 . . . . .210 B1
Harvey Rd
　Burton u T DE14 . . . . . . .254 A8
　Castle Donington DE74 . .247 B2
　Chesterfield S41 . . . . . . .96 C2
　Derby DE24 . . . . .232 E6
Harwich Rd S2 . . . . .43 F8
Harwood Ave DE14 . . . . . .253 F8
Harwood Cl S2 . . . . .43 A8
Harwood St **2** S2 . . . . . . .43 A8
Hasgill Cl DE21 . . . . .206 C3
Haskeys Cl DE22 . . . . .204 C2
Haslam's La DE21, DE22 . .205 B1
Haslam Cres S8 . . . . .56 E6
Haslam Ct
　Bolsover S44 . . . . .98 F2
　Chesterfield S41 . . . . . . .266 B4
Hasland Hall Com Sch
　S41 . . . . .115 D7
Hasland Inf Sch S41 . . . . .115 C8
Hasland Jun Sch S41 . . . .115 D7
Hasland Rd S41 . . . . .115 C8
Haslemere Ct DE21 . . . . . .219 B2
Haslemere Rd NG10 . . . . .236 B8
Haslin Rd SK17 . . . . .85 D2
Hassall Rd DE65 . . . . .227 D1
Hassock La N DE75 . . . . . .194 B7
Hassock La S DE7, DE75 . .194 C6
Hassocky La S44, S42 . . . .116 B6
Hassop Cl
　Chesterfield S41 . . . . . . .95 C6
　Dronfield S18 . . . . .57 C2
Hassop Rd
　Calver S32 . . . . .72 B1
　Derby DE21 . . . . .220 A8
　Hassop DE45 . . . . .90 D1
　Staveley S43 . . . . .78 F3
Hastilar Cl S2 . . . . .44 B8
Hastilar Cl S2 . . . . .44 B8
Hastilar Rd S2 . . . . .44 B8
Hastilar Rd S S13 . . . . . . .44 C7
Hastings Cl
　Breedon on t H DE73 . . .252 E2
　Chesterfield S41 . . . . . . .95 D6
Hastings Rd
　Buxton SK17 . . . . .85 C4
　Swadlincote DE11 . . . . . .256 B3
Hastings St DE23 . . . . .219 A1
Hasting St DE74 . . . . .247 B2
Haston Dr DE55 . . . . .170 D8
Hatchmere Cl DE21 . . . . . .206 A1
Hatfield Ave NG10 . . . . . . .223 B4
Hatfield Rd DE24 . . . . .232 F5
Hathaway Cl S42 . . . . .131 B6
Hathern Cl
　Calow S43 . . . . .96 F4
　Derby DE23 . . . . .231 E5
　Long Eaton NG10 . . . . . .236 D5
Hathersage Ave
　Derby DE23 . . . . .231 E8
　Long Eaton NG10 . . . . . .236 D5
Hathersage Cres SK13 . . .9 C2
Hathersage Dr
　Glossop SK13 . . . . .17 F8
　Somercotes DE55 . . . . . .170 B7
Hathersage Pk S32 . . . . . .53 A7
Hathersage Rd
　Bamford S32, S33 . . . . . .40 B1
　Sheffield S11, S17 . . . . .54 D6
Hathersage Sta S32 . . . . .53 A7
Hatton Cl S18 . . . . .75 D8
Hatton Crofts NG10 . . . . . .236 C6
Hatton Ct DE73 . . . . .252 A7
Hatton Dr S40 . . . . .95 B5
Haulton Dr DE74 . . . . .247 A4
Havelock Rd DE23 . . . . . . .232 A8
Havelock St
　Ilkeston DE7 . . . . .208 F7
　Ripley DE5 . . . . .169 E2
Haven Baulk Ave DE23 . . .230 C2
Haven Baulk La DE23 . . . .230 C2
Haven Cl DE24 . . . . .233 D6
Havenwood Dr DE23 . . . . .231 C5
Havercroft Terr S21 . . . . . .60 B7
Hawfield La DE15 . . . . . . .248 E4
Hawk's Dr DE15 . . . . .248 D3
Hawke St DE22 . . . . .218 C5
Hawk Green Rd SK6 . . . . .23 A3
Hawkhill Rd S32 . . . . .71 D6
Hawkinge Ho **10** S41 . . . .95 D5
Hawking La S44 . . . . .133 A7
Hawkins Ct DE7 . . . . .194 F4
Hawkins Dr DE56 . . . . .168 B3
Hawk Rd SK22 . . . . .33 E8
Hawksdale Cl DE73 . . . . . .233 A2
Hawkshead Ave
　Derby DE21 . . . . .205 D1
　Dronfield S18 . . . . .56 E1
Hawkshead Fold SK13 . . . .10 E3
Hawkshead Rd SK13 . . . . .10 C3
Hawksley Ave S40 . . . . . . .95 E4
Hawksley Dr
　Darley Dale DE4 . . . . . . .127 A4
　Rolleston DE13 . . . . .240 B4
Hawksway S21 . . . . .59 B3
Hawleys Cl DE4 . . . . .143 C6

Hawley St S18 . . . . .58 A1
Hawthorn Ave
　Breaston DE72 . . . . .235 F8
　Derby DE24 . . . . .233 A7
　Mastin Moor S43 . . . . . . .79 C4
　Netherseal DE12 . . . . . . .264 F7
　Ripley DE5 . . . . .180 D8
　Stapleford NG9 . . . . .223 D6
Hawthorn Bank
　Glossop SK13 . . . . .9 F4
　New Mills SK22 . . . . .33 B6
Hawthorn Cl
　Ashbourne DE6 . . . . .185 D8
　Chinley SK23 . . . . .34 E1
　Clowne S43 . . . . .80 D4
　Denstone ST14 . . . . .196 F6
　Doveridge DE6 . . . . .211 B1
　Hilton DE65 . . . . .228 D1
　Hope S33 . . . . .39 A4
　Mansfield Woodhouse
　NG19 . . . . .136 E5
Hawthorn Cres
　Burton u T DE15 . . . . . . .254 F7
　Findern DE65 . . . . .230 D2
Hawthorn Ct DE11 . . . . . . .267 A5
Hawthorn Dr DE24 . . . . . .155 A6
Hawthorne Ave
　Borrowash DE72 . . . . . . .221 C2
　Creswell S80 . . . . .81 E2
　Dronfield S18 . . . . .57 A3
　Glapwell S44 . . . . .134 B8
　Long Eaton NG10 . . . . . .236 C6
　Shirebrook NG20 . . . . . .119 D4
　Shirland DE55 . . . . .146 C5
　Tibshelf DE55 . . . . .148 B8
Hawthorne Cl
　Ashover DE55 . . . . .145 D8
　Barlborough S43 . . . . . . .80 A6
　Kilburn DE56 . . . . .179 F2
　Killamarsh S21 . . . . .60 D5
Hawthorne Rd NG16 . . . . .160 D3
Hawthornes Ave DE55 . . . .159 F5
Hawthorne St S44 . . . . . . .266 C1
Hawthorn Gr SK14 . . . . . . .9 D6
Hawthorn Hill S43 . . . . . . .78 F6
Hawthorn Rd
　Castle Donington DE74 . .247 B5
　Eckington S21 . . . . .59 B2
Hawthorn Rise
　Awsworth NG16 . . . . .195 B4
　Swadlincote DE11 . . . . . .255 F7
Hawthorn St DE24 . . . . . . .232 C8
Hawthorns The
　Belper DE56 . . . . .179 D5
　Chapel-en-le-F SK23 . . . .47 B4
　Little Eaton DE21 . . . . . .205 D8
　Wirksworth DE4 . . . . .165 F7
Hawthorn Way S42 . . . . . .94 F5
Hawton Cl NG19 . . . . .113 A1
Hawtrey Gdns DE24 . . . . . .233 A7
Haxby Cl S13 . . . . .44 E6
Haxby Pl S13 . . . . .44 E6
Haxby Rd S13 . . . . .44 E6
Haybrook Ct S17 . . . . .55 E5
Haycroft Cl NG19 . . . . .136 E5
Haycroft Ct DE23 . . . . .231 A7
Haydn Cl S43 . . . . .79 B4
Hayden Cl **1** SK13 . . . . . .10 C1
Haydn Fold SK13 . . . . .10 D7
Haydn Rd DE21 . . . . .219 F8
Haydock Cl
　Burton u T DE14 . . . . . . .254 A7
　Kimberley NG16 . . . . . . .195 E7
Haydock Park Rd DE24 . . .232 E8
Hayes Ave
　Breaston DE72 . . . . .235 B7
　Derby DE23 . . . . .231 D8
Hayes Cl
　Pinxton NG16 . . . . .160 C3
　West Hallam DE7 . . . . . .207 E8
Hayes Con Ctr The DE55 .170 A6
Hayes Cres DE55 . . . . .169 F7
Hayes Ct S20 . . . . .59 E6
Hayes Dr S20 . . . . .59 E6
Hayes Farm Ct DE73 . . . . .251 A4
Hayes La S45 . . . . .145 E7
Hayes The DE65 . . . . .230 C1
Hayes Wood Rd DE7 . . . . .193 A1
Hayfield Cl
　Belper DE56 . . . . .179 B5
　Dronfield S18 . . . . .56 D1
　Staveley S43 . . . . .78 F3
　Wingerworth S42 . . . . . . .114 F3
Hayfield Cres S12 . . . . . . .44 C3
Hayfield Dr S12 . . . . .44 D3
Hayfield Gdns DE21 . . . . . .231 B6
Hayfield Pl S12 . . . . .44 D3
Hayfield Prim Sch SK22 . .25 C3
Hayfield Rd
　Chapel-en-le-F SK23 . . . .47 B8
　Chinley SK23 . . . . .35 A3
　New Mills SK22 . . . . .24 C1
Hayfield Vistor Ctr* SK22 .25 C2
Hayford Pl DE22 . . . . .218 D4
Hayford Way S43 . . . . .78 E1
Hay La
　Ashover S45 . . . . .145 B7
　Scropton DE65 . . . . .226 E5
　Spout DE4 . . . . .156 F1
Hayley Cl NG16 . . . . .195 D6
Hayley Croft DE56 . . . . . . .190 F1
Hayling Cl DE7 . . . . .194 C3
Haynes Ave NG9 . . . . .209 C5
Hays Cl DE7 . . . . .194 D2
Hays The DE65 . . . . .227 C2

Heathermead Cl **2** DE21 .205 F1
Heathers Edge S32 . . . . . .53 A6
Heather Vale S41 . . . . .115 E7
Heather Vale Cl S41 . . . . . .115 C7
Heather Vale Rd S41 . . . . .115 D7
Heather Way S42 . . . . .114 F3
Heathfield DE4 . . . . .143 C7
Heathfield Ave
　Chesterfield S40 . . . . . . .95 D3
　Ilkeston DE7 . . . . .209 B8
Heathfield Cl
　Dronfield S18 . . . . .75 F8
　Wingerworth S42 . . . . . . .115 B4
Heathfield Gdns
　Buxton SK17 . . . . .85 A8
　Tibshelf DE55 . . . . .148 A7
Heathfield Nook Rd SK17 .85 E2
Heathfield Rd S12 . . . . . . .44 D4
Heath Fields Prim Sch
　DE65 . . . . .227 C1
Heath Gdns DE72 . . . . . . .236 A8
Heath Gr S17 . . . . .85 C6
Heath La
　Blackfordby DE11 . . . . . .257 C2
　Findern DE65 . . . . .242 D8
　Hartshorne DE11 . . . . . . .257 E4
　Smisby LE65 . . . . .258 B6
Heathlands Dr ST14 . . . . . .210 B1
Heathley Mews DE14 . . . . .254 C8
Heath Park Rd SK17 . . . . .85 E2
Heath Prim Sch S44 . . . . .116 F1
Heath Rd
　Burton u T DE15 . . . . . . .254 E7
　Glossop SK13 . . . . .10 C3
　Holmewood S44 . . . . . . .116 E1
　Holmewood, Williamthorpe
　S42 . . . . .132 E8
　Ripley DE5 . . . . .169 E1
　Uttoxeter ST14 . . . . .210 B1
Heath St S41 . . . . .85 B6
Heath The
　Eastwood NG16 . . . . . . .195 A8
　Glossop SK13 . . . . .10 C3
Heath View S41 . . . . .85 E1
Heath Way DE65 . . . . .227 D1
Heaton Cl S18 . . . . .56 D1
Heaton Ct **4** S40 . . . . . . .95 C2
Heaton St S40 . . . . .95 E8
Heaton St S40 . . . . .95 C2
Heavygate La DE56 . . . . . .177 F8
Hebden Cl DE23 . . . . .230 F6
Hebden Dr SK13 . . . . .17 F8
Hebrides Cl DE24 . . . . .231 D3
Heddon Bar NG19 . . . . . . .136 E3
Hedgebank Ct DE21 . . . . . .206 C3
Hedge Gr DE11 . . . . .256 B7
Hedgerow Gdns DE21 . . . .206 C3
Hedges Dr DE7 . . . . .209 A5
Hedgevale Cl DE23 . . . . . .231 A7
Hedingham Cl NE7 . . . . . .194 D1
Hedingham Way DE3 . . . . .230 D8
Hedley Cl DE55 . . . . .170 D8
Hedley Dr S43 . . . . .96 D8
Heeley Arches S2 . . . . .43 A7
Heeley Bank Rd S2 . . . . . .43 B7
Heeley City Farm* S2 . . . .43 B7
Heeley Gn S2 . . . . .43 B8
Heigham Ct DE24 . . . . .232 D3
Heights of Abraham*
　DE4 . . . . .143 A2
Heights of Abraham Cable
　Car* DE4 . . . . .143 A2
Helmsley Ave S20 . . . . . . .59 E7
Helmsley Cl S41 . . . . .95 C7
Helmton Dr S8 . . . . .43 A2
Helmton Rd S8 . . . . .43 A2
Helpston Cl DE55 . . . . .147 C1
Helston Cl
　Chesterfield S41 . . . . . . .115 B8
　Derby DE24 . . . . .233 B6
　Linton DE12 . . . . .261 D5
Helvellyn Way **3** NG10 . . .223 B2
Heming Ave S45 . . . . .132 C2
Hemington Ct DE74 . . . . . .247 C5
Hemington Hill DE74 . . . . .247 C4
Hemington La DE74 . . . . . .247 C5
Hemington Prim Sch
　DE74 . . . . .247 D5
Hemlock Cl
　Long Eaton NG10 . . . . . .223 D1
　Stapleford NG9 . . . . .223 E8
Hemlock Cl DE7 . . . . .208 D5
Hemlock La DE7 . . . . .208 D5
Hemlock Stone The*
　NG9 . . . . .209 F2
Hemper Gr S8 . . . . .56 D7
Hemper La S8 . . . . .56 D7
Hemp Yd DE6 . . . . .116 E1
Hemsley Dr NG16 . . . . .182 D3
Hemsworth Rd S8, S14 . . .43 C2
Hendon Way DE22 . . . . . . .218 B6
Henley Ave S8 . . . . .57 C8
Henley Gdns NG9 . . . . . . .209 E1
Henley Gn DE22 . . . . .217 F6
Henley Way DE7 . . . . .207 D8
Henmore Pl **10** DE6 . . . . .173 C2
Henmore Trad Est DE6 . . .173 A1
Hennymoor Cl S80 . . . . . . .82 A5
Hennymoor La S80 . . . . . . .82 C2
Henry Ave
　Mansfield Woodhouse
　NG19 . . . . .136 A5
　Matlock DE4 . . . . .143 C6
Henry Bradley Inf Sch
　S43 . . . . .96 F8

Henry Cres DE55.......... 159 C3
Henry Fanshawe Sch S18 .57 B2
Henry Prince CE Fst Sch The
  DE6 .... 184 D7
Henry St
  Chesterfield S41 .... 96 B8
  Derby DE1 .... 267 A4
  Eckington S21 .... 59 D3
  Glossop SK13............ 10 C1
  Grassmoor S42 .... 115 E3
  Ripley DE5 .... 169 D2
Henshall Ho S41......... 96 B6
Henshaw Ave DE7 ...... 208 D5
Henshaw Pl DE7......... 194 E4
Hepworth Rd DE11...... 256 E1
Herald Gr DE73......... 244 E8
Herbert St DE15 .... 248 B3
Herbert Strutt Prim Sch
  DE56 .... 178 F2
Herdings Ct S12.......... 44 A3
Herdings Rd S12......... 44 A3
Herdings View S12....... 44 A3
Hereford Ave NG19 ..... 136 D5
Hereford Cl SK17 .... 85 C4
Hereford Cres DE11 .... 256 D6
Hereford Dr S43......... 96 F8
Hereford Rd
  Buxton SK17 .... 85 C4
  Derby DE21 .... 219 D8
Hereward's Rd S14 .... 43 D1
Heritage Cl NG20....... 119 F4
Heritage Com Sch S43 ... 80 D4
Heritage Ct **4** DE56 ... 178 F3
Heritage Way DE15 ..... 248 A1
Hermitage Ave
  Borrowash DE72 .... 221 C2
  Somercotes DE55 ...... 170 C5
Hermitage Ct DE21..... 206 B1
Hermitage Gdns **1** S14 210 A1
Hermitage La DE6 ...... 184 B6
Hermitage Park Way **7**
  DE11..................... 256 A7
Hermitage Wlk DE7 .... 208 F6
Hernstone La SK17....... 49 B2
Heron Cl SK13 .... 17 F8
Heron Dr DE11 .... 256 F3
Heronswood Dr DE21 .. 220 D6
Heronway SK13.......... 10 E7
Heron Way
  Derby DE3 .... 218 A2
  Mansfield NG19......... 135 C1
Herriot Dr S40.......... 266 C1
Hessey St S13 .... 44 F6
Hewers Holt S43......... 80 B6
Hewett St NG20......... 120 D5
Hewitt Pl S26............ 61 E5
Hexham Ave DE7 .... 209 A4
Hexham Wlk DE7....... 205 E1
Heyden Bank **26** SK13 .... 9 D2
Heyden Fold **27** SK13 .... 9 D2
Heyden Terr **28** SK13 .... 9 D2
Heydon Cl DE56 .... 179 B6
Heyford Ct DE75 .... 182 A1
Heysbank Rd SK12....... 32 D5
Hey St NG10 .... 236 C4
Heywood St S43 .... 96 E8
Heywood View S43....... 80 C6
Heywood Villas **5** S43 .. 96 E8
Heyworth St DE22 ...... 218 D6
Hibbert St SK22 .... 33 B6
Hickings La NG19...... 223 E8
Hickingwood La S43 .... 81 A5
Hickinwood Cres S43 ... 80 F5
Hickleton Cl DE5 ...... 169 C1
Hickling Cl DE24....... 232 D3
Hickton Rd DE55 ...... 169 F6
Hide La SK17 .... 137 E7
Hides Gn S44 .... 99 A2
Higger La S32 .... 52 F8
Higgins Rd DE11 ...... 255 F6
Higgott La DE56 .... 167 A6
Higgott Cl DE14 .... 254 B8
Higham La
  Compstall SK14......... 15 A7
  Stonebroom DE55 ..... 146 E4
Highashes La S45....... 113 E1
Highbank S13 .... 9 F7
High Bank DE5 .... 180 F2
Highbank Rd SK13 ..... 17 F7
High Bank Rd DE15 ... 248 B3
Highbury Cl DE22 ..... 217 F6
Highbury Rd S41 .... 95 F5
Highcliffe Ave NG20... 119 D4
Highcroft Cl NG10 .... 236 E5
High Cross
  Hartington SK17 ...... 137 F5
  Linton DE11 .... 261 F7
High Cl DE4 .... 143 C6
High Edge Dr DE56 .... 179 D8
High Edge Mews DE56 . 179 A5
Higher Albert St S41... 266 B4
Higher Barn Rd SK13 ... 9 F4
Higher Dining S13 ..... 10 A2
Higher Hallsteads SK17 .47 F3
Higher La S12 .... 32 E1
Higher Noon Sun SK22 . 24 F2
Higher Sq SK13......... 10 A3
Highfield DE55 .... 108 E8
Highfield Ave
  Chesterfield S41 ...... 95 E6
  Dove Holes SK17...... 47 F1
  Mansfield NG19....... 136 B1
  Shirebrook NG20..... 119 D6

Highfield Cl
  Bakewell DE45 .... 109 C5
  Heanor DE75.......... 181 B5
  Mansfield NG19....... 136 B1
Highfield Cotts
  Alfreton DE55 .... 158 D3
  Derby DE21 .... 219 E5
Highfield Ct SK14...... 9 A4
Highfield Dr
  Bakewell DE45 .... 109 C5
  Ilkeston DE7 .... 208 B5
  Matlock DE4 .... 143 D6
  South Normanton DE55 .160 B5
Highfield Gdns
  Derby DE22 .... 218 F7
  Hollingworth SK14.... 9 D5
Highfield La
  Chesterfield S41 ..... 95 E6
  Derby DE21 .... 219 F5
  Hartington SK17 .... 137 F3
  Weston Underwood DE6 .188 F5
Highfield Mews DE21 .. 219 E5
Highfield Pl S2 .... 43 A8
Highfield Prim Sch
  NG10 .... 223 C2
Highfield Rd
  Ashbourne DE6 ...... 185 B8
  Belper DE56.......... 178 F2
  Bolsover S44 .... 99 A1
  Chesterfield S41 .... 266 A4
  Derby DE22 .... 218 F7
  Glossop SK13......... 17 D8
  Hayfield SK22 .... 25 D3
  Hulland Ward DE6 ... 175 F3
  Kilburn DE56 .... 191 F8
  Little Eaton DE21.... 205 C8
  Marple SK6 .... 23 B6
  Swadlincote DE11 ... 256 B3
  Swanwick DE55 ..... 169 D7
Highfields
  Buxton SK17 .... 67 B5
  Codnor DE5 .... 181 B8
Highfields Cres S18.... 76 A8
Highfields Dr
  Holmewood S42...... 132 D8
  Linton DE12 .... 261 C6
Highfields Lower Sch
  DE4 .... 143 C3
Highfields Park Dr DE22 .204 E1
Highfields Rd S18...... 76 A8
Highfields Sch DE4 ... 143 E7
Highfield St
  Long Eaton NG10..... 223 C2
  Swadlincote DE11 ... 256 B3
Highfields Way S42 ... 132 D8
Highfield Terr
  Chesterfield S41 ..... 95 F5
  New Mills SK22 ..... 33 A8
Highfield View Rd S41 . 95 F5
Highfield Way DE55... 180 C8
Highgate Cl S43 .... 77 D3
Highgate Dr
  Dronfield S18......... 76 C7
  Ilkeston DE7 .... 194 D3
Highgate Gn DE22 .... 218 A5
Highgate La S18 .... 76 C7
Highgate Rd SK22 .... 25 E1
Highgates DE1......... 267 B2
High Gr
  Belper DE56.......... 179 D4
  Mansfield NG19....... 136 E1
Highgrove Cl
  Burton u T DE13...... 240 C1
  Heanor DE75.......... 181 C1
Highgrove Dr DE73 ... 232 F2
High Hazel Ct S45 .... 131 D4
High Hazel Dr NG19... 136 B1
High Hazels Cl S45 ... 131 E4
High Hazels Rd S45.... 80 B5
High Hazels Wlk S45 .. 131 E4
High Hill Rd SK22 ..... 24 D1
High Holborn S80 .... 101 C7
High Holborn Rd DE5 . 170 B1
High La
  Broadbottom SK13 ... 16 E7
  Eckington S12......... 44 E1
  Holloway, Dethick Common
    DE4 .... 144 E2
  Holloway, Upper Holloway
    DE4 .... 144 E2
  Holymoorside S42..... 113 E5
  Sheffield S12 .... 58 F8
High La Central DE7 .. 193 F1
High La E DE7 .... 208 B8
Highland Cl
  Buxton SK17 .... 85 C5
  Mansfield Woodhouse
    NG19 .... 136 D3
Highland Rd S43 ...... 77 D4
Highlands Dr DE15.... 248 A4
Highlands Pl S41 ...... 76 F1
High La W DE7 .... 193 E1
High Lea Rd SK22 ..... 33 A8
High Leys Rd S43 ..... 80 E2
Highlightley La S18 ... 75 C5
Highlow Cl S40 .... 95 B5
High Mdws SK13....... 17 B7
High Meadow CE DE6 . 180 D8
High Pavement S45 ... 179 A3
High Rd DE55 .... 157 F4
High Ridge
  Mansfield NG19....... 136 F2
  Matlock DE4 .... 143 C7

High St E SK13 .... 10 D1
High St W SK13........ 10 B1
High Spannia NG16... 195 F7
High St
  Alfreton DE55 .... 159 A4
  Apperknowle S18...... 58 A1
  Barlborough S43...... 80 A7
  Belper DE56.......... 179 C3
  Bolsover S44 .... 99 A1
  Bonsall DE4 .... 142 D1
  Brimington S43 ..... 96 F7
  Brinsley NG16 ...... 171 E1
  Buxton SK17 .... 85 B7
  Calver S32 .... 72 B2
  Castle Donington DE74 .247 A2
  Chapel-en-le-F SK23 .. 47 B6
  Chellaston DE7 ..... 233 A1
  Chesterfield S41, S43 . 77 D4
  Chesterfield, Stonegravels
    S40 .... 266 B3
  Clay Cross S45 ...... 131 C3
  Clowne S43 .... 80 D3
  Codnor DE5 .... 181 B8
  Doveridge DE6........ 211 B1
  Dronfield S18......... 76 A7
  Eckington S21........ 59 D3
  Ilkeston DE7 .... 208 F8
  Kilburn DE56 .... 192 A8
  Killamarsh S21 ...... 60 D6
  Kimberley NG16...... 195 F6
  Linton DE12 .... 261 C6
  Long Eaton NG10..... 236 E8
  Longnor SK17 ...... 121 C6
  Mansfield Woodhouse
    NG19 .... 136 C3
  Marchington ST14 ... 224 E2
  Melbourne DE73 .... 252 A7
  New Mills SK22 ..... 33 C8
  Pilsley DE45.......... 91 C3
  Pleasley NG19 ...... 135 B5
  Repton DE65 .... 242 D2
  Rocester ST14 ...... 196 F3
  Sheffield, Dore S17 .. 55 D7
  Sheffield, Mosborough S20 .59 D7
  Somercotes DE55 ... 170 C8
  Somercotes, Riddings
    DE55............... 170 D5
  South Normanton DE55 .160 A6
  Stapleford NG9 ..... 223 E7
  Staveley S43 .... 78 E1
  Stonebroom DE55 ... 147 A4
  Stoney Middleton S32 .71 F3
  Swadlincote, Church Gresley
    DE11............... 256 C3
  Swadlincote, Newhall
    DE11............... 256 A6
  Swanwick DE55 ..... 169 F7
  Tibshelf DE55 ...... 148 A7
  Ticknall DE73 ...... 251 D5
  Tideswell SK17 ..... 69 C4
  Tutbury DE13 ...... 239 C6
  Whitwell S80 .... 81 F6
  Woodville DE11...... 256 F2
Highstairs La DE55 ... 146 C8
Highstones Gdns SK13 . 10 F7
High Tor* DE4 .... 143 B3
High Tor Rd DE4 ...... 143 B2
High Trees S17 .... 55 D7
Highview SK13......... 17 A7
High View Cl S41 ..... 96 D2
High View Rd DE55... 160 C7
Highway La DE6 ...... 151 F2
Highwood Ave DE56 .. 179 C1
High Wood Bank DE56 .179 C1
Highwood Cl SK13 .... 17 B8
High Wood Fold SK6... 23 C8
Highwood La S80 ..... 81 D5
Highwood Pl S21 ..... 59 C3
High Wood Way S43 .. 80 C5
Hilary Cl DE56 .... 179 E5
Hilcote La DE55 ...... 148 B1
Hilderstone Cl DE24 . 233 D6
Hillary Pl DE7 .... 208 B5
Hillberry DE5 .... 170 A1
Hillberry Rise S40..... 114 F6
Hill Brow DE1 .... 267 B2
Hill Cl
  Derby DE21 .... 220 E4
  Stanley Common DE7 .193 A1
  Turnditch SE56 ..... 177 B2
Hillcliff La
  Hulland Ward DE56 .. 176 F2
  Turnditch DE56 ..... 177 A3
Hill Cotts DE45 ...... 125 B5
Hillcrest
  Aston-on-T DE7 ..... 234 A1
  Belper DE56.......... 179 E4
  Blackwell DE55 ..... 147 E1
  Derby DE23 .... 219 B5
Hill Crest
  Crich DE4 .... 157 A1
  Shirebrook NG20..... 119 D3
Hillcrest Ave
  Burton u T DE15..... 248 A4
  Hulland Ward DE6 .. 175 F3
  South Normanton DE55 .160 A4
Hill Crest Ave DE55 .. 157 E8
Hill Crest Cl DE4...... 142 F8
Hillcrest Dr
  Codnor DE5 .... 181 B8
  Kilburn DE56 .... 192 A8
Hillcreste Dr DE73 ... 232 F3
Hillcrest Gr S43 ...... 78 F4
Hillcrest Rd S41 ...... 115 D7

Hill Crest Rd DE21 ... 219 D7
Hillcroft Dr DE7 ..... 221 C4
Hill Cross DE45 ...... 108 F8
Hill Cross Ave DE23 . 231 C7
Hill Cross Dr DE23 .. 231 B7
Hill Dr S23 .... 45 D8
Hillend SK14 .... 9 A1
Hillend La SK14........ 9 A1
Hillfield La DE13 .... 240 F1
Hillfield Rd NG9 ..... 209 F1
Hill Fields DE55 ..... 160 A3
Hillfoot Ct S17....... 55 D4
Hillfoot Rd S17....... 55 D5
Hill Gr S43 .... 78 B4
Hill Green Cl DE12 .. 260 D3
Hill Head S33......... 51 A7
Hillhead La SK17 .... 85 E1
Hillhouses La S42 ... 114 E3
Hillingdon Dr DE7 .. 209 A7
Hill La S32 .... 266 B3
Hillman Dr S43 ...... 97 C7
Hillmoor St NG19 ... 135 C3
Hillmorton DE45 .... 108 F7
Hill Nook Cl DE73 .. 233 A1
Hillock The S32....... 72 E2
Hill Pond Ave SK22 . 24 D1
Hill Rd
  Ashover S45 .... 129 F4
  Heanor DE75........ 181 D1
Hill Rise NG9 .... 209 C4
Hill Rise S32 .... 231 D8
Hillsdale Rd DE15.... 248 B5
Hillside
  Ashover S45 .... 130 A4
  Brassington DE4 .... 152 F1
  Buxton SK17 .... 85 D3
  Castle Donington DE74 .247 B4
  Chinley SK23 .... 47 B8
  Curbar S32 .... 72 E2
  Findern DE65........ 230 C2
  Holloway DE4 ...... 156 A6
  Langley Mill NG16 . 182 A3
  Middleton DE4 ..... 154 D4
  Sheffield S20 .... 59 C7
  Tutbury DE13 ...... 239 C6
  Whitwell S80 .... 81 F5
Hillside Ave
  Ashbourne DE6 ..... 173 C3
  Derby DE21 .... 220 A5
  Dronfield S18........ 76 A8
Hillside Cl
  Chesterfield S40 .... 95 D1
  Long Eaton NG10.... 236 B8
  Mastin Moor S43 ... 79 C3
Hillside Gdns DE11 .. 255 F2
Hillside Gr
  Marple SK6 .... 15 B1
  Sandiacre NG10..... 223 A6
Hillside Rd
  Derby DE21 .... 220 F4
  Linton DE12 .... 261 D7
Hillside Rise DE56 ... 178 F2
Hillside View SK22 ... 33 A8
Hill Sq The DE22 ... 205 A1
Hills Rd DE7 .... 235 C7
Hill St
  Burton u T DE15..... 254 E8
  Clay Cross S45 ..... 131 C3
  Donisthorpe DE12 .. 262 E1
  Ripley DE5 .... 169 D3
  Sheffield S2 .... 43 A8
  Swadlincote, Church Gresley
    DE11............. 256 C3
  Swadlincote DE11... 255 F6
Hill The S33 .... 51 A6
Hillstown Bsns Ctr S44 .118 F7
Hilsway
  Chellaston DE73 ... 232 F3
  Derby DE23 .... 218 B1
  Shirebrook NG20... 119 D3
Hill The
  Derby DE22 .... 205 A1
  Glapwell S44 ...... 118 A1
  Tibshelf DE56 ..... 168 B7
Hill Top
  Bolsover S44 ...... 99 A2
  Castle Donington DE74 .247 A1
  Derby DE23 .... 205 E3
Hilltop Ave NG20 ... 119 E4
Hilltop Cl S44 ...... 118 B1
Hilltop Inf Sch DE65 . 185 C8
Hilltop La
  Derby DE56......... 179 E2
  Thurvaston DE6 ... 215 D5
Hilltop Rd
  Ashover S45 .... 129 F5
  Chesterfield S41 ... 77 B2
  Dronfield S18....... 76 A8
  Glossop SK13........ 10 B3
  Pinxton NG16....... 160 C3
  Wingerworth S42 .. 114 D4
Hill Top Rd DE55 ... 170 C5
Hill Top Rise SK23 .. 45 D8
Hilltops View DE4 .. 143 D5
Hilltop Way S18 .... 76 A7
Hill View
  Duffield DE56 ..... 190 D3
  Repton DE65 ...... 242 E2

Hill View continued
  Whaley Bridge SK23 . 45 C8
Hill View Cl DE7 .... 192 B7
Hillview Ct NG19 ... 136 D4
Hill View Gr DE21 .. 220 E5
Hillview Ho **1** DE7 .. 267 B2
Hillwood Dr SK13 ... 17 F8
Hilton Cl
  Derby DE3 .... 217 D1
  Long Eaton NG10... 235 F4
  Swadlincote DE11 .. 256 A7
Hilton Gdns DE72 .. 246 A7
Hilton Ind Est DE65 . 228 D3
Hilton Park Dr DE55 . 170 C8
Hilton Prim Sch DE65 .228 D2
Hilton Rd
  Disley SK12 .... 32 B7
  Egginton DE65...... 241 B7
  Etwall DE65 .... 229 B4
Hinckley Ct DE4 .... 110 F1
Hind Ave DE72 ..... 235 C8
Hindersitch La DE4 . 156 D2
Hindscarth Cres DE21 .217 E1
Hinton Gr SK14 .... 115 A8
Hipley Cl S40 ...... 95 B6
Hipper St S40 ..... 266 B2
Hipper St W S40 .... 95 E2
Hipper St S40 ..... 266 B2
Hixon's La DE7 .... 208 B1
Hoades St S42 ..... 131 C8
Hoargate La DE6.... 200 F2
Hobart Cl
  Burton u T DE15.... 248 C2
  Derby DE3 .... 217 F2
Hobart Dr NG9 .... 209 F1
Hob Hill DE56 ..... 190 B8
Hob Hill Mdws SK13 .17 D7
Hobhouse Rd NG19 . 135 D2
Hob Hurst's Ho* DE45 .111 F7
Hobkirk Dr DE24 .. 231 E2
Hob La DE6 .... 176 C8
Hobsic Cl NG16 ... 182 D8
Hobsic La NG16..... 171 E8
Hobson Dr
  Derby DE21 .... 220 F2
  Ilkeston DE7 ..... 208 E6
Hobson Moor Rd SK14 . 9 A7
Hockerley Ave SK23 . 45 D8
Hockerley Cl SK23 . 45 D8
Hockerley La SK23 . 45 C8
Hockerley New Rd SK23 .45 D8
Hockley La
  Ashover S45 ...... 130 A1
  Wingerworth S42 .. 115 A3
Hockley Way DE55 . 159 B2
Hodder Cl DE4 .... 156 F2
Hodge Beck Cl DE24 .233 C6
Hodge Fold SK14 .. 15 F8
Hodge La
  Broadbottom SK14 . 15 F8
  Marchington ST14 . 224 A1
Hodmire La S44 ... 133 E7
Hodthorpe Cl DE21 . 206 B1
Hodthorpe Prim Sch S80 .82 C5
Hogarth Cl NG9..... 223 E6
Hogarth Rd S41 ... 223 B8
Hogarth Rise S18 .. 75 F8
Hogbarn La DE75, NG16 .181 D5
Hoggs Field NG16 . 182 F2
Hogshaw Villas Rd **1**
  SK17................. 85 C3
Hoillant Sq DE6..... 175 E3
Holbeach Dr S40.... 114 E8
Holbeck Ave S44 ... 99 C2
Holbeck Cl S41 .... 266 C4
Holbeck La S80 .... 101 D8
Holbeck St S80 .... 81 D1
Holbein Cl S18 .... 75 F8
Holborn Dr DE22... 218 A7
Holborn View DE5 . 170 B1
Holbrook Ave
  North Wingfield S42 .132 A7
  Sheffield S20........ 60 A8
Holbrook CE Prim Sch
  DE56 .... 191 D7
Holbrook Cl
  Chesterfield S40 ... 114 C8
  Pleasley NG19...... 135 A5
Holbrook Dr S13.... 44 B6
Holbrook Gn S20 .. 60 A8
Holbrook Pl S43 ... 97 C6
Holbrook Rd
  Belper DE56........ 178 F2
  Derby DE24 ...... 233 B6
  Sheffield S13 ..... 44 B7
Holbrook St DE75... 182 A2
Holbrook View S42 . 192 A8
Holbrook Way S42 . 132 A7
Holcombe St DE23 . 57 A2
Holcombe St DE23 . 219 B1
Holden Ave DE72 .. 246 A8
Holden Ct DE24 ... 233 C7
Holden Gdns **1** NG9... 223 E6
Holderness Cl DE24 . 231 D2
Holdings The DE11... 256 A1
Holdon Croft DE12 . 261 D7
Helestone Gate Rd S45 .129 D1
Holker Ave SK17 ... 85 C8
Holker Rd SK17 .... 85 C7
Holkham Cl DE7 ... 194 C3
Holland Cl DE55 ... 170 B1
Holland Mdw NG10 . 236 D5
Holland Pl **8** S2 ..... 43 A8

Holland Rd
Chesterfield S41 . . . . .76 F2
Sheffield S2 . . . . .43 A8
Hollbank Cotts DE55 . . . . . .158 B3
Hollens Way S40 . . . . .95 A5
Hollies Cl
Clifton DE6 . . . . .184 F6
Dronfield S18 . . . . .76 C8
Newton Solney DE15 . . . . .248 E8
Hollies Dr SK6 . . . . .23 A5
Hollies Farm Cl DE73 . . . . . .244 E3
Hollies La DE6 . . . . .198 C4
Hollies Rd DE22 . . . . .204 D3
Hollies The
Eastwood NG16 . . . . .182 F2
Repton DE65 . . . . .243 A1
Sandiacre NG10 . . . . .223 A5
Shirebrook NG20 . . . . .119 E2
Hollin Cl S41 . . . . .95 C8
Hollin Cross La SK13 . . . . . . .17 C8
Hollindale Dr S12 . . . . .44 C5
Hollin Dr SK23 . . . . .47 B5
Hollington Cl DE21 . . . . .219 F7
Hollington Rd ST14 . . . . . . .196 D3
Hollingworth Cres S43 . . . . .78 A1
Hollingwood Prim Sch
S43 . . . . .78 A1
Hollingworth Ave NG10 . . .223 B3
Hollingworth Prim Sch
SK14 . . . . .9 C5
Hollinhey Terr SK14 . . . . .9 C5
Hollin Hill Rd S43 . . . . .81 A3
Hollins Ave SK17 . . . . .85 B7
Hollins Bank 41 SK13 . . . . . . .9 D2
Hollins Cl 40 SK13 . . . . .9 D2
Hollinsclough CE Prim Sch
SK17 . . . . .104 D2
Hollinsclough Rake
SK17 . . . . .104 B2
Hollinsend Ave S12 . . . . .44 C5
Hollinsend Pl S12 . . . . .44 C5
Hollinsend Rd S12 . . . . .44 B5
Hollins Fold 45 SK13 . . . . .9 D2
Hollins Gdns 39 SK13 . . . . . . .9 D2
Hollins Gr 37 SK13 . . . . .9 D2
Hollins Ind Est SK13 . . . . . . .10 B5
Hollins La
Crich DE4 . . . . .157 A4
Marple SK6 . . . . .23 C8
Hollins Mews 44 SK13 . . . . . .9 D2
Hollinsmoor Rd SK6, SK22 .24 D7
Hollins Mount SK6 . . . . .23 B8
Hollins Spring Ave S18 . . . .76 A8
Hollins Spring Rd S18 . . . . .76 A8
Hollins St SK17 . . . . .85 B7
Hollins The DE4 . . . . .156 A6
Hollins Way 46 SK13 . . . . .9 D2
Hollins Wood Cl DE4 . . . . . .156 A5
Hollinwood La SK6 . . . . .23 B2
Hollinwood Rd SK12 . . . . . . .32 D6
Hollis La
Chesterfield S41 . . . . .266 C2
Denstone ST14 . . . . .196 B6
Hollis St DE24 . . . . .233 A8
Holllins Ave 47 SK13 . . . . .9 D2
Holloway Rd
Derby DE24 . . . . .232 F6
Duffield DE56 . . . . .190 E4
Hollow Cres DE15 . . . . .248 C4
Hollowford Rd S33 . . . . .38 B4
Hollowford Training &
Conference Ctr S33 . . . . . . .38 C4
Hollow Gate S33 . . . . .51 A7
Hollow La
Burton u T DE15 . . . . .248 C4
Mayfield DE6 . . . . .172 C1
Sheffield, Mosborough S20 . .59 D6
Sheffield, O'the Moor SK17 . .87 E4
Hollowood Ave DE24 . . . . . .231 C8
Hollow Rd DE73 . . . . .252 E2
Hollows The NG10 . . . . .237 A8
Holly Ave
Breaston DE72 . . . . .222 F1
Ripley DE5 . . . . .180 D8
Hollybank S12 . . . . .44 B6
Holly Bank
Glossop SK13 . . . . .17 E8
Hollingworth SK14 . . . . .9 D5
Hollybank Ave S12 . . . . .44 C6
Hollybank Cl
Sheffield S12 . . . . .44 C6
Swadlincote DE11 . . . . .256 A7
Holly Bank Cl
New Houghton NG19 . . . . . . .135 A6
South Wingfield DE55 . . . . . . .158 B3
Hollybank Cres S12 . . . . .44 C6
Holly Bank Ct DE4 . . . . .156 F1
Hollybank Dr S12 . . . . .44 D6
Hollybank Rd S12 . . . . .44 C6
Hollybank Way S12 . . . . .44 D6
Hollybrook Way DE23 . . . . .230 F6
Holly Brook Way DE23 . . . .230 F6
Holly Bush Cl DE12 . . . . .264 F7
Holly Bush La DE56 . . . . .191 A6
Holly Cl
Ashbourne DE6 . . . . .185 D8
Chesterfield S41 . . . . .77 A3
Draycott DE72 . . . . .235 A7
Killamarsh S21 . . . . .60 C5
Holly Croft DE15 . . . . .248 C2

Holly Ct
Aston-on-T DE72 . . . . .246 A7
3 Chesterfield S40 . . . . .95 C2
Derby DE3 . . . . .217 D1
2 Mansfield NG19 . . . . .136 E1
Woodville DE11 . . . . .256 F2
Holly Gdns S12 . . . . .44 C6
Holly Gn DE15 . . . . .254 F8
Holly Gr
Sheffield S12 . . . . .44 C6
Swanwick DE55 . . . . .169 F8
Holly Hill Rd NG16 . . . . .171 F6
Hollyhock Way ST14 . . . . . . .253 E6
Hollyhouse Dr DE55 . . . . . . .160 B6
Holly House La DE56 . . . . . . .178 C4
Holly House Specl Sch
S41 . . . . .77 A3
Hollyhurst La DE6 . . . . .212 B6
Hollyhurst Row DE55 . . . . . .170 F6
Holly La
Alderwasley DE56 . . . . .167 D4
Tansley DE4 . . . . .144 A4
Hollymoor Dr DE73 . . . . .232 F2
Holly Mount 2 SK13 . . . . . . .10 D1
Holly Rd
Kimberley NG16 . . . . .195 F7
Mansfield NG19 . . . . .136 F2
Uttoxeter ST14 . . . . .210 B3
Holly St DE55 . . . . .254 F8
Hollythorpe Cl S41 . . . . .115 D8
Hollythorpe Cres S8 . . . . . . .43 A4
Hollythorpe Rd S8 . . . . .43 B4
Hollythorpe Rise S8 . . . . . . .43 B4
Hollywell Ave S43 . . . . .181 B7
Hollywell Prim Sch
NG16 .195 F7
Hollywood Rd Sk6 . . . . .23 F8
Holm Ave DE21 . . . . .205 B7
Holm Cl S18 . . . . .56 D2
Holme Bank DE6 . . . . .184 D7
Holmebank Cl S40 . . . . .95 E4
Holmebank E S40 . . . . .95 F4
Holmebank View S40 . . . . . . .95 E4
Holmebank W S40 . . . . .95 E4
Holmebrook Cl S40 . . . . .95 D5
Holmebrook View S41 . . . . . .95 C6
Holme Cl
Hatton DE65 . . . . .227 C1
Holloway DE4 . . . . .156 A5
Ilkeston DE7 . . . . .194 D2
Holme Croft DE7 . . . . .207 E7
Holme Ct DE45 . . . . .109 D5
Holme Farm Ave DE55 . . . .254 F8
Holmefield Cres DE7 . . . . . .209 A8
Holmefield Rd S80 . . . . .82 A6
Holme Hall Cres S40 . . . . . . .95 B5
Holme Hall Prim Sch S40 .95 B5
Holme La
Bakewell DE45 . . . . .109 D7
Derby DE21 . . . . .220 C3
Holme Lea 2 NG10 . . . . .223 B6
Holme Park Ave S41 . . . . .95 C7
Holme Rd
Chesterfield S41 . . . . .96 A6
Matlock Bath DE4 . . . . .143 B1
Holmes Cl DE11 . . . . .256 B5
Holmes Ct DE11 . . . . .256 B5
Holmesdale Cl S18 . . . . .57 C3
Holmesdale Inf Sch S18 . . . .57 C2
Holmesdale Rd S18 . . . . .57 C3
Holmesfield Cl DE4 . . . . .144 A5
Holmesfield Dr
Derby DE3 . . . . .217 F2
Shipley DE75 . . . . .194 A8
Holmesfield Rd S18 . . . . .56 B1
Holmes Rd DE72 . . . . .235 D8
Holmes St
Derby DE23 . . . . .219 A2
Heanor DE75 . . . . .181 D2
Holmewood Ave NE7 . . . . . .194 F5
Holmewood Bsns Pk
S42 . . . . .116 C2
Holmewood Dr NG16 . . . . . .195 B8
Holmewood Ind Est S42 . .132 F8
Holmewood Ind Pk S42 . . .116 D1
Holme Woods La HD9 . . . . . . .2 F6
Holmfield
Buxton SK17 . . . . .84 E6
Derby DE23 . . . . .231 E7
Holmgate Prim Sch S45 . .131 A4
Holmgate Rd S45 . . . . .131 A4
Holm La DE55 . . . . .158 C7
Holmleigh Way DE73 . . . . . .244 F8
Holmley Bank S18 . . . . .57 A3
Holmley La S18 . . . . .57 A3
Holmoak Cl DE21 . . . . .206 B3
Holmshaw Dr S13 . . . . .44 E8
Holmshaw Gr S13 . . . . .44 E8
Holmwood Terr 2 SK17 . . . .85 C8
Holt's La DE13 . . . . .239 B6
Holt Ave DE24 . . . . .233 C6
Holt Dr DE4 . . . . .142 F7
Holt La
Lea DE4 . . . . .156 B7
Matlock DE4 . . . . .143 B5
Holtlands Dr DE24 . . . . .232 F5
Holt Rd DE4 . . . . .127 F1
Holyhead Dr DE21 . . . . .206 B3
Holymoor Rd S42 . . . . .113 E8
Holyoake Ave S13 . . . . .44 E8
Holyoake Dr NG10 . . . . .236 F7
Holyrood Ho DE24 . . . . .219 D1
Holy Rosary RC Prim Sch
DE15 .248 A3
Holy Trinity CE Prim Sch
DE4 . . . . .155 A8
Holywell DE45 . . . . .109 D4

Holywell La DE45 . . . . .125 B5
Holywell Rd DE7 . . . . .194 C3
Holywell St S41 . . . . .266 B3
Homecroft Dr NG16 . . . . . . .171 E7
Home Farm Cl DE72 . . . . . . .221 C5
Home Farm Cotts SK17 . . .105 C2
Home Farm Ct
Castle Gresley DE11 . . . . .255 D1
Selston NG16 . . . . .171 C6
Home Farm Dr DE22 . . . . . . .205 A4
Home Farm Ho DE15 . . . . . .249 A3
Home Farm Park Homes
DE13 .240 A5
Homefields Prim Sch
DE73 .232 E1
Homemoss Ho SK17 . . . . .85 A8
Homeport Mews S41 . . . . . .266 B4
Homer Dr SK6 . . . . .23 B8
Homestead NG16 . . . . .182 A4
Homestead Rd S42 . . . . .32 C6
Homestead Way SK23 . . . . . .47 C5
Honeycroft Cl DE56 . . . . . . .179 B2
Honeycroft Ct DE55 . . . . . . .160 B4
Honeyfield Dr DE5 . . . . .180 F8
Honeysuckle Cl DE11 . . . . . .256 A6
Honeysuckle Dr DE55 . . . . .160 B7
Honeysuckle View DE15 . .255 A8
Honeywall La DE6 . . . . .183 E8
Honiton Cl 11 S41 . . . . .95 F8
Honiton Ct S17 . . . . .194 C3
Hook La ST14 . . . . .210 B6
Hoole St S41 . . . . .115 D8
Hooley Cl NG10 . . . . .236 B6
Hooley St NG16 . . . . .171 F6
Hoon La DE65 . . . . .228 A3
Hoon Rd DE65 . . . . .239 D8
Hoonwell La DE6 . . . . .175 F5
Hope Ave DE3 . . . . .217 D2
Hopedale Rd S12 . . . . .44 D4
Hopefield Ave S12 . . . . .44 D4
Hope Prim Sch S33 . . . . .39 A4
Hope Rd S33 . . . . .39 D2
Hope St
Chesterfield S40 . . . . .95 E3
Derby DE1 . . . . .267 C2
Glossop SK13 . . . . .10 E2
2 Ilkeston DE7 . . . . .208 F7
Melbourne DE73 . . . . .252 A7
Hope Sta S33 . . . . .39 C3
Hope Terr DE4 . . . . .143 B2
Hopetoun St DE23 . . . . .232 A8
Hope Valley Coll S33 . . . . . . .38 F3
Hopewell Rd DE4 . . . . .143 C6
Hopewell Wlk DE7 . . . . .194 F5
Hop Inge The S26 . . . . .61 F5
Hopkins Ct NG16 . . . . .182 F3
Hopmeadow Way DE15 . . . .248 A1
Hopping Hill DE56 . . . . .190 F8
Hopping Hill Terr E
DE56 .191 A7
Hopping Hill Terr W
DE56 .191 A7
Hopping La DE45 . . . . .125 B3
Hopton Cl
Derby DE21 . . . . .206 A1
Ripley DE5 . . . . .169 F1
Hoptonwood Cl DE4 . . . . . . .154 D4
Hopwell Rd DE72 . . . . .222 A2
Horace Ave NG9 . . . . .223 D6
Hordern Cl SK13 . . . . .10 A4
Hordern La SK23 . . . . .47 B5
Horderns Park Rd SK23 . . . .47 B5
Horeston Cotts DE7 . . . . . . .192 B7
Hornbeam Cl
Brimington S43 . . . . .78 A2
Derby DE21 . . . . .205 E2
Derby DE21 . . . . .220 B6
Hornbeams The 2 ST14 .210 A1
Horncastle Rd DE21 . . . . . . .205 D1
Horner Rd 1 S7 . . . . .43 A7
Hornscroft Rd S44 . . . . .99 A1
Hornsea Rd DE21 . . . . .205 D1
Hornthorpe Rd S21 . . . . .59 C2
Horridge St DE7 . . . . .194 F4
Horsecroft Cl DE7 . . . . .194 D2
Horsedale DE4 . . . . .142 C1
Horse Fair Ave SK23 . . . . . . .47 A6
Horsehead La S44 . . . . .99 C2
Horse & Jockey Yd 7
DE6 . . . . .173 C2
Horseshoe Ave SK17 . . . . . . .47 F1
Horse Shoes The DE74 . . . .247 D4
Horsewood Rd S40 . . . . .114 B8
Horsley CE Prim Sch
DE21 .192 D6
Horsley Cl
Holbrook DE56 . . . . .191 C7
Langley Mill NG16 . . . . .182 A3
Horsleygate La S18 . . . . .74 F7
Horsleygate Rd S17, S18 . . .74 B7
Horsley La DE21 . . . . .191 E4
Horsley Rd DE21, DE56 . . . .191 F6
Horsley Woodhouse Prim
Sch DE7 . . . . .192 D6
Horton Cl
Sheffield S20 . . . . .59 E7
Swanwick DE55 . . . . .169 F8
Horton Dr S20 . . . . .59 F7
Horton St DE23 . . . . .219 C2
Horwood Ave S20 . . . . .59 F7
Hoselett Field Rd NG10 . . .236 E5
Hospital La DE3 . . . . .230 B7
Houfton Cres S44 . . . . .98 F3
Houfton Rd S44 . . . . .98 F3
Houghton Ave DE7 . . . . .194 C3
Houghton Ct SK22 . . . . .25 C2

Houghton Ct 7 DE21 . . . .205 F2
Houldsworth Cres S44 . . . . .98 F2
Houldsworth Dr S41 . . . . . . .96 E2
Hoult St DE22 . . . . .218 D4
Houndkirk Rd S11 . . . . .42 F7
Hounslow Rd DE22 . . . . .218 B6
Houston Cl DE21 . . . . .220 B6
Hoveton Cl DE24 . . . . .232 D3
Howard Cl
Glossop SK13 . . . . .10 B2
11 Long Eaton NG10 . . . . . . .223 E1
Howard Dr
Chesterfield S41 . . . . .77 A2
North Wingfield S42 . . . . .131 F5
Howards Mdw SK13 . . . . .17 B7
Howard St
Derby DE23 . . . . .218 F2
Glossop SK13 . . . . .10 C1
Howarth Cl NG10 . . . . .236 A7
Howden Cl
Derby DE3 . . . . .217 C1
Staveley S43 . . . . .78 F2
Swadlincote DE11 . . . . .256 A5
Howden Rd SK22 . . . . .24 C1
Howells Pl S43 . . . . .79 B3
Howe St DE22 . . . . .218 D5
Howitt Cres ST14 . . . . .210 B2
Howitt St
Heanor DE75 . . . . .181 F2
Long Eaton NG10 . . . . .236 E7
How La S33 . . . . .38 C3
Howth Cl DE21 . . . . .220 A4
Hoylake Ave S40 . . . . .114 C7
Hoylake Cl NG19 . . . . .136 D6
Hoylake Ct DE3 . . . . .217 C3
Hoylake Dr DE3 . . . . .217 C3
Hoyland Ct DE56 . . . . .179 E5
Hoyle Ct DE45 . . . . .109 D5
Hubert Shaw Cl DE24 . . . . .232 E4
Huckerby Rd DE7 . . . . .194 C2
Hucklow Ave
Chesterfield S40 . . . . .266 A1
North Wingfield S42 . . . . .132 A8
Staveley S43 . . . . .97 D7
Hucklow Bank 35 SK13 . . . . . .9 D2
Hucklow Cl DE21 . . . . .206 B3
Hucklow Fold 34 SK13 . . . . . . .9 D2
Hucklow Lanes 33 SK13 . . . . .9 D2
Hucknall Ave S40 . . . . .95 C4
Hudson Cl S26 . . . . .61 E7
Hudson Mount S44 . . . . .118 B8
Hudson Way DE24 . . . . .219 C3
Hufton's Ct DE75 . . . . .194 A7
Hufton's Dr DE75 . . . . .194 A7
Hugh La S33 . . . . .51 A7
Hugh St SK13 . . . . .10 B1
Hulland CE Prim Sch
DE6 . . . . .175 F3
Hulland St DE1 . . . . .267 D1
Hulland View DE22 . . . . .204 D1
Humber Cl DE24 . . . . .233 C6
Humber Rd NG10 . . . . .223 C1
Humber Rd DE65 . . . . .228 C1
Humbleton Dr DE22 . . . . . . .218 A5
Humphrey Rd S8 . . . . .56 E8
Hundall Cl 4 S40 . . . . .95 D6
Hundall La
Unstone S18 . . . . .77 A4
Hungerhill La S42, S45 . . . . .113 B4
Hunger La DE6 . . . . .188 E3
Hungry La
Bradwell S33 . . . . .51 A6
Hathersage S32 . . . . .53 B8
Hunloke Ave S40 . . . . .95 E1
Hunloke Cres S40 . . . . .95 E1
Hunloke Park Prim Sch
S42 . . . . .115 A4
Hunloke Rd S42 . . . . .132 E8
Hunloke View S42 . . . . .115 B4
Hunsdon Rd S21 . . . . .59 C3
Hunstone Ave S8 . . . . .57 A7
Hunt Ave DE75 . . . . .181 E2
Hunt Dr DE11 . . . . .256 C4
Hunter's La S13 . . . . .44 C6
Hunter's Rd DE56 . . . . .191 F8
Hunter Pk S18 . . . . .57 C1
Hunter Rd DE56 . . . . .179 D5
Hunters Chase NG19 . . . . . .136 B2
Hunters Croft DE24 . . . . . . .231 E2
Hunters Green Cl SK23 . . . .34 E1
Hunters La SK13 . . . . .16 F8
Huntingdon Ave S44 . . . . . . .99 B1
Huntingdon Ct DE73 . . . . . .252 B8
Huntingdon Dr DE74 . . . . . .247 A4
Huntingdon Gn DE21 . . . . . .219 C6
Huntingdon Rd DE15 . . . . . .254 D7
Huntingdon Way NG9 . . . . .223 F2
Huntington Wlk 2
NG10 .223 B5
Hunt La S45 . . . . .145 B8
Huntley Ave DE21 . . . . .220 F5
Huntley Cl S43 . . . . .97 B8
Hunts La DE12 . . . . .264 E8
Huntsman Rd S43 . . . . .78 F2
Huntspill Rd DE65 . . . . .228 E1
Hunts Row DE55 . . . . .157 E3
Hunt Way DE11 . . . . .256 E4
Hurdlow Gn 10 SK13 . . . . .9 D1
Hurdlow Lea 12 SK13 . . . . . . .9 D1
Hurdlow Mews SK13 . . . . .9 D1
Hurdlow Way 43 SK13 . . . . . . .9 D1
Hurds Hollow DE4 . . . . .143 A6
Hurker Rise DE4 . . . . .143 C7
Hurl Dr S12 . . . . .43 F5
Hurley Ct DE7 . . . . .207 E8
Hurlfield Ct S12 . . . . .44 A6

Hurlfield Dr S12 . . . . .43 F6
Hurlfield Rd S12 . . . . .43 F5
Hurstbrook Cl SK13 . . . . .10 E1
Hurst Cl S13 . . . . .10 E1
Hurstclough La S32, S33 . . .40 D2
Hurst Cres SK13 . . . . .17 E8
Hurst Ct DE12 . . . . .264 F4
Hurst Dr
Burton u T DE13 . . . . .240 E1
Stanley DE7 . . . . .207 C6
Hurst La DE55 . . . . .146 A5
Hurst Lea Rd SK22 . . . . .33 C7
Hurst Rd SK13 . . . . .10 F1
Hurst Rise DE4 . . . . .143 D5
Huss's La NG10 . . . . .236 F7
Hutchings Cres S43 . . . . .80 D5
Huthwaite All Saints CE Inf
Sch NG17 . . . . .148 F2
Huthwaite La DE55 . . . . .148 C2
Hut La
Ashover S45 . . . . .129 E6
Killamarsh S21 . . . . .60 F4
Hutmoor Butts S17 . . . . . . .107 A3
Hutton St DE24 . . . . .232 E6
Huxley Cl DE23 . . . . .231 F7
Hyde Bank Ct SK22 . . . . .33 C7
Hyde Bank Rd SK22 . . . . .33 C8
Hyde Park Rd DE22 . . . . .218 A6
Hyde Rd SK14 . . . . .9 A4
Hydro Cl DE4 . . . . .91 F6
Hylton Cl DE14 . . . . .254 A7
Hyndley Rd S44 . . . . .98 F3

Ian Ave DE4 . . . . .165 F7
Ians Way S40 . . . . .95 C4
Ibbotsons Croft S32 . . . . .53 A8
Ibbotsons Farm Cotts S32 .53 A8
Ibsley Cl DE24 . . . . .233 C6
Ida's Rd S21 . . . . .59 D4
Ikea Way NG16 . . . . .195 C7
Ilam Cl S43 . . . . .97 C6
Ilam Ct DE6 . . . . .185 D8
Ilam Sq DE7 . . . . .194 E5
Ilford Cl DE7 . . . . .194 D3
Ilford Ct S43 . . . . .77 D4
Ilford Rd DE22 . . . . .218 A5
Ilford Wlk DE22 . . . . .218 A5
Ilfracombe Cr 1 S41 . . . . . . .95 F8
Ilion St NG19 . . . . .135 F2
Ilkeston Com Hospl DE7 .194 D4
Ilkeston Rd
Heanor DE75 . . . . .193 F8
Sandiacre DE7, NG10 . . . . . . .223 C8
Smalley DE7 . . . . .192 F2
Stanton-by-D DE7 . . . . .208 F3
Stapleford NG9 . . . . .209 F2
Trowell NG9 . . . . .209 C5
Ilkeston Sch DE7 . . . . .208 D8
Immingham Gr S43 . . . . .78 D1
Imperial Ct DE22 . . . . .204 D5
Imperial Rd DE24 . . . . .143 B5
Inchwood Cl 4 NG9 . . . . . . .223 F2
Independent Hill DE55 . . . .158 F3
Industrial St 8 DE7 . . . . . . .194 F1
Infirmary Rd S41 . . . . .266 C4
Ingham Dr DE3 . . . . .230 D8
Ingham Rd NG10 . . . . .223 C2
Ingleborough Gdns 6
NG10 .236 A8
Ingleby Ave DE23 . . . . .231 F7
Ingleby Cl
Dronfield S18 . . . . .56 C1
Swadlincote DE73 . . . . .251 A5
Ingleby La DE73 . . . . .251 A5
Ingleby Rd
Barrow u T DE73 . . . . .244 D3
Long Eaton NG10 . . . . .235 F4
Ingle Cl DE21 . . . . .220 E5
Ingledew Cl 1 DE21 . . . . . . .205 F1
Inglefield Rd DE7 . . . . .209 A6
Ingleton Rd S41 . . . . .115 B7
Inglewood Ave DE3 . . . . . . .217 D4
Ingliston Cl DE24 . . . . .233 D6
Inkerman St NE7 . . . . .194 C5
Inkerman Rd NG16 . . . . .171 F5
Inkerman St NG16 . . . . .171 F5
Inkersall Dr S20 . . . . .59 E8
Inkersall Green Rd S43 . . . . .97 C7
Inkersall Prim Sch S43 . . . . .97 C7
Inkersall Rd S43 . . . . .97 E7
Inn La DE22 . . . . .204 B7
Inns La DE55 . . . . .157 E4
Institute La DE55 . . . . .159 A4
Instow Dr DE23 . . . . .231 D6
Intake La
Bakewell DE45 . . . . .109 E3
Cromford DE4 . . . . .156 A6
Holloway DE4 . . . . .155 E4
Intake Prim Sch S12 . . . . . . .44 C6
Intake Rd S44 . . . . .118 C3
Intakes La DE56 . . . . .188 C7
Interchange 25 Bsns Pk
NG10 .223 A4
Inveraray Cl DE24 . . . . .231 E4
Invernia Cl DE23 . . . . .231 E5
Iona Dr
Derby DE24 . . . . .231 E4
Tibshelf DE55 . . . . .147 F5
Iona Cl DE24 . . . . .231 E4
Ireland Cl S43 . . . . .78 F1
Ireland St S43 . . . . .78 F2
Ireland Trad Est S43 . . . . . . .78 F1

Ireton Cl DE56 . . . . .179 E3
Ireton Ct DE6 . . . . .165 B1
Iron Cliff Rd S44 . . . . .98 F3
Irongate S40 . . . . .266 B3
Iron Gate DE1 . . . . .267 B3
Ironside Cl S14 . . . . .43 D3
Ironside Pl S14 . . . . .43 E3
Ironside Rd S14 . . . . .43 E3
Ironside Wlk S14 . . . . .43 D2
Ironville & Codnor Park Prim
  Sch NG16 . . . . .170 F4
Ironwalls La DE13 . . . . .239 C5
Irvine Cl DE24 . . . . .231 D3
Irving Pl DE24 . . . . .232 F7
Isaac's La NG9 . . . . .223 D7
Island Cl DE11 . . . . .262 C8
Island The NG16 . . . . .182 F1
Islay Cl NG9 . . . . .209 D3
Islay Rd DE24 . . . . .231 E4
Isleworth Dr DE22 . . . . .217 F6
Ismay Rd DE21 . . . . .219 F6
Ivan Brook Cl ◆ S18 . . . . . . .56 C1
Ivanhoe Cl S42 . . . . .115 D1
Ivanhoe Ct ◆ S41 . . . . .96 A6
Iveagh Wlk DE55 . . . . .170 E5
Ivonbrook Cl DE4 . . . . .142 B8
Ivybridge Cl DE21 . . . . .206 C3
Ivy Cl
  Chesterfield S41 . . . . .77 A2
  Donisthorpe DE12 . . . . .262 E1
  Willington DE65 . . . . .242 A5
Ivycroft SK13 . . . . .9 E4
Ivy Ct
  Derby DE3 . . . . .217 D1
  Egginton DE65 . . . . .241 A5
  Hilton DE65 . . . . .228 D1
  Sheffield S8 . . . . .43 C2
Ivy Farm Cl S43 . . . . .80 E3
Ivy Gr DE5 . . . . .169 D1
Ivy House Sch DE23 . . . . . . .219 C2
Ivy La
  Eastwood NG16 . . . . .182 E2
  Elton DE4 . . . . .140 E6
Ivyleaf Way DE21 . . . . .231 B6
Ivy Lodge Cl DE15 . . . . .254 E7
Ivy Side Cl S21 . . . . .60 D6
Ivy Side Gdns S21 . . . . .60 D6
Ivy Spring Cl S42 . . . . .115 B4
Ivy Sq DE23 . . . . .219 C2
Ivywood Gdns S44 . . . . .98 A5

J

Jack's La ST14 . . . . .224 E2
Jackass La DE56 . . . . .167 B4
Jackdaw Cl DE22 . . . . .218 D5
Jacklin Cl DE14 . . . . .254 A6
Jacksdale Cl DE22 . . . . .204 D1
Jacksdale Prim Sch
  NG16 . . . . .171 B3
Jackson's La
  Heage DE56 . . . . .179 D7
  Ripley DE5 . . . . .169 A8
Jackson Ave
  Derby DE3 . . . . .218 A2
  Ilkeston DE7 . . . . .208 E8
  Sandiacre NG10 . . . . .223 A6
  Tupton S42 . . . . .131 C8
Jackson Cl DE12 . . . . .262 B3
Jackson Rd
  Bramley-Vale S44 . . . . .117 C6
  Clay Cross S45 . . . . .131 E3
  Matlock DE4 . . . . .143 B6
Jacksons Edge Rd SK12 . . . .32 B6
Jacksons La
  Belper DE56 . . . . .190 E7
  Etwall DE65 . . . . .229 C2
Jackson St
  Derby DE22 . . . . .218 C4
  Glossop, Padfield SK13 . . . . .10 C5
  Glossop SK13 . . . . .17 C7
  Mottram in t. SK14 . . . . .9 A3
Jackson Tor Rd DE4 . . . . . . .143 B6
Jackys La S26 . . . . .61 E6
Jacobean Ct DE15 . . . . .248 C4
Jagger's La S32 . . . . .52 E8
Jaggers La DE4 . . . . .128 E5
Jago Ave S41 . . . . .81 A4
James's La DE6 . . . . .215 C1
James Andrew Cl S8 . . . . . . .56 F7
James Andrew Cres S8 . . . . .56 F7
James Andrew Croft S8 . . . . .56 F7
James Ave DE55 . . . . .170 D7
James Brindley Way
  DE13 . . . . .240 F1
James Cl DE1 . . . . .218 E5
James St
  Chesterfield S41 . . . . .96 A6
  ◼ Glossop SK13 . . . . .17 C6
  Kimberley NG16 . . . . .195 F6
  Somercotes DE55 . . . . .170 C7
  Swadlincote DE11 . . . . .256 D5
James Walton Cl S20 . . . . . . .59 F7
James Walton Dr S20 . . . . . .59 F7
James Walton Pl S20 . . . . . . .59 F7
James Walton View S20 . . . . .59 F7
Jane La SK23 . . . . .34 B1
Jap La DE45 . . . . .110 E8
Jardine Ct DE72 . . . . .235 B7
Jardines La ST14 . . . . .196 D4
Jarnett The SK17 . . . . .107 B8
Jarvey's La DE22 . . . . .217 E8
Jarvis Ct DE24 . . . . .231 E2
Jarvis Rd DE24 . . . . .231 E2

Jasmin Cl NG20 . . . . .119 D6
Jasmine Cl
  Burton u T DE15 . . . . .255 A8
  Derby DE21 . . . . .220 B5
  Swanwick DE55 . . . . .169 F7
Jasmine Ct DE75 . . . . .182 B1
Jasmine Dr DE55 . . . . .148 B7
Jaspers La DE4 . . . . .153 A1
Jaunty Ave S12 . . . . .44 A8
Jaunty Cl S12 . . . . .44 B3
Jaunty Cres S12 . . . . .44 C4
Jaunty Dr S12 . . . . .44 B3
Jaunty La S12 . . . . .44 B4
Jaunty Mount S12 . . . . .44 C3
Jaunty Pl S12 . . . . .44 C4
Jaunty Rd S12 . . . . .44 C3
Jaunty View S12 . . . . .44 C3
Jaunty Way S12 . . . . .44 B4
Jawbone La DE73 . . . . .252 C8
Jaw Bones Hill S40 . . . . .115 A8
Jay Ct DE22 . . . . .218 D5
Jebb's La
  Idridgehay DE56 . . . . .176 F8
  Shottle DE56 . . . . .177 B8
Jebb Gdns S40 . . . . .95 C2
Jedburgh Cl DE24 . . . . .233 C6
Jefferson Pl DE24 . . . . .232 F7
Jeffery St ◼ S2 . . . . .43 B6
Jeffrey La S33 . . . . .51 A6
Jeffries Ave DE4 . . . . .156 F1
Jeffries La DE4 . . . . .156 F1
Jellicoe St NG20 . . . . .101 A2
Jemison Cl DE23 . . . . .230 E7
Jemison St NG19 . . . . .136 A1
Jenny's Ct DE56 . . . . .179 C5
Jephson Rd DE14 . . . . .254 B7
Jepson Rd S41 . . . . .115 C7
Jermyn Ave S12 . . . . .44 F4
Jermyn Cl S12 . . . . .44 F3
Jermyn Cres S12 . . . . .44 F4
Jermyn Dr S12 . . . . .44 F3
Jermyn Way S12 . . . . .44 F3
Jersey Rd S2 . . . . .43 A7
Jervis Ct DE7 . . . . .194 F3
Jervis Pl S43 . . . . .97 B6
Jesop Dr DE24 . . . . .231 E2
Jesses La DE56 . . . . .178 C7
Jessop Ave NG16 . . . . .170 F4
Jessop Lo DE5 . . . . .181 B7
Jessop St DE5 . . . . .181 B7
Jetting St S45 . . . . .130 A1
Jill Iain Ct ◼ NG9 . . . . .223 E5
Jinny Cl DE65 . . . . .239 C8
Joan Ave DE75 . . . . .181 E2
Jodrell Ave DE56 . . . . .179 D3
Jodrell Mdw SK23 . . . . .45 E8
Jodrell Rd SK23 . . . . .45 D8
Jodrell St SK22 . . . . .33 B7
John Bank La DE45 . . . . . . .108 F7
John Berrysford Cl DE21 . . . .219 F5
John Dalton St SK13 . . . . .9 E5
John Davies Prim Sch
  NG17 . . . . .148 F3
John Davies Workshops
  NG17 . . . . .148 F3
John Eaton's Almshouses
  S8 . . . . .43 B2
John F Kennedy Gdns
  DE21 . . . . .220 C6
John Flamsteed Com Sch
  DE5 . . . . .180 F8
John Kennedy Rd SK14 . . . . . .9 A3
John King Inf Sch NG16 . . . .160 D3
John King Workshop Mus*
  NG16 . . . . .160 D3
John Lombe Dr DE1 . . . . . . .219 A7
Johnnygate La S18 . . . . .75 A4
John O'Gaunts Way
  DE56 . . . . .179 D4
John of Rolleston Prim Sch
  DE13 . . . . .240 C4
John Port Cl DE65 . . . . .229 C4
John Port Sch DE65 . . . . . . .229 B4
Johnson Ave DE24 . . . . .232 E7
Johnson Dr DE75 . . . . .181 F2
Johnson La
  Idridgehay DE56 . . . . .176 E7
  Monyash DE45 . . . . .107 F6
Johnson Rd ST14 . . . . .210 B1
Johnson St SK23 . . . . .45 E8
Johnson Way SK23 . . . . .47 D6
John St
  Alfreton DE55 . . . . .159 A4
  Brimington S43 . . . . .96 E8
  Chesterfield S40 . . . . .95 E3
  Clay Cross S45 . . . . .131 D4
  Clowne S43 . . . . .80 D3
  Compstall SK6 . . . . .15 B3
  Creswell S80 . . . . .81 E1
  Derby DE1 . . . . .267 C2
  Eckington S21 . . . . .59 D3
  Glossop SK13 . . . . .17 C8
  Ilkeston DE7 . . . . .194 F1
  Marple SK6 . . . . .23 A5
  Matlock DE4 . . . . .143 B6
  North Wingfield S42 . . . . . . .131 E7
  Somercotes DE55 . . . . .170 C8
  Swadlincote, Albert Village
    DE11 . . . . .256 C2
  Swadlincote, Lower Medway
    DE11 . . . . .256 C5
Johnstone Cl S40 . . . . .266 A1
John Turner Rd DE4 . . . . . . .127 C3
Jolly La DE6 . . . . .175 A7
Jones St SK13 . . . . .10 A5

Jordan Ave DE13 . . . . .240 F2
Jordan St SK13 . . . . .10 E1
Jordanthorpe Ctr S8 . . . . . . .57 B6
Jordanthorpe Gn S8 . . . . . . .57 C6
Jordanthorpe Parkway
  S8 . . . . .57 C6
Jordanthorpe View S8 . . . . . .57 C7
Joseph Fletcher Dr S42 . .114 F2
Joseph St
  Belper DE56 . . . . .178 F4
  Derby DE23 . . . . .219 A1
  Eckington S21 . . . . .59 D3
  Marple SK6 . . . . .23 A6
Joseph Wright Ctr (Derby
  Coll) The DE1 . . . . .267 A4
Joseph Wright Terr DE1 . . . .267 B4
Joyce Ave NG9 . . . . .223 F3
Jubalton Cl DE24 . . . . .232 E6
Jubilee Ave DE5 . . . . .169 C1
Jubilee Bsns Pk DE21 . . . . .267 C4
Jubilee Cl DE73 . . . . .252 B7
Jubilee Cotts S44 . . . . .97 A1
Jubilee Cres
  Clowne S43 . . . . .81 A4
  Killamarsh S21 . . . . .60 E7
  Whitwell S80 . . . . .81 F6
Jubilee Ct
  Belper DE56 . . . . .179 A2
  Pinxton NG16 . . . . .160 D3
  West Hallam DE7 . . . . .207 D8
  Wirksworth DE4 . . . . .165 E7
Jubilee Gdns
  New Mills SK22 . . . . .33 C7
  Whitwell S80 . . . . .81 F5
Jubilee Parkway DE21 . . . . .267 C4
Jubilee Pk DE11 . . . . .256 F4
Jubilee Pl S80 . . . . .81 F5
Jubilee Rd
  Chapel-en-le-F SK23 . . . . . . .47 B5
  Derby DE24 . . . . .232 F4
  Whitwell S80 . . . . .81 F5
Jubilee Rise S18 . . . . .248 C3
Jubilee Sq DE6 . . . . .184 D7
Jubilee St
  Kimberley NG16 . . . . .195 E7
  New Mills SK22 . . . . .33 C7
Jubilee Terr DE12 . . . . .262 E1
Judson Ave NG9 . . . . .223 F6
Judy Hill DE4 . . . . .127 F1
Julia Cres S43 . . . . .146 F3
Julian Cl DE7 . . . . .209 B6
Julie Ave DE75 . . . . .182 B1
Julius Cl NG16 . . . . .182 B4
Jumble Rd S11 . . . . .42 F1
Junction Rd NG10 . . . . .237 A6
Junction St DE1 . . . . .218 E4
Juniper Cl S43 . . . . .78 A2
Juniper Ct NG16 . . . . .195 C8
Juniper Rise S21 . . . . .60 C5
Jura Ave DE5 . . . . .169 D2
Jury St DE1 . . . . .267 A3

K

Kariba Cl S41 . . . . .266 C3
Katherine Dr NG9 . . . . .223 F4
Katrine Wlk DE24 . . . . .231 E5
Kay Dr DE11 . . . . .255 F5
Kayes Ct ◼ NG9 . . . . .223 D7
Kean Pl DE24 . . . . .232 F7
Kearsley Rd S2 . . . . .43 A8
Keats Ave DE23 . . . . .218 A1
Keats Cl NG10 . . . . .236 B5
Keats Dr DE11 . . . . .256 C6
Keats Rd
  Chesterfield S41 . . . . .95 F8
  Stonebroom DE55 . . . . .146 F3
Keats Way S42 . . . . .115 E4
Keats Wlk DE55 . . . . .146 F3
Keble Cl
  Burton u T DE15 . . . . .248 C2
  Derby DE1 . . . . .267 C1
Kedelston st DE1 . . . . .267 A4
Kedleston Cl
  Burton u T DE15 . . . . .248 C2
  Chesterfield S41 . . . . .95 C6
  Derby DE22 . . . . .204 D1
  Long Eaton NG10 . . . . .236 A5
  Ripley DE5 . . . . .169 C3
Kedleston Ct
  ◼ Derby DE22 . . . . .204 D2
  ◼ Staveley S43 . . . . .78 E2
  Tibshelf DE55 . . . . .148 B6
Kedleston Dr
  Heanor DE75 . . . . .181 C2
  Ilkeston DE7 . . . . .194 D3
Kedleston Cl DE1 . . . . .267 A4
Kedleston Gdns DE1 . . . . . .267 A4
Kedleston Hall* DE22 . . . . .203 E5
Kedleston Old Rd DE22 . .218 D8
Kedleston Rd
  Buxton SK17 . . . . .85 C7
  Derby DE22 . . . . .218 E2
  Quarndon DE22 . . . . .204 B5
  Weston Underwood DE22 . . .203 E8
Kedleston St DE1 . . . . .267 A4
Keeling La DE4 . . . . .126 B1
Keeling Terr DE4 . . . . .126 B1
Keepers La S18 . . . . .75 E3
Kegworth Ave DE23 . . . . . . .231 C6
Kegworth Rd NG11 . . . . . . .237 E2
Keilder Cl S40 . . . . .95 D1
Kelburn Ave S40 . . . . .95 C1
Keldholme La DE24 . . . . . . .233 D6
Kelgate S20 . . . . .59 D6
Kelham Way NG16 . . . . .182 E3

Kelmoor Rd DE24 . . . . .233 B7
Kelsons Ave S17 . . . . .85 D5
Kelso Wlk DE24 . . . . .231 E2
Kelstedge La S45 . . . . .129 D5
Kelvedon Dr DE23 . . . . .231 A6
Kelvin Cl NG9 . . . . .223 C5
Kemble Pl DE24 . . . . .232 F7
Kemp Cl S21 . . . . .60 C6
Kemp Rd SK6 . . . . .23 C7
Kempton Cl NG16 . . . . .195 E7
Kempton Park Rd DE24 . . . .232 D8
Kempton Rd DE15 . . . . .248 A3
Kendal Cl SK17 . . . . .85 C4
Kendal Dr S18 . . . . .56 E1
Kendal Rd S41 . . . . .95 E8
Kendal Wlk ◼ DE21 . . . . . . .205 D1
Kendon Ave DE23 . . . . .231 E6
Kendray Cl DE56 . . . . .191 F8
Kendricks Cl DE11 . . . . .257 A7
Kenilworth Ave DE23 . . . . . .231 F8
Kenilworth Ct ◼ S41 . . . . . . .96 A6
Kenilworth Dr DE7 . . . . .208 D5
Kenilworth Rd DE5 . . . . .169 C1
Kenmere Cl S45 . . . . .131 D2
Kennack Cl DE55 . . . . .160 C6
Kennedy Ave
  Long Eaton NG10 . . . . .236 C5
  Mansfield Woodhouse
    NG19 . . . . .136 D4
Kennedy Cl DE21 . . . . .220 A7
Kennedy Dr NG9 . . . . .223 F3
Kennet Paddock NG19 . . . . .136 D3
Kennett Gr S17 . . . . .84 E6
Kennet Vale S40 . . . . .95 D5
Kenninghall Cl S2 . . . . .43 D7
Kenninghall Dr S2 . . . . .43 D7
Kenninghall Rd S2 . . . . .43 D7
Kenning St S45 . . . . .131 C3
Kensal Rise DE24 . . . . .218 B6
Kensington Ave DE75 . . . . . .181 C1
Kensington Chase S10 . . . . . .42 F8
Kensington Cl NG19 . . . . . . .136 E5
Kensington Dr S10 . . . . .42 F8
Kensington Gdns DE7 . . . . . .208 C7
Kensington Jun Sch
  DE7 . . . . .209 A7
Kensington Pk S10 . . . . .42 F8
Kensington Rd
  Burton u T DE15 . . . . .248 A3
  Sandiacre NG10 . . . . .223 A4
Kensington St
  Derby DE1 . . . . .267 A3
  Ilkeston DE7 . . . . .208 F6
Kent's Bank Rd SK17 . . . . . . .85 C6
Kent Ave NG16 . . . . .171 B4
Kent Cl S41 . . . . .95 F5
Kent Grange ◼ S8 . . . . .56 E8
Kent House Cl S12 . . . . .58 E8
Kentish Ct DE1 . . . . .219 B7
Kentmere Cl S18 . . . . .56 E1
Kentmere Way S43 . . . . .97 C8
Kent Rd
  Burton u T DE15 . . . . .254 E6
  Eastwood NG16 . . . . .195 E6
  Glossop SK13 . . . . .10 D1
  Sheffield S8 . . . . .43 B6
Kent St
  Chesterfield S41 . . . . .115 C8
  Derby DE21 . . . . .219 D7
Kenwell Dr S17 . . . . .56 B5
Kenyon Rd S41 . . . . .96 E1
Keppel Cl DE7 . . . . .194 F3
Kepple Gate DE5 . . . . .180 E8
Kernel Cl DE23 . . . . .231 A8
Kerry's Yd DE56 . . . . .191 F8
Kerry Dr DE7 . . . . .192 F6
Kerry St DE21 . . . . .219 D7
Kershaw St SK13 . . . . .17 C8
Kershope Dr DE21 . . . . .206 B3
Kerwin Cl S17 . . . . .55 C8
Kerwin Dr S17 . . . . .55 C8
Kerwin Rd S17 . . . . .55 C8
Kestrel Ave DE11 . . . . .256 F3
Kestrel Cl
  Bolsover S44 . . . . .98 F3
  Burnaston DE3 . . . . .230 B7
  Ilkeston DE7 . . . . .208 F4
  Killamarsh S21 . . . . .60 B7
  Marple SK6 . . . . .23 A3
Kestrel Dr S21 . . . . .59 B3
Kestrel Ho DE24 . . . . .231 E2
Kestrel Hts NG16 . . . . .170 F3
Kestrel View SK13 . . . . .16 F8
Kestrels Croft DE24 . . . . . . .231 E3
Keswick Ave DE23 . . . . .231 B6
Keswick Cl
  Bolsover S44 . . . . .98 F1
  Ilkeston DE7 . . . . .208 D5
  Long Eaton NG10 . . . . .223 B2
Keswick Dr S41 . . . . .95 C8
Keswick Pl S18 . . . . .56 D1
Ketton Ave S8 . . . . .43 B3
Kevin Cl DE21 . . . . .220 B8
Kew Cres
  Heanor DE75 . . . . .182 B1
  Sheffield S12 . . . . .44 A2
Kew Gdns DE22 . . . . .218 A5
Keyhaven Cl DE21 . . . . .219 D8
Keynsham Cl DE24 . . . . . . .232 E8
Keys St DE1 . . . . .267 C4
Keys St DE1 . . . . .159 B2
Keyworth Ct
  Derby DE1 . . . . .267 B4
  ◼ Glossop SK13 . . . . .17 C8
Kingsdale Lo NG10 . . . . . . .236 A5
Kingsdale Gr DE73 . . . . .244 F8
Kings Dr
  Brailsford NG16 . . . . .182 E7
  Derby DE3, DE23 . . . . .218 B2
Kingsfield Ind Est DE4 . . . . .165 E6
Kingsfield Rd DE4 . . . . .165 E7
Kingsgate S32 . . . . .72 C2
Kings Gate DE4 . . . . .247 F4
Kings Hill DE4 . . . . .153 A2
Kings Hollow Mews DE4 . .173 F7
Kingsland Cl DE21 . . . . .205 F2
Kingsley Ave
  Chesterfield S40 . . . . .114 F8
  Mansfield Woodhouse
    NG19 . . . . .136 D5
Kingsley Cl NG19 . . . . .136 D5

Kilbourne Rd DE56 . . . . .179 C4
Kilburn Dr DE7 . . . . .194 D3
Kilburn Inf Sch DE56 . . . . . .191 F8
Kilburn Jun Sch DE56 . . . . .192 A8
Kilburn La DE56 . . . . .179 E3
Kilburn Rd S18 . . . . .56 C1
Kilburn Toll Bar DE56 . . . . . .179 F1
Kilburn Way DE11 . . . . .255 F5
Kilby Ho NG10 . . . . .236 C5
Kildale Gdns S20 . . . . .59 D7
Kildare Rd DE21 . . . . .220 B4
Kildonan Gr S12 . . . . .44 C3
Kildrummy Cl DE22 . . . . . . .204 C1
Killamarsh Inf Sch S21 . . . . . .60 E7
Killamarsh Jun Sch S21 . . . . .60 E7
Killamarsh La S21, S26 . . . . .61 B6
Killingworth Ave DE24 . . . . .231 F4
Killis La
  Belper DE56 . . . . .179 D1
  Holbrook DE56 . . . . .191 D8
Kilmory Fold SK13 . . . . .10 E3
Kiln Bent Rd HD9 . . . . .3 A6
Kiln Cl DE7 . . . . .193 E1
Kiln Croft DE65 . . . . .229 C4
Kiln Hill S18 . . . . .57 C3
Kiln La
  Glossop SK13 . . . . .10 A5
  Parwich DE6 . . . . .151 D2
Kilnsey Ct DE23 . . . . .230 F6
Kiln Way DE11 . . . . .256 D3
Kilverston Rd NG10 . . . . . . .223 A6
Kilvington Ave S13 . . . . .44 B7
Kilvington Cres S13 . . . . .44 B7
Kilvington Rd S13 . . . . .44 B7
Kimberley Cl NG16 . . . . .195 F5
Kimberley Dr DE15 . . . . . . .248 C3
Kimberley Prim Sch
  NG16 . . . . .195 F6
Kimberley Rd DE72 . . . . . . .221 B2
Kinder Ave DE11 . . . . .256 A5
Kinder Cl SK13 . . . . .17 A8
Kinder Cres DE56 . . . . .168 B5
Kinder Dr SK6 . . . . .23 A6
Kinder Gr SK17 . . . . .85 A6
Kinderlee Way SK13 . . . . . . .16 B5
Kinder Rd
  Hayfield SK22 . . . . .25 E2
  Staveley S43 . . . . .97 B6
Kinder Row SK22 . . . . .25 F2
Kinder View SK22 . . . . .33 C7
Kinder Way SK17 . . . . .85 E7
Kinder Wlk DE24 . . . . .218 E4
Kinder's Cl SK17 . . . . .85 D8
King's Mead Wlk DE1 . . . . . .267 A4
King's Mill La DE72 . . . . . . .245 F5
King's Mills La DE72 . . . . . .245 F5
King's Rd SK17 . . . . .85 D8
King Alfred St DE22 . . . . . . .267 A2
King Charles Ct SK13 . . . . . . .17 C7
King Cup Cl S13 . . . . .17 C8
King Ecgbert Rd S17 . . . . . . .55 C5
King Ecgbert Sch S17 . . . . . .55 D6
King Edward Ave SK13 . . . . . .10 C1
King Edward Gdns ◼
  NG10 . . . . .223 B6
King Edward St
  Sandiacre NG10 . . . . .223 B6
  Shirebrook NG20 . . . . .119 F4
  Wirksworth DE4 . . . . .166 A8
Kingfisher Ave DE11 . . . . . . .256 F3
Kingfisher Cl DE3 . . . . .230 B7
Kingfisher Ct
  Bolsover S44 . . . . .98 F3
  Ilkeston DE7 . . . . .208 F4
Kingfisher Ho S41 . . . . .77 B3
Kingfisher Mews DE4 . . . . . . .23 A6
Kingfisher Rd NG19 . . . . . . .135 D1
Kingfisher Wlk S41 . . . . .16 F8
Kingfisher Wlk DE24 . . . . . .231 E2
King George Ave DE7 . . . . . .208 E8
King George St
  Wessington DE55 . . . . .157 E8
  Wirksworth DE4 . . . . .165 E7
King St N S41 . . . . .96 A7
King St S S40 . . . . .115 A7
Kingsbury Cl DE15 . . . . .248 A4
Kingsbury Rd DE22 . . . . . . .218 A6
Kings Cl
  Carsington DE4 . . . . .164 E8
  Clowne S43 . . . . .80 F3
  Creswell S80 . . . . .81 F1
  Heanor DE75 . . . . .181 C1
Kingsclere Ave DE21 . . . . . .206 B2
Kingsclere Wlk S40 . . . . . . .114 F8
Kings Coppice S17 . . . . .55 D6
Kings Croft DE22 . . . . .204 F4
Kingscroft Cl S17 . . . . .55 E8
Kings Ct
  Derby DE1 . . . . .267 B4
  ◼ Glossop SK13 . . . . .17 C8
Kingsdale Cl NG10 . . . . .236 A5

Kingsley Cres
Long Eaton NG10. . . . . .236 B4
Stonebroom DE55 . . . . .146 F3
Kingsley Ct NG19 . . . . 136 D5
Kingsley Rd DE22 . . . . 204 C4
Kingsley St DE24. . . . . . . .231 F5
Kingsmead Ave NG9 . . . . . .209 D2
Kingsmead CI DE1. . . . . . . 267 A4
King's Mead Ho 1 DE22 . .218 F7
Kingsmead Ind Est DE22 218 D6
Kingsmede Ave S40. . . . . . . .95 D1
Kings Mews S21. . . . . .59 E3
Kingsmoor Fields SK13 . . . .10 D3
Kingsmoor Rd SK13. . . . . . . .10 D2
Kingsmuir Rd DE22 . . . . . . 217 C3
Kings Rd
Sandiacre NG10. . . . . .223 B6
Swadlincote DE11 . . . . . . .256 B6
King St
Alfreton DE55 . . . . .158 F4
Ashbourne DE6 . . . . .173 C2
Bakewell DE45. . . . . .109 D5
Belper DE56. . . . . .178 F3
Brimington S43 . . . . .77 F1
Broadbottom SK14 . . . . .16 A8
Burton u T DE14. . . . . .254 C8
Clay Cross S45 . . . . .131 C3
Clowne S43 . . . . .80 E3
Creswell, Hodthorpe S80. . .82 C6
Creswell S80. . . . . .81 F1
Derby DE1. . . . . .267 B4
Duffield DE56. . . . . .190 E4
Eastwood NG16. . . . . .182 F2
Glossop SK13. . . . . .17 C8
Hollingworth SK14. . . . . .9 D5
Ilkeston DE7 . . . . .194 F1
Long Eaton NG10. . . . . . . .236 D8
Mansfield Woodhouse
NG19. . . . . .136 D2
Middleton DE4. . . . . .154 D5
Pinxton NG16. . . . . .160 D3
Shirebrook NG20. . . . . . . .120 D5
South Normanton DE55 . . .159 F5
Tibshelf DE55 . . . . .148 A7
Youlgreave DE45 . . . . .125 B5
Kingsthorpe CI 6 NG19. .136 C1
Kingston Ave DE7. . . . . . . .209 A4
Kingston Ct
3 Barrow Hill S43 . . . . . .78 B3
West Hallam DE7. . . . . . . .207 D8
Kingston Rd DE15. . . . . . . .248 C2
Kingston St DE1. . . . . .218 F7
Kingsway
Burton u T DE14. . . . . .254 B8
Derby DE22 . . . . .218 A5
Heanor DE75. . . . . .181 D2
Ilkeston DE7 . . . . .209 A5
Kings Way S80 . . . . .82 C6
Kingsway Cres DE56 . . . . .192 A8
Kingsway Hospl DE22 . . . .218 B4
Kingsway Ind Pk DE22 . . .218 C5
Kingsway Park CI DE22 . . .218 C5
Kingsway Ret Pk DE22 . . .218 C5
Kingswood Ave DE56. . . . .179 C6
Kingswood CI S41. . . . . .95 D8
Kingswood PI DE23. . . . . . .218 B2
King William Ctr NG16. . . .170 F4
King William St NG16. . . . .170 F4
Kinross Ave DE7. . . . . .219 C8
Kintyre Dr DE24 . . . . .231 D3
Kinver CI DE6 . . . . .184 C8
Kinver Rd DE15. . . . . .248 A4
Kipling CI S18. . . . . .76 C8
Kipling Dr DE23 . . . . .217 D1
Kipling Rd S41. . . . . .95 F8
Kirby CI S41. . . . . .115 C7
Kirby La DE4 . . . . .142 B7
Kirk's La DE56. . . . . .179 B3
Kirkby Ave
Ilkeston DE7 . . . . .208 F6
Sheffield S12. . . . . .44 A4
Kirkby Dr S12. . . . . .44 A4
Kirkby La NG16. . . . . .160 F3
Kirkby Rd S12 . . . . .44 A4
Kirkby View S12 . . . . .44 A4
Kirkby Way S12. . . . . .44 A3
Kirk CI DE5. . . . . .180 C8
Kirkcroft Ave S21. . . . . .60 D7
Kirkcroft Dr S21. . . . . .60 D6
Kirkcroft La S21. . . . . .60 D6
Kirk Dale Ave DE21 . . . . . .220 F3
Kirkdale CI S40. . . . . .115 B8
Kirkdale Gdns NG10 . . . . .236 B6
Kirkdale Rd NG10. . . . . . . .236 B6
Kirkewhite Ave NG10 . . . . .236 D7
Kirkewhite Ho NG10 . . . . .236 D7
Kirkfield Dr DE73 . . . . .233 D8
Kirk Hallam Com Tech Coll
DE7 . . . . .208 D6
Kirkham CI 5 DE75. . . . . .181 D1
Kirkham Dr NG9 . . . . .223 F2
Kirkham La DE56 . . . . .168 B7
Kirk Ireton CE Prim Sch
DE6 . . . . .165 B1
Kirkistown CI DE24 . . . . . .233 C6
Kirkland CI DE74. . . . . . . .247 A3
Kirkland Way
12 Derby DE24 . . . . .231 D3
Swadlincote DE11 . . . . . . .256 B3
Kirk Langley CE Prim Sch
DE6 . . . . .202 F2
Kirkley Dr DE75. . . . . .181 C1
Kirk Leys Ave N DE21 . . . .220 E4
Kirk Leys Ave S DE21 . . . .220 E4
Kirkman Rd DE75 . . . . .181 C4
Kirk St DE1. . . . . .219 B8
Kirkstead CI
Derby DE21 . . . . .206 B1

Kirkstead CI continued
Pinxton NG16. . . . . .160 D3
Kirkstead Jun Sch NG16 160 D3
Kirkstead Rd NG16. . . . . . .160 D3
Kirkstone Ave DE75 . . . . . .182 B1
Kirkstone Ct NG10 . . . . . . .223 B2
Kirkstone Rd
Buxton SK17 . . . . .85 D3
Chesterfield S41. . . . . .95 D8
Kirton Ave NG10 . . . . .236 D7
Kishfield La SK23 . . . . .45 A6
Kitchener Ave DE23. . . . . . .231 F7
Kitchener Terr NG20 . . . . . .101 A2
Kitson Ave NG16. . . . . .171 C4
Kiwi Dr DE24 . . . . .232 F7
Knabhall La DE4. . . . . .144 C5
Knab Rd DE4 . . . . .127 F3
Knapp Ave NG16. . . . . .182 F1
Knifesmithgate S40. . . . . . .266 B3
Knife & Steel Ct DE7 . . . . .192 C7
Knight's La DE15 . . . . .249 B5
Knighton Ct S42 . . . . .131 E6
Knighton St S42 . . . . .131 E6
Knightsbridge DE22. . . . . .218 A6
Knights CI
Beeston NG9 . . . . .223 F2
Derby DE24 . . . . .231 E2
Knights Ct DE13 . . . . .240 E2
Knights Rd DE73 . . . . .244 E8
Knightsyard Ct NG10 . . . . .236 C5
Knightwake Rd SK22 . . . . . .24 C1
Kniveton CE Prim Sch
DE6 . . . . .163 C1
Kniveton La DE6. . . . . .174 C4
Kniveton Pk DE7. . . . . .208 C7
Knob Fields DE11. . . . . . . .261 E8
Knob La DE4 . . . . .166 D5
Knoll CI DE23. . . . . .231 A8
Knoll St SK22. . . . . .33 B8
Knoll The
Chesterfield S40 . . . . .94 F2
Dronfield S18. . . . . .57 D3
Shirebrook NG20. . . . . . . .119 D3
Swadlincote DE11 . . . . . . .256 B6
Tansley DE4 . . . . .144 A5
Knowl Ave DE56 . . . . .178 E5
Knowle Ave S43. . . . . .47 B5
Knowle Gn S17 . . . . .55 C7
Knowle Rd SK6 . . . . .23 C6
Knowles CI SK17 . . . . .85 E8
Knowles Hill DE13 . . . . . . .240 B3
Knowles Ind Est SK23 . . . . .33 D3
Knowleston PI DE4 . . . . . . .143 C4
Knowles View DE11 . . . . . .256 D4
Knowle Top S20 . . . . .59 E7
Knutsford Gn DE21. . . . . . .205 D2
Kye La S26 . . . . .61 E6
Kyle CI S21. . . . . .60 B1
Kyle Gr DE21 . . . . .206 B3
Kyle Rd DE65 . . . . .240 D8
Kynance CI
Derby DE24 . . . . .233 C5
South Normanton DE55 . . .160 C6
Kynnersley Croft ST14 . . . .210 B1

L

Laburnum Ave NG20 . . . . .119 E5
Laburnum CI
Bolsover S44 . . . . .99 C1
Creswell S80 . . . . .81 F1
Darley Dale DE4 . . . . .127 B3
Sandiacre NG10. . . . . .223 B7
South Normanton DE55 . . .160 B7
Laburnum Cres
Derby DE22 . . . . .204 D4
Swannick DE55. . . . . .170 A8
Laburnum Ct S44. . . . . .97 A3
Laburnum Gr
Derby DE22 . . . . .218 B5
Killamarsh S21 . . . . .60 C5
Mansfield Woodhouse
NG19. . . . . .136 A4
Laburnum Rd
Burton u T DE15. . . . . .254 F6
Swadlincote DE11 . . . . . . .256 A6
Laburnum Way DE65. . . . . .229 C3
Laceby CI NG19. . . . . .136 E4
Lacey CI DE7 . . . . .194 A1
Lacey Fields Rd DE7. . . . . .182 B1
Ladbroke Gdns DE22. . . . . .217 F6
Ladies Spring Ct S17 . . . . . .56 A7
Ladies Spring Gr S17 . . . . . .56 A7
Ladle End La DE12. . . . . . . .253 D1
Ladybank Rd
Derby DE3 . . . . .217 C1
Sheffield S20. . . . . .59 D6
Lady Bank View S21. . . . . . .59 D4
Ladybower CI DE11 . . . . . .256 A2
Ladybower CI
Glossop SK13. . . . . .10 C1
4 Sheffield S17 . . . . .56 A5
Ladybower Dr S32 . . . . .53 A7
Ladybower La S43 . . . . .97 D8
Ladybower Rd DE21. . . . . . .220 F4
Ladycroft SK17 . . . . .66 C1
Ladycroft Paddock DE22 . .204 E4
Ladycross Inf Sch NG10 . .223 B6
Lady Field Rd S80 . . . . .62 D8
Ladyfields DE11. . . . . .256 D6
Ladyfields Way DE11. . . . . .256 A2
Ladyflatts Rd DE4. . . . . . . .165 E7
Ladygrove DE56 . . . . .168 D5
Ladygrove Cotts DE23. . . . .219 B3

Lady Grove Rd DE4 . . . . . .127 E2
Lady Hole La DE6. . . . . . . .186 B7
Lady Ida's Dr
Eckington S21 . . . . .59 C4
Sheffield S20, S21. . . . . . . .59 C5
Ladylea Rd NG10 . . . . .236 A4
Lady Lea Rd DE21, DE7 . . .192 A6
Lady Ley Hill DE21. . . . . . .192 A6
Lady Manners Sch DE45. .109 C4
Lady Mantle CI DE73. . . . . .232 E2
Lady Meadow CI ST14. . . .196 E5
Ladypit Rd SK23 . . . . .33 E4
Ladysmith Rd DE72 . . . . . .221 B2
Ladythorn Ave SK6. . . . . . . .23 A5
Ladywell CI DE13 . . . . .240 E1
Ladywell Ct DE56 . . . . .179 A3
Ladywood Ave DE56. . . . . .179 B5
Ladywood Dr S41. . . . . .95 C7
Ladywood Prim Sch DE7 208 D5
Ladywood Rd DE7 . . . . .208 C5
Lake Ave DE75. . . . . .181 C4
Lake Dr
Derby DE23 . . . . .231 F8
Doveridge DE6. . . . . .211 B1
Lake Gdns DE75 . . . . .181 C4
Lake Lands S42. . . . . .114 F2
Lakeside
12 Ashbourne DE6 . . . . . .173 C2
Bakewell DE45. . . . . .109 B7
Wingerworth S42 . . . . .114 F2
Lake Side
Doveridge DE6. . . . . .211 A1
Glossop SK13. . . . . .10 A6
Lakeside Ave NG16 . . . . . . .171 C6
Lakeside Bsns Ctr DE75 .194 A6
Lakeside CI S41. . . . . .77 C4
Lakeside Com Prim Sch
DE24 . . . . .219 E2
Lakeside Cres NG10 . . . . . .236 D5
Lakeside Dr DE23 . . . . .231 A7
Lakeside Inf Sch NG10 . . .236 C5
Lakes Rd SK6 . . . . .23 B6
Lake View Ave S40 . . . . .95 C4
Lake View Ave S40 . . . . .95 C1
Lamb Cres DE5 . . . . .169 F1
Lambcroft Rd NG16 . . . . . .160 D3
Lambe Ct DE22 . . . . .267 C1
Lambgates SK13 . . . . .10 A5
Lamb Hill CI S13. . . . . .44 D7
Lambhouse La DE56 . . . . . .177 E5
Lambley Dr DE22 . . . . .204 C2
Lambourn Ct DE22. . . . . . .205 A3
Lambourn Dr DE22 . . . . . . .205 B4
Lambourne Ave DE6 . . . . . .185 D8
Lampart La SK17 . . . . .50 D5
Lambrook CI DE3 . . . . .217 C2
Lambton CI DE7 . . . . .194 E3
Lampad CI 4 DE73 . . . . . .252 A8
Lampeter CI DE21. . . . . . . .206 B2
Lampeter St DE24 . . . . .219 E2
Lancaster Ave
Sandiacre NG10. . . . . .223 A4
Stapleford NG9 . . . . .223 E2
Lancaster Dr
Hilton DE65 . . . . .228 E2
Tutbury DE13 . . . . .239 B5
Lancaster Rd S41. . . . . .95 E8
Lancaster Rise DE56 . . . . . .179 A6
Lancaster Sports Ctr
DE1 . . . . .267 B4
Lancaster St DE24 . . . . . . .144 F1
Lancaster Wlk DE21. . . . . . .221 A6
Lancelot CI S40. . . . . .114 D8
Lancelot Dr DE13 . . . . .240 E2
Lancing Rd S2. . . . . .43 A8
Landau Forte Coll DE1 . . .267 C4
Landmere DE24 . . . . .204 D4
Landmere DE24. . . . . .231 E3
Landmere CI DE7 . . . . .194 C3
Landon CI S40. . . . . .114 B7
Landsdowne Ave S41 . . . . . .95 E6
Landsdown Gr NG10 . . . . .223 F1
Landseer CI
4 Dronfield S18. . . . . .56 E1
Sheffield S14. . . . . .43 D2
Landseer Dr
Marple SK6. . . . . .23 B7
Sheffield S14. . . . . .43 E2
Landseer PI S14. . . . . .43 E2
Landseer Wlk S14 . . . . .43 E2
Lane Head
Longnor SK17 . . . . .121 B7
Stoney Middleton S32 . . . . .71 C3
Tideswell SK17 . . . . .69 C8
Lane Head Gn S13 . . . . .37 C7
Lanehead Rd SK23. . . . . . . .45 C5
Lane Head Rd S17 . . . . .55 C4
Lanesend Cotts SK23. . . . . .46 A8
Laneside Ave NG9 . . . . .223 E2
Laneside CI SK23 . . . . .47 A5
Laneside Rd
New Mills, Rowarth SK22 . . .24 E6
New Mills SK22. . . . . .33 E7
Lanes The DE4 . . . . .155 A3
Lane The
Awsworth NG16. . . . . .195 C4
Spinkhill S21 . . . . .60 D1
Stanton in Peak DE4 . . . . .126 C5
Laneward CI DE7 . . . . .194 D4
Langdale CI S40 . . . . .94 F5
Langdale Dr
Derby DE21 . . . . .205 D1
Dronfield S18. . . . . .57 C3
Long Eaton NG10. . . . . . . .236 A6
Langdale Sq S43. . . . . .96 D8
Langdon CI 3 NG10 . . . . .223 A1
Langen Ct NG10 . . . . .236 E6
Langer CI DE14 . . . . .254 B6

Langerfield Ave S40 . . . . . .115 A7
Langer La S40, S42 . . . . . . .114 E5
Langford Rd DE3 . . . . .217 D3
Langhurst Ct S40. . . . . .95 D4
Langhurst Rd S40. . . . . .95 D4
Langley Ave
Ilkeston DE7 . . . . .194 D5
Somercotes DE55 . . . . .170 C8
Langley Bsns Pk NG16 . .182 B2
Langley CI
3 Chesterfield S40 . . . . . . .95 A5
Mansfield NG19. . . . . .135 E1
Langley Ct SK13 . . . . .10 A5
Langley Dr SK13 . . . . .17 F8
Langley Inf Sch DE75 . . . .182 A1
Langley Mill CE Inf Sch
NG16. . . . . .182 B3
Langley Mill Jun Sch
NG16. . . . . .182 A4
Langley Mill Sta NG16. . . .182 B3
Langley Pk NG16. . . . . .182 B3
Langley Rd DE21. . . . . .220 E3
Langley St DE22 . . . . .218 D6
Lang Rd DE24 . . . . .232 F6
Langsett Ave 13 SK13 . . . . .9 D1
Langsett Cl DE73 . . . . .233 A2
Langsett Gn 14 SK13 . . . . . .9 D1
Langsett Gr SK13 . . . . .9 D1
Langsett La SK13 . . . . .9 D1
Langsett Lea 15 SK13 . . . . .9 D1
Langsett Terr 14 SK13 . . . . .9 D1
Langstone Ave S44. . . . . . . .99 C1
Langton Hollow NG16. . . . .171 D6
Langton Rd The 4 DE22 . .218 E5
Langtree Ave S41. . . . . .77 A1
Langwith Bassett Prim Sch
NG20 . . . . .119 C7
Langwith Dr NG7 . . . . .194 F5
Langwith Jun Sch NG20 .100 F1
Langwith Maltings NG20 .119 F8
Langwith Rd
Bolsover S44 . . . . .118 C8
Cuckney NG20. . . . . .101 E1
Scarcliffe S44 . . . . .118 F7
Shirebrook NG20. . . . . . . .119 F5
Langwith-Whaley Thorns Sta
NG20 . . . . .100 F2
Lansbury Ave
Mastin Moor S43 . . . . .79 B4
Pilsley S45. . . . . .132 C1
Lansbury Ct S21 . . . . .59 D3
Lansbury Dr DE55. . . . . . . .160 A6
Lansbury Rd S21. . . . . .59 D2
Lanscombe Park Rd
DE22 . . . . .204 E1
Lansdowne Dr DE24 . . . . . .232 F5
Lansdowne Rd
Branston DE14. . . . . .253 D7
Brimington S43 . . . . .96 D7
Buxton SK17 . . . . .85 E8
Swadlincote DE11 . . . . . . .256 A3
Lansing Gdns DE24 . . . . . .220 B6
Lantern Gr DE21 . . . . .217 D4
Lantern Pike View SK22 . . .25 A2
Lantern View SK22 . . . . .24 B1
Lant La DE4 . . . . .144 B8
Lapwing CI DE24. . . . . .231 E2
Larch Ave
Killamarsh S21 . . . . .60 C5
Mansfield Woodhouse
NG19. . . . . .136 B5
Ripley DE5 . . . . .169 D1
Shirebrook NG20. . . . . . . .119 D4
Larch CI DE22 . . . . .204 D3
Larch Cres NG16. . . . . .182 E2
Larchdale CI DE55 . . . . . . .160 A4
Larch Dr NG10 . . . . .223 B7
Larch Rd
Eckington S21 . . . . .59 B2
Kilburn DE56 . . . . .192 B7
Swadlincote DE11 . . . . . . .255 F6
Larch Way
Chesterfield S40 . . . . .95 D5
Glossop SK13. . . . . .17 F8
Larges St DE1 . . . . .218 E5
Lark CI DE23 . . . . .231 C6
Larkfields Cres DE55. . . . . .169 F8
Larkhill DE55. . . . . .169 F8
Lark Hill DE1 . . . . .230 B7
Larkhill CI DE55 . . . . .169 F8
Larkhill Cres DE24 . . . . . . .231 F4
Larkin CI DE24. . . . . .232 A5
Larkland's Av DE7 . . . . . . .209 A4
Larklands Inf Sch DE7 . . .209 A8
Larkspur CI
Mansfield NG19. . . . . .136 D2
South Normanton DE55 . . .160 A4
Larkspur Ct DE21. . . . . . . .206 A3
Larkstone La DE6. . . . . . . .149 A1
Larpit Gn S80 . . . . .82 A5
Lascelles Rd SK17 . . . . .85 B8
Lashley Gdns DE21. . . . . . .205 F2
Latham CI DE15 . . . . .248 C2
Lathbury CI DE21. . . . . . . .205 D1
Lathkil Dr DE55. . . . . .159 F5
Lathkil Gr
Buxton SK17 . . . . .85 C5
Tibshelf DE55 . . . . .147 F6
Lathkill Ave
Derby DE24 . . . . .233 C7
West Hallam DE7. . . . . . . .207 E8
Lathkill CI
Sheffield S13 . . . . .44 C7
West Hallam DE7. . . . . . . .207 E8
Lathkill Dale DE11 . . . . . . .255 F2
Lathkilldale Cres NG10 . . .236 A5

Lathkill Dale Cvn & Camping
Site DE45. . . . . .107 C2
Lathkill Dale National Nature
Reserve* DE45. . . . . .124 C8
Lathkill Dr
Ashbourne DE6 . . . . .185 E8
Ripley DE5 . . . . .180 D6
Selston NG16. . . . . .171 F7
Lathkill Rd
Derby DE21 . . . . .219 F8
Sheffield S13 . . . . .44 C7
Latimer CI DE23 . . . . .230 E7
Latimer St DE24 . . . . .232 D6
Latrigg CI DE73 . . . . .217 E1
Lauder CI DE24 . . . . .231 E2
Launceston Rd DE24 . . . . .233 B5
Laund Ave DE56 . . . . .179 B6
Laund CI DE56. . . . . .179 A6
Laund Farm DE56. . . . . . . .179 A6
Laund Farm Mews DE56. .179 A6
Laund Hill DE56 . . . . .179 A5
Laund Nook DE56 . . . . .179 A5
Launds Ave NG16 . . . . .171 D7
Laurel Ave
Arkwright Town S44 . . . . . . .97 D3
Mansfield Woodhouse
NG19. . . . . .136 F1
Ripley DE5 . . . . .169 D1
Laurel CI
Eckington S21 . . . . .59 C2
Shirebrook NG20. . . . . . . .119 D6
Swannick DE55. . . . . .170 A8
Laurel Cres
Brimington S43 . . . . .78 A1
Long Eaton NG10. . . . . . . .236 C6
Smalley DE7. . . . . .192 F5
Laurel Dr
Aston-on-T DE72 . . . . .246 A7
Killamarsh S21 . . . . .60 C5
Laurel Garth CI S41. . . . . . .77 B3
Laurel Gr
Burton u T DE15. . . . . .254 E8
South Normanton DE55 . . .160 A4
Laurence CI S41. . . . . .77 A2
Laurie PI DE24. . . . . .232 E7
Lavant Ct 3 S43. . . . . .96 E8
Lavender CI
Burton u T DE14. . . . . .254 A8
Shirebrook NG20. . . . . . . .119 D3
Tibshelf DE55 . . . . .148 B7
Lavender Gdns DE75 . . . . .182 B1
Lavender Rd DE55 . . . . . . .170 A8
Lavender Row DE22. . . . . . .204 F1
Lavender Wlk DE55 . . . . . .157 F5
Laverdene Ave S17 . . . . .55 F5
Laverdene CI S17 . . . . .55 F4
Laverdene Dr S17. . . . . .55 F4
Laverdene Rd S17. . . . . .55 F4
Laverdene Way S17 . . . . . . .55 F5
Laverick Rd NG16. . . . . . . .171 A4
Laverock CI NG16 . . . . .171 C6
Laverstoke Ct DE22 . . . . . .218 E4
Lawman Gdns DE55 . . . . . .158 F4
Lawman Mews DE55 . . . . .159 A4
Lawn Ave
Derby DE22 . . . . .204 D2
Etwall DE65 . . . . .229 C5
Lawn CI DE75. . . . . .181 F2
Lawnfold SK13. . . . . .9 E4
Lawn Heads Ave DE23. . . .218 C2
Lawnlea CI DE23. . . . . .231 E5
Lawn Mill Rd NG16 . . . . . .195 E7
Lawn Prim Sch DE22 . . . . .204 D1
Lawns Ave DE55. . . . . .56 C1
Lawns The
Aston-on-T DE72 . . . . .246 B8
Rolleston DE13 . . . . .240 A4
Uttoxeter ST14 . . . . .210 C2
Lawnswood CI DE23 . . . . . .231 C8
Lawn The S18 . . . . .57 B2
Lawn Villas S44. . . . . .97 A2
Lawrence Ave
Awsworth NG16. . . . . .195 C4
Breaston DE72. . . . . .235 D8
Derby DE21 . . . . .220 B7
Eastwood NG16. . . . . .182 F2
Holmewood S42. . . . . .116 D1
Mansfield Woodhouse
NG19. . . . . .136 A4
Ripley DE5 . . . . .180 C8
Lawrence Dr NG16. . . . . . .182 D8
Lawrence St
Derby DE23 . . . . .231 F8
Long Eaton NG10. . . . . . . .236 E7
Sandiacre NG10. . . . . .223 B7
Stapleford NG9 . . . . .223 B7
Lawson Ave NG10. . . . . . . .236 E7
Lawson CI S40 . . . . .114 C8
Layton Dr S41. . . . . .77 B1
Lea Bank DE55 . . . . .160 A4
Leabank Rd S12. . . . . .44 A5
Leabrook CI S12. . . . . .56 C1
Leabrooks Ave NG19 . . . . .136 D5
Leabrooks Rd DE55 . . . . . .170 C8
Lea CI DE22. . . . . .204 E3
Lea Cres DE55 . . . . .170 C6
Leacroft Rd
Derby DE23 . . . . .219 B1
Winster DE4 . . . . .141 C6
Lea CI S41. . . . . .266 B4
Leadale Ave DE55. . . . . . . .170 D8
Leadale Cres NG19. . . . . . .136 E5
Leadbeater Dr S12. . . . . . . .44 A5
Leadbeater Rd S12 . . . . . . .44 A4

Leaden Knowle SK23........34 C1
Leadhill Rd S40...........95 A4
Lea Dr
  Derby, Chaddesden
  ....219 F6
  Derby, Mickleover DE3 ...217 E3
Leafenden Cl DE22........205 A3
Leafgreen La DE23........231 C6
Leafield Rd SK12...........32 C6
Leafy La DE7..............181 F1
Lea Gdns* DE4............156 A7
Leaholme Est S44..........98 D2
Leake St DE22............218 D5
Leam Cl La NG16...........171 F6
Lea Main Rd DE4...........156 B8
Leam Glen NG19...........136 D2
Leamington Cl DE23........218 D1
Leamington Dr DE55........160 B5
Leamington Rd DE14.......253 E7
Leamington St DE7.........169 F2
Leamoor Ave DE55.........170 B8
Lea Moor Rd DE4...........156 E8
Leander Cl DE23...........231 D7
Leander Ct **5** S43.........78 F2
Leander Rise DE55.........255 A8
Lean Town SK13............17 C2
Leaper St DE1.............218 E6
Leapley La DE56...........199 D3
Lea Prim Sch DE4.........156 A7
Lea Rd
  Cromford DE4............155 D6
  Dronfield S18...........57 A1
  Hayfield SK22...........25 C3
  Lea DE4................156 A7
Leas Ave NG19...........135 A5
Leashaw DE4.............156 C4
Leashaw Rd DE4..........156 C4
Leas Park Jun Sch NG19 136 C4
Leas Rd NG19.............136 D4
Lea St SK22...............33 B8
Leathersley La DE6, DE65 226 C2
Lea Vale DE55............160 A4
Leaway The NG20..........119 D3
Lea Wood Croft DE4......156 A5
Leawood Gdns DE21.......206 B3
Leawood Pump Ho*
  DE4...................155 F4
Leche Croft DE56..........256 D7
Lechlade Cl DE7..........207 D8
Ledbury Chase DE21.......220 D1
Ledbury Pl **2** DE21........205 D1
Ledo Ave DE5.............169 D2
Leebangs Rd SK14..........16 A8
Leech Ct NG16............195 B7
Lee Cres DE7.............209 B8
Lee Dale SK17.............85 C3
Leedhams Croft DE12......259 D8
Leeds Pl DE1.............267 D2
Leeds Rd S8I..............63 F7
Lee Farm Cl DE73.........232 F1
Leefield Rd SK23..........47 B5
Lee Head SK13.............16 C5
Leek Rd
  Buxton SK17.............84 E5
  Longnor SK17...........121 B6
Lee La DE75..............182 B1
Leeming La NG19, NG20...136 E7
Leeming La N NG19........136 E5
Leeming La S NG19........136 C5
Leeming Pk NG19..........136 C3
Lee Mount SK13...........17 C7
Leen Valley Dr NG20.......119 D3
Lee Rd S41................96 E2
Lees Brook Com Sports Coll
  DE21...................220 B8
Lees Brook Ho DE21.......220 A7
Lees Hall Ave S8..........43 B5
Lees Hall Pl S8...........43 B5
Lees Hall Rd S8...........43 B5
Lees House Ct S8..........43 A4
Leeside DE24.............220 A1
Lees La DE55.............159 F6
Lees Mill **4** SK22.........33 C7
Leek Nook S8.............43 A4
Lees Rd DE4..............126 E3
Lees Row SK13.............10 C5
Lees The DE72............233 D5
Leeswood Cl S41...........95 D8
Lee Vale Dr SK13..........16 D7
Lees Yd DE21.............220 D4
Legh Rd SK12.............32 A6
Leicester Dr SK13..........17 F8
Leicester Ho **2** NG9.....223 F8
Leicester St
  Burton u T DE14........254 C8
  Derby DE22.............218 E3
  Long Eaton NG10........236 E6
Leigh Rd NG9.............223 F3
Leighton Dr
  Marple SK6..............23 C8
  Sheffield S14...........43 F3
Leighton Pl S14...........43 F3
Leighton Rd S14..........43 E4
Leighton View S14.........43 E4
Leighton Way **6** DE56....178 F3
Leigh Way S42............131 F7
Leisure La SK17...........137 E5
Leman St DE22............218 E3
Lemon Gr DE11............256 B1
Lemont Rd S17.............55 E4
Leniscar Ave DE75........181 C4
Lens Rd DE22.............204 C2
Lenthall Inf Sch S18.......57 B3
Lenton St DE21............219 F6

Lenton St NG10.........223 C7
Leominster Dr DE21......206 B2
Leonard Cheshire Cl
  DE75.................182 B1
Leonard Cl
  Derby DE23............267 B1
  Sheffield S2...........44 A7
Leonard St DE1.........267 C1
Leonard Wlk DE23.......267 B1
Leopold St
  Derby DE1.............267 B2
  Long Eaton NG10.......236 D8
Leslie Ave NG16.........195 F6
Leslie Cl DE23..........230 E8
Lesser La
  Buxton SK17............85 F8
  Chapel-en-le-F SK23....65 D7
Level La SK17............84 D5
Leven Cl DE24...........231 F2
Levens Way S41...........95 E8
Leveret Cl DE73.........233 B2
Lewcote La DE7..........194 A1
Lewis Rd S13.............44 C7
Lewis St DE23...........218 F1
Lewiston Rd DE21........220 B5
Lexington Rd DE21.......220 C6
Ley Ave DE55............159 B3
Leyburn Cl
  Chesterfield S40........95 E5
  Swadlincote DE11.......256 B1
Leycote Way DE56........178 F5
Ley Croft
  Hatton DE65............227 C1
  Mansfield Woodhouse
    NG19................136 D5
Leyfield Rd S17..........55 D7
Leygate View SK22........33 B8
Ley Gdns DE55...........159 B4
Ley La
  Mansfield Woodhouse
    NG19................136 D4
  Marple SK6.............23 D8
Leyland Cl NG9..........223 F2
Leyland Ct DE1..........218 E7
Leyland Gdns DE1........218 E8
Leylands DE1............218 E8
Leylands La SK14.........15 F7
Leyland St DE1..........218 E7
Leys Ct DE56............179 D4
Leys Field Gdns DE73.....233 A2
Leys Jun Sch DE55.......159 C4
Leys La DE4.............154 B7
Leys The
  Little Eaton DE11.......191 D2
  Swadlincote DE11.......255 E6
Leyton Ct S43............77 D4
Leytonstone Dr DE22......218 A5
Lichfield Ave DE11.......256 E5
Lichfield Cl NG9.........223 E3
Lichfield Dr DE24........233 A7
Lichfield Rd
  Branston DE13, DE14....253 C4
  Chesterfield S40.......114 D8
Lichford Rd S2............43 C6
Lickpenny La DE4.........144 E4
Lidgate Ct DE21..........217 C1
Lid La
  Ashover S45............129 A6
  Roston DE6.............197 E7
Liffey Ho DE24...........232 E5
Liffs Rd DE6, SK17.......150 C7
Light Alders La SK42......32 A6
Lightfoot Rd ST14.......210 A1
Lightwood Ave **3** SK17...85 C8
Lightwood La
  Chesterfield S41.........77 E8
  Eckington, Middle Handley
    S21..................58 E1
  Eckington S8............43 F1
Lightwood Rd
  Buxton SK17............66 B1
  Eckington S21...........58 E2
Lilac Ave DE22...........218 A5
Lilac Cl
  Derby DE24.............233 A6
  Holmewood S44.........116 F2
Lilac Ct DE24............233 A6
Lilac Gr
  Bolsover S44.............99 C1
  Burton u T DE15........254 F6
  Glapwell S44...........134 B8
  Heanor DE75............181 E1
  Shirebrook NG20........119 E5
Lilac St
  Brimington S43...........78 B1
  Staveley S43............97 A8
Lilac Way
  Derby DE22.............204 D2
  Shirland DE55..........146 D1
Lilian Prime Cl DE24......233 B8
Lilley Cl NG16...........171 E6
Lilley St DE24...........233 A6
Lillymede Cl S40........114 F6
Lilybank Cl S14..........143 C5
Lilypools The DE73.......252 A7
Limbersitch La DE65......227 F6
Lime La S17..............55 D8
Lime Ave
  Derby, Breadsall Hilltop
    DE21................205 D2
  Derby DE21.............267 A1
  Duffield DE56..........190 E5
  Langley Mill NG16......182 C2
  New Mills SK22...........24 D1

Lime Ave continued
  Ripley DE5.............169 D1
  Staveley S43............78 E1
Lime Cl
  Calow S44...............97 A3
  Doveridge DE6..........224 B8
  Pinxton NG16...........160 D3
Lime Cres
  Belper DE56............179 B2
  Shirebrook NG20........120 F7
Lime Croft DE22.........204 F4
Limecroft View S42.......115 B3
Lime Ct DE15............254 E7
Limedale Ave DE21.......206 B3
Lime Gate Mews DE23 ...218 D2
Lime Gr
  Ashbourne DE6.........185 C8
  Burton u T DE15........254 E5
  Darley Dale DE4........127 C3
  Draycott DE72..........234 F7
  Long Eaton NG10........236 D8
  Sandiacre NG10..........223 D7
  South Normanton DE55..160 A5
  Stapleford NG9.........223 D5
Lime Grove Ave DE4......143 C5
Lime Grove Wlk DE4......143 B5
Limekiln Fields Rd S44 ....99 A3
Lime Kiln La
  Marple SK6..............23 A5
  Turnditch DE56.........189 B8
  Wensley DE4............142 B8
Lime Kilns The DE73......252 E1
Limekiln Way S43..........80 C6
Lime La
  Derby DE6..............206 C3
  Morley DE7, DE21.......206 D5
Lime Rd S21..............59 B2
Limerick Rd DE21.........220 B4
Limes Ave
  Derby DE23.............217 D1
  Whaley Thorns NG20....101 A2
Limes Cl The DE4.........143 C5
Limes Cres NG20.........119 D5
Limes Cl **3** DE23........217 D1
Limes Pk DE55...........169 C1
Lime St DE7.............208 F7
Limes The
  Barton in F NG11.......237 E6
  Mapperley DE7..........193 E3
Limestone Cl DE11........257 A4
Limestone Terr NG19......136 B4
Lime Terr NG10..........236 D8
Limetree Ave DE11.......256 B7
Lime Tree Ave
  Darley Dale DE4........127 B3
  Glapwell S44...........134 B8
  Killamarsh S21..........60 C5
  Mansfield Woodhouse
    NG19................136 A5
Lime Tree Bsns Pk DE4 ...143 C4
Limetree Ct S43...........96 F5
Limetree Ct DE7.........208 C6
Lime Tree Gr
  Arkwright Town S44.....97 D3
  Clay Cross S45.........131 C2
Lime Tree Pk S45..........85 D6
Lime Tree Rd DE4.........143 C5
Limetree Rise DE7.......208 C6
Lime Wlk DE56...........218 D1
Linacre Ave S45.........131 D2
Linacre Rd S40, S42......95 A5
Linacre Reservoir Nature
  Trail* S42..............94 D6
Linacres Dr DE73.........233 A2
Linacre Way SK13.........17 F7
Linbery Cl DE55..........158 B4
Lincoln Ave
  Derby DE24.............233 A8
  Sandiacre NG10........223 A4
Lincoln Cl
  Stapleford NG9.........209 E1
  Tibshelf DE55..........148 A6
Lincoln Dr NG19.........136 D6
Lincoln Gn DE73.........232 F2
Lincoln Rd DE15.........254 D7
Lincoln St
  Alfreton DE55..........158 F3
  Chesterfield S40.......115 A8
  Tibshelf DE55..........148 A6
Lincoln Way
  5 Glossop SK13.........17 F8
  North Wingfield S42.....131 F6
  Swadlincote DE11.......256 E5
Lindale Rd S41............76 E1
Lindale Way DE73........233 A2
Linden Ave
  Chesterfield S40.........95 B1
  Clay Cross S45.........131 D2
  Dronfield S18...........57 B3
Linden Cl DE56..........190 E6
Linden Ct S45...........131 D2
Linden Dr S41...........115 D6
Linden Gr
  Matlock DE4............143 C5
  Sandiacre NG10........223 A4
  Shirebrook NG20........119 F4
  Stapleford NG9.........223 C6
Linden Park Gr S40........95 D3
Linden St NG20............81 E2
Linden St
  Mansfield NG20.........136 A1
  Shirebrook NG20........119 F4
Lindford Cl DE21.........205 F3
Lindisfarne Cl **4** DE24...231 D3
Lindisfarne Dr S40........95 D1

Lindisfarne Rd S18.........76 B8
Lindley St NG16..........171 D6
Lindon Dr DE24..........233 C6
Lindrick Cl
  Derby DE3..............217 F1
  Mansfield Woodhouse
    NG19................136 D6
Lindrick Gdns S40.......114 C8
Lindrick Way S43..........80 B5
Lindsey Cl DE21..........219 E6
Lindway La DE55.........145 B1
Lingfield Rd DE14.......253 F7
Lingfield Rise DE22......217 C3
Lingfoot Ave S8..........57 B6
Lingfoot Cl S8...........57 C6
Lingfoot Cres S8.........57 C6
Lingfoot Dr S8...........57 C6
Lingfoot Pl S8...........57 B6
Lingfoot Wlk S8.........57 C6
Ling La S44..............118 C4
Linglongs Ave SK23........45 C5
Linglongs Rd SK23.........45 C5
Ling Rd S40.............114 D8
Lings Cres S42..........132 A8
Linkmel Rd NG16........182 C3
Links Cl DE24............217 F6
Links Rd
  Chapel-en-le-F SK23.....46 F5
  Dronfield S18...........56 F2
Links The NG16..........171 D6
Links View SK17...........66 D1
Linley La S12, S13........44 E5
Linnet Cl DE21..........220 F6
Linnet Hill DE3.........230 C7
Linnet Ho S41............77 A3
Linscott Cl S41..........95 D7
Linshaws Rd HD9...........3 E5
Linton Heath DE12.......261 D6
Linton Prim Sch DE12....261 D5
Linton Rd
  Chesterfield S40.......114 C8
  Linton DE11............261 E7
  Rosliston DE12.........260 E5
Linwood Cres NG16.......182 F1
Linwood Cl NG19.........136 E4
Lipp Ave S17.............60 C7
Liskeard Dr DE22.........204 D4
Lismore Ct **6** DE24.......231 D3
Lismore Gr SK17..........85 A7
Lismore Rd SK17..........85 A7
Lismore Rd
  Buxton SK17.............85 A7
  Sheffield S8............43 B5
Lissett Ave DE7.........208 E7
Lister Ave S12............44 B3
Lister Cl
  Chesterfield S41.......266 B4
  Derby DE23.............218 B3
  Sheffield S12...........44 B3
Lister Cres S12...........44 B3
Lister Dr S12.............44 B3
Lister Pl S12.............44 B3
Lister Way S12............44 A3
Liston Dr DE22..........218 F8
Litchen Cl DE7..........194 F2
Litchfield Cl NG10......237 A7
Litchurch La DE24.......219 C2
Litchurch St DE1........267 C1
Little Acre NG19.........136 E5
Little Bolehill DE4......155 A4
Little Breck S45.........160 A4
Little Brind Rd S40.......95 B7
Littlebrook Cl SK13.......10 A4
Littledale Cl DE21.......206 C3
Little Debdale La NG19 ...135 F1
Little Derby Hill DE65....230 B2
Little Eaton Prim Sch
  DE21.................205 C2
Little Edge S32...........71 C6
Little Fen DE55.........147 F5
Littlefield La
  Ellastone DE6..........183 A2
  Snelston DE6...........184 B4
Littlehall Rd DE65.......227 C7
Littlefields S14...........9 A4
Little Hallam Hill DE7....208 E6
Little Hallam La DE7.....209 A6
Little La
  Ashford in t W DE45.....89 E1
  Heanor DE5.............181 A3
  Kimberley NG16.........195 F5
  Litton SK17............69 E4
  Sheffield, Woodthorpe Estate
    S12...................44 B6
  Shirebrook NG20........119 D3
  Sutton in A NG17.......148 E2
  Thorpe Salvin S80.......63 B6
Little Liverpool DE12....260 C1
Little London DE1........267 B1
Little Longstone Cl DE3 ..217 F2
Little Lunnon NG11......237 E6
Little Meadow Rd DE73...233 A2
Littlemoor
  Chesterfield S41........95 D7
  Eckington S21...........59 E4
Littlemoor Bsns Ctr S41...59 D7
Littlemoor Cres S41.......95 D7
Littlemoor Ctr **3** S41....15 C8
Littlemoor Ctr **2** S41....95 D7
Littlemoor La
  Matlock Bath DE4.......143 F1
  Newton DE55............148 A3
Littlemoor Rd SK14........9 A2
Little Mooride DE72......246 B8
Little Morton Rd S42,
  S45...................132 A5

Little Norton Ave S8.......57 A8
Little Norton Dr S8........57 A8
Little Norton La S8........57 A8
Little Norton Way S8......57 A8
Littleover Com Sch DE23 230 F8
Littleover Cres DE23......218 D1
Littleover La DE23.......231 E8
Little Thorn Ind Est
  DE11.................256 F2
Littlewell La DE7........208 F2
Little Woodbury Dr DE23 230 F6
Little Wood Dr S12........44 A3
Littlewood La NG19.......147 B2
Little Wood La S26, S80...62 C4
Litton Bank SK13..........19 E1
Litton C E Prim Sch SK17 .69 E3
Litton Cl
  Belper DE56............179 B5
  Ilkeston DE7...........194 E4
  Staveley S43............97 C8
Litton Ct **6** S40.........95 D5
Litton Dr SK17...........69 D2
Litton Fold **46** SK13.....19 E1
Litton Gdns **17** SK13.....19 E1
Litton Mews SK13..........19 E1
Litton Rd NG19..........136 E4
Littonslack SK17..........88 E7
Liverpool St DE21........219 E8
Liversage Almshouses
  DE1...................267 C2
Liversage Pl DE1........267 C2
Liversage Rd DE1........267 C2
Liversage St DE1........267 C2
Livingstone Rd DE23......218 E1
Lloyd St DE22...........218 D5
Loadshead La S42........112 D8
Loads Rd S42............113 B7
Loake Ct **1** DE73........252 A8
Lochinvar Cl DE21........220 F4
Lock Cl DE7.............208 C6
Lockington Cl DE73.......232 F2
Lockington Rd DE74......247 D5
Lock La
  Long Eaton NG10.......236 C4
  Sandiacre NG10........223 C4
Locko Ct DE24...........220 D5
Lockoford La
  Chesterfield, Stonegravels
    S41..................96 A6
  Chesterfield, Tapton S41..96 A5
Lockoford Rd S41..........96 A5
Locko Hall DE7..........206 F2
Locko La S45............132 C3
Locko Rd
  Derby DE22.............220 F7
  Pilsley S45............132 C4
Lockside SK6.............23 A6
Lockton Ave DE75........193 E8
Lock Up Yd DE1..........267 B3
Lockwood Rd DE22........204 D4
Locomotive Way DE24 ....219 C3
Lode La DE6.............149 F4
Lodes La SK17............67 C7
Lodge Ave DE56..........185 B8
Lodge Bank SK13..........10 A6
Lodge Cl
  Calow S43...............97 A4
  Duffield DE56..........190 E3
  Etwall DE65............229 C4
Lodge Ct SK14............10 A6
Lodge Dr
  Belper DE56............178 E5
  Wingerworth S42.......115 A4
Lodge Farm Chase DE6 ...185 B8
Lodge Farm Cl S40.......114 C7
Lodge Hill DE13.........239 E3
Lodge La
  Alstonefield DE6.......149 B3
  Derby DE1.............267 A4
  Derby, Spondon DE21 ...220 D4
  Heanor DE5............181 A5
  Mackworth DE6, DE22 ...203 C5
  Shottle DE56...........177 D8
Lodge Mews DE72.........246 B7
Lodge Moor Rd S10........42 F8
Lodge Pl S43.............97 C6
Lodge Rd
  Eastwood NG16.........195 A8
  Long Eaton NG10........236 D5
  Nethersea DE7..........261 D1
Lodge Row DE7...........235 A2
Lodge St DE72............235 A2
Lodge The
  Glossop SK13............10 A6
  Tideswell SK17..........69 C3
Lodge Way SK13..........217 D1
Lodge Wlk S43.............97 C6
Loganberry Ct DE24......232 E5
Logans Rd DE11..........240 E2
Lomas Cotts SK17.........69 E1
Lombard St DE22.........217 F6
Lomond Ave DE24........231 F2
London Ho DE45..........109 D7
London Rd
  Buxton SK17.............85 C6
  Castle Donington DE72 ...247 B6
  Derby DE24.............219 C2
  Shardlow DE72...........234 E3
  Sheffield, Heeley S2......43 A6
  Sheffield, Highfield S2....43 A7
London St S2.............43 A7
London St S43.............77 D
Longacre Rd S18..........76 A
Long Acre View S20........60 A
Long Acre Way S20........60 A

Longbourne Ct NG19 . . . . . 136 F2
Longbow Cl DE13 . . . . 240 C1
Longbow Gr DE13 . . . . 240 C1
Longbridge La
  Buxton SK17 . . . . 67 B4
  Heanor DE75 . . . . 181 D3
Long Bridge La DE24 . . . . . 232 D8
Longcliff Wlk 2 S41 . . . . . . 95 C6
Longclough Dr SK13 . . . . . . 17 A8
Longcourse La S44 . . . . 98 A2
Long Croft DE72 . . . . 246 A8
Longcroft Ave
  Dronfield S18 . . . . 56 C2
  Ilkeston NE7 . . . . 194 E5
Longcroft Cl S42 . . . . 131 D8
Longcroft Cres S18 . . . . 56 C2
Longcroft Cl S40 . . . . 114 F7
Longcroft Rd S18 . . . . 56 C2
Longcroft View S80 . . . . 82 A6
Long Cswy S10, S32 . . . . 41 C5
Longdale NG19 . . . . 136 E1
Longdale Dr SK14 . . . . 9 A3
Longdale Gdns SK14 . . . . 9 A3
Longden Cl NG9 . . . . 209 F2
Longdendale Com Language
  Coll SK14 . . . . 9 C5
Longdons Row DE22 . . . . . 220 D5

Long Eaton Sch The
  NG10 . . . . 236 D7
Long Eaton Sch The (Lower
  Site) NG10 . . . . 236 C6
Long Eaton Sta NG10 . . . . 236 C5
Long Eaton Trade Ctr
  NG10 . . . . 236 F8
Longedge Gr S42 . . . . 115 B3
Longedge La S42 . . . . 114 F3
Longedge Rise S42 . . . . 115 A3
Longfield Cres DE7 . . . . . . 208 F5
Long Field Grange S41 . . . . 95 C6
Longfield La DE7 . . . . 208 F5

Longford CE Prim Sch
  DE6 . . . . 214 D8
Longford Cl
  Burton u T DE15 . . . . 248 B2
  Derby DE22 . . . . 204 D1
  Sheffield S17 . . . . 56 A5
Longford Cres S17 . . . . 56 A5
Longford Dr S17 . . . . 55 F4
Longford La
  Longford DE6 . . . . 214 F7
  Sutton-On-The-Hill DE6 . . . 215 A4
Longford Rd S17 . . . . 56 A4
Longford St DE22 . . . . 218 E8
Long Gallery DE4 . . . . 110 E6
Longhedge La
  Burton u T DE13 . . . . 239 F1
  Pleasley NG19 . . . . 134 E5
Long Hill
  Darley Dale DE4 . . . . 127 C4
  Whaley Bridge SK17, SK23 . . 65 C5
Longhurst La S6 . . . . 23 C6
Longhurst View S80 . . . . 81 F5
Long La
  Alstonefield DE6 . . . . 149 B5
  Ashover S42 . . . . 130 A6
  Broadbottom SK13 . . . . 16 C7
  Chapel-en-le-F, Combs SK23 . 46 C2
  Chapel-en-le-F SK23 . . . . . . 47 B4
  Chesterfield S21 . . . . 77 C7
  Holloway DE4 . . . . 156 B6
  Killamarsh S21 . . . . 60 F6
  Kirk Langley DE6 . . . . 202 B1
  Longford DE6 . . . . 214 C8
  Shipley DE75 . . . . 194 E7
  Shirebrook NG20 . . . . 119 E3
  Taddington SK17 . . . . 87 E5
  Thurvaston DE6 . . . . 201 D1
Longlands S44 . . . . 99 B2
Longlands Dr SK22 . . . . 33 B8
Longlands La DE65 . . . . . . 230 C1
Longlands Mews DE65 . . . . 230 C1
Longlands Rd
  New Mills SK22 . . . . 33 B8
  Swadlincote DE11 . . . . 256 D7
Longlands Villas DE56 . . . . 167 F3
Long Lane CE Prim Sch
  DE6 . . . . 201 E1
Longley La DE21 . . . . 220 D6
Longload La DE4 . . . . 154 E5
Long Mdw
  Great Cubley DE6 . . . . 198 F1
  Mansfield Woodhouse
  NG19 . . . . 136 D5
Longmeade Dr SK23 . . . . . . 47 B4
Long Meadow La SK17 . . . . 69 E1
Long Meadow Rd DE55 . . . 158 F3
Longmoor Gdns 2
  NG10 . . . . 223 A2
Longmoor La
  Breaston DE72 . . . . 222 E1
  Sandiacre NG10 . . . . 223 B4
Longmoor Prim Sch
  NG10 . . . . 223 C3
Longmoor Rd
  Glossop SK13 . . . . 17 A7
  Long Eaton NG10 . . . . 223 B3
Longnor Craft Ctr* SK17 121 B7
Longnor Gn 38 SK13 . . . . . . 9 D2
Longnor Mews 39 SK13 . . . . 9 D2
Longnor Way 37 SK13 . . . . . . 9 D2
Long Rake DE45 . . . . 123 D4
Longreave La DE45 . . . . 90 C4
Longridge La SK17 . . . . 66 F7
Longrose La DE6 . . . . 163 B2
Long Row
  Belper DE56 . . . . 178 F4
  Shardlow DE72 . . . . 235 B2
Long Row Prim Sch
  DE56 . . . . 178 F4
Long Shambles S40 . . . . . . 266 B3
Longshaw Cl
  North Wingfield S42 . . . . . . 131 F6
  Staveley S43 . . . . 97 D8
Longshaw Ct 10 S40 . . . . . . 95 D5
Longshaw Estate Trail*
  S11 . . . . 54 A4
Longshaw Estate Visitor Ctr*
  S11 . . . . 54 A4
Longshaw Gdns DE24 . . . . 233 A6
Longshaw Lo S11 . . . . 54 A4
Longside Rd S42 . . . . 112 E6
Long Sleets DE55 . . . . 160 B4
Longs Mill 4 DE1 . . . . 267 A4
Longson Rd SK23 . . . . 47 C6
Long St DE15 . . . . 248 E3
Longster La NG20, NG19 . . 120 C3
Longstock Cl DE21 . . . . . . 205 E1
Longstone Cres S12 . . . . . . 44 D4
Longstone La DE45 . . . . 89 F2
Longstone Rise DE56 . . . . 179 B6
Longstone Wlk DE1 . . . . . . 267 A2
Longthorpe Cl DE23 . . . . . 231 A7
Longwalls La DE56 . . . . . . 178 C6
Longwood Com Inf Sch
  NG16 . . . . 160 C2
Longwood Rd NG16 . . . . . 160 C2
Lonsdale Dr NG9 . . . . 223 E2
Lonsdale Gr DE4 . . . . 142 F7
Lonsdale Pl DE22 . . . . 218 D4
Lonsdale Rd
  Burton u T DE14 . . . . 254 B8
  Pilsley S45 . . . . 132 B2
  Lons Inf Sch DE5 . . . . 169 D2
Loom Cl DE56 . . . . 179 C5
Loosemore Dr S12 . . . . 43 F5
Lord Haddon Rd DE7 . . . . 194 E1
Lord Roberts Rd S40 . . . . . 266 B1
Lords Cl S44 . . . . 99 A1
Lordsmill St S41 . . . . 266 C2
Lord St
  Derby DE24 . . . . 232 D6
  Glossop SK13 . . . . 10 D1
  Hollingworth SK14 . . . . 9 D4
Lorne Cl S18 . . . . 56 D2
Lornes Dr DE15 . . . . 248 B3
Lorne St DE22 . . . . 218 F3
Lorraine Cl DE24 . . . . 232 E3
Loscoe CE Prim Sch
  DE75 . . . . 181 B3
Loscoe Ct 2 S40 . . . . 95 D5
Loscoe-Denby La DE5,
  DE75 . . . . 181 B4
Loscoe Grange DE75 . . . . 181 D3
Loscoe Rd
  Derby DE21 . . . . 206 A1
  Heanor DE75 . . . . 181 D2
Losehill Hall Study Ctr*
  S33 . . . . 38 A4
Losk Cnr S44 . . . . 118 D2
Losk La S44, NG19 . . . . . . 118 C3
Lothian Pl
  Castle Donington DE74 . . . 247 A3
  Derby DE21 . . . . 219 D7
Lothlorien Cl DE23 . . . . . . 231 B7
Loudon St DE23 . . . . 219 A3
Loudon Pl DE74 . . . . 247 A4
Loundes Rd S18 . . . . 76 E6
Loundes Wood Ave S41 . . . 95 D8
Loundsley Cl S42 . . . . 94 F4
Loundsley Green Rd S40 . . 95 C5
Lount La DE13 . . . . 239 E1
Lousie Greaves La DE21 . . 220 E6
Louvain Rd DE22, DE23 . . 218 D2
Louwil Ave NG19 . . . . 136 E5
Lovatt Cl DE13 . . . . 240 F2
Love La DE55 . . . . 147 C4
Loveys Croft DE73 . . . . . . 252 E1
Low's La DE7 . . . . 209 B2
Lowburn Rd S13 . . . . 44 C7
Low Cl DE6 . . . . 189 A2
Low Comm S21 . . . . 79 D7
Lowedges Cres S8 . . . . 56 F6
Lowedges Dr S8 . . . . 56 F6
Lowedges Pl S8 . . . . 57 A6
Lowedges Prim Sch S8 . . . 56 E6
Lowedges Rd S8 . . . . 56 E6
Lower Bagthorpe NG16 . . 171 F3
Lower Bank SK13 . . . . 17 D8
Lower Bank Cl SK13 . . . . . . 9 F3
Lower Barn Rd SK13 . . . . . . 9 F4
Lower Bloomsgrove Rd
  DE7 . . . . 194 F3
Lower Brook St SK13 . . . . . 10 B4
Lower Burch Pl S32 . . . . . . 71 E5
Lower Chapel St
  9 Ilkeston DE7 . . . . 194 F1
  Stonebroom DE55 . . . . 147 B4
Lower Clara Mount Rd
  DE75 . . . . 182 A1
Lower Dale Rd DE23 . . . . . 218 F2
Lower Dr DE55 . . . . 169 D7
Lower Dunstead Rd
  Aldercar NG16 . . . . 182 B3
  Langley Mill NG16 . . . . 182 A3
Lower Eaves View SK23 . . . 47 C5
Lower Eley St DE1 . . . . . . 267 A1
Lower Fold SK6 . . . . 23 B8
Lower Gladstone St
  DE75 . . . . 181 E2
Lower Gn DE65 . . . . 230 D1
Lower Granby St DE7 . . . . 194 F2
Lower Greenhall La SK12 32 F6
Lower Grove Rd S40 . . . . . 266 A3
Lower Hague SK22 . . . . 32 E8
Lower Hall Cl DE56 . . . . . . 178 C6

Lower Hardwick St 1
  SK17 . . . . 85 B8
Lower Higham Visitor Ctr*
  SK14 . . . . 15 A8
Lower High St DE13 . . . . . 239 C7
Lower La S23 . . . . 34 D1
Lowerlea SK12 . . . . 32 C6
Lower Macclesfield Rd
  SK23 . . . . 45 E6
Lower Mantle Cl S45 . . . . 131 D4
Lower Maples DE75 . . . . . 194 A8
Lower Market St S43 . . . . . 14 B8
Lower Meadow Prim Sch
  S8 . . . . 57 A5
Lower Middleton St DE7 195 A1
Lower Mill 1 DE5 . . . . 169 E1
Lower Nelson St 1
  DE5 . . . . 181 D2
Lower Orchard St 1
  NG9 . . . . 223 D7
Lower Park St NG9 . . . . . . 223 C6
Lower Rd DE22 . . . . 217 F8
Lower Rock St 2 SK22 . . . 33 C7
Lower Smithy La SK17 . . . 88 A3
Lower Somercotes DE55 . 170 E7
Lower Sq SK13 . . . . 10 A7
Lower Stanton Rd DE7 . . 208 F6
Lower Strines Rd SK6 . . . . 23 A5
Lower Terrace Rd SK17 . . . 69 B5
Lower Whitworth Rd
  DE7 . . . . 208 F6
Lower Wood Cotts SK17 . . 89 A7
Lowes Hill DE5 . . . . 169 D3
Lowes La DE73 . . . . 244 C7
Lowe St DE24 . . . . 232 E6
Lowfield Ave S12 . . . . 58 B8
Lowfield Com Prim Sch
  S2 . . . . 43 A7
Lowfield Cl 4 S2 . . . . 43 A7
Lowfields S43 . . . . 79 A2
Lowgates S43 . . . . 79 A2
Lowlands Lea DE75 . . . . . 181 F2
Lowlands Rd DE56 . . . . . . 179 B4
Low Lea Rd SK6 . . . . 23 B6
Low Leighton Rd SK22 . . . 33 D8
Low Mdw SK23 . . . . 45 D8
Low Pavement S40 . . . . . . 266 B3
Lowry Ct 1 S43 . . . . 9 A4
Lowry Dr
  Dronfield S18 . . . . 56 F1
  Marple SK6 . . . . 23 B8
Lows Ct DE73 . . . . 233 B2
Lowside S32 . . . . 72 B2
Lowside Cl S32 . . . . 72 B2
Loxley Cl
  Chesterfield S40 . . . . 95 B3
  Derby DE21 . . . . 206 B2
Loxley La S80 . . . . 82 A5
Loxton Ct DE3 . . . . 217 D3
Loyne Ct DE24 . . . . 231 F2
Lucas La DE65 . . . . 228 C2
Lucas Rd S41 . . . . 95 E5
Lucas Terr SK22 . . . . 25 C3
Lucas Works S18 . . . . 57 A2
Luccombe Dr DE24 . . . . . 233 D5
Lucerne Rd DE21 . . . . 206 C3
Ludborough Wlk 14
  NG19 . . . . 136 E4
Ludford Cl NG10 . . . . 236 E4
Ludgate St DE13 . . . . 239 C6
Ludgate Wlk DE22 . . . . . . 217 E6
Ludham Cl S41 . . . . 95 F7
Ludham Gdns S41 . . . . 95 F7
Ludlam Ave NG16 . . . . 195 A8
Ludlam Ho S2 . . . . 43 A6
Ludlow Cl DE21 . . . . 220 F5
Ludworth Prim Sch SK6 . . 23 B8
Luke La DE6 . . . . 201 E8
Lullington Mews DE12 . . . 262 A3
Lullington Rd
  Clifton Campville B79 . . . . 263 E3
  Overseal DE12 . . . . 262 A3
Lulworth Cl DE23 . . . . 231 D6
Lulworth Ct NG16 . . . . 195 F7
Lum's Hill Rise DE4 . . . . . 143 D6
Lumber La DE6 . . . . 176 D2
Lumb La
  Belper DE56 . . . . 178 C4
  Hazelwood DE56 . . . . 178 B2
  Northwood DE4 . . . . 127 B6
Lumford Cotts DE45 . . . . . 109 D7
Lumsdale DE4 . . . . 143 E6
Lumsdale Cres DE4 . . . . . 143 D5
Lumsdale Rd
  Matlock DE4 . . . . 143 D4
  Staveley S43 . . . . 97 C8
Lumsdale Terr DE4 . . . . . . 143 E7
Luna Croft S12 . . . . 43 F2
Lunch La SK17 . . . . 88 F8
Lundie Cl DE24 . . . . 231 D2
Lundy Rd S18 . . . . 76 B8
Lune Mdw NG19 . . . . 136 E3
Lupin Cl
  Derby DE21 . . . . 206 C3
  Shirebrook NG20 . . . . 119 D3
Lupin Way S44 . . . . 97 A3
Lupton Cres S8 . . . . 56 F6
Lupton Rd S8 . . . . 56 F6
Lupton Wlk S8 . . . . 57 A6
Lychgate Cl DE21 . . . . 205 D2
Lydden Cl S43 . . . . 96 E8
Lydford Ave S41 . . . . 96 A6
Lydford Rd DE55 . . . . 159 B5
Lydgate S32 . . . . 71 E5
Lydgate Cotts S33 . . . . 40 A6
Lydgate Dr S42 . . . . 114 E3

Lydgate La S33 . . . . 40 A6
Lydia Adns NG16 . . . . 182 E1
Lydstep Cl DE21 . . . . 206 C2
Lyle Cl NG16 . . . . 195 E7
Lymefield Terr SK14 . . . . . . 16 B7
Lymefield Visitor Ctr*
  SK14 . . . . 16 B8
Lyme Park Ctry Pk* SK12 32 E2
Lyme Pk
  Chinley SK23 . . . . 34 E2
  Disley SK12 . . . . 32 B1
Lyme Rd SK12 . . . . 32 A6
Lymewood Dr SK12 . . . . . . 32 C6
Lynam Rd DE55, DE56 . . . 168 D2
Lyncroft Ave DE55 . . . . . . 169 E1
Lyndale Dr DE5 . . . . 181 B8
Lynden Ave NG10 . . . . 236 D5
Lyndhurst Gr DE21 . . . . . . 220 A5
Lyndhurst St DE23 . . . . . . 219 A2
Lyne Ave SK13 . . . . 17 A8
Lynholmes Rd DE4 . . . . . . 143 D5
Lynholmes Rise DE4 . . . . . 143 D5
Lynmouth Dr DE7 . . . . 194 D3
Lynmouth Ho DE65 . . . . . 228 C1
Lynne Cl DE4 . . . . 17 F8
Lynton Cl DE5 . . . . 169 D3
Lynton Ct 10 S41 . . . . 95 F8
Lynton Rd DE56 . . . . 168 A3
Lynton St DE22 . . . . 218 E4
Lynwood Cl
  Branston DE14 . . . . 253 F7
  1 Dronfield S18 . . . . 56 D1
Lynwood Rd
  Branston DE14 . . . . 253 E8
  Derby DE24 . . . . 231 F4
Lysander Dr DE73 . . . . 232 E1
Lytham Cl DE21 . . . . 205 D1
Lyttelton St DE22 . . . . 218 C5

M

M1 Commerce Pk S44 . . . . 98 A4
McAdam Cl DE55 . . . . 248 B2
MacAulay St DE24 . . . . . . 232 A5
McAuley Ct DE1 . . . . 267 B4
Macclesfield Main Rd
  SK17 . . . . 84 D5
Macclesfield Old Rd SK17 84 D6
Macclesfield Rd
  Buxton SK17 . . . . 85 A6
  Horwich End SK23 . . . . 45 D6
MacDonald Cl S42 . . . . . . 115 F3
MacDonald Sq DE7 . . . . . 208 D5
McGough Mews DE24 . . . 232 A5
McGregor's Way S40 . . . . 115 B7
Machins Cl S18 . . . . 57 A2
Mackenzie St DE22 . . . . . 218 C5
Mackinley Ave NG9 . . . . . 209 E1
Macklin St DE1 . . . . 267 B3
Mackworth Cl DE11 . . . . . 256 B7
Mackworth Rd DE1, DE22 218 E6
McMahon Ave S43 . . . . 96 E6
Macnair Ct SK6 . . . . 23 A5
Macnair Mews SK6 . . . . . . 23 A5
McNeil Gr DE72 . . . . 235 A7
Macready Pl DE24 . . . . 232 F7
Maddock La DE4 . . . . 153 A1
Madehurst Gdns S2 . . . . . . 43 B7
Madehurst Rd S2 . . . . 43 B7
Madehurst Rise S2 . . . . 43 B7
Madehurst View S2 . . . . . . 43 B7
Madeley Cl DE13 . . . . 217 D1
Madeley St DE23 . . . . 219 A2
Madin Dr S43 . . . . 97 B6
Madin St
  Chesterfield S41 . . . . 266 B4
  Tupton S42 . . . . 131 D8
Madison Ave DE21 . . . . . . 219 F7
Madras Rd DE15 . . . . 248 C3
Magdala Cotts DE56 . . . . 190 E5
Magee Ct S41 . . . . 267 C4
Mag La
  Creswell NG20 . . . . 100 D5
  Idridgehay DE56 . . . . 176 D5
Magnolia Way DE55 . . . . . 170 A8
Maguire Ave SK13 . . . . 10 A6
Maidstone Dr DE24 . . . . . 232 F5
Mailholme Cl DE56 . . . . . 179 C6
Main Ave
  Derby DE22 . . . . 204 E5
  Sheffield S17 . . . . 55 E4
Main Bright Rd 8 NG19 . 136 B1
Main Bright Wlk NG19 . . 136 B1
Main Dr S42 . . . . 114 C2
Maine Dr DE21 . . . . 220 C6
Main Rd
  Bamford S33 . . . . 40 B3
  Bradwell S33 . . . . 51 A7
  Brailsford DE6 . . . . 201 F7
  Chelmorton & Flagg S42 . . 94 F4
  Chesterfield, West Handley
  S21 . . . . 77 D7
  Crich DE4 . . . . 156 D1
  Cutthorpe S42 . . . . 94 E8
  Eckington, Lightwood S21 . 58 F3
  Eckington, Ridgway S12 . . 58 E8
  Elvaston DE72 . . . . 234 A5
  Flagg SK17 . . . . 106 E6
  Grindleford DE32 . . . . 72 C7
  Hathersage S32 . . . . 53 A8
  Heath S44 . . . . 117 A2
  Holmesfield S18 . . . . 75 A8
  Jacksdale NG16 . . . . 171 B3
  Mayfield DE6 . . . . 184 D8
  Renishaw S21 . . . . 79 B8
  Ripley DE5 . . . . 169 A3
  Ripley, Pentrich DE5 . . . . . 169 C5

Main Rd continued
  Shirland DE55 . . . . 146 D1
  Smalley DE7 . . . . 192 F3
Somercotes, Leabrooks
  DE55 . . . . 170 C7
Somercotes, Pye Bridge
  DE55 . . . . 170 F6
Stonebroom DE55 . . . . . . 147 A5
Sudbury, Aston DE6 . . . . . 226 A4
Sudbury DE6 . . . . 225 F4
Taddington SK17 . . . . 88 A3
Underwood Green NG16 . . 171 F2
Unstone S18 . . . . 76 E7
Wensley DE4 . . . . 127 C1
Whaley Thorns NG20 . . . . 101 A1
Main St
  Awsworth NG16 . . . . 195 C5
  Biggin SK17 . . . . 138 C3
  Blackfordby DE11 . . . . 257 C1
  Bolsover S44 . . . . 117 F8
  Bradbourne DE6 . . . . 163 B6
  Branston DE14 . . . . 253 F7
  Breaston DE72 . . . . 235 D8
  Dreedon on t H DE73 . . . . 252 F2
  Brinsley NG16 . . . . 171 D1
  Burnaston DE65 . . . . 229 F5
  Burton u T, Stapenhill
  DE15 . . . . 254 E8
  Burton u T, Stretton DE13 240 E1
  Caldwell DE12 . . . . 260 F7
  Calver S32 . . . . 72 C1
  Chelmorton SK17 . . . . 106 A8
  Church Broughton DE65 . . 227 B8
  Clifton Campville B79 . . . . 263 F2
  Eastwood NG16 . . . . 182 F1
  Egginton DE65 . . . . 241 B5
  Elton DE4 . . . . 140 E6
  Elvaston DE72 . . . . 234 D6
  Etwall DE65 . . . . 229 B4
  Findern DE65 . . . . 230 D1
  Great Longstone DE45 . . . . 90 A4
  Hartshorne DE11 . . . . 257 B6
  Heanor DE75 . . . . 247 D5
  Hilton DE65 . . . . 228 C2
  Horsley Woodhouse DE7 . 192 C6
  Kimberley NG16 . . . . 195 F6
  King's Newton DE73 . . . . . 245 C1
  Kirk Ireton DE6 . . . . 165 B1
  Linton DE12 . . . . 261 D6
  Lockington DE74 . . . . 247 F5
  Long Eaton NG10 . . . . 236 E7
  Longford DE6 . . . . 193 E3
  Mapperley DE7 . . . . 193 E3
  Middleton DE4 . . . . 154 D4
  Moira DE11 . . . . 256 C1
  Nethersear DE12 . . . . 264 C7
  Newton DE55 . . . . 148 A4
  Newton Solney DE15 . . . . 248 A8
  Over Haddon DE45 . . . . . 109 A1
  Overseal DE12 . . . . 262 B3
  Palterton S44 . . . . 118 A5
  Repton DE65 . . . . 242 D1
  Rosliston DE12 . . . . 260 D6
  Scarcliffe S44 . . . . 118 E6
  Shirebrook NG20 . . . . 119 E3
  Smisby LE65 . . . . 258 F1
  South Normanton DE55 . . 160 B6
  Stanton-by-D DE7 . . . . . . 222 F8
  Sutton in A NG17 . . . . 148 F3
  Swadlincote DE11 . . . . . . 255 E6
  Tatenhill DE13 . . . . 253 A8
  Ticknall DE73 . . . . 251 B4
  Ticknall, Milton DE73 . . . . 243 A1
  Walton-on-T DE12 . . . . . . 253 D1
  Weston-on-T DE72 . . . . . . 245 E5
  Whaley Thorns NG20 . . . . 101 A2
  Wilson DE73 . . . . 252 E6
  Winster DE4 . . . . 141 C6
Mais Cl DE4 . . . . 144 A5
Maisies Way DE55 . . . . . . 160 D6
Maize Cl DE23 . . . . 231 A6
Majolica Mews DE11 . . . . 256 F2
Makeney Rd
  Belper DE56 . . . . 191 A6
  Duffield DE56 . . . . 190 F2
  Milford DE56 . . . . 191 C6
Makeney Terr DE56 . . . . . 191 A6
Malbon's Yd DE4 . . . . 173 C1
Malcolm Gr DE23 . . . . 230 E8
Malcolm St DE23 . . . . 219 B2
Malham Cl S40 . . . . 95 D5
Malham Gdns S20 . . . . 59 D7
Malham Gr S20 . . . . 59 E7
Malham Rd DE23 . . . . 230 F6
Malia Rd S41 . . . . 96 C6
Malin Cl DE24 . . . . 233 B5
Malinder Cl S21 . . . . 60 D6
Malinscommon La DE56. 166 C4
Malkin St S41 . . . . 266 C3
Mallard Cl NG20 . . . . 119 E3
Mallard Ct 6 S43 . . . . 78 F2
Mallard Dr S21 . . . . 60 B7
Mallard Wlk DE3 . . . . 230 C8
Mallatratt Pl NG19 . . . . . . 136 B4
Mallory Cl S41 . . . . 76 F3
Mall The S45 . . . . 131 C3
Malmesbury Ave DE11 . . 256 D6
Malpas Rd DE4 . . . . 143 B6
Malson Way S41 . . . . 95 F6
Maltby Ave DE55 . . . . 146 C5
Maltby Cl 2 DE22 . . . . . . 204 F2
Malthouse Cl
  Eastwood NG16 . . . . 182 F1
  Wirksworth DE4 . . . . 154 F3

Malthouse Ct
4 Ashbourne DE6 . . . . . . 173 C2
Chesterfield S41 . . . . . . 266 B4
Malthouse La
Ashover S45 . . . . 129 F3
Boylestone DE6 . . . . 213 C4
Froggatt S32 . . . . 72 C5
Hatton DE65 . . . . 227 D3
Nether Heage DE56 . . . . 168 B2
Wingerworth S42 . . . . . . 114 C3
Malthouse Rd
Ilkeston DE7 . . . . 208 F4
Whitwell S80 . . . . 82 A6
Maltings The
2 Barlborough S43 . . . . 173 B2
Burton u T DE15. . . . . . . 248 A1
Derby DE1 . . . . 267 B2
Derby DE22 . . . . 218 D6
Shardlow DE72 . . . . 235 B1
Malton Pl DE21 . . . . 205 D1
Malton Wlk S40 . . . . 114 F7
Malvern Ave DE16 . . . . . . 248 A1
Malvern Cl DE3 . . . . 217 D3
Malvern Gdns
5 Long Eaton NG10 . . . . 236 A8
Matlock DE4 . . . . 143 B6
Malvern Rd S40 . . . . 95 E4
Malvern Rise S40 . . . . 10 A5
Malvern Way 3 DE21 . . . 205 D1
Manchester La DE11 . . . . 257 C5
Manchester Rd
Buxton SK17 . . . . 65 F1
Chapel-en-le-F SK23 . . . . 46 E5
Glossop SK13, SK14 . . . . . 9 E7
Tideswell SK17 . . . . 69 B5
Manchester St
Derby DE22 . . . . 218 D6
Long Eaton NG10 . . . . . . 236 D6
Mandarin Way DE24 . . . . 232 F8
Manifold Ave
Ashbourne DE6 . . . . 173 D1
Staveley S43 . . . . 97 D8
Manifold Dr DE24 . . . . . . 233 B8
Manitoba Way NG16 . . . 171 F7
Manknell Rd S41 . . . . 96 A8
Manners Ave DE7 . . . . . . 194 D1
Manners Cl SK23 . . . . 34 D2
Manners Ind Est DE7 . . . 194 C1
Manners Rd DE7 . . . . 194 E1
Manners St DE7 . . . . 209 A6
Manning View DE7 . . . . . 194 F2
Mannion Cres NG10 . . . . 236 B5
Manor Ave
Brimington S43 . . . . 96 F7
Derby DE23 . . . . 218 C3
Stapleford NG9 . . . . 223 D8
Manor Bglws 4 S18 . . . . . 56 F1
Manor Cl
Brassington DE4 . . . . . . 153 A1
Newton DE55 . . . . 148 A3
Pilsley S45 . . . . 132 D1
Swadlincote DE55 . . . . . 255 A6
Manor Coll F Ed Ctr S40 266 A3
Manor Court Rd S44 . . . . 98 F3
Manor Cres
Burton u T DE15 . . . . 255 A6
Chesterfield S40 . . . . 95 D3
Dronfield S18 . . . . 56 F1
Manor Croft
Ripley DE5 . . . . 169 D3
Tatenhill DE13 . . . . 253 A8
Manor Ct
Barrow u T DE73 . . . . . . 244 B5
Breaston DE72. . . . . 235 E8
Breedon on t H DE73 . . . 252 F3
Clowne S43 . . . . 80 F3
Risley DE72 . . . . 222 D4
Somercotes DE55 . . . . . 170 E5
South Wingfield DE55 . . . 157 E3
Manor Dr
Brimington S43 . . . . 96 F7
Chesterfield S40 . . . . 95 D3
Netherseal DE12 . . . . . . 264 F6
Manor Farm S45 . . . . 132 D1
Manor Farm Barns DE21 205 E3
Manor Farm Cotts DE45. . 89 E4
Manor Farm Ct
Killamarsh S21 . . . . 60 D7
Whitwell S80 . . . . 81 F6
Manor Farm Mews
Aston-on-T DE72 . . . . . . 246 B8
Burnaston DE65 . . . . 229 F5
Long Duckmanton S44 . . . 98 A3
Manor Farm Rd DE72 . . . 246 B8
Manor Fields Dr DE21 . . . 208 D7
Manor Gr S43 . . . . 80 A6
Manor House Rd NG10 . . 236 F6
Manor Inf Sch S43 . . . . . . 96 F5
Manor La
Fritchley DE56 . . . . 168 F8
South Wingfield DE55 . . . 157 F1
Manorleigh DE72 . . . . . . 235 E8
Manor Leigh DE72 . . . . . 235 E8
Manor Park Ct DE3 . . . . . 218 B3
Manor Park Rd SK13 . . . . 10 E1
Manor Park View SK13 . . 10 E2
Manor Park Way DE3 . . . 218 B3
Manor Pk DE72 . . . . 221 B3
Manor Rd
Ashbourne DE6 . . . . 173 D3
Barlborough S43 . . . . 80 A7
Barton in F NG11. . . . . . 237 E6
Belper DE56. . . . . 178 F3
Borrowash DE72 . . . . . . 221 A1
Calow S43 . . . . 96 F6

Manor Rd continued
Chellaston DE73 . . . . . . 232 F1
Chesterfield S40 . . . . 95 C3
Derby DE23 . . . . 218 C2
Eastwood NG16 . . . . . . 182 F1
Harthill S26 . . . . 61 F8
Horwich End SK23 . . . . . . 45 E5
Ilkeston DE7 . . . . 194 E1
Killamarsh S21 . . . . 60 E5
Mansfield Woodhouse
NG19. . . . . 136 A4
South Wingfield DE55 . . . 157 F3
Swadlincote DE15 . . . . . 255 B6
Manor Sch The NG19. . . . 136 C5
Manor St S8 . . . . 10 D1
Manor View
Hartshorne DE11 . . . . . . 257 B6
Sheffield S20 . . . . 59 E7
Manse Ave S80 . . . . 100 D8
Manse Cl S80. . . . . 100 D8
Mansfeldt Cres S41 . . . . . 95 E5
Mansfeldt Rd S41 . . . . 95 E6
Mansfield Cl DE11 . . . . . . 256 D4
Mansfield Dr S12 . . . . 44 C6
Mansfield Prep Sch
NG19 . . . . 136 C3
Mansfield Rd
Alfreton DE55 . . . . 159 B4
Bramley-Vale S44 . . . . . . 117 E1
Brinsley NG16 . . . . 182 F4
Chesterfield S41 . . . . 115 F6
Clowne S43 . . . . 80 E2
Creswell S80 . . . . 81 F1
Derby DE1, DE21 . . . . . . 267 B4
Eastwood NG16. . . . . . . 182 F4
Glapwell NG19, S44 . . . 134 C8
Heanor DE75 . . . . 182 A2
Heath S44 . . . . 117 A3
Holmewood S42. . . . . . . 116 C3
Killamarsh S21 . . . . 60 F6
Mansfield Woodhouse
NG19. . . . . 136 C2
Palterton S44. . . . . 118 B6
Scarcliffe S44 . . . . 118 E5
Selston NG16. . . . . 171 F7
Sheffield S12. . . . . 44 B6
Shirebrook NG20. . . . . . 120 F1
South Normanton DE55 . . 160 D6
Tibshelf DE55 . . . . 148 B7
Whitwell S80 . . . . 82 F7
Mansfields Croft DE55 . . 229 B4
Mansfield St
Derby DE1 . . . . 267 B5
Somercotes DE55 . . . . . 170 C8
Mansfield View S12. . . . . . 44 B6
Mansfield Woodhouse Sta
NG19. . . . . 136 A3
Manton Cl
2 Burton u T DE13 . . . . 240 F1
Swadlincote DE11 . . . . . 255 F6
Manvers Ave 2 DE5 . . . . 169 E1
Manvers Ct
Chesterfield S41 . . . . 266 B4
Shirebrook NG20. . . . . . 120 A4
Manvers Rd S44 . . . . 97 A4
Manvers St
Mansfield Woodhouse
NG19. . . . . 136 A3
Ripley DE5 . . . . 169 E1
Shirebrook NG20. . . . . . 120 A4
Manystones La DE4 . . . . 153 B3
Maple Ave
Derby DE23 . . . . 231 D6
Disley SK12 . . . . 33 A6
Ripley DE5 . . . . 180 C8
Sandiacre NG10. . . . . . . 223 B7
Maplebeck Ct DE1 . . . . . 267 B5
Maple Cl
Doveridge DE6. . . . . 211 B1
Mansfield NG19. . . . . . . 136 E1
Maple Dr
Ashbourne DE6 . . . . 185 D7
Aston-on-T DE72 . . . . . . 246 A7
Belper DE56. . . . . 179 B2
Chellaston DE73 . . . . . . 233 A2
Creswell S80 . . . . 81 E2
Derby, Boulton DE24 . . . 233 A6
Killamarsh S21 . . . . 60 C5
South Normanton DE55. . 160 B4
Maple Gdns
1 Heanor DE75 . . . . . . 181 D1
Langley Mill NG16 . . . . . 182 B3
Maple Gr
Breaston DE72. . . . . 235 F8
Burton u T DE15. . . . . . . 254 E5
Derby DE22 . . . . 204 D5
Glapwell S44 . . . . 134 B8
Maple Rd
Castle Donington DE74 . . 247 A5
Swadlincote DE11 . . . . . 256 B6
Maple St S43 . . . . 97 B8
Maples The DE5 . . . . 194 A7
Mapletoft Ave NG19 . . . . 136 A1
Mapleton Ave DE21 . . . . 205 F1
Mapleton Rd
Ashbourne DE6 . . . . 173 B2
Draycott DE72 . . . . 235 A8
Maple View DE4 . . . . 143 C3
Maple Way
Branston DE14. . . . . 253 F8
Burton u T DE14. . . . . . . 254 A8
Selston NG16. . . . . 171 F7
Mapperley CE Prim Sch
DE7 . . . . 193 E3
Mapperley La DE7 . . . . . . 193 E2
Mapperley Rd S18 . . . . . . 56 C1
Marchington Cl DE22 . . . 204 E1
Marchwood Cl S40. . . . . . 95 E4

Marcie Ct DE65 . . . . 242 D2
Marcus St DE1. . . . . 219 A7
Mardale Cl S41 . . . . 76 E1
Marebrook Cvn Pk DE4 . . 156 C2
Maree Cl DE24. . . . . 231 E4
Marfleet Cl DE3 . . . . 217 D3
Margaret Ave
Derby DE21 . . . . 219 F5
Ilkeston DE7 . . . . 208 F8
Long Eaton NG10. . . . . . 223 F1
Sandiacre NG10. . . . . . . 223 B4
Margaret St DE1 . . . . 267 B5
Margery Cl DE6 . . . . 185 B8
Margreave Rd DE21 . . . . . 219 F7
Marigold Cl DE21 . . . . . . 206 B3
Marigold Pl DE11 . . . . . . 256 F4
Marina Dr
Derby, Allenton DE24 . . . 232 E5
Derby, Spondon DE21 . . . 220 D5
Marina Rd DE7 . . . . 193 B8
Marine Dr S41. . . . . 96 C3
Marion Ct SK17. . . . . 85 C6
Marjorie Rd DE21 . . . . . . 219 F8
Marjory La DE6, DE55 . . 213 C2
Mark's Cl DE21 . . . . 231 D6
Markeaton La DE22 . . . . 218 B8
Markeaton Prim Sch
DE22 . . . . 218 E7
Markeaton St DE22 . . . . 218 E6
Market Arc 2 SK13 . . . . . . 10 C1
Market Cl
Hope S33. . . . . 39 A4
Shirebrook NG20. . . . . . 119 F3
South Normanton DE55. . 160 A6
Market Head DE56 . . . . . 179 A3
Market Pl
Alfreton DE55 . . . . 158 F4
5 Ashbourne DE6 . . . . 173 C2
Belper DE56. . . . . 179 A3
Bolsover S44 . . . . 99 A1
7 Buxton SK17 . . . . 85 B7
Castleton S33 . . . . 38 C2
Chapel-en-le-F SK23 . . . . 47 B6
Chesterfield S40 . . . . 266 B3
Codnor DE5 . . . . 181 B8
Compstall SK6 . . . . 15 A2
Crich DE4. . . . . 156 F1
Cromford DE4 . . . . 155 A6
Derby DE1 . . . . 267 B3
Hartington SK17 . . . . . . 137 D5
8 Heanor DE5 . . . . 181 E1
Ilkeston DE7 . . . . 208 E8
Ironville NG16 . . . . 170 F4
Longnor SK17 . . . . 121 B6
Mansfield Woodhouse
NG19. . . . . 136 C3
Melbourne DE73 . . . . . . 252 B7
Mottram in L SK14. . . . . . 9 A3
Ripley DE5 . . . . 169 D2
Somercotes DE55 . . . . . 170 C8
Somercotes, Riddings
DE55 . . . . 170 E6
South Normanton DE55. . 160 A6
Staveley S43 . . . . 78 E2
Sutton in A NG17 . . . . . . 148 F3
Tideswell SK17 . . . . 69 C4
Wirksworth DE4 . . . . . . 165 F8
Market Sq SK17 . . . . 69 C4
Market St
Bakewell DE45. . . . . 109 D6
Broadbottom SK14 . . . . . 16 A8
Buxton SK17 . . . . 85 B7
Castle Donington DE74 . . 247 B3
Clay Cross S45 . . . . 131 D4
Disley SK12 . . . . 32 D6
Draycott DE72 . . . . 235 A7
Eckington S21 . . . . 59 E3
Glossop SK13. . . . . 10 C1
Hayfield SK22 . . . . 25 D3
Heanor DE75 . . . . 181 E1
Hollingworth SK14. . . . . . 9 D5
Ilkeston DE7 . . . . 208 F8
Ironville NG16. . . . . 170 F4
Mottram in L SK14 . . . . . . 9 A4
New Mills SK22 . . . . 33 B7
Shirebrook NG20. . . . . . 119 F4
South Normanton DE55. . 160 A5
Staveley S43 . . . . 78 E2
Sutton in A NG17 . . . . . . 148 F3
Swadlincote DE11 . . . . . 256 B4
Whaley Bridge SK23 . . . . 45 E7
Market View 5 SK17 . . . . 85 B7
Markham Cres S43 . . . . . . 78 F2
Markham Ct
Derby DE21 . . . . 205 F2
Duckmanton S44 . . . . . . 98 A5
Markham La S44 . . . . 98 B4
Markham Quay S41 . . . . 266 C2
Markham Rd
Chesterfield S40 . . . . 266 B2
Long Duckmanton S44. . . 98 B5
Markham Ret Pk S40. . . . 266 B2
Markham Rise S45 . . . . . 131 B4
Markland Ave S43 . . . . . . 81 A4
Markland Cres S43 . . . . . . 81 A4
Markland La S80, S43 . . . . 81 A2
Markland View S80. . . . . . 81 D3
Mark St NG10 . . . . 223 C6
Markland Cres DE15. . . . 255 A8
Marlborough Dr DE15. . . 179 C5
Marlborough Rd
Breaston DE72. . . . . 235 D7
Buxton SK17 . . . . 85 B8
Derby DE24 . . . . 232 C7
Long Eaton NG10. . . . . . 223 F1
Mansfield NG19. . . . . . . 135 F1

Marlow Brow SK13. . . . . . 10 A4
Marlow Cres DE7 . . . . . . 207 D8
Marlow Dr DE14 . . . . 254 A8
Marlowe Ct DE23 . . . . . . 231 F6
Marlow St
5 Buxton SK17. . . . . 85 C8
5 Glossop SK13. . . . . 10 A5
Marlpit La
Bolsover S44 . . . . 99 C3
Denstone ST14 . . . . 196 B6
Ellastone DE6 . . . . 183 A3
Sutton on t H DE6 . . . . . 228 A8
Marlpool Inf Sch DE75 . . 194 A8
Marlpool Jun Sch DE75 . . 182 A1
Marple Rd SK13 . . . . 16 E5
Marples Ave NG19 . . . . . 136 E5
Marple Sta SK6. . . . . 23 A7
Marquis Cl DE12 . . . . 262 E5
Marquis Dr DE12. . . . . . . 262 E5
Marquis Gdns DE73 . . . . 244 E8
Marrison Dr S21. . . . . 60 C6
Marsden Cl DE6 . . . . 190 E3
Marsden Dr 2 S40. . . . . . 95 D2
Marsden Row S33 . . . . . . 40 B4
Marsden St
Chesterfield S40 . . . . 266 B3
Derby DE24 . . . . 232 E7
Glossop SK13. . . . . 10 A4
Marshall Dr 1 NG9 . . . . . 223 F8
Marshall St
Alfreton DE55 . . . . 159 A3
Staveley S43 . . . . 78 E1
Marshall Way DE7 . . . . . 208 C6
Marsham Dr SK6 . . . . 23 A5
Marsh Ave
Dronfield S18. . . . . 57 B3
Hope S33. . . . . 38 F4
Ilkeston NE7 . . . . 194 E6
Marshaw Cl DE21 . . . . . . 217 E1
Marsh Cl S20. . . . . 59 C6
Marshes The S33 . . . . 38 E4
Marshfield Gr S43 . . . . . . 79 A2
Marshgreen Cl DE24 . . . . 233 D5
Marsh Green La S45 . . . . 129 F4
Marsh Hall La SK23 . . . . . 46 F5
Marsh Hollow DE6 . . . . . 200 F5
Marsh La
Belper DE56. . . . . 179 B5
Mayfield DE6. . . . . 183 D8
New Mills SK22, SK23 . . . 33 D6
Marsh Lane Cres DE56 . . 179 B4
Marsh Lane Prim Sch S21 58 E3
Marsh Lane Trad Est
S22. . . . . 33 D7
Marsh View S21 . . . . 59 B2
Marston SK17 . . . . 106 B7
Marston Brook DE65 . . . . 228 E1
Marston Cl
Belper DE56. . . . . 179 C6
Derby DE23 . . . . 231 D5
Dronfield S18. . . . . 75 D8
Marstone Cres S17 . . . . . . 55 F5
Marston La
Doveridge DE6. . . . . 211 B3
Doveridge DE6. . . . . 211 D4
Hatton DE65 . . . . 239 D8
Marston on D DE65 . . . . 228 B1
Rolleston DE13 . . . . 240 A4
Marston Montgomery Prim
Sch DE6 . . . . 211 E8
Marston Old La DE65 . . . 239 D8
Marston Rd DE65 . . . . . . 240 A8
Marston Rise DE15. . . . . . 254 F8
Martin's La DE13 . . . . . . 238 A4
Martin St S21. . . . . 59 C3
Martindale Cl S43 . . . . 97 C8
Martindale Ct DE56 . . . . 179 D5
Martin Dr DE21 . . . . 220 A8
Martin Rise S21 . . . . 59 C3
Martins La S42 . . . . 131 B8
Martlet Ave SK12 . . . . 32 C6
Marx Ct S45. . . . . 131 C3
Mary Ann St S41. . . . . 76 E4
Mary Devonshire Cotts
DE45 . . . . 91 C2
Mary Howitt Inf Com Sch
DE75 . . . . 181 D2
Maryland Ct
Stapleford NG9 . . . . 209 E1
Swadlincote DE11 . . . . . 256 A7
Maryland Rd DE21 . . . . . 220 B6
Marylebone Cres DE22 . . 218 A6
Mary St
Eckington S21 . . . . 59 D3
Whaley Thorns NG20 . . . 101 A2
Mary Swanwick Com Prim
Sch S41. . . . . 77 A3
Masefield Ave
Derby DE23 . . . . 231 E7
Holmewood S42. . . . . . . 116 D1
Swadlincote DE11 . . . . . 256 C6
Masefield Rd S13 . . . . 44 C6
Mason Cres
Sheffield S13 . . . . 44 D6
Swadlincote DE11 . . . . . 256 C6
Mason Gr S13 . . . . 44 C6
Mason Rd DE7 . . . . 194 D2
Masons Cotts S21 . . . . . . 59 A1
Masons Gr SK13 . . . . 10 A6
Masons Place Bsns Pk
DE21 . . . . 219 D6
Mason St S80 . . . . 81 F6
Masson Cl S40 . . . . 95 D5
Masson Hill View DE4 . . . 142 F7
Masson Mills Working
Textile Mus* DE4 . . . . . 155 A7
Masson Rd DE4. . . . . 143 A2

Masson Shopping Village
DE4 . . . . 155 A7
Masson Terr DE4. . . . . . . 144 A5
Masson Wlk DE22 . . . . . . 218 E4
Mastin Ave S43. . . . . 80 D5
Mather's Way S42 . . . . . . 115 D1
Matlock Bank 8 SK13 . . . . 9 E1
Matlock Bath Sta DE4. . . 143 B1
Matlock Ct NG10. . . . . . . 235 F5
Matlock Dr S43. . . . . 97 C5
Matlock Farm Pk* DE4 . . 128 D5
Matlock Gdns 5 SK13 . . . . 9 E1
Matlock Gn DE4 . . . . 143 C4
Matlock Gr SK13 . . . . 16 D1
Matlock Ho DE21 . . . . . . 220 E3
Matlock La 7 SK13 . . . . 9 E1
Matlock Pl 6 SK13 . . . . 9 E1
Matlock Rd
Ambergate DE56 . . . . . . 167 F4
Ashover S42, S45 . . . . . . 113 E3
Belper DE56. . . . . 178 F8
Brackenfield DE55 . . . . . 145 C2
Derby DE21 . . . . 205 F2
Holymoorside S40, S42. . 114 B7
Wessington DE55 . . . . . . 157 E8
Matlock Riverside Sta*
DE4 . . . . 143 A6
Matlock St DE45 . . . . 109 D5
Matlock Sta DE4 . . . . 143 B5
Matlock YH* DE4 . . . . . . 143 B1
Mattersey Ct 4 NG19. . . 136 B1
Matthew Cl S32 . . . . 9 F7
Matthews Ct NG9 . . . . . . 209 E1
Matthews Fold S8 . . . . 43 C1
Matthews La S8 . . . . 43 C1
Matthew St DE24 . . . . . . 232 F6
Matthew Way DE23 . . . . 230 E7
Matt Orch S43 . . . . 160 B4
Maugerhay S8 . . . . 43 C1
Maunleigh NG19 . . . . 136 E1
Mawfa Ave S14 . . . . 43 D2
Mawfa Cres S14 . . . . 43 D2
Mawfa Dr S14 . . . . 43 D2
Mawfa Rd S14 . . . . 43 D2
Mawfa Wlk S14 . . . . 43 D2
Mawkin La NG16. . . . . . . 160 F5
Maws La NG16. . . . . 195 E7
Mawstone La DE45. . . . . 125 B3
Maxey Pl S8 . . . . 43 A6
Max Rd DE21 . . . . 219 F8
Maxwell Ave DE22 . . . . . 218 D8
Maxwell St DE72. . . . . . . 235 F8
May Ave S41 . . . . 77 C3
Maybank Cl SK23 . . . . 35 A1
Mayfair Cres DE22 . . . . . 217 F6
Mayfair Ct DE56 . . . . 190 E4
Mayfield Ave
Heanor DE75 . . . . 181 E1
Kilburn DE56 . . . . 192 A8
Mayfield DE6 . . . . 184 C7
Mayfield Dr
Burton u T DE15. . . . . . . 255 A8
North Wingfield S42 . . . . 131 F6
Stapleford NG9 . . . . 209 F2
Mayfield Gr NG10 . . . . . . 223 E1
Mayfield Rd
Burton u T DE15. . . . . . . 248 A3
Chesterfield S40 . . . . 95 C2
Derby DE21 . . . . 219 E7
Marple SK6 . . . . 15 B1
Sheffield S10. . . . . 42 F7
Mayfield Terr
Hartlebage S32. . . . . 53 A8
Mayfield DE6. . . . . 184 D6
Mayflower Ct
Sheffield S12. . . . . 44 B6
Shirebrook NG20. . . . . . 119 E4
Mayflower Rd NG16 . . . . 195 B8
Mayhall Ave NG19 . . . . . 136 A4
Maylands DE72 . . . . 221 B1
Maylands Ave DE72 . . . . 235 E8
Maynard Rd
Chesterfield S40 . . . . 266 A1
Grindleford S32 . . . . 53 D1
Maynestone Rd SK23. . . . 34 C5
Maypole Hill DE11 . . . . . 256 A6
Maypole La DE23 . . . . . . 230 E7
May St DE7 . . . . 194 D3
May St
Derby DE22 . . . . 218 F3
Ilkeston DE7 . . . . 194 E4
Maytree Cl DE21 . . . . . . 206 C3
Mayvale Gr DE22 . . . . . . 204 D8
Mead Cl DE24 . . . . 231 F4
Mead Cres DE15 . . . . 255 A6
Meadow Ave
Buxton SK17 . . . . 67 B5
Codnor DE5 . . . . 181 B8
Meadow Bank
Glossop SK13. . . . . 16 F7
Hollingworth SK14. . . . . . 9 D6
Mansfield Woodhouse
NG19. . . . . 136 E6
South Normanton DE55. . 160 B7
Meadowbank Ct NG16 . . 182 D1
Meadowbank Way NG16. 182 D2
Meadow Brook Cl DE23 . 230 F7
Meadowbrook Ind Est
S20. . . . . 60 A4
Meadow Cl
Barlborough S43 . . . . 80 C7
Bolsover S44 . . . . 118 A4
Chesterfield S40 . . . . 95 E2
Derby DE21 . . . . 220 B8
Dove Holes SK17 . . . . 47 F1
Draycott DE72 . . . . 235 A7

Meadow Cl *continued*
Dronfield S18. . . . . .57 C4
Eastwood NG16. . . . . .182 F4
Findern DE65. . . . . .230 D2
Horsley Woodhouse DE7. . .192 D6
Repton DE65 . . . . .242 E2
Stoney Middleton S32 . . . . . .72 B3
Tibshelf DE55 . . . . .148 B7
Whaley Bridge SK23. . . . . . . .45 C8
Meadow Cots NG19 . . . . .136 C3
Meadow Cres
Castle Donington DE74 . . . .247 B2
Sheffield S20. . . . . .59 B7
Meadowcroft SK14. . . . . .9 A4
Meadow Croft S42. . . . . . . .132 D8
Meadowcroft Gdns S20. . .59 E8
Meadowcroft Glade S20 . .59 E8
Meadowcroft Rise **2** S20 .59 E8
Meadow Ct
Belper DE56. . . . . .178 F4
Chesterfield S43 . . . . .77 D4
5 Derby DE3 . . . . .217 D1
Elvaston DE72 . . . . .234 D6
Kilburn DE56 . . . . .192 A7
South Normanton DE55. . . .159 F4
Meadow End DE4. . . . . . .165 E7
Meadow Farm Com Prim Sch
DE21. .220 A4
Meadowfield S43. . . . . .45 D8
Meadowfield Cl SK13 . . . . .9 F3
Meadowgate Pk S21. . . . . .60 D7
Meadow Gdns DE75. . . . . .182 B1
Meadow Gr
Newton DE55. . . . . .148 A3
Sheffield S17 . . . . .55 E4
Meadowgrass Cl DE23 . . .231 B6
Meadow Grove Rd S17. . . .55 D4
Meadowhead S8. . . . . .56 F8
Meadow Head S8. . . . . .56 F8
Meadow Head Cl S8. . . . . .56 E7
Meadow Head Dr S8. . . . . .56 F8
Meadowhead Sch S8 . . . . .57 A7
Meadowhill Rd S41 . . . . . .115 D8
Meadow La
Burton u T DE13. . . . . .248 A8
Derby, Chaddesden DE21 . .219 F5
Derby DE1, DE21. . . . . .267 D3
Disley SK12 . . . . .32 D6
Dove Holes SK17. . . . . .47 E2
Hilton DE65 . . . . .228 C1
Long Eaton NG10. . . . . .236 F7
Newton DE55. . . . . .159 F7
Repton DE65 . . . . .243 A4
Roston DE6 . . . . .197 C2
Shirebrook NG19, NG20 . . .119 D2
Swadlincote DE11. . . . . .256 A6
Tideswell SK17 . . . . .69 B2
Meadowlands S44 . . . . .99 C2
Meadow Lane Ind Est
DE55 .159 B5
Meadowlark Gr DE21 . . . .206 A1
Meadow Nook DE24 . . . . .233 C5
Meadow Rd
Awsworth NG16. . . . . .195 C5
Clay Cross S45 . . . . .131 A5
Derby DE1 . . . . .267 C3
Derby, Wilmorton DE21,
DE24. .219 F1
Ripley DE5 . . . . .169 E1
Meadow Rise
Brassington DE4 . . . . .153 A1
Chesterfield S42 . . . . .94 F4
Church Broughton DE65 . . .227 B8
Glossop SK13. . . . . .16 F7
Meadows Com Sch The
S41. . . . . .77 B3
Meadows Croft DE56. . . . .190 D3
Meadows Dr S43 . . . . .97 F8
Meadowside
Disley SK12 . . . . .33 A6
Mayfield DE6. . . . . .184 D6
Whaley Bridge SK23 . . . . . . .45 D8
Meadows Ind Est The
DE21 .219 D5
Meadows Prim Sch
DE56. .190 D3
Meadows Rd SK22 . . . . .25 D2
Meadow St
Ilkeston DE7 . . . . .194 F1
Ironville NG16. . . . . .170 F5
New Mills SK22 . . . . .33 C8
Meadows The
Chesterfield S42 . . . . .95 A5
Dove Holes SK17. . . . . .47 F1
Great Longstone DE45. . . . . .90 A4
1 Heanor DE75 . . . . .181 E1
Killamarsh S21 . . . . .60 D6
Swanwick DE55. . . . . .169 E7
Uttoxeter ST14 . . . . .210 A2
Meadow Vale DE56. . . . . . .190 D3
Meadow View
Belper DE56. . . . . .178 F3
Bolsover S43 . . . . .80 F3
Chesterfield S40 . . . . .114 A8
Darley Dale DE4 . . . . .142 F7
Doveridge DE6. . . . . .224 C8
Holmewood S42. . . . . .132 D8
Rolleston DE13 . . . . .240 C4
South Wingfield DE55 . . . . .157 F5
Meadow View Cl DE21. . . .206 B3
Meadow View Ct DE72 . . .222 E4
Meadow View Rd
Sheffield S8. . . . . .56 F8
Swadlincote DE11. . . . . .255 F5

Meadow Way
Chellaston DE73 . . . . .233 A1
Swadlincote DE11. . . . . .256 A6
Meads The S8 . . . . .57 B8
Mead The S14 . . . . .115 C8
Meadway Dr S17 . . . . .55 D7
Meadway The S17 . . . . .55 D7
Mead Wlk DE15. . . . . .255 A6
Meakin St S41. . . . . .115 D8
Meal Hill Rd HD9 . . . . .2 F8
Meal St S22. . . . . .33 C8
Mear Dr DE72 . . . . .221 B1
Mear Greaves La DE15 . .248 B4
Mease La B79 . . . . .263 B2
Mease The DE65. . . . . .228 E1
Measham Rd
Appleby Magna DE12. . . . . .265 F1
Donisthorpe DE12 . . . . .265 D6
Moira DE12 . . . . .262 F3
Meath Ave DE21 . . . . .220 B4
Meden Ave NG19. . . . . .134 F7
Meden Bank NG19 . . . . . . .135 B5
Meden Rd NG19 . . . . .136 D4
Meden Sq NG19 . . . . .135 B5
Medina Cl DE24. . . . . .233 D5
Medlock Cl S40. . . . . .114 B7
Medlock Rd S40 . . . . .114 C8
Medway Dr DE22 . . . . .205 B5
Meerbrook Cl DE21 . . . . . .206 A1
Meerbrook Pl DE7 . . . . . . .208 C5
Meersbrook Park Rd S8 . .43 A5
Meersbrook Rd S8. . . . . . . .43 B5
Meersbrook Works **S** S2 .43 A6
Meersdale S2 . . . . .43 A6
Megaloughton La DE21 . .220 C3
Megdale DE4 . . . . .143 A6
Melandra Castle Rd SK13. .9 D2
Melandra Ct DE22 . . . . . . .218 E4
Melandra Rd SK13 . . . . .9 E3
Melanie Cl SK13 . . . . .17 A8
Melbourn Cl DE56 . . . . . . .190 E3
Melbourne Ave
Burton u T DE15. . . . . .248 C3
Dronfield S18. . . . . .56 B1
Melbourne Cl
Belper DE56. . . . . .179 A2
Derby DE22 . . . . .204 D2
Derby, Mickleover DE3 . . . . .217 F3
Melbourne Ct
Derby DE24 . . . . .219 E4
Long Eaton NG10. . . . . .235 F4
3 Staveley S43. . . . . .78 E2
Melbourne Hall & Gdns*
DE73. .252 C7
Melbourne Ho DE21 . . . . .220 E3
Melbourne Inf Sch DE73 .252 A7
Melbourne Jun Sch
DE73. .252 A7
Melbourne La
Breedon on t H DE73. . . . . .252 E1
Ticknall DE73. . . . . .251 C5
Melbourne Rd DE N G9 . .209 E1
Melbourne St
Derby DE1 . . . . .267 B1
Mansfield Woodhouse
NG19. .136 C6
Melrebak Cl DE3. . . . . .217 E1
Melfort Cl DE24. . . . . .231 F2
Melling Cl S40. . . . . .114 F8
Melling Cl S40 . . . . .114 F8
Mellington Cl S8 . . . . .43 C2
Mellor's La DE6. . . . . .191 C6
Mellor Dr ST14 . . . . .210 B1
Mellor La
Barlow S18 . . . . .75 E1
Chapel-en-le-F SK23 . . . . . . .47 A6
Mellor Prim Sch SK6. . . . .23 C6
Mellor Rd
Burton u T DE14. . . . . .254 B7
New Mills SK6, SK22. . . . . . .24 C3
Mellors Rd NG19. . . . . .135 D1
Mellor St DE24. . . . . .232 E6
Mellor Way S40. . . . . .115 A7
Melrose Cl
Chesterfield S40 . . . . .95 D3
Derby DE24 . . . . .231 E2
Melrose Ct **7** S41 . . . . . . .96 A6
Meltham La S41 . . . . .96 B6
Melton Ave
Derby DE23 . . . . .231 C6
Melbourne DE73 . . . . .252 A8

Merchant St *continued*
Shirebrook NG20. . . . . .120 A4
Mercia Cl
Eastwood NG16. . . . . .195 A8
Hatton DE65 . . . . .239 D8
Mercia Dr
Sheffield S17 . . . . .55 E6
Willington DE65. . . . . .242 B5
Mercian Cl DE7 . . . . .194 E1
Mercian Mews DE21 . . . . .220 D4
Mercian Pk DE7 . . . . .194 E1
Mere Beck DE72 . . . . .234 D6
Meredith Ct NG9. . . . . .209 E2
Mereoak La DE11, DE73 . .257 C7
Mereside Gdns SK23 . . . . .45 D6
Meridian Ct DE7 . . . . .194 E4
Merion Gr DE23 . . . . .218 A1
Merlin Ave S44 . . . . .98 F3
Merlin Cl DE56. . . . . .179 C5
Merlin Cres DE14. . . . . . . .253 F8
Merlin Gn DE24. . . . . .231 D4
Merlin Way
Burnaston DE3. . . . . .230 B7
Ilkeston DE7 . . . . .208 F4
Woodville DE11. . . . . .256 F3
Merrial Cl DE45. . . . . .109 C4
Mcrrick Cl S40 . . . . .95 D5
Merridale Rd DE23. . . . . . .231 C8
Merrill Coll DE7 . . . . .232 F4
Merrill Coll (Lower Site)
DE24 .232 E6
Merrill Way DE24 . . . . .232 D5
Merrybower Cl DE24 . . . . .231 D3
Merrydale Rd DE15 . . . . . .255 A8
Mersey Bank Rd SK13. . . . .9 F4
Merthyr Ct DE21. . . . . .206 B2
Merton La **2** DE75. . . . . . .181 F1
Merton Ct NG9 . . . . .209 E1
Mervyn Rd DE15. . . . . .248 A3
Messiter Mews DE65 . . . . .242 B5
Metcalfe Ave S21 . . . . .60 C6
Metcalfe Cl DE24 . . . . .233 B8
Meteor Ctr The DE21 . . . . .205 C1
Methley Cl S12 . . . . .43 F6
Metro Ave DE55 . . . . .148 A3
Mettesford DE4. . . . . .143 D5
Meverill Rd SK17 . . . . .69 D5
Mevril Rd SK23 . . . . .45 E5
Mevril Springs Way SK23. .45 E5
Mewies Cl DE12 . . . . .253 D1
Mews Ct DE3 . . . . .217 D4
Mews The
Burton u T DE14. . . . . .254 C8
Horsley Woodhouse DE7. . .192 C7
Little Eaton DE56. . . . . .191 B2
Melbourne DE73 . . . . .252 A7
New Mills SK22 . . . . .33 D8
Wyaston DE6. . . . . .185 B2
Meynell Cl
Burton u T DE15. . . . . .248 B1
Chesterfield S40 . . . . .95 C2
Meynell Ct
Derby DE22 . . . . .204 C2
Kirk Langley DE6 . . . . .202 F2
Meynell Rd NG10 . . . . .236 D5
Meynell Rise DE6 . . . . .173 C4
Meynell St
Derby DE23 . . . . .218 F1
Swadlincote DE11. . . . . .256 A1
Meynell Way S21 . . . . .60 C6
Michael's La DE6 . . . . .183 C5
Michael Cl S42 . . . . .115 A5
Michael House Sch
DE75. .194 A6
Michelle Cl DE24 . . . . .231 C3
Michigan Cl DE21. . . . . . . .220 C5
Michlow Cl S33. . . . . .51 A8
Michlow Dr S33 . . . . .51 A8
Michlow La S33 . . . . .51 A8
Mickleboring DE55 . . . . . .169 C1
Micklecroft Gdns DE7 . . .194 E4
Mickledon Cl **3** NG10. . .236 B8
Mickleover Ho DE3 . . . . . .230 D8
Mickleover Manor DE3. . .217 C1
Mickleover Prim Sch
DE3 . . . . .217 D2
Mickleross Cl DE3 . . . . . . .217 D4
Mickleton Cl DE11. . . . . . .256 B1
Mickley Inf Sch DE55 . . .146 C4
Mickley La
Sheffield S17, S18. . . . . .55 F4
Shirland DE55 . . . . .146 C5
Middlebeck Cl DE73 . . . . .232 F2
Middle Cl DE11. . . . . .256 B4
Middlecroft L Ctr S43. . . . .97 D7
Middlecroft Rd S43 . . . . . . .97 D7
Middlefield Cl S17 . . . . .55 C7
Middlefield Croft S17. . . . .55 C7
Middlegate Field Dr S80 . .82 A5
Middle Hay Cl S14 . . . . . . .43 E4
Middle Hay Pl S14 . . . . . . .43 E4
Middle Hay Rise S14. . . . . .43 E4
Middle Hay View S14. . . . .43 E4
Middle La
Clay Cross S45 . . . . .131 E3
Crich DE4. . . . . .156 D1
Middle Mdw S41. . . . . .96 A7
Middle Mill **2** DE1 . . . . . .267 A4
Middle Orchard St NG9 . .223 D7
Middle Ox Cl S20. . . . . .59 F6
Middle Ox Gdns S20 . . . . .59 F6
Middle Pavement S40. . . .266 B3
Middle Rd S42. . . . . .114 E1
Middle Row SK17. . . . . .89 A7
Middle Shambles S40. . . .266 B3
Middle St
Bolsover, Hillstown S44. . . .118 C8
Bolsover S44. . . . . .99 A1

Middle St *continued*
Stanton in Peak DE4 . . . . . .126 C5
Middleton Ave
Codnor DE5. . . . . .181 B6
Derby DE23 . . . . .218 C2
Middleton Com Sch DE4 .154 D4
Middleton Dr
Derby DE23 . . . . .218 C2
Staveley S43 . . . . .97 B5
Middleton La S32. . . . . .71 D3
Middleton Rd
Ilkeston DE7 . . . . .209 A5
Mansfield Woodhouse
NG19. .136 C5
Middleton St
Awsworth NG16. . . . . .195 C4
Cossall DE7 . . . . .195 A1
Derby DE23 . . . . .219 A1
Middleton Top Visitor Ctr*
DE4 . . . . .154 D3
Middleton Way DE55 . . . .170 C7
Middletown Mdws S43. . . .80 A6
Midhill Rd S2 . . . . .43 B7
Midland Ave NG9 . . . . .223 D5
Midland Cotts
5 Chesterfield S41 . . . . .115 B7
Grindleford S32. . . . . .53 D2
Pleasley NG19 . . . . .135 A6
Rowsley DE4 . . . . .110 F1
Midland Ct
Barlborough S43 . . . . .80 A5
6 Chesterfield S41. . . . . .115 B7
Midland Pl DE1. . . . . .267 D2
Midland Railway Butterley*
DE5. . . . . .169 F4
Midland Railway Ctr The*
DE5. . . . . .169 E4
Midland Rd
Chapel-en-le-F SK23 . . . . . . .47 A6
Derby DE1 . . . . .267 D1
Eastwood NG16. . . . . .182 F2
Heanor DE75. . . . . .181 E2
Swadlincote DE11. . . . . .256 B4
Midland Road Ind Est
DE11 .256 B4
Midland St NG10. . . . . .236 E8
Midland Terr
Barrow Hill S43 . . . . .78 B4
Blackwell DE55 . . . . .147 C1
4 Chesterfield S41. . . . . .115 B7
New Mills SK22 . . . . .33 C7
Midland View
7 Belper DE56. . . . . .178 F3
North Wingfield S42 . . . . . .131 F7
Midland Way S43 . . . . .80 A5
Midway DE22 . . . . .204 E2
Midway Ctr S45 . . . . .131 D4
Midway Rd DE11. . . . . .256 C5
Mikado Rd NG10. . . . . .236 C5
Milbank Cl DE22 . . . . .217 E6
Milburn Gdns DE21 . . . . . .206 B3
Milbury Cl DE21 . . . . .205 F2
Mile Ash La DE22 . . . . .204 F1
Milford DE45. . . . . .109 D6
Milford Com Prim Sch
DE56. .190 F4
Milford Ct DE45. . . . . .109 D6
Milford Dr DE7 . . . . .194 D3
Milford Rd
Duffield DE56. . . . . .190 E4
Staveley S43. . . . . .97 C5
Milford St **1** DE1. . . . . . . .218 F7
Milford The DE22 . . . . .218 F5
Milken La S45 . . . . .130 B4
Milking La S43 . . . . .80 B3
Millbank Cl DE22 . . . . .217 E6
Millbank Ave DE56. . . . . . .179 B2
Millbank Cl DE7 . . . . .194 D3
Mill Bank Cl S32. . . . . .53 A8
Mill Bank Dr ST14 . . . . . . .197 A3
Millbrook SK14 . . . . .9 D6
Millbrook Ho SK14. . . . . . . .9 E4
Mill Brow
2 Broadbottom SK14. . . .16 A8
Marple SK6 . . . . .23 D8
Mill Brow Rd SK6. . . . . .23 E8
Mill Cl
Borrowash DE72 . . . . .221 C1
Findern DE65. . . . . .230 D2
Kilburn DE56 . . . . .192 A7
Newton Solney DE15 . . . . . .248 E8
Swadlincote DE11. . . . . .256 C5
Swanwick DE55. . . . . .169 F7
Mill Cliff SK17 . . . . .85 C7
Mill Cres
Whitwell S80 . . . . .82 A6
Wingerworth S42 . . . . .115 C3
Mill Croft DE12 . . . . .217 D4
Millcross La S18 . . . . .75 E3
Mill Ct S13 . . . . .10 C1
Milldale Ave SK17. . . . . . . .84 F6
Milldale Cl
Chesterfield S40 . . . . .95 C5
Ripley DE5 . . . . .180 C6
Milldale Ct
Ashbourne DE6 . . . . .185 D8
Belper DE56. . . . . .179 B3
Milldale Rd
Derby DE21. . . . . .220 F3
Long Eaton NG10. . . . . .236 B6
Sheffield S17 . . . . .55 F5
Milldam La DE6. . . . . .186 E7
Millenium Ave DE12. . . . . .262 E5

Millennium Ct NG19. . . . . .135 E2
Millennium Cl DE7. . . . . . .194 E3
Millennium Way
Chesterfield S41. . . . . .76 F1
Derby DE24 . . . . .219 E4
Miller Ave S43. . . . . .79 C4
Millers Ct DE1. . . . . .267 B4
Millersdale Ave DE7. . . . . .194 E5
Millersdale Cl DE15 . . . . . .248 B5
Millers Dale Cl S16. . . . . . .179 C5
Millersdale Ct **1** SK13. . . .10 F1
Millers Dale Dr DE55. . . . .160 A7
Millers Gn DE4 . . . . .165 E6
Millers La DE55 . . . . .145 E2
Mill Farm Cl S32 . . . . .72 C1
Millfield DE72. . . . . .235 B2
Millfield Cl DE7. . . . . .194 C3
Millfield Croft **1** DE11. . .256 B7
Millfield Mobile Home Pk
S42. . . . . .130 F5
Millfield Rd
Ilkeston DE7 . . . . .209 A7
Kimberley NG16. . . . . .195 E7
Millfield St DE11. . . . . .257 A2
Mill Fleam DE65 . . . . .228 E1
Mill Gate DE22. . . . . .218 E6
Mill Gn
Shardlow DE72 . . . . .235 A1
Staveley S43. . . . . .78 E2
Mill Green Way S80 . . . . . .80 E4
Mill Hill
Elvaston DE24 . . . . .233 C4
Long Duckmanton S44. . . .117 B6
Repton DE65 . . . . .242 E1
Mill Hill Dr DE15. . . . . .169 F1
Mill Hill Dr DE15. . . . . .248 B4
Mill Hill La
Breaston DE72. . . . . .222 E1
Burton u T DE15. . . . . .248 B4
Derby DE1, DE23 . . . . .267 B1
Mill Hill Rd DE23 . . . . .267 A1
Mill Hill Sch DE55 . . . . . . .180 F8
Mill Holme DE55. . . . . .160 B4
Millhouse Ct DE72 . . . . . . .235 B7
Mill La
Ashbourne DE6 . . . . .173 C1
Atlow DE6 . . . . .175 A7
Ault Hucknall S44 . . . . .133 C8
Barlow S18 . . . . .75 D4
Belper DE56. . . . . .179 B3
Bolsover S44 . . . . .99 A3
Bradbourne DE6 . . . . .163 B6
Castleton S33 . . . . .38 C3
Chesterfield S40 . . . . .95 D2
Clay Cross S42, S45 . . . . . . .130 F5
Clay Cross S45 . . . . .131 B2
Codnor DE5. . . . . .181 B8
Cossall NG16. . . . . .195 C1
Derby DE3 . . . . .217 D4
Doveridge DE6. . . . . .211 A1
Dronfield S18. . . . . .57 B1
Ellastone DE6 . . . . .183 B2
Eyam S32 . . . . .71 E5
Grassmoor S42 . . . . .115 D3
Hartington SK17 . . . . .137 B4
Heath S44 . . . . .117 B1
Hilton DE65 . . . . .228 C2
Holloway DE4 . . . . .156 A5
Holmesfield S18 . . . . .74 F5
Pinxton NG16 . . . . .160 D1
Renishaw S21 . . . . .60 A2
Roston DE6 . . . . .197 D7
1 Sandiacre NG10. . . . . .223 C6
Scropton DE65. . . . . .226 F1
Scropton, Foston DE65 . . . .226 D7
Sheffield S17 . . . . .55 F5
Shirley DE6 . . . . .200 D7
Shuttlewood S44. . . . . .98 F8
Somercotes DE55 . . . . .170 C2
Sudbury DE6 . . . . .225 E1
Sutton in a N NG17. . . . . . .148 F1
Whitwell S80 . . . . .82 A6
Mill Meadow Way DE65 . .239 B7
Mill Moor Cl DE73 . . . . . . .232 F2
Millom Pl DE21. . . . . .205 D1
Mill Pond Ave SK22. . . . . . .24 D1
Mill Pond Cotts DE4 . . . . .155 A7
Millpool Cl DE11 . . . . .257 A7
Mill Rd
Cromford DE4 . . . . .155 B6
Eckington S21 . . . . .59 E4
Heanor DE75. . . . . .194 A8
Stapleford NG9 . . . . .223 D8
Mill Row DE21. . . . . .220 D5
Mills Cl DE72 . . . . .235 A7
Mills Croft DE6. . . . . .164 B1
Mills Ct S14. . . . . .156 F1
Mill St
Bakewell DE45. . . . . .109 D6
Barlow S18 . . . . .75 D3
Belper DE56. . . . . .179 A4
Chesterfield S41 . . . . .266 C3
Clowne S43 . . . . .80 E3
Coton in t E DE12 . . . . .260 D3
Derby DE1 . . . . .218 E6
Glossop SK13. . . . . .10 D1
Ilkeston DE7 . . . . .194 F1
Rocester ST14 . . . . .197 A3
Somercotes DE55 . . . . .170 C8
Stoney Middleton S32 . . . . .72 A3
Millstone Cl **1** S18 . . . . . . .56 D2
Millstone La
Ashford in t W DE45 . . . . . .108 F7

Millstone La continued
Ripley DE5 . . . . **169** C8
Mill Stream Cl S40 . . . .**95** C1
Millthorpe La S18 . . . .**75** A6
Milltown SK13 . . . .**10** D1
Mill View DE56 . . . .**178** F5
Millway NG19 . . . .**136** D1
Millway La DE6 . . . .**149** F3
Mill Wlk
Bolsover S44 . . . .**99** A3
Whitwell S80 . . . .**82** A6
Mill Yd DE55 . . . .**170** C8
Milnbank Ave SK17 . . . .**85** D8
Milner Ave
Codnor DE5 . . . .**181** B8
Draycott DE72 . . . .**235** A7
Milner Rd NG10 . . . .**236** D8
Milnhay Rd NG16 . . . .**182** C2
Milton Ave
Alfreton DE55 . . . .**159** C4
Ilkeston DE7 . . . .**194** E4
Shirland DE55 . . . .**146** C4
Swadlincote DE11 . . . .**256** C6
Milton Cl DE3 . . . .**217** C3
Milton Cres S40 . . . .**115** A7
Milton Ct 12 SK17 . . . .**85** B7
Milton La SK23 . . . .**46** B5
Milton Pl S43 . . . .**78** F2
Milton Rd
Ilkeston DE7 . . . .**194** E4
Repton DE65 . . . .**242** D2
Milton St
Derby DE22 . . . .**218** D4
Ilkeston DE7 . . . .**194** F4
Long Eaton NG10 . . . .**236** D7
Milton Terr NG10 . . . .**236** D7
Milward Rd DE7 . . . .**181** D2
Mimosa Cres DE23 . . . .**231** E5
Miners Hill DE4 . . . .**153** A1
Minimum Terr S40 . . . .**266** A2
Minninglow La DE4 . . . .**151** F8
Minster Rd DE21 . . . .**205** E2
Minster Way DE55 . . . .**169** E7
Mint Gr NG10 . . . .**236** A7
Minton Rd DE74 . . . .**246** F4
Miracle Ct DE45 . . . .**109** D6
Mires La
Great Longstone DE45 . . . .**90** B4
Tideswell SK17 . . . .**70** A3
Mires The
Birchover DE4 . . . .**126** A1
Wetton DE6 . . . .**149** A3
Miriam Ave S40 . . . .**114** A8
Miry La DE65 . . . .**227** C4
Misterton Cl DE22 . . . .**204** E2
Misterton Ct 3 NG19 . . . . . .**136** B1
Mistletoe Dr DE11 . . . .**256** F2
Mitcham Wlk DE22 . . . .**218** A6
Mitchell Ave NG16 . . . .**182** A4
Mitchells Cl DE65 . . . .**229** A4
Mitchell St
Clowne S43 . . . .**80** F4
Long Eaton NG10 . . . .**236** E8
Mitchell Terr DE7 . . . .**209** A5
Mitchell Villas S43 . . . .**77** E3
Mitchell Way S43 . . . .**77** E3
Mitre Dr DE65 . . . .**242** C2
Moat Bank DE15 . . . .**248** D2
Moat St DE11 . . . .**256** B1
Moat The DE74 . . . .**247** B4
Model Village S80 . . . .**100** E8
Model Village Prim Sch
NG20 . . . .**119** E3
Moffatt Rd S2 . . . .**43** B7
Moira Cl DE21 . . . .**220** A7
Moira Dale DE74 . . . .**247** C3
Moira Furnace Mus*
DE12 . . . .**262** E3
Moira Rd
Donisthorpe DE12 . . . .**262** F1
Moira DE11 . . . .**262** E8
Overseal DE12 . . . .**262** B3
Woodville DE11 . . . .**256** C6
Moira St DE73 . . . .**252** A7
Moisty La
Aston-on-T DE72 . . . .**246** B8
Stoney Middleton S32 . . . .**71** B3
Molineux Ave S43 . . . .**78** D1
Molineux St DE23 . . . .**219** B2
Molloy Pl 11 S8 . . . .**43** A6
Molloy St 10 S8 . . . .**43** A6
Molyneaux Bsns Pk DE4 . .**127** B3
Monarch Dr DE21 . . . .**206** D3
Monarch Way DE75 . . . .**181** D2
Moncreiff Dr DE21 . . . .**241** A1
Moncrieff Cres DE21 . . . .**220** A8
Mondello Dr DE24 . . . .**233** C6
Monk's Rd SK13 . . . .**17** A4
Monk St DE55 . . . .**159** B2
Monks Cl
Derby DE24 . . . .**231** C3
Ilkeston DE7 . . . .**209** A8
Monksdale Cl SK17 . . . .**69** B4
Monksdale La SK17 . . . .**68** F2
Monk's Dale (Nature
Reserve)* SK17 . . . .**68** E2
Monk St
Derby DE22 . . . .**267** A2
Tutbury DE13 . . . .**239** C7
Monks Way S81 . . . .**63** F7
Monkton Cl DE7 . . . .**194** D3
Monkwood Rd S41 . . . .**95** D8
Monmouth St DE21 . . . .**219** D6
Monnies End S43 . . . .**80** D5
Monsal Ave SK17 . . . .**85** D7

Monsal Cres
Staveley S43 . . . .**97** C6
Tibshelf DE55 . . . .**147** F6
Monsaldale Cl
Burton u T DE15 . . . .**248** B4
Long Eaton NG10 . . . .**236** B6
Monsal Dr
Derby DE21 . . . .**220** F3
South Normanton DE55 . . . . . .**159** F5
Monsal Gr SK17 . . . .**85** D7
Monsal Ave DE7 . . . .**194** E5
Monsaldale La DE6 . . . .**151** E2
Monsom La DE65 . . . .**242** D3
Montague Way DE73 . . . .**232** E2
Montagu St SK6 . . . .**15** B2
Monteith Pl DE74 . . . .**247** B4
Montford Mews DE74 . . . . . .**247** B4
Montgomery Cl DE65 . . . . . .**228** E2
Montpelier DE22 . . . .**204** D7
Montpelier Cl DE14 . . . .**254** B6
Montpelier Gdns 5 SK17 . . .**85** D8
Montpelier Rd SK17 . . . .**66** D1
Montpelier Rd DE56 . . . .**167** F3
Montrose Cl DE24 . . . .**231** E4
Montrose Ct NG9 . . . .**209** E1
Montrose Pl S18 . . . .**56** D2
Montrose Sq NG19 . . . .**136** B6
Monyash Cl DE4 . . . .**170** E3
Monyash CE Prim Sch
DE45 . . . .**107** C1
Monyash Cl
Derby DE21 . . . .**220** A8
Ilkeston DE7 . . . .**194** E3
Staveley S43 . . . .**97** C7
Monyash Ct 37 SK13 . . . .**9** D1
Monyash Gr 18 SK13 . . . .**9** D1
Monyash Lea 6 SK13 . . . .**9** D1
Monyash Mews 17 SK13 . . . . . .**9** D1
Monyash Pl 20 SK13 . . . .**9** D1
Monyash Rd
Bakewell DE45 . . . .**109** C5
Over Haddon DE45 . . . .**109** A2
Monyash Way
Belper DE56 . . . .**179** B5
1 Gamesley SK13 . . . .**9** E1
Moonpenny Way S18 . . . .**57** A1
Mooracre La S44 . . . .**99** D1
Moorbridge La NG9 . . . .**209** D1
Moorbrook La S33 . . . .**50** F7
Moor Cres S20 . . . .**59** C7
Moor Croft DE4 . . . .**143** E7
Moor Dr DE24 . . . .**233** B5
Moore Cl S42 . . . .**116** D1
Mooredge Dr DE4 . . . .**143** E8
Mooredge Rd DE4 . . . .**157** B2
Moorend DE45 . . . .**111** C3
Moor End DE21 . . . .**220** F6
Moor End Rd SK6 . . . .**24** A5
Moores Ave NG10 . . . .**223** C7
Moore St DE23 . . . .**219** A3
Moor Farm Ave S20 . . . .**59** B8
Moor Farm Garth S20 . . . .**59** C8
Moor Farm Rd E DE65 . . . . . .**185** F7
Moor Farm Rd W DE65 . . . . .**185** E8
Moor Farm Rise S20 . . . .**59** B8
Moorfield DE4 . . . .**143** C7
Moorfield Ave S44 . . . .**99** B1
Moorfield Cres 3 NG10 . . . .**223** B5
Moorfield Ct NG9 . . . .**209** E1
Moorfield La NG20 . . . .**100** F4
Moorfield Prec SK14 . . . .**9** D5
Moorfield Rd DE56 . . . .**191** C7
Moorfields Ave NG16 . . . . . .**182** F3
Moorfield Sq S44 . . . .**99** B1
Moorfield St SK14 . . . .**9** D5
Moorfield Terr SK14 . . . .**9** D5
Moor Furlong DE13 . . . .**240** F1
Moorgate DE22 . . . .**217** E6
Moorgate Ave NG19 . . . .**134** F7
Moorgate Cres S18 . . . .**76** B8
Moorhaigh La NG19 . . . .**135** A3
Moorhall DE45 . . . .**109** C5
Moorhay Cl S41 . . . .**95** B7
Moorhead Ave DE24 . . . .**232** F5
Moorhead Prim Sch
DE24 . . . .**232** F6
Moorings The NG12 . . . .**32** E6
Moor La
Aston-on-T DE72 . . . .**246** B8
Barrow u T DE73 . . . .**244** B8
Bolsover S44 . . . .**99** B1
Bonsall DE4 . . . .**142** B2
Calow S44 . . . .**116** C8
Dale Abbey DE7 . . . .**207** F2
Darley Dale DE4 . . . .**127** C4
Derby DE24 . . . .**232** C6
Elton DE4 . . . .**140** E5
Flagg SK17 . . . .**106** E4
Kirk Ireton DE6 . . . .**165** A3
Kirk Langley DE6 . . . .**202** F1
Little Eaton DE7 . . . .**191** E1
Ockbrook DE72 . . . .**221** C6
Osmaston DE6 . . . .**185** F5
Scarcliffe S44 . . . .**119** A8
Taddington SK17 . . . .**87** E1
Youlgreave DE45 . . . .**125** B5
Moorland Ave NG9 . . . .**223** D6
Moorland Ctr The* S33 . . . . . .**37** C8
Moorland Dr S44 . . . .**116** F2
Moorland Rd
Derby DE3 . . . .**217** D3
Hathersage S32 . . . .**53** A7
Moorlands Cl NG10 . . . .**223** B2
Moorlands Dr DE56 . . . .**184** C7
Moorlands La
Bonsall DE4 . . . .**142** B3
Froggatt S32 . . . .**72** C5
Moorlands Rd DE56 . . . .**168** B4

Moorland Terr DE4 . . . .**144** A4
Moorland View
Apperknowle S18 . . . .**58** A1
Sheffield S12 . . . .**44** A2
Moorland View Rd S40 . . . . . .**95** C1
Moorlawn Ave S42 . . . .**113** E7
Moorpark Ave S40 . . . .**114** C8
Moorpool Cres DE56 . . . .**191** C7
Moor Rd
Ashover S45 . . . .**129** F3
Breadsall DE7, DE21 . . . .**205** F5
Brinsley NG16 . . . .**182** E8
Great Longstone DE45, S32 . . .**89** F6
Moor Rise DE56 . . . .**191** C8
Moorside Cl
Cromford DE4 . . . .**155** A5
Glossop SK13 . . . .**17** B7
Sheffield S20 . . . .**59** C8
Moorside Cres DE24 . . . .**231** F4
Moorside Gdns DE72 . . . . . .**234** C1
Moorside La DE56 . . . .**191** C7
Moor St DE21 . . . .**220** E5
Moor The
Brinsley NG16 . . . .**182** D8
Middleton DE4 . . . .**154** C4
Moorthorpe Gn S20 . . . .**44** F2
Moorthorpe way S20 . . . .**44** F2
Moortop Rd S18, S21 . . . .**58** B1
Moor Valley S20 . . . .**44** F2
Moorview Cl
Brimington S43 . . . .**96** D7
Wingerworth S42 . . . .**115** B3
Moorview Ct 2 S17 . . . .**56** B5
Moor View Rd S43 . . . .**79** A2
Moorway DE21 . . . .**205** E4
Moorway Croft DE23 . . . .**231** B7
Moorway La DE23 . . . .**231** B6
Moorways Sports Ctr
DE24 . . . .**232** D6
Moorwinstow Croft S17 . . . . .**55** E7
Moorwood La S17 . . . .**55** C1
Moorwoodmoor La
DE55 . . . .**157** D6
Moray Cl NG16 . . . .**195** F7
Moray Ct S18 . . . .**56** D2
Moray Wlk DE21 . . . .**219** C8
Mordaunt Rd S2 . . . .**43** F6
Morden Gn DE22 . . . .**218** A6
Morden Rd NG16 . . . .**195** C8
Morefern Dr DE21 . . . .**205** F2
Morland Cl S14 . . . .**43** F3
Morland Dr S14 . . . .**43** F3
Morland Pl S14 . . . .**43** F3
Morland Rd
Hayfield SK22 . . . .**25** B2
Sheffield S14 . . . .**43** F3
Morledge DE1 . . . .**267** C3
Morleston St DE23 . . . .**267** C1
Morley Almshouses La
DE7 . . . .**206** B7
Morley Ave S40 . . . .**95** C4
Morley Cl
Belper DE56 . . . .**179** E6
Burton u T DE15 . . . .**248** B2
Dronfield S18 . . . .**56** C1
Morley Dr DE7 . . . .**194** D3
Morleyfields Cl DE56 . . . .**169** F1
Morley Gdns DE21 . . . .**220** B8
Morley Hall Prep Sch
DE7 . . . .**206** B1
Morley Ho
Derby, Alvaston DE24 . . . .**233** A7
1 Derby, Mickleover DE3 . **217** D1
Morley La
Little Eaton DE7, DE21 . . . . . .**205** E8
Stanley DE7 . . . .**207** B6
Morley Mews DE21 . . . .**220** A7
Morley Prim Sch DE7 . . . . . .**206** C7
Morley Rd DE21 . . . .**220** B8
Morley St
Derby DE22 . . . .**218** C5
Glossop SK13 . . . .**17** C8
Morlich Dr DE24 . . . .**231** E5
Morningside Cl DE24 . . . . . .**232** D4
Mornington Cl NG10 . . . .**223** C6
Mornington Cres DE22 . . . .**218** B6
Mornington Rd S42 . . . .**132** D8
Mornington Rise DE4 . . . . . .**143** C4
Morpeth Gdns DE21 . . . .**205** D2
Morrell Wood Dr DE56 . . . . .**179** D5
Morris Ave S41 . . . .**95** E5
Morris Dr S41 . . . .**95** E5
Mortimer Rd S6 . . . .**31** E8
Mortimer St DE24 . . . .**232** C7
Mortimer Wilson Sch
DE55 . . . .**159** A3
Morton Ave S45 . . . .**131** B4
Morton Gdns S20 . . . .**59** F6
Morton La S18, S21 . . . .**58** C1
Morton Mount S20 . . . .**59** F7
Morton Prim Sch DE55 . . . .**147** A5
Morton Rd
Pilsley S45 . . . .**147** C8
Shirland DE55 . . . .**146** D6
Morton St NG19 . . . .**135** E1
Morven Ave
Bolsover S44 . . . .**99** B1
Mansfield Woodhouse
NG19 . . . .**136** B2
Morven St S80 . . . .**100** F8
Mosborough Hall Dr S20 . . .**59** E6
Mosborough Hall Farm
S20 . . . .**59** D6
Mosborough Moor S20 . . . . . .**59** B7
Mosborough Prim Sch
S20 . . . .**59** C7
Mosborough Rd S13 . . . .**44** B7
Moscar Cross Rd S6 . . . .**31** F6

Moscow Farm Ct DE56 . .**190** F5
Mosedale Cl DE24 . . . .**232** F8
Moseley St DE5 . . . .**169** D2
Moses La DE7 . . . .**206** E7
Moses View S81 . . . .**63** F7
Mosley Dr ST14 . . . .**210** A1
Mosley Mews DE13 . . . .**240** A1
Mosley Rd SK17 . . . .**85** B6
Mossbank Cl SK13 . . . .**9** E4
Moss Beck Ct S21 . . . .**59** C2
Mossbrook Ct S21 . . . .**59** B5
Mossbrook Sch S8 . . . .**57** C8
Mosscar Cl NG20 . . . .**120** F1
Mossdale Ave S20 . . . .**59** D7
Moss Dr S21 . . . .**60** D5
Moss Edge Rd HD9 . . . .**3** C8
Moss La
Broadbottom SK14 . . . .**15** F8
Hulland Ward DE6 . . . .**175** F4
Ripley DE5 . . . .**169** D3
Moss Rd
Ilkeston DE7 . . . .**208** E7
Sheffield S17 . . . .**55** B4
Moss Rise Pl S21 . . . .**59** C3
Moss St
Derby DE22 . . . .**218** E3
Hollingworth SK14 . . . .**9** D5
Mossvale Dr DE23 . . . .**231** A6
Moss View S20 . . . .**59** C6
Moss View Rd SK23 . . . .**47** C5
Moston Wlk S40 . . . .**114** C6
Mostyn Ave DE23 . . . .**218** D1
Mottistone Cl DE24 . . . .**233** D5
Mottram CE Prim Sch
SK14 . . . .**9** A3
Mottram Fold SK14 . . . .**9** A3
Mottram Moor SK14 . . . .**9** B4
Mottram Old Rd SK14 . . . . . .**15** B8
Mottram Rd SK14 . . . .**16** A8
Moulbourn Dr DE56 . . . .**190** D4
Mouldridge La DE4 . . . .**139** F2
Moult Ave DE21 . . . .**220** E4
Moulton Cl
Belper DE56 . . . .**179** D5
Swanwick DE55 . . . .**169** F8
Mound Rd S40 . . . .**266** B1
Mountbatten Cl DE24 . . . . . .**232** E4
Mountbatten Ct DE7 . . . .**194** F3
Mount Carmel St DE23 . . . .**267** A1
Mountcastle St S41 . . . .**95** F8
Mountcastle Wlk S41 . . . .**95** F8
Mount Cres DE55 . . . .**160** A3
Mountfield Ave NG10 . . . . . .**223** A4
Mountfield Way DE24 . . . . . .**233** D6
Mountford Ave DE4 . . . .**165** E7
Mountford Cl DE21 . . . .**206** B2
Mountford Croft S17 . . . .**55** E5
Mount Pleasant
Ashford in t W DE45 . . . .**108** F8
Castle Donington DE74 . . . . . .**247** B3
Cromford DE4 . . . .**155** B7
Ilkeston DE7 . . . .**194** E4
Ripley DE5 . . . .**169** D2
Somercotes DE55 . . . .**170** D5
Youlgreave DE45 . . . .**125** C5
Mount Pleasant Ct S32 . . .**72** C8
Mount Pleasant Dr
Belper DE56 . . . .**178** E5
Heage DE56 . . . .**179** E8
Mount Pleasant La DE12 .**265** A8
Mount Pleasant Rd
Grindleford S32 . . . .**72** C8
Linton DE11 . . . .**261** E8
Repton DE65 . . . .**242** E1
Swadlincote DE11 . . . .**256** A1
Mount St
Bretby DE15 . . . .**249** A3
Compstall SK14 . . . .**15** A6
Hartshorne DE11 . . . .**257** A4
Linton DE11 . . . .**261** D8
Mount St Mary's RC Coll
S21 . . . .**60** C2
Mount St
Breaston DE72 . . . .**235** F7
Burton u T DE15 . . . .**248** A3
Derby DE1 . . . .**267** B1
Glossop SK13 . . . .**17** C8
Heanor DE75 . . . .**181** E1
Stapleford NG9 . . . .**223** E7
Mount The
Chesterfield S41 . . . .**77** A3
Stapleford NG9 . . . .**223** D6
Mount View Ave S8 . . . .**43** A3
Mount View Gdns S8 . . . .**43** A3
Mount View La S8 . . . .**43** A3
Mount View Rd S8 . . . .**43** B3
Mouselow Cl SK13 . . . .**9** F3
Mowbray Gdns DE24 . . . .**232** C8
Mowbray St DE24 . . . .**232** D8
Moy Ave DE24 . . . .**231** F2
Moyne Gdns DE73 . . . .**245** A8
Mudhurst La SK12 . . . .**32** E3
Mugginton CE Prim Sch
DE6 . . . .**188** C2
Muirfield Cl S40 . . . .**96** B6
Muirfield Dr DE3 . . . .**217** F2
Muirfield Way NG19 . . . .**136** E6
Mulberries Ct DE22 . . . .**204** E4
Mulberry Cl
Belper DE56 . . . .**179** B3
Wingerworth S42 . . . .**115** A4
Mulberry Croft
Brimington S43 . . . .**78** A1
Staveley S43 . . . .**78** A1
Mulberry Mews DE5 . . . .**180** C6
Mulberry Rd S21 . . . .**59** B2

Mulberry Way
Aston-on-T DE72 . . . .**246** A6
Hilton DE65 . . . .**228** E2
Killamarsh S21 . . . .**60** B5
Mull Ct 3 DE24 . . . .**231** D3
Mullion Pl DE24 . . . .**233** B5
Mumford Dr DE6 . . . .**185** D8
Mundella Pl S8 . . . .**43** A3
Mundella Prim Sch S8 . .**43** A3
Mundy's Dr DE75 . . . .**193** F8
Mundy CE Jun Sch DE75 .**193** F8
Mundy Cl DE21 . . . .**218** E6
Mundy St
Derby DE22 . . . .**218** E6
Heanor DE75 . . . .**181** E1
Ilkeston DE7 . . . .**194** E2
Munro Cl S21 . . . .**60** D6
Munro Ct DE24 . . . .**231** E4
Murrayfield Dr 6 DE7 . . . . . .**194** E3
Murray Park Com Sch
DE3 . . . .**217** F4
Murray Rd
Derby DE24 . . . .**217** F4
Killamarsh S21 . . . .**60** E7
Murray St DE24 . . . .**232** F8
Musard Way S21 . . . .**78** D1
Musard Way S21 . . . .**60** C6
Muse La
Boylestone DE6 . . . .**213** A2
Church Broughton DE6 . . . . . .**226** B7
Musgrave Ho S33 . . . .**40** B3
Mushroom Farm Ct
NG16 . . . .**182** D3
Mushroom La DE7 . . . .**194** F3
Muskham Ave DE7 . . . .**194** F3
Muskham Ct 8 NG19 . . . .**136** B1
Musters St NG20 . . . .**120** A4
Muswell Rd DE22 . . . .**217** E5
Mycock La SK17 . . . .**107** F5
Myers Cl DE24 . . . .**231** F4
Mynd The NG19 . . . .**136** E6
Myrtle Ave
Long Eaton NG10 . . . .**236** C6
Stapleford NG9 . . . .**223** E6
Myrtle Cl NG20 . . . .**119** D6
Myrtle Gr S43 . . . .**78** A1
Myrtle Rd S2 . . . .**43** B7
Myrtle Springs S12 . . . .**43** F5
Myrtle Springs Dr S12 . . . . . .**43** F5
Myrtle Springs Sch S12 . . . . .**43** F6
Mytham Bridge S33 . . . .**40** B1
Mytholme Cl NG10 . . . .**223** C2

N

Nabb La ST14 . . . .**196** A4
Nailers Way DE56 . . . .**179** C5
Nailor La DE4 . . . .**142** D3
Nairn Ave DE21 . . . .**219** D7
Nairn Cl DE24 . . . .**231** E3
Nairn Dr S18 . . . .**56** D1
Namur Cl DE22 . . . .**218** C3
Nan Gell's Hill DE4 . . . .**155** A3
Napier Cl DE3 . . . .**217** E4
Napier St S43 . . . .**80** B5
Napier St DE22 . . . .**218** C5
Napoleon Pk DE24 . . . .**232** E7
Narlow La DE6 . . . .**161** F2
Narrow La
Denstone ST14 . . . .**196** D6
Donisthorpe DE12 . . . .**265** E8
Ticknall DE73 . . . .**250** F4
Narrowleys La S45 . . . .**129** F3
Naseby Cl DE3 . . . .**217** C3
Naseby Dr NG10 . . . .**236** E4
Naseby Rd DE56 . . . .**179** D4
Nathaniel Rd NG10 . . . .**236** E6
National Stone Ctr* DE4 .**154** F3
National Tramway Mus*
DE4 . . . .**156** E2
Navan Rd S2 . . . .**44** A7
Navigation Home Pk
Derby DE24 . . . .**219** E1
Derby DE24 . . . .**232** E8
Neal Ct NG16 . . . .**182** A3
Neale Bank S43 . . . .**96** D7
Neale St
Clowne S43 . . . .**80** F4
Long Eaton NG10 . . . .**236** E7
Near Mdw NG10 . . . .**236** E5
Nearwell Cl SK23 . . . .**45** E6
Nearwood Dr DE21 . . . .**205** E3
Needham St DE5 . . . .**181** B8
Needham Terr DE4 . . . .**143** A7
Needwood Ave DE13 . . . .**240** C4
Need Wood Ave NG20 . . . . . .**209** D2
Needwood Ct DE13 . . . .**239** C6
Neighwood Cl NG9 . . . .**223** E2
Neilson St DE24 . . . .**232** F7
Nelper Cres DE7 . . . .**209** A5
Nelson Cl DE3 . . . .**217** F3
Nelson Pl DE55 . . . .**257** F3
Nelson St
Burton u T DE15 . . . .**248** C4
Chesterfield S41 . . . .**96** A6
Derby DE1 . . . .**267** D1
Ilkeston DE7 . . . .**194** F3
Long Eaton NG10 . . . .**236** D6
Swadlincote DE11 . . . .**256** B5
Nene Cl DE13 . . . .**240** C1
Nene Way DE65 . . . .**240** D8
Nerissa Cl DE23 . . . .**232** E2
Nesbit St S44 . . . .**118** B8
Nesfield Cl
Chesterfield S41 . . . .**95** C8
Derby DE24 . . . .**233** C7
Nesfield Ct DE7 . . . .**194** E1

Nesfield Rd DE7 . . . . **194** E1
Ness Wlk DE22 . . . . **204** E3
Nestor Cl DE73 . . . . **232** D2
Nether Ave S21 . . . . .60 C6
Nether Blindlow La
  SK17 . . . . **106** B5
Netherby Manor S17 . . . . . .36 A7
Nether Cl
  Duffield DE56 . . . . **190** E5
  Eastwood NG16 . . . . **182** F4
  Swanwick DE55 . . . . **169** F7
  Wingerworth S42 . . . . **115** A2
Netherclose St DE23 . . . . . **219** A1
Nether Croft Cl S43 . . . . . . .96 E7
Nether Croft Rd S43 . . . . . .96 E7
Netherdene Rd S18 . . . . . . .57 A1
Nether Farm Cl S43 . . . . . . .96 F5
Netherfield Cl
  Ashbourne DE6 . . . . **185** C8
  Staveley S43 . . . . .79 A2
Netherfield La DE72,
  DE74 . . . . **247** F8
Netherfield Rd
  Chapel-en-le-F SK23 . . . . . .47 D6
  Chesterfield S40 . . . . **114** A8
  Long Eaton NG10 . . . . **236** C4
  Sandiacre NG10 . . . . **223** B4
Netherfields Cres S18 . . . . .76 A8
Nether Gdns DE4 . . . . **165** F8
Nethergreen Ave S21 . . . . . .60 D7
Nethergreen Ct S21 . . . . . . .60 D7
Nethergreen Gdns S21 . . . .60 D7
Nether La
  Brassington DE4 . . . . **163** F8
  Hazelwood DE56 . . . . **190** A7
  Holbrook DE56 . . . . **191** D6
  Kirk Ireton DE6 . . . . **176** B8
Netherleigh Cl S40 . . . . .95 B3
Netherleigh Rd S40 . . . . . . .95 B3
Nethermoor Ave S21 . . . . . .60 D7
Nethermoor Cl S21 . . . . .60 D7
Nethermoor Cotts DE55 . .147 D5
Nethermoor La S21 . . . . . . .60 D7
Nethermoor La S21 . . . . . . .60 D7
Nethermoor Rd
  Tupton S42 . . . . **131** C8
  Wingerworth S42 . . . . **115** A1
Nether Park Dr DE22 . . . . **204** C3
Netherseal Rd
  Chilcote NP12 . . . . **264** F4
  Clifton Campville B79 . . . . **263** F2
Netherside S33 . . . . .51 A7
Netherside Rd DE73 . . . . . **233** B2
Nether Springs Rd S44 . . . .98 F3
Netherthorpe S43 . . . . .79 A2
Netherthorpe Airfield
  S80 .63 B5
Netherthorpe Cl
  Killamarsh S21 . . . . .60 C7
  Staveley S43 . . . . .78 F2
Netherthorpe Flash Nature
  Reserve* S43 . . . . .79 B2
Netherthorpe La S21 . . . . . .60 C7
Netherthorpe Rd ❸ S43 . . .78 F2
Nether Thorpe Rd S80 . . . . .63 B5
Netherthorpe Sch S43 . . . .79 A2
Nether Way DE4 . . . . **127** C3
Netherwood Ct DE22 . . . . **204** C3
Netlefold Cres DE73 . . . . **245** B1
Nettleton Cl DE23 . . . . **231** A6
Nettleton La S17 . . . . .85 D3
Nettleworth Inf Sch
  NG19 . . . . **136** C4
Networkcentre Barlborough
  Links S43 . . . . .80 A5
Neville Cl DE13 . . . . **240** B3
Nevinson Ave DE23 . . . . . **231** D7
Nevinson Dr DE23 . . . . **231** D7
Nevis Cl
  Chesterfield S40 . . . . .95 D4
  Derby DE24 . . . . **231** D2
Newark ❻ S20 . . . . .59 E8
Newark Rd DE21 . . . . **205** D2
New Bank St SK13 . . . . .10 A5
New Barlborough Cl S43 . .80 D5
Newbarn Cl NG20 . . . . **119** D2
New Bath Rd DE4 . . . . **155** A8
New Beetwell St S40 . . . . **266** B2
Newbery Ave NG10 . . . . . . **236** F6
Newbold Ave
  Borrowash DE72 . . . . **221** C1
  Chesterfield S41 . . . . .95 E6
Newbold Back La S40 . . . . .95 E5
Newbold CE Prim Sch
  S41 .95 E7
Newbold Cl DE73 . . . . **232** F2
Newbold Com Sch S41 . . . .95 F6
Newbold Ct ❶ S41 . . . . . . .95 D7
Newbold Dr
  Castle Donington DE74 . . **247** B5
  Chesterfield S41 . . . . .95 E6
Newbold Rd S40 . . . . .95 D6
New Bolsover Prim Sch
  S44 .98 F1
Newborough Rd DE24 . . . **233** C6
Newbound La NG17 . . . . . **134** C2
Newboundmill La NG19 . .135 A4
New Breck Rd DE56 . . . . . **179** A3
Newbridge Cl DE7 . . . . . . **207** D8
Newbridge Cres DE24 . . . **232** E4
Newbridge Ct S41 . . . . .77 A1
Newbridge Dr S43 . . . . .96 D8
Newbridge La
  Brimington S43 . . . . .96 D8
  Chesterfield S41 . . . . .77 B1
Newbridge Rd DE56 . . . . . **168** A2
Newbridge St S41 . . . . .77 A1

Newburgh Terr S32 . . . . . . .72 C2
Newbury Dr DE13 . . . . **240** C1
Newbury St DE24 . . . . **232** E8
Newby Cl DE15 . . . . **248** B1
Newby Rd S41 . . . . .95 C8
Newcastle St
  Mansfield Woodhouse
    NG19 . . . . **136** B3
  Sutton in A NG17 . . . . . . **148** F3
Newchase Bsns Pk DE23 **219** C1
New Church St S33 . . . . . . .51 A7
New City Park Homes
  DE24 . . . . **220** A1
New City Pk Homes
  DE24 . . . . **233** A8
New Cl S32 . . . . .71 C6
New Cotts
  Buxton SK17 . . . . .84 E4
  Whaley Thorns NG20 . . . . **101** F3
New Derby Rd NG16 . . . . **182** D3
Newdigate St
  Derby DE21 . . . . **232** A8
  Ikeston DE7 . . . . **209** A6
  Kimberley NG16 . . . . **195** F6
  West Hallam DE7 . . . . **207** C8
New Eaton Rd NG9 . . . . . . **223** E5
Newell Way DE4 . . . . **127** C3
New England Way NG19 . .135 C3
New Fall St NG17 . . . . **148** F3
Newfield Cres S17 . . . . .55 C7
Newfield Croft S17 . . . . . . .55 C8
Newfield Farm Cl S14 . . . . .43 E5
Newfield Green Rd S2 . . . . .43 D6
Newfield La S17 . . . . .55 C7
Newfield Pl S17 . . . . .55 C7
Newfield Rd DE15 . . . . **248** B4
Newfield Sec Sch S8 . . . . . .43 C3
Newgate Cl DE73 . . . . **233** B2
Newhall Com Jun Sch
  DE11 . . . . **255** E6
Newhall Inf Sch DE11 . . . . **255** F7
Newhall Rd DE11 . . . . **256** C5
New Hall Rd S40 . . . . .95 D2
Newham Ave DE5 . . . . **169** C1
Newham Cl DE75 . . . . **182** A1
Newhaven Ave NG19 . . . . **136** B3
Newhaven Cl S40 . . . . .95 B1
Newhaven Cvn & Camping
  Pk SK17 . . . . **138** B4
New Haven Gdns S17 . . . . .55 E4
Newhaven Rd DE21 . . . . . **220** B6
Newhay DE13 . . . . **240** F1
New High St SK17 . . . . .85 D8
Newholme Hospl DE45 . . **109** D7
New Horwich Rd SK23 . . . . .45 E4
New Houses
  Chesterfield S41 . . . . .96 C3
  Tideswell SK17 . . . . .88 E8
New Inn La DE21 . . . . **205** C7
New La
  Bradwell S33 . . . . .50 E6
  Hilcote DE55 . . . . **148** C1
New Lamb Inn Sta*
  DE55 . . . . **170** C3
Newland Dale S41 . . . . . . **266** B4
Newland Gdns S41 . . . . . . .95 E5
Newlands Ave
  Chesterfield S40 . . . . .95 C3
  Sheffield S12 . . . . .44 A6
Newlands Barns DE22 . . . **189** E3
Newlands Cl
  Ripley DE5 . . . . **169** E2
  Swadlincote DE11 . . . . . . **256** A2
Newlands Cres DE55 . . . . **148** A3
Newlands Dr
  Glossop SK13 . . . . .9 F4
  Heanor DE75 . . . . **181** E3
  Sheffield S12 . . . . .44 A6
  Somercotes DE55 . . . . . . **170** D5
Newlands Gr S12 . . . . .44 B6
Newlands Ho DE55 . . . . . . **170** D4
Newlands Inn Sta* DE55 **170** D5
Newlands Rd
  Sheffield S12 . . . . .44 A6
  Somercotes DE55 . . . . . . **170** C4
Newlands The DE1 . . . . . . **267** A3
New Lane Galleries
  DE55 . . . . **159** A4
New Lawn Rd DE7 . . . . . . **208** E8
New Linden St NG20 . . . . **120** A4
New Lumford DE45 . . . . . . **109** C7
Newlyn Dr
  Derby DE23 . . . . **231** F8
  Somercotes DE55 . . . . . . **160** C6
Newlyn Pl S8 . . . . .43 A3
Newman Dr DE14 . . . . **254** B8
Newmanleys Rd NG16 . . . **194** F8
Newmanleys Rd S NG16 . .194 E8
Newmanleys Road (South)
  NG16 . . . . **182** E1
Newmarket Ct DE24 . . . . **219** E1
Newmarket Dr DE24 . . . . **232** E8
Newmarket La S45 . . . . . . **130** F3
New Market St SK17 . . . . . .85 B6
Newmarket Way NG9 . . . . **223** F2
New Mill La NG19 . . . . **136** E3
New Mills Central Sta
  SK22 . . . . .33 B7
New Mills Heritage Ctr*
  SK22 . . . . .33 B7
New Mills Newtown Sta
  SK22 . . . . .33 B8
New Mills Prim Sch SK22 .33 B8
New Mills Rd
  Broadbottom SK13 . . . . . . .16 A4
  Hayfield SK22 . . . . .25 B3

New Mills Sch & Sixth Form
  Ctr SK22 . . . . .33 C8
New Mount Cl DE23. . . . . **231** D5
Newness Ct DE4 . . . . **143** C6
New Park Cl SK22 . . . . .33 D7
New Park Pl DE24 . . . . **219** D3
Newport Cres NG19 . . . . . **135** E1
Newport Ct DE24 . . . . **233** C5
Newquay Pl DE24 . . . . **233** C5
New Queen St S41 . . . . . . **266** B4
New Rd
  Apperknowle S18 . . . . .58 A1
  Bamford S33 . . . . .40 B5
  Barlborough S43 . . . . .80 B7
  Barton in F NG11 . . . . **237** F6
  Belper DE56 . . . . **178** D4
  Bradwell, Bradwell Hills S33 .51 B6
  Bradwell S33 . . . . .51 A4
  Coton in t E DE12 . . . . **260** D3
  Crich DE4 . . . . **168** A8
  Derby DE22 . . . . **205** A1
  Eyam S32 . . . . .71 F5
  Flash SK17 . . . . **103** A3
  Glossop SK13 . . . . .9 F7
  Grindleford S32 . . . . .72 B5
  Heage DE56 . . . . **179** D8
  Hilton DE65 . . . . **228** E2
  Holmesfield S18 . . . . .75 A5
  Holymoorside S42 . . . . . . **113** D7
  Horwich End SK23 . . . . . . .45 E6
  Idridgehay DE56 . . . . **176** F4
  Ironville NG16 . . . . **170** F3
  Middleton DE4 . . . . **154** B5
  Ridgeway DE56 . . . . **168** B4
  Somercotes NG16, DE55 . .170 D2
  Stapleford NG9 . . . . **209** D1
  Swadlincote DE11 . . . . . . **255** E6
  Uttoxeter ST14 . . . . **210** A1
  Weston Underwood DE6 . **188** D1
  Whaley Bridge, Bridgemoor
    SK23 . . . . .33 F1
  Whaley Bridge SK23 . . . . . .34 A1
  Wingerworth S42 . . . . **114** E3
  Wirksworth DE4 . . . . **155** A3
  Woodville DE11 . . . . **256** E2
  Youlgreave DE45 . . . . **125** C5
New Road Ind Est NG9 . . **209** D1
New Row NG16 . . . . **171** A5
New School Cl S20 . . . . . . .59 C7
New School Gr S20 . . . . . . .59 C7
New School Rd S20 . . . . . . .59 C7
New Scott St NG20 . . . . . . **101** A2
Newshaw La SK13 . . . . .9 F4
New Sq S40 . . . . **266** B3
New St
  Alfreton DE55 . . . . **159** A4
  Bakewell DE45 . . . . **109** D6
  Bolsover S44 . . . . .99 A3
  ❸ Broadbottom SK14 . . . . .16 A8
  Buxton SK17 . . . . .67 B5
  Chesterfield S40 . . . . **266** B2
  Derby DE1 . . . . **267** C2
  Donisthorpe DE12 . . . . . . **262** E1
  Draycott DE72 . . . . **235** A7
  Grassmoor S42 . . . . **115** F3
  Hilcote DE55 . . . . **160** C8
  Little Eaton DE21 . . . . **205** C8
  Long Eaton NG10 . . . . **236** E8
  Matlock DE4 . . . . **143** C5
  New Mills SK22 . . . . .33 D7
  North Wingfield S42 . . . . **131** F6
  Ockbrook DE72 . . . . **221** C4
  Pilsley S45 . . . . **132** D1
  Ripley DE5 . . . . **169** E1
  Rosliston DE12 . . . . **260** D6
  Sheffield, Holbrook S20 . . .60 A8
  Shirland DE55 . . . . **146** C2
  Somercotes DE55 . . . . . . **170** C8
  South Normanton DE55 . .160 A6
  Stanley DE7 . . . . **207** C6
  Stonebroom DE55 . . . . . . **147** B3
  Sutton in A NG17 . . . . . . **148** F3
  Swadlincote DE11 . . . . . . **256** B2
  Swanwick DE55 . . . . **169** E7
  Whitwell S80 . . . . .81 E5
New Station Rd S44 . . . . . . .99 B1
Newstead Ave
  Derby DE21 . . . . **219** F6
  Sheffield S12 . . . . .44 E3
Newstead Cl
  Dronfield S18 . . . . .56 C1
  Sheffield S12 . . . . .44 E3
Newstead Dr S12 . . . . .44 E2
Newstead Gr S12 . . . . .44 E3
Newstead Pl S12 . . . . .44 E2
Newstead Rd
  Long Eaton NG10 . . . . **223** C3
  Sheffield S12 . . . . .44 F3
Newstead Rd N DE7 . . . . **194** D3
Newstead Rd S DE7 . . . . . **194** D3
Newstead Rise S12 . . . . . . .44 F2
Newstead Terr ❸ SK17 . . . .85 B6
Newstead Way S12 . . . . . . .44 E2
New Street Bus Link S20 . .60 A8
New Terr
  Pleasley NG19 . . . . **134** F5
  Sandiacre NG10 . . . . **223** B6
Newton Comm Prim NG16 .195 A8
Newton's Wlk DE22 . . . . . **218** E8
Newton Cl
  Belper DE56 . . . . **179** C6
  Newton Solney DE15 . . . . **248** E8
Newton ❶❻ S41 . . . . .95 F8
Newtondale Ave NG19 . . .136 E1

Newton Dr NG9 . . . . **223** E6
Newton La
  Bretby DE15 . . . . **249** A5
  Newton Solney DE15 . . . . **248** E7
  Tibshelf DE55 . . . . **147** F6
Newton Leys DE15 . . . . . . **248** C4
Newton Park Cl ❷ DE11 . .256 A7
Newton Pk DE15 . . . . **248** A3
Newton Prim Sch DE55 . . **148** A3
Newton Rd
  Burton u T DE15 . . . . **248** A5
  Tibshelf DE55 . . . . **147** F4
Newtons Croft Cres S43 . . .80 B6
Newtons La NG16 . . . . **195** B4
Newton Solney CE Inf Sch
  DE15 . . . . **248** E8
Newton Wonder Cl DE7 . .245 B1
Newtonwood La DE55,
  NG17 . . . . **148** C5
Newtown Prim Sch SK22 . .33 B6
New Tythe St NG10 . . . . . **236** F7
New Westwood NG16 . . . **171** D4
New Whittington Com Prim
  Sch
  Chesterfield S43 . . . . .77 D3
  Chesterfield S43 . . . . .77 D4
New Wye St SK17 . . . . .85 C8
New Zealand La DE56 . . . **190** E2
New Zealand Sq DE22 . . . **218** C5
Nicholas Cl DE21 . . . . **220** E6
Nicholas St S41 . . . . **266** B4
Nicholson's Row NG20 . . **119** F3
Nicholson Ct
  ❾ Sheffield S8 . . . . .43 B6
  Tideswell SK17 . . . . .69 C4
Nicholson Pl ❼ S8 . . . . . . .43 B6
Nicholson Rd S8 . . . . .43 A6
Nicklaus Cl DE14 . . . . **254** A7
Nicola Gdns DE23 . . . . . . **231** D4
Nicolas Cl SK17 . . . . .85 E8
Nidderdale Ct DE24 . . . . . **233** D6
Nields Way SK6 . . . . .23 D4
Nightingale Ave NG19 . . . **135** A4
Nightingale Bsns Pk
  DE24 . . . . **232** D8
Nightingale Ct
  Chesterfield S41 . . . . **266** B4
  Clay Cross S45 . . . . **131** E2
  Holloway DE4 . . . . **155** F6
  Ripley DE5 . . . . **169** D1
Nightingale Dr
  Mansfield NG16 . . . . **135** E1
  Woodville DE11 . . . . **256** F3
Nightingale Jun & Inf Schs
  DE24 . . . . **232** D2
Nightingale Mews DE11 . **267** D2
Nightingale Rd DE24 . . . . **232** C8
Nikolas Rd S21 . . . . .60 B1
Nimbus Way NG16 . . . . . . **195** F7
Nine Ladies Stone Circ*
  DE4 . . . . **126** D3
Ninelands Rd S32 . . . . .53 A7
Nix's Hill DE55 . . . . **159** B2
Noble St DE1 . . . . **267** D1
Nodder Rd S13 . . . . .44 C7
Nodin Hill La DE56 . . . . . . **168** B3
Noe La S33 . . . . .40 A2
Noel-Baker Com Sch
  DE24 . . . . **232** F4
Noel St DE22 . . . . **218** D6
No Man's Heath Rd DE12 **264** F3
No Man's La DE7, DE27 . . **222** D7
Nook End Rd DE75 . . . . . . **181** D1
Nook La S44 . . . . .97 B3
Nook The
  Barrow u T DE73 . . . . **244** A6
  Heanor DE75 . . . . **181** C4
  Holbrook DE56 . . . . **191** C7
  Shirebrook NG20 . . . . **119** D3
  Stoney Middleton S32 . . . .72 A4
Nooning La DE72 . . . . **234** E8
Norbriggs Prim Sch S43 . .79 B3
Norbriggs Rd S43 . . . . .79 C2
Norburn Dr S21 . . . . .60 D6
Norbury CE Prim Sch
  DE6 . . . . **197** C7
Norbury Cl
  Chesterfield S40 . . . . .95 B5
  Derby DE22 . . . . **204** D1
  Dronfield S18 . . . . .56 D1
Norbury Cres DE23 . . . . . **231** C5
Norbury Ct ❷ DE22 . . . . . **204** D2
Norbury Hollow DE6 . . . . **183** D1
Norbury Way
  Belper DE56 . . . . **179** C6
  Sandiacre NG10 . . . . **223** A6
Norfolk Ave S42 . . . . **115** F2
Norfolk Cl S40 . . . . **114** B8
Norfolk Com Prim Sch
  S2 . . . . .43 D8
Norfolk Ct NG19 . . . . **136** E5
Norfolk Gdns DE22 . . . . . **218** F8
Norfolk Park Ave S2 . . . . . .43 D8
Norfolk Rd
  Burton u T DE15 . . . . **254** D7
  Long Eaton NG10 . . . . **223** F1
Norfolk Sq ❸ SK13 . . . . . .10 C1
Norfolk St
  Derby DE23 . . . . **219** B2
  Glossop SK13 . . . . .10 D1
Norfolk Wlk NG10 . . . . . . **223** B5
Norgreave Way S20 . . . . . .59 E7
Norman Ave DE23 . . . . . . **231** E7
Norman Cres DE7 . . . . **194** E3
Normandy Rd DE65 . . . . . **228** E2
Normanhurst Pk DE4 . . . . **127** E1
Norman Keep DE13 . . . . . **239** C6

Norman Rd
  Ripley DE5 . . . . **169** C1
  Somercotes DE55 . . . . . . **170** E7
  Tutbury DE13 . . . . **239** C6
Norman St
  Ilkeston DE7 . . . . **194** E3
  Kimberley NG16 . . . . **195** F7
Normanton Ave S21 . . . . . **159** C3
Normanton Brook Rd
  DE55 . . . . **160** D7
Normanton Hill S13 . . . . . . .44 F6
Normanton Ho ❸ SK17 . . .85 A7
Normanton House Prim Sch
  DE23 . . . . **231** E7
Normanton Jun Sch
  DE23 . . . . **231** E7
Normanton La DE23 . . . . **231** E8
Normanton Lo DE23 . . . . **231** E8
Normanton Rd DE1 . . . . . **267** B1
Normanton Spring Ct S13 .44 F6
Normanton Spring Rd
  S13 .44 F5
Normanton Village Inf Sch
  DE23 . . . . **231** F8
Northacre Rd DE21 . . . . . **206** B2
Northam Dr DE5 . . . . **169** C2
North Ave
  Ashbourne DE6 . . . . **173** B2
  Derby, Darley Abbey DE22 . .205 A3
  Derby DE3 . . . . **217** E2
  Sandiacre NG10 . . . . **223** A6
North Brook Rd SK13 . . . . . .9 E4
North Church St DE45 . . . **109** D6
North Cl
  Derby DE3 . . . . **217** E3
  Glossop SK13 . . . . .9 F7
  South Normanton DE55 . . **159** F5
  Unstone Green S18 . . . . . . .76 E6
  Willington DE65 . . . . **242** B5
Northcliffe Rd DE22 . . . . . **173** B2
Northcote Ave S2 . . . . .43 B6
Northcote Rd S2 . . . . .43 B6
Northcote St NG10 . . . . . . **236** E7
North Cres
  Duckmanton S44 . . . . .98 A5
  Killamarsh S21 . . . . .60 E8
North Derbyshire Tertiary
  Coll (Markland Campus)
  S80 .81 E3
Northedge La S42 . . . . **130** B7
North End DE4 . . . . **154** F1
Northern Ave S2 . . . . .43 E7
Northern Comm S18 . . . . . .56 B2
Northern Dr NG9 . . . . **209** D3
Northern Rd DE75 . . . . . . **181** D2
North Farm Cl S26 . . . . . . .61 E7
Northfield
  Derby DE24 . . . . **231** D3
  Kilburn DE56 . . . . **179** F2
Northfield Ave
  Ilkeston DE7 . . . . **194** E1
  Long Eaton NG10 . . . . **236** B4
  Mansfield Woodhouse
    NG19. . . . . **136** A4
  Rocester ST14 . . . . **197** A4
Northfield Cl ST14 . . . . . . **210** A2
Northfield Cres NG4 . . . . **223** F4
Northfield Jun Sch S18 . . .57 C3
Northfield La
  Mansfield Woodhouse
    NG19. . . . . **135** F4
  Mansfield Woodhouse
    NG19. . . . . **136** B5
  Palterton S44 . . . . **118** C6
Northfield Pk NG19 . . . . . **136** B5
Northfield Prim Sch
  NG19 . . . . **136** B5
Northfield Rd NG9 . . . . . . **223** F4
Northfields
  Clowne S43 . . . . .80 F3
  Long Eaton NG10 . . . . **236** B4
Northgate DE11 . . . . **267** B4
North Gate S44 . . . . .98 E3
Northgate Ho S21 . . . . .59 D3
Northgate St ❹ DE7 . . . . **194** F1
North Gr S44 . . . . .98 A6
North La
  Belper, Milford DE56 . . . . **190** E7
  Brailsford DE56 . . . . **187** E4
  Old Brampton S42. . . . . . . .94 D4
Northlands
  ❹ Buxton SK17 . . . . .85 D8
  Harthill S26 . . . . .61 E7
North Leys DE6 . . . . **173** B1
Northmead Dr DE3 . . . . . **218** B3
North Mill DE56 . . . . **178** F5
Northmoor Cl S43 . . . . .96 F7
North Moor View S43 . . . . .96 F7
North Par
  Derby DE1 . . . . **267** A4
  Matlock Bath DE4 . . . . . . **143** A1
North Rd
  Buxton SK17 . . . . .66 D1
  Calow S44 . . . . .96 F3
  Clowne S43 . . . . .80 E4
  Glossop SK13 . . . . .10 C3
  Hayfield SK22 . . . . .25 D3
  Long Eaton NG10 . . . . **236** C6
North Row DE22 . . . . **205** A1
Northside S42 . . . . **115** D1
North Side S42 . . . . **115** D1
North St
  Alfreton DE55 . . . . **159** B3
  Blackwell DE55 . . . . **147** F2

North St continued
Bramley-Vale S44 . . . . **117** D1
Burton u T DE15 . . . . **248** B3
Clay Cross S45 . . . . **131** B5
Cromford DE4 . . . . **155** A6
Derby DE1 . . . . **267** B5
Derby DE23 . . . . **218** C2
7 Ilkeston DE7 . . . . **194** F1
Langley Mill NG16 . . . . **182** B3
Melbourne DE73 . . . . **252** A7
North Wingfield S42 . . . . . . **131** E6
Pinxton NG16 . . . . **160** D3
Shirebrook NG20 . . . . **120** D4
Somercotes DE55 . . . . **170** D6
South Normanton DE55 . . . **159** F5
Swadlincote DE11 . . . . **256** B5
Whaley Thorns NG20 . . . . . **101** A2
North Terr 1 S41 . . . . **115** B7
Northumberland Rd
DE15 . . . . **254** D7
Northumberland St
DE23 . . . . **218** F2
North Ave
Crich DE4 . . . . **168** A8
Derby DE23 . . . . **218** C1
North View St S44 . . . . **98** F1
Northway Dr DE1 . . . . **218** E4
North Wingfield Inf & Jun
Sch S42 . . . . **131** F7
North Wingfield Rd S42 . . **115** E3
Northwood Ave
Darley Dale DE4 . . . . **127** C3
Derby DE21 . . . . **219** E7
Northwood La
Ellastone DE6 . . . . **183** C5
Northwood DE4 . . . . **127** A6
Northwood Rise DE6 . . . . . **185** B8
Northwood St NG9 . . . . . . **223** D8
Norton Ave
Chesterfield S40 . . . . **114** A8
Sheffield S14 . . . . **43** E2
Shuttlewood S44 . . . . **98** F6
Norton Church Glebe S8 . . **43** C1
Norton Church Rd S8 . . . . . **43** B1
Norton Free CE Prim Sch
S8 . . . . **43** C1
Norton Green Cl S8 . . . . **43** C1
Norton Hall S8 . . . . **43** B1
Norton Hall Ct S8 . . . . **43** B1
Norton La S8 . . . . **43** C1
Norton Lawns S8 . . . . **43** C1
Norton Lees Cl S8 . . . . **43** A3
Norton Lees Cres S8 . . . . . . **43** A4
Norton Lees Glade S8 . . . . . **43** A4
Norton Lees La S8 . . . . **43** A4
Norton Lees Rd S8 . . . . **43** A4
Norton Lees Sq S8 . . . . **43** A3
Norton Mews S8 . . . . **43** C1
Norton Park Ave S8 . . . . **57** B8
Norton Park Cres S8 . . . . . . **57** A8
Norton Park Dr S8 . . . . **57** A8
Norton Park Rd S8 . . . . **57** B8
Norton Park View S8 . . . . . . **57** B8
Norwell Cl 2 NG16 . . . . . **136** B1
Norwich Cl NG19 . . . . **136** D5
Norwich St DE21 . . . . **219** D7
Norwood Ave S41 . . . . **115** C6
Norwood Cl
Chesterfield S41 . . . . **115** E6
Derby DE22 . . . . **218** A5
Norwood Cres S21 . . . . **60** F7
Norwood Ind Est S21 . . . . . **60** E8
Norwood Pl S21 . . . . **60** F7
Nothills Cl DE73 . . . . **233** A1
Nottingham Canal Nature
Reserve The* DE7,
NG16 . . . . **195** C1
Nottingham Cl S42 . . . . . . **115** B3
Nottingham Dr S42 . . . . . . **115** B3
Nottingham East Midlands
Airport Aeropark*
DE74 . . . . **247** A4
Nottingham La NG16 . . . . **170** F5
Nottingham Rd
Alfreton DE55 . . . . **159** B2
Ashby-de-la-Z LE65 . . . . . . **258** F1
Belper DE56 . . . . **179** B4
Borrowash DE72 . . . . **221** D2
Breedon on t H DE73 . . . . . **252** D1
Codnor DE5, NG16 . . . . **181** C8
Derby, Chaddesden DE21 . . **219** E6
Derby DE1, DE21 . . . . **267** C4
Derby, Spondon DE21 . . . . **220** E3
Eastwood, Bailey Grove
NG16 . . . . **182** E2
Eastwood, Giltbrook NG16 **195** C8
Ilkeston DE7 . . . . **209** A6
Long Eaton NG10 . . . . **236** F8
Ripley DE5 . . . . **169** E2
Selston NG16 . . . . **171** F6
Stapleford NG9 . . . . **223** E7
Tansley DE4 . . . . **144** B4
Trowell NG9 . . . . **209** E5
Nowill Ct 2 S8 . . . . **43** A6
Nowill Pl 3 S8 . . . . **43** A6
Nun's St DE1 . . . . **218** E6
Nunbrook Gr DE4 . . . . **143** B4
Nunn Brook Rd NG17 . . . . **148** E2
Nunn Brook Rise NG17 . . **148** E2
Nunn Cl NG17 . . . . **148** E2
Nunsfield Dr DE24 . . . . . . **233** B7
Nunsfield Rd SK17 . . . . **66** C1
Nursery Ave
Sandiacre NG10 . . . . **222** F5
West Hallam DE7 . . . . **207** E7

Nursery Cl
Borrowash DE72 . . . . **221** B2
4 Glossop SK13 . . . . **17** C8
Swadlincote DE11 . . . . **256** B6
Nursery Croft DE4 . . . . . . **165** E6
Nursery Dr
Bolsover S44 . . . . **98** F2
Buxton SK17 . . . . **66** C2
Nursery Gdns DE55 . . . . . . **160** C4
Nursery Hollow DE7 . . . . . **208** E6
Nursery La SK17 . . . . **84** E6
Nutbrook Cres DE7 . . . . . . **208** D4
Nuthall Circ DE7 . . . . **208** C4
Nuthall Cl DE55 . . . . **158** F3
Nuttall St DE55 . . . . **158** F3
Nuttall Terr S44 . . . . **117** D1
Nutwood Cl DE22 . . . . **205** A3

O

Oadby Dr S41 . . . . **115** C7
Oadby Rise DE23 . . . . **231** E6
Oakamoor Cl S40 . . . . **95** A5
Oak Apple Cres DE7 . . . . . **208** E6
Oak Ave
Aldercar NG16 . . . . **182** B5
Disley SK12 . . . . **33** A6
Ripley DE5 . . . . **180** D7
Sandiacre NG10 . . . . **223** A7
Shirebrook NG20 . . . . **119** D4
Oak Bank SK12 . . . . **33** A6
Oak Bank Ave S41 . . . . **77** B2
Oakbank Ct S17 . . . . **55** E5
Oak Cl
Brimington S43 . . . . **96** D7
Chapel-en-le-F SK23 . . . . . . **47** C5
Derby DE22 . . . . **204** E4
Duffield DE56 . . . . **190** E2
Killamarsh S21 . . . . **60** C5
Linton DE11 . . . . **261** E7
Mottram in L SK14 . . . . **9** A4
Ockbrook DE72 . . . . **221** C5
Pinxton NG16 . . . . **160** C3
Oak Cres
Ashbourne DE6 . . . . **185** C7
Derby DE23 . . . . **231** C8
Wingerworth S42 . . . . **114** F3
Oakdale Cl S45 . . . . **131** E2
Oakdale Gdns DE21 . . . . . . **206** B3
Oakdale Rd DE55 . . . . **160** A4
Oakdell S18 . . . . **57** D7
Oak Dr
Alfreton DE55 . . . . **159** B4
Derby, Boulton DE24 . . . . . **233** A6
Derby DE3 . . . . **217** E2
Doveridge DE6 . . . . **211** B1
Eastwood NG16 . . . . **182** E2
Hilton DE65 . . . . **228** D2
Mansfield Woodhouse
NG19 . . . . **136** C2
Oaker Terr DE4 . . . . **142** A7
Oakerthorpe Rd DE4 . . . . . **155** B2
Oakey's Row NG16 . . . . **170** F5
Oakes Park Sch S8 . . . . **43** C2
Oakes Park View S14 . . . . . **43** D1
Oakes The S8 . . . . **43** B1
Oakfield Ave S40 . . . . **95** B1
Oakfield Ct DE7 . . . . **193** A2
Oakfield Dr NG10 . . . . **223** B3
Oakfield Rd
Glossop SK13 . . . . **9** E3
Stapleford NG9 . . . . **223** D7
Oakfields Gr DE21 . . . . **220** D3
Oakfields DE13 . . . . **238** A4
Oak Grove SK17 . . . . **55** E4
Oakham Cl DE21 . . . . **205** D1
Oakham Way DE7 . . . . **194** E3
Oakhill Rd S18 . . . . **57** C3
Oakhurst Cl DE56 . . . . **178** D6
Oak La DE6 . . . . **212** D4
Oakland Ave
Long Eaton NG10 . . . . **236** C5
Sutton in A NG17 . . . . **148** F2
Oakland Cres DE55 . . . . . . **170** D5
Oakland Croft NG17 . . . . . **148** F3
Oaklands SK22 . . . . **25** C3
Oaklands Ave
Derby DE23 . . . . **231** C5
Heanor DE75 . . . . **182** A2
Marple SK6 . . . . **23** C8
Oaklands Cl DE55 . . . . **180** D1
Oaklands Rd DE65 . . . . **229** C4
Oakland St DE55 . . . . **159** B4
Oaklands The DE55 . . . . . . **160** A4
Oaklands Way DE73 . . . . . . **252** B8
Oakland Terr NG10 . . . . . . **236** C5
Oaklea SK17 . . . . **85** C5
Oaklea Way S42 . . . . **131** B6
Oakleigh Ave
Derby DE21 . . . . **219** F6
Mansfield Woodhouse
NG19 . . . . **136** E4
Oakleigh Dr DE11 . . . . **255** F5
Oakley's Rd NG10 . . . . **236** E7
Oakley's Rd W NG10 . . . . . **236** D6
Oakley Ave S40 . . . . **95** E4
Oak Lodge Dr NG16 . . . . . . **195** F7
Oakmeadows DE55 . . . . . . **160** B4
Oakover Dr DE22 . . . . **204** D2
Oak Rd
Denstone ST14 . . . . **196** D5
Derby DE72 . . . . **233** F4
Grassmoor S42 . . . . **115** F3
Matlock DE4 . . . . **143** C5
Shardlow DE72 . . . . **234** A5

Oak Rd continued
Sheffield, Gleadless Townend
S12 . . . . **44** A2
Oakridge DE21 . . . . **220** B7
Oakridge Cl NG19 . . . . **136** F1
Oakridge Pk DE74 . . . . **247** A5
Oaks Ave
Creswell S80 . . . . **100** C8
Hayfield SK22 . . . . **25** D2
Oaks Barn DE45 . . . . **109** A2
Oaksedge La DE4 . . . . **144** A5
Oaks Farm La S44 . . . . **97** A2
Oakside Way DE21 . . . . **206** B3
Oaks La
Ashover S45 . . . . **129** C5
Cutthorpe S18, S42 . . . . **94** A8
Oak Sq DE11 . . . . **255** F2
Oaks Rd DE65 . . . . **242** B5
Oak St
Brimington S43 . . . . **78** A1
Derby DE23 . . . . **219** A2
Glossop SK13 . . . . **10** C1
Sheffield, Heeley S8 . . . . **43** A7
Sheffield S20 . . . . **59** C8
Swadlincote DE11 . . . . **256** A2
Oakstedge La S45 . . . . **145** B7
Oaks The
Glossop SK13 . . . . **17** A7
Little Eaton DE21 . . . . **205** C8
Oaktree Ave DE24 . . . . **232** B7
Oak Tree Ave S44 . . . . **134** B8
Oak Tree Cl
Arkwright Town S44 . . . . **97** D3
Swanwick DE55 . . . . **170** A8
Oak Tree Cotts S44 . . . . **97** A1
Oak Tree Cres NG19 . . . . . **136** B4
Oak Tree Ct DE72 . . . . **221** D1
Oak Tree Gdns DE4 . . . . . . **144** A4
Oaktree Rd DE55 . . . . **160** C8
Oak Tree Rd S43 . . . . **80** E2
Oakvale Ho DE23 . . . . **219** A2
Oakwell Cres DE7 . . . . **208** E8
Oakwell Dr
Crich DE4 . . . . **156** F1
Ilkeston DE7 . . . . **208** E8
Oakwood SK13 . . . . **16** F8
Oakwood Cl
Derby DE65 . . . . **231** D2
Hatton DE65 . . . . **239** C8
Oakwood District Ctr
DE21 . . . . **206** A1
Oakwood Dr
Darley Dale DE4 . . . . **142** E8
Derby DE21 . . . . **206** B2
Oakwood Inf Sch DE24 . . . **233** A6
Oakwood Jun Sch DE24 . . . **233** A6
Oakwood Rd SK12 . . . . **32** D6
Oakwood Way S43 . . . . **79** B4
Oakworth Cl 1 S20 . . . . **59** E6
Oakworth Dr S20 . . . . **59** D6
Oakworth Gr S20 . . . . **59** D6
Oakworth View S20 . . . . **59** D6
Oat Hill DE4 . . . . **165** F7
Oats Orch S20 . . . . **59** D6
Oberon Cl DE7 . . . . **232** E1
Occupation Cl S43 . . . . **80** A6
Occupation La
North Wingfield S42 . . . . . . **131** E7
Sheffield, Birley S12 . . . . **44** F3
Woodville DE11 . . . . **256** D1
Occupation Rd
Chesterfield S41 . . . . **95** F8
Moira DE11 . . . . **262** C8
New Houghton NG19 . . . . . **134** F7
Ochbrook Ct DE7 . . . . **194** F3
Ockbrook Sch DE72 . . . . . . **221** C5
Octavia Cl DE24 . . . . **232** E2
Octavia St S40 . . . . **266** A3
Oddfellows Cotts 15 SK17 . **85** B7
Oddfellows Rd S32 . . . . **53** A7
Oddfellows Row S32 . . . . . . **53** A7
Oddfellow Terr DE45 . . . . . **109** D6
Oddford La DE4 . . . . **127** D2
Odom Ct S2 . . . . **43** B6
Offcote Cres 1 DE6 . . . . . **173** D3
Offerton Ave DE23 . . . . . . **231** F8
Offridge Cl S43 . . . . **80** F2
Off Spring Bank SK22 . . . . **33** C8
Ogden St SK14 . . . . **16** B8
Ogston La DE55 . . . . **146** B4
Ogston New Rd DE55 . . . . **145** E4
Okeover Ave DE6 . . . . **173** D1
Oker Ave DE4 . . . . **127** B3
Oker Dr DE4 . . . . **127** B3
Oker La DE4 . . . . **142** D6
Oker Rd DE4 . . . . **142** B7
Old Bakery Cl
Chesterfield S41 . . . . **77** A2
Hognaston DE6 . . . . **164** B1
Old Bank DE6 . . . . **184** D8
Old Barn Cl DE21 . . . . **205** D8
Old Brick Works La S41 . . . . **96** A6
Oldbury Cl DE21 . . . . **206** A2
Old Chester Rd DE1 . . . . . . **219** A8
Old Church Ct DE22 . . . . . **204** C5
Old Coach Rd DE4 . . . . **143** F4
Old Coalpit La SK17 . . . . **86** F1
Old Colliery La S42 . . . . . . **132** E8
Old Coppice Side DE75 . . . **193** E7
Old Court House Shops 4
SK17 . . . . **85** B8
Old Cross SK13 . . . . **10** E2
Old Dam La SK17 . . . . **49** F4
Old Derby Rd
Ashbourne DE6 . . . . **185** D8
Eastwood NG16 . . . . **182** D3
Olde Derwent Ave DE4 . . . **143** B4

Olde English Rd DE4 . . . . . **143** B4
Old End DE12 . . . . **265** F1
Olders Valley DE11 . . . . **256** E4
Old Fall St NG17 . . . . **148** F3
Old Farm Ct NG11 . . . . **237** E6
Old Farmhouse The
DE45 . . . . **109** D6
Oldfield Dr DE11 . . . . **256** C5
Oldfield La
Egginton DE65 . . . . **241** A8
Hognaston DE6 . . . . **164** B2
Kirk Ireton DE6 . . . . **164** F2
Snelston DE6 . . . . **184** B3
Wensley DE4 . . . . **142** A8
Old Forge Bsns Pk 5 S2 . . **43** A7
Old Forge Cl DE65 . . . . **241** A5
Old Gate HD9 . . . . **2** F7
Old Gate Ave DE72 . . . . . . **245** C6
Old Hackney La DE4 . . . . . **142** F8
Old Hall Ave
Derby, Alvaston DE24 . . . . . **233** D7
Derby DE23 . . . . **218** B1
Duffield DE56 . . . . **190** E3
Old Hall Cl
Darley Dale DE4 . . . . **127** C3
Glossop SK13 . . . . **10** C2
Pilsley S45 . . . . **132** C2
Old Hall Ct DE55 . . . . **169** E7
Old Hall Dr
Horwich End SK23 . . . . **45** E4
Willington DE65 . . . . **242** B5
Old Hall Gdns
Stoney Middleton S32 . . . . . **72** A4
Swadlincote DE11 . . . . **256** A2
Old Hall Jun Sch S40 . . . . . **95** C2
Church Broughton DE65 . . **227** B8
Marple SK6 . . . . **23** C5
Mottram in L SK14 . . . . **9** A5
Whitwell S80 . . . . **81** F6
Old Hall Mills Bsns Pk
DE21 . . . . **205** C7
Old Hall Rd
Chesterfield S40 . . . . **95** D3
Derby DE23 . . . . **218** C1
Old Hall Sq 3 SK13 . . . . . . **10** A5
Old Hartshay Hill DE5 . . . **169** C2
Oldhay Ct S17 . . . . **55** D6
Old Hay Gdns S17 . . . . **55** C6
Old Hay La S17 . . . . **55** C6
Old Hill DE6 . . . . **173** C1
Old Hillcliff La DE6 . . . . . . **177** A3
Old House Mus* DE45 . . . **109** C6
Old House Rd S40 . . . . **95** C2
Old Houses S41 . . . . **96** C3
Oldicote La DE15 . . . . **248** E3
Oldknow Rd SK6 . . . . **23** A6
Old La
Derby DE22 . . . . **205** A2
Idridgehay DE56 . . . . **176** F3
Sheffield S20 . . . . **60** A7
Shottle DE56 . . . . **177** A5
Wirksworth DE4 . . . . **154** F2
Old Lime Ct DE4 . . . . **143** C5
Old Longhill Rd SK17 . . . . . **65** B4
Old Manor Rd NG19 . . . . . **136** C3
Old Mansfield Rd DE21 . . . **205** C1
Old Market Pl DE55 . . . . . . **160** A6
Old Mill Cl
Duffield DE56 . . . . **190** E3
Mansfield NG19 . . . . **136** E1
Old Mill Dr S40 . . . . **95** A8
Old Mill La
Calver S32 . . . . **72** D2
Mansfield NG19 . . . . **136** E1
Old Mill Lane Ind Est
NG19 . . . . **136** C1
Old Park Ave S8 . . . . **56** D7
Old Park Rd S8 . . . . **56** D7
Old Peveril Rd S44 . . . . **98** A4
Old Pit La DE7 . . . . **193** A6
Old Pond The DE75 . . . . . . **194** A8
Old Post Office Row S33 . . . **40** B4
Old Quarry Cl S43 . . . . **80** C6
Old Rd
Branston DE14 . . . . **253** E7
Buxton SK17, SK23 . . . . **65** C5
Chesterfield S40 . . . . **95** C3
Darley Dale DE4 . . . . **127** C1
Furness Vale SK23 . . . . **33** D4
Glossop SK13 . . . . **10** A7
Heage DE56 . . . . **179** E8
Horwich End, New Horwich
SK23 . . . . **45** E6
Mottram in L SK14 . . . . **9** A5
Oldridge Cl S40 . . . . **95** B6
Old School Cl
Bramley-Vale S44 . . . . **117** D1
Holymoorside S42 . . . . **113** D7
Tideswell SK17 . . . . **69** C4
Old School Ho The S42 . . **113** D7
Old School La
Awsworth NG16 . . . . **195** C5
Chesterfield S44 . . . . **96** F2
Pleasley NG19 . . . . **135** A5
Old School Mews DE7 . . . . **246** B8
Old School The DE55 . . . . . **228** C2
Old Ship La S40 . . . . **266** B3
Old Smithy Row SK22 . . . . . **33** C7
Old St SK14 . . . . **16** B8
Old Station Cl
Etwall DE65 . . . . **229** B4
Rowsley DE4 . . . . **126** F8
Old Station Yd S43 . . . . **96** C8
Old Storth La DE55 . . . . . . **160** B4
Old Swanwick Colliery Rd
DE55 . . . . **158** F1

Old Tennis Courts The
SK17 . . . . **85** B8
Old Terr NG19 . . . . **134** F4
Old Vicarage Cl DE23 . . . . **218** C1
Old Vicarage La DE22 . . . . **204** C5
Old Vicarage Sch The
DE22 . . . . **205** A3
Old Waterworks The
DE73 . . . . **243** A4
Oldwell Cl S17 . . . . **55** D4
Old Whittington La S18 . . . **76** E6
Olive Ave
Long Eaton NG10 . . . . **223** E1
Shirebrook NG20 . . . . **119** D6
Olive Cres S12 . . . . **44** A2
Olive Gr DE21 . . . . **219** F5
Olive Grove Rd S2 . . . . **43** B8
Oliver Cl DE75 . . . . **182** B2
Oliver Rd S20 . . . . **59** D7
Oliver St S41 . . . . **266** C3
Oliver Rd DE7 . . . . **208** C6
Olive St DE23 . . . . **218** E4
Olive Terr 1 SK14 . . . . **16** A8
Olivet Rd S8 . . . . **43** A3
Olivier St DE23 . . . . **219** B1
Ollersett Ave SK22 . . . . **33** D8
Ollersett Dr SK22 . . . . **33** D8
Ollersett Ho S3 . . . . **33** D8
Ollersett La SK22 . . . . **33** D8
Olton Rd DE3 . . . . **217** C4
Onslow Rd DE3 . . . . **217** E4
Onward Cotts SK17 . . . . **85** E8
Opal Cl DE21 . . . . **206** A2
Openacre NG16 . . . . **170** F4
Openwoodgate DE56 . . . . . **179** D3
Openwood Rd DE56 . . . . . . **179** E3
Orange Cl NG20 . . . . **119** F6
Orange St DE55 . . . . **159** B4
Orchard Ave
Castle Donington DE74 . . . **247** A3
Whaley Bridge SK23 . . . . . . **45** D7
Orchard Bsns Pk
Ilkeston DE7 . . . . **194** D1
Sandiacre NG10 . . . . **223** C6
Orchard Cl
Barlborough S43 . . . . **80** A7
Belper DE56 . . . . **191** B8
Bolsover S44 . . . . **99** B1
Breadsall DE21 . . . . **205** D4
Breaston DE72 . . . . **235** F8
Clowne S43 . . . . **80** E3
Derby DE23 . . . . **231** C7
Elvaston DE24 . . . . **233** D4
Hilton DE65 . . . . **228** D1
Melbourne DE73 . . . . **252** A7
Ockbrook DE72 . . . . **221** C4
Ripley DE5 . . . . **181** A7
Shirebrook NG20 . . . . **119** E5
Sudbury DE6 . . . . **225** E5
Uttoxeter ST14 . . . . **210** B1
Walton-on-T DE12 . . . . **253** D1
West Hallam DE7 . . . . **207** E7
Willington DE65 . . . . **242** B6
Orchard Com Prim Sch
DE74 . . . . **247** A3
Orchard Cotts DE56 . . . . . . **190** E4
Orchard Cres
Glapwell S44 . . . . **134** B8
Swanwick DE55 . . . . **169** D7
Orchard Ct
Derby DE21 . . . . **220** E5
Doveridge DE6 . . . . **211** B1
Langley Mill NG16 . . . . **182** B3
South Normanton DE55 . . . **159** F4
Orchard Dr
Creswell S80 . . . . **81** E2
Gamesley SK13 . . . . **9** E1
Orchard La DE6 . . . . **185** D1
Orchard Lee S26 . . . . **61** E6
Orchard Pl S21 . . . . **60** D6
Orchard Rd
Compstall SK6 . . . . **15** B2
Darley Dale DE4 . . . . **142** E8
Matlock Bath DE4 . . . . **143** A1
Somercotes DE55 . . . . **170** C6
Whaley Bridge SK23 . . . . . . **45** D7
Orchard Rise DE75 . . . . . . **181** F2
Orchard Sq S18 . . . . **56** D2
Orchard St
Derby DE1 . . . . **267** A4
Derby, Mickleover DE3 . . . **217** D1
Ilkeston DE7 . . . . **208** F7
Kimberley NG16 . . . . **195** F6
Langley Mill NG16 . . . . **182** B3
Long Eaton NG10 . . . . **236** E7
Mansfield NG19 . . . . **136** B1
Swadlincote DE11 . . . . **255** F6
Orchards The
Derby DE22 . . . . **204** D3
Jacksdale NG16 . . . . **171** B4
Orchards Way S40 . . . . **95** D1
Orchard The
Belper DE56 . . . . **179** A4
Codnor DE5 . . . . **170** B1
Disley SK12 . . . . **32** D6
Horsley Woodhouse DE7 . . **192** D6
Stanton-by-D DE7 . . . . **222** F8
Uttoxeter ST14 . . . . **210** A4
Youlgreave DE45 . . . . **125** C5
Orchard View
Bolsover S44 . . . . **117** F8
Mansfield Woodhouse
NG19 . . . . **136** B3
Orchard View Rd S40 . . . . . **95** C4
Orchard Way
Chellaston DE73 . . . . **232** F2
Sandiacre NG10 . . . . **223** A3

Orchid Cl
Burton u T DE15........ 255 A8
Calow S44 ....97 A3
Orchid Way NG20 .... 119 D3
Ordish Ave DE21 .... 219 F5
Ordley La DE6 .... 183 F8
Ordley Wlk DE65 .... 228 D1
Oregon Way DE21....... 220 C6
Orford Ave SK12 .... 32 D6
Organ Way SK14 .... 9 D5
Oriel Ct DE1............... 267 C1
Orient Way DE24......... 219 E2
Orkney Cl DE24......... 231 D3
Orly Ave DE74 .... 247 A2
Ormesby Cl S18........... 56 C1
Ormond Cl
Chesterfield S40 .... 114 B7
Sheffield S8 ....57 B6
Ormond Dr S8.............57 B6
Ormonde St NG16 .... 182 B4
Ormonde Terr NG16 ..... 182 B4
Ormond Rd S8 ....57 B7
Ormond Way S8 ....57 B7
Ormsby Rd S41 ....95 F7
Ormskirk Rise DE21..... 220 F4
Orpean Way NG9 .... 223 E2
Orpen Dr S14............. 43 E2
Orpen Ho S14 .... 43 D2
Orpen Way S14 .... 43 E2
Orton Way DE56 .... 179 B6
Orwins Cl 8 S41 ....95 D7
Osborne Cl NG10 .... 223 B4
Osborne Croft S26........ 61 F6
Osborne Ct DE21 .... 205 D4
Osborne Pl SK13.......... 10 A5
Osborne Rd DE23 ...... 219 C3
Osborne St
Burton u T DE15........ 248 A3
Derby DE23............. 267 D1
Osbourne Gdns DE15 ... 248 A3
Oscar Ct S43 ....77 D3
Osiers Cl DE22........... 204 C1
Osleston La DE6 .... 215 D7
Osmaston CE Prim Sch
DE6 .... 185 F4
Osmaston Cl NG10 ...... 235 F5
Osmaston Park Ind Est
DE24 .... 232 E8
Osmaston Park Rd DE23,
DE24 .... 232 C7
Osmaston Rd DE23, DE24 219 B2
Osmaston St NG10....... 223 C5
Osmaton Park Ind Est
DE24 .... 219 D1
Osmund Ct S21........... 59 C3
Osmund Rd S21 ....59 C3
Osprey Cl
Burton u T DE15........ 248 D4
Derby DE24 .... 231 E2
Osterly Gn DE22......... 218 A5
Oswestry Cl DE21....... 206 B3
Othello Dr DE73......... 232 D2
Otterburn Dr DE22...... 204 C2
Otter St
Derby DE1 .... 219 A7
Hilton DE65 .... 228 D1
Otter Way NG19 .... 135 D1
Oulton Cl DE24 .... 232 D4
Oundle Dr
Ilkeston DE7 .... 209 B7
Mansfield NG19........ 135 D1
Ousley La DE6 .... 183 C5
Outfield Rd DE15 .... 254 F8
Outgang La
Mansfield Woodhouse
NG19 .... 136 D4
Pleasley NG19 .... 135 C6
Out La S42, S44 .... 132 F6
Outlands Rd S33.......... 50 F6
Outram Cl DE72 .... 221 B1
Outram Ct DE5 .... 169 E2
Outram Dr DE11........ 256 D4
Outram Rd S41 ....95 F6
Outram St DE5 .... 169 E2
Outram Way DE24 ...... 231 E2
Outseats Dr DE55 ...... 159 B3
Oval Cl DE23 .... 231 C8
Oven Hill Rd SK22, SK23 ..34 A5
Overcroft Rise S17........55 D4
Overdale DE4............ 143 D5
Overdale Ave SK17........85 D8
Overdale Cl NG10 .... 236 A6
Overdale Dr S14 ....17 B8
Overdale Gdns S17 ....55 D6
Overdale Rd
Derby DE23 .... 218 E2
New Mills SK22 .... 32 F6
Overdale Rise S17 ....55 C6
Overend Cl S14 .... 43 D4
Overend Dr S14 .... 43 D4
Overend Rd S14 .... 43 D4
Overend Way S14........ 43 D4
Over La
Baslow DE45 ....91 E6
Belper DE56............ 179 E5
Hazelwood DE56 ...... 178 A2
Overlees S18 ....79 B5
Overmoor View DE55...148 B7
Over Rd DE45 ....91 E6
Overseal Prim Sch DE12 262 B4
Oversetts Ct DE11 ...... 255 F6
Oversetts Rd DE11...... 255 E5
Overstone Cl DE56...... 179 D4
Overton Cl S43 ....78 F3
Owen Ave NG10 .... 237 A7
Owen Falls Ave S41......96 C3
Owers Ave DE75........ 193 F7
Owlcotes View S44...... 118 A8

Owler Bar Rd S11..........54 B4
Owler Car La S18..........57 F5
Owlers La DE23 .... 218 C2
Owlers The SK23..........45 E6
Owlston Cl NG16.......... 182 F3
Owlswick Cl DE23........ 231 A8
Owlthorpe Ave S20 ....59 B8
Owlthorpe Cl S20.........59 B8
Owlthorpe Dr S20.........59 B8
Owlthorpe Gr S20.........59 B8
Owlthorpe La S20.........59 B8
Owlthorpe Rise S20.......59 B8
Oxbury Rd NG16 .... 195 F8
Ox Cl S45 .... 131 D3
Ox Close Ave S17..........56 A5
Oxclose Dr 2 S18 ....56 C1
Oxclose La
Alsop en le D DE6 ...... 150 C2
Dronfield S18.............56 C1
Mansfield NG19........ 135 D3
Mansfield Woodhouse
NG19. .... 136 A3
Oxclose Park Gdns S20 ..59 F6
Oxclose Park Rd S20......59 F6
Oxclose Park Rd N S20 ...59 F7
Oxclose Park View S20 ...59 F6
Oxcroft Est S44............99 D7
Oxcroft Ind Est S44 ....99 A8
Oxcroft La
Bolsover S44 ....99 B6
Elmton S44 ....99 E8
Oxcroft View S44 ....99 B8
Oxcroft Way S43...........80 B5
Oxenhope Cl DE23 ...... 230 E7
Oxford Cl S43 ....96 F5
Oxford Rd S43 ....96 F8
Oxford St
Blackwell DE55 .... 147 E1
Bramley-Vale S44 ...... 117 F1
Derby DE1 .... 267 C1
Derby, Spondon DE21 ... 220 E5
Eastwood NG16........ 182 F2
4 Ilkeston DE7........ 208 F7
Long Eaton NG10...... 236 D8
Mansfield Woodhouse
NG19. .... 136 C1
Ripley DE5 .... 169 D1
Swadlincote DE11 ..... 256 A1
Ox Hill S20 ....60 A5
Oxley Rd DE15........... 248 A3
Oxmead DE6............. 184 D7
Oxpasture La NG20 .... 100 B5
Oxton Rake Rd S18 ....94 A8
Oxwich Ct DE21......... 206 B2
Oyster Cl DE14 .... 254 B7
Ozier Holt NG10 .... 236 C6

Palatine Gr DE23 .... 230 F7
Palerow La DE56 .... 166 E3
Palissy Cl DE11 .... 256 D4
Palladium Dr DE23 ..... 231 A6
Pall Mall DE21........... 205 E4
Palm Cl DE23 .... 218 A1
Palmer Cl DE14 .... 254 B8
Palmer Cres 3 S18.......57 B1
Palmer Dr
Stapleford NG9 .... 223 D5
Swanwick DE55 .... 169 E7
Palmersgate S40 .... 266 B3
Palmerston Ct DE73 .... 252 B7
Palmerston Rd 4 DE7 .. 208 F8
Palmerston St
Derby DE23 .... 218 L1
Underwood Green NG16 .171 F2
Westwood NG16 .... 171 C4
Palterton La S44........ 117 D7
Palterton Prim Sch S44 .118 B5
Pankhurst Pl S45....... 131 C3
Parade The
4 Derby DE23 .... 217 D1
Sheffield S12 ....44 A6
Paradise St SK13 ....10 A5
Parcel Terr DE22 .... 218 D5
Pares Way DE72 .... 221 C5
Pargate Cl DE5 .... 180 D6
Park Ave
Ashbourne DE6 .... 173 D1
Awsworth NG16........ 195 B5
Castle Donington DE74 ..246 F3
Darley Dale DE4 .... 127 C3
Dronfield S18.............57 B2
Eastwood NG16........ 182 E3
Furness Vale SK23...... 33 D3
Glapwell S44 .... 118 C1
Mansfield Woodhouse
NG19. .... 136 C4
Ripley DE5 .... 169 F1
Scropton DE65 .... 227 A5
Shirebrook NG20........ 119 E4
Stanley DE7 .... 207 C6
Uttoxeter STA14 ...... 210 B2
Park Cl
Chesterfield S40 .... 115 A7
Glossop SK13............10 D2
Kilburn DE56 .... 192 A8
Linton DE12 .... 261 C6
Little Eaton DE21...... 205 B8
Matlock DE4 .... 143 D4
Ripley DE5 .... 169 C2
Shirland DE55 .... 146 E1
Stanton-by-D DE7 .... 222 F8
Park Cotts DE4 .... 127 A5
Park Cres
Chapel-en-le-F SK23 .....47 B5
Doveridge DE6 .... 211 B1
Eastwood NG16........ 182 F4
Furness Vale SK23...... 33 D3
Glossop SK13............ 10 B3
Heage DE56 .... 179 E8
Ilkeston DE7 .... 209 A8
Park Ct
Heanor DE75............ 181 F1
Swadlincote DE11 ..... 256 C5
Park Dene Dr SK13 ....10 C2
Park Dr
Chesterfield S41 .... 266 C1
Derby DE23 .... 218 C1
Ilkeston DE7 .... 208 F7
Sandiacre NG10........ 223 A3
Swanwick DE55 .... 169 F6
Park Edge S32.............52 F8
Parker's La NG19 .... 136 C3
Parker Ave S44 ....96 F3
Parker Cl DE1 .... 267 A4
Parker Ctr DE21 .... 219 B8
Parker Rd SK17...........69 C4
Parker Gdns NG9 .... 223 F8
Parkers La S17 ....55 D8
Parker St DE1 .... 218 F7
Park Farm S18 ....56 C2
Park Farm Ctr DE22.... 204 D2
Park Farm Ctr DE22.... 204 D2
Park Farm Mews S21 ....60 D7
Parkfield Cres DE12.....265 F1
Parkfield Ct SK17.........85 A7
Parkfield La DE6......... 184 D4
Parkfield Pl S2 ....43 A8
Parkfields S43 ....80 E3
Parkfields Dr DE22 ..... 218 E8
Parkfields View DE56.... 179 E8
Parkgate
Derby DE21 .... 219 B2
Dronfield S18.............57 C2
Parkgate Cl S20 ....59 A8
Parkgate Croft S20 ....59 A8
Parkgate Dr S20 ....59 A8
Parkgate La S21, S43 .....77 E5
Park Gr DE22............ 218 E7
Park Grange Cl S2 ....43 C8
Park Grange Dr S2 ....43 C8
Park Grange Mount S2 ...43 C8
Park Grange Rd S2 ....43 C8
Park Grange View S2 .....43 D8
Park Hall S40 ....266 B3
Park Hall Ave S40, S42 ..114 B8
Park Hall Cl S40 ....114 B7
Park Hall Farm DE55 .... 180 A3
Park Hall Gdns
Chesterfield S40 ....114 B7
Mansfield Woodhouse
NG19. .... 136 C5

Parkhall La S21 ....60 D2
Park Hall La
Mapperley DE7 .... 193 D2
West Hallam DE7...... 207 C8
Park Hall Rd
Denby Village DE5 ..... 180 A3
Mansfield Woodhouse
NG19. .... 136 C5
Parkham Rd NG16...... 195 F7
Park Head Rd DE4 ...... 143 B5
Park Hill
Awsworth NG16........ 195 B5
Eckington S21 ....59 E3
Park Hill Cl SK22 .... 24 C1
Park Hill Dr DE23 ...... 231 F7
Park Ho DE56........... 179 A3
Parkhouse Cl S45........ 131 B4
Parkhouse Dr DE55..... 159 E5
Park House Prim Sch
S45...................... 132 B4
Parkhouse Rd S42, S45 . 132 A4
Parkin St DE55 .... 159 B4
Park Jun & Inf Schs The
NG20 ....119 E5
Park La
Castle Donington DE74 ..246 E3
Chesterfield S41 ....95 F7
Darley Dale DE4 .... 127 D2
Derby, Allestree DE22 .. 204 F4
Derby, Normanton Park
DE23.................... 218 C1
Hayfield SK22 .... 25 D5
Heage DE56 .... 179 F8
Holbeck NG20, S80 .... 101 C6
Over Haddon DE45, DE4 . 110 C1
Pinxton NG16.......... 160 C2
Ripley DE5 .... 169 A7
Shirland DE55 .... 159 A8
Shirley DE6 .... 200 D8
South Wingfield DE55 .. 157 D1
Stanton in Peak DE4 ... 126 C5
Tutbury DE13 .... 239 B6
Weston-on-T DE7...... 245 E4
Parkland Ave SK22.......24 C1
Parkland Dr S43 ....115 A2
Parkland Mews NG10 ... 236 D8
Parklands Dr DE73...... 245 A8
Parklands Inf Sch NG10 . 223 B1
Park Leys Ct DE21 ..... 220 E4
Park Mews
Derby DE22 .... 218 F8
Mansfield Woodhouse
NG19. .... 136 C4
Somercotes DE55 ..... 170 D6
Park Mill Dr DE55....... 159 C2
Park Pale The DE13 .... 239 C5
Park Rd
Ashbourne DE6 .... 173 C2
Bakewell DE45.......... 109 D5
Belper DE56............ 179 A2
Buxton SK17 ....85 A8
Chapel-en-le-F SK23 .....47 B5
Chesterfield S40 ....266 A2
Derby DE3 .... 217 D2
Derby, Spondon DE21 .. 220 D5
Donisthorpe DE12 ..... 262 E2
Duffield DE56........... 190 D3
Glossop SK13............ 10 A4
Heage DE56 .... 179 E8
High Lane SK12 .... 32 A6
Homewood S42.......... 131 A6
Horwich End SK23...... 45 D6
Ilkeston DE7 .... 208 F7
Mansfield Woodhouse
NG19. .... 136 B3
New Mills SK22 .... 33 C7
Over Haddon DE45 .... 110 B2
Overseal DE12........... 262 A6
Ripley DE5 .... 169 C1
Shirebrook NG20........119 E5
Stapleford NG9 .... 223 E8
Swadlincote, Church Gresley
DE11.................... 256 C2
Swadlincote, DE11, DE15 . 255 D5
Tupton S42.............. 131 C7
Park Rise S18 ....75 A8
Park Row
Bretby DE15............ 249 B1
Clay Cross S45 .... 131 D4
Parks Ave S45 .... 157 F3
Parkside
Buxton SK17 ....85 A8
Chesterfield S41 ....96 A7
Heage DE56 .... 179 E8
Renishaw S21 ....60 B1
Park Side
Belper DE56............ 179 A3
Somercotes DE55 ..... 170 D7
Parkside Ave NG10..... 236 B8
Parkside Cl NG16....... 160 C8
Parkside Com Sch S40 .. 266 A2
Parkside Dr
Ironville NG16...........170 F4
Long Eaton NG10...... 236 B8
Parkside Jun Sch DE6 .. 173 C2
Parkside Rd S41 .... 266 B6
Parkside View S40 ....95 B6
Park Spring Dr S2 ....43 C8
Park Spring Pl S2 ....43 C8
Park Spring Way S2 .....43 C8
Park St
Alfreton DE55 .... 158 F3
Barlborough S43 ....80 B7
Breaston DE72 .... 235 F8
Chesterfield S40 ....115 A7
Derby DE1 .... 267 D2

Park St continued
Heanor DE75............ 181 D2
Long Eaton NG10...... 223 C1
Mansfield Woodhouse
NG19. .... 136 B3
Ripley DE5 .... 169 E1
Stapleford NG9 .... 223 D6
Swadlincote DE11 ..... 256 A6
Uttoxeter ST14 .... 210 C1
Wessington DE55 ..... 157 E8
Parkstone Ct DE21 ..... 217 C2
Parkstone Delph S12 ....44 A2
Park Studios S40 ....266 A2
Park Terr DE4 .... 127 A5
Park The
Darley Dale DE4 .... 127 D3
Duffield DE56........... 190 E3
Ironville NG16........... 170 E3
Mansfield Woodhouse
NG19. .... 136 C1
Mayfield DE6 .... 184 C8
Parkview DE21 .... 205 C8
Park View
9 Ashbourne DE6 .... 173 C2
Aston-on-T DE72 ..... 246 B7
Bakewell DE45.......... 109 D5
Barlborough S43 ....80 B7
Chesterfield S41 ....115 D7
Clowne S43 ....80 F5
Heanor DE75............ 181 D1
Northwood DE4 .... 127 A5
Pleasley NG19 .... 135 A5
Somercotes DE55 ..... 170 D5
Whaley Thorns NG20 .. 100 F2
Park View Ave S20 ....59 E7
Park View Cl DE22 ..... 204 F4
Park View Ct S8 ....43 A2
Park View Dr SK23.......47 B6
Park View Ho DE21 .... 219 C6
Parkview Prim Sch DE21 206 A2
Park View Rise SK22 ....24 C1
Parkville Cl SK17 ....85 D5
Parkway
Chellaston DE73........ 232 E1
New Mills SK22 ....24 C1
Whitwell S80 ....82 B6
Park Way DE65 .... 229 C4
Parkway Ct S8............56 F7
Parkway The DE72 ..... 127 C3
Parliament Cl DE22 ....218 E4
Parliament St
Derby DE22 .... 218 E4
Swadlincote DE11 ..... 255 F6
Parson's Wlk B79....... 263 F2
Parsonage Cl S20 ....59 D6
Parsonage Croft DE45 .. 109 C5
Parsonage Gdns SK6.....23 A4
Parsons Cl
Hartington SK17 ...... 137 D5
Swadlincote DE11 ..... 256 A1
Parsons Gate S33.........40 A6
Parsons Gr DE5 .... 180 C2
Parsons La S33 ....39 D3
Parthenon Cl NG19 .... 134 F5
Partington Ct 2 SK13....10 F1
Partington Pk SK13.......9 E3
Partridge Cl S21 ....93 B3
Partridge Dr DE11 ..... 256 F3
Partridge Way DE3 ..... 218 A3
Parwich Cl S40 ....95 A5
Parwich La DE4.......... 151 E7
Parwich Prim Sch DE6 .. 151 D2
Parwich Rd S42 .... 131 F5
Pasteur Ave DE5........ 169 C2
Pasture Gr S21 ....59 C3
Pasture La
Brassington DE4 .... 152 D1
Flagg SK17............. 106 D6
Hilcote DE55 .... 148 C1
Long Eaton NG10...... 237 A5
Stonebroom DE55 .... 147 A3
Pasture Rd NG9 .... 209 D1
Pastures Ave DE23 ..... 230 F7
Pastures Hill DE23 ..... 218 B1
Pastures The
Duffield DE56........... 190 E4
Eastwood NG16........ 195 B8
Mansfield Woodhouse
NG19. .... 136 E5
Repton DE65 .... 242 C2
Swadlincote DE11 ..... 255 F5
Weston-on-T DE72..... 245 F5
Patchwork Row NG20 .. 119 F4
Paterson Ave DE21..... 220 B6
Patmore Sq DE23 ...... 231 F7
Paton Gr S43 ....96 D8
Patrick Cl DE12 .... 261 D5
Patten Ct DE24 .... 232 A5
Patterdale Cl 2 S18 ......56 E1
Patterdale Rd DE24 .... 220 A1
Pattison St S44 ....98 F6
Pauiet High Sch DE6 ... 254 F7
Pavilion Cl S43 ....80 E2
Pavilion Ct DE7 .... 207 D7
Pavilion Gdns
Buxton SK17 ....85 B7
New Houghton NG19 .. 134 F8
Pavilion Mans 3 SK17 ...85 B7
Pavilion Rd DE23 ...... 231 C8
Pavilion Workshops S42 116 D1
Paxton Cl
Derby DE3 .... 217 C1
Matlock DE4 .... 143 A6
Paxton Ct S14 ....43 F4
Paxton Rd S41...........96 C5

Payler Cl S2. . . . . .44 A8
Payne St DE22. . . . . 218 D6
Peach Ave
  Selston NG16. . . . . .171 C6
  South Normanton DE55. . .160 B7
Peach St
  Derby DE22 . . . . 218 D5
  Heanor DE75 . . . . 181 D1
Peacock Cl
  Glossop SK13. . . . . .9 E4
  Killamarsh S21 . . . . .60 D6
Peacock Gr DE23. . . . . . . .231 B6
Peacock Pl DE7 . . . . 194 D4
Peacock Way DE55 . . . . .169 F8
Peacroft Ct DE65 . . . . . . 228 D2
Peacroft La DE65 . . . . . . 228 D2
Peafield La NG19 . . . . . . 136 F4
Peafield Lane Prim Sch
  NG19 . . . . .136 F3
Peak Ave DE56 . . . . .170 B6
Peak Cavern* S33. . . . . . .38 B2
Peak Cl S45 . . . . 132 C1
Peakdale Cl
  Long Eaton NG10. . . . . . .236 A6
  Ripley DE5. . . . . 180 D6
Peakdale Cres S12. . . . . . .44 E5
Peak Dale Prim Sch SK17 .67 B5
Peakdale Rd
  Glossop SK13. . . . . .9 E3
  Marple SK6. . . . . .23 A4
Peak District Mus of Mining*
  DE4 . . . . .143 A1
Peak Dr DE23, DE24 . . . . 232 A7
Peak Forest CE Prim Sch
  SK17. . . . . .49 A3
Peak Ho SK13 . . . . .10 A5
Peakland View DE4 . . . . .127 C3
Peaknaze Cl SK13. . . . . . .17 B8
Peak Pl S43 . . . . .97 D7
Peak Rd SK22 . . . . .33 D8
Peak Sch S23. . . . . .34 F2
Peaks The SK23. . . . . .46 C5
Peak The NG20 . . . . 119 E3
Peaktor La DE4 . . . . 126 E7
Peak View
  Clowne S43 . . . . .80 D5
  Glossop SK13. . . . . .9 F4
  South Normanton DE55. . .159 F5
Peak View Cl S32 . . . . .72 B2
Peak View Dr DE6. . . . . . 173 C1
Peak View Rd S40 . . . . . . .95 D5
Peak Village Outlet Sh Ctr
  DE4 . . . . .110 F1
Pearce La S42 . . . . 114 D3
Pearl Bank DE6 . . . . 211 F8
Pearl Way S41. . . . . .9 A2
Pearson Croft S41. . . . . . .95 C6
Pearson Trad Est S41 . . . .96 B8
Pear Tree Ave
  Ripley DE5. . . . . 180 D8
  Swadlincote DE11 . . . . . .255 F7
  Wingerworth S42 . . . . . . .114 E3
Peartree Cl DE74 . . . . . . 247 A3
Peartree Ct
  Derby DE21 . . . . 205 D1
  Etwall DE65. . . . . 229 B4
Pear Tree Dr
  Linton DE12 . . . . 261 C6
  Shirebrook NG20 . . . . . . .119 E6
Peartree La NG17 . . . . . . 134 B1
Pear Tree Rd
  Derby DE23 . . . . 219 A1
  Pilsley S45. . . . . 132 C1
Peartree Sta DE23 . . . . . .232 B7
Pease Cl DE55 . . . . 159 B3
Peasehill DE5 . . . . 180 F8
Pease Hill DE55. . . . . 159 B3
Peasehill Rd DE55 . . . . . . 180 E8
Peasunhurst La S45. . . . . 113 A1
Peatburn Ave DE75 . . . . . 181 C1
Peatfield Ct NG9 . . . . . . 209 D1
Peatfield Rd
  Killamarsh S21 . . . . .60 F7
  Stapleford NG9 . . . . 209 D1
Peat La DE4, DE56. . . . . . 166 D4
Peats Cl DE6 . . . . 165 B1
Peckham Gdns DE22. . . . .218 A5
Pedley Ave 4 S20 . . . . . . .59 E8
Pedley Dr S20 . . . . .59 E8
Pedley St DE7 . . . . 208 F7
Peebles Ct DE24 . . . . 231 E2
Peel Cres NG19 . . . . 135 D2
Peel Gdns S18. . . . . .56 F1
Peel St
  Derby DE22 . . . . 218 D6
  Glossop SK13. . . . . .10 C5
  Langley Mill NG16 . . . . . .182 B3
  Long Eaton NG10. . . . . . .236 E8
  South Normanton DE55. . .160 B6
Pegers Cl DE21 . . . . 206 B2
Peggars Cl DE21 . . . . 218 E4
Pegasus La S44. . . . . .99 B1
Pegasus Sch DE12 . . . . . . 260 F7
Pegasus Way DE65 . . . . . .228 E2

Peggars Cl S43 . . . . .80 B6
Peggs Wlk DE23 . . . . 231 E7
Peggy La DE55 . . . . 146 B6
Pegwell Ct DE23 . . . . 231 D7
Pelham Ave DE7 . . . . 194 E1
Pelham St
  Derby DE22 . . . . 218 F4
  Ilkeston DE7 . . . . 194 E1
Pemberton The DE55. . . . 160 B4
Pembleton Dr NG19. . . . . 135 D1
Pembrey Cl NG9 . . . . 209 D2
Pembroke Cl S40. . . . . . . .95 C1
Pembroke Ct S41. . . . . . . .95 F7
Pembroke Rd
  Dronfield S18. . . . . .76 A8
  Shireoaks S81 . . . . .63 F7
Pembroke St DE21 . . . . . . 219 D8
Penalton Cl DE24 . . . . . . 232 E6
Pencroft Gr DE23 . . . . . . 231 C5
Pendean Cl DE55 . . . . . . 147 E1
Pendennis Cl DE24. . . . . .233 B6
Pendine Cl DE55 . . . . 160 C6
Pendlebury Dr DE3 . . . . . 217 E1
Pendleside Way DE23 . . . 230 E7
Pendleton La DE56 . . . . . 166 F7
Penfold Way DE55 . . . . . . 147 B5
Penge Rd DE22 . . . . 218 A7
Penhaligan's Cl DE7 . . . . 232 F1
Peniston Rise DE21 . . . . . 205 D6
Peniston Rise DE7 . . . . . . 252 A7
Penkridge Rd DE11 . . . . . 256 B1
Penmore Cl S41 . . . . 115 C8
Penmore Gdns 4 S41 . . . .96 C1
Penmore La S41 . . . . 115 C8
Penmore St S41 . . . . 115 C8
Penncroft Dr S45 . . . . . . 131 D2
Penncroft La S45 . . . . . . 131 D3
Pennie Cl NG10 . . . . 236 D4
Penniment La NG19. . . . . 135 B2
Pennine Ave DE55 . . . . . . 170 C7
Pennine Cl
  Long Eaton NG10. . . . . . .223 A1
  Mansfield Woodhouse
    NG19. . . . . .136 C4
  Newton DE55 . . . . .148 A3
  Sutton in Ashfield NG17. . .148 E4
  Tibshelf DE55 . . . . .147 F6
Pennine Dr
  Selston NG16. . . . . .171 F7
  South Normanton DE55. . .159 F5
Pennine Rd SK13 . . . . .17 A8
Pennine View
  Heage DE56. . . . . .179 E8
  Palterton S44. . . . . 118 A5
Pennine Way
  Chesterfield S40 . . . . . . .95 C5
  Grassmoor S42. . . . . .115 F3
  Swadlincote DE11 . . . . . .256 A3
Pennine Way Jun Sch
  DE11 . . . . .256 A2
Pennine Wlk S42 . . . . 115 F3
Penn La DE73 . . . . 252 B7
Penn Moor Rd NG10. . . . .236 A6
Penns Rd S2 . . . . .43 C6
Penn St DE56. . . . . 179 A4
Penny Acres Prim Sch
  S18. . . . . .74 F8
Pennycress Cl DE23. . . . . 231 A7
Pennycroft La ST14. . . . . 210 C1
Pennycroft Rd ST14. . . . . 210 A1
Penny Engine La S21 . . . . .59 E4
Pennyfields Bvd NG10. . . .236 B7
Penny Gn S80 . . . . .82 A5
Penny La S17 . . . . .55 C5
Penny Long La DE22 . . . . 218 E8
Pennyunk La S45. . . . . . . .89 E1
Pennywell Dr S42. . . . . . . 113 D7
Penrhyn Ave DE23 . . . . . . 218 D1
Penrith Pl DE21. . . . . 205 D2
Penrose Cres S44 . . . . . . .98 D3
Penryn Cl DE55. . . . . 160 C6
Pentagon The DE21 . . . . .219 C6
Pentewen Cl DE24 . . . . . . 204 E2
Penthorpe Cl S12. . . . . . . .44 B6
Pentland Cl
  5 Chesterfield S40 . . . . . .95 C5
  Derby DE21 . . . . 206 A2
Pentland Gdns NG10 . . . . 223 A1
Pentland Rd S18. . . . . . . .56 D1
Pentrich Ct 1 S40 . . . . . . .95 D5
Pentrich Rd
  Ripley DE5. . . . . 169 D2
  Swanwick DE55. . . . . 169 D7
Pentridge Dr DE7. . . . . . . 194 C3
Penzance Rd DE24. . . . . . 233 B5
Pepper La DE7 . . . . 208 E1
Percival Cl SK17 . . . . 138 D3
Percy St
  Derby DE22 . . . . 218 E3
  Ilkeston DE7 . . . . 208 F7
Percy Wood Cl DE65 . . . . 228 C2
Peregrine Cl
  Burton u T DE15. . . . . . . 248 D3
  Derby DE24 . . . . 231 D4
Peregrine Way S26 . . . . . .61 E5
Perlethorpe Ave NG19 . . . 136 A1
Pershore Dr DE14. . . . . . . 254 A8
Perth Cl
  Burton u T DE15. . . . . . . 248 C2
  Derby DE3 . . . . 217 E4
  Mansfield Woodhouse
    NG19. . . . . .136 C5
Perth Dr NG9 . . . . 209 F1
Perth St DE21 . . . . 205 D1
Peter Baines Ind Est
  DE22. . . . . .267 A1
Peterborough St DE21 . . . 219 E8

Peterdale Cl S43. . . . . .96 E8
Peterdale Rd S43. . . . . . . .96 E8
Peterhouse Terr 1
  DE23 . . . . .219 A2
Peterleas The DE12 . . . . . 262 E1
Peterlee Pl DE24 . . . . 233 A5
Peter Morn Hill S80. . . . . . .81 E4
Peters Ave S45 . . . . 131 B4
Peters Ct DE65 . . . . 227 D1
Petersgate NG10. . . . . . . 223 A1
Petersgate Cl NG10. . . . . 223 A2
Petersham Ct 7 NG10 . . .223 B2
Petersham Dr DE24 . . . . . 233 C6
Petersham Rd NG10 . . . . . 223 A1
Peter St
  Ashbourne DE6 . . . . 173 C1
  Glossop SK13. . . . . .10 A5
Peterway DE55 . . . . 170 D8
Pettifor Terr DE55 . . . . . . 147 C1
Pettyclose La S41, S43. . . .96 D5
Petty Close La DE6 . . . . . 202 C1
Petworth Ave NG9 . . . . . . 223 F3
Pevensey Ave S41 . . . . . . .95 E6
Pevensey Ct S41 . . . . .95 E7
Peveril Ave
  Borrowash DE72 . . . . 221 C2
  New Mills SK22 . . . . .24 C1
Peveril Castle* S33. . . . . . .38 C2
Peveril Cl
  Castleton S33 . . . . .38 C2
  Darley Dale DE4 . . . . 127 C3
  Somercotes DE55 . . . . . . 170 C6
Peveril Cres
  Long Eaton NG10. . . . . . .235 F5
  West Hallam DE7 . . . . . . .207 E8
Peveril Ct
  1 Glossop SK13. . . . . . . .17 F8
  Ripley DE5. . . . . 169 C1
Peveril Dr
  Ilkeston DE7 . . . . 194 D2
  Somercotes DE55 . . . . . . 170 C6
Peveril Gdns SK12 . . . . . . .33 A6
Peveril Ho SK17 . . . . .85 A6
Peveril Mews SK12 . . . . . . .33 A6
Peveril Rd
  Bolsover S44 . . . . .98 F3
  Buxton SK17 . . . . .85 E7
  Castleton S33 . . . . .38 C2
  Chesterfield S41 . . . . . . .95 F7
  Eckington S21 . . . . .59 E3
  Tibshelf DE55 . . . . .147 F6
Peveril St DE24 . . . . 232 D6
Pewit Cl S42 . . . . 132 D8
Pewit La DE55 . . . . 147 C6
Pheasant Field Dr DE21. . 221 A6
Pheasant Hill NG19 . . . . . 136 A1
Philip Howard Rd SK13 . . .17 C8
Philips Croft DE56 . . . . . . 190 E4
Philipway DE55. . . . . 170 D8
Phoenix Ct S12 . . . . .44 E1
Phoenix Rd S12 . . . . .44 E1
Phoenix St DE1 . . . . 267 B4
Phyllis Gr NG10. . . . . 236 F7
Piccadilly La DE4 . . . . . . .96 C3
Piccadilly Rd S41. . . . . . . .96 C3
Pickard Cres S13 . . . . .44 D8
Pickard Dr S13 . . . . .44 D8
Pickard La DE56 . . . . 168 D1
Pickburns Gdns DE56 . . . 191 F8
Pickering Ave NG16. . . . . 182 F2
Pickering Rise DE21 . . . . . 205 D1
Pickford Pl SK23. . . . . .47 B6
Pickleys La DE6 . . . . 202 B3
Pickton Cl S40 . . . . .95 D2
Pictor Gr SK17 . . . . .85 D7
Pic Tor La DE4 . . . . 143 B4
Pictor Rd SK17 . . . . .85 D7
Piddocks Rd DE15 . . . . . . 255 B5
Pighills La S18 . . . . .57 B4
Pig La DE4 . . . . 111 B4
Pike's La SK13. . . . . .17 B8
Pike Cl
  Chesterfield S40 . . . . . . .95 B5
  Hayfield SK22 . . . . .25 C3
Pike View Cl SK23. . . . . . . .34 E2
Pilgrim Ct S81 . . . . .63 F7
Pilgrims Way DE24. . . . . . 231 C3
Pilhough La DE4 . . . . 126 D6
Pilhough Rd DE4 . . . . 126 E5
Pillar Butts DE4 . . . . 165 E8
Pilsley CE Prim Sch S45 . .91 C2
Pilsley Cl DE56 . . . . 179 C6
Pilsley Prim Sch S45. . . . 132 C1
Pilsley Rd
  Clay Cross S45 . . . . 131 E3
  Stonebroom DE55. . . . . . 147 B6
Pimlico
  Derby DE22 . . . . 218 B6
  Ilkeston DE7 . . . . 208 E8
Pimm's Rd DE6 . . . . 217 A8
Pinchom's Hill Rd DE56. . 179 B3
Pinch The DE6 . . . . 150 B2
Pindale Ave S43 . . . . .97 C7
Pindale Rd S33 . . . . .38 F4
Pine Ave NG16. . . . . 182 A3
Pine Cl
  Burton u T DE14. . . . . . . 254 A8
  Creswell S80 . . . . .81 F1
  Derby DE21 . . . . 220 F6
  Etwall DE65 . . . . 229 C4
  Killamarsh S21 . . . . .60 C5
  Mansfield Woodhouse
    NG19. . . . . .136 C5
  Ripley DE5. . . . . 169 D1
  Shirebrook NG20. . . . . . . 119 E6
  Smalley DE7. . . . . 192 F5
Pine Croft DE56 . . . . 185 D7
Pinecroft Ct DE21. . . . . . . 206 B1

Pine Gr DE11 . . . . 255 F6
Pine St S43 . . . . .97 A8
Pines The DE72. . . . . 235 B7
Pine Tree Wlk NG16. . . . . 182 E2
Pine View
  Chesterfield S40 . . . . . . .95 B3
  Clay Cross S45 . . . . 131 E3
Pine Wlk DE11. . . . . 261 E7
Pinewood DE5 . . . . 181 B7
Pinewood Cl DE55 . . . . . . 159 C3
Pinewood Rd
  Belper DE56. . . . . .178 E6
  Burton u T DE15. . . . . . . 254 F6
  Matlock DE4 . . . . .143 B7
Pinfold Sch S13 . . . . .9 E4
Pinfold Cl
  Holymoorside S42 . . . . . . 113 C8
  Repton DE65 . . . . 242 D2
  Tutbury DE13 . . . . 239 C5
Pinfold Cres SK17. . . . . . .69 C3
Pinfold Gdns NG19. . . . . . 136 F2
Pinfold Hill S32. . . . . .72 E2
Pinfold La
  Bradley DE6. . . . . .187 A8
  Repton DE65 . . . . 242 D2
  Stapleford NG9 . . . . .223 E7
Pinfold Rd SK17 . . . . .69 A8
Pinfold St S21 . . . . .59 D3
Pinfold The
  Belper DE56. . . . . .179 C5
  Elvaston DE72 . . . . .233 F4
  Glapwell S44 . . . . .118 B1
  Middleton DE45 . . . . .124 E3
Pinfold Trad Est NG9. . . . 223 E7
Pinfold View DE45 . . . . . . 109 C5
Pingle Cl DE22 . . . . 204 E4
Pingle Cres DE56 . . . . . . 178 F5
Pingle Farm Rd DE11. . . . 255 F5
Pingle Grange S43 . . . . . . .96 E7
Pinglehill Way DE73 . . . . 233 B2
Pingle La
  Belper DE56. . . . . .178 E6
  Carsington DE4 . . . . .164 E7
Pingle Rd S21 . . . . .60 E7
Pingle Sch The DE11. . . . 256 A5
Pingle The
  Derby DE21 . . . . 220 F4
  Long Eaton NG10. . . . . . .236 D8
  Melbourne DE73 . . . . . . .252 A7
Pingot Rd SK22 . . . . .33 D8
Pingott La SK13 . . . . .10 A5
Pingreaves Dr DE73. . . . . 233 A2
Pintail Dr DE24 . . . . 231 D4
Pinxton Gn NG16 . . . . 160 E3
Pinxton La
  Kirby-in-A NG17. . . . . . . .160 F6
  South Normanton DE55. . .160 E5
Piper Ave S45 . . . . 131 E4
Piper La S42 . . . . .94 E3
Pipers Ct NG16 . . . . 170 F3
Pipeyard La S21. . . . . .59 C2
Pippenwell Rd SK17 . . . . . 106 A7
Pippin Gdns DE24 . . . . . . 232 F7
Pippin Hill DE5 . . . . 180 E1
Pipworth La S21. . . . . .59 F4
Pitch Cl S43 . . . . .80 E2
Pit Close La DE73. . . . . . . 233 A1
Pit La
  Codnor DE5. . . . . .181 A7
  Crich DE4, DE55 . . . . .157 B6
  Ripley DE5. . . . . 169 E1
  Sheffield S12 . . . . .44 A6
  Shipley DE75 . . . . .194 B6
  Shirland DE55 . . . . .158 D8
  Stonebroom DE55 . . . . . .147 A5
Pits La DE6 . . . . 151 E1
Pittar St DE22 . . . . 267 A2
Pitt Hill NG20. . . . . 100 F2
Pittlemere La SK17 . . . . . .50 A1
Pitt St S21 . . . . .59 C2
Pittywood Rd DE4 . . . . . . 165 E7
Placket La DE4 . . . . 141 B6
Plackett Cl
  Breaston DE72. . . . . .235 D8
  Stapleford NG9 . . . . .223 F8
Plains La DE56 . . . . 178 B4
Plainspot Rd NG16. . . . . . 171 E2
Plain The DE6 . . . . 203 A6
Plaistow Green Rd DE4 . . 156 F2
Plantain Gdns DE23 . . . . 231 C5
Plantation Cl
  Chesterfield S40 . . . . . . .95 A5
  Whitwell S80 . . . . .82 A6
Plantation Rd 7 S8 . . . . . .43 A6
Plantations The 9 NG10 . 236 A8
Plantin Rise S20 . . . . .59 E7
Plantin The S20. . . . . .59 E7
Plant La NG10 . . . . 236 A4
Platform Ct DE21 . . . . 220 D5
Platts Ave DE55 . . . . 181 C1
Platt St
  Glossop SK13. . . . . .10 B5
  Pinxton NG16. . . . . .160 D1
Playhouse Theatre*
  DE1 . . . . .267 C2
Pleasant Ave S44 . . . . 118 B7
Pleasant Cl S12. . . . . .44 B6
Pleasant Rd S12. . . . . .44 B6
Pleasant St S12 . . . . .44 B6
Pleasant View S45 . . . . . . .15 B3
Pleasley Springs NG19 . . . 135 B8
Plimsoll Ct DE22. . . . . 267 A1
Plimsoll St DE22 . . . . 218 C6
Ploughfield Cl DE23. . . . . 231 B6
Plough Gate DE22 . . . . . . 204 E2
Plover Ave DE11 . . . . 256 F3
Plover Cl SK13. . . . . .17 F6
Plover Ct S43 . . . . 230 B7

Plover Way S44. . . . . .96 F3
Plowman Ct NG9 . . . . 223 D6
Plowright Cl S14 . . . . .43 D5
Plowright Dr S14 . . . . .43 D5
Plowright Mount S14 . . . . .43 D5
Plowright Way S14 . . . . . . .43 D5
Plucksbridge Rd SK6 . . . . .23 B3
Plumbley Hall Mews S20 . .59 C6
Plumbley Hall Rd S20. . . . .59 C6
Plumbley La S20 . . . . .59 B6
Plumbleywood La S12,
  S20. . . . . .58 F6
Plummer Rd DE11 . . . . . . 256 A5
Plumptre Cl NG16. . . . . . . 182 F1
Plumptre Rd NG16. . . . . . 182 F1
Plumptre Way NG16. . . . . 182 F1
Plymouth Ave NG16. . . . . 160 E2
Plymouth Ct 7 S41. . . . . . .95 F8
Pocknedge La S42. . . . . . 113 D8
Podnor La SK6 . . . . .24 A6
Pole's Rd DE6 . . . . 217 A8
Pole La SK22, SK6. . . . . . . .24 B4
Pollards Oaks DE72 . . . . . 221 C1
Polly Froggatt La S32 . . . . .72 B2
Polyfields La S44 . . . . 118 B8
Pomegranate Theatre*
  S41. . . . . .266 C3
Pomeroy Cotts SK17 . . . . 106 B4
Pond Cotts DE4. . . . . 143 E6
Pond End DE74 . . . . 247 B6
Pond La
  Tupton S42. . . . . .131 D8
  Wingerworth S42 . . . . . . .114 E4
Pondor La SK6 . . . . .24 A6
Pond Rd DE56 . . . . 191 C7
Pond St S40 . . . . 266 B2
Pondwell Cnr S43 . . . . .96 F7
Pondwell Dr S43 . . . . .96 F7
Ponsonby Terr DE1. . . . . . 218 E5
Pontefract St DE24 . . . . . 232 D7
Pontypool Cl DE21 . . . . . . 206 B2
Pool's La S21 . . . . .77 C7
Pool Cl
  Elvaston DE24 . . . . 233 C4
  Pinxton NG16. . . . . .160 D2
Poolclose Row NG16. . . . . 160 D2
Poole's Cavern* SK17. . . . .85 A6
Poole St DE24 . . . . 232 E6
Poolsbrook Ave S43 . . . . . .98 A8
Poolsbrook Country Pk*
  S43. . . . . .97 F7
Poolsbrook Cres S43. . . . . .98 A8
Poolsbrook Prim Sch S43 . .98 A5
Poolsbrook Rd S43 . . . . . . .98 A5
Poolsbrook Sq S43 . . . . . . .98 A8
Pool St DE11 . . . . 256 D2
Pope Carr Rd DE4 . . . . . . 143 C5
Poplar Ave
  Chesterfield S40 . . . . . . .95 B2
  Derby DE5 . . . . 220 E5
  Moira DE12 . . . . .262 E2
  New Mills SK22 . . . . .24 D1
  Ripley DE5. . . . . 180 D8
  Sandiacre NG10. . . . . . . .223 A7
  Swadlincote DE11 . . . . . .256 B6
Poplar Cl
  Derby DE24 . . . . 233 B7
  Dronfield S18. . . . . .76 C7
  Killamarsh S21 . . . . .60 C5
  Poplar Cres DE6 . . . . 185 D8
Poplar Dr
  Chesterfield S42 . . . . 115 C1
  Glapwell S44 . . . . .134 B8
  Pleasley NG19. . . . . .135 B4
  Poplar Nook DE22. . . . . . 204 F4
Poplar Rd
  Breaston DE72. . . . . .235 F8
  Eckington S21 . . . . .59 C2
  South Normanton DE55. . .160 B7
Poplar Row DE22 . . . . 205 A1
Poplar St NG19. . . . . 136 C3
Poplars The
  Derby DE22 . . . . 204 F4
  Whitwell S80 . . . . .82 A5
Poplar Way
  High Lane SK6 . . . . .32 A7
  Ilkeston DE7 . . . . 208 D5
Poppy Cl NG20 . . . . 119 D3
Poppyfields DE5 . . . . 180 D7
Poppy Gdns DE55 . . . . . . 148 B7
Porlock Cl 2 NG10 . . . . . . 236 A8
Porlock Ct DE21 . . . . 206 A2
Porteous Ct DE4 . . . . 127 D3
Porter's La
  Derby DE21 . . . . 205 F3
  Findern DE65. . . . . 230 D1
Porter Ho 9 S43 . . . . .78 E2
Porterhouse Rd DE5 . . . . 169 F1
Porter La DE4 . . . . 154 E3
Porter Pl DE21. . . . . 220 D5
Porter Rd DE23 . . . . 218 F2
Porters Farm Ct ST14 . . . 224 E1
Porter's La DE21 . . . . 205 F3
Porter St S43. . . . . .78 E2
Porthcawl Pl DE21 . . . . . . 206 C2
Portico Rd DE23 . . . . 231 A6
Portis St DE21 . . . . 220 D3
Portland Ave
  Bolsover S44. . . . . .99 B1
  Burton u T DE14. . . . . . . 254 A7
  Creswell S80 . . . . .81 E1

Portland Cl
Chesterfield S41 . . . . .266 B4
Derby DE33 . . . . .217 D2
Portland Court Mews
NG19 . . . . .136 C4
Portland Cres
Bolsover S44 . . . . .99 B1
Mansfield Woodhouse
NG19 . . . . .136 D3
Stapleford NG9 . . . . .223 E6
Portland Gr SK23 . . . . .34 E2
Portland Rd
Beeston NG9 . . . . .223 F1
Eastwood NG16 . . . . .195 B8
Ilkeston DE7 . . . . .194 F3
Long Eaton NG10 . . . . .236 B4
New Mills SK22 . . . . .24 D1
Shirebrook NG20 . . . . .119 F4
Whaley Thorns NG20 . . . . . .101 A3
Portland Sq DE45 . . . . . . .109 D6
Portland St
Clowne S43 . . . . .81 A4
Derby DE23 . . . . .232 A8
Etwall DE65 . . . . .229 B4
Mansfield Woodhouse
NG19 . . . . .136 C3
New Houghton NG19 . . . . . .135 A7
Whitwell S80 . . . . .81 F6
Portland Terr NG20 . . . . . .101 A2
Portreath Dr DE22 . . . . . . .204 E3
Port Way DE21, DE56 . . . .191 D5
Portway Cl DE22 . . . . .205 A4
Portway Dr DE13 . . . . . . .239 C5
Portway Inf Sch DE22 . . . .204 E4
Portway Jun Sch DE22 . . . .204 E4
Portwood Ind Est DE11 . . .256 A1
Postmans La S42 . . . . .116 C4
Post Office Row SK17 . . . . .69 E3
Post St SK13 . . . . .10 B5
Posy La DE72 . . . . .246 A7
Potato Pit La
Dale Abbey DE7 . . . . .208 A1
Stanton-by-D DE7 . . . . .222 A8
Potlocks The DE65 . . . . . . .242 C6
Potter Rd SK13 . . . . .9 E3
Potters Cl S41 . . . . .77 C2
Potters Croft
Clifton Campville B79 . . . . . .263 E2
Swadlincote DE11 . . . . .256 A5
Potters La DE4, DE56 . . . . .157 B5
Potters Nook S81 . . . . .63 F7
Potter St
Derby DE21 . . . . .220 D4
Melbourne DE73 . . . . .252 B7
Potters Way DE7 . . . . .209 A8
Pottery La DE73 . . . . .252 B7
Pottery Cl DE56 . . . . .179 C5
Pottery La DE5 . . . . .180 C3
Pottery La E S45 . . . . .96 B8
Pottery La W S41 . . . . .96 A7
Pottery Prim Sch DE56 . . .179 C4
Poulter Ctry Pk* NG20 . . .100 C2
Poulter St NG20 . . . . .100 F1
Pounder La DE4 . . . . .142 D2
Powell Dr S21 . . . . .60 C6
Powell St DE23 . . . . .218 E2
Pown St SK17 . . . . .137 A6
Powtrell Pl DE7 . . . . .209 B6
Poynter Cl DE75 . . . . .181 C1
Poynton Wood Cres S17 . . .56 A4
Poynton Wood Glade S17 . .56 A4
Poyser Ave DE21 . . . . .220 A7
Poyser La DE6 . . . . .203 A1
Pratt Cl NG19 . . . . .135 D1
Pratthall La DE4 . . . . .166 A6
Premier Ave DE6 . . . . .185 B8
Prescot Cl DE3 . . . . .217 C1
Press La S42 . . . . .130 D6
Prestbury Cl DE21 . . . . . . .206 B1
Preston Ave DE55 . . . . . . .159 B4
Preston St S8 . . . . .43 A7
Prestwick Way DE73 . . . . .232 E2
Prestwold Way S41 . . . . . .115 C7
Prestwood La ST14 . . . . . .196 F8
Prestwood Park Dr
DE11 . . . . .256 D5
Pretoria St S44 . . . . .98 F6
**Pride Park Stad (Derby
County FC)*** DE24 . . . . . .219 E3
Pride Parkway DE24 . . . . .219 D3
Pride Pl DE24 . . . . .219 D3
Pride Point Dr DE24 . . . . .219 D2
**Priestcliffe Lees (Nature
Reserve)*** SK17 . . . . .88 B7
Priestcliffe Rd SK17 . . . . . .87 F4
Priestfield Gdns S41 . . . . . .95 B7
Priestland Ave DE21 . . . . .220 D4
Priestley Ave DE55 . . . . . .146 C5
Primary Cl DE56 . . . . .179 A4
Prime Ind Est DE23 . . . . . .219 C2
Prime Ind Pk DE23 . . . . . .219 C2
Prime Parkway DE1 . . . . . .267 C4
Primrose Ave NG16 . . . . . .171 F2
Primrose Bank DE65 . . . . .229 C5
Primrose Bsns Pk DE55 . . .147 F1
Primrose Cl
Derby DE21 . . . . .205 F3
Killamarsh S21 . . . . .60 E7
South Normanton DE55 . . . .160 B7
Primrose Cotts
Hazelwood DE56 . . . . .190 C7
Risley DE72 . . . . .222 D3
Primrose Cres ⬛ SK13 . . . .17 B8
Primrose Ct
Hayfield SK22 . . . . .25 D3
Mansfield Woodhouse
NG19 . . . . .136 F4

Primrose Dr
Burton u T DE14 . . . . .254 A8
Morley DE7 . . . . .206 C8
Primrose Hill
Blackwell DE55 . . . . .147 F1
Glossop SK13 . . . . .17 B8
Ilkeston NE7 . . . . .194 E3
Primrose La
Glossop SK13 . . . . .17 B8
Hayfield SK22 . . . . .25 C5
Killamarsh S21 . . . . .60 E7
Marple SK6 . . . . .24 A4
Tideswell SK17 . . . . .69 C3
Primrose Mdw DE11 . . . . .256 B7
Primrose Rise NG16 . . . . . .195 B8
Primrose St DE7 . . . . .194 E3
Primrose Terr ⬛ SK13 . . . .17 B8
Primrose Vale Cotts SK22 .25 C4
Primrose Way NG20 . . . . . .119 F6
Primula Cl NG20 . . . . .119 D3
Primula Way DE23 . . . . . .231 D4
Prince's Rd SK17 . . . . .85 D8
Prince's St DE23 . . . . .219 B1
Prince Charles Ave
DE22 . . . . .218 A6
Prince Edward Prim Sch
S12 . . . . .44 A7
Prince of Wales Rd S2 . . . . .44 B7
Princes Dr DE23 . . . . .218 B2
Princes Rd SK23 . . . . .34 E2
Princess Ave
Linton DE12 . . . . .261 C5
South Normanton DE55 . . . .160 A5
Princess Cl
Heanor DE75 . . . . .181 D2
Woodville DE11 . . . . .256 F2
Princess Ct S2 . . . . .44 B8
Princess Dr
Borrowash DE72 . . . . .221 A2
Sandiacre NG10 . . . . .223 B4
Princess Pl S45 . . . . .131 C2
Princess Rd
Dronfield S18 . . . . .57 B2
Uttoxeter ST14 . . . . .210 A1
Princess St
Brimington S43 . . . . .96 F8
Chesterfield S40 . . . . .266 A4
Glossop SK13 . . . . .17 C8
Swadlincote DE11 . . . . .261 F8
Princes St NG16 . . . . .182 F3
Princess Way DE13 . . . . . .240 E1
Prince St
Ilkeston DE7 . . . . .194 E4
Long Eaton NG10 . . . . .236 D4
Printers Dr SK15 . . . . .4 A6
Printers Fold SK14 . . . . .9 D5
Printers Pk SK14 . . . . .9 D5
Priors Barn DE72 . . . . .221 D2
Priorway Ave DE72 . . . . . .221 D2
Priorway Gdns DE72 . . . . .221 C1
Priory Cl
Chellaston DE73 . . . . .245 A8
Ilkeston DE7 . . . . .208 C6
Swadlincote DE11 . . . . .256 A6
Tutbury DE13 . . . . .239 B5
Yeaveley DE6 . . . . .199 D5
Priory Ct S26 . . . . .61 E5
Priory Gdns
Derby DE21 . . . . .205 F3
Swannick DE55 . . . . .170 A8
Priory Lands DE13 . . . . . . .240 F2
Priory Rd
Alfreton DE55 . . . . .159 B5
Eastwood NG16 . . . . .182 F1
Mansfield Woodhouse
NG19 . . . . .136 B3
Priory Sq NG19 . . . . .136 B3
Pritchard Dr NG9 . . . . .223 E6
Pritchett Dr DE23 . . . . . . .230 E8
Private Dr S43 . . . . .78 A1
Progress Ct DE45 . . . . .109 D6
Prospect Ave DE55 . . . . . .159 C4
Prospect Cotts S43 . . . . .80 E5
Prospect Ct
⬛ Sheffield S17 . . . . .56 B5
Sutton in A NG17 . . . . .148 E1
Prospect Dr
Belper DE56 . . . . .178 F2
Matlock DE4 . . . . .143 A6
Sheffield S17 . . . . .55 F5
Shirebrook NG20 . . . . .119 E3
Prospect Gdns DE56 . . . . .169 E7
Prospect Ho S43 . . . . .78 F1
Prospect Pl
Derby DE23 . . . . .219 E4
Sheffield S17 . . . . .56 A5
Prospect Rd
Chesterfield S41 . . . . .76 F2
Denby Village DE5 . . . . .180 A1
Dronfield S18 . . . . .57 C3
Heanor DE75 . . . . .194 A8
Pilsley S45 . . . . .132 C1
Sheffield, Bradway Bank
S17 . . . . .56 A5
Sheffield, Lowfield S2 . . . . . .43 A7
Prospect St DE55 . . . . .159 B4
Prospect Terr
Bakewell DE45 . . . . .109 C6
Chesterfield S40 . . . . .95 E4
Crich DE4 . . . . .168 A8
Providence Ct DE11 . . . . . .256 F2
Providence Pl
Alfreton DE55 . . . . .158 F3
⬛ DE56 . . . . .194 E1
Providence Rd NG16 . . . . .171 A4
Providence St DE55 . . . . . .180 E8
Provident St ⬛ DE23 . . . . .219 A2

Pryor Mede S26 . . . . .61 E5
Pudding Bag La S45 . . . . . .129 F4
Puddle Hill DE4 . . . . .142 C1
Pulborough Gdns DE23 . . .231 A6
Pullman Cl S43 . . . . .78 F3
Pullman Rd DE21 . . . . .219 F4
Pump Cl DE41 . . . . .143 C3
Pump La DE6 . . . . .224 B8
Pump Yd DE56 . . . . .177 B2
Punch Bowl Pk SK17 . . . . . .85 A8
Purbeck Ave S40 . . . . .95 D4
Purbeck Cl
Long Eaton NG10 . . . . .236 A8
Mansfield Woodhouse
NG19 . . . . .136 C6
Purchase Ave DE75 . . . . . .181 C2
Purdy Mdw NG10 . . . . .235 F5
Pursglove Dr SK17 . . . . .69 D4
Pursglove Rd SK17 . . . . .69 C4
Putney Cl DE22 . . . . .217 E5
Pybus St DE22 . . . . .218 D6
Pye Bridge Ind Est DE55 .170 F6
Pyegrove SK13 . . . . .10 F1
Pyegrove Rd SK13 . . . . .10 E1
Pye Hill Rd NG16 . . . . .171 A4
Pykestone Cl ⬛ DE21 . . . .205 F2
Pym Leys NG10 . . . . .235 F5
Pynot Rd S41 . . . . .77 B2
Pytchley Cl DE56 . . . . .179 D4

Q

Quadrant Mews ⬛ SK17 . . .85 B8
Quadrant The
Buxton SK17 . . . . .85 B8
Sheffield S17 . . . . .55 E5
Quaker Cl DE73 . . . . .252 A7
Quantock Cl DE24 . . . . . . .231 D2
Quantock Rd NG10 . . . . . .223 A1
Quantock Way S40 . . . . .95 B5
Quarndon Hts DE22 . . . . . .204 C1
Quarndon View DE20 . . . . .204 C2
Quarn Dr DE22 . . . . .204 C3
Quarn Gdns DE1 . . . . .218 F7
Quarn St DE1 . . . . .218 E6
Quarn Way DE1 . . . . .218 F6
Quarry Bank DE4 . . . . .143 B7
Quarry Bank Rd S41 . . . . . .96 C2
Quarry Berry La DE42 . . . .264 F1
Quarry Cl SK13 . . . . .10 D1
Quarry Hill
Eckington S21 . . . . .58 D2
Sheffield S17 . . . . .59 A8
Stanton-by-D DE7 . . . . .223 A8
Quarry Hill Ind Est DE7 . . .208 F5
Quarry Hill Rd DE7 . . . . . . .208 F5
Quarry La
Alton S42 . . . . .130 C5
Brackenfield DE55 . . . . .145 D6
Chesterfield S40 . . . . .95 C2
Matlock DE4 . . . . .143 E7
Stonebroom DE55 . . . . .146 F3
Quarry Rd
Apperknowle S18 . . . . .58 A1
Belper DE56 . . . . .178 F2
Bolsover S44 . . . . .99 A3
Hayfield SK22 . . . . .24 F2
Killamarsh S21 . . . . .60 C7
Morley DE7 . . . . .192 B1
New Mills SK22 . . . . .33 D7
Sheffield, Totley Brook S17 . .55 E8
Somercotes DE55 . . . . .170 C2
Quarry Vale Gr S12 . . . . . . .44 C4
Quarry Vale Rd S12 . . . . . . .44 C4
Quarry Ave S45 . . . . .85 D8
Queen's Cres S41 . . . . .266 A4
Queen's Dr
Belper DE56 . . . . .178 E5
Glossop SK13 . . . . .10 F1
Ilkeston DE7 . . . . .208 E8
Swadlincote DE11 . . . . .256 B6
Queen's Park Sports Ctr
S40 . . . . .266 A2
Queen's Rd SK17 . . . . .85 D8
Queen's Sq NG16 . . . . .182 F2
Queen's Way S42 . . . . .115 D1
Queen's Wlk
Tupton S42 . . . . .115 C1
Whaley Thorns NG20 . . . . . .101 A1
Queen Ann Ct S14 . . . . .43 E3
Queen Elizabeth's Gram Sch
DE6 . . . . .173 C3
Queen Elizabeth's Sch
NG19 . . . . .136 A1
Queen Elizabeth Ct
⬛ Ashbourne DE6 . . . . . . .173 B2
Sheffield S14 . . . . .43 E3
Queen Elizabeth Way
DE7 . . . . .208 C5
Queen Mary Cl S2 . . . . .44 A7
Queen Mary Cres S2 . . . . . .44 A8
Queen Mary Ct
Derby DE1 . . . . .218 F7
Sheffield S2 . . . . .44 A8
Queen Mary Gr S2 . . . . .43 E3
Queen Mary Mews S2 . . . . .44 A7
Queen Mary Rd
Chesterfield S40 . . . . .95 B1
Sheffield S2 . . . . .44 A8
Queen St N S41 . . . . .96 A8
Queens Ave
Heanor DE75 . . . . .181 D2
Ilkeston DE7 . . . . .209 A5
Stanley DE7 . . . . .207 C6
Queensbury Chase DE23 . .231 A6
Queens Cl S80 . . . . .82 C5

Queens Ct
Burton u T DE14 . . . . .254 B8
Buxton SK17 . . . . .85 D8
Creswell S80 . . . . .81 F2
Derby DE22 . . . . .218 E8
Derby DE72 . . . . .235 A7
Queen's Ct SK6 . . . . .23 A6
Queens Dr
Brinsley NG16 . . . . .182 E7
Derby DE23 . . . . .218 C2
Sandiacre NG10 . . . . .223 B4
Queensferry Gdns DE24 . .232 E4
Queensgate Dr DE73 . . . . .244 F8
Queens Gdns S2 . . . . .43 C8
Queensland Cl DE3 . . . . . . .217 E4
Queensland Cres DE15 . . .248 C2
Queens Mews S2 . . . . .43 C8
Queens Rd
Creswell S80 . . . . .82 C6
Sheffield, Lowfield S2 . . . . . .43 B8
Queens Rd N NG16 . . . . . .182 F2
Queens Rd S NG16 . . . . . . .182 F1
Queens Ret Pk S2 . . . . .43 B8
Queens Stables S2 . . . . .43 C8
Queen St
Belper DE56 . . . . .179 A3
Brimington S43 . . . . .77 F1
Chesterfield S40 . . . . .266 A4
Clay Cross S45 . . . . .131 C3
Creswell S80 . . . . .81 F1
Derby DE1 . . . . .267 B4
Eckington S21 . . . . .59 E3
Glossop SK13 . . . . .17 B8
Hadfield SK13 . . . . .10 A4
Ilkeston DE7 . . . . .208 E8
Ironville NG16 . . . . .170 F4
Langley Mill NG16 . . . . .182 C3
Long Eaton NG10 . . . . .236 E7
Longnor SK17 . . . . .121 B6
Marple SK6 . . . . .23 A6
Middleton DE4 . . . . .154 D5
Pilsley S45 . . . . .132 D1
Pinxton NG16 . . . . .160 C3
Ripley DE5 . . . . .181 A7
Sheffield, Mosborough S20 . .59 C7
Somercotes DE55 . . . . .170 D8
South Normanton DE55 . . . .159 F5
Staveley S43 . . . . .97 D8
Swadlincote DE11 . . . . .256 B6
Tideswell SK17 . . . . .69 C4
Queens View S2 . . . . .43 C8
Queensview Dr DE55 . . . . .181 A7
Queensway
Castle Donington DE74 . . . .246 F4
Derby DE22 . . . . .204 F2
Holmewood S42 . . . . .116 E1
Pilsley S45 . . . . .132 C1
Stonebroom DE55 . . . . .146 F3
Queens Wlk S42 . . . . .116 E1
Queen Victoria Dr DE11 . . .256 B5
Queen Victoria Rd
Sheffield S17 . . . . .55 F5
Tupton S42 . . . . .115 C1
Quenby La DE5 . . . . .169 E1
Quernd Rd SK23 . . . . .47 C6
Quick Cl DE73 . . . . .252 A7
Quick Hill Rd DE24 . . . . . . .231 D2
Quillings Way DE72 . . . . . .221 D1
Quilow La DE6 . . . . .185 E3
Quintin Rd DE24 . . . . .233 A8
Quixhill Bank ST14 . . . . . . .196 D8
Quixhill La ST14 . . . . .196 D8
Quoit Gn S18 . . . . .57 A1
Quorn Cl DE15 . . . . .248 A1
Quorndon Cres NG10 . . . . .236 D5
Quorn Dr ⬛ S40 . . . . .95 A5
Quorn Rise DE23 . . . . .231 E6

R

Rabown Ave DE23 . . . . .231 D8
Racecourse Ind Est
DE21 . . . . .219 C8
Racecourse Mount S41 . . . .95 F8
Racecourse Rd
Chesterfield S41 . . . . .76 F1
Chesterfield S41 . . . . .95 F8
Radbourne Comm ⬛ S18 . .56 D1
Radbourne Gate DE3 . . . . .217 D5
Radbourne La DE22 . . . . . .217 E6
Radbourne St
Derby DE22 . . . . .218 C6
Mansfield Woodhouse
NG19 . . . . .136 E4
Radburn Cl NG9 . . . . .209 E1
Radcliffe Ave DE21 . . . . . . .219 F7
Radcliffe Dr DE22 . . . . .218 A6
Radford Mdw DE74 . . . . . .246 F3
Radford Rd DE7 . . . . .192 F6
Radford St DE24 . . . . .232 F7
Radleigh Gr DE11 . . . . .257 A2
Radleigh Grange DE11 . . . .257 A2
Radmanthwaite Rd
NG19 . . . . .135 D3
Rad Mdws NG10 . . . . .236 C6
Radnor Pl NG19 . . . . .136 E1
Radnor St DE21 . . . . .219 D7
Radstock Gdns DE21 . . . . .205 E1
Radstone Cl DE21 . . . . . . .206 B2
Raeburn Cl S14 . . . . .43 E2
Raeburn Dr
Beeston NG9 . . . . .223 E2
Marple SK6 . . . . .23 B8
Raeburn Pl S14 . . . . .43 E3

Raeburn Rd S14 . . . . .43 E3
Raeburn Way S14 . . . . .43 E2
Raglan Ave DE22 . . . . .218 C5
Raglan St DE55 . . . . .159 A4
Railway Ave S80 . . . . .100 D8
Railway Cotts
Bolsover S44 . . . . .98 C2
Derby DE24 . . . . .232 A6
Derby, Stenson DE24 . . . . . .243 A8
Egginton DE65 . . . . .241 B7
Holmewood S42 . . . . .116 F1
Kimberley NG16 . . . . .195 F6
Temple Normanton S41 . . . .116 A5
Railway Row NG16 . . . . . . .170 F4
Railway Side DE11 . . . . . . .256 B1
Railway St
Glossop SK13 . . . . .10 C1
Hadfield SK13 . . . . .10 A5
**Railway Techical Centre Bsns
Pk** DE24 . . . . .219 D2
Railway Terr
Buxton SK17 . . . . .85 C8
⬛ Chesterfield S41 . . . . . .115 B7
Derby DE1 . . . . .267 D2
Disley SK12 . . . . .32 D6
Rain's La DE4 . . . . .154 C4
Rainham Gdns DE24 . . . . .233 A5
Rainier Dr DE21 . . . . .220 A6
Rake Head Rd HD9 . . . . .2 E7
Rake La DE45 . . . . .124 D3
Rakes La DE6 . . . . .162 A6
Rakes Rd DE45 . . . . .107 C1
Rake The DE45 . . . . .123 B6
Raleigh Cl DE7 . . . . .194 F3
Raleigh Rd S2 . . . . .43 B6
Raleigh St DE22 . . . . .218 C6
Ralley Cl S42 . . . . .132 D8
Ralph Dr DE55 . . . . .170 D7
Ralph Rd S43 . . . . .79 A2
Ralston Croft S20 . . . . .59 E6
Ralston Gr S20 . . . . .59 D6
Ralston Pl S20 . . . . .59 D6
Rambler Cl DE11 . . . . .256 A5
Ramblers Dr DE21 . . . . . . .206 C3
Ramper Ave S43 . . . . .80 E2
Ramscliff Ave DE12 . . . . . .265 F8
Ramsdean Cl DE21 . . . . . . .219 D8
Ramsden Cl SK13 . . . . .10 D2
Ramsden La HD9 . . . . .3 B7
Ramsden Rd HD9 . . . . .3 C7
Ramsey Ave S40 . . . . .95 D1
Ramsey Cl NG9 . . . . .209 E2
Ramshaw Cl S41 . . . . .95 C7
Ramshaw Rd S18 . . . . .76 E6
Ramshaw Way DE22 . . . . . .218 E4
Ramsley Ct ⬛ S40 . . . . .95 D5
Randal Cres SK23 . . . . .45 E5
Randall Dr DE11 . . . . .256 B4
Randall Pl ⬛ S2 . . . . .43 A8
Randall St S21 . . . . .59 B2
Randolph Rd DE23 . . . . . . .231 F8
Ranelagh Gdns DE22 . . . . .218 B2
Raneld Mount S40 . . . . . . .114 C8
Rangemoor La DE6 . . . . . . .183 D6
Rangemore Cl DE3 . . . . . . .217 E4
Rangewood Rd DE55 . . . . .159 F4
Ranmoor Cl S41 . . . . .115 C6
Ranmoor Hill S32 . . . . .52 E8
Ranmoor La S32 . . . . .52 F8
Rannoch Cl
Derby DE22 . . . . .204 E3
Derby, Spondon DE21 . . . . .220 F5
Ranworth Cl DE24 . . . . . . .232 D3
Ratcliffe Ave DE14 . . . . . . .254 B8
Ratcliffe Cl S41 . . . . .115 C7
Ratcliffe La S80 . . . . .82 D6
Ratcliffe St NG16 . . . . .182 F2
Rauche St DE23 . . . . .267 C2
Raven Ave DE55 . . . . .147 F5
Ravencar Rd S21 . . . . .59 B3
Raven Cl DE55 . . . . .170 C6
Raven Oak Cl DE56 . . . . . . .179 A3
Ravens Cl SK13 . . . . .16 F8
Ravenscourt Rd DE22 . . . .218 C6
Ravenscroft Ave S13 . . . . . .44 E8
Ravenscroft Cl S13 . . . . . . .44 E8
Ravenscroft Cres S13 . . . . .44 E8
Ravenscroft Ct S13 . . . . . . .44 E8
Ravenscroft Dr
Derby DE21 . . . . .219 F6
Sheffield S13 . . . . .44 E7
Ravenscroft Oval S13 . . . . .44 E7
Ravenscroft Pl S13 . . . . . . .44 E8
Ravenscroft Rd S13 . . . . . . .44 E7
Ravenscroft Way S13 . . . . .44 E8
Ravensdale Ave NG10 . . . .223 B8
Ravensdale Cl S43 . . . . .97 C5
Ravensdale Cotts SK17 . . . .89 A8
Ravensdale Inf & Jun Schs
DE3 . . . . .217 E3
Ravensdale Rd
Derby DE22 . . . . .204 C3
Dronfield S18 . . . . .56 D1
Ravenside Ret Pk S40 . . . . .266 B2
Raven St DE22 . . . . .218 E3
Ravenstor Rd DE4 . . . . .154 F2
Ravenstor YH* SK17 . . . . .154 F2
Ravenswood Rd S40 . . . . . . .95 A5
Ravenwood Cl DE7 . . . . . . .207 D5
Rawdon Cl DE74 . . . . .247 A4
Rawdon St DE24 . . . . .262 E5
Rawdon Side DE11 . . . . . . .256 D4
Rawdon St DE23 . . . . .218 F2
Rawlins Ct S18 . . . . .57 C4

Rawlinson Ave DE23 . . . . . 232 A7
Rawson Gn DE56 . . . . 179 F1
Ray's Ave DE75 . . . . 181 E1
Rayleigh Ave S43 . . . . 96 D8
Raynald Rd S2 . . . . 44 A8
Rayneham Rd DE7 . . . . 194 C4
Raynesway
  Derby, Alvaston DE21 . . . . 233 B8
  Derby DE21 . . . . 220 A2
Raynesway Park Dr
  DE21 . . . . 220 B1
Ray Rushin Bsns Pk The
  DE21 . . . . 220 B1
Ray St DE75 . . . . 181 E1
Reader St DE21 . . . . 220 E5
Realm Cl DE73 . . . . 244 E8
Rebecca Ho DE41 . . . . . . 218 E5
Recreation Cl
  Blackwell DE55 . . . . 147 E1
  Clowne S43 . . . . 80 E4
Recreation Dr DE20 . . . . . 119 F2
Recreation Gd The
  (Chesterfield FC) S40 . 266 A4
Recreation Rd
  Calow S43 . . . . 96 F5
  New Houghton NG19 . . . . 134 F7
  Sandiacre NG10 . . . . 223 B6
  Shirebrook NG20 . . . . . . 119 E6
  Tideswell SK17 . . . . 69 C4
  Wirksworth DE4 . . . . 165 E7
Recreation St NG10 . . . . . 236 F7
Recreation Terr NG9 . . . . 223 D6
Recreation View NG20 . . 119 E6
Rectory Cl
  Breedon on t H DE73 . . . . 252 E2
  Eckington S21 . . . . 59 E4
  Long Duckmanton S44 . . . 98 A3
Rectory Dr S42 . . . . 114 E4
Rectory Farm Mews
  DE72 . . . . 245 E4
Rectory Gdns
  Aston-on-T DE72 . . . . . . 246 A7
  Harthill S26 . . . . 61 E6
  Killamarsh S21 . . . . 60 D6
  Long Duckmanton S44 . . . 98 A3
Rectory La
  Appleby Magna DE12 . . . . 265 E1
  Breadsall DE21 . . . . 205 D5
  Kirk Ireton DE6 . . . . 165 B1
Rectory Mews DE65 . . . . . 241 B4
Rectory Pl NG11 . . . . 237 E6
Rectory Rd
  Breaston DE72 . . . . 235 E8
  Clowne S43 . . . . 80 E4
  Killamarsh S21 . . . . 60 D5
  Long Duckmanton S44 . . . 98 A4
  Staveley S43 . . . . 78 E2
Reculver Cl DE21 . . . . 231 D7
Redacre Cl S44 . . . . 99 C2
Red Barn Cl DE55 . . . . . . 148 B3
Redbarn La DE55 . . . . . . 148 B3
Redbridge Cl NG20 . . . . . 119 F2
Redbrook Ave S41 . . . . . . 115 B8
Redbrow Hollow S66 . . . . 15 A2
Redbury Cl DE1 . . . . 218 E4
Redcar Gdns **6** DE21 . . 205 D1
Reddish Ave S43 . . . . 45 C6
Reddish La SK23 . . . . 45 C6
Reddish Rd SK23 . . . . 45 C6
Redens The NG10 . . . . . . 236 B4
Redfern Ave DE5 . . . . 169 E2
Redfern Cl SK13 . . . . 10 A6
Redfern Rd ST14 . . . . 210 A1
Redfern St S42 . . . . 131 C7
Redgap La SK17 . . . . 86 A8
Redgate St S13 . . . . 10 C4
Redgate St NG16 . . . . 160 D2
Redgrove Way S40 . . . . . . 114 C8
Red Hill DE4 . . . . 144 C4
Redhill Ct DE56 . . . . 179 E7
Redhill Foundation Prim Sch
  DE72 . . . . 221 C5
Redhill La DE13 . . . . 239 B5
Red Hill La DE4 . . . . 144 D3
Redhill Lodge Rd **6**
  DE11 . . . . 256 A7
Redhouse Cl S43 . . . . 77 D4
Redhouse La SK12 . . . . . . 32 E7
Redhouse Stables Working
  Carriage Mus* DE44 . 127 D1
Red La
  Belper DE56 . . . . 191 B6
  Brinsley NG16 . . . . 171 E1
  Chesterfield S41 . . . . 77 C1
  Disley SK12 . . . . 32 C5
  Repton DE65 . . . . 249 F6
  South Normanton DE55 . . 159 F3
Redland Cl
  Derby DE24 . . . . 231 F4
  Ilkeston DE7 . . . . 194 F3
Red Lion Hill DE4 . . . . . . 153 A1
Red Lion Row S32 . . . . . . 72 C8
Red Lion Sq DE75 . . . . . . 181 E1
Red Lo SK2 . . . . 32 A6
Redmires Dr DE73 . . . . . . 233 A2
Redmires Rd S10 . . . . 42 B8
Redmoor Cl
  Burton u T DE15 . . . . . . 248 B3
  Codnor DE5 . . . . 170 B1
Redmoor La
  Disley SK12 . . . . 33 A4
  Nether Heage DE56 . . . . . 33 B6
Rednall Cl S40 . . . . 95 A5
Red Rose Ct S16 . . . . 254 E7
Redruth Pl DE24 . . . . 233 C5

Redshaw St DE1 . . . . 218 E7
Redstart Cl DE21 . . . . . . 220 F6
Redthorn Rd S13 . . . . 44 F8
Redvers Buller Rd S40 . . 266 B1
Redway Croft **5** DE73 . 252 A8
Redwing Croft DE23 . . . . 231 D7
Redwood Ave S21 . . . . . . 60 C5
Redwood Cl S43 . . . . 97 B8
Redwood Dr DE15 . . . . . . 255 A8
Redwood Inf Sch DE24 . . 231 F3
Redwood Jun Sch DE24 . . 231 F3
Redwood Rd DE24 . . . . . . 231 E3
Reedman Rd NG10 . . . . . . 236 B4
Reeves Ave S45 . . . . 132 C1
Reeves Rd DE23 . . . . 219 B1
Regal Gate DE11 . . . . 244 F8
Regency Cl
  Derby DE23 . . . . 231 D7
  4 Glossop SK13 . . . . . . 10 C1
Regent Ct
  Ironville NG16 . . . . 170 F4
  Swadlincote DE11 . . . . . . 256 B2
Regent Gdns S41 . . . . . . 266 B4
Regents Ho **8** DE14 . . . 253 F7
Regent St
  Clowne S43 . . . . 80 D4
  Derby DE1 . . . . 267 C1
  Glossop, Padfield SK13 . . . 10 A3
  Glossop SK13 . . . . 10 D1
  Ilkeston DE7 . . . . 208 F7
  Kimberley NG16 . . . . 195 F6
  Langley Mill NG16 . . . . . . 182 B3
  Long Eaton NG10 . . . . . . 236 D8
  Stapleford NG9 . . . . 223 C5
  Swadlincote DE11 . . . . . . 256 B2
Reginald Rd N DE21 . . . . 219 F7
Reginald Rd S DE21 . . . . 219 F6
Reginald St DE23 . . . . . . 219 B2
Regis Cl DE21 . . . . 206 B2
Reigate Dr DE22 . . . . 204 C1
Reigate Prim Sch DE22 . . 217 F7
Reliant Cl DE11 . . . . 256 E1
Rembrandt Dr S18 . . . . . . 56 E1
Rempstone Dr S41 . . . . . 115 C7
Renals St DE23 . . . . 267 B1
Reney Ave S8 . . . . 56 D6
Reney Cres S8 . . . . 56 D6
Reney Dr S8 . . . . 56 D6
Reney Rd S8 . . . . 56 E7
Reney Wlk S8 . . . . 56 D6
Renfrew St DE21 . . . . 219 E7
Renishaw Hall* S21 **59** F1
Renishaw Hall (Mus & Craft
  Ctr)* S21 . . . . 59 F2
Renishaw Rd S43 . . . . 79 B8
Renishaw Dr DE11 . . . . . 255 F5
Renshaw Dr DE11 . . . . . . 255 F5
Renishaw Prim Sch S21 . . 79 B8
Repton Cl DE7 . . . . 208 F7
Repton Ct **8** NG19 . . . . 136 E4
Repton Dr DE7 . . . . 209 B7
Repton Pl S18 . . . . 56 C1
Repton Prep Sch DE65 . . 243 C2
Repton Prim Sch DE65 . . 242 E2
Repton Rd
  Appleby Magna DE12 . . . . 265 F5
  Hartshorne DE11 . . . . . . 256 F8
  Long Eaton NG10 . . . . . . 235 F4
  Newton Solney DE65 . . . . 248 F8
  Willington DE65 . . . . 242 A5
Repton Sch DE65 . . . . . . 242 C3
Reservoir Hill DE12 . . . . . 262 D6
Reservoir Rd DE55 . . . . . 146 A5
Reservoir Rd SK23 . . . . . . 45 D7
Reservoir Terr S40 . . . . . . 95 F4
Resthaven Dr DE11 . . . . . 256 E1
Resthaven DE11 . . . . 256 B5
Retford Cl DE21 . . . . 205 D2
Revill Cl DE7 . . . . 194 C2
Revill Cres NG9 . . . . 223 F8
Revolution House Mus The*
  S41 . . . . 77 A2
Reynard Cres S21 . . . . . . 79 B8
Reynards La SK17 . . . . . . 137 E4
Reynolds Ave DE5 . . . . . . 169 F1
Reynolds Cl S18 . . . . 75 E8
Reynolds Dr SK6 . . . . 23 B8
Rhein O' Thorns NG20 . . 120 E5
Rhodes Ave S41 . . . . 95 F5
Rhodes Cotts S43 . . . . . . 80 F4
Rhodes Ho DE15 . . . . 248 C3
Rhodesia Rd S40 . . . . 95 C2
Rhodes St SK13 . . . . 10 B5
Rhodeswood Dr SK13 . . . . 10 A6
Rhuddlan Pl SK23 . . . . . . 34 D1
Ribble Cl DE65 . . . . 240 D8
Ribblesdale DE7 . . . . 208 C5
Ribblesdale Dr DE22 . . . . 204 C2
Ribblesdale Dr S12 . . . . . . 44 F1
Ribblesdale Rd NG10 . . . 236 A5
Ribble Way DE65 . . . . . . 170 D8
Riber Bank **11** SK13 . . . . 9 E1
Riber Cl
  20 Gamesley SK13 . . . . . 9 E1
  Long Eaton NG10 . . . . . 236 D5
  Staveley S43 . . . . 97 C5
  West Hallam DE7 . . . . . . 207 E8
Riber Cres S42 . . . . 131 B5
Riber Ct **11** S40 . . . . 95 D5
Riber Fold **16** SK13 . . . . . 9 E1
Riber Gn **10** SK13 . . . . . . 9 E1
Riber Rd
  Lea DE4 . . . . 156 A8
  Matlock DE4 . . . . 143 C2
Riber Terr S40 . . . . 266 A2
Riber View Cl DE4 . . . . . . 144 A5
Richard La SK17 . . . . 69 C3
Richards Ct **2** S2 . . . . . . 43 B6

Richardson Dr DE7 . . . . . 192 F6
Richardson Endowed Prim
  Sch DE7 . . . . 192 F6
Richardsons La DE55 . . . 170 C5
Richardson St DE22 . . . . 218 D6
Richards Rd S2 . . . . 43 B6
Richard Wakefield CE Prim
  Sch DE13 . . . . 239 C6
Richmond Ave
  Derby DE23 . . . . 231 C8
  Ilkeston DE7 . . . . 194 F4
  Long Eaton DE72 . . . . . . 236 A8
  Sandiacre NG10 . . . . 223 A4
  Sheffield S13 . . . . 44 F8
Richmond Ct
  Chesterfield S40 . . . . 114 C8
  Derby DE23 . . . . 231 A7
  Glossop SK13 . . . . 10 A5
  West Hallam DE7 . . . . . . 207 D8
Richmond Ct
  5 Barrow Hill S43 . . . . . 78 B3
  Repton DE65 . . . . 242 D2
  Sheffield S13 . . . . 44 D7
Richmond Dr
  Duffield DE56 . . . . 190 D5
  Mansfield Woodhouse
    NG19 . . . . 136 D2
Richmond Farm Mews
  S13 . . . . 44 D7
Richmond Gdns S41 . . . . 266 B4
Richmond Gr S13 . . . . 44 E8
Richmond Hall Ave S13 . . 44 D8
Richmond Hall Cres S13 . 44 D7
Richmond Hall Dr S13 . . . 44 D7
Richmond Hall Rd S13 . . . 44 D8
Richmond Hall Way S13 . 44 D7
Richmond Ho S13 . . . . . . 44 D7
Richmond Ho DE65 . . . . . 228 C1
Richmond Pl S13 . . . . 44 D7
Richmond Rd
  Derby, Chaddesden
    DE21 . . . . 219 F6
  Derby, Rose Hill DE23 . . . 219 A1
  Sheffield S13 . . . . 44 D7
Richmond Terr SK6 . . . . . 23 B1
Rickmans Cnr Cvn Site
  DE12 . . . . 262 A6
Ricroft Rd SK6 . . . . 15 B3
Riddings DE22 . . . . 204 E4
Riddings Cl S2 . . . . 44 A7
Riddings Croft S41 . . . . . . 95 C6
Riddings Inf Sch DE55 . . 170 D6
Riddings Jun Sch DE55 . . 170 D6
Riddings La S32 . . . . 72 D4
Riddings St DE22 . . . . . . 218 F3
Ridd Way S42 . . . . 115 A3
Ridge Ave SK6 . . . . 23 A4
Ridge Cl SK13 . . . . 9 E3
Ridge Cres SK6 . . . . 23 A3
Ridgedale Rd S44 . . . . . . 118 A8
Ridgedale View DE56 . . . 169 D2
Ridge End Fold SK6 . . . . . 23 A2
Ridgehill Ave S12 . . . . 44 B5
Ridgehill Gr S12 . . . . 44 B5
Ridge Rd
  Eckington S21 . . . . 58 E2
  Marple SK6 . . . . 23 A3
Ridge The
  Blackwell DE55 . . . . 147 E1
  Marple SK6 . . . . 23 A3
Ridge Top La S22 . . . . 25 C2
Ridgeway
  Chellaston DE73 . . . . . . 245 A8
  Clowne S43 . . . . 80 F2
  Dronfield S18 . . . . 57 D3
  Heanor DE75 . . . . 193 F8
  Shirebrook NG20 . . . . . . 119 F5
Ridgeway Ave
  Bolsover S44 . . . . 99 C2
  Derby DE23 . . . . 231 D6
Ridgeway Craft Ctr* S12 . 58 E8
Ridgeway Cres S12 . . . . . 44 A6
Ridgeway Ct DE23 . . . . . . 218 D2
Ridgeway Dr
  Ilkeston DE7 . . . . 208 B5
  Sheffield S12 . . . . 44 A6
Ridgeway Inf Sch DE23 . . 231 D6
Ridgeway La DE56 . . . . . . 168 C4
Ridgeway Moor S12 . . . . . 58 E6
Ridgeway Prim Sch S12 . . 58 E8
Ridgeway Rd
  Burton u T DE15 . . . . . . 254 E7
  Sheffield S12 . . . . 44 A5
Ridgeways The SK22 . . . . 25 D2
Ridgeway W S43 . . . . 80 E2
Ridgewood Ct DE21 . . . . . 205 E2
Ridgewood Dr DE4 . . . . . 143 B6
Riding The SK12 . . . . 32 C6
Riding Bank DE73 . . . . . . 251 F6
Riding Hill Ave NG20 . . . 119 D3
Ridings Rd SK13 . . . . 9 F5
Ridings The
  Mansfield NG19 . . . . 136 A1
  Ockbrook DE72 . . . . 221 D5
Rigga La DE56 . . . . 191 E1
Riggotts Way S42 . . . . 94 E8
Riggs La DE6 . . . . 212 A7
Rigley Ave **8** DE7 . . . . . 194 F1
Rigsby Ct DE3 . . . . 217 C3
Riley Ave DE55 . . . . 157 D8
Riley Back La S32 . . . . 71 E6
Riley La DE55 . . . . 169 A6
Rimsdale Cl DE24 . . . . . . 231 E3
Ringer La S43 . . . . 80 E3
Ringer Way S43 . . . . 80 E3

Ringinglow Rd S10, S11 . . 42 E4
Ring-o-Bells La SK12 . . . . 32 D6
Ringstone Way S43 . . . . . 45 D8
Ringwood Ave
  Chesterfield S41 . . . . 95 E7
  Compstall SK14 . . . . 15 A8
  Staveley S43 . . . . 97 C8
Ringwood Cl **3** DE21 . . 219 E8
Ringwood Rd S43 . . . . . . 96 F8
Ringwood View S43 . . . . . 96 F7
Rink Dr DE11 . . . . 256 B3
Ripley Ho DE21 . . . . 220 E3
Ripley Hospl DE5 . . . . . . 169 D1
Ripley Jun Sch DE5 . . . . 180 D8
Ripley Jun Sch DE5 . . . . 180 D8
Ripley Rd
  Bullbridge DE56 . . . . . . 168 D5
  Heage DE56 . . . . 169 A1
Ripon Cres DE21 . . . . . . 219 E8
Ripon Gdns SK17 . . . . 85 D5
Risborow Cl DE65 . . . . . 229 D4
Rises The SK13 . . . . 9 F5
Rise The
  Derby DE22 . . . . 204 E2
  Horwich End SK23 . . . . . . 45 C6
  Swadlincote DE11 . . . . . . 255 F5
Risings The SK22 . . . . 24 B1
Risley Ct DE7 . . . . 194 F3
Risley La DE72 . . . . 222 D2
Risley Lower Gram CE Prim
  Sch DE72 . . . . 222 E4
Rivendale Cvn Pk DE6 . . 150 E6
Rivenhall Cl DE23 . . . . . . 230 F7
Riverbank DE4 . . . . 110 F1
Riverbank The DE65 . . . . 242 B5
Riverbank Way SK13 . . . . 17 F7
Rivercroft Cl ST14 . . . . . . 197 A3
River Ct S17 . . . . 56 A7
Riverdale S32 . . . . 72 C7
Riverdale Cl DE15 . . . . . . 248 B5
Rivermead Ho DE65 . . . . 267 B5
Riversdale DE56 . . . . 168 B4
Riversfield Dr ST14 . . . . . 196 F3
Riverside
  Baslow DE45 . . . . 91 D6
  Walton-on-T DE12 . . . . . 253 C1
Riverside Bsns Pk DE45 . 109 C7
Riverside Cl
  Calver S32 . . . . 72 D1
  Glossop SK13 . . . . 10 D1
Riverside Cres
  Bakewell DE45 . . . . 109 D6
  Holymoorside S42 . . . . . 113 F7
Riverside Ct
  Ambergate DE56 . . . . . . 167 F3
  Baslow DE45 . . . . 91 E6
  Calver S32 . . . . 72 D2
  Derby DE24 . . . . 219 D4
Riverside Dr
  Branston DE14 . . . . 253 F7
  Calver S32 . . . . 72 D2
Riverside Rd DE21 . . . . . 219 D4
Riverside Studios S18 . . . 57 B1
Riverside Way
  Bolsover S44 . . . . 98 E2
  Mansfield Woodhouse
    NG19 . . . . 136 D5
River St DE1 . . . . 267 B4
River View
  Aldercar DE55 . . . . 171 A6
  Belper DE56 . . . . 190 F7
  Chesterfield S40 . . . . 115 A8
  Long Eaton NG10 . . . . . . 236 A3
  Longnor SK17 . . . . 121 B6
  Tideswell SK17 . . . . 88 D7
Riverview Cres **2** SK13 . 17 C7
Rivington Rd **8** NG9 . . . 223 E7
Roadmeadow Dr DE6 . . . 185 D8
Robert Cl S18 . . . . 76 E5
Robert Rd S8 . . . . 57 A7
Roberts Ave NG17 . . . . . 148 F2
Roberts Dr DE55 . . . . 159 B4
Robertson Ave S44 . . . . . . 98 A4
Robertson Rd SK17 . . . . . 85 B6
Roberts St DE7 . . . . 209 A6
Robert St DE1 . . . . 267 C4
Robert Sutton RC Sch
  DE15 . . . . 255 A7
Robey Dr NG16 . . . . 182 F3
Robian Way DE11 . . . . . . 256 A6
Robin's Cross La DE65 . . 249 F7
Robincroft S42 . . . . 114 F7
Robincroft Rd S42 . . . . . 114 D4
Robin Croft Rd DE22 . . . 204 C2
Robinettes La NG16 . . . . 195 D5
Robin Hood Cl NG16 . . . . 182 F1
Robin Hood Pl DE11 . . . . 256 C2
Robin Hood Prim Sch
  NG19 . . . . 136 B3
Robin Hood Rd DE4 . . . . 156 C2
Robinia Cl DE21 . . . . 206 C3
Robinlands La S33 . . . . . . 38 B4
Robin Rd DE1 . . . . 218 F7
Robins Cl DE7 . . . . 233 D5
Robinscross DE72 . . . . . . 221 C2
Robinson's Hill DE73 . . . . 251 F6
Robinson Ind Est DE23 . . 219 B2
Robinson Rd DE11 . . . . . 256 A6
Robinson Way SK17 . . . . . 60 C6
Robinwood Lo DE55 . . . . . 9 E1
Robridding Rd S45 . . . . . 129 A4
Robson Cl DE24 . . . . 246 F4
Roby Lea DE4 . . . . 246 F4
Rocester Way S42 . . . . . . 131 F6
Roche **9** S42 . . . . 59 E8
Rochester Cl
  Derby DE24 . . . . 233 A5

Rochester Cl continued
  Long Eaton NG10 . . . . . . 236 A7
Rochley Cl DE21 . . . . 205 F2
Rock Bank
  Buxton SK17 . . . . 85 C3
  Horwich End SK23 . . . . . . 45 E6
Rockbourne Cl DE24 . . . . 233 D6
Rockcliffe Cl DE11 . . . . . 256 B1
Rock Cres S45 . . . . 131 A5
Rockets The DE21 . . . . . . 191 E4
Rockfield Rd SK17 . . . . . . 85 D8
Rockford Ct NG9 . . . . 209 E1
Rockhall Terr SK22 . . . . . . 25 E2
Rock Ho DE4 . . . . 155 A6
Rock House Cl DE55 . . . . 147 F5
Rockhouse Rd DE24 . . . . 233 A6
Rockingham **11** S20 . . . . 59 E8
Rockingham Cl
  Chesterfield S40 . . . . 95 C3
  Derby DE22 . . . . 205 A4
  3 Dronfield S18 . . . . . . 56 C1
Rock La S44 . . . . 116 E6
Rocklands The NG20 . . . . 119 E4
Rockley Cl S40 . . . . 114 F7
Rockley Way NG20 . . . . . 119 E4
Rockmay Ho DE55 . . . . . 170 E6
Rock Mill Bsns Pk S32 . . . 71 E4
Rock Mill La SK22 . . . . . . 33 B7
Rock Side NG16 . . . . 195 F6
Rockside Cotts S43 . . . . . 80 E4
Rockside Hall DE4 . . . . . 143 C6
Rockside Hydro DE4 . . . . 143 C6
Rockside Stps DE4 . . . . . 143 C6
Rockside The DE4 . . . . . . 143 C7
Rock Sq S32 . . . . 71 D4
Rock St S32 . . . . 33 C7
Rocks The DE4 . . . . 144 A5
Rock Terr
  Bakewell DE45 . . . . 109 C6
  Buxton SK17 . . . . 85 B6
Rock The DE45 . . . . 109 C6
Rockvale Terr DE4 . . . . . 143 B1
Rockvale Villas DE4 . . . . 143 B1
Rock View SK17 . . . . 88 A7
Rodge Croft S41 . . . . 77 A3
Rodger's La DE55 . . . . . . 159 A5
Rodknoll La S42 . . . . 93 D2
Rod Moor Rd S17, S18 . . . 56 B4
Rodney Cl DE65 . . . . 228 E2
Rodney Ho DE24 . . . . 232 E6
Rodney Way DE7 . . . . . . 194 F3
Rodney Wlk DE23 . . . . . . 230 E7
Rodsley Cl S40 . . . . 95 B5
Rodsley Cres DE23 . . . . . 231 D5
Rodsley La
  Rodsley DE6 . . . . 199 F7
  Yeaveley DE6 . . . . 199 E5
Rodwood Ave S43 . . . . . . 80 A7
Roe's La DE4 . . . . 157 A1
Roebuck Pl SK23 . . . . 47 B6
Roecar Cl S41 . . . . 77 B2
Roe Cross Ind Est SK14 . . 9 A5
Roe Cross Rd SK14 . . . . . . 9 A5
Roe Farm La DE21 . . . . . 219 C7
Roe Farm Prim Sch
  DE21 . . . . 219 E8
Roehampton Dr
  Derby DE22 . . . . 218 A7
  Stapleford NG9 . . . . 209 D2
Roe's Ct DE24 . . . . 157 A2
Roe Wlk DE23 . . . . 219 A1
Rogers Ave S80 . . . . 81 D1
Rogers Ct DE65 . . . . 227 D1
Rolaine Cl NG19 . . . . 136 D2
Rolleston Cres NG16 . . . . 195 F8
Rolleston Dr NG16 . . . . . 195 B8
Rolleston La DE13 . . . . . 239 D5
Rolleston Rd DE13 . . . . . 240 B1
Rollins La S65 . . . . 15 A1
Roman Bank NG19 . . . . . 136 D3
Roman Rd DE1 . . . . 219 B7
Roman Way DE72 . . . . . . 221 C1
Romeley Cres S43 . . . . . . 80 D3
Romeley La S43 . . . . 80 B3
Romford Way **4** S43 . . . . 78 B3
Romney Dr S18 . . . . 56 E1
Romney Gdns S2 . . . . 43 B6
Romorantin Pl NG10 . . . . 236 C7
Romsley Cl DE3 . . . . 217 D4
Rona Cl DE24 . . . . 231 E4
Ronald Cl DE23 . . . . 230 E7
Rood La
  Clowne S43 . . . . 80 E3
  Idridgehay DE56 . . . . . . 176 F6
Rookery The DE11 . . . . . 255 F5
Roosevelt Ave
  Derby DE21 . . . . 220 B6
  Long Eaton NG10 . . . . . . 236 C5
Roost The S32 . . . . 53 A6
Roper Ave DE5 . . . . 193 F7
Roper Hill S10 . . . . 42 D7
Ropewalk Ind Ctr DE7 . . 195 A1
Ropewalk The
  Heanor DE75 . . . . 193 F8
  Ilkeston DE7 . . . . 195 A1
  Stanley Common DE7 . . . 193 B1
Rosamond's Ride DE23 . . 231 D8
Rosamond Ave S17 . . . . . . 56 A6
Rosamond Cl S17 . . . . 56 A6
Rosamond Ct S17 . . . . 56 A6
Rosamond Dr S17 . . . . 56 A6
Rosamond Glade **5** S17 . 56 A6
Rosamond Pl S17 . . . . 56 A6
Rose Ave
  Borrowash DE72 . . . . . . 221 C1
  Burton u T DE13 . . . . . . 241 A2
  Calow S44 . . . . 97 A3
  Clowne S43 . . . . 81 A5

Rose Ave *continued*
Ilkeston DE7 . . . . .194 E2
Rose Bank Cl SK14. . . . . .9 D5
Roseberry Ct DE21. . . . . .206 B1
Rose Cl DE73 . . . . .232 E1
Rose Cottage Dr NG17 . . .148 F2
Rose Cotts
Bonsall DE4 . . . . .142 C1
Chesterfield S41. . . . . .96 C2
Rose Cres S43 . . . . .79 C4
Rosecroft Gdns DE11 . . . .256 C3
Rose Ct
Clay Cross S45 . . . . .131 A4
Long Eaton NG10. . . . . .223 B1
Rosedale Ave
Chesterfield S40 . . . . .115 B8
Derby DE24 . . . . .233 A6
Rosedale Cl NG10. . . . . .236 B6
Rosedale View S40. . . . . .114 B7
Rosedale Way NG19. . . . . . .136 F2
Rosedene View DE12. . . . . .262 C4
Rose End Ave DE4. . . . . .155 A6
Rose Garth Cl S41. . . . . .96 C1
Rose Gdns S44 . . . . .97 D2
Rosehealth Ct DE23. . . . . . . .231 E5
Rose Hill
Chesterfield S40 . . . . .266 B3
Sheffield S20. . . . . .59 B8
Woodville DE11 . . . . .256 E3
Rose Hill Ave S20. . . . . .59 B8
Rosehill Bsns Ctr DE23. .219 A2
Rose Hill Cl S44. . . . . .99 A8
Rose Hill Dr S20. . . . . .59 B8
Rose Hill E S40. . . . . .266 B3
Rosehill Int Sch DE23. . . . .219 B3
Rose Hill Mews S20. . . . . . . .59 B8
Rose Hill St DE22. . . . . .219 A2
Rose Hill View S20. . . . . .59 B8
Rose Hill W S40 . . . . .266 A3
Rose La
Mansfield Woodhouse
NG19. . . . . .136 C3
Ticknall DE73. . . . . .251 A4
Roseland La DE4 . . . . .166 D5
Roseleigh Cres DE11 . . . . . .255 F6
Rosemary Cl **1** S8 . . . . .43 A3
Rosemary Dr DE24. . . . . .233 A5
Rosemoor La DE21. . . . . .206 B1
Rosemount Ct DE22. . . . . . .204 C3
Rosengrave St DE1. . . . . .267 B2
Rose Tree La DE11 . . . . .255 F7
Rosette Ct DE21. . . . . .206 B2
Rose Valley DE11. . . . . .256 A5
Rose Way S21 . . . . .60 D5
Rosewood Cl
Derby DE24 . . . . .233 B7
South Normanton DE55 . . . .160 B7
Rose Wood Cl S41. . . . . .95 D8
Rosewood Rd DE15 . . . . . . .254 F6
Roseybank SK23 . . . . .34 B1
Rosier Cres DE55 . . . . .170 A8
Rosling Way S44. . . . . .97 D2
Rosliston CE Prim Sch
DE12. . . . . .260 C6
Rosliston Forestry Visitor
Ctr* DE12. . . . . .260 C8
Rosliston Rd
Burton u T DE15. . . . . .254 D3
Burton u T DE15. . . . . .254 E6
Walton-on-T DE12 . . . . .259 E8
Rosliston Rd S DE15 . . . . . .254 E5
Roslyn Cres S32 . . . . .53 A7
Roslyn Rd S32. . . . . .53 A7
Rossell Dr NG9. . . . . .223 E5
Rossendale DE7 . . . . .194 E4
Rossendale Cl S40. . . . . .114 E8
Rosser Ave S12. . . . . .43 F2
Rossington Dr DE23. . . . . . .230 F6
Rosslyn Gdns DE24 . . . . . . .233 A6
Ross Wlk DE21. . . . . .205 E1
Roston Cl **3** S18 . . . . .56 D1
Rosyth Cres DE73 . . . . .232 E1
Rothay Cl S18 . . . . .75 E8
Rothbourne Croft DE6 . . .151 D2
Rothbury Ave NG9 . . . . .209 D2
Rothbury Pl DE21. . . . . .205 E1
Rother Ave S43 . . . . .96 D8
Rother Cl S40. . . . . .114 E8
Rother Croft S42 . . . . .131 D8
Rotherham Cl S21 . . . . .60 F8
Rotherham Rd
Bolsover S44. . . . . .99 C2
Eckington S20, S21. . . . . .59 F6
Killamarsh S21. . . . . .60 F8
New Houghton NG19. . . . . . .134 F7
Scarcliffe S44. . . . . .118 D7
Shirebrook S44, NG19. . . . . .118 D3
Spinkhill S43. . . . . .61 D2
Rotherham Rd N S20 . . . . . .59 F8
Rother Jun Sch S40 . . . . . .115 A8
Rotherside Rd S21. . . . . .59 F4
Rother St S45 . . . . .132 C2
Rothervale Rd S40. . . . . .115 A8
Rother Valley Ctry Pk*
S21. . . . . .60 C8
Rother Valley Way S20 . . . .60 B8
Rother Way S41. . . . . .96 B6
Rotherwood Rd S21. . . . . . . .60 E7
Rothesay Cl DE24 . . . . .231 E4
Rothey Gr S40. . . . . .94 F5
Rothwell Ho DE65 . . . . .228 D1
Rothwell La DE56. . . . . .179 B4
Rothwell Rd DE3 . . . . .217 D3
Rough Heanor Rd DE3 . .218 A2
Rough La DE6 . . . . .186 E4
Roughlow La DE6. . . . . .183 D1

Roughpiece La DE4 . . . . . . .166 D5
Roughton Cl DE4 . . . . .230 D8
Round Hill Cl SK13. . . . . .9 F3
Roundhouse Rd DE24 . . . .219 C4
Round Way SK22. . . . . .33 D8
Rouse St S45 . . . . .132 D1
Rousseau Ct DE6 . . . . .173 D1
Routh Ave DE74 . . . . .247 B2
Rowallan Way DE73. . . . . . .232 E1
Rowan Ave
Ripley DE5 . . . . .180 D8
Stapleford NG9 . . . . .209 E2
Rowan Cl
Creswell S80. . . . . .81 E2
Darley Dale DE4 . . . . .127 B3
Derby, Cherrytree Hill
DE21. . . . . .220 B5
Derby, Sinfin DE24. . . . . .231 D3
Ilkeston DE7. . . . . .208 F5
Mansfield NG19. . . . . .136 D1
Rowan Croft NG17. . . . . . . .148 F4
Rowan Ct ST14 . . . . .196 F4
Rowan Dr
Kilburn DE56. . . . . .192 B8
Selston NG16. . . . . .171 D6
Shirebrook NG20. . . . . .119 D5
Shirland DE55 . . . . .146 D1
Rowan Park Cl DE23 . . . . .231 D7
Rowan Rd
Eckington S21. . . . . .59 C1
Mastin Moor S43 . . . . .79 D2
Rowan Sch The S17. . . . . . . .55 E6
Rowan Tree Cl
Ashbourne DE6 . . . . .185 D8
Killamarsh S21. . . . . .60 C5
Rowan Tree Dell S17. . . . . .55 E3
Rowan Tree Rd S21. . . . . . . .60 C5
Rowan Wlk SK13. . . . . .9 E4
Rowarth Ave **13** SK13 . . . . . .9 D2
Rowarth Bank **9** SK13 . . . . .9 D2
Rowarth Cl **10** SK13 . . . . .9 D2
Rowarth Fold **12** SK13. . . . . .9 D2
Rowarth Way **11** SK13. . . . . .9 D2
Rowbury Dr DE21. . . . . .248 B2
Rowdale Cres S12 . . . . .44 D5
Rowditch Ave DE22 . . . . . . .218 D4
Rowditch Cotts DE1. . . . . . .218 D4
Rowditch Pl DE22. . . . . .218 D4
Rowena Cl DE24 . . . . .232 F7
Rowland Ct DE55 . . . . .158 F4
Rowland Rd **3** S2. . . . . .43 A8
Rowland St
Alfreton DE55 . . . . .159 A4
Derby DE24 . . . . .232 E6
Rowley Cl DE11. . . . . .256 D5
Rowley Ct DE11. . . . . .256 B4
Rowley Gdns DE23. . . . . . . .231 C7
Rowley La DE23 . . . . .231 C7
Rowley Mill **3** DE1 . . . . . . .218 E5
Rowsley Ave
Derby DE23 . . . . .231 D8
Long Eaton NG10 . . . . .236 A5
Rowsley CE Prim Sch
DE4 . . . . .126 F8
Rowsley Cl SK13 . . . . .9 E2
Rowsley Cres S43. . . . . .97 C8
Rowsley Gn SK13 . . . . .9 E2
Rowsley Gr SK13. . . . . .9 E2
Rowsley Mews SK13 . . . . . . .9 E2
Rowsley South Sta*
DE4 . . . . .127 A5
Rowsley Wlk SK13 . . . . .9 E2
Row The
Great Cubley DE6 . . . . .198 E1
Lea DE4. . . . . .156 B8
Rowthorne La S44. . . . . .170 A8
Rowthorne La S44. . . . . .134 B7
Rowton Grange Rd SK23 . .47 B5
Roxburgh Ave DE71. . . . . . .219 F7
Roxton Ave **2** S8. . . . . .56 F8
Roxton Ct NG16. . . . . .195 F7
Royal App DE73. . . . . .244 F8
Royal Ave NG10. . . . . .223 D1
Royal Cl DE72 . . . . .221 B1
Royal Croft Dr DE45. . . . . . .91 E6
Royal Crown Derby Visitor
Ctr* D23 . . . . .267 C1
Royale Cl S21 . . . . .59 E3
Royal Gate DE56. . . . . .179 D3
Royal Gr DE21 . . . . .206 D3
Royal Hill Rd DE21. . . . . . . .220 D6
Royal Oak Ct S43 . . . . .79 D4
Royal Oak Pl DE45. . . . . . . .109 D5
Royal Rd SK12 . . . . .32 D5
Royal Sch for the Deaf
DE22 . . . . .218 D6
Royal Scot Rd DE24. . . . . . .219 E2
Royal Way DE24 . . . . .219 E3
Roydon Ct DE23. . . . . .217 C3
Royle Ave SK13 . . . . .10 C1
Royle Bsns Pk DE15. . . . . .254 E3
Royston Cl
Ashbourne DE6 . . . . .185 C8
Chesterfield S40 . . . . .114 B7
Royston Dr DE56. . . . . .179 D5
Rubens Cl
Dronfield S18. . . . . .56 F1
Marple SK6. . . . . .23 C8
Ruby Ho S8 . . . . .43 A4
Ruby Paddocks NG16 . . . .195 F5
Rudyard Ave DE21. . . . . . . .220 F6
Rufford Cl S41. . . . . .95 E1
Rufford Dr NG19. . . . . .136 E3
Rufford Rd NG10. . . . . .236 B4
Ruffstone Cl DE56. . . . . .191 C7
Rugby Ave DE55. . . . . .159 C3
Rugby Cl DE14. . . . . .254 C8

Rugby St DE24. . . . . .219 E1
Rugeley Ave NG10 . . . . .237 A7
Ruislip Cl NG16. . . . . .195 E7
Rupert Rd DE21. . . . . .220 A7
Rupert St
Ilkeston DE7 . . . . .195 A1
Pilsley S45. . . . . .132 B3
Rushcliffe Ave DE21. . . . . . .219 F6
Rushcliffe Gdns DE21 . . . .219 F6
Rushdale Ave
Derby DE23 . . . . .231 D6
Sheffield S8. . . . . .43 B5
Rushdale Mount **4** S8. . . . .43 A5
Rushdale Rd S8. . . . . .43 A5
Rushdale Terr **3** S8 . . . . . . .43 A5
Rusham Mount S40 . . . . . . .114 F6
Rushes The
Glossop SK13. . . . . .9 F4
Mansfield Woodhouse
NG19. . . . . .136 D5
Rushleigh Ct S17. . . . . .55 D7
Rushley Ave S17. . . . . .55 D8
Rushley Cl S17. . . . . .55 D8
Rushley Dr S17. . . . . .55 D7
Rushley Rd S17. . . . . .55 D8
Rush Leys NG10 . . . . .236 D5
Rushmere S13. . . . . .17 E8
Rushpool Ave NG19 . . . . . .136 D3
Rushpool Cl NG19 . . . . .136 F2
Rushton Cl DE13. . . . . .239 C6
Rushton Dr SK6. . . . . .23 A5
Rushup Cl DE22. . . . . .205 A5
Rushup La SK17, SK23 . . . .48 D8
Rushycroft SK14 . . . . .9 A4
Ruskin La NG10, DE72. . . .222 E6
Ruskin Rd NG10 . . . . .236 B5
Ruskin Rd
Derby DE1. . . . . .218 F7
Mansfield NG19. . . . . .135 D1
Ruskin Sq S8 . . . . .43 A6
Ruskin Way DE23 . . . . .231 B8
Rusk The S43 . . . . .80 B6
Russell Cl **1** NG10. . . . . . . .223 D1
Russell Gdns S42 . . . . .131 B6
Russell St
Compstall SK6. . . . . .15 A3
Derby DE24 . . . . .219 C1
Long Eaton NG10. . . . . .223 D1
Swadlincote DE11 . . . . .256 C3
Russet Cl
Derby DE21. . . . . .206 B1
Hatton DE65. . . . . .227 C1
Russet Ct DE23 . . . . .218 E2
Ruston Cl
Chesterfield S40 . . . . .95 B6
Swadlincote DE11 . . . . .256 B4
Rutherford Rise **8** DE21 .205 F2
Ruthyn Ave S43. . . . . .80 A7
Rutland Ave
Baslow S44 . . . . .99 A1
Borrowash DE72 . . . . .221 C2
Matlock DE4 . . . . .143 C6
Ripley DE5. . . . . .181 A7
Rutland Cl DE15 . . . . .254 D6
Rutland Ct
Ilkeston DE7 . . . . .194 D1
Matlock DE4 . . . . .143 C6
Rutland Dr DE3. . . . . .217 A1
Rutland Gr NG10 . . . . .223 C5
Rutland Mews DE45. . . . . . .109 E6
Rutland Pl DE56 . . . . .168 B4
Rutland Rd
Chesterfield S40 . . . . .266 A5
Westwood NG16 . . . . .171 C4
Rutland Sq DE45. . . . . .109 D6
Rutland St
Chesterfield S41. . . . . .77 A2
Derby DE23 . . . . .219 A1
Ilkeston DE7. . . . . .194 F2
Matlock DE4 . . . . .143 C6
Rutland Terr
Barlow S18. . . . . .75 D7
Ilkeston DE7 . . . . .194 F2
Rutland Way S23 . . . . .34 C2
Ryan Cl DE24 . . . . .231 E3
Rycroft CE Mid Sch
ST14. . . . . .196 E4
Rycroft Cl DE22 . . . . .218 C3
Rydal Ave NG10. . . . . .223 B2
Rydal Cl
Derby DE22 . . . . .204 E1
Dronfield S18. . . . . .56 D1
Rydal Cres S41 . . . . .95 E8
Rydal Way S45 . . . . .131 B3
Ryde Ho DE24 . . . . .233 C7
Ryder Cl DE11. . . . . .255 E2
Rye Butts DE73 . . . . .232 F1
Rye Cl DE21. . . . . .205 E3
Rye Cres S45 . . . . .131 D3
Ryecroft DE4 . . . . .127 D2
Ryecroft Glen Rd S17. . . . . .56 A8
Ryecroft St NG9 . . . . .223 E8
Ryecroft View S17. . . . . .55 D8
Rye Ct S45 . . . . .131 D3
Ryedale Gdns DE23 . . . . . .231 C5
Rye Flatt La S40. . . . . .95 C2
Rye Flatts La DE65. . . . . . . .227 D1
Ryegrass Cl DE56 . . . . .179 D4
Ryegrass Rd DE21 . . . . .206 C2
Ryehill Ave S40. . . . . .95 A2
Ryemere Cl NG16 . . . . .182 E2
Ryemere Ct NG16. . . . . .182 E2
Rykneld Cl DE23 . . . . .230 E6
Rykneld Ct S45. . . . . .131 C3
Rykneld Dr DE23. . . . . .230 E7
Rykneld Prim Sch DE14. .253 E7
Rykneld Rd DE23 . . . . .230 E6

Rykneld Rise S42. . . . . .115 A3
Rykneld Sq S40. . . . . .266 B3
Rykneld Way DE23 . . . . .230 E6
Rykneld Hill DE5 . . . . .180 B2
Rykneld Rd DE56, DE7. . .192 B8
Rylah Hill S44 . . . . .118 A5
Rymill Dr DE21 . . . . .205 F1
Ryton Way DE65 . . . . .228 D1

S

Sacheveral La DE4. . . . . .140 F4
Sacheverall Ave NG16. . . .160 D3
Sacheverel St DE1 . . . . .267 B2
Sackerville Terr S21. . . . . . . .60 B7
Sackville Cl S40 . . . . .114 F6
Sackville St DE23 . . . . .231 F8
Saddlers Cl NG19 . . . . .136 F1
Saddlers Croft S42. . . . . . . .131 F7
Saddletree View S43 . . . . . . .79 B4
Saddleworth Wlk DE24. . .232 E3
Sadler Gate DE1 . . . . .267 B3
Saffron Dr DE21. . . . . .206 A1
Sage Mews SK23 . . . . .47 B8
St Agnes Ave DE22. . . . . . . .204 D4
St Aidan's Ave S2. . . . . .43 D8
St Aidan's Dr S2. . . . . .43 E8
St Aidan's Pl S2 . . . . .43 E8
St Aidan's Rd S2 . . . . .43 E8
St Aidan's Way S2. . . . . .43 E8
St Alban's RC Prim Sch
DE21. . . . . .219 F6
St Albans Cl
Holmewood S42. . . . . .132 E8
Long Eaton NG10. . . . . .236 E5
St Albans Rd DE22 . . . . . . .218 D3
St Albans St S2. . . . . .33 C8
St Alkmund's Cl DE56. . . .190 E4
St Alkmund's Way **1** DE1. .267 B4
St Alkmunds Way DE56. .190 E4
St Andrew's CE Jun Sch
DE21. . . . . .9 F4
St Andrew's CE Methodist
Prim Sch S18 . . . . .56 D1
St Andrew's CE Prim Sch
Clifton Campville B79 . . . . .263 E2
Stanley DE7. . . . . .207 B5
St Andrew's Cl B79 . . . . . . .263 F2
St Andrew's Cl DE7 . . . . . . .194 D1
St Andrew's Dr
Ilkeston DE7 . . . . .208 E8
Swanwick DE55. . . . . .169 F7
St Andrews Cl DE55. . . . . . .170 A7
St Andrews Cl SK13. . . . . . . .10 A4
St Andrews Rise S40. . . . . .114 C8
St Andrews Sch DE21 . . . .205 E1
St Andrews View DE21. . . .205 E1
St Andrews Wlk SK22 . . . . .33 D8
St Ann's Cl SK23 . . . . .46 F6
St Anne's CE Prim Sch
DE45. . . . . .91 E5
St Anne's Cl
Baslow DE45. . . . . .91 E5
Derby DE1. . . . . .218 E6
Staveley S43 . . . . .97 E8
St Anne's La DE74 . . . . .247 B3
St Anne's RC Prim Sch
SK17. . . . . .85 C4
St Anne's Well (Micrarium)*
SK17. . . . . .85 B8
St Annes Ave **4** SK14 . . . . .16 A8
St Anselm's Sch DE45. . . .109 C6
St Augustines Ave S40. . . .115 A8
St Augustines Cres S40 . .115 A8
St Augustine Dr S40 . . . . . .266 B1
St Augustines Mount
S40. . . . . .266 B1
St Augustines Rd S40. . . . .115 A8
St Augustines Rise **1**
S40. . . . . .115 A8
St Augustine St **3** DE23 .218 F1
St Barnabas Ho **12** S2. . . . .43 A8
St Barnabas La **4** S2. . . . . .43 A8
St Barnabas Rd **5** S2. . . . .43 A8
St Bartholomew's CE Sch
SK17. . . . . .121 B7
St Benedict RC Sch &
Performing Arts Coll
DE22. . . . . .204 E1
St Benedicts Cl S2 . . . . .43 D8
St Bride's Farm DE7 . . . . . .251 D7
St Bride's Wlk DE22 . . . . . .218 B6
St Catherine's Rd DE11. .255 F5
St Catherines Prep Sch
SK6. . . . . .23 B7
St Chad's CE Inf Sch
DE23 . . . . .218 F2
St Chad's Cl
Denstone ST14 . . . . .196 D6
Draycott DE72. . . . . .235 A7
St Chad's Rd DE23 . . . . . . .218 F2
St Chad's Way S41. . . . . .96 A8
St Charles's RC Prim Sch
SK13. . . . . .9 E5
St Charles Cl SK13. . . . . .9 F5
St Christopher's Way
DE24 . . . . .219 D3
St Clare's Cl DE22 . . . . .218 D2
St Clare's Sch DE22 . . . . . .218 A2
St Cuthbert's Rd DE22 . . .218 C3
St David's Cl DE22 . . . . .218 D3
St David's Rise S40 . . . . . . .114 D8
St Davids Cl NG16 . . . . .170 F3
St Davids Rd B79 . . . . .263 F2
St Edmund's Ave NG19. . .136 C3

St Edmund's CE Prim Sch
NG19. . . . . .136 C3
St Edmund's Cl DE22. . . . .204 F4
St Edward's CE Prim Sch
DE74 . . . . .247 B3
St Edward's RC Prim Sch
DE11. . . . . .256 B5
St Edward's Rd DE74 . . . . .247 B3
St Edwards Cl DE11. . . . . . .255 E5
St Elizabeth's RC Prim Sch
DE56. . . . . .178 F5
St Elizabeth Cl S2 . . . . .43 B8
St Elphin's Sch DE4. . . . . . .127 E1
St Giles CE Prim Sch
New Mills SK22 . . . . .33 C8
Swadlincote DE11 . . . . .256 B5
St George's Cl DE22 . . . . . .204 F3
St George's Pl **1** DE56. . .178 F4
St George's RC Prim Sch
DE23. . . . . .231 C7
St George's Dr **3** NG9. . . .223 F2
St George's Ho DE22. . . . .204 F3
St Georges Rd SK22. . . . . . .33 C8
St Giles CE Prim Sch
Killamarsh S21. . . . . .60 C6
Matlock DE4 . . . . .143 C3
St Giles Cl S40 . . . . .115 B8
St Giles Rd DE23 . . . . .218 F1
St Giles Sch DE21. . . . . .205 C1
St Giles Wlk DE4 . . . . .143 C4
St Helen's St
Chesterfield S41. . . . . .266 B4
Darley Dale DE4 . . . . .127 B3
Grindleford S32. . . . . .72 D8
St Helen's Cres NG19 . . . .209 C4
St Helen's Croft S32. . . . . . .72 D8
St Helen's Dr NG16 . . . . . .171 D7
St Helen's La DE4. . . . . .166 A7
St Helen's St
Chesterfield S41. . . . . .266 B4
Derby DE1. . . . . .267 A4
St Helens Ave NG16. . . . . .160 C4
St Hugh's Cl DE22 . . . . .205 A2
St James' CE Jun Sch
DE23. . . . . .219 B3
St James CE Inf Sch
DE23 . . . . .267 C1
St James' Dr NG16 . . . . . . .182 D8
St James' Rd DE23 . . . . . . .218 F1
St James's Ct SK17 . . . . .85 C3
St James's Sq SK22 . . . . . . .33 C8
St James's Rd **3** NG9 . . .223 C6
St James' St
14 Buxton SK17. . . . . .85 B7
Derby DE1. . . . . .267 B3
Derby, Rose Hill DE23 . . . .219 A1
St James' Terr SK17. . . . . . . .85 B7
St James Ave DE7 . . . . .209 A7
St James CE Prim Sch
SK13. . . . . .17 B8
St James Cl
Belper DE56 . . . . .179 D4
2 Chesterfield S41. . . . . . . .96 C1
Glossop SK13. . . . . .17 C7
Willington DE65. . . . . .242 C5
St James Ct
Ashbourne DE6 . . . . .173 D3
Sandiacre NG10. . . . . .223 B3
St James Sq
Chesterfield S40 . . . . .266 B3
Chesterfield S40 . . . . .266 B3
St James' Terr NG9 . . . . . . .223 D6
St John's **4** SK17. . . . . .85 A7
St John's CE Prim Sch
Belper DE56 . . . . .179 B5
Ripley DE5. . . . . .169 F1
Stapleford NG9 . . . . .223 E7
St John's Cl
Brinsley NG16 . . . . .171 D1
Derby DE22 . . . . .204 D3
St John's Cres S43 . . . . .80 F3
St John's Dr
Derby DE21. . . . . .220 B5
Kilburn DE56. . . . . .192 A8
Swadlincote DE11 . . . . .255 F5
St John's Mount S41. . . . . .95 F8
St John's Rd
Belper DE56 . . . . .179 A4
Buxton SK17. . . . . .85 A7
Chesterfield S41. . . . . .95 F8
Dronfield S18. . . . . .76 E7
Ilkeston DE7. . . . . .209 A7
Matlock Bath DE4 . . . . .143 B3
Smalley DE7. . . . . .192 F5
Tideswell SK17 . . . . .69 C4
St John's St
Long Eaton NG10. . . . . .236 D7
Wirksworth DE4 . . . . .165 F8
St John Fisher RC Prim Sch
DE24 . . . . .233 C8
Saint John Houghton RC Sch
DE7 . . . . .208 C2
St Johns Cl
Bamford S33. . . . . .40 B3
Chesterfield S40 . . . . .114 B7
Ripley DE5. . . . . .169 F2
St Johns Rd S43 . . . . .78 D1
St Johns Road Bsns Ctr
S41. . . . . .115 B7
St John St SK22 . . . . .25 C3
St Joseph's Convent Sch
S41. . . . . .266 A4

St Joseph's RC Prim Sch
Derby DE23 . . . . 267 A4
Matlock DE4 . . . . 143 D6
Shirebrook NG20 . . . . 119 F5
Staveley S43 . . . . 97 D8
St Joseph's St DE44 . . . . . . 143 C5
St Katherines Cl DE4 . . . . . 110 E1
St Katherine's Ct DE22 . . . 218 D6
St Laurence CE Prim Sch
NG10 . . . . 236 E6
St Laurence Ct NG10 . . . . . 236 E6
St Laurence Gdns 10
DE56 . . . . 178 F4
St Lawrence Ave S44 . . . . . 118 C8
St Lawrence Cl DE75 . . . . . 181 F2
St Lawrence Rd S42 . . . . . . 131 F6
St Lawrence View S80 . . . . . 81 F5
St Leonards Dr S41 . . . . 96 C1
St Leonards Pl DE55 . . . . . 146 E1
St Luke's CE Prim Sch
Glossop SK13 . . . . 10 C1
Shireoaks S81 . . . . 63 F7
St Lukes Cl 2 S41 . . . . 95 F8
St Lukes View S81 . . . . 63 F7
St Margaret's Dr S40 . . . . . 266 A3
St Margaret's RC Prim Sch
SK13 . . . . 16 D8
St Mark's Rd
Chesterfield S40 . . . . 95 E3
Derby DE21 . . . . 219 D6
St Marks Cl DE4 . . . . 155 A6
St Martin's Cl S41 . . . . 95 D6
St Martin's Rd SK6 . . . . 23 A6
St Martin's Sch DE24 . . . . 232 F8
St Martin's Wlk S80 . . . . . . 82 C6
St Martins Ct DE55 . . . . . . 158 F4
St Mary's Ave DE72 . . . . . . 235 A7
St Mary's CE Fst Sch
ST14 . . . . 210 B1
St Mary's Cl
Chinley SK23 . . . . 34 E2
Derby DE24 . . . . 233 A6
Newton Solney DE15 . . . . 248 E8
St Mary's Cres ST14 . . . . . 210 B1
St Mary's Dr Cl DE1 . . . . . 267 B4
St Mary's Dr DE13 . . . . . . 240 F2
St Mary's Gate
Chesterfield S41 . . . . 266 C3
Derby DE1 . . . . 267 B3
Wirksworth DE4 . . . . 165 F8
St Mary's Pl S41 . . . . 266 C3
St Mary's RC High Sch
S41 . . . . 95 C7
St Mary's Rd
Disley SK12 . . . . 32 D5
Glossop SK13 . . . . 17 C8
New Mills SK22 . . . . 33 B8
St Mary's View DE4 . . . . . 143 D7
St Mary's Wlk NG16 . . . . . 171 B3
St Mary & All Saints Church
(Crooked Spire)* S40 . . 266 B3
St Mary's Ct SK14 . . . . 9 C5
St Mary's RC Prim Sch 10
DE22 . . . . 204 F1
St Mary St DE7 . . . . 208 E8
St Marys Wharf Rd DE1 . . 219 B7
St Matthew's Cl S21 . . . . . . 60 B1
St Matthew's St DE14 . . . . 254 C8
St Matthew's Wlk 4
DE22 . . . . 204 F2
St Mawes Cl DE22 . . . . . . 204 D4
St Mellion Cl DE13 . . . . . . 217 F1
St Michael's CE Prim Sch
S32 . . . . 53 A8
St Michael's Cl
Holbrook DE56 . . . . 191 C6
Shirley DE6 . . . . 200 D8
Willington DE65 . . . . 242 B5
St Michael's Dr
Appleby Magna DE12 . . . . 265 F1
South Normanton DE55 . . 160 A7
St Michael's La DE1 . . . . . 267 B4
St Michaels Cl
Crich DE4 . . . . 156 F2
Derby DE24 . . . . 233 C7
St Michaels View
Derby DE24 . . . . 233 C7
Selston NG16 . . . . 171 F5
St Nicholas Cl DE21 . . . . . 204 D2
St Nicholas Pl DE11 . . . . . 267 A5
St Norbert Dr DE7 . . . . . . 208 D4
St Oswald's CE Inf Sch
DE6 . . . . 173 B1
St Oswald's Hospl DE6 . . . 173 A1
St Oswald Cres DE6 . . . . . 173 C1
St Pancras Way DE7 . . . . . 267 C5
St Paul's Rd DE1 . . . . 219 A7
St Pauls Ave S41 . . . . 115 D6
St Pauls Ct NG16 . . . . 195 F6
St Peter's CE Fst Sch
ST14 . . . . 210 B1
St Peter's CE Jun Sch
DE23 . . . . 218 C1
St Peter's CE Prim Sch
DE12 . . . . 264 F6
St Peter's Churchyard
DE1 . . . . 267 B3
St Peter's Cl DE56 . . . . . . 179 A4

St Peter's Rd
Buxton SK17 . . . . .66 D1
Chellaston DE73 . . . . 233 A1
Thorpe Salvin S80 . . . . 62 E7
St Peter's St DE1 . . . . 267 B3
St Peter & St Paul Sch
S41 . . . . 96 D3
St Peters Cl S44 . . . . 98 A4
St Peters Croft DE56 . . . . 179 A4
St Peters Ct DE24 . . . . . . 233 A8
St Peter's Way DE1 . . . . . 267 B2
St Philip's Dr S41 . . . . . . 115 B8
Saint Philip Howard Comp
Sch SK13 . . . . 10 B1
St Philip Howard RC Comp
Sch SK13 . . . . 17 B8
St Quentin Cl
Derby DE21 . . . . 218 C3
Sheffield S17 . . . . 56 B5
St Quentin Dr S17 . . . . 56 B5
St Quentin Mount S17 . . . . 56 B5
St Quentin Rise S17 . . . . . . 56 B5
St Quentin View S17 . . . . . 56 B5
St Ronan's Ave DE56 . . . . 190 E2
St Stephen's Cl DE23 . . . . 231 D6
St Stephen's Ct DE11 . . . . 256 E3
St Stephens Cl DE72 . . . . 221 B1
St Swithin's Cl DE22 . . . . 218 D3
St Swithuns Ct DE56 . . . . 179 A2
St Theresa's RC Prim Sch
S2 . . . . 44 B7
St Thomas' St S40 . . . . 95 C2
St Thomas Cl DE55 . . . . . 147 E5
St Thomas More RC Sch
SK17 . . . . 85 B8
St Thomas of Canterbury RC
Prim Sch S8 . . . . 56 F8
St Thomas RC Prim Sch
DE7 . . . . 208 E6
St Thomas Rd DE23 . . . . . 219 A1
St Vincent Cl NG10 . . . . . . 236 E6
St Werburgh's CE Prim Sch
Derby DE21 . . . . 220 D5
Hanbury DE13 . . . . 238 A4
St Werburgh's View
DE21 . . . . 220 D5
St Wilfrid's Rd
11 Sheffield S2 . . . . 43 A8
West Hallam DE7 . . . . 207 E8
St Wystan's Rd DE22 . . . . 218 C3
St Wystans Sch DE65 . . . . 242 C2
Salcey Cl DE55 . . . . 169 F7
Salcey Dr NG9 . . . . 209 D2
Salcey Sq S40 . . . . 95 D1
Salcombe Ct 12 S41 . . . . . . 95 F8
Salcombe Rd DE55 . . . . . 159 C5
Sale & Davys CE Sch
DE73 . . . . 244 A6
Sales Ave S42 . . . . 131 C8
Sale La DE15 . . . . 248 C4
Sale St DE23 . . . . 219 B2
Salisbury Ave
Burton u T DE15 . . . . 248 D3
Chesterfield S41 . . . . 95 E7
Dronfield S18 . . . . 76 A7
Salisbury Cl NG19 . . . . . . 136 D4
Salisbury Cres S41 . . . . 95 F7
Salisbury Dr
Belper DE56 . . . . 179 D5
Swadlincote DE11 . . . . . . 256 E5
Salisbury Ho 13 SK17 . . . . .85 C7
Salisbury La DE73 . . . . . . 252 B7
Salisbury Rd S18 . . . . 76 B8
Salisbury St
Derby DE1 . . . . 267 B1
Glossop SK13 . . . . 10 A5
Long Eaton NG10 . . . . . . 236 E7
Sallfield La DE6 . . . . 183 E8
Sallywood Cl DE24 . . . . . 231 D2
Salturn Pl DE21 . . . . 205 C1
Salter Cl DE74 . . . . 246 F4
Saltergate S40 . . . . 266 B3
Saltergate La S33 . . . . 40 B2
Salters La DE4 . . . . 142 F8
Salvin Cres S43 . . . . 80 E4
Samantha Ct DE21 . . . . . . 206 B1
Sampson's La NG19 . . . . . 135 B3
Sampsons Yd NG17 . . . . . 148 F3
Samuel Cl S2 . . . . 43 D7
Samuel Ct DE5 . . . . 180 D8
Samuel Dr S2 . . . . 43 D7
Samuel Pl S2 . . . . 43 D7
Samuel Rd S2 . . . . 43 D8
Samuel St SK14 . . . . 9 C4
Sancroft Ave DE21 . . . . . . 220 E6
Sancroft Rd DE21 . . . . . . 220 F6
Sandalwood Cl DE24 . . . . 233 C7
Sandalwood Rd DE11 . . . . 254 E6
Sandbach Cl DE21 . . . . . . 206 A1
Sandbed La DE56 . . . . . . 179 C2
Sandby Croft S14 . . . . 43 E2
Sandby Dr S14 . . . . 43 E2
Sandby La
Marple SK6 . . . . 23 B8
Sheffield S14 . . . . 43 E2
Sandcliffe Pk DE11 . . . . . 256 D7
Sandcliffe Rd DE11 . . . . . 256 D6
Sandcroft Cl DE11 . . . . . . 256 D5
Sanderling Heath DE3 . . . 230 B7
Sanderman Ho DE11 . . . . 256 E3
Sanders Cl DE7 . . . . 194 C2
Sanderson Rd DE21 . . . . . 220 B6
Sandfield Cl DE21 . . . . . . 220 B8
Sandfield Rd 1 NG9 . . . . . 223 E2
Sandford Ave NG10 . . . . . 236 E7
Sandford Brook DE21 . . . 228 C1
Sandgate Ave NG19 . . . . . 136 D4
Sandgate Cl DE24 . . . . . . 233 A6

Sandgate Rd NG19 . . . . 136 D4
Sandhall La DE56 . . . . . . 166 F5
Sandham La DE5 . . . . 169 C1
Sandhill La
Broadbottom SK6 . . . . 16 A2
Marple SK6 . . . . 15 E1
Sandhills Rd S44 . . . . 99 C1
Sandiacre Rd NG9 . . . . . . 223 C6
Sandiway
Chesterfield S40 . . . . 114 C8
Glossop SK13 . . . . 17 F7
Sand La DE6 . . . . 211 B1
Sandlands The DE11 . . . . . 256 D6
Sandlands Way NG19 . . . . 136 F2
Sandown Ave DE3 . . . . . . 217 C3
Sandown Cl
Burton u T DE14 . . . . 254 A7
Eckington S21 . . . . 59 B2
Sandown Rd
Beeston NG9 . . . . 223 F2
Derby DE24 . . . . 232 E8
Sandpiper La DE3 . . . . . . 230 B6
Sandringham Ave DE15 . . 248 A1
Sandringham Cl
Calow S44 . . . . 97 A4
5 Chesterfield S41 . . . . . . 96 A8
Swadlincote DE11 . . . . . . 256 B5
Sandringham Ct
13 Buxton SK17 . . . . 85 B7
Mansfield Woodhouse
NG19 . . . . 136 B6
Sandringham Dr
Derby DE21 . . . . 220 F5
Heanor DE75 . . . . 181 C2
Mansfield Woodhouse
NG19 . . . . 136 B6
Sandringham Ho DE24 . . . 219 D1
Sandringham Pl DE7 . . . . 208 D5
Sandringham Rd
Calow S44 . . . . 97 A4
Derby DE21 . . . . 205 E1
Mansfield Woodhouse
NG19 . . . . 136 B6
Sandiacre NG10 . . . . 223 B4
Sands Cl S14 . . . . 43 E4
Sandstone Ave S40 . . . . . 114 B8
Sandwell Cl NG10 . . . . . . 236 A6
Sandwood Cl DE55 . . . . . 148 A3
Sandybank Cl SK13 . . . . 9 E4
Sandybrook Cl DE6 . . . . . 173 C4
Sandybrook Country Pk
DE6 . . . . 173 B5
Sandybrook Hall DE6 . . . 173 B5
Sandy Cl S80 . . . . 81 F5
Sandycliffe Cl NG19 . . . . 136 F1
Sandyford La DE56 . . . . . 166 F4
Sandyhill Cl DE73 . . . . . . 233 A2
Sandy La
Broadbottom SK13 . . . . . . 16 A4
Caldwell DE12 . . . . 261 A8
Chinley SK23 . . . . 35 B3
Crich DE4 . . . . 167 F8
Farley DE4 . . . . 128 D1
Horsley DE21, DE7 . . . . . 192 A3
Matlock DE4 . . . . 143 D8
Whitwell S80 . . . . 81 F5
Sandypits La DE65 . . . . . . 229 D4
Sanforth St S41 . . . . 96 A6
Sankey Dr DE21 . . . . 206 C1
Santolina Dr DE21 . . . . . . 205 F1
Sapperton Cl DE23 . . . . . 231 D5
Sappertonfield La DE65,
DE65 . . . . 213 D3
Sapperton La DE65 . . . . . 213 E1
Sapphire Dr DE5 . . . . 180 B2
Sarah Cl DE55 . . . . 147 F5
Sark Rd S2 . . . . 43 A7
Saundby Ave NG19 . . . . . 135 D1
Saundersfoot Way DE21 . . 206 C2
Savage La S17 . . . . 55 D7
Save Penny La DE56 . . . . 191 A5
Saville Cl NG9 . . . . 223 E8
Saville House Sch NG19 . . 136 B3
Savoy The 2 SK17 . . . . 85 B7
Saw Inf Sch NG10 . . . . . . 236 A5
Sawley Jun Sch NG10 . . . 236 A5
Sawley Rd
Breaston DE72 . . . . 235 E6
Draycott DE72 . . . . 235 B7
Sawmand Cl NG10 . . . . . 236 C6
Sawmills Ind Pk DE75 . . . 181 D3
Saw Pit Ind Est DE55 . . . 148 C6
Sawpit La DE65 . . . . 227 C2
Saw Pit La DE55 . . . . 148 B5
Saxon Cl
Breedon on t H DE73 . . . . 252 F2
Burton u T DE15 . . . . 254 F7
Saxon Croft DE65 . . . . . . 242 D3
Saxondale Ave DE3 . . . . . 217 C4
Saxon Gr S42 . . . . 242 A5
Saxon Rd S2 . . . . 43 B8
Saxon St DE15 . . . . 254 F7
Saxton Ave DE75 . . . . 181 F2
Saxton Cl S41 . . . . 115 C8
Scaddows La DE73 . . . . . 250 E3
Scalby Cl NG16 . . . . 182 D2
Scaliot Cl SK22 . . . . 33 B8
Scalpcliffe Rd DE15 . . . . 248 A2
Scarborough Ave DE7 . . . 208 E8
Scarborough Rise DE21 . . 205 E1
Scarcliffe Cl DE24 . . . . . . 232 E3
Scarcliffe Lanes NG20 . . . 119 C7
Scarcliffe Prim Sch S44 . . 118 F6
Scarcliffe Terr NG20 . . . . 101 A2
Scargill CE Prim Sch
DE7 . . . . 207 D7
Scargill Rd DE7 . . . . 207 E8
Scargill Wlk NG16 . . . . . . 182 F3

Scarsdale Ave
Derby, Allestree DE22 . . . 204 D3
Derby, Littleover DE23 . . . 218 C2
Scarsdale Cl S18 . . . . 76 B8
Scarsdale Cres S43 . . . . . . 96 D7
Scarsdale Cross 1 S18 . . . . 57 B1
Scarsdale Hospl S40 . . . . 266 B4
Scarsdale Pl 3 SK17 . . . . . 85 B7
Scarsdale Rd
2 Chesterfield S41 . . . . . . 96 A8
2 Dronfield S18 . . . . 57 B1
Duffield DE56 . . . . 190 E3
Scarsdale St S44 . . . . 117 E8
Scarthin DE4 . . . . 155 A6
Schofield Cl DE4 . . . . 110 F1
Sch of Nursing (Univ of
Nottingham) DE1 . . . . . 267 C2
School Ave S20 . . . . 59 F7
School Board La S40 . . . . . 95 E3
School Cl
Blackwell DE55 . . . . 147 C1
Darley Dale DE4 . . . . 127 C3
Fenny Bentley DE6 . . . . . 162 A1
Moira DE11 . . . . 256 C1
Newton DE55 . . . . 148 B3
Sheffield S20 . . . . 59 F7
Shirland DE55 . . . . 146 D2
Stonebroom DE55 . . . . . . 146 F4
School Croft DE55 . . . . . . 170 D6
School La
Arkwright Town S44 . . . . . 97 D3
Ashbourne DE6 . . . . 173 B1
Baslow DE45 . . . . 91 E5
Beeley DE4 . . . . 111 B4
Brackenfield DE55 . . . . . 145 C2
Castle Donington DE74 . . 247 A4
Chellaston DE73 . . . . . . 233 A2
Compstall SK6 . . . . 15 B4
Crich DE4 . . . . 157 A1
Dronfield S18 . . . . 57 A1
Eckington S21 . . . . 58 E3
Hassop DE45 . . . . 91 A5
Hathersage S32 . . . . 53 A8
Heage DE56 . . . . 168 D2
Mansfield Woodhouse
NG19 . . . . 136 C3
Old Brampton S42 . . . . . . 93 F3
Over Haddon DE45 . . . . . 109 B1
Ripley DE5 . . . . 169 D1
Rolleston DE13 . . . . 240 A3
Rowsley DE4 . . . . 126 F8
Sheffield, Greenhill S8 . . . . 56 F7
Sheffield S8 . . . . 43 C1
South Normanton DE55 . . 160 B4
Stanton-by-D DE7, NG10 . 222 F8
Stanton in Peak DE4 . . . . 126 C5
Sudbury DE6 . . . . 225 E4
Taddington SK17 . . . . 87 F3
School Lane Cl S8 . . . . 43 C1
Schoolpiece La DE65 . . . 227 F7
School Rd
Buxton SK17 . . . . 67 B5
Chesterfield S41 . . . . 96 A7
Uttoxeter ST14 . . . . 210 A1
School Sq DE7 . . . . 207 E7
School St
Eckington S21 . . . . 59 D3
Moira DE12 . . . . 262 F2
Sheffield, Mosborough S20 . 59 D7
Swadlincote DE11 . . . . . . 256 B2
School Woods Cl DE75 . . . 194 A6
School Yd The DE11 . . . . . 267 B4
Scotches The DE56 . . . . . 178 F5
Scotia Cl S2 . . . . 43 F8
Scotia Dr S2 . . . . 43 F8
Scotland St S80 . . . . 81 F6
Scotswood Rd NG19 . . . . 136 B6
Scott Cl S42 . . . . 115 E3
Scott Cres DE55 . . . . 146 F3
Scott Dr
Belper DE56 . . . . 179 C5
Somercotes DE55 . . . . . . 170 D8
Scott St DE23 . . . . 218 F1
Scotts The DE11 . . . . 261 D8
Scotty Brook Cres SK13 . . . 17 E8
Scowerdons Cl S12 . . . . . . 44 F5
Scowerdons Dr S12 . . . . . . 44 F5
Scratta La S80 . . . . 63 C2
Screetham La DE4 . . . . . . 112 C1
Scropton Old Rd DE65 . . . 239 C8
Scropton Rd DE65 . . . . . . 239 B8
Scropton Wlk DE24 . . . . . 232 E3
Sea Breeze Terr S13 . . . . . 44 D8
Seaburn Rd NG9 . . . . 223 E2
Seaford Way DE7 . . . . 194 F5
Seagrave Ave S12 . . . . 44 B4
Seagrave Cl DE21 . . . . . . 220 B8
Seagrave Cres S12 . . . . . . 44 B4
Seagrave Dr
Chesterfield S41 . . . . 115 C7
Sheffield S12 . . . . 44 B4
Seagrave Rd S12 . . . . 44 B4
Seale St DE1 . . . . 267 B5
Sealey Cl DE65 . . . . 228 D2
Seals Rd DE12 . . . . 262 E1
Seal View DE12 . . . . 262 D1
Sealwood La
Linton DE12 . . . . 261 E4
Overseal DE12 . . . . 261 E4
Seamer Rd NG16 . . . . 195 F7
Seanor La S45 . . . . 131 D8
Searl St DE1 . . . . 218 F6
Searson Ave S44 . . . . 99 A1
Searston Ave S42 . . . . 132 D8

Seascale Cl 5 DE21 . . . . 205 D1
Seaton Cl DE3 . . . . 217 C3
Seaton Ct 9 S41 . . . . 95 F8
Sebastian Cl SK6 . . . . 23 B7
Second Ave
Branston DE14 . . . . 253 E8
Chellaston DE73 . . . . 245 A8
Risley DE72 . . . . 222 F5
Sedbergh Cres S43 . . . . . . 95 D8
Sedgebrook Cl 2 DE21 . . 205 F2
Sedgebrook St NG19 . . . . 136 E3
Sedgefield Gn DE23 . . . . 217 C1
Sedgefield Rd
Branston DE14 . . . . 253 F7
Burton u T DE14 . . . . 254 A8
Sedgemoor Cl S40 . . . . 95 B4
Sedgemoor Rd NG10 . . . . 236 E5
Sedgemoor Way DE21 . . . 231 A5
Sedgwick Cl NG16 . . . . . . 160 D2
Sedgwick St
Jacksdale NG16 . . . . 171 B3
Langley Mill NG16 . . . . . 182 B3
Sefton Ave NG3 . . . . 223 F6
Sefton Cl DE15 . . . . 248 B1
Sefton Rd DE21 . . . . 219 F6
Sefton St SK13 . . . . 17 C8
Sefton Way DE56 . . . . . . 190 D4
Selborne St DE24 . . . . . . 219 D2
Selby Cl
Beeston NG9 . . . . 223 F8
Chesterfield S40 . . . . 114 C8
Selhurst Rd S41 . . . . 95 C7
Selig Par S12 . . . . 44 C2
Selina Cl DE74 . . . . 247 A4
Selina St DE73 . . . . 252 A7
Selkirk St DE21 . . . . 219 E7
Selly Oak Gr S8 . . . . 57 C6
Selly Oak Rd S8 . . . . 57 C6
Selmer Ct S43 . . . . 96 D8
Selston Arts & Com Coll
NG16 . . . . 171 F7
Selston CE Inf Sch NG16 . 171 E6
Selston Rd NG16 . . . . 171 B5
Selworthy Cl DE21 . . . . . . 206 A2
Selwyn St
Bolsover S44 . . . . 118 C8
Derby DE24 . . . . 218 C6
Senners La SK17 . . . . 87 A2
Sepycoe La DE6 . . . . 214 D7
Serina Ave DE23 . . . . 231 D8
Serlby Dr S26 . . . . 61 F5
Serlby La S26 . . . . 61 F6
Serpentine Wlk S8 . . . . 57 B8
Setcup La S21 . . . . 59 D2
Sett Cl SK22 . . . . 33 B8
Settlement The DE72 . . . 221 C5
Setts Way S42 . . . . 115 B4
Sevenlands Dr DE24 . . . . 233 C4
Sevenoaks Ave DE22 . . . . 217 F6
Seven Oaks Rd DE7 . . . . . 209 A1
Severals S80 . . . . 223 F7
Severnale Cl DE22 . . . . . . 205 B5
Severn Cl DE13 . . . . 240 C1
Severn Cres S42 . . . . 132 A5
Severn Dr DE65 . . . . 240 D8
Severn Sq S43 . . . . 78 C4
Severn St DE24 . . . . 232 F8
Sewell Rd S20 . . . . 59 F6
Sexton St SK13 . . . . 9 F7
Seymour Cl DE22 . . . . . . 218 C5
Seymour La S43 . . . . 79 C1
Seymour Rd NG16 . . . . . . 182 F1
Shacklecross Cl DE72 . . . 221 C1
Shady Gr DE65 . . . . 228 C2
Shaef Cl DE65 . . . . 228 E2
Shaftesbury Ave
Chesterfield S40 . . . . 95 D3
Long Eaton NG10 . . . . . . 236 B4
Mansfield NG19 . . . . 135 E2
Sandiacre NG10 . . . . 223 A5
Shaftesbury Cres DE23 . . 219 B1
Shaftesbury St S DE23 . . 219 B1
Shaftesbury St DE23 . . . . 219 B2
Shafton Cl S41 . . . . 131 E4
Shafton Wlk S45 . . . . 131 E4
Shakespeare Ave
Creswell S80 . . . . 81 D1
Mansfield Woodhouse
NG19 . . . . 136 B4
Shirland DE55 . . . . 146 C4
Shakespeare Cl
Clay Cross S42 . . . . 131 B6
Repton DE65 . . . . 242 D1
Swadlincote DE11 . . . . . . 256 C6
Shakespeare Cres S18 . . . 76 C7
Shakespeare Ct 4 DE6 . . 173 B2
Shakespeare Dr DE55 . . . 159 B4
Shakespeare Mdws
DE65 . . . . 242 D1
Shakespeare Rd NG16 . . . 195 C5
Shakespeare St
Derby DE24 . . . . 232 A5
Grassmoor S42 . . . . 115 E3
Holmewood S42 . . . . 116 D1
Long Eaton NG10 . . . . . . 223 D1
Shaldon Dr DE23 . . . . . . 218 D1
Shalfleet Dr DE24 . . . . . . 233 C5
Shallcross Ave SK23 . . . . . 45 E4
Shallcross Cres SK23 . . . . 45 E4
Shallcross Hall Barns
SK23 . . . . 45 E4
Shallcross Mill Rd SK23 . . 45 E5
Shallcross Rd SK23 . . . . . 45 E4
Shambles The S40 . . . . . . 266 B3
Shamrock Pl S43 . . . . 79 C4
Shamrock St DE23 . . . . . 218 E1
Shandwick Ct 10 DE24 . . 231 D3
Shanklin Dr NG9 . . . . 223 D7

Shanklin Ho DE24 . . . . 233 C7
Shannon Cl DE23 . . . . 231 D6
Shannon Ho DE24 . . . . 232 E5
Shannon Sq DE21 . . . . 220 B4
Shap Cl **7** S40 . . . . 95 C5
Shardlow Bsns Pk DE72 . 234 D1
Shardlow Prim Sch
DE72 . . . . 234 E2
Shardlow Rd
 Aston-on-T DE72 . . . . 246 B7
 Derby DE24, DE74 . . . . 233 C6
Sharman Cl S18 . . . . 58 A1
Sharman Wlk S18 . . . . 58 A1
Sharp Cl
 Ilkeston DE7 . . . . 208 C6
 Long Eaton NG10 . . . . 236 C6
Sharp Ave S8 . . . . 56 E8
Sharpswood Manor
DE11 . . . . 256 E4
Sharrard Cl S12 . . . . 44 B5
Sharrard Dr S12 . . . . 44 B5
Sharrard Gr S12 . . . . 44 B6
Sharrard Rd S12 . . . . 44 B5
Shatton La
 Bamford S33 . . . . 40 A1
 Thornhill S32, S33 . . . . 51 E7
Shaw's Row S40 . . . . 95 D2
Shaw's Yd DE56 . . . . 191 F8
Shawcroft **8** DE6 . . . . 173 C2
Shawcroft Ave DE55 . . . . 170 C5
Shawfield Rd SK13 . . . . 9 F3
Shaw La
 Belper DE56 . . . . 191 B7
 Glossop SK13 . . . . 9 F3
 Holloway DE4 . . . . 156 C8
 Marston Montgomery DE6 198 A1
Shaw St E DE7 . . . . 209 A6
Shaw St W DE7 . . . . 209 A6
Shaws Gn DE22 . . . . 218 D6
Shaws Hill DE4 . . . . 156 D1
Shaw St
 Chesterfield S41 . . . . 96 A8
 Derby DE22 . . . . 218 E6
 Dronfield S18 . . . . 57 C4
 Glossop SK13 . . . . 17 C8
 Holmewood S42 . . . . 116 D1
 Mottram in L SK14 . . . . 9 A4
 Somercotes DE55 . . . . 170 C6
Shaw The SK13 . . . . 10 A3
Shaw Wood Cl DE55 . . . . 157 F3
Shaw Wood View DE55 . . . 157 F3
Sheaf Bank S2 . . . . 43 A7
Sheaf Bank Bsns Pk S2 . 43 A7
Sheardhall Ave SK12 . . . . 32 E5
Sheards Cl S18 . . . . 56 F1
Sheards Dr S18 . . . . 56 E1
Sheards Way S18 . . . . 56 F1
Shearsby Dr NG19 . . . . 136 F2
Shearwater Cl DE23 . . . . 231 D7
Sheepbridge Bsns Ctr
S41 . . . . 76 E2
Sheepbridge La S41 . . . . 76 E2
Sheepcote Hill S21 . . . . 60 D6
Sheepcote Rd S21 . . . . 60 C6
Sheephill Rd S11, S17 . . . . . . 42 F1
Sheep La DE55 . . . . 158 C8
Sheeplea La S45 . . . . 129 E8
Sheepwash La S45 . . . . 145 B8
Sheets Stores Ind Est
NG10 . . . . 236 D5
Sheffield Coll (Norton Coll)
 The S8 . . . . 57 B7
Sheffield Coll The
 (Frecheville Ctr) S12 . . 44 C4
Sheffield Pl DE1 . . . . 267 D2
Sheffield Rd
 Baslow DE45 . . . . 92 B7
 Chapel-en-le-F SK23 . . . . 47 E7
 Chesterfield S41 . . . . 96 A6
 Creswell S80, S43 . . . . 81 D3
 Dronfield S18 . . . . 56 F3
 Eckington S20, S21 . . . . 59 E5
 Glossop SK13 . . . . 10 F1
 Hathersage S32 . . . . 53 A7
 Killamarsh S21 . . . . 60 D2
 Renishaw S21, S43 . . . . 79 D8
 Sheffield S20 . . . . 44 F2
 Unstone S18, S41 . . . . 76 E3
Shelden Cl **4** SK13 . . . . 9 D1
Shelden Fold **3** SK13 . . . . 9 D1
Shelden Mews SK13 . . . . 9 D1
Shelden Pl **5** SK13 . . . . 9 D1
Sheldon Cl NG10 . . . . 223 B3
Sheldon Ct DE24 . . . . 232 E3
Sheldon Gdns DE4 . . . . 156 F1
Sheldon Rd
 Chesterfield S40 . . . . 95 B5
 Heanor DE75 . . . . 181 C5
Shelford Cl DE3 . . . . 217 C3
Shelford La DE4 . . . . 156 B7
Shelley Ave NG19 . . . . 136 B4
Shelley Dr
 Derby DE24 . . . . 232 A5
 Dronfield S18 . . . . 76 C7
Shelley Gr DE55 . . . . 146 F3
Shelley Rd DE11 . . . . 256 C5
Shelley St S42 . . . . 116 D1
Shelmory Cl DE24 . . . . 232 E5
Shelton Cl NG19 . . . . 135 E1
Shelton Dr DE24 . . . . 232 F3
Shelton Gate Cl DE24 . . 232 E5
Shelton Jun & Inf Sch
DE24 . . . . 232 D4
Shenington Way DE21 . 206 B2
Shepherd's La DE23 . . . . 251 D6
Shepherd St DE23 . . . . 218 C1
Shepley's Yd S40 . . . . 266 B3

Shepley St
 Chesterfield S40 . . . . 95 D2
 Glossop SK13 . . . . 10 F2
 Hadfield SK13 . . . . 9 E3
Shepton Cl DE7 . . . . 194 D3
Sheraton Way SK17 . . . . 66 B1
Sherbourne Ave S41 . . . . 95 E8
Sherbourne Dr
 Belper DE56 . . . . 179 D5
 Burton u T DE14 . . . . 254 A7
 Hilton DE65 . . . . 228 C1
Sherbrooke Rd SK12 . . . . 32 D6
Sherbrook Gr SK17 . . . . 85 C5
Sheridan Ct NG9 . . . . 209 F1
Sheridan St DE24 . . . . 231 F5
Sheriff Dr DE4 . . . . 143 B6
Sheringham Cl DE65 . . . . 228 C2
Sherriff's Lea NG9 . . . . 223 E2
Sherroside Cl DE22 . . . . 204 D4
Sherston Cl DE21 . . . . 206 B2
Sherwin Rd NG9 . . . . 209 F1
Sherwin St DE22 . . . . 218 E8
Sherwood Ave
 Borrowash DE72 . . . . 221 D2
 Creswell S80 . . . . 81 D1
 Derby, Chaddesden DE21 . . 219 F7
 Derby, Littleover DE23 . . . . . 231 D5
 Hope S33 . . . . 39 A3
 Pinxton NG16 . . . . 160 D3
 Shirebrook NG20 . . . . 119 E4
Sherwood Chase S17 . . . . 55 E5
Sherwood Copse SK17 . . . . . 69 C4
Sherwood Ct NG19 . . . . 136 B2
Sherwood Dr NG20 . . . . 119 E3
Sherwood Fold SK13 . . . . 16 D7
Sherwood Foresters
 Regiment Meml* DE4 . 156 E3
Sherwood Pl **2** S18 . . . . 56 D1
Sherwood Rd
 Buxton SK17 . . . . 85 C5
 Dronfield S18 . . . . 56 D1
 Killamarsh S21 . . . . 60 E7
 Matlock DE4 . . . . 143 C4
 Tideswell SK17 . . . . 69 C3
Sherwood Rise
 Eastwood NG16 . . . . 182 F1
 Mansfield Woodhouse
 NG19 . . . . 136 A1
Sherwood St
 Bolsover S44 . . . . 117 F8
 Chesterfield S40 . . . . 266 C1
 Derby DE22 . . . . 218 E3
 Mansfield Woodhouse
 NG19 . . . . 136 B2
 Newton DE55 . . . . 148 B4
 Shirland DE55 . . . . 146 C5
 Somercotes DE55 . . . . 170 C8
 Sutton in A NG17 . . . . 148 F3
Shetland Cl
 Derby DE21 . . . . 219 C7
 Mansfield NG19 . . . . 136 F1
Shetland Rd
 Dronfield S18 . . . . 76 B8
 Tibshelf DE55 . . . . 147 F5
Shields Cres DE74 . . . . 246 F3
Shieling The DE65 . . . . 227 C2
Shilling Way NG10 . . . . 236 A7
Shiloh Rd SK22, SK6 . . . . 24 B6
Shilo Way NG16 . . . . 195 B4
Shining Cliff YH* DE56 . 167 D5
Shinwell Ave S43 . . . . 97 B7
Shipley Cl DE14 . . . . 254 B8
Shipley Common La DE7 194 D4
Shipley Country Park Visitor
 Ctr* DE75 . . . . 193 E7
Shipley Ctry Pk* DE7 . . . . 194 D7
Shipley Ctry Pk* DE7 . . . . 194 A4
Shipley La DE7, DE75 . . . . . . 193 F5
Shipley View DE7 . . . . 192 F6
Shipley Wlk DE24 . . . . 232 E3
Shipman Ct S20 . . . . 59 D7
Shippen Rural Bsns Ctr The
 S18 . . . . 75 E2
Shippon La S32 . . . . 72 B2
Shirebrook Bsns Pk
 NG20 . . . . 120 A3
Shirebrook Cl NE7 . . . . 194 F6
Shirebrook Ct S21 . . . . 43 A6
Shirebrook Dr
 Glossop SK13 . . . . 17 E8
 Glossop SK13 . . . . 17 F8
Shirebrook Rd S8 . . . . 43 A6
Shirebrook Sch NG20 . . . 119 D5
Shirebrook Sta NG20 . . . 120 A4
Shiregate Gdns DE23 . . 231 A5
Shire Hill Hospl SK13 . . . . . . 10 E3
Shire La S44 . . . . 116 F4
Shireoaks DE56 . . . . 178 D5
Shireoaks Cl DE23 . . . . 231 C7
Shireoaks Comm S81 . . . . . . 63 F7
Shireoaks Rd
 Dronfield S18 . . . . 57 C2
 Shireoaks S81 . . . . 63 F6
Shireoaks Row S81 . . . . 63 E7
Shireoaks Sta S81 . . . . 63 F7
Shires The NG19 . . . . 136 F1
Shire Way SK13 . . . . 10 E3
Shirland Ct DE24 . . . . 232 E3
Shirland Prim Sch DE55 146 D2
Shirland St S41 . . . . 266 B4
Shirley Cl
 Castle Donington DE74 . . . 247 A4
 Chesterfield S40 . . . . 95 B5
 Hope S33 . . . . 39 A4
Shirley Cres DE72 . . . . 235 D8
Shirley La DE6 . . . . 200 B6
Shirley Pk DE72 . . . . 246 B7

Shirley Rd
 Derby DE21 . . . . 205 F1
 Ripley DE5 . . . . 169 D1
 Swanwick DE55 . . . . 169 F7
Shirley St NG10 . . . . 236 A4
Shop La DE56 . . . . 168 C2
Shop Stones DE72 . . . . 221 C5
Shoreham St S2 . . . . 43 A8
Short Ave DE22 . . . . 204 F5
Shortbrook Bank **10** S20 . . 59 E8
Shortbrook Cl S20 . . . . 59 F8
Shortbrook Com Prim Sch
 S20 . . . . 59 F8
Shortbrook Croft **6** S20 . . 59 E8
Shortbrook Dr S20 . . . . 59 E8
Shortbrook Rd S20 . . . . 59 E8
Shortbrook Way **11** S20 . . 59 E8
Shortbrook Wlk **12** S20 . . 59 E8
Short Cl S42 . . . . 113 D7
Shortheath DE21 . . . . 262 C3
Shortheath Rd DE12 . . . . 262 E3
Short Hill DE73 . . . . 252 E6
Short La DE74 . . . . 246 F4
Short Lands DE56 . . . . 179 A4
Shortlands The DE4 . . . . 143 B3
Short Row **4** DE56 . . . . 178 F4
Shorts La S17 . . . . 55 B6
Short St
 Belper DE56 . . . . 179 B4
 Burton u T DE15 . . . . 254 E7
Short Street Inf Sch
 DE15 . . . . 254 E7
Shorwell Gdns DE24 . . . . 233 C5
Shottle Wlk DE24 . . . . 232 E3
Shotwood Cl DE13 . . . . 240 A4
Shotwoodhill La DE13 . . 240 A5
Shrewsbury Cl DE21 . . . . 206 C2
Shrewsbury Rd DE13 . . . . . . 240 F2
Shrewsbury St SK13 . . . . 10 C1
Shrewsbury St SK13 . . . . 55 D4
Shropshire Ave
 Derby DE21 . . . . 219 E7
 Westwood NG16 . . . . 171 C4
Shropshire Dr SK13 . . . . 17 F8
Shrubbery The DE11 . . . . . . 257 A2
Shuckstone La DE4 . . . . 156 F6
Shudehill Cl SK22 . . . . 25 D3
Shunters Drift S43 . . . . 80 B6
Shuttlewood Rd S44 . . . . 99 A4
Shutts La DE45 . . . . 109 C4
Sickleholme La S18 . . . . 107 F4
Sickleholme S33 . . . . 40 B1
Sidcup Ct S43 . . . . 78 B4
Siddalls St DE15 . . . . 248 B3
Siddals La DE22 . . . . 204 F4
Siddals Rd DE1 . . . . 267 C2
Siddons St DE24 . . . . 233 A7
Side End La SK23 . . . . 45 A2
Sides La DE6 . . . . 184 B5
Sidings The
 Chinley SK23 . . . . 34 E2
 Derby DE21 . . . . 220 A4
 Kimberley NG16 . . . . 195 F6
 Whaley Bridge SK23 . . . . 45 E8
Sidings Way DE55 . . . . 147 C1
Sidlaw Cl **6** S40 . . . . 95 C5
Sidmouth Cl DE24 . . . . 233 C7
Sidmouth **11** S41 . . . . 95 F8
Sidney Robinson Bsns Pk
 DE24 . . . . 219 D1
Sidney St
 Derby DE1 . . . . 219 B3
 Kimberley NG16 . . . . 195 F6
 Long Eaton NG10 . . . . 236 D6
Siggate S33 . . . . 38 D1
Silken Holme DE55 . . . . 160 B4
Silk Hill SK23 . . . . 45 F8
Silk Mill La DE13 . . . . 239 C6
Silk St S13 . . . . 10 E1
Silkstone Cl
 Sheffield S12 . . . . 44 E4
 Swadlincote DE11 . . . . 256 B1
Silkstone Cres S12 . . . . 44 E4
Silkstone Dr S12 . . . . 44 D4
Silkstone Pl S12 . . . . 44 E4
Silkstone Rd S12 . . . . 44 E4
Silver Birch Cres DE55 . 159 C8
Silverburn Dr DE21 . . . . 206 A2
Silverdale NG9 . . . . 223 E5
Silverdale Ave NG19 . . . . . . 136 B4
Silverdale Cl
 Chellaston DE73 . . . . 233 A2
 Chesterfield S41 . . . . 76 E1
Silverhill Cl DE13 . . . . 240 C1
Silverhill La NG17 . . . . 148 F8
Silverhill Prim Sch DE3 217 C3
Silverhill Rd DE21 . . . . 220 E3
Silver Hill Rd DE23 . . . . 219 A2
Silver La
 Elvaston DE72 . . . . 234 A5
 Marchington S14 . . . . 224 F1
Silverlands SK17 . . . . 85 D7
Silverlands Rd SK13 . . . . 17 B8
Silverlands Cl SK17 . . . . 85 C7
Silverlands Pk SK17 . . . . 85 C7
Silver Mill Rd S21 . . . . 43 A8
Silverton Dr DE24 . . . . 231 C2
Silver Well Dr S43 . . . . 97 D8
Silvey Gr DE21 . . . . 220 D4
Simcoe Leys DE73 . . . . 233 A2
Simcrest Ave S21 . . . . 60 D5
Simmondley Gr S13 . . . . 17 A8
Simmondley La S13 . . . . 17 A8
Simmondley New Rd
 SK13 . . . . 17 A7
Simmondley Prim Sch
 SK13 . . . . 17 A7
Simon Fields Cl DE7 . . . . 193 A2
Simons Cl SK13 . . . . 17 A7

Simons Wlk SK13 . . . . 17 A8
Sims Ave DE1 . . . . 218 E5
Sims Croft S41 . . . . 77 C3
Sinclair Cl
 Derby DE24 . . . . 231 E4
 Heanor DE75 . . . . 193 D8
Sinfin Ave DE24 . . . . 232 D3
Sinfin Central Bsns Pk DE23,
 DE24 . . . . 231 F5
Sinfin Com Sch DE24 . . . 231 E3
Sinfin District Ctr DE24 . 231 E3
Sinfin Fields Cres DE24 . 232 D5
Sinfin La
 Barrow u T DE73 . . . . 244 A6
 Derby DE23, DE24 . . . . 231 F4
Sinfin Moor La DE73 . . . . . . 232 E2
Sinfin Moor Sch DE24 . . 231 F5
Sir Francis Ley Ind Pk
 DE23 . . . . 219 C1
Sir Frank Whittle Rd
 DE21 . . . . 219 C7
Sir Harold Jackson Prim Sch
 S17 . . . . 56 B5
Sir Henry's La DE73 . . . . 252 A4
Sir Joseph's La DE4 . . . . 127 B4
Sir William Hill Rd
 Eyam S32 . . . . 71 C8
 Grindleford S32 . . . . 53 B1
Sir William Terr S32 . . . . 72 C8
Siskin Cl DE3 . . . . 230 B7
Siskin Dr DE24 . . . . 231 D4
Sisley Ave NG9 . . . . 223 E6
Sister's La DE72 . . . . 221 C5
Sitch La
 Hayfield SK22 . . . . 24 F3
 Kirk Ireton DE4 . . . . 165 A4
 Wensley DE4 . . . . 142 D7
Sitwell **14** S20 . . . . 59 E8
Sitwell Ave S40 . . . . 266 A1
Sitwell Cl DE21 . . . . 220 D4
Sitwell Dr DE56 . . . . 192 A8
Sitwell Grange La S45 . 147 D8
Sitwell St
 Derby DE1 . . . . 267 B2
 Derby, Spondon DE21 . . . . . 220 E4
 Eckington S21 . . . . 59 C3
Sitwell Villas DE55 . . . . 146 E5
Skeavington's La DE7 . . 194 E5
Skeldale Dr S40 . . . . 115 B8
Skelton Rd S8 . . . . 43 A5
Skelwith Cl S41 . . . . 95 D8
Ski 2000 Ilkeston NG16 . 195 B1
Skiddaw Cl **2** S40 . . . . 95 C6
Skiddaw Dr DE3 . . . . 217 E1
Skinner St S80 . . . . 81 D2
Skinners Way DE11 . . . . 256 D5
Skipness Cl DE73 . . . . 232 E2
Skipton Cl DE7 . . . . 194 D3
Skipton Dr DE24 . . . . 205 C1
Skye Gdns DE55 . . . . 147 F5
Skylark Way DE24 . . . . 231 D4
Slack's La S45 . . . . 132 C2
Slackey La DE12 . . . . 262 C4
Slack La
 Ashover S45 . . . . 129 C2
 Brailsford DE6 . . . . 187 D1
 Chesterfield S40 . . . . 95 B3
 Derby, Allestree DE22 . . . . . 204 F2
 Derby, New Zealand DE22 . 218 D5
 Hartshorne DE11 . . . . 257 B6
 Heath S44 . . . . 116 F2
 Mayfield DE6 . . . . 184 C8
 Nether Heage DE56 . . . . . . 168 C3
 Ripley DE5 . . . . 169 D1
 Shipley DE75 . . . . 193 E8
 Somercotes DE55 . . . . 170 B5
 Wessington DE55 . . . . 157 D8
Slack Rd DE7 . . . . 193 F3
Slacks Cotts SK17 . . . . 84 E4
Slacks La SK22 . . . . 25 C5
Slade Cl
 Etwall DE65 . . . . 229 C4
 Ilkeston DE7 . . . . 209 A5
 South Normanton DE55 . . 160 B4
Slade Farm DE73 . . . . 251 A4
Slade Fields ST14 . . . . 210 B1
Slade Hollow La DE6 . . . 201 A3
Slade La
 Weston Underwood DE6 . 202 E7
 Wilson DE73 . . . . 252 F6
Slade Lands Dr DE73 . . . 233 A2
Slag La S43 . . . . 77 D6
Slaidburn Cl DE24 . . . . 231 D2
Slaley La DE4 . . . . 154 C8
Slaney Cl DE24 . . . . 232 E7
Slant Cl SK13 . . . . 17 E8
Slant La
 Mansfield Woodhouse
 NG19 . . . . 136 B4
 Shirebrook NG20 . . . . 119 D4
Slatelands Ave SK13 . . . . 17 B8
Slatelands Rd SK13 . . . . 17 B8
Slate Pit Dale S42 . . . . 113 E4
Slatepit La S18, S42 . . . . 93 C8
Slater Ave DE22 . . . . 218 E6
Slater Cres DE4 . . . . 165 F7
Slater St S45 . . . . 131 D3
Slate St S2 . . . . 43 B8
Slayley Hill S43 . . . . 80 C4
Slayley View S43 . . . . 80 C5
Slayley View Rd S43 . . . . 80 B6
Slaypit La S80 . . . . 63 A1
Sledgegate La DE4 . . . . 156 B7
Sledmere Cl DE24 . . . . 233 C7
Sleepy La DE73 . . . . 245 C1
Sleetmoor La DE55 . . . . 170 B8
Sleights La NG16 . . . . 160 C2
Slindon Croft DE24 . . . . 233 D6

Slipperlow La SK17 . . . . 87 F2
Sloade La S12 . . . . 58 D7
Sloane Rd DE22 . . . . 218 A6
Smalldale Cotts SK17 . . . . . . 67 D7
Smalldale Head Rd S33 . . 50 F7
Smalldale Rd
 Buxton SK17 . . . . 67 C7
 Sheffield S13 . . . . 44 D4
Smalley Dr DE21 . . . . 206 B3
Smalley Mill Rd DE21,
 DE7 . . . . 192 B4
Small Gate NG19 . . . . 136 E6
Small Knowle End SK17 . . 67 C6
Small Meer Cl DE73 . . . . 232 F1
Small Thorn Pl DE11 . . . . . . 256 E1
Smeath Rd NG16 . . . . 171 F2
Smeckley Wood Cl S41 . . 76 C2
Smedley's Ave NG10 . . . . . . 223 B5
Smedley Ave
 Ilkeston DE7 . . . . 209 A7
 Somercotes DE55 . . . . 159 D1
Smedley Ct DE65 . . . . 241 B5
Smedley Pl SK13 . . . . 10 E2
Smedley St E DE4 . . . . 143 C5
Smedley St W DE4 . . . . 143 B7
Smedley St DE4 . . . . 143 B6
Smeeton St DE75 . . . . 182 B1
Smelter Wood Ave S13 . . . 44 E7
Smelter Wood Cl S13 . . . . . . 44 E7
Smelter Wood Cres S13 . . 44 E7
Smelter Wood Ct S13 . . . . . 44 E7
Smelter Wood Dr S13 . . . . . 44 E7
Smelter Wood La S13 . . . . . 44 E7
Smelter Wood Pl S13 . . . . . 44 E7
Smelter Wood Rd S13 . . . . 44 E7
Smelter Wood Rise S13 . . 44 E7
Smelter Wood Way S13 . . 44 E7
Smeltinghouse La S18 . . . 75 E3
Smisby La DE65 . . . . 258 A1
Smisby Way DE24 . . . . 232 E3
Smith Ave
 Codnor DE5 . . . . 170 B1
 King's Newton DE73 . . . . . . 245 B1
 Staveley S43 . . . . 97 C7
Smithbrook Cl SK23 . . . . 47 C6
Smith Cres S41 . . . . 96 D1
Smith Dr NG16 . . . . 182 A3
Smithfield Ave
 Chesterfield S41 . . . . 115 C7
 Trowell NG9 . . . . 209 D4
Smithfield Rd S12 . . . . 44 A3
Smith-Hall La DE6 . . . . 176 A1
Smith Hall La DE6 . . . . 188 A7
Smith Rd DE4 . . . . 143 B6
Smiths La DE55 . . . . 146 C7
Smithson Ave S44 . . . . 99 B1
Smithurst Rd NG16 . . . . 195 B7
Smithy Ave S45 . . . . 131 C4
Smithy Brook Rd S21 . . . . . . 79 C8
Smithy Cl
 Glossop SK13 . . . . 10 D1
 Parwich DE6 . . . . 151 D1
Smithy Croft S18 . . . . 56 D2
Smithy Fold SK13 . . . . 10 D1
Smithy Hill S33 . . . . 51 A7
Smithy Knoll Rd S32 . . . . 72 C2
Smithy La
 Clifton Campville B79 . . . . . 263 E4
 Marple SK6 . . . . 15 F1
 Taddington SK17 . . . . 88 A3
Smithy Mdws S32 . . . . 53 A8
Smithy Pl S42 . . . . 115 F2
Smuse La DE4 . . . . 143 E4
Snake La DE56 . . . . 190 E4
Snake Pass SK13 . . . . 11 B1
Snake Rd
 Bamford S33 . . . . 29 D6
 Derwent S33 . . . . 30 B2
 High Peak S33 . . . . 28 D8
Snake Woodland Forest
 Wlk* S33 . . . . 19 F3
Snape Hill S18 . . . . 57 A3
Snapehill Cl S18 . . . . 57 A3
Snape Hill Cres S18 . . . . 57 A3
Snape Hill Dr S18 . . . . 57 B3
Snape Hill La S18 . . . . 57 A2
Snapes La DE6 . . . . 184 B1
Snelsmoor La DE73 . . . . . . 233 B2
Snelston Cl S18 . . . . 56 D1
Snelston Cres DE23 . . . . 218 D2
Snipe Cl S42 . . . . 113 D7
Snipesmoor La DE6 . . . . 185 F7
Snitterton Rd DE4 . . . . 143 A5
Snowberry Ave DE56 . . . . . 179 B3
Snowdon La S21 . . . . 58 B2
Snowdrop Dr NG19 . . . . 136 F4
Snowdrop Valley DE4 . . . . 168 A8
Snowfield View DE4 . . . . . . 165 E6
Soaper La S18 . . . . 57 A3
Soarbank Cl NG16 . . . . 195 E7
Soar Way DE55 . . . . 228 D1
Society Pl DE23 . . . . 219 A2
Soft Water La S33 . . . . 51 A7
Soldier's Croft DE45 . . . . . 107 C2
Solney Cl DE11 . . . . 255 F3
Soloman Pk NG16 . . . . 195 B2
Soloman Rd DE7 . . . . 195 B2
Solomons View SK17 . . . . . . 85 C7
Solway Cl DE21 . . . . 206 A2
Solway Rise S18 . . . . 56 D2
Somerby Way **3** DE21 . . 205 F2
Somercotes Hill DE55 . . . 170 D8
Somercotes Inf Sch
 DE55 . . . . 170 C6
Somercotes Rd S12 . . . . 44 D5

Somerlea Park Jun Sch
DE55 . . . . 170 C8
Somerleyton Dr DE7 . . . 209 A4
Somersal Cl DE24 . . . . . 232 E3
Somersal Cl S40 . . . . . . 95 A1
Somersall La S40 . . . . . 95 A1
Somersall La S40 . . . . . 95 A1
Somersal Park Rd S40 . . 95 A1
Somersall Willows S40 . . 95 A1
Somersby Ave S40 . . . . 114 B8
Somerset Cl
  Buxton SK17 . . . . 85 C4
  Long Eaton NG10 . . . . 237 A8
Somerset Dr S43 . . . . . . 97 A8
Somerset Rd DE15 . . . . 254 D6
Somerset St DE21 . . . . 219 D7
Somme Rd DE22 . . . . . 204 B3
Sookholme Cl NG20 . . . 119 F3
Sookholme La NG20 . . . 120 E3
Sookholme La NG20 . . . 119 F3
Soresby St S40 . . . . . . 266 B3
Sorrel Dr DE11 . . . . . . 256 E4
Sough La
  Calver S32 . . . . 72 B2
  Taddington SK17 . . . . . 87 D2
  Wirksworth DE4 . . . . . 154 F2
  Wirksworth, Steeple Grange
  DE4 . . . . 155 B2
Soughley La S10 . . . . . . 42 C8
Sough Rd DE55 . . . . . . 160 B7
Souter Cl S43 . . . . 43 A6
Southard's La S80 . . . . 62 E5
South Ave
  Buxton SK17 . . . . 85 B7
  Chellaston DE73 . . . . . 232 F3
  Derby, Darley Abbey DE22 . 205 A2
  Derby DE23 . . . . 218 D1
  Derby, Spondon DE21 . . 220 E4
  Shirebrook NG20 . . . . 119 F3
South Brae Cl DE23 . . . 231 D7
South Broadway St
  DE14 . . . . 254 C8
Southbrook Cl SK13 . . . . 9 E4
South Church St DE45 . . 109 D5
South Cl
  Glossop SK13 . . . . 9 F7
  Unstone Green S18 . . . 76 E6
Southcote Dr S18 . . . . . 56 D1
South Cres
  Bolsover S44 . . . . 99 B1
  Duckmanton S44 . . . . 98 A5
  Killamarsh S21 . . . . . . 60 E7
Southcroft
  Alfreton DE55 . . . . . . 159 A3
  1 Buxton SK17 . . . . . . 85 A7
  Derby DE23 . . . . 231 D4
South Ct S17 . . . . 55 E6
South Darley CE Prim Sch
  DE4 . . . . 142 B7
Southdown Ave S40 . . . 95 C5
Southdown Cl DE24 . . . 231 C2
South Dr
  Chellaston DE73 . . . . . 232 F3
  Derby, Cherrytree Hill
  DE21 . . . . 220 A5
  Derby, Littleover DE23 . 218 F7
  Swadlincote DE11 . . . . 255 F5
South East Derbyshire Coll
  Heanor DE75 . . . . 181 F1
  Ilkeston DE7 . . . . 208 F7
Southend S42 . . . . 115 F2
South End DE4 . . . . . . 155 A7
South Farm Ave S26 . . . 61 E6
Southfield Ave S41 . . . . 115 D6
Southfield Cl S80 . . . . . 81 F5
Southfield Dr
  Dronfield S18 . . . . 76 C8
  South Normanton DE55 . 160 C5
Southfield La S80 . . . . . 82 A4
Southfield Ind Site S80 . 82 A4
Southfield Mount S18 . . 76 C8
Southfields
  Clowne S43 . . . . 80 F3
  Long Eaton NG10 . . . . 236 F3
Southfields Ave NG16 . . 160 D4
Southgate S21 . . . . 59 E3
Southgate Bglws S80 . . . 81 C7
Southgate Bsns Ctr
  DE23 . . . . 267 B1
Southgate Cl DE3 . . . . 217 C3
Southgate Cres S43 . . . 80 F5
Southgate Ct S21 . . . . . 59 E3
Southgate Way S43 . . . 78 B4
South Head Dr SK23 . . . 47 C7
South Hill
  Ashover DE55 . . . . . . 145 F7
  Rolleston DE13 . . . . . 240 D4
South Hill La DE55 . . . . 145 F6
South Lodge Ct S40 . . . 95 C1
South Marlow St SK13 . . 10 A4
Southmead Way DE3 . . 218 B3
South Mews 10 SK17 . . . 85 B7
Southmoor Cl S43 . . . . 96 F4
South Oak St DE14 . . . 254 B8
South Par DE4 . . . . . . 143 A1
South Park Ave DE4 . . . 127 C3
South Pl
  Chesterfield, Brampton
  S40 . . . . 95 D2
  Chesterfield, Stonegravels
  S40 . . . . 266 B2
  Ripley DE5 . . . . 169 D1
South St N S43 . . . . . . 77 D3
South St
  Ashbourne DE6 . . . . . 173 C1

South St *continued*
  Blackwell DE55 . . . . . 147 F2
  Buxton SK17 . . . . 85 B7
  Chesterfield S40 . . . . . 266 B2
  Derby DE1 . . . . 218 E5
  Draycott DE72 . . . . . . 235 A7
  Eastwood, Bailey Grove
  NG16 . . . . 182 E2
  Eastwood, Giltbrook NG16 . 195 C8
  Ilkeston DE7 . . . . 208 F8
  Long Eaton NG10 . . . . 236 E7
  Melbourne DE73 . . . . . 252 A7
  Pilsley S45 . . . . 132 D1
  Sheffield S20 . . . . 59 D6
  Somercotes DE55 . . . . 170 D5
  Swanwick DE55 . . . . . 169 E7
  Woodville DE11 . . . . . 257 A1
South Uxbridge St DE14 . 254 B8
South View
  Bamford S33 . . . . 40 B4
  Chesterfield S41 . . . . . 95 D7
  Derby DE23 . . . . 218 C1
  Mayfield DE6 . . . . 184 D6
  New Mills SK22 . . . . . . 33 B8
  Pilsley S45 . . . . 91 C2
  Sheffield S20 . . . . 60 A7
  Whitwell S80 . . . . 81 F5
South View Rd SK13 . . . 17 F7
South View Wlk ST14 . . 196 F3
Southwark Cl DE22 . . . 218 B5
Southwell Rise NG16 . . 195 B7
South Wingfield Prim Sch
  DE55 . . . . 157 F4
Southwood 2 SK17 . . . 85 A7
Southwood S18 . . . . . . 76 B7
Southwood Dr S43 . . . . 80 F3
Southwood St DE24 . . . 232 F8
Southworth Rd DE73 . . 252 E2
Sovereign Dr DE14 . . . 254 B8
Sovereign Gr NG10 . . . 236 B7
Sovereign Way
  Derby DE21 . . . . 206 D3
  Heanor DE75 . . . . 181 D1
Sowbrook Brook DE7 . . 208 D4
Sowbrook La DE7 . . . . 208 E3
Sowter Rd DE1 . . . . . . 267 B4
Sowters Row S40 . . . . 266 B3
Spa Brook Cl S12 . . . . . 44 F4
Spa Brook Dr S12 . . . . . 44 F5
Spa Croft DE55 . . . . . . 147 E5
Spa Ct DE1 . . . . 267 A1
Spa La
  Chesterfield, Hady S41 . 266 C2
  Chesterfield, Hady S41 . 266 C3
  Derby DE1 . . . . 267 A1
Spalden Ave DE6 . . . . . 173 C3
Spang La NG17 . . . . . . 148 E4
Spanker La DE56 . . . . . 168 B2
Spanker Terr DE56 . . . . 168 C2
Sparrowbusk Cl S43 . . . 80 B6
Sparrow Cl
  Derby DE24 . . . . 231 D4
  Ilkeston DE7 . . . . 209 A5
Spa View Ave S12 . . . . 44 F3
Spa View Dr S12 . . . . . 44 F3
Spa View Pl S12 . . . . . 44 F3
Spa View Rd S12 . . . . . 44 F3
Spa View Terr S12 . . . . 44 F3
Spa View Way S12 . . . . 44 F3
Speedwell SK13 . . . . . . 9 F7
Speedwell Cavern* S33 . . 37 F2
Speedwell
  Derby DE21 . . . . 206 C3
  Glossop SK13 . . . . 9 F7
  Woodville DE11 . . . . . 256 F4
Speedwell Ind Est S43 . . 78 F2
Speedwell Inf Sch S43 . . 78 E1
Speedwell La NG16 . . . 195 E6
Speetley View S43 . . . . 80 B7
Speighthill Cres S42 . . . 114 E4
Spenbeck Dr DE22 . . . 205 A5
Spencer Ave
  Belper DE56 . . . . 179 B4
  Derby DE24 . . . . 232 D4
  Sandiacre NG10 . . . . . 223 B6
  Staveley S43 . . . . 79 B2
Spencer Cl
  Ashbourne DE6 . . . . . 185 C8
  Burton u T DE13 . . . . . 240 D1
Spencer Cres NG9 . . . . 223 F8
Spencer Dr DE55 . . . . . 170 D7
Spencer Gr SK17 . . . . . 85 B6
Spencer Ho
  Derby, Crewton DE24 . . 233 A8
  Derby, Spondon DE21 . . 220 C7
Spencer Rd
  Belper DE56 . . . . 179 B4
  Buxton SK17 . . . . 85 B6
  Chapel-en-le-F SK23 . . . 46 F6
  Sheffield S2 . . . . 43 A7
Spencer St
  Bolsover S44 . . . . 117 F8
  Chesterfield S40 . . . . . 266 B4
  Derby DE24 . . . . 233 A8
  Stanley Common DE7 . . 193 A1
Spend La DE6 . . . . 161 E2
Sperry Cl NG16 . . . . . . 171 F6
Spilsbury Cl DE65 . . . . 242 C5
Spindletree Dr DE21 . . 205 F2
Spinkhill Ave S13 . . . . . 44 C8
Spinkhill Dr S13 . . . . . . 44 D8
Spinkhill Immaculate
Conception Prim Sch
  S21 . . . . 60 C2
Spinkhill La S21 . . . . . . 60 B2
Spinkhill Rd
  Killamarsh S21 . . . . . . 60 E4

Spinkhill Rd *continued*
  Sheffield S13 . . . . 44 D8
Spinkhill View S21 . . . . 60 B1
Spinnerbottom SK22 . . . 24 F2
Spinners Way S56 . . . . 179 C5
Spinneybrook Way DE3 . 217 D4
Spinney Cl
  Derby DE22 . . . . 205 A2
  Glossop SK13 . . . . 10 C2
  Mansfield Woodhouse
  NG19 . . . . 136 E6
Spinney Cres NG9 . . . . 223 F3
Spinney Dr NG10 . . . . . 223 C2
Spinney Hill DE73 . . . . 252 A7
Spinney Lo
  Repton DE65 . . . . 242 C2
  Tutbury DE13 . . . . 238 E6
Spinney Rd
  Branston DE14 . . . . . . 253 F8
  Derby, Chaddesden DE21 . 219 F7
  Derby DE22 . . . . 218 E3
  Ilkeston DE7 . . . . 208 E6
  Long Eaton NG10 . . . . 223 C2
  Ripley DE5 . . . . 169 D3
  Shirebrook NG20 . . . . 119 D3
  Stanton-by-D NG10 . . . 222 F8
Spire Hollin DE45 . . . . . 10 C2
Spire Hollin Ho SK13 . . . 10 C2
Spital Brook Cl S41 . . . . 96 C1
Spital Gdns S41 . . . . . . 96 C2
Spital La S41 . . . . 96 C1
Spitewinter La S18, S42 . 93 D8
Spittal DE74 . . . . 247 A4
Spittal Gn S44 . . . . . . 118 A8
Spittal Hill DE74 . . . . . 247 A4
Spondon Rd DE7 . . . . . 207 D2
Spondon Sch DE21 . . . . 220 C4
Spondon Sta DE21 . . . . 220 D3
Spooner Dr S21 . . . . . . 60 C6
Spooner La S32 . . . . . . 72 C5
Spoonley Wood Ct DE23 . 230 F7
Sporton Cl DE55 . . . . . 160 A7
Sporton La DE55 . . . . . 160 B7
Spotswood Cl S14 . . . . 43 E4
Spotswood Dr S14 . . . . 43 E5
Spotswood Mount S14 . . 43 E4
Spotswood Pl S14 . . . . 43 D4
Spotswood Rd S14 . . . . 43 D5
Spout La
  Spout DE56 . . . . 166 C3
  Tansley DE4 . . . . 144 A5
Spridgeon Cl 2 NG10 . . 223 B2
Springbank SK13 . . . . . 9 F5
Spring Bank
  Buxton SK17 . . . . 67 C4
  Great Longstone DE45 . . 90 A4
Springbank Gdns SK22 . . 33 B8
Spring Bank Rd
  Chesterfield S40 . . . . . 266 A3
  New Mills SK22 . . . . . . 33 C8
Spring Cl
  Belper DE56 . . . . 178 E6
  Breaston DE72 . . . . . . 235 C8
  Renishaw S21 . . . . 79 C7
  Swadlincote DE11 . . . . 256 A1
  Wirksworth DE4 . . . . . 154 F2
Spring Close Dell S14 . . 43 F4
Spring Close Mount S14 . 43 F4
Spring Close View S14 . . 43 F4
Spring Cottage Rd DE12 . 262 D5
Spring Ct 4 NG9 . . . . . 223 E7
Spring Ct Mews SK14 . . 9 D5
Springdale Ct DE3 . . . . 217 E1
Spring Dale Gdns NG9 . 209 D3
Springfarm Rd DE15 . . . 248 A1
Springfield
  Broadbottom SK13 . . . . 16 C6
  Derby DE23 . . . . 218 B2
Springfield Ave
  Ashbourne DE6 . . . . . 185 D8
  Chesterfield S40 . . . . . 95 D3
  Heanor DE75 . . . . 181 B6
  Long Eaton NG10 . . . . 236 F8
  Sandiacre NG10 . . . . . 223 B3
  Shirebrook NG20 . . . . 119 E5
Springfield Cl
  Bradwell S33 . . . . 51 A7
  Clowne S43 . . . . 80 E3
  Crich DE4 . . . . 157 A1
  Eckington S21 . . . . 59 C3
  Glossop SK13 . . . . 9 E4
  Swadlincote DE11 . . . . 256 B6
Springfield Cres
  Bolsover S44 . . . . 98 F3
  Somercotes DE55 . . . . 170 D7
Springfield Ct NG9 . . . . 209 F7
Springfield Dr DE56 . . . 190 D3
Springfield Gdns DE7 . . 194 F2
Springfield Jun Sch
  DE11 . . . . 256 C5
Springfield Prim Sch
  DE21 . . . . 220 D5
Springfield Rd
  Barlow S18 . . . . 75 D3
  Bradwell S33 . . . . 51 A8
  Chellaston DE73 . . . . . 232 F2
  Derby, Cherrytree Hill
  DE21 . . . . 220 B5
  Etwall DE65 . . . . 229 B3
  Holmewood S42 . . . . . 132 E8
  Repton DE65 . . . . 242 D7

Springfield Rd *continued*
  Swadlincote DE11 . . . . 256 B6
Springfield Rise DE4 . . 143 C6
Springfield Terr
  Burton u T DE15 . . . . . 248 A1
  Hayfield SK22 . . . . 25 D2
  Ripley DE5 . . . . 169 E1
Springfield View DE5 . . 169 D2
Spring Gardens Ctr The
  SK17 . . . . 85 B8
Spring Garden Terr DE7 . 194 F2
Spring Gdns
  Buxton SK17 . . . . 85 C8
  Derby DE21 . . . . 219 F7
  Glossop SK13 . . . . 10 A5
  Ripley DE11 . . . . 257 A8
Spring Hill
  Kimberley NG16 . . . . . 195 F5
  Mansfield Woodhouse
  NG19 . . . . 136 B3
  Whitwell S80 . . . . 82 A6
Springhill Way DE5 . . . 181 A8
Spring Hollow DE56 . . . 190 C8
Spring House Cl S42 . . . 94 F5
Spring La
  Elmton S80 . . . . 99 F6
  Heanor DE75 . . . . 181 E1
  Sheffield S2 . . . . 43 E8
  Shireoaks S80, S81 . . . . 63 F5
Springmeadow S15 . . . . 16 D7
Spring Mount SK22 . . . . 33 C8
Spring Pl S40 . . . . 266 B3
Spring Rd DE55 . . . . . . 170 E6
Spring Rise SK13 . . . . . 16 F7
Spring St
  Broadbottom SK14 . . . . 16 A8
  Derby DE22 . . . . 267 A2
  Glossop SK13 . . . . 9 C5
  Hollingworth SK14 . . . . 9 C5
  Swadlincote DE11 . . . . 262 A8
  Whitwell S80 . . . . 82 A6
Spring The NG10 . . . . . 236 D5
Springvale Cl S45 . . . . . 131 D2
Springvale Rd S45 . . . . 131 D2
Spring Vale Rd
  Brimington S43 . . . . . . 96 E8
  Hayfield SK22 . . . . 25 D2
Spring Water Ave S12 . . 44 F3
Spring Water Dr S12 . . . 44 F3
Springwell Com Sch S43 . 97 D7
Springwell Hill S21 . . . . 77 F6
Springwell Park Dr S43 . 97 D7
Springwell St NG17 . . . 148 F2
Springwood S13 . . . . . . 16 F8
Spring Wood Cl S41 . . . 95 C8
Springwood Ct S43 . . . . 77 D4
Springwood Dr
  Derby DE21 . . . . 206 B2
  Mansfield Woodhouse
  NG19 . . . . 136 C2
Springwood Farm Rd
  DE11 . . . . 256 B7
Springwood Gdns DE56 . 179 A4
Springwood Rd S8 . . . . 43 A6
Springwood St S42 . . . 116 B4
Sprinkswoods La DE6 . . 184 E5
Spruce Ave NG16 . . . . . 171 D6
Spurr St S12 . . . . 60 C5
Square The
  Boylestone DE6 . . . . . 213 C4
  Bretby DE15 . . . . 249 B3
  8 Buxton SK17 . . . . . . 85 B8
  Clay Cross S45 . . . . . 131 E3
  Derby, Darley Abbey DE22 . 205 A1
  Derby DE3 . . . . 217 D1
  Elmton S80 . . . . 100 A8
  Eyam S32 . . . . 71 E5
  Hartington SK17 . . . . . 137 D5
  Marchington ST14 . . . . 224 E2
  Middleton DE45 . . . . . 124 A5
  Monyash DE45 . . . . . . 107 C2
  Whitwell S80 . . . . 81 F6
Squires La S33 . . . . . . 38 C3
Squires Way DE23 . . . . 231 A6
Squirrel La DE73 . . . . . 252 E4
Squirrel Wlk DE12 . . . . 262 B3
Stable Cl DE4 . . . . 156 B5
Stable Cotts DE4 . . . . . 155 A6
Stable La DE6 . . . . 149 B1
Stable Mews DE11 . . . . 256 F2
Stables Ct S44 . . . . 99 C1
Stables St DE22 . . . . . . 218 D5
Stables The DE65 . . . . . 228 F1
Stacey Rd NG10 . . . . . . 135 D2
Staden Bsns Pk SK17 . . . 85 E5
Staden La SK17 . . . . 85 E6
Stadium Bsns Ct DE24 . 219 E4
Stadium Ind Pk NG10 . . 236 B5
Stadium View DE24 . . . 219 E3
Stadmoor Ct DE73 . . . . 232 F1
Staffa Dr DE55 . . . . 147 F5
Stafford Cl
  Dronfield S18 . . . . 56 C2
  8 Glossop SK13 . . . . . 17 F8
  Smalley DE7 . . . . 192 F6
Stafford Cres DE4 . . . . 165 F2
Stafford Ho DE24 . . . . . 232 E6
Stafford St
  Derby DE1 . . . . 267 A3
  Long Eaton NG10 . . . . 236 F8
  New Mills SK22 . . . . . . 24 C1
Staines Cl DE3 . . . . 217 C2
Stainforth St NG19 . . . 136 C2
Stainsbro' La DE4, DE6 . 165 B6
Stainsby Ave
  Heanor DE75 . . . . 193 E8
  Horsley Woodhouse DE7 . 192 E6

Stainsby Cl S42 . . . . . 132 F8
Stainsby Gr NG17 . . . . 148 F2
Stainsby Mill* S44 . . . . 133 D7
Staithes Wlk DE21 . . . . 205 C1
Staker La DE3 . . . . 230 D6
Stalybridge Ctry Pk* SK15 . 4 A2
Stalybridge Rd
  Mottram in L SK14 . . . . 9 A4
  Mottram in L SK14 . . . . 9 A4
Stamford Cl NG10 . . . . 236 E4
Stamford St
  Awsworth NG16 . . . . . 195 C4
  Derby DE24 . . . . 232 D6
  Heanor DE75 . . . . 181 E2
  2 Ilkeston DE7 . . . . . 194 E1
Stamps Cl DE15 . . . . . 248 C3
Stanage Gn DE3 . . . . . 217 F1
Stanage Rise S12 . . . . . 44 E5
Stanage Way S40 . . . . . 94 F5
Stancliffe Ave DE4 . . . . 127 C3
Stancliffe Hall Sch DE4 . 127 B5
Stancliffe View DE4 . . . 127 B3
Standing Butts Cl DE12 . 259 D8
Standlow La DE6 . . . . . 163 C2
Stand Park East S41 . . . 96 B1
Stand Rd S41 . . . . 95 F7
Stanedge Rd DE45 . . . . 109 B6
Stanford Rd S18 . . . . . . 56 C1
Stanford Way S40 . . . . 114 B8
Stanhope Glade DE15 . . 256 A8
Stanhope Gn DE15 . . . . 248 F1
Stanhope Rd
  Derby DE3 . . . . 217 E3
  Sheffield S12 . . . . 44 C5
  Swadlincote DE11 . . . . 256 B3
Stanhope St
  Bramley-Vale S44 . . . . 117 E1
  Burton u T DE15 . . . . . 248 B3
  Derby DE23 . . . . 219 A2
  Ilkeston DE7 . . . . 209 A6
  Long Eaton NG10 . . . . 236 D8
  Stanton-by-D NG10 . . . 222 E8
Stanier Way
  Derby DE21 . . . . 220 A3
  Renishaw S21 . . . . 60 B1
Staniforth Ave S21 . . . . 59 B3
Stanleigh Gdns DE12 . . 265 E8
Stanleigh Ho DE12 . . . . 265 E8
Stanleigh Rd DE12 . . . . 262 B4
Stanley Ave
  Ripley DE5 . . . . 169 E2
  Staveley S43 . . . . 97 B7
Stanley Cl
  Derby DE22 . . . . 218 F8
  Ilkeston DE7 . . . . 208 E7
  Netherseal DE12 . . . . . 264 F7
  Woodville DE11 . . . . . 256 F3
Stanley Common CE Prim
  Sch DE7 . . . . 193 B1
Stanley Cres ST14 . . . . 210 A2
Stanley Ct NG16 . . . . . 182 F1
Stanley Hall La SK12 . . . 32 C6
Stanley La S44, NG17 . . 133 D2
Stanley Rd
  Derby, Allenton DE24 . . 232 F6
  Derby, Cherrytree Hill
  DE21 . . . . 220 A5
  Sheffield S8 . . . . 43 B5
Stanley St
  Chesterfield S41 . . . . . 96 C2
  Derby DE22 . . . . 218 D5
  Ilkeston DE7 . . . . 208 F7
  Killamarsh S21 . . . . . . 60 D7
  Long Eaton NG10 . . . . 236 E7
  Somercotes DE55 . . . . 170 D8
  Swadlincote DE11 . . . . 262 A8
Stanshope La DE6 . . . . 149 C2
Stanstead Rd DE3 . . . . 217 C3
Stanton Cl DE4 . . . . . . 127 B3
Stanton Cres DE56 . . . 179 B4
Stanton Gate DE7 . . . . 209 C1
Stanton Hill DE73 . . . . 251 C5
Stanton in Peak CE Prim Sch
  DE4 . . . . 126 C5
Stanton La
  Ellastone DE6 . . . . . . 183 C4
  Mayfield DE6 . . . . 172 A2
Stanton Moor View DE4 . 142 F7
Stanton Pl NG19 . . . . . 134 F7
Stanton Prim Sch DE15 . 255 B5
Stanton Rd
  Ashbourne DE6 . . . . . 185 D8
  Burton u T DE15 . . . . . 254 F7
  Ilkeston DE7 . . . . 208 F7
  Sandiacre NG10 . . . . . 223 A7
Stanton St
  Derby DE23 . . . . 218 F1
  New Houghton NG19 . . 134 F7
Stanton Vale Sch NG10 . 236 C4
Stanton View DE45 . . . 109 C4
Stanwood Dr S40 . . . . . 114 B8
Stanyforth St SK13 . . . . 10 A4
Stapleford La NG9 . . . . 223 F3
Stapleford Rd NG9 . . . . 209 D3
Stapleton Rd DE7 . . . . . 194 E4
Starch La NG10 . . . . . . 223 C7
Starcross Ct DE21 . . . . 217 C3
Starflower Way DE7 . . . 217 F5
Starkholmes Rd DE4 . . 143 C2
Starkie Ave DE74 . . . . . 246 F3
Starthe Bank DE75 . . . . 181 F1
Starth La DE4 . . . . 144 A3
Start La SK23 . . . . 45 B7
Statham Ave S42 . . . . . 131 C8
Statham St DE22 . . . . . 218 E7

Station App
Ambergate DE56 . . . . .167 F4
Buxton SK17 . . . . .85 B8
Derby DE1 . . . . .267 B4
Duffield DE56 . . . . .190 F4
Hathersage S32 . . . . .53 A7
Station Back La S41 . . . .266 C3
Station Cl
Chellaston DE73 . . . . .232 F1
Kilburn DE56 . . . . .179 F1
Station Cotts DE6 . . . . . .225 E2
Station Ct 3 DE7 . . . . . .194 E1
Station Dr DE12 . . . . . . .262 F4
Station Hill NG19 . . . . . .136 B3
Station La
Chesterfield S41, S43 . . . . . .77 C2
Codnor DE5 . . . . .181 B6
Walton-on-t DE12 . . . . .253 D1
Station La Ind Est S41 . . .77 B2
Station New Rd S42 . . . .131 D7
Station Rd
Ashbourne DE6 . . . . .173 B1
Awsworth NG16 . . . . .195 C5
Bakewell DE45 . . . . .109 E6
Bamford S33 . . . . .40 B2
Barrow Hill S43 . . . . .78 B3
Bolsover S44 . . . . .98 F2
Borrowash DE72 . . . . .221 B1
Breadsall DE21 . . . . .205 E4
Brimington, Hollingwood
 S43 . . . . .78 A2
Brimington S43 . . . . .96 D8
Burton u T DE13 . . . . .253 A1
Buxton SK17 . . . . .85 B7
Castle Donington DE74 . . . .247 C5
Chapel-en-le-F SK23 . . . . . .47 B6
Chellaston DE73 . . . . .232 F1
Chesterfield, Old Whittington
 S41 . . . . .77 A1
Chesterfield S41 . . . . .266 C3
Chinley SK23 . . . . .34 D2
Clowne S43 . . . . .80 E4
Darley Dale DE4 . . . . .127 C2
Derby Village DE65 . . . . . . .180 B3
Derby DE3 . . . . .217 D3
Derby, Spondon DE21 . . . . .220 D3
Dove Holes SK17 . . . . .47 F1
Draycott DE72 . . . . .235 B7
Duffield DE56 . . . . .190 F4
Furness Vale SK23 . . . . .33 D4
Glossop SK13 . . . . .10 A5
Great Longstone DE45 . . . . .89 F3
Hathersage S32 . . . . .53 A7
Hatton DE65 . . . . .239 D8
Hayfield, Birch Vale SK22 . . .25 A2
Hayfield SK22 . . . . .25 D2
Hope S33 . . . . .39 B3
Ilkeston DE7 . . . . .194 F1
Ironville NG16 . . . . .170 F3
Killamarsh S21 . . . . .60 A6
Kimberley NG16 . . . . .195 F6
Langley Mill NG16 . . . . . . .182 B2
Little Eaton DE21 . . . . .205 C7
Long Eaton NG10 . . . . .236 F8
Marple SK6 . . . . .23 A7
Marple, Strines SK6, SK2 . . .23 D1
Melbourne DE73 . . . . .252 C8
New Mills SK22 . . . . .33 B3
North Wingfield S42 . . . . . .131 E6
Pilsley S45 . . . . .132 D1
Renishaw S21 . . . . .60 A2
Rolleston DE13 . . . . .240 C4
Sandiacre NG10 . . . . .223 C5
Scarcliffe S44 . . . . .118 F6
Selston NG16 . . . . .160 E1
Sheffield S20 . . . . .59 E7
Shirebrook NG20 . . . . .119 E6
Spinkhill S21 . . . . .60 D2
Stanley DE7 . . . . .207 C6
Stonebroom DE55 . . . . . . .147 B5
Tibshelf DE55 . . . . .147 F6
West Hallam DE7 . . . . .207 C8
Whaley Bridge SK23 . . . . . . .34 A1
Whitwell S80 . . . . .82 A5
Woodville DE11 . . . . .256 F2
Station St
Ashbourne DE6 . . . . .173 B1
Cossall DE7 . . . . .195 A1
Glossop SK13 . . . . .10 D1
Long Eaton NG10 . . . . .236 E7
Mansfield Woodhouse
 NG19 . . . . .136 B3
Swadlincote DE11 . . . . .261 F8
Station View NG10 . . . . .223 C6
Station Wlk 1 SK17 . . . . .85 D8
Station Yd DE7 . . . . .252 C8
Staton La S18 . . . . .58 A1
Staunton Ave DE23 . . . . .231 E6
Staunton Cl
Castle Donington DE74 . . . .247 A4
Chesterfield S40 . . . . .115 A6
**Staunton Harold Resr Visitor
Ctr*** DE73 . . . . .251 F5
Staunton La DE7 . . . . . . .251 A1
Staveley Cl DE24 . . . . . . .232 E3
Staveley Jun Sch S43 . . . .78 E1
Staveley La
Barrow Hill S21, S43 . . . . . . .78 A5
Eckington S21 . . . . .59 E2
Staveley S21 . . . . .78 E7
Staveley Rd
Chesterfield S43 . . . . .77 E3
Long Duckmanton S44 . . . . .97 E4
Poolsbrook S43 . . . . .98 A8
Sheffield S8 . . . . .43 A7
Staverton Dr DE3 . . . . . .217 D4
Stead Mews S21 . . . . .59 D3
Stead St S21 . . . . .59 D3

Steam Mill La DE5 . . . . .170 A1
Steel's La S44 . . . . .118 B6
Steele Ave S43 . . . . .97 B6
Steele Ct SK17 . . . . .85 A8
Steel La S44 . . . . .99 D3
Steeping Cl S43 . . . . .96 E8
Steep La S42 . . . . .114 A4
Steeple Cl DE21 . . . . .205 E2
Steeple Dr DE5 . . . . .180 E8
Steeple End Fold SK22 . . .25 D2
Steeplegate S40 . . . . .266 B3
Steeple Grange DE4 . . . . .154 F3
Steeple Grange Light Rly*
 DE4 . . . . .154 F4
Steep Turnpike DE4 . . . . .143 C5
Steetley La S80 . . . . .63 E3
Stenson Ave DE23 . . . . . .231 E6
Stenson Ct DE5 . . . . .169 F1
**Stenson Fields Prim Com
 Sch** DE24 . . . . .231 D2
Stenson Rd DE23, DE24 . .231 D4
Stenton Rd S8 . . . . .56 F7
Stephenson Cl S40 . . . . . .95 B2
Stephenson Pl
Chesterfield S40 . . . . .266 B3
Clay Cross S45 . . . . .131 D3
Stephenson Rd S43 . . . . . .78 E1
Stephensons Way DE21 . .220 A3
Stephens Rd DE14 . . . . . .254 B8
Stepping Cl DE22 . . . . . . .218 E5
Stepping La DE22 . . . . . . .218 E5
Sterland St S40 . . . . .95 E3
Sterling Cl DE5 . . . . .180 B2
Sterndale Cl SK17 . . . . . . .69 E3
Sterndale Ho 3 DE7 . . . .267 B2
Sterndale La SK17 . . . . . . .69 E3
Sterndale Moor SK17 . . . .105 E6
Sterndale Rd NG10 . . . . .236 B6
Sterry Cl S43 . . . . .80 E2
Stevenage Cl DE24 . . . . . .232 F5
Steven Cl NG19 . . . . .223 F4
Stevens La DE72 . . . . .235 B8
Stevenson Ave DE72 . . . . .235 B8
Stevenson Ho S41 . . . . . . .96 B6
Stevenson Jun Sch NG9 . .223 F8
Stevenson Pl DE23 . . . . . .231 B8
Stevenson Rd DE6 . . . . . .224 B8
Stevens Rd NG10 . . . . . . .223 A5
Steward Gate S33 . . . . . . .40 A6
Stewart Cl
Burton u T DE14 . . . . .254 A6
Derby DE21 . . . . .220 E6
Stewart St DE55 . . . . .170 D5
Stile Croft DE4 . . . . .154 D5
Stiles Cl SK13 . . . . .9 E5
Stiles Rd DE24 . . . . .233 B8
Stillman Cl S41 . . . . .115 C8
Stinting La
Mansfield NG19 . . . . .136 E2
Shirebrook NG20 . . . . .119 D3
Stirland St DE5 . . . . .170 B1
Stirling Cl
Castle Gresley DE11 . . . . . .255 F1
Derby DE21 . . . . .219 D8
Stirling Ct S41 . . . . .266 B4
Stirling Gr NG16 . . . . . . .195 E7
Stirling Way S2 . . . . .44 A8
Stockbrook Rd DE22 . . . .218 D3
Stockbrook St DE22 . . . . .218 E4
Stockdove Cl DE24 . . . . . .231 D4
Stocker Ave DE24 . . . . . . .233 D7
Stock La S14 . . . . .224 C1
Stockley La S44 . . . . .117 C1
Stockley View S44 . . . . . .118 B8
Stockport Rd
Broadbottom SK14 . . . . .15 D8
Marple SK6 . . . . .23 A6
Stocks Brow SK13 . . . . . . .10 A7
Stocks Green Cl S17 . . . . . .55 D4
Stocks Green Dr S17 . . . . .55 D4
Stocks Rd NG16 . . . . .195 E7
Stocks The SK13 . . . . .10 A7
Stockton Dr DE24 . . . . . . .34 E1
Stockwell Ct S40 . . . . . . .114 F7
Stoddard Dr DE75 . . . . . .181 F2
Stodhart Flats SK23 . . . . . .47 C8
Stoke Cl DE56 . . . . .179 A2
Stollard St S45 . . . . .131 D4
Stone Bank Ct S18 . . . . . . .57 B1
Stonebench La SK17 . . . . .106 C3
Stone Bench Way SK17 . . .85 E8
Stonebridge La NG20 . . . .101 A1
Stonebroom Ind Est
 DE55 . . . . .147 B4
Stonebroom La DE55 . . . .147 B5
Stonebroom Prim Sch
 DE55 . . . . .147 A4
Stonechat Cl DE3 . . . . . . .218 A3
Stone Cl
Derby DE21 . . . . .220 E6
Dronfield S18 . . . . .57 C3
Stonecliff Terr SK17 . . . . . .85 C8
Stone Cotts DE6 . . . . .184 E8
Stonecroft Rd S17 . . . . . . .55 F5
Stonedale Cl S20 . . . . .59 D7
Stone Fronts DE73 . . . . . .251 A4
Stonegravels Croft 7
 S20 . . . . .59 E6
Stonegravels La S41 . . . . . .96 A5
Stonegravels Way S20 . . . .59 F6
Stonehedges SK23 . . . . . . .45 C8
Stoneheads Rise SK23 . . . .45 D8
Stonehill Rd DE4 . . . . . . .247 B2
Stone Hill Rd DE23 . . . . . .218 F1
Stoneholes Dr S45 . . . . . .131 E2
Stone La
Chesterfield S43 . . . . .77 D4

Stone La continued
Sheffield S13 . . . . .44 F5
Stoneleigh Way DE55 . . . .169 F8
Stoneley Cl S12 . . . . .44 B1
Stoneley Cres S12 . . . . . . .44 B1
Stoneley Dell S12 . . . . . . .44 B1
Stoneley Dr S12 . . . . .44 B1
Stone Low S18 . . . . .57 C2
Stonelow Cl S18 . . . . .57 B2
Stonelow Jun Sch S18 . . . .57 C2
Stonelow Rd S18 . . . . .57 C2
Stone Mdws NG10 . . . . . .236 C5
Stonepit La DE6 . . . . .164 A3
Stone Rd S18 . . . . .57 C3
Stoneridge S13 . . . . .9 F5
Stone Row
Chesterfield S40 . . . . .95 D2
Marple SK6 . . . . .23 A6
Stonerows La S45 . . . . . . .145 C6
Stonesby Cl DE21 . . . . . . .205 F2
Stonesdale Ct 1 DE24 . . .233 C6
Stones La DE4 . . . . .156 F1
Stone St S20 . . . . .59 D7
Stones The S33 . . . . .38 B2
Stonewell La SK17 . . . . . .137 D5
Stoney Cl DE45 . . . . .109 D4
Stoneycroft La S42 . . . . . .114 A5
Stoney Cross DE21 . . . . . .220 E3
Stoneydale Cl DE7 . . . . . .209 A5
Stoneyfield Bank DE56 . . .179 A5
Stoney Flatts Cres DE23 . .231 B6
Stoney Furlong Rd DE45 . .91 E6
Stoney Gate Rd DE21 . . . .220 D3
Stoney Hill DE4 . . . . .155 B2
Stoney La
Appleby Magna DE12 . . . . .265 F1
Ashover S42 . . . . .130 C3
Brinsley NG16 . . . . .182 D6
Derby DE21 . . . . .220 E5
Hognaston DE6 . . . . .164 A2
Selston NG16 . . . . .171 E7
Trowell NG9 . . . . .209 B5
**Stoney Middleton CE Prim
 Sch** S32 . . . . .71 F3
Stoney Way DE4 . . . . .143 C4
Stoney Wood Dr DE4 . . . .156 C1
Stonyhurst Ct DE24 . . . . .232 E3
Stony Ridge Rd S11 . . . . . .54 C5
Stoodley Pike Gdns
 DE22 . . . . .204 C2
Stoops Cl S40 . . . . .95 D6
Stoppard Cl DE7 . . . . .194 D2
Storer La DE4 . . . . .166 B3
Stores Rd DE21 . . . . .267 D4
Storforth La S41 . . . . .115 B7
Storforth Lane Terr S41 . .115 C8
Storforth Lane Trad Est
 S40 . . . . .115 B8
Stormont Cl DE15 . . . . . . .160 B4
Stormont Gr S43 . . . . .97 C7
Stornoway Cl 9 DE24 . . .231 D3
Storrs Rd S40 . . . . .95 B2
Storth Bank S13 . . . . .16 F7
Storthfield Way DE55 . . . .160 B4
Storth La DE55 . . . . .160 B4
Storth Meadow Rd SK13 . .16 F7
Stort Sq NG19 . . . . .136 D2
Stour Cl
Brimington S43 . . . . .96 E8
Hilton DE65 . . . . .240 E8
Stourdale Cl NG10 . . . . . .236 A6
Stourport Dr DE73 . . . . . .233 A3
Stow Cl 6 NG19 . . . . .136 E3
Stowmarket Dr DE21 . . . .219 D8
Stradbroke Ave S13 . . . . . .44 D7
Stradbroke Cl S13 . . . . . . .44 E7
Stradbroke Cres S13 . . . . .44 E7
Stradbroke Dr S13 . . . . . . .44 E7
Stradbroke Pl S13 . . . . . . .44 E7
Stradbroke Prim Sch S13 . .44 D7
Stradbroke Rd S13 . . . . . . .44 E6
Stradbroke Rise S40 . . . . .114 C8
Stradbroke Way S13 . . . . . .44 E7
Stradbroke Wlk S13 . . . . . .44 D7
Strand DE1 . . . . .267 B3
Strand Arc DE1 . . . . .267 B3
Stranfaer Cl DE55 . . . . . . .170 A7
Stranraer Cl NG19 . . . . . .136 C6
Stratford Cl DE65 . . . . . . .242 D1
Stratford Rd DE21 . . . . . .205 D2
Stratford St DE7 . . . . .194 F4
Strathallan Cl DE4 . . . . . .127 C4
Strathaven Ct DE21 . . . . . .220 E5
Strathglen Cl NG16 . . . . . .195 C7
Strathmore Ave DE24 . . . .233 A6
Stratton Rd S44 . . . . .99 A2
Strawberry Bank NG17 . . .148 E4
Strawberry La
Blackfordby DE11 . . . . .257 B1
Rosliston DE12 . . . . .260 D5
Strawberry Lee La S17 . . . .55 B5
Straw La
Clay Cross DE55 . . . . .146 D8
Shirland DE55 . . . . .146 D8
Streatham Rd DE22 . . . . . .218 B6
Street Farm La S26 . . . . . . .61 E6
Streetfield Cres S20 . . . . . .59 D6
Streetfields S20 . . . . .59 D6
Street Forest Walks The*
 S17 . . . . .64 C4
Street La DE5 . . . . .180 B6
Street Lane Prim Sch
 DE5 . . . . .180 B5
Street The SK10, SK17 . . . .64 C5
Strelley Ave DE5 . . . . .180 C8
Stretfield Rd S33 . . . . .39 B1

Strettea La DE55 . . . . . . .146 C2
Stretton Brook Sch
 DE13 . . . . .240 C1
Stretton Cl DE3 . . . . .217 D1
**Stretton Handley CE Prim
 Sch** DE55 . . . . .145 D7
Stretton Rd
Clay Cross S45 . . . . .131 C1
Shirland DE55 . . . . .146 C8
Stonebroom DE55 . . . . . . .146 E5
Stretton View DE12 . . . . .265 F6
Striding Edge Cl 4
 NG10 . . . . .223 B2
Strines Rd
Marple SK6 . . . . .23 B3
New Mills SK6 . . . . .32 D8
Strines Sta SK6 . . . . .23 D1
Stroma Cl DE24 . . . . .231 F4
Strutt's Park Ho 2 DE22 .218 F7
Strutt St
Belper DE56 . . . . .178 F3
Derby DE23 . . . . .219 A2
Stuart Cl S41 . . . . .96 C6
Stuart St DE1 . . . . .267 B4
Stubben Edge La S45 . . . .130 C2
Stubbing Rd S40 . . . . .114 F7
Stubbins La S33 . . . . .34 D2
Stubbins Wood NG20 . . . .119 C6
Stubbins Wood La NG20 . .119 C6
Stubbin Wood Sch NG20 . .119 F6
Stubley La S18 . . . . .56 E2
Stubley Croft S18 . . . . .56 D2
Stubley Dr S18 . . . . .56 E2
Stubley Hollow S18 . . . . . .56 F3
Stubley La S18 . . . . .56 E2
Stubley Pl S18 . . . . .56 E2
Stubwood Hollow ST14 . .196 D5
Stubwood La ST14 . . . . . .196 D4
Studbrook Cl DE74 . . . . . .246 F3
Studfarm Cl DE73 . . . . . . .252 E2
Studios The S40 . . . . .95 E3
Studland Cl NG19 . . . . . . .136 D6
Sturge Croft 3 S2 . . . . . . .43 B6
Sturges La DE72 . . . . .233 F4
Sturston Rd DE6 . . . . .173 C1
Sudbury Ave
Ilkeston DE7 . . . . .209 B7
Sandiacre NG10 . . . . .223 A6
Sudbury Cl
Chesterfield S40 . . . . .95 B5
Derby DE1 . . . . .218 E5
Sudbury Ct NG10 . . . . . . .235 F4
Sudbury Dr NG17 . . . . . . .148 E2
**Sudbury Hall & Mus of
 Childhood*** DE6 . . . . . . .225 D5
Sudbury Mews NG16 . . . .182 E1
Sudbury Pk DE6 . . . . .225 D7
Sudbury Prim Sch DE6 . . .225 E4
Sudbury St DE1 . . . . .218 E5
Sudhall Cl S41 . . . . .95 D8
Suff La NG16 . . . . .160 C3
Suffolk Ave DE21 . . . . . . .219 E7
Suffolk Rd DE15 . . . . .254 D7
Sugworth Rd S6 . . . . .31 F6
Sulleys Field DE22 . . . . . . .204 D7
Sullivan Cl DE23 . . . . .231 E7
Summerbottom SK14 . . . . .16 A8
Summerbrook Ct DE22 . . .218 F4
Summer Cross SK17 . . . . . .69 B4
Summer Dr DE4 . . . . .165 E7
Summerfield Cres S43 . . . .96 E8
Summerfield Rd
Chesterfield S40 . . . . .266 A1
Dronfield S18 . . . . .57 B3
Summerfields Way DE7 . . .194 D3
Summerfields Way S
 DE7 . . . . .194 D2
Summer La
Sheffield S17 . . . . .55 D4
Wirksworth DE4 . . . . .165 E8
Summerley Lower Rd S18 . .57 F2
Summerley Rd S18 . . . . . . .57 F2
Summerskill Gn S43 . . . . . .97 C7
Summerville Cl DE23 . . . . .231 B6
Summer Wood Ct DE23 . . .231 D7
Summerwood La S18 . . . . . .56 F3
Summerwood Pl S18 . . . . .56 F2
Summit Dr NG20 . . . . .119 E4
Sumners Pl SK13 . . . . .10 B1
Sumner St SK13 . . . . .17 C8
Sunart Cl DE24 . . . . .231 F2
Sundew Cl DE21 . . . . .220 F4
Sundial Cl DE6 . . . . .201 E8
Sundial Wlk DE6 . . . . .201 E8
Sundown Cl DE24 . . . . . . .231 D6
Sundown Cl SK22 . . . . .33 A8
Sundown Pl S13 . . . . .44 F8
Sundown Rd S13 . . . . .44 F8
Sunflower Cl
Derby DE24 . . . . .220 A1
Shirebrook NG20 . . . . .119 D3
Sun La DE4 . . . . .156 F1
Sunlea Cres SK13 . . . . .17 B8
Sunlaws St SK13 . . . . .17 B8
Sunlea Cres NG9 . . . . .223 F5
Sunningdale Ave
Derby DE21 . . . . .220 D5
Heanor DE75 . . . . .193 F8
Sunningdale Cl
Burton u T S42 . . . . .115 C1
Chesterfield S40 . . . . .114 E8
Sunningdale Dr
Glossop SK13 . . . . .10 E1
Ilkeston DE7 . . . . .208 B5
Sunningdale Rise S40 . . . .114 C8
Sunninghill Cl DE7 . . . . . .207 D8
Sunnybank DE4 . . . . .110 F1

Sunny Bank
Great Longstone DE45 . . . . .90 A4
Mayfield DE6 . . . . .184 C7
Tibshelf DE55 . . . . .147 F5
Sunny Bank Gdns DE56 . .178 F2
Sunny Bank La S17 . . . . . . .69 C4
Sunny Banks 3 SK13 . . . . .17 B8
Sunny Brook Cl S43 . . . . . .80 E3
Sunnyfield SK17 . . . . .85 F1
Sunny Gr DE21 . . . . .220 A5
Sunny Hill DE56 . . . . .190 F7
Sunnyhill Ave DE23 . . . . . .231 E6
Sunnyhill Inf Sch DE23 . . .231 E7
Sunnyside
Swadlincote DE11 . . . . .255 E7
Whitwell S80 . . . . .82 A6
Sunnyside Cl DE11 . . . . . .255 E7
Sunnyside St S14 . . . . .210 B1
Sunnyside Terr S44 . . . . . .143 A8
Sunny Springs S41 . . . . . .266 B4
Sunnyvale Ave S17 . . . . . . .55 E4
Sunnyvale Rd S17 . . . . .55 D4
Sun St
Derby DE22 . . . . .267 A2
Woodville DE11 . . . . .256 F2
Surbiton Cl DE22 . . . . . . .218 A6
Surbiton Ct DE7 . . . . .207 D8
Surgery La DE4 . . . . .157 A1
Surprise Villas S32 . . . . . . .53 A7
Surrey St
Derby DE22 . . . . .267 A2
Glossop SK13 . . . . .10 C1
Sussex Cir DE21 . . . . .219 E8
Sussex Cl NG16 . . . . .195 A8
Sussex Rd DE15 . . . . .254 E6
Sussex Way NG10 . . . . . . .223 B5
Sutherland Rd DE23 . . . . .219 A1
Sutton Ave DE73 . . . . .232 F3
Sutton Cl DE22 . . . . .218 D6
Sutton Cres S43 . . . . .97 C7
Sutton Cl NG16 . . . . .182 F2
Sutton Dr DE24 . . . . .232 E3
Sutton Hall Rd S44 . . . . . .117 E8
Sutton Ho DE24 . . . . .233 C5
Sutton La
Etwall DE65 . . . . .229 B5
Hatton DE65 . . . . .227 E4
Long Duckmanton S44 . . . .116 F3
Sutton Rd
Church Broughton DE65 . . .227 D7
Sutton in A NG17 . . . . .148 F3
Suttons Ave DE11 . . . . . . .256 E3
Suttons Bsns Pk DE11 . . . .256 E3
Sutton Scarsdale Hall*
 S44 . . . . .117 A6
Suttons La SK6 . . . . .23 A5
Sutton View
Bolsover S44 . . . . .118 B8
Temple Normanton S42 . . . .116 B4
Sutton Way SK13 . . . . .10 A5
Swaddale Ave S41 . . . . .96 B6
Swaddale Cl S41 . . . . .96 B6
Swadlincote La DE11, DE12 .255 E3
Swadlincote Rd DE11 . . . .256 E3
Swadlincote Ski Ctr
 DE11 . . . . .255 E4
Swaines Mdw DE11 . . . . . .165 C8
Swainspark Ind Est DE12 .262 B6
Swalebank Cl S40 . . . . . . .115 B8
Swaledale Ct 2 DE24 . . . .233 C6
Swaledale Cl S18 . . . . .218 A3
Swallow Croft DE5 . . . . . .180 D6
Swallow Cl S41 . . . . .180 D6
Swallowdale Rd DE24 . . . .233 C6
Swallow Fold SK13 . . . . . . .16 F8
Swallow Ho DE1 . . . . .218 C5
Swallow House Cres
 SK22 . . . . .25 C3
Swallow House La SK22 . . .25 C3
Swallow Rd DE11 . . . . . . .256 F3
Swanbourne Cl 1 S41 . . . .96 C1
Swan Hill DE3 . . . . .230 B6
Swan La NG19 . . . . .136 B3
Swanmore Rd DE23 . . . . . .231 A8
Swann Yd NG17 . . . . .148 F3
Swanson Ave NG17 . . . . . .148 F3
Swans Rest DE11 . . . . .255 F6
Swanwick Ave NG20 . . . . .119 F3
Swanwick Gdns DE21 . . . .206 A1
Swanwick Hall Sch DE55 .169 F7
Swanwick Junc Sta*
 DE55 . . . . .170 A3
Swanwick Prim Sch
 DE55 . . . . .169 D6
Swanwick Rd DE55 . . . . . .170 B7
Swanwick St S41 . . . . .77 C2
Swarkestone Dr DE23 . . . .231 C5
Swarkestone Rd
Barrow u T DE73 . . . . .244 B6
Chellaston DE73 . . . . .244 F8
Swathwick Cl S42 . . . . . . .114 E4
Swathwick La S42 . . . . . . .114 C4
Swayfield Cl DE3 . . . . .217 C3
Sweetbriar Cl DE24 . . . . . .233 A5
Swift Bank SK13 . . . . .16 F8
Swift Cl
Derby DE3 . . . . .218 A3
Woodville DE11 . . . . .256 F3
Swift Cl NG16 . . . . .182 F2
Swinburne St DE1 . . . . . . .267 B1
Swinderby Dr DE21 . . . . . .206 B1
Swindon Cl NG16 . . . . . . .195 C2
Swiney Way NG9 . . . . .223 F2

Swinger La S45. . . . . 129 C7
Swinney Bank DE56. . . . . 179 A5
Swinney La DE56. . . . . . . 179 A5
Swinscoe Hill DE6. . . . . . 172 B2
Swinscoe Ho 🟦 DE1. . . 267 B2
Swinscoe Way S40. . . . . . 95 A5
Swinson Cl ST14. . . . . . . 197 A3
Swithland La S11. . . . . . . 115 C7
Sycamore Ave
  Chesterfield S40. . . . . . . 95 E2
  Creswell S80. . . . . 81 E2
  Derby DE22. . . . . 204 D3
  Dronfield S18. . . . . 57 A3
  Findern DE65. . . . . 230 E1
  Glapwell S44. . . . . 134 B8
  Ripley DE5. . . . . 180 D8
  Swadlincote DE11. . . . . 256 A7
Sycamore Cl
  Bolsover S44. . . . . 99 C2
  Burton u T DE15. . . . . . 254 E5
  Buxton SK17. . . . . 66 B1
  Etwall DE65. . . . . 229 B1
  Linton DE12. . . . . 261 D5
  Mapperley DE7. . . . . . . 193 F3
  New Mills SK22. . . . . 24 C1
  Pinxton NG16. . . . . 160 D3
  Selston NG16. . . . . 171 D7
  Shirland DE55. . . . . . . 146 C4
Sycamore Cotts DE6. . . . 151 D1
Sycamore Cres NG10. . . 223 A7
Sycamore Ct
  Derby DE21. . . . . 220 E5
  Willington DE65. . . . . . 242 B5
Sycamore Dr
  Calow S44. . . . . 96 E3
  Ilkeston DE7. . . . . 209 B7
  Killamarsh S21. . . . . 60 C5
Sycamore La
  Awsworth NG16. . . . . . 195 C5
  Brimington S43. . . . . 78 A1
  Burton u T DE15. . . . . . 254 F6
  Castle Donington DE74. 247 B5
  Chapel-en-le-F SK23. . . . 47 B4
  Hayfield SK22. . . . . 24 F2
  Long Eaton NG10. . . . . 236 C5
  Mansfield Woodhouse
    NG19. . . . . 136 C5
  Matlock DE4. . . . . 143 B6
  Mayfield DE6. . . . . 184 C7
Sycamore St
  Sheffield S20. . . . . 59 C8
  Shirebrook NG20. . . . . 120 F6
Sycamores The
  Eastwood NG16. . . . . . 182 E1
  Glossop SK13. . . . . 9 F3
  Sheffield S13. . . . . 44 C6
  South Normanton DE55. 160 B5
Sycamore Terr SK22. . . . . 25 D3
Syda La S42. . . . . 93 E1
Syday La S21. . . . . 60 D1
Sydenham Rd DE22. . . . 218 A7
Sydney Cl
  Derby DE3. . . . . 217 F3
  Mansfield Woodhouse
    NG19. . . . . 136 C6
Sydney Rd DE72. . . . . . . 235 A7
Sydney St S40. . . . . 95 E3
Sydnope Hall DE4. . . . . 128 A5
Sydnope Hill DE4. . . . . . 128 A5
Syerscote La DE12. . . . . 263 B2
Sylvan Cl S41. . . . . 266 C1
Sylvan Cliff SK17. . . . . . . 85 C7
Sylvan Dr S42. . . . . 131 A6
Sylvan Pk SK17. . . . . 85 C8
Sylvia Rd S18. . . . . 76 D5
Sywell Cl DE55. . . . . 169 F8

T

Tabley Gdns SK6. . . . . 23 A4
Taddington Cl 🟦 DE21. . 219 E8
Taddington Pl 🟦 SK13. . . 9 E1
Taddington & Priestcliffe
  Sch SK17. . . . . 87 F3
Taddington Rd
  Chesterfield S40. . . . . . . 95 B5
  Derby DE21. . . . . 205 F1
Taft Ave NG10. . . . . 223 B6
Tagg La DE45. . . . . 107 A1
Taggs Knoll S33. . . . . 40 B4
Taghole La DE6. . . . . . . 188 E2
Tailby Dr DE65. . . . . 242 A5
Talbot Cres S41. . . . . . . 115 D7
Talbot Dr NG9. . . . . 209 D2
Talbot Pl DE12. . . . . 265 E8
Talbot Rd SK13. . . . . 10 C2
Talbot Sch S8. . . . . 43 C2
Talbot St
  Chesterfield S41. . . . . . 115 D7
  Derby DE1. . . . . 267 A3
  Glossop SK13. . . . . 10 C1
  Pinxton NG16. . . . . 160 C2
  Swadlincote DE11. . . . . 256 A1
Talgarth Cl DE21. . . . . . 206 C2
Tall Trees Park (Cvn Pk)
  NG19. . . . . 136 C2
Tallys End S43. . . . . 80 A6
Tamar Ave DE22. . . . . . 204 D4
Tamworth Rd
  Appleby Magna DE12. . 265 E2

Tamworth Rd continued
  Castle Donington DE72,
    NG10. . . . . 235 D1
  Long Eaton NG10. . . . . 236 C5
Tamworth Rise DE56. . . 190 E4
Tamworth St DE56. . . . . 190 E3
Tamworth Terr DE56. . . 190 E3
Tamer's La DE65. . . . . . 242 C3
Tansley Ave DE7. . . . . . . 193 A1
Tansley Ct S41. . . . . 95 E6
Tansley Dr S40. . . . . 95 A5
Tansley House Gdns
  DE4. . . . . 144 A4
Tansley Prim Sch DE4. . 144 A4
Tansley Rd S42. . . . . 131 F5
Tansley Rise 🟦 DE4. . . 205 F1
Tansley Way S43. . . . . . . 97 C6
Tansley Wood Ho DE4. . 143 E5
Tants Mdw DE55. . . . . . 191 F6
Tantum Ave DE75. . . . . 181 C4
Tanyard Cl DE74. . . . . . 247 B4
Tap La S40. . . . . 266 A3
Taplow Cl DE3. . . . . 217 C2
Tapton Bsns Ctr S41. . . . 266 C3
Tapton La S41. . . . . 266 C3
Tapton Lock Hill S41. . . . 96 B6
Tapton Lock Visitor Ctr*
  S41. . . . . 96 B6
Tapton Terr S41. . . . . . . 266 C4
Tapton View Rd S41. . . . . 96 C5
Tapton View Rd S41. . . . . 95 F5
Tapton Way S43. . . . . 96 F3
Tarina Cl DE73. . . . . 233 A1
Tarn Cl NG16. . . . . 182 B4
Tarnside Fold 🟦 SK13. . . 17 A7
Tarquin Cl DE13. . . . . . 240 E2
Tasman Cl DE3. . . . . 217 F3
Tatenhill La
  Branston DE14. . . . . . 253 D7
  Tatenhill DE13. . . . . . . 253 A8
Tatham's La DE7. . . . . . 194 E2
Tattersall Wlk 🟦 NG19. . 136 E4
Tattle Hill DE7. . . . . 207 F2
Tatwin Ct DE73. . . . . . . 252 F2
Taunton Cl DE24. . . . . . 233 C8
Taverners Cres DE23. . . 231 C8
Tavern Rd SK13. . . . . 9 E3
Tavistock Ave DE5. . . . . 169 D2
Tavistock Cl 🟦 DE24. . 231 D3
Tavistock Ct S41. . . . . . . 95 F8
Tavistock Sq DE55. . . . . 159 B5
Tawney Croft DE4. . . . . 144 A4
Tawny Way DE23. . . . . . 231 A7
Taxal & Fernilee CE Prim Sch
  SK23. . . . . 45 C6
Taxal Moor Rd SK23. . . . 45 C3
Tayberry Ct DE24. . . . . . 232 E7
Tay Cl
  Derby DE24. . . . . 231 D2
  Dronfield S18. . . . . 56 D2
Taylor's La
  Spout DE4. . . . . 166 B4
  Trusley DE6. . . . . 215 E6
Taylor Cres
  Chesterfield S41. . . . . . . 96 D1
  Stapleford NG9. . . . . . . 223 F8
Taylor Ct DE6. . . . . 173 C1
Taylor La DE75. . . . . 181 D4
Taylors La S14. . . . . 196 D4
Taylor St
  Derby DE24. . . . . 219 E2
  Hollingworth SK14. . . . . . 9 D4
  Ilkeston DE7. . . . . 194 F1
Tayside Cl DE24. . . . . . . 231 D3
Tay Wlk DE22. . . . . 204 E3
Tealby Wlk 🟦 NG19. . . 136 E4
Teal Cl NG20. . . . . 119 D3
Tean Cl DE15. . . . . 248 A1
Teasel Dr DE11. . . . . . . 256 F4
Tedder Ave SK17. . . . . . . 85 D3
Tedgness Rd S32. . . . . . . 53 E1
Tedworth Ave DE21. . . 231 D2
Teesdale Rd
  Long Eaton NG10. . . . . 236 A6
  Sheffield S12. . . . . 58 F8
Telford Cl DE3. . . . . 217 E1
Telford Cres S43. . . . . . . 78 F2
Telford Rd SK6. . . . . 23 A4
Telmah Cl DE13. . . . . . . 240 D1
Temperance Hill DE55. . 145 E7
Temperance Sq SK14. . . . 9 A4
Temperance St 🟦 SK14. . 16 A8
Templar Cl DE24. . . . . . 231 E3
Temple Ave SK13. . . . . . . 10 C5
Templebell Cl DE23. . . . 231 A6
Temple Ct SK17. . . . . 85 A6
Temple Normanton Bsns Pk
  S41. . . . . 116 A4
Temple Normanton Prim Sch
  S42. . . . . 116 C4
Temple Rd
  Buxton SK17. . . . . 85 A6
  Matlock Bath DE4. . . . 143 A1
Temple St
  Derby DE23. . . . . 219 A3
  Glossop SK13. . . . . 10 C5
Temple View SK17. . . . . . 85 C7
Temple Wlk DE4. . . . . . 143 A1
Tenant St DE1. . . . . 267 B3
Tenby Dr DE21. . . . . . . 206 C2
Ten Foot Cl SK13. . . . . . . 10 B2
Tennessee Rd DE21. . . . 220 B7
Tennyson Ave
  Chesterfield S40. . . . . . 266 A3
  Mansfield Woodhouse
    NG19. . . . . 136 C2
  Swadlincote DE11. . . . . 256 C6
Tennyson Rd S80. . . . . . . 81 D1

Tennyson Sq NG16. . . . . 195 C4
Tennyson St
  Derby DE24. . . . . 232 D7
  Holmewood S42. . . . . . 116 D1
  Ilkeston DE7. . . . . 194 E3
  Shirland DE55. . . . . . . 146 C5
Tennyson Way S42. . . . . 115 E3
Tenter Cl NG10. . . . . . . 236 D5
Tenter La DE56. . . . . . . 168 D1
Tern Ave DE11. . . . . 256 F3
Terrace La NG19. . . . . . 134 F5
Terrace Rd
  Buxton SK17. . . . . 85 B7
  Chapel-en-le-F SK23. . . . 47 B6
  Tideswell SK17. . . . . 69 C4
Terret Gr SK17. . . . . 84 D5
Terrey Rd S17. . . . . 55 E5
Terr The DE21. . . . . 219 E7
Terry Pl DE24. . . . . 232 F6
Tetford Wlk 🟦 NG19. . 136 E4
Teversal Ave S44. . . . . . 135 B4
Tevery Cl NG9. . . . . 223 E8
Teviot Pl DE21. . . . . 206 A2
Tewkesbury Ave NG19. . 136 D4
Tewkesbury Cres DE21. . 219 D8
Tewkesbury Dr NG16. . . 195 E7
Tewkesbury Rd NG10. . . 236 E4
Thackeray Rd DE55. . . . 146 F3
Thackeray St DE24. . . . . 232 A5
Thame Ct 🟦 S43. . . . . . . 96 E8
Thames Cl DE22. . . . . . . 217 F5
Thames Way DE65. . . . . 228 D1
Thanet Dr DE24. . . . . . . 233 A6
Thanet St S45. . . . . 131 D3
Thatch Cl DE22. . . . . . . 204 F2
Thatchers La DE4. . . . . . 144 A3
Thatchmarsh Cl NE7. . . 194 F6
Theatre La S41. . . . . 266 C3
Theatre Wlk DE1. . . . . . 267 C3
Theatre Yd S40. . . . . . . 266 B3
Thickley Cl NG20. . . . . . 119 F4
Thimble Hill DE6. . . . . . 188 F7
Thirlmere Ave DE22. . . 204 E3
Thirlmere Cl 🟦 NG10. . 223 B2
Thirlmere Dr S18. . . . . . . 57 A2
Thirlmere Rd
  Chesterfield S41. . . . . . . 95 C7
  Long Eaton NG10. . . . . 223 B2
Thirsk Pl DE24. . . . . 232 D7
Thirteen Row S44. . . . . 118 A6
Thistle Bank NG19. . . . . 136 F4
Thistle Cl
  Eastwood NG16. . . . . . 195 B8
  Woodville DE11. . . . . . 256 F4
Thistledown Cl DE22. . . 205 A2
Thistle Gr DE73. . . . . . . 232 E1
Thistlegreen Cl DE75. . . 182 B1
Thistle Rd DE7. . . . . 209 A4
Thomas Chambers 🟦
  SK13. . . . . 17 C7
Thomas Cl NG16. . . . . . 170 F3
Thomas Cook Cl DE73. . 252 A7
Thomas Ct DE11. . . . . . 218 E4
Thomas St
  Compstall SK6. . . . . 15 B2
  Glossop SK13. . . . . 10 E1
Thompson Cl
  🟦 Chesterfield S41. . . . 96 A8
  Swadlincote DE11. . . . . 256 E4
Thompson St
  Chesterfield S41. . . . . . . 96 A8
  Langley Mill NG16. . . . 182 B3
Thomson Dr DE5. . . . . . 181 B7
Thomson Wlk DE5. . . . . 181 A8
Thoresby Ave
  Clowne S43. . . . . 81 A4
  Shirebrook NG20. . . . . 119 E4
Thoresby Cl
  Derby DE21. . . . . 206 B1
  Ripley DE5. . . . . 169 C1
Thoresby Cres DE72. . . . 234 F7
Thoresby Pl S43. . . . . 97 C6
Thoresby Rd
  Long Eaton NG10. . . . . 236 C6
  Mansfield Woodhouse
    NG19. . . . . 136 A3
Thorn Ave NG19. . . . . . 135 F1
Thornborough Cl S2. . . . . 43 C7
Thornborough Pl S2. . . . . 43 C7
Thornborough Rd S2. . . . 43 C7
Thornbridge Ave S12. . . . 44 D3
Thornbridge Cl S12. . . . . 44 D3
Thornbridge Cres
  Chesterfield S40. . . . . . 115 A6
  Sheffield S12. . . . . 44 D3
Thornbridge Dr S12. . . . . 44 D3
Thornbridge Gr S12. . . . . 44 D3
Thornbridge La S12. . . . . 44 D3
Thornbridge Pl S12. . . . . 44 D3
Thornbridge Rd S12. . . . . 44 D3
Thornbridge Rise S12. . . 44 D3
Thornbridge Way S12. . . 44 D3
Thornbrook Cl SK23. . . . 47 C5
Thornbrook Rd SK23. . . 47 C6
Thorn Cl
  Buxton SK17. . . . . 85 E8
  Derby DE22. . . . . 204 D4
Thorncliffe Ave DE4. . . . 127 A6
Thorncliffe Rd SK13. . . . . 9 F4
Thorncliffe Terr SK17. . . . 85 A7
Thorndene Cl S41. . . . . . 96 A6
Thorndike Ave DE24. . . 233 A7
Thorndon Cl DE3. . . . . . 230 D8
Thorndon Way S40. . . . 114 C8
Thorn Dr NG16. . . . . . . 195 B8
Thorne Cl S42. . . . . 94 F4
Thornecliffewood SK14. . . 9 D5

Thornell Cl SK23. . . . . . . 47 C5
Thornescroft Gdns DE14 254 B8
Thorness Cl DE24. . . . . . 233 C5
Thornewill Dr DE13. . . . 247 F1
Thorneywood Rd NG10. . 236 F8
Thornfield Ave S40. . . . . . 95 B1
Thornfield Sch S41. . . . . . 95 A5
Thornfield Sq NG10. . . . 236 E8
Thornhill Dr DE55. . . . . 160 B6
Thornhill La S33. . . . . . . 39 F4
Thornhill Rd DE23. . . . . 218 C1
Thornley Pl DE6. . . . . . . 173 C1
Thornsett SK22. . . . . 24 E2
Thornsett Ave SK17. . . . . 85 E8
Thornsett Cl S40. . . . . . . 95 A5
Thornsett Gdns S17. . . . . 55 F8
Thornsett Prim Sch SK22 24 E3
Thornsett Trad Est SK22. . 24 E2
Thorn St
  Derby DE23. . . . . 218 F2
  Woodville DE11. . . . . . 256 F2
Thorn Street Mews DE11. . 256 F2
Thornton Pl 🟦 S18. . . . . 56 C1
Thornton Rd DE7. . . . . . 222 F1
Thorntree Cotts DE4. . . 154 F2
Thorntree Ct S40. . . . . . 114 F7
Thorn Tree Gdns NG16. . 182 F4
Thorn Tree La DE11,
  DE15. . . . . 255 F7
Thornway SK6. . . . . 32 A7
Thornwood Ct SK17. . . . . 85 A8
Thorpd Cl S2. . . . . 43 A8
Thorpe's Rd
  Heanor DE75. . . . . 181 D1
  Shipley DE75. . . . . 193 D8
Thorpe Ave
  Dronfield S18. . . . . 57 C4
  Whitwell S80. . . . . 81 F5
Thorpe Cl
  Burton u T DE15. . . . . . 248 C2
  Stapleford NG9. . . . . . . 95 F8
  Stapleford NG9. . . . . . . 223 D7
Thorpe Croft DE4. . . . . 156 B5
Thorpe Downs Rd DE11. 256 B1
Thorpe Dr DE3. . . . . 217 E3
Thorpe Hill Dr DE75. . . . 193 E8
Thorpe House Ave S8. . . . 43 B4
Thorpe House Rd S8. . . . 43 B4
Thorpe House Rise S8. . . 43 B4
Thorpelands Ave NG19. . 136 E1
Thorpelands Dr DE22. . . 204 E1
Thorpe Leys NG10. . . . . 236 D5
Thorpe Rd
  Eastwood NG16. . . . . . 182 F4
  Harthill S26. . . . . 62 A7
Thorpe St
  Glossop SK13. . . . . 10 C2
  Ilkeston DE7. . . . . 194 E3
Thorpe View DE6. . . . . . 185 C8
Thorpe Way DE56. . . . . 179 B5
Thorpleigh Rd S43. . . . . . 79 B2
Three Gates DE6. . . . . . 178 F2
Thrift Rd DE14. . . . . 254 B8
Throstle Nest Way S41. . 201 F8
Thrumpton Ave NG10. . 237 A7
Thrumpton Hall* NG11. . 237 B3
Thrushton Cl DE65. . . . . 230 C2
Thruxton Cl DE24. . . . . . 233 C6
Thunderpit La S32. . . . . . 71 A3
Thurgarton Ct DE6. . . . . 173 D1
Thurgaton Way S15. . . . 148 A3
Thurlby Ct 🟦 NG19. . . . 136 E4
Thurlow Ct DE21. . . . . . 206 A1
Thurman St DE7. . . . . . . 209 A2
Thurrows Way DE73. . . . 233 B2
Thurstan Ave S8. . . . . . . 56 E8
Thurston Ave DE55. . . . 170 D8
Thurstone Furlong DE73. 232 E1
Thurvaston La
  Longford DE6, DE65. . . 214 C3
  Thurvaston DE6. . . . . . 215 A8
Thurvaston Rd DE6. . . . 197 F1
Thyme Cl DE23. . . . . . . 231 D4
Tiber Cl DE24. . . . . 233 D5
Tibshelf Bsns Pk DE55. . 148 C6
Tibshelf Inf Sch DE55. . . 148 A7
Tibshelf Rd
  Blackwell DE55. . . . . . 147 C1
  Holmewood S42. . . . . . 132 E7
Tibshelf Sch DE55. . . . . 148 A7
Tickham Ave DE24. . . . . 231 C2
Tickhall La DE56. . . . . . 180 B1
Ticknall Rd DE11. . . . . . 257 B7
Ticknall Wlk DE23. . . . . 231 E6
Tideswell Bank 🟦 SK13. . . 9 E1
Tideswell Cl S40. . . . . 95 C8
Tideswell Ct 🟦 S40. . . . . 95 C8
Tideswell Gn DE11. . . . . 255 E5
Tideswell La S32. . . . . 71 B6
Tideswell Rd DE21. . . . . 205 F1
Tideswell Wlk 🟦 SK13. . . 9 E1
Tiger Yd 🟦 DE6. . . . . . . 173 B2
Tilbury Pl DE24. . . . . . . 233 A5
Tilford Gdns NG9. . . . . . 223 F6
Tiller Ct DE23. . . . . 231 B6
Tilley Gn DE11. . . . . 255 E5
Tillotson Cl 🟦 S8. . . . . . 43 A6
Tillotson Rise S8. . . . . . . 43 A6
Tilton Dr DE7. . . . . 208 C5
Timber La S45. . . . . 132 D5
Timberbrook Cl DE21. . . 194 D5
Timsbury Ct DE21. . . . . 205 E2
Tinderbox La DE65. . . . . 229 F5
Tinker Croft DE7. . . . . . 208 E7
Tinkerley La DE6. . . . . . 160 D1
Tinkley La S42. . . . . 130 D1

Tinsell Brook DE65. . . . . 228 E1
Tinsley Rd DE756, NG16. . 182 D1
Tintagel Cl
  Burton u T DE13. . . . . . 240 E2
  🟦 Derby DE23. . . . . . 219 B2
Tintwistle CE Prim Sch
  SK13. . . . . 9 F6
Tissington Cl S40. . . . . . . 95 B5
Tissington Cl S40. . . . . . . 10 A7
Tipnall Rd DE74. . . . . . . 247 A3
Tipper's La DE65. . . . . . 227 A8
Tip Tree Cl NG16. . . . . . 195 F7
Tiree Cl
  Derby DE24. . . . . 231 F4
  Stapleford NG9. . . . . . . 209 D2
Tibshelf DE55. . . . . 147 F5
Tissington Bank 🟦 S13. . . 9 D1
Tissington Cl S40. . . . . . . 95 B5
Tissington Dr DE21. . . . 206 B3
Tissington Gn 🟦 SK13. . . 9 D1
Tissington Terr 🟦 S13. . . 9 D1
Titchfield Ave NG19. . . . 136 D3
Titchfield St
  Creswell S80. . . . . 81 F1
  Whitwell S80. . . . . 81 E2
Tithe Barn Cl SK17. . . . . 69 C3
Tithebarn La DE6. . . . . 215 C5
Tiverton Cl DE3. . . . . . . 217 D4
Tiverton Ct 🟦 S41. . . . . . 95 F8
Tivoli Gdns DE1. . . . . . . 218 E7
Toadmoor La DE56. . . . 167 F3
Tobermory Way DE24. . 231 D3
Toddbrook Cl SK23. . . . . 45 D6
Todd St SK13. . . . . 17 D8
Toll Bar Ave S12. . . . . . . 43 E5
Toll Bar Cl S12. . . . . 43 E5
Toll Bar Dr S12. . . . . 43 E5
Toll Bar Rd S12. . . . . 43 E5
Tollbridge Rd S43. . . . . . 79 B2
Tollemache Cl SK14. . . . . . 9 A5
Tollemache Rd SK14. . . . . 9 A5
Tollgate Cotts DE6. . . . . 184 E8
Toll House Mead S20. . . . 59 C7
Tom Brads Croft SK23. . . 45 E8
Tom La
  Chapel-en-le-F SK23. . . . 46 D5
  Staveley S44. . . . . 97 F5
Tomlinson Bsns Pk DE65 226 F4
Tomlinson Ct DE24. . . . 232 F7
Tomlinson Ind Est DE21. 205 C2
Tomlinsons Cotts DE21. . 205 C2
Tomwood Rise SK13. . . . 16 C6
Tonbridge Dr DE24. . . . 233 A5
Tonge La DE73. . . . . 252 F3
Tongue La S17. . . . . 205 E7
Tongue Lane Ind Est SK17 85 E7
Tooth St DE11. . . . . 256 E1
Top Cotts SK17. . . . . 88 F7
Top Hagg La DE56. . . . . 168 A6
Tophill La S43. . . . . 153 D8
Tophole Rd S33. . . . . 50 F4
Top La
  Crich DE4. . . . . 156 D1
  Mansfield NG19. . . . . . 135 A3
  Old Brampton S42. . . . . 93 E3
  Shottle DE56. . . . . 166 C1
Topley Gdns DE21. . . . . 205 F2
Top Lons DE6. . . . . 176 B8
Top Manor Cl DE72. . . . 221 C5
Top Mdw DE21. . . . . . . 256 B7
Toppham Dr S8. . . . . 56 F6
Toppham Rd S8. . . . . 56 F6
Toppham Way S8. . . . . . . 56 F6
Top Pingle Cl S43. . . . . . 96 E7
Top Rd
  Calow S44. . . . . 97 A3
  Top Row NG16. . . . . . . 171 A5
Topshill La DE6. . . . . . . 165 B2
Tor Ave DE55. . . . . 170 C6
Tor Cl DE4. . . . . 143 B2
Torfield Cotts DE4. . . . . 127 B3
Torksey Wlk 🟦 NG19. . . 136 E4
Torquay Ct 🟦 S41. . . . . . 95 F8
Torr Cl SK17. . . . . 85 D5
Torrance Way S42. . . . . 114 D1
Torridon Cl DE24. . . . . . 231 E4
Tor Rise DE4. . . . . 143 B3
Torr St SK17. . . . . 85 B7
Torrs Valley SK22. . . . . . 33 C7
Torr Top St SK22. . . . . . . 33 C7
Torrvale Rd SK22. . . . . . . 33 B7
Torside Mews SK13. . . . . 10 A6
Torside Way SK13. . . . . . 10 A5
Tors Spring DE4. . . . . . . 168 A8
Tors The SK14. . . . . 156 F1
Tor View Rise DE4. . . . . 155 A6
Torwood Dr S8. . . . . 56 E7
Totley All Saints CE Prim Sch
  S17. . . . . 55 D4
Totley Ave 🟦 SK13. . . . . . 9 D1
Totley Brook Cl S17. . . . . 55 D5
Totley Brook Croft S17. . . 55 D5
Totley Brook Glen S17. . . 55 D5
Totley Brook Gr S17. . . . 55 D5
Totley Brook Rd S17. . . . 55 D5
Totley Brook Way S17. . . 55 D5
Totley Cl 🟦 SK13. . . . . . . 9 D1
Totley Gdns 🟦 SK13. . . . . 9 D1
Totley Gn 🟦 SK13. . . . . . . 9 D1
Totley Grange Cl S17. . . . 55 D4
Totley Grange Rd S17. . . 55 D4
Totley Hall Croft S17. . . . 55 D3
Totley Hall Dr S17. . . . . . 55 D3
Totley Hall La S17. . . . . . 55 D4
Totley Hall Mead S17. . . 55 D4
Totley La S17. . . . . 56 A5

Totley Lanes 43 SK13 . . . . 9 D1
Totley Mews 43 SK13 . . . . 9 D1
Totley Mount S43 . . . . 96 D8
Totley Pl 46 SK13 . . . . 9 D1
Totley Prim Sch S17 . . . . 55 D4
Toton Bispham Drive Jun
 Sch NG9 . . . . 223 E3
Toton La NG9 . . . . 223 E6
Touchstone Cl DE73 . . . . . . 232 D2
Toulmin Dr DE11 . . . . 256 B4
Tower Bsns Pk S45 . . . . . . 131 C4
Tower Cl
 Sheffield S2 . . . . 43 C8
 Somercotes DE55 . . . . 170 C8
Tower Cres S44 . . . . 118 B8
Tower Dr S2 . . . . 43 C8
Tower Ho S2 . . . . 43 C8
Tower Rd
 Burton u T DE15 . . . . 248 B2
 Hartshorne DE11 . . . . 257 A6
Towers La S32 . . . . 40 E1
Tower St DE24 . . . . 232 D7
Town End
 Apperknowle S18 . . . . 58 A1
 Bolsover S44 . . . . 99 A1
 Buxton SK17 . . . . 66 E1
 Kirk Ireton DE6 . . . . 165 B1
 Shirland DE55 . . . . 146 D2
Town End Jun Sch DE55 . 147 E5
Town End Rd DE72 . . . . 235 B7
Townfield La S33 . . . . 39 E1
Town Fold SK6 . . . . 23 B7
Town Gate S33 . . . . 51 A7
Town Hall Yd 8 DE6 . . . . . 173 C2
Townhead S32. . . . . 71 C6
Town Head Rd S33 . . . . 173 C3
Townlands La S33 . . . . 39 F4
Townhead Rd S17 . . . . 55 C7
Town La
 Bradwell S33 . . . . 51 A7
 Broadbottom SK13 . . . . 16 D6
 Newton DE55 . . . . 148 A3
Townscliffe La SK6 . . . . 23 C6
Townsend Gr DE73 . . . . 233 A2
Townside Cl NG10 . . . . 236 B4
Town St
 Brassington DE4 . . . . 153 A1
 Duffield DE56 . . . . 190 F3
 Holbrook DE56 . . . . 191 C6
 Marple SK6 . . . . 23 B7
 Pinxton NG16 . . . . 160 E3
 Sandiacre NG10 . . . . 223 B5
Town The DE21 . . . . 205 C7
Town View NG16 . . . . 195 F7
Towson Ave NG16 . . . . 182 C2
Trafalgar Rd NG10 . . . . 236 D6
Trafalgar Sq NG10 . . . . 236 E7
Trafalgar Terr NG10 . . . . . . 236 E7
Traffic St DE1 . . . . 267 C2
Traffic Terr
 Barrow Hill S43 . . . . 78 B4
 Chesterfield S41 . . . . 115 B7
Trafford Way DE23 . . . . 231 C8
Trails* S33. . . . . 40 A8
Trail View SK13 . . . . 10 B5
Tramway The DE11 . . . . 255 F7
Tranmere Ave S41 . . . . 131 D3
Transvaal Terr S44 . . . . 118 B5
Traso Bsns Pk S18 . . . . 57 D1
Travers Rd NG10 . . . . 223 B6
Travey Rd S2 . . . . 44 A7
Treak Cliff Cavern* S33 . 37 E3
Tredcroft St S18 . . . . 17 B8
Tredegar Dr DE21 . . . . 206 B2
Treeneuk Cl S40 . . . . 95 B3
Trefoil Ct DE23 . . . . 231 A7
Tregaron Cl DE21 . . . . 206 C2
Tregony Way DE24 . . . . 231 D3
Trelawney Rd S45. . . . . 131 D3
Trenchard Dr SK17 . . . . 85 D3
Trent Ave
 Buxton SK17 . . . . 85 C4
 Willington DE65 . . . . 242 C5
Trent Bridge Ct DE23. . . 231 C8
Trent Cl
 Derby DE24 . . . . 231 D2
 Willington DE65 . . . . 242 C5
Trent Coll NG10 . . . . 236 C8
Trent Cotts NG10 . . . . 236 F6
Trent Dr DE23 . . . . 231 D6
Trent Gr
 Alfreton DE55 . . . . 159 A2
 Dronfield S18. . . . . 57 B3
Trent Ho NG10 . . . . 236 A4
Trent La
 Castle Donington DE74 . . 247 A5
 King's Newton DE73 . . . . . . 245 C1
 Long Eaton NG10 . . . . 236 F5
 Newton Solney DE15 . . . . . 248 E8
 Weston-on-T DE72. . . . . 245 F4
Trent Lane Ind Est DE74 . 247 A8
Trenton Dr DE21 . . . . 220 B6
Trenton Gn DE21 . . . . 220 B6
Trenton Green Dr DE21 . 220 B6
Trent Rd DE7 . . . . 208 D4
Trent Rise DE21 . . . . 220 F4
Trent St
 Derby DE24 . . . . 233 A7
 Long Eaton NG10 . . . . 236 E8
Trent Wlk 1 NG19 . . . . 136 E4
Tresillian Cl DE22 . . . . 204 E2

Tressall Cl DE7 . . . . 209 A8
T V DE6 . . . . 172 B1
Twayblade DE14 . . . . 254 B8
Tweeds Muir Cl 5 DE21. . 205 F2
Twentylands DE13 . . . . 240 D4
Twentywell Ct S17 . . . . 56 A7
Twentywell Dr S17 . . . . 56 B6
Twentywell La S17 . . . . 56 B6
Twentywell Rd S17 . . . . 56 B6
Twentywell Rise S17 . . . . 56 B6
Twentywell View S17 . . . . 56 B6
Twiggs Row DE4 . . . . 143 A7
Twin Oaks Cl DE23 . . . . 230 F7
Twisses Bank DE6 . . . . 213 A2
Twyford Cl
 Heanor DE75 . . . . 193 C8
 Swadlincote DE11 . . . . 255 F2
 West Hallam DE7 . . . . 207 D8
 Willington DE65 . . . . 242 C5
Twyford Rd
 Barrow u T DE73 . . . . 244 A6
 Long Eaton NG10 . . . . 235 F4
 Willington DE65 . . . . 242 B6
Twyford St DE23 . . . . 267 B1
Tylney Rd S40 . . . . 114 B8
Tyndale Chase DE24 . . . . . 231 C2
Tyndale Cl S40 . . . . 114 B8
Tynefield Ct DE65 . . . . 229 B2
Tynefield Dr DE65 . . . . 229 B2
Tynefield Mews DE65 . . . . 229 B2
Tynsel Parkes CE Fst Sch
 ST14. . . . . 210 A1
Tythe Barn La DE6 . . . . 215 C5
Tythe The DE11 . . . . 256 B7

Tuxford Cl DE21 . . . . 206 B1

U

Uffa Magna DE3 . . . . 217 C1
Uldale Gr DE11 . . . . 256 C1
Ulley Cres S13 . . . . 44 B7
Ulley Rd S13 . . . . 44 B7
Ullswater Ave S20 . . . . 59 E6
Ullswater Cl
 Derby DE21 . . . . 205 D2
 Dronfield S18. . . . . 56 E2
 Grassmoor S42 . . . . 59 E6
Ullswater Dr
 Derby DE21 . . . . 220 C5
 Dronfield S18. . . . . 56 E2
Ullswater Pk S18 . . . . 56 E2
Ullswater Pl S18 . . . . 56 E2
Ulverston Rd S41 . . . . 95 D7
Undercliffe DE45. . . . . 109 D6
Underhall DE4 . . . . 127 D2
Underhill Ave DE23 . . . . 231 F7
Underhill Cl DE23 . . . . 231 E6
Underhill La S43 . . . . 80 B6
Underpass The DE1 . . . . . . 267 C4
Undertown La DE6. . . . . 197 D6
Underwood CE Prim Sch
 NG16 . . . . 171 F1
Underwood Terr
 Chelmorton SK17 . . . . 106 A8
 Darley Dale DE4 . . . . 143 A7
Union Rd
 Ilkeston DE7 . . . . 208 F7
 New Mills SK22 . . . . 33 C7
 Swadlincote DE11 . . . . 256 B5
Union St
 Ashbourne DE6 . . . . 173 B2
 Glossop SK13. . . . . 17 C8
 Harthill S26 . . . . 61 E6
 Long Eaton NG10 . . . . 236 E8
 Melbourne DE73 . . . . 252 A7
 South Normanton DE55. . . 159 F5
Unity Cl DE11. . . . . 256 A1
Unity Wlk S13 . . . . 17 C7
Univ of Derby DE22 . . . . . . 204 D1
Univ of Derby (Green Lane
 Campus) DE1 . . . . .85 D3
Univ of Derby (Green Lane
 Campus) DE1 . . . . 267 B2
Univ of Derby (Sch of Health
 & Com Studies) DE23. . 218 D7
Univ of Sheffield SK17 . . 104 B8
Univ of Sheffield (Research
 Labs) SK17. . . . . .85 B1
Unstone Dronfield By-Pass
 S18. . . . . 76 E7
Unstone Hill S18 . . . . 76 D7
Unstone Jun Sch S18 . . . . . 76 F7
Unstone Rd S41 . . . . 76 F4
Unstone St Mary's Inf Sch
 S18. . . . . 76 F7
Unthank La S18 . . . . 54 D4
Upchurch Cl DE3 . . . . 217 C3
Upland Rise S40 . . . . 95 D1
Uplands Ave DE23 . . . . 231 C6
Uplands Gdns DE23 . . . . . . 218 E2
Uplands Rd
 Compstall SK14 . . . . 15 A6
 Glossop SK13. . . . . 17 D8
Upper Albert Rd S8. . . . . . . 43 B5
Upper Bainbrigge St
 DE23 . . . . 219 A3
Upper Barn Cl DE75. . . . . . 181 E2
Upper Blindlow La SK17 . 106 A6
Upper Boundary Rd
 DE22 . . . . 218 E4

Upper Croft
 Clay Cross S45 . . . . 131 E3
Tupton S42. . . . . 131 D8
Upper Croft Cl S43 . . . . 96 E7
Upper Dale Rd DE23 . . . . . 218 F1
Upper Dunstead Rd
 NG16 . . . . 182 B4
Upper End Rd SK17 . . . . . . 67 C4
Upper Greenhill Gdns
 DE4 . . . . 143 C6
Upper Hall Cl DE56 . . . . . . 191 C6
Upper Hollow DE23 . . . . 218 C1
Upper King St S43 . . . . 77 F1
Upper La DE6. . . . . 175 E4
Upper Lum Cl S41 . . . . 96 D2
Upper Mantle Cl S45. . . . . 131 C4
Upper Marehay Rd DE5 . . 180 D6
Upper Moor Rd DE24 . . . . 232 E6
Upper Moor St S40 . . . . 95 B2
Upper Nelson St 3
 DE75 . . . . 181 D2
Upper Newbold Cl S40. . . 95 B7
Upper Orchard St 2
 NG9 . . . . 223 E7
Upper School La S18 . . . . . 76 B8
Upperthorpe Rd S21 . . . . . 60 D4
Upperthorpe Villas S21 . . 60 D5
Uppertown La DE4 . . . . 142 C1
Upper Town La DE4 . . . . . . 126 B1
Upper Valley Rd S8 . . . . 43 B5
Upper Wellington St
 NG10 . . . . 223 C1
Upperwood Rd DE4 . . . . . . 143 A1
Upper Yeld Rd DE45. . . . . . 109 C4
Upton Cl
 Castle Donington DE74 . . 247 B4
 Heanor DE75. . . . . 182 A1
Upton Mount NG19 . . . . . . 135 E1
Upwood Cl S40 . . . . 95 A5
Upwoods Rd DE6 . . . . 211 A1
Utah Cl DE65 . . . . 228 E2
Uttoxeter New Rd DE22 . 218 C3
Uttoxeter Old Rd DE22 . . 218 E5
Uttoxeter Rd
 Derby DE3 . . . . 217 E1
 Hatton DE65 . . . . 227 B2
 Hilton DE65 . . . . 228 C2
 Scropton DE65 . . . . 226 C4
 Scropton, Foston DE65 . . . 226 F3
Uxbridge St DE14 . . . . 254 C8

V

Vale Cl
 Bolsover S44 . . . . 99 A1
 Dronfield S18. . . . . 57 B1
Vale Ct NG19 . . . . 136 B3
Vale Dr NG20 . . . . 119 F2
Vale House Dr SK13 . . . . . . 10 A5
Vale Mills DE22 . . . . 218 F3
Valemount SK13 . . . . 10 A5
Valentine Ave NG16 . . . . . . 171 E7
Vale Rd
 Hartshorne DE11 . . . . 257 A3
 Mansfield Woodhouse
 NG19 . . . . 136 B4
 Swadlincote DE11 . . . . 256 B6
Valerian Cl S43. . . . . 85 C7
Valerie Rd DE72 . . . . 246 A7
Vale The DE7 . . . . 194 E3
Vallance St NG19 . . . . 136 B4
Valley Cl S45 . . . . 132 B4
Valley Cotts S44 . . . . 117 F8
Valley Cres S41 . . . . 96 C2
Valley Dr
 Chapel-en-le-F SK23 . . . . . . 47 C6
 Ilkeston DE7 . . . . 208 F7
Valley Gdns S14 . . . . 15 E8
Valley Park Com Sch S14 . 43 F2
Valley Rd
 Barlow S18 . . . . 75 D3
 Bolsover S44 . . . . 118 A8
 Broadbottom SK14 . . . . 15 E8
 Chesterfield S41 . . . . 96 C2
 Clay Cross S45 . . . . 131 A4
 Derby, Cherrytree Hill
 DE21 . . . . 220 B5
 Derby DE23 . . . . 218 D1
 Glossop SK13. . . . . 16 F8
 Hayfield SK22 . . . . 25 E2
 Ilkeston DE7 . . . . 208 E5
 Killamarsh S21 . . . . 60 D7
 Kimberley NG16. . . . . 195 D7
 Mastin Moor S43 . . . . 79 C4
 Overseal DE12. . . . . 262 A3
 Sheffield, Heeley S8 . . . . . . 43 A6
 Shirebrook NG20. . . . . 119 E5
Valley Rise
 Barlow S18 . . . . 75 D3
 Swadlincote DE11 . . . . 256 B5
Valley View
 Alton S42. . . . . 130 C5
 Belper DE56 . . . . 179 A2
 Ilkeston DE7 . . . . 208 E5
Valley View Cl
 Chesterfield S41 . . . . 115 E7
 Eckington S21 . . . . 59 C2
Valley View Dr DE7. . . . . . . 193 B1
Valley View Rd DE55 . . . . . 170 D4
Valley View Wlk ST14 . . . . 197 A3
Vancouver Ave DE21 . . . . . 220 D4
Vancouver Dr DE15 . . . . . . 248 C3
Vanguard Rd NG10 . . . . . . 236 D5
Vanguard Trad Est S40 . . . 115 B7
Varley Ho S41 . . . . 96 B6
Varley St DE24 . . . . 232 D6
Vaughan Pl NG20 . . . . 119 E6

Vaughan Rd SK23 . . . . 45 E5
Vauxhall Ave DE22 . . . . 218 A4
Velvet Mill SK17 . . . . 69 B4
Ventnor Ho DE24 . . . . 233 C7
Ventura Ct S43 . . . . 24 D1
Venture Cres DE55 . . . . 159 A2
Venture Rd S41 . . . . 76 F1
Venture Way S41 . . . . 76 F1
Verbena Dr DE23 . . . . 231 D4
Vere Cl DE65 . . . . 242 B5
Vermont Dr DE21 . . . . 220 C6
Verney St NG19 . . . . 134 F7
Verney Way NG19 . . . . 134 F7
Vernon Cotts DE4 . . . . 154 F1
Vernon Ct
 Bakewell DE45. . . . . 109 D5
 Shirebrook NG20 . . . . 120 A4
Vernon Dr
 Bakewell DE45. . . . . 109 B7
 Derby DE21 . . . . 220 B7
Verngate DE11 . . . . 218 E5
Vernon Gn DE45 . . . . 109 B7
Vernon La S45 . . . . 129 C4
Vernon Rd
 Chesterfield S40 . . . . 95 D3
 Sheffield S17 . . . . 55 F6
Vernon Rise S42 . . . . 115 F2
Vernon St
 Derby DE1 . . . . 218 E5
 Ilkeston DE7 . . . . 194 F4
 Shirebrook NG20 . . . . 120 A4
Vernon Street Ind Est
 NG20 . . . . 120 A4
Verona Way DE24 . . . . 232 E2
Veronica Dr NG16 . . . . 195 C8
Vestry Rd DE21 . . . . 205 E3
Vetchfield Cl DE24 . . . . 231 F2
Viadevana DE12 . . . . 262 E3
Via Gellia Rd DE4 . . . . 154 C7
Vicarage Ave
 Derby DE23 . . . . 218 E2
 Ilkeston DE7 . . . . 194 D4
Vicarage Cl
 Belper DE56 . . . . 179 A4
 Burton u T DE15. . . . . 248 B4
 Heath S44 . . . . 117 B2
 Holmesfield S18 . . . . 75 A8
 Shirebrook NG20. . . . . 119 E3
 Smalley DE7. . . . . 192 F6
 Swanwick DE55. . . . . 169 E7
Vicarage Croft DE4 . . . . . . 110 E1
Vicarage Ct DE3 . . . . 217 C1
Vicarage Dr
 Derby DE21 . . . . 220 A7
 Uttoxeter ST14 . . . . 210 A4
Vicarage Gdns
 Clay Cross S45 . . . . 131 C2
 Heanor DE75 . . . . 181 F1
 Swadlincote DE11 . . . . 256 C4
Vicarage La
 Ashford in t W DE45 . . . . . 108 E8
 Duffield DE56 . . . . 190 E4
 Hayfield SK22 . . . . 25 C3
 Ironville NG16 . . . . 170 F4
 Little Eaton DE21 . . . . 205 C8
 Sheffield S17 . . . . 55 D7
Vicarage Mews DE55. . . . . 170 E6
Vicarage Rd
 Belper DE56 . . . . 190 F8
 Chellaston DE73 . . . . 232 F2
 Derby DE1 . . . . 217 C2
 Swadlincote DE11 . . . . 256 C4
 Woodville DE11 . . . . 256 E2
Vicarage St DE7 . . . . 194 D4
Vicarage Wlk DE12 . . . . . . 260 C6
Vicar La
 Chesterfield S40 . . . . 266 B3
 Tibshelf DE55 . . . . 148 A6
Vicarwood Ave
 Derby DE22 . . . . 204 F1
 Holbrook DE56. . . . . 191 C7
Victor Ave DE22 . . . . 218 F8
Victor Cres NG10 . . . . 223 C4
Victoria Ave
 Borrowash DE72 . . . . 221 B2
 Buxton SK17 . . . . 85 D8
 Draycott DE72 . . . . 235 A7
 Glossop SK13. . . . . 10 A5
 Heanor DE75 . . . . 181 D1
 Staveley S43 . . . . 79 A3
Victoria Cl DE3 . . . . 217 E4
Victoria Cotts DE45 . . . . . . 109 D6
Victoria Cres DE15 . . . . . . 248 C3
Victoria Ct
 6 Glossop SK13. . . . . 17 C8
 Long Eaton NG10 . . . . 236 D7
 Matlock DE4 . . . . 143 C6
Victoria Dr
 Blackwell DE55 . . . . 147 E1
 Woodville DE11. . . . . 256 E1
Victoria Gr SK12 . . . . 32 A5
Victoria Hall Gdns DE4 . 143 C6
Victoria Ho S80 . . . . 81 F1
Victoria Mews 2 SK13 . . 17 C8
Victoria Park Rd
 Buxton SK17 . . . . 85 D7
 Calow S43 . . . . 96 F5
Victoria Rd
 Bamford S33 . . . . 40 A3
 Draycott DE72 . . . . 235 A7
 Pinxton NG16. . . . . 160 D3
 Ripley DE5 . . . . 169 E2
 Sandiacre NG10. . . . . 223 B6
 Selston NG16 . . . . 171 F6
Victoria St N S41 . . . . 76 F2

Victoria St
Victoria St W S40 . . . . .95 C2
Victoria Sq 15 DE6 . . . . . .173 C2
Victoria St
Alfreton DE55 . . . . .159 B4
Bolsover S44 . . . . .118 B8
Brimington S43 . . . . .77 F1
Castle Donington DE74 . .247 B5
Chesterfield S41 . . . . .266 B4
Clay Cross S45 . . . . .131 C3
Creswell S80 . . . . .81 F1
Derby DE1 . . . . .267 B3
Dronfield S18 . . . . .56 F2
Glossop SK13 . . . . .17 C8
Ilkeston DE7 . . . . .194 F3
Ironville NG16 . . . . .170 F4
Langley Mill NG16 . . . . . .182 C3
Long Eaton NG10 . . . . . . .236 B5
Melbourne DE73 . . . . . . .252 A7
New Mills SK22 . . . . .33 B6
Ripley DE5 . . . . .169 F2
Shirebrook NG20 . . . . . . .119 F4
Somercotes DE55 . . . . . .170 C8
South Normanton DE55 . .160 A6
Stapleford NG9 . . . . .223 D7
Victoria Terr
Great Longstone DE45 . . . .89 F4
Selston NG16 . . . . .160 F1
Tibshelf DE55 . . . . .148 B7
Victoria Way DE24 . . . . .219 E3
Victoria Wlk S42 . . . . . .115 D1
Victor Rd S17 . . . . .55 F7
Victory Ave DE5 . . . . . . .169 F1
Victory Cl NG10 . . . . . . .236 E5
Victory Dr NG19 . . . . . . .136 F1
Victory Rd DE24 . . . . . . .232 B6
Viewdales Cl DE6 . . . . . .175 F2
View Rd S2 . . . . .43 A7
Viking Bsns Ctr DE11 . .256 F3
Vikinglea Cl S2 . . . . .44 B8
Vikinglea Dr S2 . . . . .44 B8
Village Ct DE56 . . . . .190 F3
Village St DE23 . . . . .231 F8
Village The
Dale Abbey DE7 . . . . .207 F2
West Hallam DE7 . . . . . . .207 E7
Villas Rd
Ambergate DE56 . . . . . . .167 F3
Bolsover S44 . . . . .98 E2
Villa St DE72 . . . . .235 B7
Villas The
Bolsover S44 . . . . .99 B2
Whaley Thorns NG20 . . . .101 A3
Villa The SK14 . . . . .9 E5
Villiers Cl S2 . . . . .43 E6
Villiers Dr S2 . . . . .43 E6
Vincent Ave
Derby DE1 . . . . .220 E3
Ilkeston DE7 . . . . .208 F8
Vincent Cl DE56 . . . . . . .192 A8
Vincent Cres S40 . . . . . . .95 B2
Vincent La S40 . . . . .95 B2
Vincent St DE23 . . . . . . .218 F1
Vine Cl DE23 . . . . .231 B7
Vine Cres NG10 . . . . . . .223 B6
Vine Farm Cl DE7 . . . . . .208 D5
Vineyard Terr DE4 . . . . .127 C4
Viola Cl DE21 . . . . .206 C3
Violet Ave NG16 . . . . . . .195 B8
Violet Cl
Donisthorpe DE12 . . . . . .262 E1
Shirebrook NG20 . . . . . . .119 D3
Violet La DE15 . . . . .254 F8
Violet St DE23 . . . . .218 F1
Violet Way DE15 . . . . . . .255 A8
Virginsalley La DE4 . . . . .184 D2
Vista The NG9 . . . . .223 E5
Vivian St
Derby DE1 . . . . .219 B8
Shuttlewood S44 . . . . .98 F6
Vulcan St DE23 . . . . .219 B1
Vyse Dr NG10 . . . . .236 C6

W

Wade Ave
Derby DE23 . . . . .218 C2
Ilkeston DE7 . . . . .209 B7
Wadebridge Gr DE24 . . .233 C5
Wade Dr S43 . . . . .217 E2
Wade St DE23 . . . . .218 C1
Wadsworth Ave S12 . . . . .44 D5
Wadsworth Cl S12 . . . . . .44 D5
Wadsworth Dr S12 . . . . . .44 D5
Wadsworth Rd
Sheffield S12 . . . . .44 C5
Stapleford NG9 . . . . .223 F8
Wagstaff La NG16 . . . . . .171 B4
Wagtail Cl DE24 . . . . . . .231 D4
Wain Ave
Chesterfield S41 . . . . .266 C3
North Wingfield S42 . . . . .132 A7
Wainfleet Cl DE7 . . . . . . .194 C3
Waingroves Prim Sch
DE5 . . . . .181 A7
Waingroves Rd
Codnor DE5 . . . . .181 B6
Ripley DE5 . . . . .181 A8
Wainhouse Brow SK22 . . .25 D3
Wains Cl SK17 . . . . .47 F1
Wain Way S42 . . . . .132 A7
Wainwright Ave
Mansfield NG19 . . . . .135 D1
Sheffield S13 . . . . .44 D8

Wainwright Cres S13 . . . . .44 D8
Wakami Cres DE24 . . . . .233 A3
Wakefield Ave DE13 . . . .239 B6
Wakefield Croft DE7 . . . .194 C3
Wakefield Ct DE74 . . . . .247 C4
Wakelyn Cl
Hilton DE65 . . . . .228 C2
Shardlow DE72 . . . . .234 F1
Walbrook Rd DE23 . . . . .218 F1
Walcote Cl DE56 . . . . . . .179 D5
Waldene Dr DE24 . . . . . .233 A6
Walden Rd S2 . . . . .43 B7
Waldley La DE6 . . . . .211 D7
Waldorf Ave DE24 . . . . . .233 A7
Waldorf Cl DE24 . . . . . . .233 A7
Walford Rd
Killamarsh S21 . . . . .60 C6
Rolleston DE13 . . . . .240 D3
Walgrave Cl DE56 . . . . . .179 B6
Walgrove Ave S40 . . . . . .95 E1
Walgrove Rd S40 . . . . . . .95 D1
Walk Cl DE72 . . . . .235 A7
Walkdale Brow SK13 . . . . .17 B7
Walker Ave DE5 . . . . . . .169 E2
Walker Brow SK17 . . . . . .47 F1
Walker Cl DE7 . . . . .209 A4
Walker Gr 2 NG9 . . . . . .223 E6
Walker La DE1 . . . . .267 A4
Walkers La S21 . . . . .60 D6
Walker St SK13 . . . . .10 A4
Walk Mill Rd SK22 . . . . . .25 D2
Walk The DE56 . . . . .192 B8
Wallace Gdns NG9 . . . . .223 F1
Wallace St DE22 . . . . . . .218 C5
Wall Ditch DE6 . . . . .149 B2
Wallfields Cl DE65 . . . . . .230 D2
Wallis Cl DE72 . . . . .235 A7
Wallis Ho DE11 . . . . .256 E3
Wall Rd DE14 . . . . .254 A7
Walls La S80 . . . . .81 A8
Wall St
Bolsover SK17 . . . . .85 D8
Ripley DE5 . . . . .169 D2
Walnut Ave
Derby DE24 . . . . .233 B7
Shireoaks S81 . . . . .63 F7
Walnut Cl
Aston-on-T DE72 . . . . . . .246 B8
Barrow u T DE73 . . . . . . .244 A6
Burnaston DE65 . . . . .229 F5
Chesterfield DE73 . . . . . . .245 A8
Ilkeston DE7 . . . . .209 A7
Repton DE65 . . . . .243 A2
Swadlincote DE11 . . . . . . .256 A5
Walnut Dr S21 . . . . .60 C5
Walnut Rd DE56 . . . . . . .179 B3
Walnut St DE24 . . . . .232 C7
Walpole St DE21 . . . . . . .219 D6
Walseker La S26 . . . . .61 C7
Walsham Ct DE24 . . . . . .232 E4
Walter Evans CE Prim Sch
DE22 . . . . .204 F2
Walters Ave NG16 . . . . . .182 E6
Walters Cres NG16 . . . . .171 D6
Walter St
Derby DE1 . . . . .218 E7
Draycott DE72 . . . . .234 F8
Walters Wood S43 . . . . . .45 F5
Waltham Ave DE24 . . . . .231 F4
Waltham Croft S41 . . . . .115 C7
Walthamstow Dr DE24 . .218 B6
Waltheof Rd S2 . . . . .44 A8
Walton Ave DE24 . . . . . .232 E4
Walton Back La
Chesterfield S40 . . . . .114 B7
Holymoorside S42 . . . . . . .113 F7
Walton Cl
Chesterfield S40 . . . . .114 B8
Dronfield S18 . . . . .56 C2
Swadlincote DE11 . . . . . . .256 A3
Walton Dr
Chesterfield S40 . . . . .95 E1
Derby DE23 . . . . .231 E7
Walton Fields Rd S40 . . . .95 D2
Walton Hill DE74 . . . . . . .247 A4
Walton Holymoorside Prim
Sch S42 . . . . .113 D7
Walton Hospl S40 . . . . . .114 E8
Walton-on-Trent CE Prim
Sch DE12 . . . . .259 D8
Walton Rd
Burton u T DE15 . . . . . . .254 D5
Chesterfield S40 . . . . .95 D1
Derby DE21 . . . . .219 F5
Walton St NG10 . . . . .223 B2
Walton Way S42 . . . . . . .114 E4
Walton Wlk S40 . . . . .266 A2
Wansfell Cl DE3 . . . . .217 E1
Wapentake La DE6 . . . . .165 C2
Warburton Cl S2 . . . . .43 C7
Warburton Gdns S2 . . . . .43 C7
Warburton Rd S2 . . . . . . .43 C7
Ward's La
Barrow u T DE73 . . . . . . .244 F3
Breaston DE72 . . . . .235 D8
King's Newton DE73 . . . . .245 A2
Ward Dr DE5 . . . . .170 D7
Wardgate Way S40 . . . . . .95 A5
Ward La
Barlborough S43 . . . . .80 B8
Disley SK12 . . . . .32 F4

Wardlow Ave
Derby DE21 . . . . .220 A8
17 Gamesley SK13 . . . . .9 D1
Wardlow Cl S40 . . . . .114 F8
Wardlow Fold 21 SK13 . . . .9 D1
Wardlow Gdns 18 SK13 . . . .9 D1
Wardlow Gr 22 SK13 . . . . . .9 D1
Wardlow Mews
19 Gamesley SK13 . . . . .9 D1
22 Gamesley SK13 . . . . .9 D1
Wardlow Rd
Ilkeston DE7 . . . . .194 E3
Sheffield S12 . . . . .44 D5
Wardlow Wlk
18 Gamesley SK13 . . . . .9 D1
20 Gamesley SK13 . . . . .9 D1
Ward St
Derby DE22 . . . . .218 E4
Tupton S42 . . . . .131 D8
Wards Yd S18 . . . . .57 A1
Wardwick DE1 . . . . .267 B3
Warehouse La S33 . . . . . .38 D4
Warhurst Fold 2 SK13 . . .10 A5
Warke Flatt DE74 . . . . . . .247 B6
Warmbrook DE4 . . . . . . .165 F8
Warmbrook Rd SK23 . . . . .47 C6
Warminster Cres S8 . . . . .43 A4
Warminster Dr S8 . . . . . . .43 B3
Warminster Gdns S8 . . . . .43 A3
Warminster Pl S8 . . . . . . .43 B2
Warminster Rd S8 . . . . . . .43 A3
Warmwells La DE5 . . . . . .180 D6
Warner St
Chesterfield S41 . . . . .266 C1
Derby DE22 . . . . .267 A1
Derby, Mickleover DE3 . . .217 D1
Warney Rd DE4 . . . . .127 D2
Warren Ave NG9 . . . . . . .223 D7
Warren Ave Extension
NG9 . . . . .223 D7
Warren Cl
Burton u T DE13 . . . . . . .240 E1
Pilsley S45 . . . . .132 C2
Warren Cres S21 . . . . .58 E2
Warren Ct NG9 . . . . .223 D7
Warrendale Ct DE73 . . . .233 A2
Warren Dr DE12 . . . . . . .261 C6
Warren Hill 7 DE11 . . . . .255 E5
Warren La
Castle Donington DE74,
DE72 . . . . .236 B2
Warren Lea SK6 . . . . .15 B2
Warren Rise S18 . . . . .57 C3
Warren Wlk S21 . . . . .58 E2
Warsop Rd NG19 . . . . . . .136 D3
Warwick Ave DE23 . . . . .218 D1
Warwick Cl
Branston DE14 . . . . .253 F8
Glossop SK13 . . . . .17 F8
Swadlincote DE11 . . . . . . .256 E5
Warwick Ct DE55 . . . . . . .170 B8
Warwick Dr DE7 . . . . .194 C3
Warwick Gdns DE56 . . . .179 D5
Warwick Rd
Long Eaton NG10 . . . . . . .237 A7
Somercotes DE55 . . . . . . .159 C1
Warwick St
Chesterfield S40 . . . . .115 B7
Derby DE24 . . . . .219 D2
Wasdale Ave 6 S20 . . . . . .59 E6
Wasdale Cl S20 . . . . .59 E6
Washbrook La DE6 . . . . . .161 F4
Washford Rd DE65 . . . . . .240 E8
Wash Gn DE4 . . . . .166 B8
Wash Hills Cl DE4 . . . . . .153 A1
Washouse Bottom SK17 . .69 E8
Wash House La S40 . . . . . .95 C2
Washington Ave DE21 . . .220 B6
Washington Cl DE73 . . . .252 A7
Washington Cotts DE72 . .221 D1
Washington Dr NG9 . . . . .209 F1
Washington Terr DE41 . . .143 E7
Watburn Rd SK22 . . . . . . .24 D1
Watchorn Cl DE11 . . . . . .256 D5
Watchorn Cotts DE55 . . .158 F3
Watchorn La DE55 . . . . . .158 F2
Watercress La S45 . . . . . .131 D2
Waterdown Cl NG19 . . . .136 D5
Waterfoot Cotts SK14 . . . . .9 A4
Waterfoot La SK23 . . . . . .45 D6
Waterford Dr DE21 . . . . .220 B6
Watergo La DE22 . . . . . . .230 D7
Wateringbury Gr 1 S43 . . .78 F2
Watering La DE56 . . . . . . .191 D6
Water La
Bakewell DE45 . . . . .109 D6
Bamford S33 . . . . .40 A3
Bolsover S44 . . . . .117 E8
Cromford DE4 . . . . .155 A6
Eyam S32 . . . . .71 E6
Hollingworth SK14 . . . . . . .9 D5
Middleton DE4 . . . . .154 C5
Pleasley NG19 . . . . .135 B3
Sheffield S17 . . . . .55 F7
Shirebrook NG20 . . . . . . .119 E1
South Normanton DE55 . .160 B6
Tideswell SK17 . . . . .68 F8
Wirksworth DE4 . . . . .165 F7

Waterloo St continued
Doe Lea S44 . . . . .117 F1
Water Mdws DE73 . . . . . .244 D6
Watermeade S21 . . . . .59 B2
Water Meadow La S40 . . .95 B7
Watermeadow Rd DE24 . .233 A5
Watermeadows The
NG10 . . . . .236 A8
Watermint Cl DE24 . . . . .231 B6
Water Orton Cl NG9 . . . .223 E3
Waterpark Rd DE6 . . . . . .224 B8
Waters Edge SK6 . . . . .23 B8
Waters Edge La SK23 . . . .47 C5
Waterside
Burton u T DE15 . . . . . . .254 E7
Disley SK12 . . . . .32 E7
Furness Vale SK23 . . . . . . .33 E3
Glossop SK13 . . . . .10 A6
Ironville NG16 . . . . .170 F4
Marple SK6 . . . . .23 A5
Willington DE65 . . . . .242 A6
Waterside Bsns Pk SK13 . . .9 F6
Waterside Cl
Derby DE21 . . . . .205 A2
Sandiacre NG10 . . . . .223 B3
Waterside Com Jun Sch
DE15 . . . . .254 E7
Waterside Ho DE11 . . . . .267 B4
Waterside Rd
Burton u T DE15 . . . . . . .254 D7
Disley SK12 . . . . .32 E7
Waterside Ret Pk DE7 . . .195 A1
Water St
Bakewell DE45 . . . . .109 D5
Buxton SK17 . . . . .85 B8
Glossop SK13 . . . . .10 E2
Waterswallows La SK17 . . .66 F4
Waterswallows Mews
SK17 . . . . .66 E1
Waterswallows Rd SK17 . .66 E1
Waterthorpe Cl 4 S20 . . .59 F8
Waterthorpe Gdns 8 S20 .59 F8
Waterthorpe Glade 9
S20 . . . . .59 F8
Waterthorpe Glen 2 S20 .59 F8
Waterthorpe Rise 1 S20 . .59 F8
Waterton Cl DE21 . . . . . .241 A1
Waterway The NG10 . . . .223 B2
Watery La
Bretby DE15 . . . . .249 C3
Clifton DE6 . . . . .184 C7
Ellastone DE6 . . . . .183 B4
Holme HD9 . . . . .2 F8
Scropton DE65 . . . . .226 C2
Swadlincote DE11 . . . . . . .255 D5
Thurvaston DE6 . . . . .215 D5
Watford Bridge Ind Est
SK22 . . . . .24 D1
Watford La SK22 . . . . .24 C2
Watford Lo SK22 . . . . .24 C1
Watford Rd
Buxton SK17 . . . . .84 F8
New Mills SK22 . . . . .24 C2
Watkin Ave SK13 . . . . .9 E4
Watkinson St DE75 . . . . .181 D2
Watson Ave DE7 . . . . .181 F2
Watson La S42 . . . . .114 C3
Watson Rd DE7 . . . . .194 C2
Watson St DE1 . . . . .218 E6
Watten Cl DE24 . . . . .231 F2
Watts Gn DE45 . . . . .108 F8
Waveney Cl DE22 . . . . . . .205 B5
Waverley Dr DE4 . . . . . . .232 D7
Waverley St
Long Eaton NG10 . . . . . . .236 E8
Tibshelf DE55 . . . . .148 B7
Wayfaring Rd DE21 . . . . .206 A1
Wayford Ave S41 . . . . . . .266 C1
Wayside S43 . . . . .96 D8
Wayside Cl S42 . . . . .132 A7
Wayside Ct S43 . . . . .96 D8
Wayzgoose Dr DE21 . . . .219 C6
Weaddow La DE45 . . . . . .124 F2
Weakland Cl S12 . . . . .44 F3
Weakland Cres S12 . . . . . .44 F3
Weakland Dr S12 . . . . .44 F3
Weakland Way S12 . . . . . .44 F3
Weather Hill La HD9 . . . . . .3 E8
Weathern Field DE12 . . . .261 D5
Weaver Cl
Ashbourne DE6 . . . . .185 C8
Crich DE4 . . . . .156 F1
Weaver Rd ST14 . . . . .210 B2
Weavers Cl
Belper DE56 . . . . .179 C5
Borrowash DE72 . . . . .221 D1
Weavers Croft DE56 . . . .180 E8
Weavers Ct SK14 . . . . .9 A4
Weavers Gn DE56 . . . . . .217 C1
Weavers The ST14 . . . . . .196 D6
Weaving Ave S33 . . . . .38 C2
Webbs Orch SK23 . . . . . . .45 D8
Webster's Terr DE4 . . . . .143 D4
Webster Ave NG16 . . . . . .182 F1
Webster Croft S41 . . . . . . .77 B2
Webster St S40 . . . . .95 E5
Webster St DE1 . . . . .267 A2
Wedgwood Cl DE15 . . . . .248 B1
Wedgwoods La S45 . . . . .130 A5
Wedneshough NG10 . . . .119 F2
Weightman Dr NG16 . . . .195 B7
Weir Bank DE15 . . . . .254 E6
Weirfield Rd DE22 . . . . . .205 A2
Weirside DE6 . . . . .184 D7

Welbeck Ave
Buxton SK17 . . . . .85 C6
Ilkeston DE7 . . . . .208 D5
Welbeck Cl
Dronfield S18 . . . . .56 C2
Staveley S43 . . . . .97 D6
Welbeck Ct
1 Chesterfield S40 . . . . . . .95 C2
Clowne S43 . . . . .80 F3
1 Staveley S43 . . . . .78 E2
Welbeck Dr S42 . . . . .114 E4
Welbeck Gdns
Beeston NG9 . . . . .223 F3
Bolsover S44 . . . . .99 C2
Welbeck Gr DE22 . . . . . . .204 D3
Welbeck Rd
Bolsover S44 . . . . .99 B2
Long Eaton NG10 . . . . . . .223 C3
Mansfield Woodhouse
NG19 . . . . .136 C3
Welbeck St
Creswell S80 . . . . .81 E1
Whitwell S80 . . . . .82 B6
Welburn Cl NG19 . . . . . . .136 F2
Welbury Gdns S20 . . . . . . .59 E6
Welch Ave NG9 . . . . .223 E8
Welfare Ave S40 . . . . .95 D3
Welfare Cl NG20 . . . . .119 E3
Welfitt Gr NG20 . . . . .101 B2
Welland Cl
Burton u T DE15 . . . . . . .248 A5
Derby DE3 . . . . .217 D4
Welland Rd DE65 . . . . . . .228 D1
Well Banks DE6 . . . . .165 B1
Wellcarr Rd S8 . . . . .43 A2
Well Cl DE6 . . . . .175 E3
Welldon St DE5 . . . . .181 A4
Wellesley Ave DE23 . . . . .231 D7
Wellfield DE4 . . . . .143 C6
Wellfield Cl S12 . . . . .44 E1
Wellfield Ct DE4 . . . . .143 C6
Well Gate DE53 . . . . .112 C6
Wellgate La DE45 . . . . . .109 B1
Wellhead Rd 4 S8 . . . . . . .43 A6
Wellington Cres DE11 . . .267 D2
Wellington Ct
1 Belper DE56 . . . . .178 F3
Eastwood NG16 . . . . .182 F2
Wellington Mews DE55 . .146 D2
Wellington Pk S55 . . . . . .146 D2
Wellington Pl NG16 . . . . .182 F2
Wellington Rd DE14 . . . . .253 E8
Wellington St
Chesterfield S43 . . . . .77 D3
Derby DE1 . . . . .267 D2
Eastwood NG16 . . . . .182 F3
Heanor DE75 . . . . .181 E3
Long Eaton NG10 . . . . . . .223 C2
Matlock DE4 . . . . .143 C6
Ripley DE5 . . . . .169 E1
Stapleford NG9 . . . . .223 D6
Well La
Belper DE56 . . . . .190 F7
Blackfordby DE11 . . . . . . .257 B1
Kegworth DE74 . . . . .202 B5
Shirland DE55 . . . . .146 C1
Well Rd S8 . . . . .43 A6
Well Row SK14 . . . . .16 A8
Wells Cl NG19 . . . . .136 D4
Wells Ct DE23 . . . . .230 F7
Wellspring Cl
Barlborough S43 . . . . .80 B6
Sheffield S42 . . . . .115 B4
Well Spring Cl S43 . . . . . . .96 F7
Wellspring Dale NG9 . . . .223 E5
Wells Rd DE3 . . . . .217 E2
Wells St S44 . . . . .118 C8
Well St
Brassington DE4 . . . . .152 F1
Derby DE1 . . . . .267 B5
Elton DE4 . . . . .140 E7
New Mills SK22 . . . . .33 B8
Ripley DE5 . . . . .169 D1
Wellwood Rd DE11 . . . . .256 A6
Well Yd
Belper DE56 . . . . .179 A5
Holbrook DE56 . . . . .191 C6
Welney Cl DE3 . . . . .230 D8
Welshpool Pl S40 . . . . .95 D3
Welshpool Rd DE21 . . . . .205 D1
Welton Ave DE56 . . . . . . .179 B6
Welwyn Ave
Derby, Alleton DE24 . . . . .232 E4
Derby DE22 . . . . .204 D3
Mansfield Woodhouse
NG19 . . . . .136 C4
Welwyn Cl
Chesterfield S40 . . . . .95 D3
Sheffield S12 . . . . .44 B8
Welwyn Ct S12 . . . . .44 B8
Welwyn Rd S12 . . . . .44 B8
Wembley Gdns DE22 . . . .218 A6
Wendover Cl DE7 . . . . . . .217 C1
Wenham La NG17 . . . . . . .148 F4
Wenlock Cl
Chesterfield S40 . . . . .95 D4
Derby DE21 . . . . .219 C8
Wenlock Cres S40 . . . . . . .95 D4
Wenlock Dr S42 . . . . .115 D2
Wenlock Wlk S42 . . . . . . .115 F3
Wensley Ct DE21 . . . . . . .220 F3

Wensley Rd
North Wingfield S42 . . . . . . **131** F5
Winster DE4 . . . . **141** D6
Wensley Way S43 . . . . **97** C8
Wentworth Ave S40 . . . . . . **114** E8
Wentworth Cl
Derby DE3 . . . . **217** F2
Mansfield NG19 . . . . **136** F2
Wentworth Croft DE75 . . **182** A3
Wentworth Ct NG16 . . . . . . **195** E6
Wentworth Dr DE13 . . . . . . **240** D1
Wentworth Ho ■ DE1 . . . . **218** E5
Wentworth Rd S18 . . . . **56** C1
Wentworth St DE7 . . . . **195** A2
Werburgh Cl DE21 . . . . **220** D4
Werburgh St DE22 . . . . **267** A2
Werneth Low Ctry Pk* SK14 . . . . **15** A7
Werneth Low Rd SK14 . . . . **15** B6
Werneth Rd DE7 . . . . **194** E4
Wesleyan Chapel La SK17 . **88** A3
Wesleyan Chapel Wlk NG9 . . . . **223** D7
Wesley Cl SK23 . . . . **47** C6
Wesley Ho ■ S43 . . . . **85** D8
Wesley La DE7 . . . . **221** C5
Wesley Pl NG9 . . . . **223** E7
Wesley Rd
Ambergate DE56 . . . . **167** F3
Derby DE24 . . . . **233** D6
Stonebroom DE55 . . . . **146** F3
Wesley St
Glossop SK13 . . . . **10** E2
Hadfield SK13 . . . . **10** A5
Ilkeston DE7 . . . . **194** E4
Langley Mill NG16 . . . . **182** C3
Wessex Cl ■ S43 . . . . **96** F8
Wessex Dr NG16 . . . . **195** A8
Wessex Gdns S17 . . . . **55** D5
Wessington Bank ■ SK13 . . **9** E2
Wessington Dr S43 . . . . **97** C8
Wessington Fold ■ SK13 . . . **9** E2
Wessington La ■ SK13 . . . . . **9** E2
Wessington La DE55 . . . . . . **158** A6
Wessington Mews
Derby DE22 . . . . **204** E1
Gamesley SK13 . . . . **9** E2
Wessington Prim Sch
DE55 . . . . **157** A8
Wessington Rd DE11 . . . . . . **255** F2
West Ave
Chellaston DE73 . . . . **232** E3
Derby DE1 . . . . **267** A4
Draycott DE72 . . . . **234** F8
Hilton DE65 . . . . **228** C2
Ripley DE5 . . . . **169** C1
Sandiacre NG10 . . . . **223** A6
Stapleford NG9 . . . . **223** E8
West Bank
Matlock Bath DE4 . . . . **143** A1
Toadmoor DE56 . . . . **168** A2
Winster DE4 . . . . **141** B5
West Bank Ave
Crich DE4 . . . . **156** F1
Derby DE22 . . . . **218** F8
Mansfield NG19 . . . . **136** B1
West Bank Cl DE22 . . . . **218** E8
Westbank Ct S18 . . . . **57** C4
West Bank Lea NG19 . . . . . . **136** B1
West Bank Link NG19 . . . . . **136** B1
West Bank Rd DE22 . . . . . . **204** E5
West Bars S40 . . . . **266** A3
Westbourne DE55 . . . . **147** A4
Westbourne Cl NG19 . . . . . . **136** E4
Westbourne Ct S40 . . . . **95** F5
Westbourne Gr S40 . . . . **95** B3
Westbourne Pk DE22 . . . . . **217** F7
Westbridge Rd S43 . . . . **80** A7
Westbrook Cl
Chapel-en-le-F SK23 . . . . **47** C5
Chesterfield S40 . . . . **94** F2
Westbrook Dr S40 . . . . **94** F2
Westbury Ct DE22 . . . . **218** E3
Westbury Gdns DE56 . . . . . **179** C5
Westbury St DE22 . . . . **218** E3
Westby La NG16 . . . . **195** D3
West Cl DE22 . . . . **204** E2
West Cres
Duckmanton S44 . . . . **98** A5
Matlock DE4 . . . . **143** A6
West Croft Ave DE23 . . . . . **231** D5
West Croft Cl DE45 . . . . . . **125** B5
Westcroft Cres S20 . . . . **59** E8
West Croft Ct S43 . . . . **97** B5
Westcroft Dr S20 . . . . **59** E7
West Croft Dr S43 . . . . **97** B5
Westcroft Gdns S20 . . . . **59** E8
Westcroft Glen S20 . . . . **59** E7
Westcroft Gr S20 . . . . **59** E7
Westcross Ave NG9 . . . . **223** E8
Westdale Cl TN G10 . . . . **236** A5
Westdale Rd
Mansfield NG19 . . . . **136** B1
Westwood NG16 . . . . **171** C4
Westdene Ave DE24 . . . . . . **232** D5
West Dr
Derby DE3 . . . . **217** D2
Doveridge DE6 . . . . **211** B1
Glossop SK13 . . . . **9** E7
West Edge Cl S45 . . . . **129** D4
West End
Alfreton DE55 . . . . **159** A3
Barlborough S43 . . . . **80** A7
Baslow DE45 . . . . **91** E5
Brassington DE4 . . . . **152** F1
Broadbottom SK14 . . . . **15** F8
Elton DE4 . . . . **140** E6

West End *continued*
Pinxton NG16 . . . . **160** C4
Wirksworth DE4 . . . . **165** E8
West End Cl DE55 . . . . **159** A3
West End Cres DE7 . . . . . . **208** D8
West End Dr
Ilkeston DE7 . . . . **208** D8
Shardlow DE72 . . . . **234** E1
West End St NG9 . . . . **223** C5
West End View S21 . . . . **59** C2
Westerlands NG9 . . . . **223** F6
Western Ave DE55 . . . . **169** D7
Western Dr DE75 . . . . **193** F8
Western La SK23 . . . . **46** A8
Western Rd
Derby DE3 . . . . **217** E2
Derby, Rose Hill DE23 . . . . . **219** A3
Western View S45 . . . . **90** A4
Western Villas DE56 . . . . . . **167** F3
Westfield Ave
Chesterfield S40 . . . . **95** B1
■ Heanor DE75 . . . . **181** F1
West Field Bank S43 . . . . **80** A7
Westfield Cl
Chesterfield S40 . . . . **95** B2
Ilkeston DE7 . . . . **208** C6
Westfield Cres S20 . . . . **59** C8
Westfield Ctr S20 . . . . **59** E8
Westfield Dr
Blackwell DE55 . . . . **147** E1
Ilkeston DE7 . . . . **194** D2
Westfield Gdns S40 . . . . **95** B2
Westfield Gr DE22 . . . . **218** D4
Westfield Inf Sch S40 . . . . . . **95** B2
Westfield La
Barlborough S43 . . . . **79** F7
Chesterfield S21 . . . . **77** E8
Westfield Northway S20 . . . . **59** E8
Westfield Rd
Dronfield S18 . . . . **76** C8
Killamarsh S21 . . . . **60** C5
Swadlincote DE11 . . . . **256** B6
Westfield Sch S20 . . . . **59** D8
Westfield Southway S20 . . . . **59** E8
Westgate DE1 . . . . **218** E6
West Gate
Holme HD9 . . . . **3** F8
Long Eaton NG10 . . . . **236** F7
Westgate ST14 . . . . **196** F3
West Gr DE22 . . . . **232** D5
Westgreen Ave DE24 . . . . . **232** D5
Westhall Rd DE3 . . . . **217** D3
West Hill DE5 . . . . **181** B7
Westhill La S42 . . . . **115** E3
West Hill Pk NG19 . . . . **136** B3
West Ho S8 . . . . **43** A4
West Horderns SK23 . . . . **47** B5
Westhorpe Dr NG10 . . . . . . **236** C8
Westhouses Prim Sch
DE55 . . . . **147** C1
Westland Dr NG16 . . . . **160** C3
Westland Gdns S20 . . . . **59** D8
Westland Gr ■ S20 . . . . **59** E8
Westland Rd ■ S20 . . . . **59** E8
Westlands The ST14 . . . . . . **196** D6
West Lawn DE55 . . . . **230** D2
Westlea DE4 . . . . **143** D6
West Lea
Chesterfield S40 . . . . **95** B2
Clowne S43 . . . . **80** D4
West Lea Cotts S43 . . . . **80** D4
Westlea View S43 . . . . **80** D4
West Lees Rd S33 . . . . **40** B4
Westleigh NG19 . . . . **136** D6
Westleigh Ave DE22 . . . . . . **218** C6
West Lodge La S40 . . . . **95** E5
Westley Cres DE21 . . . . **191** D2
Westminster Ave ■ NG10 . . . . **223** C5
Westminster St DE24 . . . . . **232** F8
Westmoor Rd S43 . . . . **96** F4
Westmorland Cl DE21 . . . . . **219** C6
Westmorland Way NG16 . . . **171** B3
Weston Bank DE6 . . . . **197** F1
Weston Cl S40 . . . . **95** A5
Weston Cres NG10 . . . . **235** F4
Weston Ct DE72 . . . . **245** E4
Westonhill Chalet Pk
DE72 . . . . **245** C4
**Weston-on-Trent CE Prim
Sch** DE72 . . . . **245** E4
Weston Park Ave DE72 . . . . **232** E3
Weston Park Gdns DE72 . . . **232** D3
Weston Rd
Aston-on-T DE72 . . . . **246** A7
Weston-on-T DE72 . . . . **245** F6
Weston Rise DE73 . . . . **245** A8
Weston Spot Cl DE5 . . . . . . **180** D7
Weston St
Heanor DE75 . . . . **194** A8
Swadlincote DE11 . . . . **256** B3
West Park Ct NG10 . . . . **236** D7
West Park Rd DE22 . . . . **218** E8
West Park Sch DE21 . . . . . . **220** D5
West Rd
Buxton SK17 . . . . **85** B6
Derby DE21 . . . . **220** D5
West Road Ho ■ SK17 . . . . . **85** B6
West Row DE21 . . . . **205** A1
West Service Rd DE21 . . . . . **220** B3
West St
Bramley-Vale S44 . . . . **117** D1
Burton u T DE15 . . . . **248** B3
Chesterfield S40 . . . . **266** A4
Clay Cross S45 . . . . **131** A4
Clowne S43 . . . . **81** A5
Creswell S80 . . . . **81** D1
Dronfield S18 . . . . **56** F2

West St *continued*
Eckington S21 . . . . **59** C2
Glossop SK13 . . . . **9** F7
Heanor DE75 . . . . **181** D2
Ilkeston DE7 . . . . **208** E7
Langley Mill NG16 . . . . **182** B3
Shirebrook NG20 . . . . **120** D4
Somercotes DE55 . . . . **170** D6
South Normanton DE55 . . . **159** F5
Stonebroom DE55 . . . . **146** F3
Swadlincote DE11 . . . . **256** B4
Whaley Thorns NG20 . . . . . . **101** A3
West Terr ■ DE7 . . . . **194** F1
Westthorpe Fields Rd
S21 . . . . **60** C4
Westthorpe Rd S21 . . . . **60** D5
West Towers Mews SK6 . . . **23** A4
West View
Barlborough S43 . . . . **80** A6
Bolsover S44 . . . . **118** B8
Hulland Village DE6 . . . . . . **175** E2
Mayfield DE6 . . . . **184** D6
Parwich DE6 . . . . **151** E1
Rocester ST14 . . . . **197** A3
Staveley S43 . . . . **78** E1
Tibshelf DE55 . . . . **147** F6
West View Cl S17 . . . . **55** F6
West View La S17 . . . . **55** F6
West View Rd S41 . . . . **95** C6
Westward Cl ST14 . . . . **210** B1
West Way DE55 . . . . **159** C1
Westwell Pl S20 . . . . **59** C6
Westwick Cres S8 . . . . **56** D7
Westwick Gr S8 . . . . **56** E7
Westwick La S42 . . . . **94** D2
Westwick Pk S8 . . . . **76** D3
Westwick Rd S8 . . . . **56** E7
Westwick St DE7 . . . . **209** B6
Westwood Ave S43 . . . . **97** C8
Westwood Cl S43 . . . . **97** C5
Westwood Dr
Derby DE24 . . . . **232** D5
Staveley S43 . . . . **97** C5
Westwood Drive Gdns
S43 . . . . **97** B5
Westwood Gdns DE55 . . . . **147** B5
Westwood Inf Sch NG16 . . **171** C4
Westwood La S43 . . . . **97** A6
Westwood Pk DE11 . . . . **255** F5
Westwood Rd S44 . . . . **97** A4
Wetherby Cl NG16 . . . . **195** E7
Wetherby Ct DE14 . . . . **253** F7
Wetherby Rd DE24 . . . . **232** E7
Wetheral Rd DE14 . . . . **248** C2
Wetlands La S43, S44 . . . . . . **96** E4
Weyacres DE7 . . . . **221** C1
Weybridge Cl DE7 . . . . **207** D8
Whaley Bridge Prim Sch
SK23 . . . . **45** E7
Whaley Bridge Sta SK23 . . . **45** E8
Whaley La SK23 . . . . **45** C8
Whaley Rd NG20 . . . . **101** A2
Whaley Thorns Heritage Ctr*
NG20 . . . . **101** A3
Whaley Thorns Prim Sch
NG20 . . . . **101** A3
Wharf Cl SK23 . . . . **45** E7
Wharfedale Cl DE22 . . . . . . **205** B4
Wharfedale Rd NG10 . . . . . **236** A6
Wharf Hos DE13 . . . . **253** A1
Wharf La
Eckington S12 . . . . **44** C2
Shottle DE56 . . . . **177** D4
Staveley S43 . . . . **79** A3
Wharford La DE73 . . . . **245** E8
Wharf Rd
Pinxton NG16 . . . . **160** D2
Whaley Bridge SK23 . . . . **45** E7
Wharf Road Ind Est
NG16 . . . . **160** D2
Wharf The DE72 . . . . **235** A2
Wharmby Ave NG19 . . . . . . **135** D3
Wharncliffe Cl SK13 . . . . **9** E4
Wharncliffe Rd DE7 . . . . . . **208** E8
Wharton Dr S41 . . . . **266** C4
Whatstandwell Sta DE4 . . . **156** C1
Wheal La SK17 . . . . **107** D7
Wheatbridge Rd S40 . . . . . **266** A3
Wheatbridge Ret Pk S40 . . **266** A2
Wheatcroft SK13 . . . . **9** E4
Wheatcroft Cl
Clay Cross S45 . . . . **131** D2
Wingerworth S42 . . . . **115** A4
Wheatcroft La DE4 . . . . **157** A7
Wheatcroft Way DE21 . . . . **205** C2
Wheatfield Cres NG19 . . . . **136** E5
Wheatfield Way DE65 . . . . **242** D5
Wheatfields SK23 . . . . **47** C7
Wheatfield Way S42 . . . . **94** F5
Wheathill Cl
Calow S44 . . . . **96** F4
Chesterfield S42 . . . . **94** F5
Wheathill Gr DE23 . . . . **231** A6
Wheathill La S41 . . . . **96** D4
Wheatland Cl DE24 . . . . . . **231** C2
Wheatlands La DE45 . . . . . . **91** C5
Wheatlands Rd
Burton u T DE15 . . . . **254** E7
Wingerworth S42 . . . . **114** E4
Wheatley Ave S43 . . . . **159** C1
Wheatley Cl NG19 . . . . **136** E1
Wheatley Gdns DE4 . . . . . . **127** D2
Wheatley La DE15 . . . . **248** C6
Wheatley Rd DE4 . . . . **127** D3
Wheatsheaf Cl
Derby DE21 . . . . **206** C2
Horwich End SK23 . . . . **45** E6

Wheatsheaf La DE4 . . . . . . **156** F1
Wheatsheaf Rd SK23 . . . . . . **45** E6
Wheeldon Ave
Belper DE56 . . . . **179** B4
Derby DE22 . . . . **218** E2
Wheeldon Cl NE7 . . . . **194** F6
Wheeldon Cres S43 . . . . **96** D3
Wheeldon Manor DE22 . . . **218** E8
Wheeldon Way DE6 . . . . . . **175** E3
Wheelwright Way DE24 . . . **219** D3
Whenby Cl DE3 . . . . **217** C2
Whernside Cl DE24 . . . . . . **233** D6
Wheston Bank SK17 . . . . **69** B4
Wheston Ct ■ S40 . . . . **95** D5
Whetmorhurst La SK6 . . . . . **23** E4
Whilton Cres DE7 . . . . **207** D8
Whinacre Cl DE56 . . . . **179** D4
Whinacre Cl S8 . . . . **57** B6
Whinacre Pl S8 . . . . **57** A6
Whinacre Wlk S8 . . . . **57** A6
Whinbush Ave DE24 . . . . . . **232** E5
Whinney Bank NG19 . . . . . **136** D4
Whinney Hill NG19 . . . . **136** D4
Whisperwood Cl S44 . . . . . . **98** A5
Whistlestop Cl DE24 . . . . . . **217** D4
Whiston St DE23 . . . . **219** A2
Whitaker Gdns DE23 . . . . . **218** C1
Whitaker Mews ST14 . . . . . **196** F3
Whitaker Rd DE23 . . . . **218** B2
Whitaker St DE23 . . . . **219** A2
Whitburn Rd NG9 . . . . **223** E3
Whitby Ave DE21 . . . . **205** C1
Whitcombe Pl DE5 . . . . **169** D2
Whitebank Cl S41 . . . . **266** C1
Whitecar La DE55, S45, . . . **145** D7
Whitecotes Cl S40 . . . . **114** E8
Whitecotes La S40 . . . . **114** E8
Whitecotes Pk S40 . . . . **114** E8
Whitecotes Prim Sch
S40 . . . . **114** F8
Whitecroft Rd SK6 . . . . **23** C1
Whitecross Ave SK17 . . . . **69** C4
Whitecross Gdns DE1 . . . . . **218** E7
Whitecross Rd DE55 . . . . . . **170** D7
Whitecross Rd SK17 . . . . **69** D5
Whitecross St DE1 . . . . **218** E6
White Edge Cl S40 . . . . **95** D5
White Edge Dr DE45 . . . . . . **91** E6
Whitefield La
Ashover S45 . . . . **129** A5
Chinley SK17 . . . . **106** E8
White Gate Rd HD9 . . . . **3** D7
Whitegates SK14 . . . . **9** A1
White Gates DE5 . . . . **181** B8
Whitegates Way NG17 . . . . **148** E2
Whitehall Barn S33 . . . . **51** A6
White Hart Cnr S21 . . . . **59** E4
White Hart Yd DE56 . . . . . . **191** F8
Whitehaven Gr DE73 . . . . . **233** A3
Whitehead Cl DE7 . . . . **194** D2
Whitehead Dr NG16 . . . . . . **182** D8
Whitehead St ◢ S43 . . . . **78** E5
White Horse La DE55 . . . . . **145** D7
Whitehough Head La
SK23 . . . . **106** E8
Whitehouse Cl DE24 . . . . . . **232** D3
Whitehouse Rise DE56 . . . . **178** E6
Whitehouses S41 . . . . **266** C1
Whitehurst St DE24 . . . . . . **232** D7
White Knowle Cl SK17 . . . . . **85** C5
White Knowle Pk SK17 . . . . . **85** C5
White Knowle Rd SK17 . . . . . **85** C5
White La
Eckington S12 . . . . **44** C2
Shottle DE56 . . . . **177** D4
Whitelea La DE4 . . . . **144** B6
White Leas S40 . . . . **95** B4
Whiteleas Ave S42 . . . . **132** A7
Whiteleas Rd S43 . . . . **45** D3
Whiteley Rd DE5 . . . . **180** F7
White Lion Sq DE7 . . . . **208** F7
White Lodge La DE45 . . . . . . **91** F6
Whitelow La
Ible DE4 . . . . **153** E7
Sheffield S17 . . . . **55** B5
Whitely Cl ■ NG9 . . . . **223** E8
Whitemoor Hall DE56 . . . . **179** D5
Whitemoor La DE56 . . . . . . **179** D5
White Rd
New Mills SK22 . . . . **24** C2
Staveley S43 . . . . **79** A3
Whites Cl DE55 . . . . **159** A2
Whites Croft View S43 . . . . . **80** B6
White La DE55 . . . . **147** F1
Whitesmead Cl SK12 . . . . **32** D5
White St DE22 . . . . **218** E7
White Thorns Cl S8 . . . . **57** B5
White Thorns Dr S8 . . . . **57** B5
White Thorns View S8 . . . . . . **57** B6
White Tor Rd DE4 . . . . **143** C2
Whiteway DE22 . . . . **204** E2
Whitewell Gdns DE24 . . . . **233** C5
Whitewells La DE56 . . . . . . **178** C8
Whitewells Rd DE56 . . . . . . **167** E2
White Woods Way DE4 . . . . **143** B3
Whitfield Ave SK13 . . . . **17** C7
Whitfield Cross SK13 . . . . . . **17** D7
Whitfield La DE45 . . . . **108** A3
Whitfield Pk SK13 . . . . **17** C7
Whitfield Wells SK13 . . . . . . **17** D7
Whiting Ave ◢ NG9 . . . . . . **223** F8
White Bank Rd DE22 . . . . . **204** C4
Whitle Rd SK22 . . . . **24** C1
Whitley Way DE6 . . . . **185** E8
Whitley Wlk SK13 . . . . **16** F8
Whitmore Ave S42 . . . . **115** E2
Whitmore Rd DE21 . . . . . . **219** F6

Whitstable Cl DE23 . . . . . . **231** D7
Whittaker La DE21 . . . . **191** D7
Whitt Cl DE72 . . . . **221** C1
Whiting Mews S41 . . . . **76** F2
Whittington Hill S41 . . . . . . **77** A2
Whittington La S18 . . . . **76** F5
Whittington Rd S43 . . . . **77** F4
Whittington St DE24 . . . . . **232** C7
Whittington Way S41 . . . . . . **77** A1
Whitting Valley Rd S41 . . . . **77** B1
Whittlebury Dr DE23 . . . . . **230** F7
Whitwell Bank ■ SK13 . . . . . . **9** D2
Whitwell Cl
◢ Gamesley SK13 . . . . **9** D2
Ilkeston NE7 . . . . **194** E6
Whitwell Fold ■ SK13 . . . . . . **9** D2
Whitwell Gn ◢ SK13 . . . . **9** D2
Whitwell Lea ◢ SK13 . . . . **9** D2
Whitwell Prim Sch S80 . . . . **82** A5
Whitwell Rd S80 . . . . **63** A4
Whitwell Sta S80 . . . . **82** A5
Whitworth Ave DE4 . . . . . . **127** C3
Whitworth Cl DE11 . . . . . . **262** E4
Whitworth Hospl DE4 . . . . **142** F8
Whitworth Rd
■ Chesterfield S41 . . . . **96** A6
Darley Dale DE4 . . . . **127** B4
Ilkeston DE7 . . . . **208** F7
Wholey Pl S45 . . . . **131** C3
Whysall Rd NG10 . . . . **236** B7
Whysall St DE7 . . . . **208** E2
Whyteleafe Gr DE21 . . . . . . **206** B1
Wichal Farm Cl DE5 . . . . . . **180** D7
Wicken Low La SK17 . . . . . **103** D1
Wickersley Cl ■ DE22 . . . . **204** F2
Wickets The DE15 . . . . **254** F8
Wickfield Cl S12 . . . . **44** F5
Wickfield Dr S12 . . . . **44** F5
Wickfield Gr S12 . . . . **44** F5
Wickfield Pl S12 . . . . **44** F5
Wickfield Rd S12 . . . . **44** F5
Wickins Pl S43 . . . . **79** B3
Wicksteed Cl DE56 . . . . **179** D5
Widdop Cl S13 . . . . **44** D8
Widdop Croft S13 . . . . **44** D8
Widdybank Cl DE22 . . . . . . **204** C2
Widecombe Ct 24 S41 . . . . . . **95** F8
Widnall St DE11 . . . . **256** C4
Widmerpool St NG16 . . . . . **160** C2
Wigley Prim Sch S42 . . . . . . **93** E4
Wigley Rd S43 . . . . **97** C6
Wigmore Ct DE3 . . . . **217** C3
Wikeley Way S43 . . . . **96** D7
Wilberforce Rd NG19 . . . . . **135** D2
Wilcock Ho DE21 . . . . **219** C6
Wilcox Ave NG19 . . . . **136** B5
Wildaygreen La S18 . . . . **75** B2
Wilden Croft S43 . . . . **96** C8
Wilderbrook La DE56 . . . . . **178** A8
Wilders Lea Ct DE56 . . . . . **179** A2
Wildersley Rd DE56 . . . . . . **179** A1
Wildhay Brook DE65 . . . . . **228** C1
Wildhay La DE6 . . . . **183** C7
Wild Hill NG17 . . . . **148** E7
Wildpark La DE6 . . . . **157** B4
Wildpark La DE6 . . . . **262** D6
Wildsmith St DE24 . . . . . . **233** A8
Wild St DE22 . . . . **218** D5
Wilfred St DE23 . . . . **219** B2
Wilhallow La NG16 . . . . **171** E2
Wilkin Hill S18 . . . . **75** E2
Wilkins Dr DE24 . . . . **232** E7
Wilkinson Cl
Chesterfield S40 . . . . **115** A6
Duffield NG19 . . . . **135** A5
Wilkinson Dr S43 . . . . **97** B7
Willbury Dr S12 . . . . **44** A6
Willcock Rd DE14 . . . . **254** A7
Willersley Ct ■ S41 . . . . **95** D7
Willersley Ho NG10 . . . . . . **236** A5
Willersley La
Matlock Bath DE4 . . . . **155** C8
Matlock DE4 . . . . **143** C1
Willesden Ave DE22 . . . . . . **218** A7
Willetts Rd DE21 . . . . **220** D3
William Allitt Sch DE11 . . . **255** E7
William Ave NG16 . . . . **182** F2
William Cl
Duffield DE56 . . . . **190** D4
Sheffield S20 . . . . **59** D6
William Cres S20 . . . . **59** D6
**William Gilbert Endowed
Prim Sch** DE56 . . . . **190** E4
William Holmes Almshouses
DE5 . . . . **169** F2
William Howitt Jun Com Sch
DE75 . . . . **181** D2
William Levick Prim Sch
S18 . . . . **56** C2
William Lilley Inf Sch
NG9 . . . . **223** D6
William Nadin Way DE11 . **255** F4
William Newton Cl DE65 . . **241** B5
William Rd NG9 . . . . **223** D7
William Rhodes Prim Sch
S40 . . . . **266** A4
William St N S41 . . . . **76** F2
William St DE5 . . . . **170** D6
**William Shrewsbury Prim
Sch** DE13 . . . . **240** E1
Williamson Ave SK17 . . . . . . **66** C1
Williamson Cres SK23 . . . . . **45** D8
Williamson Rd SK23 . . . . . . **45** D8
William St
Belper DE56 . . . . **178** F4

William St continued
Chesterfield S41 . . . . .96 A6
Derby DE1 . . . . .218 E6
Eckington S21 . . . . .59 D3
Long Eaton NG10 . . . . .223 C2
Williamthorpe Cl S42 . . . .132 A7
Williamthorpe Ind Pk
S42 .116 D2
Williamthorpe Ponds (Nature
Reserve)* S42 . . . . .116 E2
Williamthorpe Rd S42 . . . .132 B7
Willington Prim Sch
DE65 . . . . .242 B5
Willington Rd
Etwall DE65 . . . . .229 D3
Findern DE65 . . . . .242 D8
Repton DE65 . . . . .242 B4
Willington Sta DE65 . . . . . .242 A6
Willn St DE23 . . . . .218 F1
Willoughby Almshouses
NG16 . . . . .195 C1
Willoughby Ave NG10 . . . .223 C3
Willoughby Cl DE72 . . . . . .235 F8
Willoughby Ct DE72 . . . . . .222 D4
Willoughby Ho DE11 . . . . .256 C4
Willow Ave
Long Eaton NG10 . . . . .223 D1
Ripley DE5 . . . . .180 D7
Shirebrook NG20 . . . . .119 D5
Stapleford NG9 . . . . .223 D6
Willowbath La DE4 . . . . . . .165 F7
Willowbrook Cl DE65 . . . . .228 C2
Willowbrook Grange
DE73 . . . . .233 A1
Willow Cl
Aldercar NG16 . . . . .182 B4
Alfreton DE55 . . . . .159 B5
Aston-on-T DE72 . . . . .246 B7
Creswell S80 . . . . .81 F1
Derby DE21 . . . . .204 F2
Pilsley S45 . . . . .132 C1
South Normanton DE55 . . .160 B5
Stanley Common DE7 . . . . .193 A2
Willow Croft DE24 . . . . . . .233 C4
Willowcroft Rd DE21 . . . . .220 E4
Willow Ct
Ashbourne DE6 . . . . .185 D7
Calow S44 . . . . .97 A3
Swadlincote DE11 . . . . .256 C4
Willow Dr
Chapel-en-le-F SK23 . . . . . . .47 B5
Mastin Moor S43 . . . . .79 C4
Swadlincote DE11 . . . . .255 F7
Willow Farm Bsns Pk
DE74 . . . . .247 B6
Willow Farm Ct DE65 . . . . .230 D2
Willowfields DE65 . . . . . . .228 D2
Willow Garth Rd S41 . . . . . .95 C8
Willow Gr
Belper DE56 . . . . .179 A2
Willington DE65 . . . . .242 A6
Willowherb Cl DE24 . . . . . .231 F2
Willow Ho DE21 . . . . .219 C6
Willow Meadow Rd DE6 . .185 D7
Willow Park Way DE72 . . . .246 A7
Willowpit La DE65 . . . . . . .228 E5
Willow Pl DE15 . . . . .254 E7
Willow Rd
Castle Donington DE74 . . . .247 B5
Killamarsh S21 . . . . .60 C5
Willow Rise NG10 . . . . .223 B5
Willow Row DE1 . . . . .267 A4
Willows Ave DE55 . . . . .159 B5
Willows Ct DE5 . . . . .169 C1
Willowside DE11 . . . . .230 D1
Willowslade DE21 . . . . .220 D3
Willow St DE55 . . . . .146 C1
Willows The
Hulland Ward DE6 . . . . .175 F3
Pleasley NG19 . . . . .135 A6
Willow Tree Dr S43 . . . . . . .80 F2
Willow Way DE7 . . . . .127 B3
Willridding La DE6 . . . . . . .183 C7
Will Shore's La DE4 . . . . . .162 C6
Willson Ave DE23 . . . . .231 D8
Willson Dr DE55 . . . . .170 C7
Willson Rd DE23 . . . . .231 C8
Wilmans Wlk SK13 . . . . . . .10 A1
Wilmington Ave DE24 . . . .233 B5
Wilmore Rd DE24 . . . . .232 B5
Wilmot Ave
Derby DE21 . . . . .219 F5
Weston-on-T DE72 . . . . .245 E5
Wilmot Dr DE7 . . . . .192 F6
Wilmot Rd
Belper DE56 . . . . .179 A4
Swadlincote DE11 . . . . .256 B3
Wilmot St
Derby DE1 . . . . .267 B2
Heanor DE75 . . . . .181 E1
Ilkeston DE7 . . . . .194 E1
Long Eaton NG10 . . . . .236 A5
Matlock DE4 . . . . .143 B6
Wilmslow Dr DE21 . . . . . . .206 B1
Wilne Ave NG10 . . . . .236 A4
Wilne Cl NG10 . . . . .235 F4
Wilne La
Breaston DE72 . . . . .235 D4
Shardlow DE72 . . . . .235 B2
Wilne Rd
Draycott DE72 . . . . .235 B5
Long Eaton NG10 . . . . .235 F4
Wilshaw Cl SK23 . . . . .47 C5
Wilson's Terr SK13 . . . . . . .17 B8

Wilson Ave
Blackwell DE55 . . . . .147 E1
Clowne S43 . . . . .80 F5
Heanor DE75 . . . . .181 B4
Wilson Cl
Burnaston DE65 . . . . .230 C8
Clay Cross S45 . . . . .131 D2
Wilson La S44 . . . . .117 B2
Wilson Pl 6 S8 . . . . .43 A7
Wilson Rd
Derby DE21 . . . . .219 F8
Dronfield S18 . . . . .57 C4
Eastwood NG16 . . . . .182 F1
Wilson Rise DE73 . . . . .252 E6
Wilson St
Alfreton DE55 . . . . .159 B4
Derby DE1 . . . . .267 B2
Dronfield S18 . . . . .76 B8
Mansfield NG19 . . . . .135 D2
Pinxton NG16 . . . . .160 D3
Wilstorpe Bsns & Enterprise
Coll NG10 . . . . .223 B1
Wilsthorpe Rd
Breaston DE72 . . . . .235 F8
Derby DE21 . . . . .220 A7
Long Eaton NG10 . . . . .236 B7
Wilton Cl DE24 . . . . .231 C2
Wilton Pl DE7 . . . . .194 F1
Wilton St 5 DE7 . . . . .194 F1
Wiltra Gr DE56 . . . . .190 F3
Wiltshire Ave NG16 . . . . . .171 B4
Wiltshire Dr SK13 . . . . .17 F8
Wiltshire Rd DE21 . . . . . . .220 B6
Wimbledon Rd DE22 . . . . .218 A7
Wimborne Cres S41 . . . . . .95 F7
Wimbourne Cl DE73 . . . . . .233 A2
Wimpole Gdns DE22 . . . . .218 B6
Wimsey Way DE55 . . . . . . .159 B2
Wincanton Cl DE24 . . . . . .219 D1
Winchcombe Dr DE15 . . . .248 B1
Winchcombe Way DE21 . .206 B2
Winchester Cl S42 . . . . . . .115 A3
Winchester Cres DE7 . . . . .209 A8
Winchester Dr
Burton u T DE14 . . . . .254 C8
Linton DE12 . . . . .261 D5
Mansfield Woodhouse
NG19 . . . . .136 D2
Swadlincote DE11 . . . . .256 D6
Winchester Rd S41 . . . . . . .95 E7
Windermere Ave
Dronfield S18 . . . . .56 E1
Ilkeston DE7 . . . . .208 D5
Windermere Cl NG10 . . . . .223 A1
Windermere Cres DE22 . . .204 E3
Windermere Dr DE21 . . . . .220 F5
Windermere Gdns NG10 . .223 B2
Windermere Rd
Chesterfield S41 . . . . .95 D7
Clay Cross S45 . . . . .131 B3
Long Eaton NG10 . . . . .223 B2
Winders Cnr S43 . . . . .80 B5
Winding Wheel The*
S41 .266 C3
Windlea Rd DE55 . . . . .170 C6
Windley Cres DE22 . . . . . .204 F1
Windley Dr DE7 . . . . .194 D3
Windley La
Idridgehay DE56 . . . . .176 E5
Turnditch DE56 . . . . .177 A1
Windley DE56 . . . . .189 E7
Windmill Ave DE56 . . . . . .192 A8
Windmill Cl
Bolsover S44 . . . . .99 A3
Castle Donington DE74 . . . .247 B2
Elvaston DE24 . . . . .233 D4
Ockbrook DE72 . . . . .221 C5
6 Uttoxeter ST14 . . . . . . .210 B1
Windmill Dr S14 . . . . .43 C4
Windmill Greenway S20 . . .59 E5
Windmill Hill La DE22 . . . .218 C6
Windmill La
Alderwasley DE56 . . . . .166 F6
Ashbourne DE6 . . . . .173 C4
Belper DE56 . . . . .179 A4
Eyam S32 . . . . .71 C6
Snelston DE6 . . . . .184 C2
Unstone S18 . . . . .77 A6
Windmill Rd DE65 . . . . . . .229 B3
Windmill Rise
Belper DE56 . . . . .179 A5
Somercotes DE55 . . . . .170 D7
South Normanton DE55 . . .159 F5
Windmill Way
Wilmill Side DE11 . . . . .256 A1
Windmill View DE56 . . . . .179 E8
Windmill Way S42 . . . . .96 C8
Windrush Cl DE22 . . . . . . .205 B5
Windrush Ct 4 S43 . . . . . . .96 E8
Windrush Rd DE65 . . . . . . .240 D8
Windses Est S32 . . . . .53 D2
Windsmoor Rd NG16 . . . . .182 D8
Windsor Ave
Derby DE23 . . . . .231 B8
Melbourne DE73 . . . . .252 A8
Windsor Cl
6 Ashbourne DE6 . . . . . . .173 D3
Borrowash DE72 . . . . .221 C1
Chesterfield S40 . . . . .95 C1
Heanor DE75 . . . . .181 E3
Swadlincote DE11 . . . . .256 A6
Swanwick DE55 . . . . .170 A7
Windsor Cres
Ilkeston DE7 . . . . .208 E4
Stapleford NG9 . . . . .223 D6
Windsor Ct
Derby DE5 . . . . .217 D3
Long Eaton NG10 . . . . .236 E7

Windsor Ct continued
Sandiacre NG10 . . . . .223 B4
West Hallam DE7 . . . . .207 D8
Windsor Dr
Derby DE21 . . . . .221 A6
Dronfield S18 . . . . .56 C1
Wingerworth S42 . . . . .114 E4
Windsor Park Rd SK17 . . . .85 D8
Windsor Rd
Buxton SK17 . . . . .85 C8
Linton DE12 . . . . .261 D5
Uttoxeter ST14 . . . . .210 A1
Windsor St NG9 . . . . .223 E7
Windsor Wlk 7 S41 . . . . . .96 C1
Windy Fields Rd S42 . . . . .113 D7
Windy House La S2 . . . . . . .43 A8
Windy Knowle SK22 . . . . . .25 A3
Windy La DE12 . . . . .191 C1
Windyridge S42 . . . . .121 B6
Winfield Gr S26 . . . . .15 B1
Wingerworth Ave S8 . . . . . .56 D8
Wingerworth Cotts S42 . . .15 B3
Wingerworth Park Rd
DE21 . . . . .220 E5
Wingerworth St S42 . . . . . .115 E3
Wingerworth Way S40 . . . .114 F7
Wingfield Cl 8 S18 . . . . . . .56 C1
Wingfield Cres S12 . . . . . . .44 C5
Wingfield Dr
Derby DE21 . . . . .205 F1
Ilkeston DE7 . . . . .194 D3
Wingfield Gr SK13 . . . . .17 F7
Wingfield Rd DE55 . . . . . . .157 F3
Wingfield Manor Ho*
DE55 . . . . .157 E2
Wingfield Rd
Alfreton DE55 . . . . .158 E3
Tupton S42 . . . . .131 D8
Wingfield View S45 . . . . . .131 E4
Winhill Rd SK22 . . . . .24 C1
Winkpenny La DE55 . . . . . .147 F5
Winnat Pl S43 . . . . .97 C7
Winnats S33 . . . . .37 E2
Winney Cl
Chesterfield S40 . . . . .95 D5
Glossop SK13 . . . . .17 F8
Winney Hill S26 . . . . .61 E5
Winney La S26 . . . . .61 E3
Winnings The S80 . . . . .101 E8
Winnington Rd SK6 . . . . . . .23 A7
Winn La DE6 . . . . .174 F7
Winshill Inf Sch DE15 . . . .248 B3
Winslow Ave SK14 . . . . .9 A2
Winslow Gn DE21 . . . . .220 C6
Winster CE Prim Sch
DE4 .141 D6
Winster Cl
Belper DE56 . . . . .179 B5
Clay Cross S42 . . . . .131 A5
Winster Ct S41 . . . . .96 A5
Winster Gr 3 DE11 . . . . . . .255 E5
Winster Gr S17 . . . . .85 E7
Winster La DE4 . . . . .140 F7
Winster Market Ho*
DE4 .141 C6
Winster Mews SK13 . . . . . . .9 E2
Winster Rd
Derby DE21 . . . . .205 E1
Staveley S43 . . . . .97 C8
Winster St S43 . . . . .85 E7
Winster Way NG10 . . . . . . .235 F5
Winston Cl NG9 . . . . .223 E8
Winterbourne Dr NG9 . . . .209 E1
Winter Closes NG16 . . . . . .171 F1
Wintercroft La DE6 . . . . . .161 E1
Wintergreen Dr DE23 . . . .230 F6
Winyard Ct 2 S40 . . . . .95 D5
Wire La DE55 . . . . .148 B3
Wirestone La S45 . . . . .129 A3
Wirksmoor Rd SK22 . . . . . .33 B7
Wirksworth Hall Gdns
DE4 .165 B8
Wirksworth Heritage Ctr
Mus* DE4 . . . . .154 F1
Wirksworth Ind Ctr DE4 . .154 F3
Wirksworth Inf Sch DE4 . .154 F1
Wirksworth Jun Sch
DE4 .155 A1
Wirksworth Rd
Duffield DE56 . . . . .190 B4
Holloway DE4 . . . . .156 B2
Ilkeston DE7 . . . . .208 C4
Kirk Ireton DE6 . . . . .165 B2
Shottle DE56 . . . . .177 C3
Wisbech C5 S40 . . . . .114 E8
Wisgreaves Rd DE24 . . . . .232 F8
Wishing Stone Way DE4 . .143 E6
Wiston Way S41 . . . . .115 C7
Witham Cl
Chesterfield S41 . . . . .96 C6
Hilton DE65 . . . . .228 E2
Witham Cl S40 . . . . .95 C3
Witham Dr DE23 . . . . .231 D6
Witney Cl DE24 . . . . .232 C8
Witney St S43 . . . . .43 A8
Wittering Cl NG10 . . . . . . .236 E5
Witton Ct DE24 . . . . .231 D4
Woburn Cl
Blackwell DE55 . . . . .147 E1
Swanwick DE55 . . . . .169 F7
Woburn Cotts DE4 . . . . . . .143 B7
Woburn Croft NG10 . . . . . .223 A4
Woburn Ho DE55 . . . . .147 E1
Woburn La NG19 . . . . .135 C4
Woburn Pl
Derby DE22 . . . . .218 B5
Pleasley NG19 . . . . .135 C4

Woburn Rd NG19 . . . . . .135 C4
Wolds Rd DE4 . . . . .143 D7
Wolds Rise DE4 . . . . .143 C7
Wolfa St DE22 . . . . .267 A2
Wolfcote Cl S45 . . . . .131 D1
Wolfe Cl S40 . . . . .95 D1
Wolfscote Dale DE11 . . . . .255 F2
Wolfscote Gr DE21 . . . . . . .205 E1
Wollaton Dr S17 . . . . .56 A5
Wollaton Dr S17 . . . . .56 A5
Wollaton Rd
Derby DE21 . . . . .219 F8
Sheffield S17 . . . . .56 A5
Wollaton Rd N 5 DE21 . . . .205 F1
Wollen Cl S80 . . . . .81 F1
Wolseley Rd 2 S8 . . . . .43 A7
Wolverley Grange DE24 . .233 D6
Wood's Hospl SK13 . . . . . . .10 C3
Woodale Cl DE23 . . . . .230 F6
Woodall La DE55 . . . . .61 D6
Woodall Rd S21 . . . . .60 F5
Wood Ave
Creswell S80 . . . . .81 D1
Sandiacre NG10 . . . . .223 A6
Woodbank Ct S17 . . . . .56 A7
Woodbeck Ct DE21 . . . . . . .206 B2
Woodbine Cl DE14 . . . . . . .253 E6
Woodbine Terr DE23 . . . . . .47 A6
Woodborough Rd NG19 . . .135 E1
Woodbourne Rd SK22 . . . . .33 A5
Woodbridge Cl
Chellaston DE73 . . . . .232 F1
Heanor DE75 . . . . .182 B1
Woodbridge Jun Sch
DE55 . . . . .159 A3
Woodbridge Rise S40 . . . .114 B8
Woodbrook S40 . . . . .45 E8
Woodbrook Ct SK23 . . . . . .45 E7
Woodchester Dr DE24 . . . .233 D6
Wood Cl S42 . . . . .114 D4
Woodcock Gr SK13 . . . . . . .10 E1
Woodcock Rd SK13 . . . . . . .11 A1
Woodcock Sq DE23 . . . . . .230 C8
Woodcote Way DE23 . . . . .231 A7
Wood Croft DE21 . . . . .231 D8
Wood End Dr DE56 . . . . . . .156 B6
Wood End La DE73 . . . . . . .244 D1
Wood End Rd DE75 . . . . . . .181 E2
Woodfall La
Duffield DE56 . . . . .190 A1
Windley DE22 . . . . .189 E3
Wood Farm Ct NG11 . . . . . .237 D2
Wood Farm La DE11 . . . . . .256 E4
Woodfield Cl SK13 . . . . .9 F5
Woodfield Dr
Ripley DE5 . . . . .170 A1
Swadlincote DE11 . . . . .256 C5
Woodfield Rd
Pinxton NG16 . . . . .160 D4
South Normanton DE55 . . .159 F4
Woodford Rd DE22 . . . . . . .218 A7
Woodford Way S43 . . . . . . .78 B4
Woodgate Dr DE73 . . . . . . .233 A1
Wood Gdns SK22 . . . . .25 C3
Woodhall Dr DE23 . . . . . . .230 E8
Woodhall House Farm
S26 . . . . .61 C6
Woodhead La S45 . . . . .130 D1
Woodhead Rd
Glossop SK13 . . . . .10 D5
Holme HD9 . . . . .2 E6
Sheffield, Highfield S2 . . . . .43 A8
Sheffield S12 . . . . .44 B8
Tintwistle SK13 . . . . .10 B8
Woodhouse Ct NG19 . . . . .136 C2
Woodhouse La
Barlborough S43 . . . . .79 E5
Bolsover S44 . . . . .98 E3
Mastin Moor S43 . . . . .79 C5
Scropton DE65 . . . . .226 F7
South Normanton DE55 . . .159 E5
Winster DE4 . . . . .141 C6
Woodhouse Rd
Kilburn DE56, DE7 . . . . .192 A7
6 Mansfield NG19 . . . . . .136 B1
Rowsley DE4 . . . . .126 F7
Sheffield S12 . . . . .44 B8
Woodhouse St S41 . . . . . . .256 D3
Woodhouse Station Ent Ctr
NG19 . . . . .136 B3
Woodhurst Cl DE21 . . . . . .219 D8
Wood La
Belper DE56 . . . . .190 F7
Creswell S80 . . . . .100 C8
Crich DE4 . . . . .157 B2
Hayfield DE13 . . . . .238 A4
Hayfield SK22 . . . . .25 C3
Holloway DE4 . . . . .144 A1
Horsley Woodhouse DE7 . .192 D5
Ible DE4 . . . . .153 E6
Idridgehay DE6, DE56 . . . .176 E8
Kniveton DE6 . . . . .163 A1
Pleasley NG20 . . . . .119 D1
Ripley DE5 . . . . .168 F3
Scarcliffe S44 . . . . .118 F6
Shirebrook NG20 . . . . .120 F7
Swadlincote DE11 . . . . .256 A7
Woodland Ave
Borrowash DE72 . . . . .221 C2
Breaston DE72 . . . . .235 F8
Ilkeston DE7 . . . . .194 D4
Sutton in A NG17 . . . . .148 E4
Woodland Dr
Rocester ST14 . . . . .196 F3
Scropton DE65 . . . . .226 D4
Sheffield S12 . . . . .44 B2
Woodland Gr
Barlborough S43 . . . . .80 A6
Clay Cross S42 . . . . .131 B6
Clowne S43 . . . . .81 A4

Woodland Gr continued
Mansfield Woodhouse
NG19 . . . . .136 C3
Woodland Pl S17 . . . . .55 F5
Woodland Rd
Derby DE22 . . . . .218 E8
Mansfield NG19 . . . . .136 F1
Sheffield S8 . . . . .43 B3
Swadlincote DE15 . . . . .255 B4
Woodlands
Brimington S43 . . . . .96 D7
Great Longstone DE45 . . . . .89 F3
Wirksworth DE4 . . . . .165 E8
Woodlands Ave
Breaston DE72 . . . . .235 F8
Ilkeston DE7 . . . . .232 E4
Woodlands Brow DE6 . . . .173 C4
Woodlands Cl
Glossop SK13 . . . . .9 F6
Little Eaton DE21 . . . . .205 B8
Melbourne DE73 . . . . .252 A8
Thorpe DE6 . . . . .161 C7
Woodlands Com Sch
DE22 . . . . .204 D4
Woodlands Cres DE12 . . . .262 B4
Woodlands La
Chellaston DE73 . . . . .245 A8
Quarndon DE22 . . . . .204 D6
Woodlands Rd
Chapel-en-le-F SK23 . . . . . . .47 B1
Derby DE22 . . . . .204 E5
High Lane SK12 . . . . .32 A6
New Mills SK22 . . . . .33 A8
Overseal DE12 . . . . .262 B4
Woodlands The
6 Mansfield NG19 . . . . . .136 B1
Melbourne DE73 . . . . .252 B8
Tatenhill DE13 . . . . .253 A8
Whaley Thorns NG20 . . . . .101 A3
Woodlands View DE7 . . . . .193 A2
Woodlands Way DE73 . . . .252 B8
Woodlands Yd DE73 . . . . . .245 A8
Woodland View
Buxton SK17 . . . . .85 C8
Chilcote DE12 . . . . .264 F3
Crich DE4 . . . . .167 E8
Hathersage S32 . . . . .53 A7
Horwich End SK23 . . . . .45 F7
Sheffield, Abbeydale Park
S17 .56 A7
Sheffield, Charnock Hill S12 .44 B2
Whaley Thorns NG20 . . . . .101 A3
Woodland Views ST14 . . . .224 C2
Woodland Way
Clay Cross S42 . . . . .131 B6
Eastwood NG16 . . . . .182 E2
Woodland Wlk S40 . . . . . . .94 F5
Woodlea Gr DE21 . . . . .205 C8
Woodlea Rd SK13 . . . . .17 B7
Woodleigh Cl S40 . . . . .94 F5
Woodmans Croft DE65 . . .227 E3
Woodmere Dr S41 . . . . .77 C4
Woodminton Dr DE73 . . . .232 F3
Woodnook Cl S42 . . . . .95 A4
Wood Nook Cl NG16 . . . . . .171 F6
Woodnook Gr S21 . . . . .58 E2
Woodnook La S42 . . . . .94 F5
Woodnook Way S42 . . . . . .94 F4
Woodpecker Hill DE7 . . . . .208 A2
Wood Rd
Derby, Chaddesden
DE21 . . . . .220 A8
Derby, Oakwood DE21 . . . .205 F1
Derby, Spondon DE21 . . . .221 A6
Woodridge The DE56 . . . . .190 F6
Woodrising Cl DE21 . . . . . .206 B3
Woodroffe Wlk DE21 . . . . .231 E7
Woodrove Ave S13 . . . . .44 B7
Woodrove Cl S13 . . . . .44 B7
Wood St N DE55 . . . . .159 C5
Woodseat Gr ST14 . . . . . . .197 A4
Woodseats La SK13 . . . . . . .16 B4
Woodshop La DE73 . . . . . . .244 D6
Woodside
Buxton SK17 . . . . .85 C7
Carsington DE4 . . . . .164 E7
Eastwood NG16 . . . . .182 E3
Horsley DE7 . . . . .192 D3
Woodside Ave
Holmesfield S18 . . . . .75 A8
Killamarsh S21 . . . . .60 F7
Ripley DE5 . . . . .180 D8
Woodside Cl
Bakewell DE45 . . . . .109 D5
Chesterfield S40 . . . . .95 B4
Woodside Cres
Ilkeston DE7 . . . . .194 D5
Long Eaton NG10 . . . . .236 B8
Woodside Dr
Bakewell DE45 . . . . .109 D5
Derby DE22 . . . . .205 A4
Woodside Pl S45 . . . . .131 B4
Woodside Rd
Sandiacre NG10 . . . . .223 B5
Shirebrook NG20 . . . . .119 E5
Shireoaks S81 . . . . .63 F7
Woodside St SK22 . . . . .33 B6
Woodside View S43 . . . . . . .75 A8
Woods La
Burton u T, Stapenhill
DE15 . . . . .254 F7
Derby DE22 . . . . .267 A3
Woods Mdw DE72 . . . . .246 A8
Woodsome Pk S42 . . . . . . .116 D2
Woodsorrel Dr DE21 . . . . .206 B3
Wood St
Alfreton DE55 . . . . .159 C5
Codnor DE5 . . . . .181 B4

Wood St *continued*
Derby DE1 . . . . .267 C4
Eastwood NG16 . . . . .182 F3
Glossop SK13 . . . . .17 C8
Hollingworth SK14 . . . . .9 D5
Holmewood S42 . . . . .116 E1
Ilkeston DE7 . . . . .194 F1
New Mills SK22 . . . . .33 B7
Ripley DE5 . . . . .169 D2
Somercotes DE55 . . . . .170 C8
Swadlincote DE11 . . . . .256 B2
Wirksworth DE4 . . . . .165 F8
Woodstock Cl DE22 . . . . .204 D4
Woodstock Ct ⑤ S41 . . . . . .96 A6
Woodstock Dr S41 . . . . . .115 C8
Woodstock Rd NG9 . . . . . .223 F3
Woodstock Rise S41 . . . . .115 C8
Woodthorne Ave DE24 . . .232 E4
Woodthorpe Ave
Clay Cross S45 . . . . .131 A4
Derby, Chaddesden DE21 . . .219 F6
Woodthorpe CE Prim Sch
S43 . . . . .79 C1
Woodthorpe Cl S44 . . . . . . .98 F7
Woodthorpe Cres S13 . . . . .44 C8
Woodthorpe Prim Sch
S13 . . . . .44 C7
Woodthorpe Rd
Sheffield S13 . . . . .44 C7
Shuttlewood S44 . . . . .98 F8
Staveley S43 . . . . .79 C2
Woodvale Cl S40 . . . . .114 A8
Wood View S21 . . . . .79 A8
Woodview Cl S42 . . . . .114 F2
Woodview Gdns DE22 . . . . .218 F8
Wood View Ho S21 . . . . . . .59 C3
Woodview Rd DE11 . . . . . . .255 E5
Woodville CE Jun Sch
DE11 . . . . .256 F2
Woodville Inf Sch DE11 . . .256 F2
Woodville Rd
Hartshorne DE11 . . . . .257 A5
Overseal DE12 . . . . .262 B4
Woodward's Pl DE11 . . . . .256 C3
Woodwards Cl DE72 . . . . . .221 D1
Woodward Way DE11 . . . . .256 D4
Woodyard Cl DE11 . . . . . . .255 F1
Woodyard La DE65 . . . . . . .226 F5
Wooley Cl S42 . . . . .131 B7
Wooliscroft Cl DE7 . . . . . . .194 C2
Woollaton La SK17 . . . . . . .138 D2
Woolley's Yd DE4 . . . . .141 C6
Woolley Bridge Rd
Glossop SK13 . . . . .9 F5
Hadfield SK13 . . . . .9 F5
Woolley Cl SK14 . . . . .9 D4
Woolley La
Hollingworth SK14 . . . . .9 D4
Hollingworth SK14 . . . . .9 D6

Woolley Mill La SK13 . . . . . .9 E7
Woolley Rd DE4 . . . . .143 B6
Woolrych St DE23 . . . . . . .218 F2
Woolsthorpe Cres DE7 . . .208 D4
Woolstitch Pk DE12 . . . . . .264 E7
Woosnam Cl DE14 . . . . . . .254 A6
Worcester Ave NG19 . . . . .136 C6
Worcester Cl S45 . . . . .131 E4
Worcester Cres DE21 . . . . .219 E8
Worcester Gr SK13 . . . . .17 F8
Worcester Mews NG19 . . .136 C6
Worcester Rd DE15 . . . . . .254 E6
Wordsworth Ave
Derby DE24 . . . . .231 F5
Mansfield Woodhouse
NG19 . . . . .136 B4
Swadlincote DE11 . . . . .256 C6
Wordsworth Dr DE24 . . . . .232 A5
Wordsworth Pl S18 . . . . . . .76 C7
Wordsworth Rd
Awsworth NG16 . . . . .195 C5
Chesterfield S41 . . . . .95 F8
Works La S44 . . . . .97 B3
Worksop Rd
Mastin Moor S43 . . . . .79 D4
Thorpe Salvin S80 . . . . .62 E7
Whitwell S80 . . . . .81 F6
Works Rd S43 . . . . .78 B2
Worrall Ave NG10 . . . . . . .223 E1
Worthington La DE73 . . . . .252 F1
Wortley Ave NG9 . . . . .209 D3
Wortley Cl DE7 . . . . .209 A8
Wortley Ct S33 . . . . .51 B7
Wragley Way DE24 . . . . . .231 D2
Wreakes La S18 . . . . .56 F2
Wren Cl DE11 . . . . .256 F3
Wren Ct NG10 . . . . .236 A3
Wren Nest Cl SK13 . . . . .17 B8
Wren Nest Rd SK13 . . . . . . .10 B1
Wren Nest Terr SK13 . . . . . .10 C1
Wren Park Cl
Belper DE56 . . . . .178 E5
Chesterfield S40 . . . . .114 F7
Eckington S12 . . . . .58 E8
Findern DE65 . . . . .230 D1
Wren Park Prim Sch
DE3 . . . . .218 A2
Wrenpark Rd S42 . . . . .114 D4
Wren Way DE3 . . . . .230 B7
Wretham Cl DE3 . . . . .230 D8
Wright Ave DE5 . . . . .169 F1
Wright Cres DE6 . . . . .185 D8
Wright St DE5 . . . . .181 B8
Wroxham Ct DE24 . . . . . . .232 D4
Wulfric Cl S2 . . . . .43 F8
Wulfric Pl S2 . . . . .43 F8
Wulfric Rd
Eckington S21 . . . . .59 C3
Sheffield S2 . . . . .44 A8

Wyaston Cl DE22 . . . . .204 E1
Wyaston Gdns DE6 . . . . . .185 D7
Wyaston Rd DE6 . . . . .185 C6
Wyatts Way DE5 . . . . .169 F3
Wybersley Rd SK6 . . . . .32 A8
Wychwood Dr NG9 . . . . . .209 D2
Wycliffe Rd DE55 . . . . .159 A4
Wycombe Grange NG19 . .136 F2
Wye Bank DE45 . . . . .109 E5
Wye Bank Gr DE45 . . . . . .109 E4
Wye Cl DE65 . . . . .240 D8
Wye Croft Ct DE45 . . . . . .109 D5
Wye Dale DE11 . . . . .255 F2
Wyedale Cl
Bakewell DE45 . . . . .109 E4
Buxton SK17 . . . . .85 B6
Wyedale Cres DE45 . . . . . .109 E4
Wyedale Ct ⑤ S41 . . . . .95 E7
Wyedale Dr DE45 . . . . . . .109 E4
Wyedale View DE45 . . . . . .109 E4
Wye Gr SK17 . . . . .85 A7
Wye Head Cl SK17 . . . . . . .84 F7
Wye Ho SK17 . . . . .66 B1
Wyelands Cl SK17 . . . . .84 F7
Wye Mill SK17 . . . . .89 A6
Wye St
Buxton SK17 . . . . .85 C8
Derby DE24 . . . . .233 A8
Wye Terr DE4 . . . . .126 F8
Wyming Brook Dr S10 . . . . .42 B8
Wyndale Dr DE7 . . . . .208 C6
Wyndham Cres DE15 . . . . .248 C3
Wyndham St DE24 . . . . . .233 A7
Wynd The S21 . . . . .79 C7
Wynton Ave DE24 . . . . . . .232 F8
Wyntor Ave DE4 . . . . .141 C6
Wynyard Cl DE7 . . . . .194 C3
Wysall Cl NG19 . . . . .135 E1
Wystan Ct DE65 . . . . .242 D2
Wyston Brook DE65 . . . . . .228 D1
Wythburn Rd S41 . . . . .95 C2
Wyver La DE56 . . . . .178 F6
Wyvern Ave NG10 . . . . . . .236 D5
Wyvern Bsns Pk DE21 . . . .220 A4
Wyvern Cl
Eastwood NG16 . . . . .195 A4
Matlock DE4 . . . . .143 A6
Wyvern Gdns S17 . . . . .55 E6
Wyvernside DE21 . . . . .219 F4
Wyvern Way DE21 . . . . . . .220 A4

Y

Yard Cl DE11 . . . . .256 B4
Yardley Cl DE55 . . . . .169 F8
Yardley Way DE56 . . . . . . .179 D4
Yard The ④ SK13 . . . . .10 C1
Yarmouth Ho DE24 . . . . . .233 C7

Yarncliff Cl S40 . . . . .95 D5
Yarrow Cl
Burton u T DE15 . . . . .248 B2
Derby DE24 . . . . .231 E2
Yarwell Cl DE21 . . . . .205 D1
Yates Ave DE72 . . . . .246 A7
Yates Rd SK22 . . . . .33 C7
Yates St DE23 . . . . .219 A1
Yeardsley Ave SK23 . . . . . . .33 D3
Yeardsley Gn SK23 . . . . .45 D8
Yeardsley La SK23 . . . . .33 D3
Yeld Cl DE45 . . . . .109 C4
Yeldersley Cl S40 . . . . .95 B5
Yeldersley La
Brailsford DE6 . . . . .187 B2
Osmaston DE6 . . . . .186 E6
Yeld Rd DE45 . . . . .109 D5
Yeld The DE45 . . . . .109 C5
Yelt La DE6 . . . . .224 D8
Yeoman Park Sch NG19 . .136 C4
Yeoman St DE4 . . . . .142 D1
Yeovil Cl DE24 . . . . .233 C7
Yerley Hill DE6 . . . . .172 C6
Yewdale Gr DE21 . . . . .206 C3
Yews Cl DE73 . . . . .233 A1
Yew Tree Ave DE72 . . . . . .221 D5
Yew Tree Cl
Ashover S45 . . . . .129 F3
Darley Dale DE4 . . . . .127 B3
Derby DE24 . . . . .233 C7
Yew Tree Cotts DE72 . . . . .222 E3
Yewtree Cres DE15 . . . . . .254 F7
Yew Tree Cl DE65 . . . . .227 C2
Yew Tree Dr
Chesterfield S40 . . . . .114 A8
Clay Cross S42 . . . . .131 B6
Killamarsh S21 . . . . .60 C5
Shirebrook NG20 . . . . .119 D5
Sutton in A NG17 . . . . .148 F2
Yew Tree Gdns DE12 . . . . .260 C6
Yew Tree Hill DE4 . . . . . . .156 B5
Yew Tree La
Bradley DE6 . . . . .186 E8
Elvaston DE72 . . . . .233 F4
Yewtree Rd DE11 . . . . .255 F7
Yew Tree Rd
Hatton DE65 . . . . .227 D1
Rosliston DE12 . . . . .260 C6

York Pl
North Wingfield S42 . . . . . .132 B7
Shireoaks S81 . . . . .63 F7
York Rd
Derby DE21 . . . . .219 F7
Long Eaton NG10 . . . . .223 C1
Shirebrook NG20 . . . . .119 E3
Swadlincote DE11 . . . . .256 B2
Yorkshire Way SK13 . . . . . . .17 F8
York St
Chesterfield S41 . . . . .115 C7
Derby DE1 . . . . .218 E5
Glossop SK13 . . . . .10 C1
York Terr
Glossop SK13 . . . . .17 C8
Pinxton NG16 . . . . .160 C1
Youlgreave Cl DE21 . . . . . .205 F1
Youlgreave Cres SK13 . . . . . .9 D1
Youlgreave Dr S12 . . . . .44 D5
Youlgreave YH* DE45 . . . .125 C5
Young St DE23 . . . . .218 F1
Yoxall Dr DE22 . . . . .218 C4
Ypres Rd DE22 . . . . .204 C2

Z

Zetland Cres DE24 . . . . . . .231 C2
Zion Ho DE11 . . . . .256 C1

Name and Address	Telephone	Page	Grid reference

PHILIP'S MAPS
the Gold Standard for drivers

◆ **Philip's street atlases cover every county in England, Wales, Northern Ireland and much of Scotland**

◆ Every named street is shown, including alleys, lanes and walkways

◆ Thousands of additional features marked: stations, public buildings, car parks, places of interest

◆ Route-planning maps to get you close to your destination

◆ Postcodes on the maps and in the index

◆ Widely used by the emergency services, transport companies and local authorities

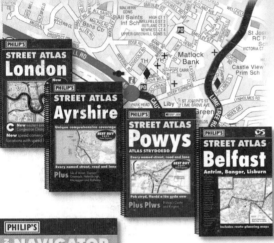

For national mapping, choose
Philip's Navigator Britain
the most detailed road atlas available of England, Wales and Scotland. Hailed by Auto Express as 'the ultimate road atlas', the atlas shows every road and lane in Britain.

'The ultimate in UK mapping'
The Sunday Times

Street atlases currently available

England
Bedfordshire and Luton
Berkshire
Birmingham and West Midlands
Bristol and Bath
Buckinghamshire and Milton Keynes
Cambridgeshire and Peterborough
Cheshire
Cornwall
Cumbria
Derbyshire
Devon
Dorset
County Durham and Teesside
Essex
North Essex
South Essex
Gloucestershire and Bristol
Hampshire
North Hampshire
South Hampshire
Herefordshire Monmouthshire
Hertfordshire
Isle of Wight
Kent
East Kent
West Kent
Lancashire
Leicestershire and Rutland
Lincolnshire
Liverpool and Merseyside
London
Greater Manchester
Norfolk
Northamptonshire
Northumberland
Nottinghamshire
Oxfordshire
Shropshire
Somerset
Staffordshire
Suffolk

Surrey
East Sussex
West Sussex
Tyne and Wear
Warwickshire and Coventry
Wiltshire and Swindon
Worcestershire
East Yorkshire Northern Lincolnshire
North Yorkshire
South Yorkshire
West Yorkshire

Wales
Anglesey, Conwy and Gwynedd
Cardiff, Swansea and The Valleys
Carmarthenshire, Pembrokeshire and Swansea
Ceredigion and South Gwynedd
Denbighshire, Flintshire, Wrexham
Herefordshire Monmouthshire
Powys

Scotland
Aberdeenshire
Ayrshire
Dumfries and Galloway
Edinburgh and East Central Scotland
Fife and Tayside
Glasgow and West Central Scotland
Inverness and Moray
Lanarkshire
Scottish Borders

Northern Ireland
County Antrim and County Londonderry
County Armagh and County Down
Belfast
County Tyrone and County Fermanagh

How to order
Philip's maps and atlases are available from bookshops, motorway services and petrol stations. You can order them from the publisher by phoning **0207 531 8473** or online at **www.philips-maps.co.uk**
For bulk orders only, e-mail philips@philips-maps.co.uk